THE EVANGELIST
AND THE IMPRESARIO

New Studies in American Intellectual and Cultural History

Dorothy Ross and Kenneth Cmiel, Series Editors

THE EVANGELIST
AND THE IMPRESARIO

RELIGION, ENTERTAINMENT,
AND CULTURAL POLITICS
IN AMERICA,
1884–1914

Kathryn J. Oberdeck

The Johns Hopkins University Press

Baltimore and London

©1999 The Johns Hopkins University Press
All rights reserved. Published 1999
Printed in the United States of America on acid-free paper

2 4 6 8 9 7 5 3 1

The Johns Hopkins University Press
2715 North Charles Street
Baltimore, Maryland 21218-4363
www.press.jhu.edu
Library of Congress Cataloging-in-Publication Data
will be found at the end of this book.
A catalog record for this book is available from the British Library.
ISBN 0-8018-6060-1

Publication of this work has been supported by a grant from the
Oliver M. Dickerson Fund. The Fund was established by Mr. Dickerson
(Ph.D., Illinois, 1906) to enable the publication of selected works in American
history, designated by the executive committee of the Department
of History of the University of Illinois at Urbana-Champaign.

To
Mrs. Anna Irvine Buck,
in fond memory,
and to
Fiona Jean,
with love

CONTENTS

Contents

PREFACE AND ACKNOWLEDGMENTS

T HE HISTORICAL TRAJECTORIES traced in this book found an echo in my own
tour through many of the far-flung locales its main character, Alexander
Irvine, passed through. I have therefore organized my acknowledgments in the
form of a tour as well, in order to recognize some of the continuities and changes
between the world he shared with Sylvester Poli and ours while revisiting the
places in that world where friends, colleagues, and relative strangers have helped
me complete this project. However, I would not want the resulting sequence
to diminish the central importance of people whose generosity with the stories
and documents of their family members made this book possible. One of these,
Mrs. Anna Irvine Buck, is recognized in the dedication to this book for the
friendly, hospitable, and inspiring assistance she gave me in gathering her father's documents and sharing her memories of him. I am also grateful to Ms.
Jeanne Poli for sharing documents and stories of her grandfather's life. As for
inaccuracies and infelicities in these pages, they are of course all my own.

This project started in New Haven, Connecticut, in the midst of a labor campaign that attested eloquently to continuities and changes in local labor relations
since the time when Alexander Irvine learned his gospel of work. Its early stages
as a research project coincided with the early victories won by Local 34, Yale University's union of clerical and technical employees. Local 34's negotiations with
Yale University involved intensive efforts to muster support among university students and faculty for the wage and occupational safety concerns of university employees. Irvine would have recognized such attempts to bridge fissures between
town and gown and across class divides as akin to his own work helping Yale students understand trade union aims eighty years before. He might have been
more surprised at Local 34's membership and aims. Ethnically and racially di-

verse and made up predominantly of women, Local 34 targeted the disparity between male and female wages that Irvine and the labor movements of his time
only rarely questioned. Their union victory contributed to wider changes in New
Haven society and politics that had transformed the New Haven Irvine knew: the
city's social geography was transformed by urban renewal after his death, and
by the 1980s and 1990s it had lost many of its manufacturing jobs. Its politics were
marked by the grassroots campaign of the city's first African-American mayor,
John Daniels. The lively movements that helped produce these changes provided indispensable dimensions to my education in New Haven.

I am even more indebted to the academic advisors and colleagues in New
Haven who supported this project. My advisor, David Montgomery, had faith in
an unusual proposal and a steady stream of invaluable suggestions for research
and writing. The other members of my dissertation committee, Jean-Christophe
Agnew and Nancy F. Cott, provided steady support and indispensable advice
throughout. Amy Kaplan offered incisive readings of earlier versions of the analysis of literary realism that appears in the Introduction; Ken Fones-Wolf offered
useful suggestions on an earlier version of Chapter 1; and Jon Butler provided
helpful criticisms after the dissertation was completed. I am especially grateful
to the members of my dissertation reading group—Jacqueline Dirks, Regina
Kunzel, and Catherine Stock—for their friendship, encouragement, and excellent counsel throughout this project. Many other New Haven friends and colleagues contributed ideas, lent interested ears, and otherwise aided this project,
including Cecelia Bucki, Micaela Di Leonardo, Jeanne Lawrence, Christopher
Lowe, Charles Musser, Adolph Reed, Karen Sawislak, Marian Smith, Glenn
Wallach, Linda Watts, John Willoughby, Lynne Zeavin, and members of the
Greater New Haven Labor History Association. I am also grateful to the staffs
of Sterling Memorial Library, the Yale Divinity School Library, the New Haven
Colony Historical Society, the Historical Manuscripts and Archives Division of
the University of Connecticut at Storrs, the New Haven Public Library, and the
New York Public Library for the Performing Arts for their generous assistance.
In addition to Ms. Poli, Reverdy Whitlock provided me with information about
his father and aunt, who had been members of Irvine's circle in New Haven.

I made two fruitful trips to Northern Ireland and England to research this
project, during which I visited many of the precincts where Alexander Irvine
spent his childhood and youth, and where he pursued his transatlantic ministry
later in life. Northern Ireland was profoundly stirring for its considerable beauty
and terrible divisions, which at the time of my visits in 1987 and 1992 were
painfully apparent. Irvine would have been greatly moved by the impressive and

hopeful strides toward peace made more recently by the parties to these conflicts. The kind people who offered me assistance and hospitality enhanced my understanding of Irvine's homeland, past and present. Mr. R. Woods, Principal Administrative Officer of the Antrim Borough Council, was immensely helpful in making arrangements for me to examine Irvine manuscripts held by the Council, and his staff was very gracious—and generous with tea and biscuits—during my research. Mr. Woods also arranged my first meeting with Alastair Smyth, author of the *Story of Antrim* and introductions to several modern editions of Irvine's chimney-corner stories, who kindly took time from a busy schedule to share with me his own considerable knowledge of Irvine's life as well as documents relating to Irvine's life that he had collected. Gillian O'Rourke provided me with helpful information on today's "Chimney Corner" by correspondence. My Antrim accommodations in 1988 with Mr. and Mrs. Jackson and in 1992 with Hazel McMinn provided me with much more than their advertised "bed and breakfast" led me to expect. In Belfast my research was substantially aided by several members of the faculty in Economic and Social History at Queen's University, especially Dr. David Hempton, and Dr. Liam Kennedy. Dr. Alun C. Davies introduced me to Professor George Shepperson, who has been extremely generous in sharing his interest in and knowledge of Alexander Irvine over the years. Finally, I am grateful to the library staffs at the Greystone Library in Antrim, the Public Record Office of Northern Ireland, the Public Record Office at Kew, and the British Library for their help.

The core of my research on Irvine took place in California, where he spent his final years. For me this provided a special kind of intellectual homecoming, as California was where I grew up and first acquired the taste for history that fueled this book. I cannot overemphasize my debt to Mrs. Buck, as well as her daughter Anna Giarretto, who has remained a steadfast supporter of this project throughout, and has provided great encouragement with her interest and assistance. In Santa Barbara Sasha and Wilda Irvine kindly offered me access to further Irvine documents. Peter Blodgett at the Huntington Library helped me in finding Irvine-related documents in their collections and ultimately assisted in transferring the Alexander Irvine papers to the library after Mrs. Buck's death. Paul Lichterman, Nina Eliasoph, David Morrison, and Vicki Symonds were kind enough to provide me with places to stay during my research. So was my own family, Chuck, Jean, and Carol Oberdeck to whom, along with my aunt, Doris Oberdeck, I am especially grateful for support, concern, interest, and patience through this project and much that preceded it.

Other sojourns that were not directly related to research on Irvine but contributed significantly to this book took place in Durban, South Africa, and Paris, France. In Durban my mother-in-law, Mrs. Wendy Munro, graciously suffered my preoccupation with Irvine and Poli and took considerable interest in my labors despite the fact that while visiting I disappeared to the University of Natal library to work on portions of the manuscript. The library overlooked Durban harbor, which offered a spectacle of international trade to stimulate my descriptions of the global networks that Irvine and Poli had traveled a century ago. In Paris Marian Smith and Carl Woideck made me feel at home among friends, and Marian offered generous guidance into the good graces of the staff of the Bibliotheque Nationale.

I am extremely grateful for the financial support lent to this project by the American Association of University Women, in the form of a dissertation grant, the Whiting Foundation, the Michigan Society of Fellows, the Cushwa Center for the Study of American Catholicism, for a Hibernian Research Award, and the Research Board of the University of Illinois.

A previous version of portions of Chapters 3 and 4 appeared in an article in *American Quarterly*, a previous version of portions of Chapters 2 and 5 appeared in *Radical History Review*, and a previous version of portions of Chapters 6 and 7 in the collection *Labor Histories: Class, Politics, and the Working-Class Experience* edited by Bruce Laurie, Eric Arnesen, and Julie Greene and published by University of Illinois Press. I am grateful to these sources for permission to use this material again, and to the editors of the journals and book for their comments.

This project became a book in the Midwest, where Irvine's mix of evangelism and politics resounded especially deeply with an indigenous mix of faith and fight. While I have been teaching at the University of Michigan and, currently, at the University of Illinois, friends and colleagues have offered many kinds of support that combined into a similar mixture of spirit and commitment. In Ann Arbor, members of "the group"—especially Laura Downs, Susan Johnson, Sueanne Caulfield, and Valerie Kivelson—offered a rare mixture of acute criticism and moral support in the early stages of revision. Members of the Fellows Seminar at the Michigan Society of Fellows also provided helpful comments on previous versions of these chapters. At the University of Illinois several research assistants contributed substantially to the final data gathering; I am very grateful to Jon Coit, Dawn Flood, Andrew Nolan, and Steve Vaughan in this regard. The "History Workshop" at the University of Illinois offered discerning readings of portions of the manuscript. In addition, I am grateful for the support and advice of individual friends and colleagues in Urbana, especially Leslie Reagan, Daniel

Preface and Acknowledgments

Schneider, Diane Koenker, and Harry Liebersohn. In its final stages, much of the manuscript received an especially careful and acute reading from Jim Barrett, for whose generous advice I am particularly grateful. Two New Haven friends whose intellectual comradeship has continued into my years in the Midwest—Jacqueline Dirks and Karen Sawislak—also read portions of the manuscript and provided comments that were, as ever, thoughtful and thought-provoking.

At the Johns Hopkins University Press, my editor, Bob Brugger, has provided good-humored support throughout the publication process. I am also very grateful to series editor Dorothy Ross for her careful and constructive critique of the manuscript before its final revisions. In copyediting Maria denBoer saved me from several infelicities.

My greatest debts are at home, where William Munro has taken time from his own teaching and research to be my closest and most patient critic, often my companion in discovery, always a loyal supporter of this project. His humor, insight, wisdom, and affection have made this a better book and have sustained me immeasurably in writing it.

Our daughter, Fiona, born just as this book was being completed, did not contribute so much to writing it as to helping me focus, finally, on the profoundly human aspirations it traces. I close this preface with an account of a sad moment that attended her arrival only because this otherwise personal story bears so closely on the questions that tie the concerns of the book to some of my hopes for her. As I completed the final revisions of the manuscript, we learned that we had lost Fiona's twin. Like any joyfully expectant parents, we felt this loss keenly, and struggled to reconcile ourselves to it. In this we found that some available interpretations—though offered by kind people to whom we remain extremely grateful—complicated our search for meaning by posing two stark alternatives: a scientifically meaningful world in which our remaining baby had survived a kind of Darwinian struggle, or a spiritually meaningful world in which our loss was part of a providential plan. We could not accept that life was either so cold-blooded or so preordained. As I pondered why these alternatives were not enough for me, though, I was struck by their similarity to the alternatives Alexander Irvine had faced a hundred years ago in comprehending his life trajectory, and I felt with new sympathy their human dimension. So I dedicate this book to Fiona in hopes that she may find something like what I identify with these historical actors in seeking: a meaning for life that combines reasoned inquisitiveness and spiritual peace with the vital activity of human endeavor and a commitment to extending broadly the goods it pursues.

THE EVANGELIST
AND THE IMPRESARIO

PIETY, PLEASURE, AND THE PUBLIC SPHERE
Cultural Politics and the Problem of Realism

WHAT IS CULTURE, and who has the authority to define it? Does it consist in universal standards to which people aspire along shared hierarchies of cultivation? Or are there multiple cultures that render life meaningful for groups with incommensurable ideals? If culture comprises shared hierarchies, who determines what their standards should be, and how? If there are multiple cultures, who says who belongs within the bonds of one or another? And are these conceptions of culture mutually exclusive, or are there hierarchies within and between distinctive cultures?

These sound like questions from late-twentieth-century American culture wars, but they were already in vigorous dispute a century ago. This book is about those century-old debates over the meaning of culture and about people who entered them in ways that shaped American cultural politics in the twentieth century. It is a history of intellectual arguments over the meaning of culture itself— not just over whether some forms of culture are good, bad, or just different from one another, as the recent wars would often have it, but over the stakes involved in conceiving of culture in these terms. It finds these arguments not in arenas conventionally associated with intellectual discourses, but in class conflicts over culture that took place at the labile border of religion and entertainment in late-nineteenth- and early-twentieth-century America.

That religion and entertainment should have combined to produce any kind of meaningful cultural debate during this period may strike readers as surprising, in light of the available history on these social arenas. Many historians see cultural debate losing its critical edge precisely when and where religion and entertainment met in late-nineteenth-century America—for example, in church services adapted to theatrical techniques that congregations knew from the realm of popular culture, or vaudeville theaters that sanitized their performances to appease religious critics. Such developments seem to have dulled a robust Protestant heritage full of heady contests over the conundrums of culture. In colonial America, John Winthrop exhorted the Puritan settlers of Massachusetts Bay to achieve the summit of a sacred hierarchy, Roger Williams pondered the spiritual significance of Native American cultural diversity, and the landed elite of the Chesapeake dramatized their cultural superiority by making their churches sites of hierarchical pageantry. Evangelical upheavals in the late eighteenth and early nineteenth centuries challenged these patterns of Protestant cultural authority by claiming legitimacy for untutored religious enthusiasts who often expressed spiritual conviction in theatrical terms. Still, these upheavals also addressed important questions about the character and boundaries of culture, especially as they extended spiritual authority across lines of gender and race. But after evangelical fervor resolved itself into the respectable denominations, and these began to lose hold on congregations lured by expanding commercial entertainment, mixtures of religion and popular culture seem, in many historical accounts, to have become more manipulative than incisive. Some historians associate such mixtures with a late-nineteenth-century surrender to "therapeutic" concerns about individual spiritual comfort that dissolved questions about cultural value or community bonds. Popular entertainments that sought to accommodate Protestant respectability in this period also appear as questionable sources of meaningful cultural commentary. As impresarios tried to banish transgressive performances that defied standards of civilized "decency," cultural historians suggest, popular culture became an arena of safe, uncontroversial sensation.[1]

Departing from such interpretations, this book focuses on ministers, worshipers, entertainers, and audiences for whom religion and entertainment comprised an arena of vibrant conflict over the meaning of class distinctions—and over categories of race, ethnicity, and gender that complicated those distinctions. It examines traditions of Protestant evangelical uplift from the perspective of people who encountered them as subordinate beneficiaries, but who also had alternative visions of the virtues that any broadly applicable cultural hierarchy should enshrine at its summit. Popular entertainments like vaudeville helped shape such alternatives by ridiculing and reformulating pious cultural hierarchies that they also endorsed. While popular culture demonstrated the malleability of cultural hierarchy, economic and political conflicts mobilized working-class audiences to criticize publicly the hierarchies that Protestant elites and reformers recommended, and to pose alternative cultural ideals. In the course of these conflicts, workers helped transform cultural hierarchies they encountered at the intersection of religion and theater, and made this juncture a dynamic arena of cultural politics.

Piety, Pleasure, and the Public Sphere

There were high stakes in these assertions of cultural privilege and defiance. Their champions shaped and reshaped the boundaries of an expanding public sphere that legitimated cultural authority itself. As provocatively described by sociologist Jürgen Habermas, the public sphere developed during the eighteenth century into a distinct arena of debate located between "society," where individuals negotiated competing economic interests, and the state, with its threat of arbitrary authority that the bourgeois "public" was trying to bring under control. In the public sphere, individuals met as ostensibly equal participants in rational discussion about common cultural and political concerns. But this "equality" was compromised by exclusive boundaries of class, gender, and race maintained, in part, through hierarchical cultural standards defining what constituted "rational" discourse. This tension in Habermas's historical formulation of the public sphere has prompted historians to inquire into the ways that workers, women, or racial and ethnic minorities affected debates over culture and politics that cultural elites regarded as their own preserve.[2]

At the turn into the twentieth century, the juncture of religion and popular culture was a dynamic location for just such encounters. Both champions and critics of the cultural hierarchies implicit in American middle-class Protestantism wondered how to make this religious tradition meaningful to industrial workers who seemed to inhabit alien cultures comprising trade unionist solidarities, immigrant institutions, and frivolous entertainments. Meanwhile, workers themselves found alternative satisfactions in entertainments that maintained pious hierarchies even while they acknowledged perspectives critical of the cultural standards those hierarchies promoted. Encouraged by such entertainments to reformulate concepts of culture that they encountered in religious teaching and challenged on the field of industrial conflict, workers who were also worshipers and entertainment audiences, along with their allies and adversaries, helped redraw the boundaries of the public sphere.

To capture the cultural transformations at stake in this process, I have constructed this book as a guided tour rather than a social survey. Its scope is no less wide for this, for I employ two tour guides who established varied and far-flung connections within the arenas of religion, popular culture, and class politics they helped to shape. The main narrative follows the trajectory of Alexander Irvine, a Protestant minister of plebeian Irish origins whose American career led him into labor activism, socialist politics, popular authorship, and eventually a stint on the vaudeville stage. Irvine's theatrical ambitions brought him into contact with the book's second guide, Italian-American vaudeville manager Sylvester Poli, who used his skills as a wax sculptor to establish himself as a theatrical entrepreneur with an impressive circuit of vaudeville houses spread across New

England and the mid-Atlantic states. Though Irvine did not tour Poli's theatrical circuit until 1913, he had already drawn extensively on the formulas and themes of Poli's entertainment world as a working-class missionary and popular author. By charting connections across the converging paths of the two men's careers, this book shows how Irvine, Poli, and the communities who joined their intersecting projects of evangelism and popular entertainment also helped transform the cultural vocabularies of class distinction in their era. In this sense, the approach developed here is less one of recounting biographies than of tracing cultural trajectories—mapping influences and alliances that shaped the careers of men who revised the terms of public sphere debate.[3]

Irvine and Poli formulated their earliest conceptions of cultural distinction in the course of their journeys from Ireland and Italy to America, which are the focus of Part I. The education they received along the way reveals cross-national cultural currents that informed American cultural debates. Irvine constructed his missionary ambitions out of strains of evangelical fervor that had shaped Protestant religious practice on both sides of the Atlantic throughout much of the nineteenth century. He embraced evangelical uplift and self-improvement as means of transcending the poverty and ignorance of his Ulster childhood, and followed his evangelical aspirations into the Royal Marines and a mission to the American working class. But, throughout this journey, his conceptions of faith, learning, and labor also reproduced the plebeian camaraderie he had enjoyed in the cramped cobbler's cottage he had shared with his siblings and parents. Finding plebeian mixtures of pleasure and piety at odds with the methods favored by institutions of Protestant uplift that employed him in the United States, Irvine set out to reconcile the two through a growing engagement with labor and social reform movements.

Meanwhile, Sylvester Poli's European apprenticeship in the art of wax sculpture also drew on cultural practices reaching back to the earlier nineteenth century, when museums dedicated to the education of an expanding public used wax effigies to celebrate newly minted ideals of national "civilization." As they developed over the course of the century, these popular traditions generated complex commentaries on "civilized" cultural standards. Poli and other entertainment impresarios popularized and combined multiple hierarchies—drawn from nationalist, imperialist, religious, and evolutionary discourses—as measures of the relative "civilization" of individuals, social classes, nations, and "races." As Poli's wax exhibits and vaudeville enterprises demonstrate, these hierarchies became key components in popular representations of industrial conflicts that divided his audiences. The ethnic caricatures that dominated the vaudeville programs Poli began to mount in the 1890s ridiculed their subjects for being "unrefined" while poking fun at prevailing standards of "refinement." Like Irvine's missionary work, Poli's entertainments appealed to audiences who wrestled with the very transatlantic notions of "uplift" and "civilization" that had shaped his own early encounters with cultural hierarchy.

As they pursued their careers in America, Irvine and Poli engaged political and economic conflicts that transformed these terms of cultural debate. These conflicts are the focus of Part II, which is set in the city of New Haven, Connecticut, where Poli made his home and vaudeville headquarters from 1892 until his death, and where Irvine spent eight years as a minister involved in labor conflicts that pivotally reshaped his mission. In New Haven, Irvine participated in a series of political and shop floor disputes that exposed him to distinctively working-class perspectives on cultural hierarchy. His laborite allies distinguished between democratic Christian cultivation and the "so-called culture" associated with the "civilized" conceits of a privileged elite. Irvine incorporated this perspective into his own evangelism through popular cultural techniques such as the stereopticon. His laborite gospel also echoed the way that hierarchies of civilization were celebrated and ridiculed in Poli's entertainments.

As both men discovered, however, the contested cultural values they addressed made for delicate negotiations of the politics of culture. Venturing to parlay entrepreneurial success into cultural authority, Poli played patron to rival audiences to which his varied programs of "high-toned acts" and ethnic caricatures appealed. His careful maneuvers around New Haven's ethnic divisions reveal cultural disputes that also confounded Irvine's efforts to reconstruct cultural authority according to proletarian solidarities, which often fractured along lines of ethnicity and race. The gender dynamics of New Haven cultural politics posed further dilemmas for Irvine and Poli. Irvine complicated his appeal to female parishioners by asserting masculine bravado against a fear of "feminized" religion he shared with other clerics. Meanwhile, the "vaudeville trust" that swallowed Poli's enterprises encouraged the proliferation of acts featuring flamboyant female stars. Defying "civilized" standards to which Poli had long paid ambivalent homage, these actresses helped to shift the terms in which he wielded cultural authority. Both men negotiated such authority by engaging the concerns of popular audiences who connected conflicts over labor and civic life with the meaning of worship and recreation.

While these local struggles are indispensable to understanding Irvine's and Poli's careers, the cultural debates in which the two men participated had much wider cultural significance. Part III focuses on the popular stories and theatrical performances that won Irvine national audiences in the 1910s and considers how these stories illuminate broad transformations in the conceptualization of culture and social difference. For Irvine, the periodical press and the vaudeville stage offered laboratories of proletarian self-construction where he refashioned the cultural lessons of New Haven's class conflicts into narratives of his own developing class consciousness. He learned to tell and sell his life story in terms of an evolutionary vernacular that recast the hierarchies of civilization he had pondered throughout his career as an opposition between the vital brutalities of the social pit and the enervating refinements of bourgeois comfort. Irvine not only mastered this vocabulary; he reworked and transformed it as the politics of class distinction provoked new insights into public debates over the meaning of culture. As he moved into national prominence as a socialist propagandist, Irvine applied questions and insights generated in the realm of class politics to the reformulation of his life story. He reconceptualized notions of ethnicity, race, and gender implicit in the overlapping hierarchies of "civilization" he had encountered over the course of his mission. Recoiling from the racist implications of the popular evolutionary terms in which he had cast his first autobiography, *From the Bottom Up*, Irvine rewrote his story as a popular stage-Irish memoir entitled *My Lady of the Chimney Corner*. This revised self-construction identified his adult proletarian affiliations and religious convictions as the product of ethnic loyalties enshrined in his mother's plebeian Irish wisdom.[4] Inspired by socialist infighting over the racial boundaries of class solidarity and conceived on the model of ethnic caricatures long prevalent in Poli's vaudeville entertainments, *My Lady* illuminates popular, working-class sources of a broader turn from evolutionary hierarchies to pluralist communities in American conceptualizations of culture. To cap his career in popular self-representation, Irvine went on to dramatize the class conflicts that had provoked his reconceptualization of culture in a one-act play that toured Poli's vaudeville circuit.

By identifying Irvine's self-representations and the entertainment practices on which they drew as crucibles of class identity, the final chapters of this book invoke recent perspectives that locate class distinction in language and culture. Historians who embrace such poststructuralist views often set themselves in opposition to those who look for "objective" sources of class division in the relations of capitalist production.[5] But recent studies of popular narrative and class identity suggest more nuanced approaches to this dispute. Analyzing popular narratives as instances of "historically situated authorial consciousness" as well as sites for the production of class and gender identity, for example, Judith Walkowitz has demonstrated how cultural constructions of class develop out of social pressures generated by class conflict. Other scholars have emphasized how working-class autobiographers transformed prevailing narratives of class distinction as they tried to make sense of their own experiences.[6] This study builds on such rapprochements between cultural and social history by showing how the narratives Irvine forged at the intersection of evangelical religion, popular culture, and socialist politics contributed to wider transformations in representations of class distinction in the public sphere. It maps a process whereby popular audiences and working-class activists contributed to a broader shift in concepts of culture and civilization that led from narratives of Protestant self-improvement to evolutionary narratives and finally to visions of twentieth-century cultural pluralism. By tracing this process through the interpenetration of religion, entertainment, and class politics, I show how the debates among diverse groups engaged in these arenas—including trade unionists and theologians, evangelists and entertainers—contributed to changing narratives of culture.

My emphasis on narrative is not exclusively an analytical concern, however. As a narrative in its own right, this book is an account of how Alexander Irvine— informed by evangelical enthusiasms, labor militancy, and the representations of cultural distinction portrayed on Sylvester Poli's stages—came to tell certain historically specific kinds of stories about his own cultural encounters with class distinction. In constructing that account, I have tried to be faithful to the pleasures of narrative that made stories vital to the ways the two men and their audiences debated the meaning of culture. Told around the chimney corner, through wax exhibits, at church, on stage, or on the lecture platform, good stories were the means of imparting and transforming the conceptions of culture and class distinction at issue in the public sphere Irvine and Poli inhabited. Intriguing narratives helped foster the considerable acclaim both men won for their contributions to the arenas of religion, popular culture, and class politics. Though changing fashions and social structures of cultural debate rendered them more obscure by the late twentieth century, Irvine and Poli remain important ambassadors to a vibrant public sphere that generated cultural contests to come. Out of respect for this status, I have aimed to tell their stories well by subordinating analytical jargon that speaks to our cultural conundrums instead of theirs.

Piety and Pleasure in American Cultural History

That Irvine's and Poli's stories speak to current cultural questions and analytical debates is nevertheless part of their interest. Their trajectories inform several arenas of contemporary scholarship in cultural history. To begin with, by showing how Irvine's Protestant evangelicalism and Poli's immigrant Catholicism contributed to a wider public sphere that also embraced popular enter-

tainment, their stories reveal important bridges between religion and other areas
of cultural history. In the process, the story of their intertwined careers helps to
develop and revise several trends in scholarship on American religion. The first
of these has belatedly addressed Herbert Gutman's call for historians to devote
more attention to Protestant themes in American working-class culture and politics as well as to the distinction between working-class criticisms of Protestant
institutions and those posed by the more familiar, middle-class social gospel.
Though recent work has begun to answer Gutman's call, American historians
have left this field relatively fallow, in marked contrast to the field of British history, where debate over the role of Protestant piety in working-class popular culture and politics has been a prominent theme. For America, in-depth study of
religious belief within working-class daily life long remained the province of historians of immigrant groups. These historians often emphasize the autonomous
values that set ethnic communities off from dominant political and cultural hierarchies. The cultural conflicts revealed in Irvine's and Poli's trajectories
demonstrate how religious struggles between class- and ethnically defined communities from various religious traditions spoke to public discourses that were
nominally Protestant in character.[7]

These conflicts, in turn, illuminate a plebeian legacy of evangelical Protestantism that has remained largely unexamined. Literature on evangelical Christianity in nineteenth-century America was long constrained by a "social control"
interpretation linking evangelicalism to the social aims of an aspiring middle
class.[8] Though it accurately represented some of the purposes to which employers and civic elites put evangelical culture, this interpretation obscures a
much more complicated history. As explored in the work of Nathan Hatch,
Richard Cawardine, Jama Lazerow, and Susan Juster, evangelicalism's cross-
Atlantic culture turns out to have had varied meanings for workers and bosses,
women and men, and to have fed democratic political and social sensibilities
even as it promised otherworldly salvation.[9] Irvine's story extends the multiple
meanings of this evangelical tradition into the late nineteenth and twentieth centuries. At this point the structure and scope of evangelical revivalism had certainly changed, transformed in part by the mass revivals of Dwight Moody and
Ira Sankey, whose influence was important in Irvine's conversion. But the ambiguous social character of the evangelical message continued. It has been obscured by narratives that read into the nineteenth century divisions between
"urban" and "rural" sensibilities, or scientific modernism and Fundamentalist
antimodernism, which developed later. Irvine's trajectory defies such divisions,
demonstrating how conflicts over evangelicalism's democratic traditions con-

tinued to shape nodes of urban industrial life, such as popular culture and working-class politics, which are often seen as antithetical to evangelical appeals.

In its relations to Poli's entertainment world, Irvine's evangelical career also illuminates understudied aspects of the intersection between religion and popular culture. Historians differ in their interpretation of the efforts of religious leaders to appropriate popular cultural techniques. Some see in such efforts the seeds of a distinctively twentieth-century "therapeutic culture" while others trace a longer history of compromise between piety and pleasure. Whereas the former treat compromise with commercial culture as an abdication of religion's transcendent refuge from worldly preoccupations, the latter recognize in the commercial diffusion of religious pastimes sources of critical, popular commentaries on more orthodox pieties.[10] Indeed, R. Laurence Moore has pointed to vaudeville as a site in which working-class audiences integrated their class-specific values into a broader, national commercial culture that religious authorities were also trying to shape.[11] The cultural perspectives at issue among the various groups involved in this process, and the nature of their influence, however, remain more obscure. Irvine's mission elucidates such perspectives among the popular audiences he engaged, who argued with local religious leaders over cultural tastes they associated with entertainments available at Poli's vaudeville theaters. As he took these arguments into national arenas of cultural politics, Irvine worked them into popular narratives that transformed prevailing concepts of culture itself. His trajectory thus helps demonstrate how the evangelical values with which he began were contested within and integrated into, rather than abandoned by, an expanding public sphere that embraced popular culture.

This perspective on the juncture of religion and popular culture has important implications for the history of entertainment as well. Because of the claims that Poli and other vaudeville managers made for their shows' "refinement," vaudeville has come to play a crucial role in the narratives through which cultural historians account for the wide propagation of turn-of-the-century hierarchies that rank culture in terms of high and low, refined and vulgar. Viewing the mixture of religion and commercial culture from the vantage point of entertainment, they emphasize how vaudeville impresarios blunted the edge of a more irreverent popular culture by incorporating the perspective of middle-class refinement and Sunday school piety. Displacing segmented nineteenth-century audiences who had jeered one another's tastes across class lines and then retreated to group-specific entertainments, they argue, vaudeville entrepreneurs assembled heterogeneous audiences governed by uniform evaluations of "refinement" associated with Protestant pieties.[12]

There is much in the content and context of Poli's vaudeville shows to confirm this narrative. But, as it intersects with Irvine's, Poli's story also complicates
the picture in revealing ways. Though hardly "authentic" and often derogatory,
vaudeville caricatures did not just ridicule subordinate groups according to universalizing cultural standards. They also appealed to cultural tastes that questioned such standards. Poli's efforts to transform vaudeville celebrity into local
cultural authority permit rare glimpses of the cultural contests that his shows addressed. While aspiring to a cultural refinement he associated with the local Yankee elite, Poli catered to a range of tastes that his audiences disputed within and
across New Haven's class and ethnic boundaries. In this context, Poli found the
emerging standardization of refinement something of a paradox. Urged by corporate pressures to cast "refinement" as a single standard of feminine propriety,
Poli eventually came to wield cultural authority in terms less clearly attuned to
local cultural divisions where he had negotiated cultural legitimacy.

To explore this paradox of cultural authority, this book develops a novel approach to the study of vaudeville shows and their audiences. Several deftly researched works document the character of vaudeville performances.[13] Often,
however, they emphasize nationally renowned stars, especially those whose reputations retained a retrospective gloss after vaudeville's decline in the 1930s. Such
interpretations slight the wide range of acts presented to vaudeville audiences
who attended local theaters week in and week out and saw shows made up of for-
gotten performers appealing to historically specific tastes as well as those who
survived the shifting vogues of popular and scholarly fascination. In order to capture this dimension of theatrical experience, I assembled a sample of acts, cate-
gorized by type and topic, which appeared at Poli's New Haven theaters over
three six-year periods. This information allowed me to observe the shifting relations between the diverse themes apparent in Poli's shows.[14]

The significance of these changing programs lies not only in the acts that
composed them, but also in their audiences' contests outside the theater. By setting Poli's shows in the context of his entrepreneurial and civic appeals to communities divided along lines of class, ethnicity, and gender, this book reveals how
vaudeville's unstable cultural standards spoke to wider public controversies over
cultural ideals. While no single manager's local strategies can exhaustively document these resonances between theater and everyday life, we must also beware
of seeking vaudeville's significance only through the strategies of managers like
Benjamin Franklin Keith, who led the corporate consolidation of vaudeville,
or through culture industry hubs like New York, which have received the most
attention from vaudeville scholars. Discussions of vaudeville conceived in these
terms neglect the concerns of subordinate groups who saw important cultural

stakes in their contests with one another and with locally prominent elites or celebrities like Poli. Such contests shaped audience encounters with national culture industries. As Poli maneuvered among New Haven's elites, working-class audiences, and ethic communities, as well as his corporate associates nationwide, he provided a trail that connects the content of vaudeville shows to local and national contests that rendered such content meaningful.

The account of vaudeville and its audiences that emerges from this approach builds on but also recasts cultural studies scholarship that focuses on oppositional meanings in entertainment. Such scholarship has challenged intellectual paradigms that associated popular culture with ideological false consciousness imposed by powerful culture industries on passive audiences. Instead, many cultural studies scholars draw on the more fluid concept of "hegemony" outlined in the work of Antonio Gramsci. Gramsci reflected on the processes of popular knowledge and "common sense," often shaped by popular culture institutions, which produce a broad-ranging consensus that legitimates power relations between social groups or classes. Rather than seeing this popular knowledge as consisting in illusory notions imposed by dominant elites, he sketched a more complex account of a "hegemonic" culture that legitimates existing power relations by compromising with the alternative values that subordinate groups propose. The result is a fragmentary, contradictory, and shifting constellation of perspectives on prevailing social relations that contains, to some extent, its own critique. Historians and other scholars of popular culture have provocatively applied this vision of hegemony in interpretations of popular entertainment that emphasize alternative meanings available to diverse audiences rather than a general acceptance of prevailing cultural standards. This book contributes to such interpretations by exploring themes and narratives its main characters shared with audiences and critics who embraced competing social ideals.[15]

The approach developed here departs from some work in cultural studies, however, in elaborating the social uses to which Irvine, Poli, and their audiences put the varied meanings they found in entertainments like vaudeville. That is, it ventures beyond the focus of cultural studies scholarship that seeks cultural politics primarily within entertainment. While this focus follows wider scholarly currents that have usefully broadened the definition of politics beyond party formation or voting, it can obscure important political dimensions of cultural practices. Scholarship conceived in these terms illuminates what popular cultural representations might mean to various audiences, but neglects political, economic, and social constraints that shape such meanings.[16] Rather than focusing on entertainment as an arena of political resistance in itself, this book seeks the politics of culture in wider conflicts that connected amusements like vaudeville with other realms of public life, such as industrial conflict, local politics, and a national socialist movement. In addition to illuminating debates to which Sylvester Poli's theatrical fare appealed, this approach shows how vaudeville engaged with changing hegemonic ideals as it developed into a corporate culture industry.

To consider how entertainment and religion informed the political and civic conflicts Irvine and Poli engaged is also to invoke arguments over the significance of the class distinctions—as well as ethnic, racial, and gender divisions—across which they and their audiences waged these conflicts. As I have noted, the class-conscious, proletarian terms in which Irvine defined his own cultural politics have become the subject of sharp conceptual debate among historians. Some cultural historians have charged social history with a naive view of a "real," "material," or "social" bedrock of class experience that gets expressed in culture and consciousness. They argue that culture and language produce the categories of "class" and the "social" in which social historians seek "real" sources of consciousness. Social historians unconvinced by such arguments refuse to abandon social and material facts as the foundation of historical truth, irrespective of what contemporaries or later theorists may say.[17] By focusing on what Irvine, Poli, and their audiences did think and say about class and other social distinctions, this book addresses such debates in ways that suggest a historical synthesis.

Language, culture, and narrative are central to understanding how these historical actors experienced not only class divisions but also boundaries of ethnicity, race, and gender that complicate any simple correlation of class consciousness with collective material interest. Irvine, Poli, and their audiences wove these divisions into cultural images and popular narratives that reveal much about the complexity of their social vision. But they also persistently questioned and rearranged these narratives, often provoked by class struggles that workers conceived in explicitly collective and material terms. These terms did not produce working-class "interests" as monolithic totalities founded on economic "realities"; for class identity remained fractured by shifting hierarchies of race, ethnicity, gender, and "culture." But material and political battles over class-based issues such as wages, control of production, or ownership of public utilities did shape and change the way that Irvine, in particular, envisioned the loyalties implied in his own popular narratives of class identity. From the perspective of Irvine's changing popular self-representations, and the techniques they borrowed from Poli's entertainment world, we can see not only how popular narratives shaped class identities, but also how class struggles and class politics transformed those narratives.

The Meanings of Class, the Politics of Realism, and the Public Sphere

The contested relations between narrative and class find further illumination in Irvine's and Poli's engagement with the problems of "realism" that recent critics have identified at the heart of the enterprise of social history. The decades during which Irvine and Poli launched their American careers were also the heyday of an American literary "realism" that found echoes in the entertainment techniques the two men deployed in more popular cultural arenas. According to the creeds of its most programmatic enthusiasts, American literary realism promised to mend the era's increasingly fractious class relations through a renunciation of sentimentality and melodrama in the name of "the facts." This was an effort akin to the attempt to see "reality" operating beneath the obfuscations of "culture" with which cultural historians currently charge social historians. In practice, and even in creed, however, literary realists never achieved this renunciation. They returned again and again to popular culture to explore the significance of class and other social distinctions they depicted. Revealingly, popular theater became an especially potent figure for these conundrums. Through their treatment of the entertainment sphere where Irvine and Poli met, realist authors betrayed misgivings about the authority of their representations of social distinction. In the process they raised haunting and persistent questions about the class politics of culture for which Irvine's and Poli's careers provide some provisional answers. A brief consideration of three such authors—William Dean Howells, Stephen Crane, and Theodore Dreiser—will serve to introduce realist problems that Irvine and Poli help to illuminate.

For these authors, realism involved an interrogation of popular culture, particularly popular theater, in search of "real" relations of class, but also profound uncertainty about the nature of those relations. This is a more complicated rendering of "realism" in relation to class distinctions and their cultural constructions than more recent debates between social and cultural history have often allowed. Howells, Crane, and Dreiser did try to craft authoritative accounts of "real" class relations. Without abandoning the notion that popular entertainments like theater could obscure such relations, however, they also pondered the ways in which popular cultural constructions of class distinction were themselves vividly real to their characters. As such, they captured an intermingling of social conflict and popular cultural narrative that figures prominently in the cultural politics of class that Alexander Irvine and Sylvester Poli engaged at the level of "popular" rather than "literary" realism.

Popular theater served as a figure for anxieties about the class relations of realist representation from the first announcement of realism as an American literary creed. In the 1880s, William Dean Howells formulated this creed as an attack on both elitist hierarchy and cheap sensation in culture. In the "Editor's Study" columns for *Harper's Monthly*, where he mounted this attack, Howells proposed that realist "truth" could reveal ordinary human commonalities so that readers "may be all humbled and strengthened with a sense of their fraternity." But, while he championed literature that did not disdain the lives of "the mass," Howells also had qualms about a growing mass culture. The "literary elect," he insisted, could not foster a common humanity by succumbing to "savage tastes" that the "unthinking multitude" satisfied through "melodrama, impossible fiction, and the trapeze" as well as the circus, the burlesque, and the minstrel show. The common humanity Howells associated with realism required more active moral purposes from writers and readers than these entertainments demanded.[18]

As Howells tried to foster such moral purposes through realism, he often portrayed theater as an ambiguous cultural force that not only threatened realism's "common morality," but also asserted an inescapable "common culture" of its own. His *Harper's* columns portrayed theater as institutionally antirealist because "so much money has to be put in the frame of the picture that only the well-known chromo-effects in sentiment, character and situation can be afforded in the picture." But he also saw a more truthful drama growing out of "vernacular" stage characters—the rural Yankee, the "negro minstrel," the Irish "bhoy"— that were staples of nineteenth-century American popular theater and the basis of vaudeville. He found such vernaculars most convincingly portrayed by Edward Harrigan, a former minstrel and variety actor who expanded his short sketches of Lower East Side immigrant life into full-length plays during the 1880s. At his best, Howells suggested, Harrigan approached the highest achievement of realist art, in which "the illusion is so perfect that you lose the sense of being in the theatre; you are out of that world of conventions and traditions, and in the presence of the facts." But even Harrigan lapsed into sensation and romance, producing a forced, "sentimental" commonality in which he "quite forgets his realism." For Howells, entertainments like Harrigan's—and, later, Poli's—offered a cultural commons that competed with the one realist literature provided.[19]

This competition between entertainment and "realism" developed more ominous dimensions in Howells's fiction, particularly the novels *Annie Kilburn* and *A Hazard of New Fortunes*. These novels depict social worlds riven by misunderstandings and contests across class lines, yet inhabited by central characters who strive for a common morality to bridge such divides. In *Annie Kilburn*, the title character desires to "do good" in her hometown by reaching from her position in the town's native elite to help its working-class factory hands. Her efforts are subverted by a plan hatched by the town's fashionable suburbanites: a program of amateur theatricals to raise funds for a "Social Union" that the privileged will run for the cultural benefit of the working class. At the public performance of the theatricals, elites and workers mix poorly, demonstrating that a slight theatrical culture is inadequate to produce authentic common experiences. However, the alternative, Christian social vision offered in the novel is hardly more compelling. Howells associates this vision with the Reverend Julius Peck, an ardent critic of the Social Union that the theatricals are designed to support. Peck convinces Annie Kilburn that the rich cannot create sympathetic relations for the poor with their money, and she eventually helps found a Social Union organized and run by working people themselves, as he advises. While the minister undermines self-serving notions of charity among his privileged parishioners, however, he proves inept at sympathizing with the factory hands. He cannot see that pretensions to "refinement"—the very cultural presumptions of the privileged—are part of working-class aspiration, as local workers confirm by subscribing enthusiastically for tickets to the theatricals' most exclusive seats. They thereby contribute substantially to the fund with which Annie helps found a more authentic Social Union at the end of the novel. Its origin in the success of the theatricals leaves doubts as to the opposition between "real" and "theatrical" commonality, as if Howells recognized in the morals of his realist creed the same impracticality he attributed to Peck's Christian ideals.[20]

In A Hazard of New Fortunes, Howells explored similar ambiguities within the social divisions of urban industrial life. Hazard focuses on a group of characters concerned with a literary journal in New York City. Its editor, Basil March, comes closest to articulating Howellsian realist principles, but also demonstrates the difficulty of achieving realist representation untinged by theatrical sentimentality. As he gathers impressions of the city for his own literary sketches, March regards the elevated as "better than the theater, of which it reminded him," as it offers slices of life through passing windows. And when he and his wife become overwhelmed by the moral complexities of living in a city filled with destitute beggars, March demonstrates the fragility of his own realist morals by recommending that they forget such problems by going to the theater. Again, however, Howells offers rather paltry alternatives to theatrical culture. As in Annie Kilburn, he finds these alternatives in the moral purposes of Christian characters who strive to meet the poor on their own cultural ground rather than romanticizing or vilifying them from "above." But, like the Reverend Peck, Hazard's Christian Socialists are also faulty realists. One, Conrad Dryfoos, dies futilely in a violent railway strike in which he intervenes because he sentimentally imagines that the other, Miss Vance, wants him to stop the mayhem. When the Marches encounter Miss Vance at the end of the novel in the garb of a Protestant sister, "the peace that passeth understanding" seems to look at them from her eyes. But they cannot be certain she has resolved her sense of responsibility for Conrad's death. "Well," Basil March philosophizes, "we must trust that look of hers," putting faith in appearances which, as he has remarked of a beggar they met at the beginning of the novel, may well be mere playacting.[21]

Howells's realist misgivings about how theatricality featured in the contemporary experiences of class distinction foreshadowed directions taken by younger realists writing in the 1890s. In novels such as Stephen Crane's *Maggie: A Girl of the Streets* and Theodore Dreiser's *Sister Carrie*, popular theater becomes a central medium of social distinctions, so much so that some critics imply that Crane and Dreiser dispensed with Howells's concerns about class relations in order to refashion realism as a struggle with the dilemmas of commercial culture. Rather than focusing on the portrayals of working-class poverty for which previous generations praised these novels, such critics emphasize how Crane and Dreiser depicted capitalism as a market system generating speculative desires and self-transformations.[22] But, while it is true that Crane and Dreiser no longer conceived of realism as a means of expanding genteel literary practices to embrace working-class experiences, they still worried over the class relations of representation implicit in the alternative realist projects they took on. As with Howells, moreover, Christian sympathy offered a foil for the ambiguous cultural authority they wielded. In rebellion against his family's middle-class Protestant pieties, Crane pictured in *Maggie* a tenement environment hermetically sealed against elite cultural pretension or middle-class evangelical sentimentality. In *Sister Carrie*, Dreiser resorted to evolutionary expertise to explain the appeal of the theater's seductive cultural hierarchies for working-class youths from pious backgrounds such as his dour Catholic father had tried to create. Together, the two narratives register anxieties about competing notions of cultural class relations with which Alexander Irvine and Sylvester Poli also contended.

In Crane's novel, Maggie Johnson attends a series of popular theaters that inspire her to believe she can rise above her tenement home and factory job, but only ensnare her more deeply in the miseries of her enclosed working-class world. This narrative parodied Protestant pieties Crane had repudiated. As in his father's 1869 handbook *Popular Amusements*, which outlined conventional

Methodist perspectives on recreation, the theater appears in *Maggie* as an arena that fosters class distinctions through outrages on female purity. But, rather than dragging youths of "high social position" to the level of "lower class morality," as in the elder Crane's treatise, the theaters in *Maggie* sustain the monotonous shabbiness of the tenement environment. They exact Maggie's moral "ruin" by tantalizing her with a false promise that there is a cultural "up" and "down."[23]

However, the cultural politics of class were more complicated than Crane's filial defiance alone addressed. By the time Crane was writing *Maggie*, reformers of the sort who employed Alexander Irvine sought to reclaim the tenements for Protestant morals rather than shunning their inhabitants. *Maggie* refuses this approach to social division as well. It takes as a specific target tenement house reformer Jacob Riis, whom Crane had seen offer stereopticon lectures while reporting on Jersey shore society events for the *New York Tribune* in 1892. In his lectures, Riis used photographs that he had carefully constructed to make tenement disorder and darkness appear as the product of a casual, amateurish photograph practice that registered facts of nature rather than the idealizations of art. Alternating these photographs with images of the light, orderly world of Fifth Avenue, he offered himself as a guide who could make the tenement world comprehensible in terms of his affluent audiences' own moral boundaries and categories. Throughout *How the Other Half Lives*, the book based on his tenement investigations, Riis noted "lines" that distinguished the moral nuances of class distinction: the line between the honest poor and lazy shirkers, the clothes line, the color line. Crane countered this conceit by parodying one of Riis's favorite symbols of moral distinction, the "womanhood pure and undefiled" that mysteriously "blossoms forth" in the tenements. Maggie Johnson "blossoms in a mud puddle," growing into a "rare and wonderful production of tenement life: a pretty girl." Rather than becoming a "gleam of hope" allied to a reforming adventurer, Maggie is pretty only in the eyes of other tenement dwellers, who ensnare her in an encompassing misery unrelieved by the moral distinctions of Riis's reform narrative.[24]

Maggie's theatrical scenes complicate Crane's parodies of his father and Jacob Riis by betraying his uncertainty about the realist techniques he deploys to depict tenement life as an autonomous cultural world. The oft-cited discrepancy between Crane's highly mannered descriptive prose and the vulgar language of his characters is central to his realist strategy.[25] His descriptive prose is lofty, as in his portrayal of a group of fighting boys as "tattered gamins" with "small convulsed faces" on which "shone the grins of true assassins." His characters speak a coarse language far removed from the eloquence of his descriptions, as in the case of Maggie's lover Pete describing an altercation uptown: "'Oh, gee,' I says, 'oh gee, go teh hell and git off deh eart',' like dat." This disparity serves as a version of what art historians Charles Rosen and Henry Zerner identify as the realist "double claim," first to abstract beauty—"uninfluenced by the world that is represented"—and, second, to absolute truth—"undistracted by aesthetic [or moral] preconceptions." Making this claim through *Maggie*'s disparate languages, Crane guaranteed his repudiation of the moral "meanings" that evangelistic Protestants like his father and moral reformers like Riis imposed on "lower class" life.[26]

However, the theatrical scenes in the novel throw into question the viability of the distinction between "elevated" and "crude" culture on which Crane's double claim depends. From the beginning of the novel, Maggie looks to the theater as a spectacle of aesthetic distinctions that might lead to a "rose-tinted" future, distant from her tenement existence. But these distinctions prove illusory: they excite Maggie in ways that only enhance her appeal for the men who prey on her at the theater. Similarly, the languages of the novel also produce illusory distinctions. These linguistic distinctions communicate a vain hope of narrative escape from the distortions of moral "treatments" of the tenement world. But, just as Maggie's theatrical experiences never evade her tawdry tenement existence, so Crane's characters never present themselves to the narrator or reader unembellished by his descriptive art. By discrediting the claim to "objectivity" through which Crane mocks his father and Jacob Riis, *Maggie*'s theatrical scenes acknowledge that he imposes his own significance on the tenement scenes he depicts.

The novel's pervasive theatricality suggests that, despite Crane's "realist" claims, his vision of the tenement world's cultural autonomy amounts to a minutely directed stage set that he controls. Its characters enact a hierarchy of mastery over the theatrical realm that supports this vision of narrative authority. Entrapped by a theatrical spectacle that overawes her, Maggie occupies the bottom of this hierarchy. Pete does better by associating himself, in Maggie's eyes, with the illusory distinctions of the theatrical realm and thus seducing her. Nell, for whom Pete abandons Maggie, outdoes him in theatrical calculations by plying him with liquor and women and absconding with his money. Finally, by reducing Nell to a mere gesture in its descriptive eloquence—"a woman of brilliance and audacity"—the novel's narrative voice outdramatizes her and asserts its own theatrical authority.[27]

As other scenes reveal, however, the narrator's theatrical mastery is incomplete. Particularly when portraying Maggie's drunken mother Mary, the novel's narrative voice slips into theatrical excess, merging with the histrionic vulgarity in which Mary indulges. Mary's condemnation of her ruined daughter provides an especially vivid example:

> Maggie's mother paced to and fro, addressing the doorful of eyes, expounding like a glib showman at a museum. . . . "Dere she stands," she cried, wheeling suddenly and pointing with dramatic finger. "Dere she stands! Lookut her! Ain' she a dindy? An' she was so good as to come home to her mother, she was! Ain' she a beaut'? Ain' she a dindy? Fer Gawd's sake!"[28]

Here moral reform stalks its object as a "glib showman"—a showman who struts in the costume of moral righteousness, exhibiting vice with "dramatic finger." Equating moral and theatrical treatments of the tenements, Mary's burlesque reduces both of them to futility. In her character, the "otherness" Crane attributes to lower-class life subsumes any significance a narrator proposes for it. She stands as Crane's admission of the fragile narrative mastery afforded by his theatrical treatment of an "autonomous" working-class culture.

Sister Carrie also follows the trajectory of a young working woman who looks to the theater to escape to cultural realms beyond her lowly station. Unlike Maggie Johnson, however, Carrie Meeber finds that aesthetic distinctions displayed in the theater aid her in escaping the privations of working-class existence. A visit to the theater eases Carrie's move from the "round of toil" she shares in her sister's drab Chicago flat, where she pays rent earned as a factory hand, to a more morally ambiguous but materially alluring existence living, unmarried, with the flashy salesman Charles Drouet. Another theatrical outing shifts Carrie's aspirations from the "round of pleasure" Drouet represents to the "higher" cultural level associated with the elegant saloon manager George Hurstwood. After Hurstwood transports Carrie from Chicago to New York, new rounds of theatrical pleasure make her discontented with the pleasures he provides. Ultimately, Carrie tries to escape the disappointment that theatrical spectacles generate about each new level on the hierarchy she ascends by becoming part of the spectacle herself. A mode of experiencing class difference, theatricality in *Sister Carrie* also becomes a way of achieving status mobility, and perhaps of transcending the shifting values of the hierarchy of status.[29]

Dreiser's anxiety about this treatment of class distinction turns on the problem of identifying the "real" sources of Carrie's theatrical and social rise. While she appears to climb a flimsy hierarchy made up of fluctuating status gradations, the novel's narrative voice repeatedly intervenes to displace this dazzling spectrum with a truer calculation of human worth. It derives this calculation from an evolutionary knowledge that locates "our civilization" at a "middle stage, scarcely beast, in that it is no longer wholly guided by instinct, scarcely human, in that it is not yet wholly guided by reason." So, too, in Carrie, "instinct and reason, desire and understanding were at war for the mastery." The novel's narrative voice claims to see through her desires to more fundamental forces determining her fate. It attributes her artistic yearnings to the "underworld of toil from which she had so recently sprung," which she transforms through art into a genius that renders her "representative of all desire." This is an aggregate not measurable by the relative standards that render a Drouet or a Hurstwood attractive. Carrie's genius springs instead from the substantial achievements of proletarian labor, which produces more enduring values. Basing its appreciation for these values on an understanding of evolution to which Alexander Irvine would also lay claim, Sister Carrie's narrative voice deploys this understanding in ways that mediate conundrums of religion and theater Dreiser had experienced as a youth. Dreiser experienced his father's immigrant, working-class Catholicism as an obstacle to the delights he and his siblings associated with theatrical entertainment. Evolutionary science provided an alternative conception of human motivation that dispersed both his father's religious obsessions and the theater's chimerical hierarchies.[30]

For all its flourishes of scientific authority, however, Sister Carrie's narrative voice remains diffident about its knowledge concerning the sources of Carrie's rise. This uncertainty surfaces with particular poignancy in the narrator's explanation of Carrie's attraction to Drouet early in the novel. Instead of displacing theatrical spectacle, this explanation seems to magnify its power:

> If it were not for the artificial fires of merriment, the rush of profit-seeking trade, and pleasure-selling amusements . . . if our streets were not strung with signs of gorgeous hues and thronged with hurrying purchasers, we would quickly discover how firmly the chill hand of winter lays upon the heart; how dispiriting the days during which the sun with-holds a portion of our allowance of light and warmth. We are more dependent upon these things than it is often thought. We are insects produced by heat, and pass without it.[31]

The ambiguity of this passage turns on the words "these things." Ostensibly they refer to the "light and warmth" of the sun, but the richly described "artificial fires of merriment" contend far more powerfully as objects of human dependence.

Read as identifying these "artificial fires" as the "heat" that humans require, the passage produces a concise statement of the uncertainty at the heart of the evolutionary knowledge that Dreiser's narrative voice deploys. "If it were not for the glitter of the theatre and all the allurements of status arrayed there, we would know the forces which truly move us, which determine human life and relations. We would know that these are determined by the glitter of the theatre and the allurements of status arrayed there." The narrative voice of *Sister Carrie* pretends to evolutionary knowledge that uncovers "real" class experience beneath the illusory, theatrical distinctions of status. But it also fears that, upon probing this reality, it may find only the status distinctions that its knowledge supposedly overturned.

Considered together, *Maggie* and *Sister Carrie* map conceptions of cultural class relations that were widely contested in Irvine's and Poli's time and continue to receive varied treatment from American social and cultural historians. Crane pictured class distinctions in terms of a working-class cultural autonomy that Irvine's laborite allies and Poli's popular audiences often wielded for themselves. Trade unionists and ethnic leaders emphasized the peculiar cultural values cultivated within the communities they claimed to represent, though usually they portrayed these autonomous cultures as far less stifling than Maggie's tenement world. Dreiser's alternative vision of class distinctions as a hierarchy of status gradations also found expression among the working-class allies and audiences Irvine and Poli engaged. The middle-class Protestant reformers Crane parodied had no corner on hierarchical notions of self-improvement: workingmen's praying bands and labor movements also subscribed to such ideals, often redefining them to suit their own conditions. Popular theaters like Poli's displayed such competing conceptions of cultural hierarchy to audiences who also subscribed to notions of cultural autonomy. In short, Irvine and Poli participated in cultural politics of class distinction that combined conceptions of cultural hierarchy and cultural autonomy in ways that complicated not only the portrayals of class distinction offered by literary realists, who registered such challenges in the uncertainty of their texts, but also more recent reconstructions of American cultural history. These reconstructions offer informative pictures of the autonomous cultural standards that working men and women developed and of the shared cultural hierarchies that diverse audiences increasingly accepted.[32] While Irvine's and Poli's stories confirm both of these pictures, they also reveal the extent to which visions of class autonomy and cultural hierarchy intermingled within the cultural arenas they traversed.

Introduction

Such juxtapositions of cultural autonomy and cultural hierarchy character-ized the "popular realism" that Irvine, Poli, and their audiences generated. Pop-ular realism shared many themes and techniques with the literary and reformist "realisms" that Howells, Riis, Crane, and Dreiser developed. Like Howells and Riis, Poli mixed verisimilitude with moral purpose. His vaudeville advertisements also echoed literary realists' claims that they authentically represented workers' and immigrants' autonomous cultural worlds, though derogatory vaudeville sketches about these groups demonstrated the complex cultural politics involved in such claims. In his sermons and literary self-representations, Irvine deployed realist strategies for representing working-class culture as well, including the stereopticon lecture and the undercover exploration. These methods shared in Dreiser's ambivalence about the chimerical hierarchies of popular culture: like Dreiser, Irvine and other investigative realists drew on evolutionary realism to discover the "real" determinants of class distinction. The difference between pop-ular realism and other realist deployments of these themes and methods lay in their approaches to cultural authority. In contrast to Howells, Riis, Crane, and Dreiser, Irvine and Poli did not stake their authority on any particular approach to the relation between cultural hierarchy and autonomy. Their performances and self-representations played to audiences who harbored multiple, sometimes conflicting perspectives on the cultural distinctions they addressed. Indeed, in Poli's commercial entertainment realm, such appeals to diverse audiences were practically the definition of success. This commercialization posed difficulties for the aesthetic or moral distinctions Poli and Irvine tried to assert through pop-ular realism, as Poli discovered when his vaudeville circuit was absorbed by a syn-dicate that figured the politics of "refinement" differently than he had, and Irvine found out when he tried to use vaudeville to convey socialist ideals. Still, by jux-taposing diverse perspectives on cultural hierarchy, popular realism reworked such hierarchies into cultural perspectives relevant to broader arenas of debate, including local politics, labor conflict, and socialist agitation.

Such debates made popular realism an important source for transformations of cultural concepts that informed widely ranging discourses of social distinction. This is especially true of the evolutionary imagery that Poli's entertainments and Irvine's popular self-representations shared with wider currents of popular real-ism as well as literary realism and academic social science. Such imagery de-ployed categories of "savagery" and "civilization" that displaced older, Protestant narratives of working-class uplift and interwove cultural hierarchies of class with scientific notions of racial, ethnic, and gender difference. Narratives of class dis-tinction that literary and popular realists improvised out of this mix reshaped conceptions of class in ways that give credence to current scholarly perspectives on the cultural construction of class. But, as debated and reworked among audiences for popular realism, such narratives also reveal the volatility of cultural constructions of class. Irvine, Poli, and their audiences deployed "savagery" and "civilization" to define diverse social differences, but often transformed the meanings of these terms in ways that demonstrate popular realism's contribution to broader twentieth-century reconceptualizations of class and culture.

These popular sources of intellectual transformation reveal important and unexplored dimensions of the public sphere Irvine and Poli shared with contemporary literary realists. In their engagement with popular realism, Irvine and Poli serve as guides to relationships within this sphere that authors like Howells, Crane, and Dreiser registered only as challenges to their own authority. Howells constructed his realist creed to defend as well as revise cultural standards associated with the genteel periodicals that employed him, which distributed refined literary culture to cultivated audiences. As he conceived it, realism would reunite readers tempted by commercial entertainment in a public sphere that took account of broader interests and needs than the genteel periodicals had acknowledged, but would also maintain that sphere's "standards" against commercialized sentiment. Crane and Dreiser, in contrast, constructed their realist projects in a literary public sphere steeped in commercial popular entertainment. Having begun as writers for the newspapers and mass market journals that fed such forces, their problem was not so much to defend and reform the boundaries of polite discourse that Howells patrolled, but to construct cultural authority out of the conventions of the commercial popular sphere in which they worked.[33] The tensions in their narratives betray an awareness that, as realist authors, they could not lay undisputed claim to the representation of class difference—that, in a widening public sphere, their representations contended with alternative notions of what class autonomy or cultural hierarchy could mean.

Irvine's and Poli's careers illuminate such alternatives among diverse groups who found in commercial culture and popular realism new access to public debates that had previously excluded them. As such, their stories revise the scenario of decline associated with commercial entertainment in Habermas's portrait of the public sphere. Though the market had been important in distributing cultural products to the newly formed publics of the late eighteenth century in Habermas's account, by the mid-nineteenth century and after, cultural industries conceived their products primarily as commodities for mass audiences seeking private comfort rather than public debate. In the process, characteristics of public sphere debate such as rational discourse and equal access dissolved as such debates addressed wider publics and their interests through commercial media and the bureaucratic state.[34] For Irvine and Poli and their audiences, however, culture industries like vaudeville also addressed public debates over cultural hierarchy among groups of workers, immigrants, and women, who had found more exclusive arenas of public debates closed to them. The commercial imperatives of vaudeville circumscribed the way Irvine and Poli engaged these debates, as we will see. However, such imperatives did not prevent them or their audiences from finding in entertainment interpretations and critiques that could take on important political implications in social arenas that surrounded the vaudeville theater.

As Irvine's career illustrates, religion was one arena in which the forms and themes of commercial culture provoked considerable public controversy. Though Habermas slighted religion in general and Protestantism in particular in his account—relegating it to the realm of domestic intimacy that informed but remained distinct from political issues discussed in public—other scholars taking up his ideas have reasserted the significance of religious discourses for the debates that shaped and transformed the public sphere. This is especially important for discussions of the public sphere in nineteenth-century America, where evangelical religion provided widely shared terms for debating slavery, women's rights, and labor reform, and was often intertwined with the Enlightenment rationalism that Habermas associates with public debate.[35] By the time Irvine arrived in the United States in the late 1880s, evangelical Protestantism was addressing new challenges posed by Darwinian science, escalating industrial conflict, and competing commercial entertainment. But it continued to provide a shared language for contests over the standards and inclusiveness of public debate. While leaders of evangelical institutions worried over competition from commercial amusements and circumscribed such entertainments in their own organizations, the populations they sought to reach, such as workingmen, were incorporating commercial popular culture into forms of worship they advanced as acceptable public demonstrations of piety. Their innovations provided contexts in which a figure like Irvine could use the forms and techniques of vaudeville to attract allies for public contests over the meaning of Christianity in industrial life. In the process, Irvine connected popular realism to wider intellectual transformations that reworked American concepts of class distinction, moving them away from Protestant hierarchies of self-improvement and toward modern notions of cultural relativism.

Irvine's evangelism and Poli's entertainment career also illuminate the plural character of the "publics" they traversed, a dimension of the public sphere that many scholars have criticized Habermas for neglecting. Historians of women, the working class, and African Americans, in particular, have noted that by portraying a single public sphere dominated by bourgeois standards of debate, Habermas overlooked the alternative "counterpublics" fashioned by subordinate groups who found themselves excluded from that debate. Coming together in female moral crusades, workingmen's parties, or black churches, these groups addressed questions the bourgeois public sphere ignored. In the process, they challenged that sphere's presumptions to "equality" and often questioned the standards of debate it enshrined by conducting their own discussions in forms deemed "uncivilized" by cultural elites who patrolled the "official" public sphere. To conceive of the "public sphere" in such plural terms also revises Habermas's account of its "decline." Historians of twentieth-century public culture suggest that counterpublics continue to provide alternatives to the commercialized, bureaucratic discourses that Habermas sees as dissolving the critical significance of public debate.[36] Irvine and Poli and the audiences they courted reveal this process of popular public critique at work in an era when the degrading influences involved in Habermas's "transformation" were just beginning. Already inspired by commercial popular entertainment to criticize the exclusive cultural standards of Protestant uplift, their audiences also formed "counterpublics" who questioned the hierarchies of popular amusements. Examining how ethnic organizations, socialist parties, and female audiences made sense of the politics of popular realism, this book contributes to a wider reevaluation of the public sphere as a divided arena in which commercial entertainment only complicated ongoing politics of unequal cultural power.

However, while this book recognizes multiple, overlapping venues where civic elites and workers, worshipers and entertainment audiences, men and women, immigrants and the native-born debated alternative standards of public discussion, I have not set out to map a set of autonomous publics and counterpublics among these groups. Rather, I seek to comprehend the terms in which they debated shared concepts of cultural hierarchy or autonomy. Through such terms and the narratives constructed from them, Irvine, Poli, and their audiences shaped and transformed, on a popular level, the significance of distinctions of class, race, ethnicity, and gender for public debates about culture. In the process, they helped forge the terms in which later-twentieth-century scholars conceive of the public as a cultural and political problem. Their stories illuminate the interests at stake in the cultural conflicts they engaged by revealing shared tropes of hierarchy and autonomy that various groups negotiated across the social distinctions they encountered in daily life.

encounters reveal what Howells, Crane, and Dreiser feared—that all ..npts to reconcile the tensions between cultural hierarchy and cultural autonomy through privileged access to standards of "art" or "science" were subject to challenge by social actors who saw their own well-being and self-respect at stake. These privileged spheres of culture were not the preserve of a bounded public that dissolved on contact with popular commercial culture or the class politics of industrial struggle. Instead, they included wide-ranging narratives of social distinction that Irvine, Poli, and their audiences put to diverse purposes forged on the stage and shop floor, in the trade union and in the pulpit. In these venues, they debated how the means of self-improvement and community life were distributed across distinctions of class, race, ethnicity, and gender—and how they could or should be distributed. The story that follows is a story of these debates. As reflected in the chapter titles, I have tried to tell that story in the terms Irvine, Poli, and their contemporaries used, as a way of understanding how these terms of cultural politics, and the social conflicts that shaped them, affected our own.

PART I

TRANSATLANTIC TRAJECTORIES
Learning Cultural Hierarchy in an Age of Empire

CHAPTER ONE

"A CELTIC PILGRIMAGE"

Culture, Class, and Evangelism in
Alexander Irvine's Global Apprenticeship

ALEXANDER IRVINE AND SYLVESTER POLI began their American careers in New York City during the 1880s, within a few years of one another, and quickly became immersed in the cultural conundrums of class. In Irvine's case, evangelical narratives that explained the plight of homeless men in terms of individual moral failing gradually gave way to questions about how material inequalities produced the impoverished lives to which he ministered. As a sculptor for New York's finest wax museum, Poli used the Haymarket anarchists—central players in an especially dramatic episode of America's increasingly antagonistic industrial conflicts—as the subject of a traveling exhibit that helped raise capital for his own entertainment enterprises. As they fashioned these public representations of class difference, the two men moved from New York's evangelical and entertainment industries to journeys across the Midwest and New England in pursuit of American careers equal to their ambitions. Along the way they attracted allies and audiences who demonstrated the complexities of American class distinction.

Neither Irvine nor Poli arrived in New York unprepared to ponder these complexities. Each carried some twenty-five years of experience with representations of cultural hierarchy and cultural autonomy in late-nineteenth-century Ireland, Britain, and Europe. Public cultures with intersecting agendas of revolution, nationalism, class conflict, evangelical ferment, and imperialism had shaped the cultural repertoires from which both men forged the ambitions they brought to the New World. In this respect, they did not encounter new cultural politics of hierarchy and autonomy in America so much as they refocused their own renditions of cultural hierarchies that linked the United States to wider currents of transatlantic cultural conflict and exchange. The two chapters that make up Part I address this global character of Irvine's and Poli's early education in the politics of culture and its relation to their early careers in America.

Irvine's pilgrimage from the Ulster town of Antrim to
work in the United States. This pilgrimage passed through
arenas that supplied Irvine with competing cultural standards.
the Antrim cobbler's shop where he spent his childhood; the cur-
evangelical revivalism that spanned the Atlantic; the British Royal
nes that taught Irvine to read and showed him a wider world; the tenement
neighborhoods of New York's Lower East Side where he worked as a missionary during his first years in America; and the winds of evangelical fervor, working-class mobilization, and Populist politics that blew across the American Midwest at the end of the nineteenth century. As he navigated the cultural currents
at play in these arenas, Irvine became acquainted with many of his era's most
perplexing cultural contests "from the bottom up," as his own autobiography
styled the perspective he personified. This is what makes his journey so illuminating. It mixed a startling range of types of knowledge, combining popular and
high culture in "traditional" and "modern" forms that defied boundaries others
drew between these categories. In the process, Irvine's trajectory participated in
wider intersections between plebeian cultural constructs and debates emanating from academic intellectual sources.

This is especially true of the evangelical ideals that loomed large in Irvine's
adolescent aspirations. These ideals carried Irvine far beyond the cramped cabin
where he spent his youth, bringing him in contact with men whose innovations
in religious thought and practice helped define some of the central cultural
debates of the age. As Irvine charted a course through these contests—over the
relation between secular and biblical truth, between Protestant morality and
economic deprivation, between piety and pleasure—he outlined the legacy of
a plebeian evangelical tradition that was much broader and longer than his own
trajectory. The ideals of this tradition shared much with the hierarchical cultural
values of Protestants who enjoyed greater educational and material privileges
than someone like Irvine. But, in the hearts and minds of working people on
both sides of the Atlantic, these ideals had taken on democratic and collective
meanings that Irvine echoed throughout his missionary career. His "Celtic pilgrimage"[1] is valuable in large part for showing how someone of his obscure origins
could make this tradition into a mission that addressed the economic, political,
and cultural contests associated with class difference in his maturity. This
achievement grew out of an international commerce in religious and political
ideas that began shaping Irvine's aspirations long before he imagined crossing
the Atlantic himself.

Cobbler's Shop Culture

Alexander Irvine spent his childhood in a twelve-by-sixteen-foot cottage crowded with the tools of a cobbler's trade and the domestic life of a family of ten. Jamie Irvine's workbench occupied the single window in the front room. A second window illuminated a small back room almost filled by the bed that Jamie shared with his wife Anna. The smallest Irvines slept in a loft above the bedroom; as younger children moved into the loft, older ones made beds on the dried mud floor. For meals, Anna pulled a table into the middle of the floor and set it with crockery kept in small dressers arranged along the walls. She surrounded the table with a bench and several stools—the Irvines owned no chairs. The main focus of family life was the wide, open fireplace that took up one end of the front room. The emblem of the cobbler's shop culture as Irvine memorialized it in his most famous memoir, *My Lady of the Chimney Corner,* this was the source of tea, broth, bread, and storytelling.[2] Between them, the cobbler's bench and chimney corner comprised a cultural crossroads that molded his developing ambitions.

In Irvine's memory, the multifaceted culture of the cobbler's shop was sharply distinguished from that of the "quality" who owned the local land and governed the town. Among other cultural prerogatives, "quality" enjoyed the privilege of officially representing the locality's interests to the world beyond it, and the world beyond to the locality. The family and visitors who gathered at the Irvines' partook only marginally of these concerns. Many of them encountered the daily newspapers that featured such information as parts of a cash nexus rather than as organs of common knowledge. Among the Irvines, only Anna and two or three of her oldest children could read. The ninth of twelve children, among whom eight survived to adulthood, Alexander was illiterate until after he left Antrim. But, from the age of nine or ten, he peddled newspapers to supplement his father's trade. As he later explained:

> Our people never bought any. They had no particular desire for either national or world news. . . . Our substitute for these essential elements of civilization make an amazing catalogue . . . our people, being limited in information, resorted to gossip, fairy tales, superstitions, racial and religious prejudices. Our music was the barrel organ, the German band, the street ballad singer, our drama the Punch and Judy show and maybe, once a year, a magic lantern in a church or hall—even then only a few saw them. Books were written to inspire us how to live or how not to live, but our people read no books.

The varieties of "news" available within Jamie Irvine's shop reveal the distinctive kinds of knowledge from which Irvine devised hopes he later reconstructed through the written word.[3]

Jamie's dwindling income offered one form of knowledge about the wider world. Outside the small market-town of Antrim—seventeen miles east in Belfast and, on greater scale, in the economies of England and Scotland—industrial production was overtaking the craft of shoemaking. In *My Lady* Irvine cast Anna as a prophet of this change: one scene depicts her reading from a weekly paper about the advent of machine-made shoes. In his autobiography, however, Irvine suggested that the family learned of this transformation without the help of written explanation:

> My father was a shoemaker, but something had gone wrong with the making of shoes. Improvements in machinery are pushed out into the commercial world, and explanations follow. A new shoemaker had arrived—a machine—and my father had to content himself with the mending of the work that the machine produced.

Whether or not Anna's reading heralded this shift, the Irvines could have registered its implications in their everyday interactions. The number of shoemakers in County Antrim fell 38 percent between 1871 and 1901. In the town of Antrim itself, the changed conditions of the trade altered the relations among those who continued to pursue it.[4]

Early in his career, Jamie Irvine attached himself to the shops of Antrim's master shoemakers. In these years the family enjoyed the benefits of Jamie and Anna's departure from the town of Crumlin ten miles away, where they were born, raised, wed, and then ostracized for their Protestant-Catholic marriage. While both towns lost trade and population during the second half of the nineteenth century, Antrim at least maintained the custom provided by semiannual agricultural fairs, by legal business transacted at its courthouse, and by its significance as the market center for the surrounding countryside. At first the couple lived in the home of Jamie's employer, but by the 1850s and 1860s the Irvine family enjoyed a modicum of independence in a series of small rented homes. These cabins were situated in "entries" nearby some of the town's prominent shoemakers—those who got listed in the trade and post-office directories. At the time of Alexander's birth in 1863 the family lived in "Rooney's Entry" near the establishment of shoemaker Andrew Rooney; soon afterward they moved to "Adair's Entry," named probably for the William Adair who lived on the street entrance but also nearby the workshop of shoemaker John Adair (today it is known as Pogue's entry). Jamie Irvine himself would never achieve the status of Rooney or Adair, with a shop listed in the local directory. The move from making shoes to cobbling machine-made uppers and soles placed him in a more dependent relation to another stratum of businessmen. In Alexander's childhood, Jamie took in cobbling from Barney McQuillan, one of two tradesmen who dealt in shoes and leather from the center of town.[5]

In the wake of this change, the family turned to sources of income that added new elements to their mix of knowledge and entertainment. Gone, until Alexander wistfully reconstructed it in adulthood, was the intertwining of work and family life when Jamie made boots with his older sons, singing "Black-Eyed Susan" toward the chimney corner where Anna prepared waxed ends. Once reduced to cobbling for McQuillan, Jamie found barely enough work for himself. He was often reduced to casual agricultural labor. At such times he profited from the dearth of laborers in the surrounding countryside and the corresponding rise in agricultural wages. Still, a pressing need for ready cash sent Alexander to peddling newspapers instead of attending the parish school, while older sons and daughters departed for places better equipped to offer employment. Their letters and visits provided new information about the world "over the hills and far away," as it was known in the cobbler's cottage. Often written for the correspondents by friends, such letters described the lives of a young woman clerking in a Belfast commercial firm, two laborers and a coal miner in Scotland, and, eventually, a marine educating himself aboard the flagship of Britain's Mediterranean fleet and then venturing to America as a missionary.[6]

As they departed on these journeys, the Irvine children joined a stream of migrants and emigrants who provided the cobbler's shop with news of the world beyond its ken. Some of this information came from America, whence many Ulster emigrants proceeded directly. Ulster had contributed the bulk of Irish emigrants to America in the eighteenth century, as descendants of Presbyterian farmers escaped conditions that threatened the economic and religious independence their ancestors had sought on Irish soil. The more prosperous of these journeyed in family groups, fleeing entrepreneurial landlords intent on transforming tenants into laborers in Ulster's developing linen industry. In the nineteenth century, new machines encroached not only on shoemaking but also on the weaving through which Ulster cottiers gained access to land, for which they competed with the children of small farmers. By this time, lower passage fares and established chain migrations allowed emigrants of more modest means a greater chance of material advancement in the New World. News of their success usually carried on the common life the emigrant had left behind, through remittances to assist in rent payments or farm improvements. Sometimes emigrants tried to include Irish relatives in new solidarities, either by sending passage to the New World or by supporting political struggles in Ireland. Only occasionally did they tell of a phenomenal individual success, such as that enjoyed by the former Antrim laborer who returned as a "Mr." during Alexander Irvine's childhood. At a lecture by this fortunate native son, Irvine discovered a new hero—a rail-splitter named Lincoln, who inspired him to believe that he could participate in the world described in the newspapers he sold.[7]

American influences like this one drew Irvine into vital currents of transatlantic social thought, political protest, and, eventually, religious ferment. Antrim itself had been the site of a particularly climactic scene provoked by Irish and American political cross-fertilization. The 1798 Battle of Antrim pitted United Irishmen emboldened into declaring an Irish republic by the rhetoric of both the American and the French Revolutions against government-supported military brigades. Though in early stages it combined Presbyterians and Catholics, the abortive revolt ultimately helped fuel the sectarian antagonism that has plagued Irvine's homeland since. It also stoked the British wariness of Irish political autonomy that resulted in the 1800 Act of Union. Over the next century Irvine's countrymen continued to draw on American ideas and dollars to combat the economic, political, and religious inequities that the Union symbolized.

The Fenian Brotherhood, a revolutionary nationalist society conceived and funded in America, continued such cross-Atlantic links during the mid-nineteenth century. In *My Lady of the Chimney Corner*, Irvine commemorated this history in the character of a Fenian farmer who aided Anna and Jamie during the famine years of the 1840s. Fenians were still active in America and Ireland during Irvine's youth, and among Protestants the name remained a favored epithet to disparage Irish-Catholic tenant and nationalist movements. But the Land League developed by Fenian veterans to organize Catholic tenant-farmers into a social movement would have found few adherents in the Irvines' area. Anna hailed from a modestly successful Catholic farming family, but most of the farmers living around Antrim were Presbyterians. They had their own heritage of resistance to English rule, but by the late nineteenth century many found in the Orange Order a common cause with Anglican elites in opposition to Irish nationalism.[8] The young Alexander thus had little knowledge of the transatlantic political ferment that the Land League generated in his adolescence. He would encounter its effects in America, still a long journey away.[9]

Migrants crossing the Irvine threshold usually ventured on shorter or more circuitous travels than those undertaken by voyagers bound directly for the New

World.[10] With no American relatives to send them the price of transatlantic passage, the Irvine children joined an already numerous class of "spalpeens" wandering around the province and back and forth to Scotland, seeking jobs as farm laborers, industrial workers, or miners. Set loose from rural and village homes by Ulster's rising rents and declining linen trade, such migrants found the Irvine hearth a convenient resting place to exchange stories while watching Jamie mend their much used footwear. They congregated in even greater numbers on agricultural fair days in May and November, when farmers came to town seeking hands for the next season's labor. In the course of their visits they supplemented the Irvine family's entertainment with stories of their journeys across the land and sea and up and down the social hierarchy, and with variations on tales of wee people and Celtic heroes already familiar to chimney corner audiences. Sometimes a ballad singer or fiddler appeared in the Irvines' entryway and provided musical interludes in the storytelling. On other occasions Anna read from a weekly paper of adventure and romance tales.[11]

These contributions to the cobbler's shop's entertainment formed a pattern of "traditional" and "modern" recreation that was widespread in the nineteenth century. Visiting bards lured to town to seek employment taught cobbler's shop audiences distinctive twists that storytellers from other towns gave to familiar legends. Meanwhile, the formulas of adventure and melodrama that prevailed in the story papers introduced Anna's listeners to entertainment fare popular in larger cities. The Antrim street offered glimpses of this urban fare as well, when a traveling dramatic troupe set up for an annual week-long stint of theatrical melodrama. Thus, as Alexander journeyed into the urban, industrial landscape of Britain and America, he did not move from a "traditional" culture to a "modern" destination, but between different arrangements of the traditional and the modern, the rural and the urban, the Old World and the New. His mission would deploy increasingly strategic versions of such cultural mixtures learned in the cobbler's shop's public sphere writ small.[12]

In the absence or weariness of storytellers and musicians, cobbler's shop entertainment often turned to religious topics. Married across Ireland's warring sects, Anna and Jamie had limited patience for religious prejudice; but their visitors, neighbors, and children reveled in it. Since the Irvines had a vague association with the Anglican parish church (the children were baptized there), orange-tinted vituperation of "papish" characteristics predominated among their visitors. But, cobble stones being no great respecters of credal differences, the pope's defenders needed to have their footwear mended as well. Ensuing arguments between orange and green translated one of Antrim's most readily available street recreations into verbal sport. Excluded from many benefits claimed for the Protestant ascendancy or the Catholic Church by those who represented their district to the wider world, the propertyless and untutored still borrowed queen, Church, or pope to inspire fistic battles that enlivened evenings and fair days.[13]

Catholic participants in these battles probably bore a closer, more sympathetic relation to their religious institutions and leaders than the Protestants enjoyed with their "learned men." In ministering to impoverished Irish Catholics and sharing to some extent their struggle against the English, the Catholic Church had become an important symbol for a distinctively Irish way of life. Building on this relationship, Antrim's Father O'Loughlin took special pains to protect the interests of his poorest parishioners from the predations of local Protestant magistrates during Alexander Irvine's childhood. As Roman Catholic chaplain of the Antrim Workhouse, O'Loughlin protested vehemently to the Board of Commissioners of the Poor Law regarding the domineering attitudes of the local, Protestant Board of Guardians toward him and his flocks. He complained that the Guardians insulted him, banned Catholic Testaments in the workhouse, and discharged Catholic orphans into non-Catholic homes.[14]

Whatever his sympathies with his parishioners, however, O'Loughlin enjoyed a freedom of movement that linked him more closely to his highly placed Protestant rivals than to Antrim's Catholic poor. He managed to escape further insults from the Protestant gentry by removing to a Brooklyn parish in 1870, just as the man who would become vicar of the local Anglican church during Alexander Irvine's adolescence, Reverend John Gordon Holmes, was sampling posts in Canada and New York.[15] Installed in Antrim in 1874, the parson frustrated the more zealous supporters of Protestant ascendancy by refusing to allow Orange Order flags to fly from the church steeple. But he did appeal to popular sectarianism by preaching unwavering Protestant superiority. Only after his own protracted journey across the waters that men such as Holmes and O'Loughlin bridged more easily would Irvine decide that the daily life of his youth, with its potatoes and stirabout, fairie stories and fights, had provided more bonds with his Catholic mates than either had with the gowned representatives of their divided creeds.[16]

The Irvine family did not completely lack examples of solidarities that cut across sectarian divisions, but such examples remained somewhat remote. There was local grocer John Kirk, whom Antrim townsfolk deemed "quare" because he worshiped at a Presbyterian church but supported Home Rule. Kirk expressed wider Presbyterian traditions of intellectual, religious, and economic independence that fed a fluctuating tenant right movement in the countryside. However, this remained a rare extension of Presbyterian radical traditions, which Alexander was unlikely to encounter among his poor neighbors. Numerically dominant in the area—census figures showed over half the population in the Antrim Poor Law Union were nominally Presbyterians, while the Church of Ireland claimed not quite 10 percent and the Catholic Church not quite 20 percent—Presbyterians were concentrated among thriving farmers and more prosperous tradesmen.[17]

Other fractures in the politics of religious sectarianism were symbolized by the Orange leader William Johnston of Ballykillbeg, whose countenance was a familiar image to the young Alexander from commemorative plates and cups proudly displayed in the Irvine household. As a parliamentary candidate in 1868, Johnston appealed to Belfast working-class defenders of outlawed Orange demonstrations in their struggle against the elite members of the Grand Orange Lodge of Ireland, who preferred to focus their efforts on resisting the imminent disestablishment of the Church of Ireland. Orangeism offered its working-class adherents opportunities to flaunt their version of ascendancy before working-class Catholics, which was more important to them than defending the legal status of the established church.[18] While such struggles contributed artifacts to the cobbler's shop culture, however, the Irvine family had little truck with emergent public cultures of Protestant class consciousness. Though it served as a local market for surrounding farms, Antrim was becoming a backwater of nineteenth-century social and economic development. Other towns in the county grew and gained new industries during the late nineteenth century, while in Antrim old manufactories like the paper mill and the cornmill closed, the local bleachworks were incorporated into the huge Belfast York Street Linen Company, and the working population deserted the town for industrial centers like Belfast and Glasgow.[19]

Among the plebeian communities that remained, poverty and illiteracy reinforced customary relations of patronage and subordination. Poor, untutored Anglicans were apt to feel such subordination especially acutely. Of all local denominations, the Church of Ireland spanned the greatest range of social conditions, from the lords of Antrim's Massareene Castle to the day laborers of the Irvine household. Illiteracy among Anglicans was second only to that among Roman Catholics, and nearly twice that among farming Presbyterians and shopkeeping Methodists.[20] As a result, families like the Irvines absorbed little class feeling from their brushes with cultures of popular print, piety, or proletarian feeling that raised questions about the social hierarchy they inhabited. In autobiography, story, and memoir, Alexander Irvine portrayed his family's unquestioning acquiescence in their lot. "Loyalty to the *status quo* used to be a fetish with us," he recalled, "submission to authority was our eleventh commandment and discontent was treason or worse." And, in another place:

> Beaconsfield was our political demigod, Gladstone, Mephistopheles, and Parnell our Catiline. We never heard them, never saw them, never read anything they said. Our learned men knew, and that was sufficient for us. We were taught to be content with that condition of life that God had mapped out for us. We were.[21]

Even so, such authorities also remained somewhat distant from the Irvines' day-to-day affairs. In Alexander Irvine's fond memory, this distance was measured in the contempt that sectarian prejudice received from the chimney corner and the cobbler's bench. In *My Lady*, Irvine pictured Anna complaining that sectarians used Bible texts to fight each other rather than to find "pace of the heart." Jamie expressed more earthly doubts regarding religious divisions, replying to a neighbor's hatred of the pope, "That's blether, Ben; it's worse nor blether, it's a ha' penny pistol cocked in people's faces, until they come t' believe it's a loaded revolver. . . . If th' Queen lived at wan en ov th' street, an' the Pope at th' other, it wouldn't make onny difference t' me. Their oul' boots wud niver come down our entry t' git mended. No, 'deed they wudn't!"[22] The undertone of class feeling in this remark conflicts with the absence of such sentiments that Alexander Irvine usually attributed to his family—it seems to owe much to the gospel of work that he absorbed during his ministry in America. In the context of the Irvine family's relation to religious practices and institutions more generally, however, it gives voice to the specifically plebeian terms in which beliefs and distinctions upheld by local authorities were assimilated by the Antrim poor.

With respect to religion, in particular, the Irvines willingly used resources tendered by local Protestant authorities, but they did not feel any obligation to adopt wholesale the pieties, prejudices, or practices such agents sought to inculcate. For the everyday purposes of the Irvine household, religious teaching became a form of entertainment. In the exchanges of stories between family members and visitors gathered around the hearth, the weekly offering of the Methodist tract distributor took its place as a narrative resource alongside tales of adventure and romance Anna read from the *Weekly Budget*, or those constructed out of her own and her guests' received fund of Celtic lore. Meanwhile, loyalties to local religious institutions were determined in part by the allure of the entertainments they could provide. Christmas brought an annual demonstration of this contingency, as customary (if not regular) attendants at the parish church Sunday school drifted off to the rival Methodist establishment. No theological nicety prompted the shift: the Methodists gained their Yuletide popularity from their custom of giving a Christmas soiree, complete with free coffee, buns, and an address by a missionary with a tale of adventurous escape from savage heathens. Alexander remembered retaining his Wesleyan connection long enough every year to enjoy the Methodist watch night service. This "doleful, somber occasion" appealed to his imagination, coloring it with vivid images of hellfire that helped reconcile him to the cold pavement under his feet. In later life he catalogued this among the "thrills" of his childhood, a category that also included a lecture on *Pilgrim's Progress* illustrated with a magic lantern.[23]

In adulthood, Alexander Irvine fashioned a poignant vignette featuring a visit from the local tract distributor, Miss Clarke, in order to capture the distinctive shape his family gave to the religious blandishments offered by their more prosperous townsfolk. According to Irvine's recollections, the tract *Buy Your Own Cherries!* had provided an enjoyable contribution to the Irvines' evening entertainment when Anna read it to assembled family and guests. The story details the meteoric rise of a young workingman after a local publican refuses him a cherry from the full bowl on her counter. Recognizing the advantages of buying his own cherries rather than buying hers with his patronage, he rapidly improves his family's food and clothing, moves them to a finer neighborhood, rises from employee to manager to a life of leisure, educates his children for professional careers, and becomes an active church member. Within the world of the cobbler's shop Irvine recreated in *My Lady of the Chimney Corner*, the story outlined the improvements Anna hoped to transfer from her own education to her husband and children. Daily struggles for bread, tea, and a modicum of order in a close and teeming cabin, along with the liquor she used to assuage her disappointments, kept Anna from offering much more than cheerful stories and Bible lessons. But she might still borrow from the narratives of the tract society to impart some of what she wished to offer, adding it to the fairy legends and commercial story papers that provided her stock of sunny visions of transformation.

What made the tract a part of the cobbler's shop culture was Anna's sympathy with the needs and desires that insulated its participants from the condescensions of the tract distributor and the church authorities. In Irvine's vignette, Anna articulates this division for the cobbler's shop as a whole. When Miss Clarke arrives to collect the tract, young Alexander is commissioned by the family to go to the door and return it. The pious Methodist sees in their exchange an opportunity to expound on the ethics of private property that make *buying* cherries more virtuous than picking them from the wild trees around Antrim, as Alexander does. But Anna cuts this lesson short and gently rebukes Miss Clarke, pointing out that "because we've no choice ye come down here like a petty sessions-magistrate an' make my bhoy feel like a thief because he goes like a crow an' picks a wild cherry or a sloe that wud rot on the tree." She finishes with her own Bible lesson from Luke 13 and 19, admonishing "d'ye think He cares less fur boys than birds?" Whatever her improving visions, Anna enforced a distinction between those friends who entered her cottage at will to share its plebeian camaraderie and others, like the vicar and the tract distributor (sister of bleaching green managers and the workhouse matron), who prudently knocked at the door. Though she borrowed Miss Clarke's wares to instruct her audiences, Anna still wanted "no glory here or hereafter that Jamie [who "glunched" at donning a dickey to attend his children's baptisms and never learned to read] cannot share."[24]

Through such uses of religion, the Irvines shaped recreational relief and moral teaching to the cultural possibilities and material horizons of the cobbler's shop. Despite the limited horizons the shop afforded, the components of this culture were remarkably diverse. They made up a complex web of traditional oral culture, the cultures of popular commercial theater and print, and transatlantic cultures of piety and protest. As they wove this web to the dimensions of their own needs and desires, the participants in the cobbler's shop culture took part in the expansive public sphere whose contours Alexander Irvine would probe and contest for the rest of his life. Still, the material confines of their lives limited their agency within this sphere. Audiences for Anna's blend of piety and pleasure might well spread her homilies and humor on their travels; her son Alexander was probably only the most widely published popularizer of the chimney corner's cultural fare. But Anna, Jamie, and their children and neighbors did not have the authority or the resources to distribute their cultural perspective as systematically as Miss Clarke, let alone widely connected local luminaries such as O'Loughlin or Holmes. Limited by its material dependence on the diminishing income of cobbling, the Irvines' culture was also "cobbled" out of currents of piety and pleasure they had little power to direct and control. Their mixture of these cultural elements was a fragile one, open to new patterns and meanings as their relations with one another and with the wider public sphere in which they participated shifted around them. Alexander Irvine's evangelical conversion irrevocably altered his own connection to the cobbler's shop culture.

Religious Calling

The town of Antrim nestles against the northeast edge of Lough Neagh, the largest lake in the British Isles. In adulthood, Irvine cursed the stone walls that hid the Lough from his boyhood view, reserving this vista for aristocrats welcomed to the castle grounds rimming the shore. Walls could not contain every visual pleasure that Lough Neagh offered, however. At sunset the light refracted over its waters into the clouds might produce a celestial canvas of breathtaking color. Just such a spectacle helped arouse in adolescent Alexander an emotional sensation to which he later traced his religious mission. Employed as a scarecrow in a potato field owned by James Chaine—a local gentryman and owner of extensive bleaching greens—Irvine had ample time to hum hymn tunes while pondering the scene around him. When one evening a stunning Antrim sunset enhanced these pleasures, the young farm laborer was moved to tears and prayer by the effect. A "sense of awe" and "convincement of love" moved him to "indescribable ecstasy." As he reflected in retrospect, the warm glow of this inner vision "seemed to raise me from the condition of an inert clod of clay to soul-consciousness."[25]

Arising the morning after this potato field epiphany with the sense of awe intact, Irvine recalled, he became dissatisfied with his ragged and unwashed aspect. New exertions at hygiene, along with his promotion to stableboy at Mr. Chaine's, enhanced his personal grooming and introduced him to boiled linen. Both inner and outer transformations pointed him toward an active participation in the parish Sunday school, where he could enhance his knowledge of religion and sport a white shirt and collar. There the capacity for recitation, instilled by years of listening to fairy stories at home, stood him in good stead for memorizing Bible verses. He exhausted the grades of the Sunday school and prepared for his June 1880 confirmation with his illiteracy posing a handicap but no debilitating impediment, though he experienced it as a matter of shame. When he sought to join the vicar's Bible class, for example, Irvine found that co-religionists more accustomed to clean shirts and studious habits would not tolerate his illiteracy and the humble social status it betrayed. His attempt to join a newly formed YMCA brought a similar rebuff. But Irvine remained firm in his new cultural aspirations.[26]

These aspirations were fed in part by the new association with "quality" Irvine enjoyed at the Chaine estate, where the material life of the gentry made tangible the refinements of spiritual knowledge he sought at church. Irvine's new posi-

tion afforded glimpses of luxury and ease beyond his previous imaginings—
"a world of beauty for God's good people." Meanwhile his duties as groom
revealed a troubling gap between the comfort arranged for the master's horses
and that available for humans within the economies of a crowded cobbler's shop.
Responding to his new awareness of class differences within the confines set by
Antrim's social hierarchy, Irvine copied the ways of other eager flunkies. He
traded on his attachment to the master's house, associated with the best-dressed
working youths of the town, and attached himself to a sect that shaped his religious belief into a conviction that he could participate in the privileges of the
aristocracy by sharing their theological superiority. Though insufficient to elevate him into the vicar's Bible class or the Antrim YMCA, the logic of this superiority at least raised Irvine above the Catholics, which seemed a status worth
fighting for.[27]

In later life, Irvine represented his religious awakening and the social striving it provoked as episodes that separated him decisively from previous entertainments and associations. In retrospect it appeared a bittersweet division. He
could not regret the intimate sense of divine presence he had discovered in
Chaine's potato field, for he identified this as the primary source of all that gave
his life its greatest interest and purpose. But the way he had adapted his piety to
the contours of Antrim's social and religious distinctions inspired remorse. In
adulthood he was ashamed that haughty respectability and sectarian zeal had set
him against the cobbler's shop and its pleasures, and in the final chapters of *My
Lady* he sought restitution. In these scenes he depicted his youthful rectitude
as an alliance with forces of righteousness like the tract distributor and vicar who
supplied the cobbler's shop with religious material but disdained its plebeian
camaraderie. "'Are you wiser nor Mr. Holmes (the vicar), an' William Brennan
and Miss McGee?'" he recalled asking his mother. "'Them's th' ones that think
as I do—I mane I think as they do.'" By the fond light of Irvine's memory, Anna
recommended a more generous religious spirit. "No," she responded, "'deed I'm
not as wise as aany of thim, but standin' outside a wee bit I can see things that
can't be seen inside. Forby they haave no special pathway t' God that's shut t' me,
nor yer oul' father nor Willie Withero."[28] But the pious young Alexander felt
himself too exalted to help the old stonebreaker Withero shoulder his hammers
on the road to Antrim. As Jamie admonished in *My Lady*, "some o' ye young
upstarts whin ye git a dickey on an' a choke-me-tight collar think yer jist ready
t' sit down t' tay wi' God!"[29]

This mixture of personal rapture and social snobbery illuminates some of the
complex heritage conferred by the spirit of evangelical enthusiasm that nour-

ished Irvine's potato field afflatus. Though the precise moment of Irvine's conversion is difficult to pinpoint, it clearly occurred sometime during or in the wake of the revivals conducted throughout Britain by American evangelist Dwight L. Moody and his musical co-worker Ira Sankey. Moody and Sankey toured Ireland's largest cities—Belfast, Londonderry, and Dublin—in the fall of 1874; whether they passed through Antrim or not, their far-reaching influence would certainly have been felt there. At the very least, Irvine became acquainted with the simple hymns that Sankey popularized on this tour; his descriptions of his own religious awakening and its consequences suggest that he gleaned more than music from the Americans' religious crusade. The intimate sensation of Christian belief and forgiveness that Irvine recalled echoed the personal change of heart that Moody urged to massive meetings as well as in more private interchanges he held with the anxious in his inquiry rooms. In this respect, Moody followed generations of evangelists who had complained that arid theological doctrines prevented preachers from inspiring their congregations and who insisted on enthusiastic and often extempore preaching. He translated these legacies into simple, dramatic exhortation in order to free Christian feeling from the web of doctrinal disputes that had begun to fragment Protestant denominations along the new faults opened up by evolutionary science and historicist Bible criticism. But Moody did not mean to disrupt denominational and social hierarchies that earlier evangelists had challenged. He aimed to inspire converts to join or renew connections with existing churches. As a young convert, Irvine demonstrated this dimension of Moody's revivalism by moving rapidly from religious awakening to diligent—even fanatical—attachment to the forms and fashions of the parish church.[30]

Still, sectarian pieties like Irvine's developed in the context of competing meanings for nineteenth-century evangelical experience, both in mid-Victorian Antrim and on the global path of missionary zeal his conversion opened to him. Fifteen years before, County Antrim had been the font of a much more enthusiastic and unconventional revival than Moody offered, complete with popular reports of prostrations and stigmata frowned upon by church authorities. Inspired at its outset by accounts of lay revivals in the United States, the 1859 Ulster Revival and its offshoots in Scotland and England harked back to the more convulsive evangelicalism of the late eighteenth and early nineteenth centuries. In those inspired days, untutored enthusiasts roamed North America, Britain, and Ireland rebuking orthodox churches for arcane doctrines and restrictive membership that distanced ordinary people from the saving Word. Extending broad transatlantic traditions of democratic dissent, and enlivening them through the spread of the American camp meeting, such revivals helped swell the ranks of what Eric Hobsbawm styled the "labour sects." These churches, best exemplified by the Primitive Methodists, thrived throughout the first half of the century by committing themselves to an unpretentious, enthusiastic, and popularly accessible ministry. By the late nineteenth century, the forms of mass evangelism pioneered in the 1820s by Charles Grandison Finney and reformulated in the 1870s and 1880s by Moody and Sankey contributed to the decline of these more unruly and plebeian evangelical practices. But their legacy was by no means vanquished on either side of the Atlantic.[31]

It is in part because Irvine at first conformed so closely to Moody's revivalism that his story helps illuminate these complex evangelical legacies. Moody's revivalism contributed substantially to a transformation in revivalist culture that cast a long shadow on the interpretation of evangelical religion itself. Whereas social and denominational elites on both sides of the Atlantic often shunned the democratic enthusiasms stirred by earlier evangelists, they welcomed Moody and Sankey as antidotes to threatening social disorder and working-class restiveness. Moody organized his revivals like business enterprises, placed no importance on spells of fainting, and admonished those inspired to overly enthusiastic repetitions of "Amen" or "hallelujah" that "I can do all the hollering."[32] This reputation for restraint and the shift it signaled in evangelical culture has encouraged many social and religious historians to associate evangelical religion with "social control" and working-class submissiveness. According to such interpretations, nineteenth-century Protestant evangelicalism was primarily the religious tool of a politically aspirant middle class, whose economic individualism found pious expression in the evangelical emphasis on personal faith, and who discovered in revivals techniques of moral education required to transform subordinates into reliable employees. Many historians regard such religious teaching as unsuited to the daily lives, common culture, or collective economic interests of the working class; only those willing to exchange more sturdy proletarian solidarities for a bloodless bourgeois ideology, they argue, were attracted. While accurately reflecting some of the worldly purposes that evangelical culture has served—indeed, Moody himself castigated the proletarian politics that Irvine eventually embraced—such stock images obscure a more complicated, contested, and interesting public culture of nineteenth-century evangelicalism.[33] Initiated into piety along a path shaped by Moody's teaching, yet venturing to recast the revivalist's largely conservative social message, Irvine helps trace such contests across the broad social terrain his pilgrimage traversed.

Irvine began following Moody's path beyond the confines of Antrim soon after he was confirmed in the parish church. At his first stop along this journey, Irvine barely supported himself as a coachman and delivery boy for a Belfast clothes merchant. The highlight of this period, he recalled later, was "listening to 'Roarin' Hugh Hanna' thunder his preachments from the pulpit of St. Enochs." This excitement compounded the evangelical tangles Irvine had entered. Hanna was renowned for taking the enthusiasm of open air preaching to sectarian extremes: refusing to bow to magisterial requests that he desist from such preaching in the face of Catholic hostility, he helped incite riots between Catholics and Protestants in 1857. He also participated enthusiastically in the Ulster Revival of 1859. By the time of Irvine's Belfast sojourn, Hanna continued to draw large crowds to his revivalist, anti-Catholic rites and also won invitations to air his views in Scotland and North America. During the mid-1880s he thundered not only against the Catholic religion but also its association with the Land League and the American prophet of a single tax on land, Henry George. Echoing evangelical arguments that relied on the Bible to refute evolutionary science, Hanna advanced scriptural evidence for the primacy of private property in order to dismiss George's "economic science." In Hanna's example, Irvine encountered an extreme version of prevalent conservative evangelical approaches to social questions.[34]

By the time Hanna was lambasting Henry George, however, Irvine had moved on to other teachers. Following long-established paths of migration traveled by the spalpeens he had met in Jamie's cobbler's shop and many before them, he had departed Belfast to work alongside his coal mining brothers in Scotland. Irishmen made up more than two-thirds of the miners in Scottish mines by 1848, according to one estimate. Because they were often used as strikebreakers and were overwhelmingly Catholic, many Scottish miners held them in contempt.[35] For the Protestant Irvine, however, ethnic enmity was less troubling than the misery he endured as a miner's helper, which posed new complications to his spiritual and educational project. The sweaty underground labor of the pit and the crush of Scotland's sordid working-class housing left him little strength or liberty to pursue his aims. He now recalled with bitter longing the summer he had spent on Chaine's seaside property, where he had enjoyed a room and bed of his own. As he worked in the mines, Irvine remembered later, his goals of education and spiritual growth took the shape of ideals utterly opposed to the world of industrial work he had entered. He was encouraged in this view by a scholarly urban missionary who introduced him to further conundrums of evangelical culture.

Wearily searching Glasgow for inspiration to revive his flagging spiritual aspirations, Irvine chanced upon a Sunday evening service in the working-class suburb of Possilpark. He returned several times to hear the impressive young preacher speaking there, but every time he fell asleep. Asked for an account of himself, he explained his goals and conditions. His newfound teacher advised him to leave the coal pits to pursue his education.[36]

This Possilpark mentor was Henry Drummond, an ardent admirer of Dwight Moody who had accompanied the American evangelist on his tours of England, Scotland, and Ireland in the 1870s. The central attraction of Moody's message for Drummond was its vital interest in the individual, an interest that Drummond saw suffocated by academic debates over theology. Yet Drummond was also very involved in the central theological disputes of his day. The mission he had begun in Possilpark in 1878 competed with his labors as lecturer in natural science at Free Church College, where he worked toward the rapprochement between Protestant theology and evolutionary science for which he is best remembered. Thus, the education to which Drummond encouraged Irvine was not the stern insistence on a biblical inerrancy opposed to modern science that is often associated with late-nineteenth-century evangelical culture. In the 1880s such lines were not clearly drawn: though Dwight Moody had little sympathy with efforts to square theological doctrine and evolutionary thought, he maintained long friendships with thinkers like Drummond who were engaged in this project and featured them in his own educational institutions despite the criticism of more orthodox associates. In this milieu, evangelical converts like Irvine could make use of the democratization of the Word that was so central to the evangelical heritage without confining their ambitions for intellectual self-improvement to scriptural truth.[37]

There were limits to this democratization of knowledge, however. Drummond's amalgam of science and faith produced a "programme of Christianity" that made salvation and wisdom available to individuals who distinguished themselves from their fellows. While optimistic in its vision of human progress toward the Kingdom of God, this perspective accorded little place for militant demands made by working-class collectivities for increased leisure to pursue the aspirations Drummond approved. Indeed, Drummond calculated that the spiritual and intellectual enhancements he offered would ameliorate such disturbances. He taught that Christianity's "wider extension of horizon" tended to diminish worldly preoccupations and thus "to abolish unrest." In place of agitation, "[p]ersonal conversion means for life a personal religion, a personal trust in God, a personal debt to Christ, a personal dedication to his cause. These, brought about how you will, are supreme things to aim at, supreme losses if they are missed. Sanctification will come to masses only as it comes to individual men."[38]

Though often recommended by late-nineteenth-century evangelism, this was not the only conclusion to which plebeian conversion could lead. Another famous visitor to the Scottish coal mines explored the avenues of evangelistic self-improvement in the 1880s, but developed them in directions Irvine would not consider until the following decade. Keir Hardie had been working the mines thirteen years and was just beginning his career as a union leader at the time Irvine arrived in the pits. Young Hardie shared in many of the cultural currents that drove Irvine: converted in the wake of the Moody–Sankey mission to Scotland in the 1870s, he was an avid temperance worker who often attributed working-class distress to such individual moral failings as intemperance and improvidence. While he never completely abandoned this evangelical orientation, Hardie's involvement in the union struggles of Scottish miners during the 1880s decisively shifted his assessment of the alliances that could best facilitate improvements in miners' lives. The shift found its most fervent expression in what Fred Reid has termed Hardie's "conversion to Socialism": his developing conviction, fueled by contact with Social Democrats, that improvement in both the material and the moral conditions of working-class life awaited collective political control over the processes of production.[39] Hardie's experiences demonstrate the distinctive shape given to evangelicalism by turn-of-the-century working-class organizations. Since the ideological tendencies of the mainstream evangelicalism articulated by Moody and Drummond went against the grain of these principles, the deployment of evangelical language within working-class movements constituted an important alternative direction for the meaning of evangelical faith. Emphasis on trade union solidarity as a means toward self-improvement made the process of improvement a decisively collective rather than individual project.[40]

However, no one representing any of the Scottish miners' organizations that were forming at the time approached Irvine. Nor did he seek these out, his own developing class feeling remaining one of aspiration toward the cultural capacities he associated with Antrim's vicar and Possilpark's missionary. Drummond did not believe Irvine could, as a coal miner, realize the cultural possibilities opened by his conversion, and neither did Irvine. Setting out on Drummond's advice to seek work more congenial to his spiritual and educational aspirations, Irvine soon found a venue that seemed ideally suited to his purposes: the British Royal Marines.

The Education of a Marine

Somewhat less common than coal mining for a youth of Alexander Irvine's background, sea-soldiering offered him a hold on the cultural accoutrements he associated with his social "betters." His timing and choice of service were extremely apt for such self-improving purposes. Dependent on men from plebeian backgrounds who sought employment and adventure on its lower decks, the Navy had been enhancing the tenure and educational opportunities available to its ordinary recruits since the 1850s. The Marines had long enjoyed special favor in this respect, as officers depended on their loyalty and discipline to enforce each ship's social order at sea. Moreover, to the soldierly duties of the ordinary marine were added opportunities for ritual attendance on those above their station, as when they waited on officers dining in the wardroom or attended to the personal needs of the cadets of the midshipmen's' mess. Irvine served in both capacities, and in the process reveled in a new propinquity with men familiar with the cultural skills he admired. His seven years in uniform appear in Irvine's memoirs as a decisive transition in which he "evened the score" with those who enjoyed educational privileges his poverty in Antrim had denied him.[41]

Early on, Irvine's new career proved congenial to these aspirations. His initial training provided the access to reading and writing for which he had hungered since leaving Antrim as well as an array of lectures, prayer groups, and sermons. To enjoy these treats, he had to endure the derision of more ribald recruits and overcome self-consciousness about his ignorance and Irish brogue. But the rewards were tangible, especially when they came in the form of new access to advisors who had been more distant models in the past. Soon after arriving at corps headquarters in Portsmouth, Irvine attended a lecture by J. W. Kirton, the author of *Buy Your Own Cherries!*, and sought a private interview. Kirton recommended Dinah Maria Mulock's *John Halifax, Gentleman*. Irvine found the program of self-mastery advocated in Kirton's tract tantalizingly amplified by Mulock's story of a ragged orphan who, by honesty and fortitude, becomes the dignified owner of a prospering mill and the wise master of a graceful estate. One passage proved especially inspirational to a newly literate marine still daunted by the task of acquiring a knowledge of books. Early in John Halifax's development, he is asked by his benefactor's crippled son what he would do if he had to get over a high, thick yew hedge. The reply became Irvine's motto of self-education: "He smiled—there was no 'giving up' in that smile of his. 'I'll tell you what I'd do—I'd begin and break it, twig by twig, till I forced my way through, and got out safe at the other side.'" Irvine made prodigious progress by applying this method to learning.[42]

1. Alexander Irvine as a self-improving marine, at age nineteen.
Photo from Alexander Irvine, *From the Bottom Up: The Life Story of
Alexander Irvine* (New York: Doubleday-Page, 1910).

Advancing self-confidence soon brought him into further contact with
another early mentor, Henry Drummond. Having found a name for his potato
field ecstasy, Irvine began to speak publicly of his "conversion" whenever he had
the chance. Ordered to London with a dispatch to the Horse Guards, he seized
the opportunity for a week's leave to tell the story of his transformation to the
city's costermongers and unemployed. Introduced to an officer interested in such
work, he was invited to a meeting in the town house of a duke, "the most gorgeous place I had ever been in." The social intercourse of such a gathering was
beyond him, but he ventured out of his corner when Professor Drummond
appeared as the afternoon's speaker. Drummond expounded upon the philosophy he had been following when Irvine met him in Possilpark—"The Programme of Christianity." Irvine later recalled that the speech provided his first

inkling that religious fervor should relate to everyday life as well as otherworldly aims. He responded by more strenuous efforts both to cultivate his faith and to acquire secular knowledge.[43]

Still, for the most part, Irvine's program of maritime self-improvement held largely to the pious path that Dwight Moody's wide influence recommended. He found supportive fellow travelers among a group of Plymouth Brethren with whom he became associated on board HMS *Alexandra*, the Mediterranean flag-ship to which he was drafted in January 1883. Arising in the 1820s out of dissatisfactions with the worldliness of the Anglican Church, the Brethren sought to return to a purer, apostolic Christianity through lay preaching, an insistence on the inerrancy of the saving Word, and the experience of conversion as an emotional rebirth. Brethren organizations participated extensively in the complex heritage of evangelical enthusiasm and discipline from which Irvine was beginning to draw. The Ulster Revival of the 1850s swelled their ranks with converts who found their anti-ecclesiastical, gathered churches a respite from the formality of other denominations. In the next decades, the Brethren's otherworldly, premillennial expectation of Christ's return helped direct Dwight Moody away from the more optimistic and reformist postmillennialism that had focused mid-century revivalism on human efforts to improve the world. In this respect the Brethren, and especially their leader John Nelson Darby, provided a crucial link between the cultures of nineteenth-century evangelicalism, with their diverse enthusiasms for piety, reform, democracy, and improvement, and the more conservative and otherworldly perspective of twentieth-century Fundamentalism, which rejected the world as a wrecked vessel and looked for salvation in Christ's return. In the late nineteenth century, however, evangelical Protestants might share the Brethren's emphasis on personal testimony and missionary zeal without wholly embracing their dour predictions for the future, as Irvine's experience demonstrated.[44]

Irvine reveled in the Brethren's biblical expertise and joined wholeheartedly in the one earthly project they endorsed: the effort to win converts. In a context in which religious devotion generally met, at best, with disinterest and derogatory jibes, such support for Irvine's efforts to convey the awe he had felt in an Antrim potato field was attractive indeed. Even so, many of the cultural and social avenues Irvine found open to him as a marine did not accord with Brethren piety. The founders of the Plymouth Brethren sect had renounced earthly comforts to prepare for the Lord's imminent arrival, and adherents had little patience for secular culture or genteel refinement. But Irvine remained eager to master as much as he could of the culture of "quality" that had remained out of his reach in Antrim. Fellow Bible students might admonish when they found him devouring *Adam Bede* by fighting lamp, but they could not quench his thirst for worldly as well as spiritual accomplishment. Irvine's situation aboard the *Alexandra* was well suited to such purposes. Employed as body servant to the ship's paymaster and waiter in the officers' wardroom, he was excused from military and naval duty and came in contact with men whose conversation quickly expanded his vocabulary and the horizons of his curiosity. With only four hours a day required for his official tasks, he could make substantial use of the ship's library and school. He hid behind stanchions to avail himself of the junior officers' lessons, studied the histories of the lands the *Alexandra* visited, and found young officers-in-training willing to teach him foreign languages.[45]

While Irvine strove to emulate the culture of the *Alexandra*'s officers, these were not the only influences that tried the Brethren's patience. After all, Irvine's intercourse with officers, though regular, was necessarily of a distant and subservient character. Messmates and other comrades of the lower deck provided the main companionship available to an ordinary recruit. Here piety was something of a disadvantage, especially since in Irvine's case it extended to temperance principles that led him, under Brethren counsel, to refuse his daily ration of rum. Such scruples disappointed his messmates, whose custom it was to exchange this commodity. But most of them were mollified by the conviviality that Irvine supplied by means of the Irish fairy stories and ready laughter that pained his religious comrades. For Irvine, this was early training in the combination of earnest evangelism and plebeian culture that he would come to wield more strategically in the coming decades.

When Irish folklore did not suffice to reconcile Irvine's lower-deck companions to his moral ideals, he could resort to more pugnacious methods, which scandalized the Brethren still further. Irvine had learned the art of boxing in order to stand up to a training-depot sergeant who thought he was too focused on mental self-development, and he struggled against the impulse to use this skill to enhance his status among the enlisted men of the *Alexandra*. When a particularly surly member of his mess, Billy Creedan, provoked him with profanity reflecting lewdly on his mother, Irvine abandoned the stricture of his morals, met the challenge with his fists, and achieved new shipboard stature as a bruiser. He regretted these manly exhibitions as lapses in the virtue and refinement he was trying to cultivate. But they did provide tantalizing openings for his missionary ambitions, as other enlisted men seemed to extend their respect for his skill in the ring to his religious ideas. Such mixtures of manly performance and missionary zeal were also important preparations for Irvine's mission, during which he joined other prominent evangelists in pondering the meaning of Christianity for modern manhood.[46]

Officers of
H.M.S. Alexandra
on a Picnic
at Cattaro
in Hungary

Mr. Wood
Chief Engineer
Mr. Dewar
Paymaster

Younger, Colonel Philips servant

J.
O.
G.
I.

Heaven's
Light, Our
Guide

HOLY BIBLE

GOD
Save the Queen,

L
O
L
3.2.3

Protestant
Constitution of
England

King William's Own 323

2. During his Mediterranean tour with the Royal Marines,
Alexander Irvine recorded in his notebook his respect for the social
hierarchies of military life and reverence for the conventional
pieties of British Protestantism. Photo from Alexander Irvine,
"From the Bottom Up: IV, The Gordon Relief Expedition,"
The World's Work 18, no. 6 (1909).

For the time being, religious piety, cultural ambition, and youthful bravado hung in a balance that Irvine recorded poignantly in the only contemporary account of this period of his life that remains: a chronicle entitled *Three Days in the Holy Land*. This narrative describes Irvine's experiences as he tagged along with a company of officers on a tour of Jerusalem, Bethlehem, and other scriptural sites in late August 1884. The religious enthusiasm that made such a pilgrimage especially meaningful to Irvine is the most pervasive theme of his account. As soon as the company's caravan left the port of Jaffa, Irvine explains, he retrieved his Bible and began hunting for scriptural references to the towns they passed, often pitting his faith in the literal truth of such stories against the lore provided by their guide. Where the scenery did not lend itself to Bible study, Irvine and his rank-and-file comrade Hugh Best entertained themselves by singing Moody and Sankey hymns that enhanced the reverent mood in which they approached Jerusalem.

This mood blossomed into exaltation as Irvine toured Jerusalem, Gethsemane, and Bethlehem over the next two days. Reveling in his recently acquired skills of reading and writing, Irvine captured his feelings by setting down in print the Sunday school reminiscences, Bible verses, and hymns that had provided his earliest knowledge of the saving Word. At Calvary, "my thoughts went back to when I was an attentive listener to the Bible stories read by my dear teacher Miss L. Fleming ten years ago. I stood there with my Bible under my left arm and my notebook and pencil in the right hand. I was in a reverie of thought." Other tales of his pilgrimage reveal the aggressive proselytism that had come to characterize his faith in the military. Counseled about his efforts to hire a horse by an old Jewish man who was heading to worship one evening, Irvine grasped at the opportunity for a prize convert and began haranguing the friendly stranger about the gospel:

> seeing that the Israelite could speak English very well, I resolved to have a talk with him on another subject, so I said is that a Bible in your hand, he made no answer, I said again, did you ever read the New Testament, to this he replied don't pay the Arab too much for the Horse, Jack, I asked him two or three other questions about religion, but he would not say one word about it.

But such tantalizing opportunities were infrequent. Most of *Three Days in the Holy Land* describes sacred places visited, reverent memories stirred, and favorite hymns intoned.[47]

While predominant, religious reverence competes with other themes in Irvine's Holy Land narrative. Several vignettes attest to his pride in mastering knowledge not gleaned from scriptural study. Irvine's facility with languages proved particularly useful, as many of the priests presiding over the sites of Christ's birth, life, and death spoke Italian, which he translated for his companions. Elsewhere, Irvine's description and commentary emulates the flowery prose of the Victorian literary marketplace, which he had also been sampling liberally since learning to read. Upon first seeing the city of Jerusalem as he approached on horseback, Irvine noted, "I stopped my horse, and raised my Helmet aloft in the direction of the City, and shouted at the top of my voice to my comrade; Jerusalem, Jerusalem, when my Comrade Hugh came up we rode leisurely up the road." Later, referring to an encounter with an *Alexandra* midshipman on whom he attended as a servant, Irvine described it as a discussion with "my gallant young master, A.H. Williamson." At mealtime Irvine and Hugh did not simply eat but did "ample justice to a very good dinner." Irvine was putting his recently acquired literary culture to ambitious use.

For the most part, such secular culture harmonized with Irvine's religious beliefs, but the trip also served to demonstrate that biblical truth as interpreted by the Plymouth Brethren was not universally accepted. Irvine recorded repeated arguments about the information offered by the guides. Indeed, he prefaced the account with an apologetic comment that "In giving a description of the places and the traditions connected with them, I can only relate it as it was related to me by the guide or dragoman who always accompanied us, although they do not always accord with Scripture." Though his narrative affirmed that Irvine gave greater credence to scriptural teachings, such difficulties betrayed wider conflicts over religious culture that lay on Irvine's horizon.[48]

Alongside religious faith and secular knowledge, a consciousness of social rank provided perhaps the most worldly of the themes that preoccupied Irvine in recounting his trip to the Holy Land. Granted special leave to participate, along with Best, in a tour designed principally for the upper echelons of the naval hierarchy, Irvine expressed an acute awareness of his lowly station. He described frequent efforts to propitiate those above his rank. At the very beginning of the trip, he was charged with the care of Admiral John Hay's luggage and refused to part with it until assured of its safe delivery at the admiral's hotel. Irvine also recalled beating a hasty retreat from a dining room full of officers to wait outside with Best until their superiors had finished eating. As his reference to his "gallant young master" suggests, Irvine accepted this social order in good humor. He even struggled to avoid embarrassing those above his rank with behavior they might find demeaning. He recounted one episode in Bethlehem when he and Best indulged themselves in a generous snack of grapes and then, seeing the admiral coming down the street, bolted into an alley as "we did not like to let him see us with such a huge bunch of grapes in our hands, because it looked so unsoldier-like." Such self-representations reveal Irvine's eagerness to avoid offending his superiors, but also display the hearty camaraderie he willingly indulged in with other recruits when social obsequies did not intervene. Manifesting itself in high-spirited donkey races with Best and the gifts purchased for his messmates, such fellow feeling provided a counterpoint to Irvine's hierarchical social observances.[49]

Soon after his trip to the Holy Land, Irvine seized on a further adventure that seems to have provoked his first misgivings about the hierarchies he had accepted in the military. Perhaps it was the exaltation of visiting scenes of scriptural stories that inspired this new purpose: to participate in the Gordon Relief Expedition. General Charles Gordon had gone to Khartoum in early 1884 to oversee the evacuation of Egyptian soldiers and civilians stranded by the victories of the Mahdist revolt in the Sudan. He was soon hemmed in by revolutionary troops of Muhammed Ahmad, a religious leader who claimed to be the Mahdi, the "expected one" of Sufi Islam, come to purify Muslim practice and wage a *jihad* to prepare the way for the millennium. Gordon's plight proved irksome to the halfhearted imperialists who sent him. An idiosyncratically pious officer who often weighed the wisdom of his commanders against the will of God, Gordon had a habit of precipitously shifting the terms of his command. No sooner did he arrive in Khartoum than he telegraphed back to Westminster that the "Mahdi must be smashed up." Having recently taken over the reluctant administration of Egypt, Gladstone and his cabinet were largely uninterested in committing further resources to the Sudan than those required to extract their unpredictable envoy. However, as a military hero and devout Christian, Gordon commanded the sympathy of the British public, monarch, and fighting forces, who were eager to see him saved and, later, avenged.

Irvine shared in this sympathy. He had caught a thrilling glimpse of Gordon as the popular soldier-saint was on his way to the Sudan the previous January. By December, news of the siege of Khartoum, combined with Gordon's reputation as a Christian, had captured Irvine's imagination as few military causes could. He offered his savings to take the place of the valet of a marine officer who had been called to serve under General Gerald Graham in the desert west of Suakin.[50] Irvine sped to Suakin just a month before the Mahdi captured Khartoum in January 1885, then remained another four months attached to Graham's staff.

In some respects this episode reinforced the self-improving reverence Irvine had demonstrated toward officers of the *Alexandra*. What impressed him most about Graham, he recalled, was the commander's "chaste use of English." Fired with concern for the evangelist-warrior on the Nile, however, Irvine also became more interested in soldierly duties. Graham's forces engaged in perpetual skirmishes with the Hadendowa Beja followers of Osman Digna, the Mahdi's strongest military leader in the eastern Sudan. Though Irvine did not figure in any battles himself, he became fascinated with the campaign and temporarily abandoned Bible and history books to map army and enemy encampments and speculate on military tactics. At one point this attention to the campaign won Irvine a commission to deliver marching orders to advance forts, and he learned later that his terrified progress through the furze bushes had figured in dispatches and might mean a promotion. This was as close to military glory as Irvine's marine experience was to take him, and served during World War I as testimony to younger soldiers that he had "done his bit in Egypt." For these purposes, Christian faith, cultural aspiration, and military duty seemed briefly to coalesce.[51]

As recalled in Irvine's autobiography, however, this introduction to imperial warfare also raised troubling questions. Demonstrations of the fury with which the British executed their belated Sudanese campaign made Irvine wonder. According to his reminiscence:

> There was somewhat of a mixture of my sentiment and feeling on this war. I wanted Gordon released, I wanted the war ended and the Soudanese beaten; but when I contrasted the spirit of the campaign with the spirit of Jesus, I often wished that I could lend my assistance to these black men of the desert who were fighting for the thing under their feet, and the home life of their tribe. But it was not until I was completely out of the desert that I was possessed of a loathing and disgust for the game of war as such. This disgust grew until I had completely ridden myself not only of the war spirit, but of the paraphernalia of the soldier.[52]

It is difficult to gauge how much of this sympathy Irvine actually experienced in the desert, since he left no contemporary record of this experience. The final sentences of this passage suggest that his second thoughts about the military developed only gradually. But in the larger context of Irvine's career, the Sudan seems to have provoked distressing doubts.

Despite misgivings in Westminster, the Sudan campaign contributed to the expanding imperial odyssey and its popular culture of racial superiority and exotic fascination—issues that Irvine would wrestle with for years. The grudging respect Irvine recalled for the forces of Osman Digna was itself popularized in more jingoistic terms by Kipling's famous tribute to the courage of the Beja "fuzzy wuzzies":

So 'ere's to you Fuzzy-Wuzzy, at your 'ome in the Soudan;
You're a pore benighted 'eathen but a first-class fightin' man
An' 'ere's to you, Fuzzy-Wuzzy, with your 'ayrick 'ead of 'air—
You big black boundin' beggar—for you broke a British square!

But, as Carolyn Steedman suggests in her reading of the autobiography of work-ing-class soldier and policeman John Pearman (which Pearman composed at the time Irvine was beginning his marine training), popular jingoism should not be too profusely attributed to the mass of fighting men. Both Pearman and Irvine, it is true, found terms to express their disaffection with imperial service only after their military careers had ended, and even then never completely lost their affec-tion for the discipline or camaraderie of military life. Still, their memoirs recall misgivings, perhaps inchoately felt, about aiding imperial exploits that paralleled in racial terms the inequities of class they knew at home. In Irvine's reminiscent identification with the Mahdist rebels there may well have been an added reli-gious dimension, a sympathy for people whose courage the British military defined as "fanaticism," a dismissal with which he was familiar. Irvine's stories about his own life suggest that his experience in the Sudan at least raised ques-tions about the narratives of class aspiration he had been following. Soon after his return to Britain, he began to struggle to imagine the trajectory along which his own life would progress. Christian piety, military duty, and self-improvement no longer melded into a satisfying plot.[53]

Perhaps this was partly because Irvine found, on returning to England and Ire-land, that some narratives that he could make out of his military education were complete. During his after-campaign furlough in early 1886, Irvine returned to Antrim to see his family and deliver his first lecture—not counting the testa-ments of faith he had uttered to the down and out of the London wharves. As he later described it, the event filled the town hall with local notables curious about the transformation of a young man who a few years before had been unable to read or write his own name. They were joined by Sunday school teach-ers who had taught him Bible verses, Sunday school scholars to whom he had passed on this knowledge, and the newsboys of the town whom he had person-ally rounded up. Irvine spoke to this crowd of Gordon and Khartoum and of his experiences on the desert, winning accolades and thanks from the town officers. Such a re-retelling of his desert adventures wove them into what Steedman has described as a standard narrative of the working-class soldier: he is rewarded for years of service to imperial causes from which he feels estranged by returning home to a society in which he is accorded new stature. This had been one of

Irvine's ambitions—to "even the score"—and the public acknowledgment signaled its achievement. But, in Irvine's account, this conclusion to his military adventure had an ambiguous denouement, since his new stature implied an alienation from his hometown. According to his recollection, he ended his speech by enjoining his audience to be kind to the newsboys: "It is too late now to help me," he admonished. "I am beyond your reach." If Irvine's struggle with Antrim's privations was over, there remained a question of what to reach for next.[54]

Irvine spent two years attempting to answer that question through further education, only to find that the wider worlds to which his new status seemed to entitle him were no more accommodating than Antrim. He finished his furlough with a brief period as a passman at Oxford, but felt woefully out of place, more at sea in his efforts to make progress in his studies than he had been in the Navy. Still—like Hardy's Jude in Christminster—Irvine eagerly sought counsel from the very authorities who represented the hierarchy that excluded him. He requested an audience with Benjamin Jowett, the Master of Balliol, and for the rest of his life remained reverently impressed by the few minutes that keeper of culture and refinement spent with him. He returned to the naval garrison at Portsmouth, where he continued his schooling. By 1887 he had secured a second degree certificate of education in the military schools and had been promoted to corporal. But the hierarchy and restriction of military life had become unbearable. In 1888 he deserted the Navy and headed for America.[55]

Though Irvine's own accounts and contemporary evidence suggest that he made the move out of frustration with the career trajectories and social hierarchies he had embraced in Britain, there was a further difficulty that seemed to push him toward new adventures. In 1886 Irvine had wed a young woman from Alverstoke, near Portsmouth, named Ellen Mary Skeens. This effort to bring his social striving to a domestic culmination was understandable, especially in light of his recent immersion in Victorian literature, which favored marriage as an essential ingredient in narratives of upward mobility. Throughout his Mediterranean tour, moreover, Irvine had resisted ubiquitous temptations in order to hold to the "purity, continence, and self-mastery" demanded by his religious beliefs. When he fell in love upon return, marriage no doubt seemed an appropriate solution to sexual desires as well as domestic ideals. By the time of Irvine's departure for America, the couple had two sons, William and Gordon.[56]

This was the first of many romantic and domestic experiments that failed to live up to Irvine's expectations. The precise difficulties Irvine encountered with "Nellie" remain obscure, for he never mentioned her in published work, and private documents of their life together seem to have disappeared. Perhaps she was more content with her own background as the daughter of a cabman and a mother who did not write her own name than he had become with his similarly modest beginnings. Perhaps the rigors of immigrant adventure did not appeal to her as they did to Irvine. According to their oldest son, Nellie accompanied her husband and children to America. In 1891, however, she was in Alverstoke to give birth to her third son, and by 1894 she appears to have died or abandoned the family. Irvine's public silence about their lives together suggests a profound disappointment attached to this first romantic adventure, and underscores his lifelong troubles in relating to women. This struggle, too, would shape the mission on which he embarked across the Atlantic.[57]

Working the Gospel in New York

Alexander Irvine made his first trip across the Atlantic as a steerage passenger eager for learning, for evangelism, and for labor that would allow him to study, preach, and support his growing family. Like many immigrants, he discovered that the circumstances in which he sought employment imposed their own calculus of means and ends. When employed, Irvine had to shape his projects of intellectual and spiritual development around the demands of the jobs that he found. Tenants of the office building where he ran an elevator glowered at his open Greek grammar when he failed to respond promptly to their calls for a lift. As a milk-wagon driver, Irvine mumbled Greek roots as he maneuvered the underground shafts and dumbwaiters that separated his kind from the domestic life of the well-to-do. From wagon-driver he moved to a relatively lucrative position as clerk for a publisher who was compiling a new English dictionary. But he did not enjoy the material fruits of this position long. He had taken it to convince a mission society that he was more spiritually than financially motivated to enter mission work.[58]

As he moved from job to job, Irvine sustained the evangelical ambitions championed by Moody and Drummond. Wage-labor represented a status to be surmounted through individual effort, with evangelical faith providing the guiding light for material and cultural aspiration. Irvine found support in this view from institutions and individuals to whom he looked for encouragement. Soon after his arrival, he recalled in his autobiography, he became active in the work of a Methodist chapel that offered opportunity for study and preaching. When asked by the clerk of a wholesale house where he worked as a porter how he spent his Sundays, Irvine proudly reported teaching a Bible class, leading a people's meeting, and preaching. Impressed by this recital and by Irvine's trusty Greek grammar, the clerk introduced him to Dr. A. F. Schauffler of the New York City Mission and Tract Society. A pioneering institution of evangelical service to the poor of New York, the Society at first seemed well suited to Irvine's mission of offering to others the religious solaces he associated with his liberation from poverty and ignorance. He began work as the Society's lodging house missionary in the early 1890s.[59]

As lodging house missionary, Irvine linked his ambitions to a branch of the contested legacy of nineteenth-century evangelicalism as it had developed in America. Founded before the great revivals of the 1830s, the New York City Tract Society had discovered in the expansive theology of revivalist Charles Grandison Finney an inspiration for revised methods of evangelism. Finney's postmillennialist notion that Christians had to prepare the way for Christ's return inspired followers to conquer vice and degeneracy, while the egalitarian element in his theology emboldened them to believe that they could be the instruments of mass conversions among the poor and unchurched. Accordingly, the Society's workers went from merely distributing tracts to taking an active interest in the devotional life of the households they visited. They soon established special services, Sunday schools, and Bible classes in growing tenement neighborhoods, where living conditions inspired them to dispense food, money, and clothing along with religious literature and instruction. The organization's development into the New York City Mission and Tract Society in the 1860s reflected this expanding project. Paid city missionaries and slum missions also provided answers to the challenge posed by growing numbers of Catholic immigrants arriving from Germany and Ireland. By the time Irvine started his work on the Lower East Side many mission churches dotted its landscape, including the Broome Street Tabernacle, where he led the weary feet of willing converts. Irvine's appointment as lodging house missionary represented the latest of the New York City Mission and Tract Society's innovations to keep up with the evangelistic challenges of urban industrial life.[60]

In his missionary work, Irvine aimed to convert homeless and jobless isolates of the Bowery. By his own accounts, official and autobiographical, he gained many loyal followers, but his years among these men also fundamentally altered the methods and goals of his mission. Irvine's qualms proceeded in part from the peculiar purposes served by the version of evangelicalism that the City Mission and Tract Society espoused. Though egalitarian with respect to its designation of potential converts and the agents of their conversion, the Society was more hierarchical when it came to determining who was worthy of temporal assistance. Petitioners for aid had to adopt the ethic of individual self-improvement to which their benefactors attributed worldly success. In assessing such improvements, evangelical workers enacted cultural class relations with which American literary realists wrestled. Sauntering into the domain of the "other half," they proceeded to search for the lines of distinction between those who belonged to their own moral world and those lost to the peculiar morality of the ghetto—a realm they regarded as increasingly alien to their evangelical faith.[61]

When first employed as city missionary, Alexander Irvine worked with a will at fostering these distinctions. Bible in hand, he wandered the lodging houses from afternoon until early morning offering the armor of God against the individual failings of drink and debauchery. Irvine's earliest reports to the City Mission and Tract Society attest to his convictions about the effects of such failings on his congregations. "In these services," he declared, "we reach all nationalities, religions, professions—all sorts and conditions of men. . . . The great majority of them reduced to the level of the common tramp through strong drink."[62] Here, in the first extended example of Irvine's written self-expression since the journal of his trip to the Holy Land, it is apparent that in some ways he had not changed much from the pious marine who shunned a water bottle that had been filled with beer. In his daily work, Irvine followed potential converts from bunkhouse to underground restaurant to saloon, tirelessly recommending an alternative round of faith and self-mastery. He also engaged in social crusades that complemented his missionary work, such as Reverend Charles Parkhurst's Society for the Prevention of Crime. In 1892, Parkhurst determined to expose and eradicate the extortion of protection fees from saloons and brothels by members of the police force. Irvine donned a costume of poverty to visit local saloons so that he could serve as a witness before the Grand Jury convened to pursue Parkhurst's allegations. He also became chairman of a committee of Parkhurst's City Vigilance League, a movement spearheaded by the leading lights of the City Mission Society.[63]

Even as Irvine served the religious and civic causes devised by these evangelical leaders, however, men of the lodging houses were teaching him to revise his missionary methods. A group of bunkhouse converts stirred him by producing a ready volunteer to take up his challenge that he could prove their fundamental laziness by accompanying one of them in the pursuit of a job. Pondering this man's example, Irvine began to see material relations confounding the moral calculus in terms of which evangelicalism figured failure and success.

This revised assessment of Bowery life showed up in Irvine's reports on his work. Placing the moral label of "tramp" in quotation marks, he began to emphasize his converts' material requirements:

> In and around Bowery, Park Row and Chatham Square there are not less than 15,000 men, and the majority of these are denominated "bums," "tramps," etc. The public shun them as if they were lepers, and the police watch them as criminals. Their hands seem to be against every man, and every man's hand seems to be against them. Yet they are a part of our social fabric and demand some consideration. . . . The greatest difficulty which confronts me, is the difficulty of preaching and talking to, and living amongst men who are half naked and starving. . . . I would like to sit at the feet of any man who can go in amongst these men and preach the gospel without giving.[64]

Increasingly, Irvine referred to unemployment instead of willful self-abuse to account for the worldly fate of his lodging house congregations.

Beyond documenting the changes occurring in his own missionary self-conception, this shift in Irvine's depiction of his converts speaks to ongoing divisions in the American heritage of evangelical Protestantism. As in the British context Irvine had left behind, and stimulated by some of the same sources, nineteenth-century American evangelicalism embraced diverse perspectives on the moral economy of industrial capitalism. The middle-class morality of the City Mission Society was but one of these. Throughout the century, evangelical spokesmen supported causes, such as agrarianism and the eight-hour day, which expressed distinctively artisanal moral concerns. Artisans themselves entered some of evangelicalism's chief moral battles, such as the war against drink, with organizations fashioned on their own developing ethics of group solidarity. It is difficult to say how much of this plebeian evangelical culture had influenced the Bowery converts to whom Irvine attributed his changing conception of evangelical reform. Artisanal evangelicals were committed to sensibilities of morality and respectability that many men on the Bowery had comprehensively betrayed. But, at the very least, their interactions with Irvine suggest the appeal of evangelical themes to those who refused, even after religious rebirth, to attribute their material difficulties wholly to moral failings.[65]

Irvine's sympathy with such plebeian strains of evangelical culture ran athwart official City Mission policy. When he preached to wealthy men that they should establish cooperative work projects for unemployed converts, a City Mission superintendent admonished that he should confine himself to saving souls. But Irvine could no longer conceive of souls as distinct from work and wages.[66] It would be a decade before he forged the relations between them into a "gospel of work" inspired by both evangelicalism and trade union solidarity. But he was beginning to fashion new methods that acknowledged the moral distinctions and cultural discriminations he discovered among the denizens of the Lower East Side.

A downtown Presbyterian church abandoned by its fashionable congregation served as the first depot for these new methods. The City Mission Society transferred Irvine's lodging house work to the Church of Sea and Land at 61 Henry Street because other mission preachers resented his attempts to combine his "tramps" with the "family" life of their more settled churches. While somewhat miffed at this rebuke, Irvine soon reveled in the opportunities the Henry Street church offered.[67] Establishing himself as the church's director of religious work, he discovered new colleagues and guides to missionary technique. The New York Kindergarten Association selected the Sea and Land Church as its first outpost on the Lower East Side, and Irvine also allied with the idealistic college graduates of the expanding University Settlement nearby.[68]

Irvine especially admired the settlement workers' efforts to enrich their own arcane cultural heritage rather than merely imposing the Protestant pieties and cultural prejudices in which they had been trained. He liked their enthusiasm for both sharing with tenement dwellers the cultural privileges they imported from uptown and learning from the lives and tastes of their newfound neighbors. However, Irvine's path also diverged from the settlement's treatment of tenement neighborhoods as laboratories for cultural experimentation by trained "experts." Though this perspective did not completely overshadow the efforts of such workers to understand tenement communities on their own terms, it did express a preoccupation with revisions of the settlement workers' own elite cultural legacy. This approach was different than Irvine's, as he sought to lay claim to elite cultural privileges from which he had originally been excluded.[69]

Still, the imperative to learn from the experiences of immigrant laborers did lead settlement workers to revise the moral categories of city mission work along lines useful to Irvine. While the City Mission Society reported campaigns to convert New York's growing Russian Jewish population to Christianity, for example, the University Settlement Society enlisted cooperation for its art exhibit from diverse religious groups. The Settlement also extended relief during a cloakmakers' strike led by Jewish unionists. Settlement workers thus provided an arena in which Irvine could investigate the economic sources of poverty his City Mission employers had declared outside his purview. Irvine teamed up with the

Settlement to organize a lecture series at his church that examined contemporary social life from a variety of perspectives. Joseph Barondess, union leader of the Russian Jewish cloakmakers, was one of their guests. In addition, the lecture series brought Irvine into brief contact with Henry George, the prophet of the single tax who had embraced the cause of Irish land reform and raised such hackles with Hugh Hanna. Other speakers included Charles Spahr, assistant editor of the reformist *Outlook*, who studied lopsided distributions of American wealth; Daniel De Leon, leader of the Socialist Labor Party; and Franklin Henry Giddings, academic champion of cooperation and profit sharing and leading light in the American Economic Association and American Academy of Political and Social Science.[70]

Irvine also took very seriously the settlement ideal of learning from the neighborhood immediately surrounding his post at the Church of Sea and Land. His growing inclination "to work *with* the people around me instead of *for* them" helped enhance the doubts about sectarianism and cultural supremacism that the Plymouth Brethren and the Gordon Relief Expedition had provoked. As he recalled later, he began to abhor the conviction that tenement houses full of striving people could be damned because they did not take the missionaries' Christ as their Messiah—and thus, implicitly, to rethink the aggressive proselytism he had pursued in the Holy Land ten years before. Looking around him, Irvine saw that the inhabitants of the Lower East Side required neither missionary morals nor settlement refinements to uplift their souls. As he phrased the revelation later, he recognized that the soul of the East Side lay not in the churches but in the efforts of immigrant intellectuals and sidewalk Socialists to inspire their neighbors:

> They were not merely making them discontented with conditions, but they were offering a programme of reconstruction—a programme that included a trowel as well as a sword.
>
> The soul of the East Side expressed itself in the Yiddish press, daily, weekly, and monthly, and in Yiddish literature, and in the spoken word of the propagandist whose ideal, though limited in literary expression, made him a flame of living fire.[71]

In Yiddish political and cultural life Irvine encountered familiar transatlantic patterns of the traditional and the modern, of the "civilized" and the popular. Many Russian Jewish intellectuals aimed both to appeal to working-class audiences and to elaborate a program of cultural self-development to "improve" them. They advocated Yiddish literature and drama featuring "realistic" European and American Jewish types who made everyday immigrant problems of business, home, and generational divisions the stuff of moral lessons. But such fare competed with historical romances and comic operas with which Yiddish theater had begun in European productions and continued on the Bowery. In this turmoil of cultural debate, Irvine could glimpse cultural complexities that lay ahead on his own path from the church to the stage.[72]

Irvine's four years on the Bowery thus shaped his evangelistic purposes in a number of ways. He retained the profoundly personal ideal of conversion he had inherited from the tradition in which Moody preached, but shifted the ethics and methods that accompanied this message of individual salvation. He no longer held individual sinners alone responsible for their fates, but began to inquire into the economic and environmental causes of their plight. And he experimented with new ways to convey these combined religious and social messages so as to appeal to his audience's taste for entertainment. He dispensed not only with the stern piety of the Plymouth Brethren, but also with their sectarian prejudices against other creeds. He stressed instead the solace of Christian teaching as it spoke to the variety of needs and cultures he found around him. He might well have continued to elaborate these missionary approaches in New York's metropolitan context had not the disruption of his domestic life interrupted his mission and, briefly, obscured his faith.

Little is recoverable about this crisis. Irvine's son William recalled that he had originally come to the United States with his parents, and handed out tracts for his father in a Bowery church as a child. But Nellie must have returned to England to give birth to her youngest son about the time her husband was beginning missionary work. None of Irvine's children recalled clearly, or passed on to their own children, what happened to her. Late in life, Irvine complained that his mission salary was insufficient to support a family, and referred obliquely to an emotional crisis that precipitated his move from New York to Omaha. He also complained of repeated betrayals by women, and of his unrealized wish to have the companionship of a woman who possessed the qualities he attributed to Anna of *My Lady of the Chimney Corner*. If his commitment to ill-paid missionary work prompted Nellie to return home to bear his child, she may have felt any unfaithfulness began on his side. Whether it ended in death or desertion, Irvine's marriage to Nellie was symptomatic of more general difficulties with the gender politics of domestic life. His anguish in the wake of his "domestic tragedy" also suggests the depth of his emotional investment in the Victorian family romance he found so difficult to realize in life. As described in both of his later autobiographies, the early months of his next missionary venture in Omaha were clouded by suicidal despair. Only when friends raised money for him to take a vacation in the mountains of Colorado, Irvine recalled, was "the door of my soul opened again."[73]

Public and Private on the Prairie

Once his despair had lifted, Irvine found Omaha full of inspirations for his mission. In the 1890s, the city was at the center of a dynamic political culture emerging out of new coalitions involving struggling chapters of the Knights of Labor and Eugene V. Debs's militant American Railway Union. This ferment of labor politics was stirred further by battles in the Central Labor Council between Socialists committed to political activism and craft unionists championing the "pure and simple unionism" of the emerging American Federation of Labor (AFL). Irvine's years in Omaha also coincided with the final chapter in the political rise and fall of American Populism — and its brief link with the Democratic politics of William Jennings Bryan. As he continued to refine his missionary role within this political environment, Irvine experimented with political affiliations that would later compel as well as confound his mission. After he tired, temporarily, of these political challenges, Irvine resorted to small-town Midwestern preaching.[74]

Irvine began his work in Omaha along much the same moral reform lines as he had abandoned in New York. Announcing his ambitions as Congregational city mission worker in local newspapers, Irvine inflated his connection with Charles Parkhurst in order to propose a moral purification crusade for Omaha. Shocked to find citizens funding public education by condoning and taxing houses of prostitution, Irvine laid out a plan to canvass the forces of Christian voluntarism that churches might contribute to an anti-vice campaign. At the same time, he attached himself to a squatters' colony on the banks of the Missouri. Here he experimented with the missionary possibilities of the stereopticon, a device already familiar to him in his City Mission work and, earlier, from the magic lantern lectures of his childhood and marine service. Whereas the City Mission lantern shows had been restricted to the illumination of biblical scenes, Irvine now lectured on his experience in Egypt, and on art, biography, and history. As his work progressed he began to interest students at nearby Tabor College, and engaged them in settlement-like projects at his "Chapel of the Carpenter." Elia Peattie, who wrote exposés and a women's column for Bryan's

Omaha World Herald, helped Irvine organize a middle-class congregation in addition to his parish on the "bottoms," and for a while he ran both churches. He drew on the innovations of his working-class evangelism by setting up his stereopticon in his middle-class parish for illustrated sermons on "Problems of the Cities," "Child Life in the Slums of New York," "The Gospel Among the Criminals of New York," and "Child Life on the Bottoms."[75]

These presentations interested some parishioners in the work of Irvine's settlement, but Irvine struggled in vain to convince Omaha's middle-class Congregationalists that they should eradicate their vice district. Turning to politics, he pushed his moral crusade in meetings of the Knights of Labor and the People's Party. Both organizations had links to Irvine's evangelical heritage through leaders who had taken the plebeian appeal of evangelical Protestantism as the foundation for political activism in behalf of the worldly concerns of workers and farmers. The Populists listened to Irvine most sympathetically, and he joined a local faction of the Party that insisted on loyalty to the cooperative economic principles of the 1892 Omaha Platform. This faction struggled feebly against Republican political interests, who founded a new "citizens movement" in hopes of foiling the appeal of the bimetalist Populist platform. Irvine managed to get a resolution condemning the school system's financial dependence on vice passed in the city's Populist convention of 1895, but then lost interest in Populism's political wrangles.[76]

In the meantime, he encountered Midwestern political and cultural notorieties who inspired him with new visions of the shape his American mission might take. At a local chautauqua settlement Irvine could hear William Jennings Bryan defending bimetalism one week and the next week listen to the Reverend George D. Herron, professor of applied Christianity at Iowa College. Irvine later befriended Bryan in New Haven, but for the time being he was especially impressed by Herron. Herron's conception of the gospel pointedly contradicted the otherworldly focus of Irvine's previous mentors and gave voice to values Irvine was beginning to weave into his own ministry. Herron insisted that "[t]here is no falser conception of religion than that which speaks of the works of the world as hindrances to spiritual growth; as vocations secular and profane. The drudgery of the world is worship; it is communion and creation with God." Besides offering an example of Christian socialism to fuel Irvine's developing mission, Herron surrounded himself with students of American economics and labor who were also convinced that the Christian gospel had something to say about the morality of industrial production, and vice versa. Among visitors to the

Summer School of Applied Christianity organized by Herron during the period Irvine associated with him were economist Richard T. Ely and social scientist John R. Commons, both Christian academic students of the American labor movement.[77]

While stimulated by such Midwestern contacts, Irvine sought in vain for an institutional base on which to forge a link between biblical teaching and the world of work. When his political battles in Omaha made further activity in that city impracticable, Irvine moved to a small-town parish in Avoca, Iowa. Here he entered religious terrain that was reshaping his own heritage of popular evangelical Christianity to very different ends than he was pursuing.

During these years, Billy Sunday traversed Iowa's small towns while constructing a style of popular revivalism that shared much with Irvine's evangelical methods but very little with his social objectives. Like Irvine, Sunday sustained the anecdotal style and personal address that had characterized Moody's revivals, but updated these evangelical legacies with theatrical techniques and masculine postures calculated to appeal to a new generation of potential converts. Though he never went on stage—he regarded popular theater as morally dangerous—Sunday was compared to vaudeville actors with whom both he and Irvine shared themes and techniques. In enactments of turn-of-the-century strenuosity and vigor—a style Irvine also eventually adopted—Sunday was the more impetuous of the two. But he held to a vision of "reform" focused on the moral transformation of individuals, rejecting the ideas of collective social transformation toward which Irvine was moving in the 1890s. Even when he moved from small-town revivals to the massive metropolitan extravaganzas that won him national fame, Sunday continued to extol the personal faith and moral virtue he associated with the values of the rural Midwest. He linked "traditional American" ideals of temperance, piety, and self-reliance to literal scriptural teaching, which he belligerently defended against the false gospel of liberal theology and "this godless social service nonsense." This combination of small-town individualism, political conservatism, and the premillennialist dispensationalism that emerged later as "Fundamentalism" has often been associated with a developing urban-rural split in the evangelical heritage.[78] Irvine encountered symptoms of this split as he tried to pursue his own mission on Sunday's training ground. In Avoca, he discovered that the new ideas of evangelism and religious work he had begun to devise in New York and practiced in Omaha did not appeal to a small town in Iowa. In 1897 he moved on to manage a temperance hotel in Cleveland, Ohio, but his mission was also at odds with the pieties of the Women's Christian Temperance Union members who worked there.[79]

As Irvine's subsequent crusades would show, however, the fracturing of the evangelical tradition embraced much more than a division between rural and urban life, or "traditional" and "modern" values. Heirs to evangelicalism's democratic heritage were not confined to Billy Sunday's small-town constituencies, or their city-bound sons and daughters. They inhabited the very nodes of urban industrial life in which historians have judged Sunday's message to be increasingly irrelevant—such as militant trade unions and popular theaters. Conversely, the democratic cultural traditions of the small-town Midwest were fertile ground not just for Fundamentalism, but for socialism as well. Moreover, Sunday's chosen enemies within the urban landscape were profoundly divided among themselves—between learned theologians and pious workers, reform-minded settlement workers and fun-loving theater audiences—as to who best comprehended and spoke for their values. These complex conflicts over culture and piety belie interpretations of the era that pit backward-looking rural Fundamentalists against progressive urban liberals—interpretations that slight the complexities of Fundamentalist culture as well as the cultural debates into which Irvine ventured. Like the cobbler's shop that had shaped Irvine's earliest strivings, the urban arenas of religious reform, working-class politics, and popular culture to which he traveled were complicated mosaics of "traditional" and "modern" ideals.

As he struggled in the Midwest to locate a mission equal to his ambitions, Irvine could take solace from a rebuilt domestic circle. His sons joined him and he soon remarried. His second wife, Clara Maude Hazen, was the culturally accomplished daughter of a prominent lawyer and Democratic politician in Council Bluffs, Iowa. An able musician who was also known for her elocution skills, she could soothe the dissatisfied Alexander by sharing the cultural refinements he had learned to enjoy in the course of his journey out of Antrim. Irvine may well have imagined that in Maude he had found a companion who would uncomplainingly provide intellectual camaraderie and mystical sympathy to sustain his religious and social struggles.[80]

The complications that doomed such fantasies appeared quickly. Tiring of the smug versions of evangelical culture practiced in his Avoca parish and at the temperance institution in Cleveland, Irvine set out in search of new venues for his mission. In New Haven, where he moved to serve as religious director for the local YMCA in 1898, he began to draw the working-class audiences he sought, but apparently Maude did not relish their company. Increasingly, Irvine relegated the domestic concerns he associated with women and children to a corner of life less important than the public questions of economic and political justice he was integrating into his evangelism. However, this division of life into gendered spheres did not resolve the problems women posed for Irvine's career, either at home or in public forums. Throughout his years in New Haven and after, Irvine struggled with the problem of how women fit into a mission that was forged in the midst of widespread dispute over the "woman question." These conundrums colored the way he came to represent his own identification with the struggles of workingmen.

Irvine's approach to these questions shared much with the popular theatrical world, where anxieties about the morals of urban life were also played out. In New Haven, Irvine relied increasingly on theatrical practices like the stereopticon show to draw church-shy members of the working class. Moreover, he immersed himself in the sort of class and ethnic rivalries that were central to the appeal of popular theater during this period. Vaudeville's representations of class were particularly rich with commentary on the kinds of cultural divisions Irvine had been reevaluating in the course of his journey from Antrim. It provided an arena in which ethnic and regional identities were probed, ridiculed, and remade, against the background of nationalist and imperial hierarchies that fed on the very military adventures out of which Irvine had snatched his education. In their efforts to draw ever wider audiences that crossed class, ethnic, and gender lines, moreover, vaudeville managers were particularly concerned with how women fit into their entertainments. Their theaters thus provided public arenas for speculation about issues Irvine had pondered over the course of his developing mission. Sharing such an arena with his own prospective constituents, Irvine would draw upon its imagery and ideas as he continued to remake the cultural and religious aspirations he had forged since his youth in Jamie's cobbler's shop. As an introduction to the relations and practices of the entertainment world, we turn next to the early career of Sylvester Poli, who became one of its chief luminaries in New Haven.

Chapter Two

"WE GAVE THEM REALISM"
Sylvester Poli's Theatrical World

BY THE TIME ALEXANDER IRVINE ARRIVED in the United States, Sylvester Poli had been courting commercial success in the field of American entertainment for several years. Poli had arrived in 1881 in order to help prepare wax figures for a new museum in New York. The Eden Musée opened in March 1884 with a collection that included scenes drawn from the imperial arenas Irvine was busy patrolling as a Royal Marine. Within months of its debut, the museum was displaying General Gordon and the Mahdi, and they were still listed in its catalog the year before Irvine arrived in New York. The Eden's subjects also included imperial ventures mounted by European nations, and eventually by the United States.[1] But the museum did not only depend on the far-flung interests of empire. Industrial and cultural conflicts at home also furnished dramatic incidents and celebrities that could be profitably represented in wax. These themes, united through the wax museum's pervasive evolutionary hierarchy of civilization, characterized the exhibits Poli produced and prepared him for the world of American popular theatrical entertainment.

When Poli described his years as a wax sculptor as an era in which "we gave them realism," he stressed the mimetic cast of late-nineteenth-century popular wax exhibits, but gestured as well at the multiple perspectives engaged by the popular entertainment world where he made his career. "Whenever we could," Poli's recollection continued, "we'd get the actual clothes worn by the subjects."[2] This was true whether the subject was a policeman killed in a fight with a gangster or a group of working-class radicals condemned to death for their beliefs. That families of both the policeman and the death row inmates donated their loved ones' effects to enhance the verisimilitude of a wax display suggests that popular realism catered to diverse sympathies. Of course, it may be objected that Poli's very role as a showman renders suspect any interpretation of this realism as culturally significant, since by definition a showman delights the widest audience he can for the largest profit. However, the interpretation developed here maintains that "popular realism" was an influential cultural construct that developed out of just such entrepreneurial concerns, as showmen expanded popular access to exclusive hierarchical celebrities and cultural traditions. Poli's early career shows how entrepreneurial strategies in the entertainment world helped produce important forms of cultural discourse on which a mission like Alexander Irvine's—aimed at a critique of business interests—could usefully draw.

From the beginning of his entertainment career, Poli engaged events and themes that helped make the cultural hierarchies of the popular public sphere especially volatile, and thus amenable to perspectives like those Irvine was developing. The wax museums where Poli worked were steeped in a heritage of revolutionary conflict that had thrown established social hierarchies into question and continued to challenge the boundaries of nations and their publics throughout the nineteenth century. They emphasized national chauvinism and imperial pride as themes that might unite audiences divided by this revolutionary heritage. But they also featured images of urban diversity, class conflict, and competing political loyalties that gave rise to contending views of the cultural hierarchies embodied in their exhibits. Wax sculpture thereby provided Poli with training in a rhetoric of popular realism that he developed further in the vaudeville shows that he began to mount in the 1890s. These theatrical programs drew at once on hierarchical cultural ideals and on perspectives of groups who criticized them "from below." In the process, they gave voice and dramatic form to contests over cultural hierarchy that Alexander Irvine's mission was just beginning to address.

The World in Wax: Poli's Training in Popular Realism

Sylvester Zeffarino Poli was born in Piano Di Coreglia, a suburb of the Tuscan town of Lucca, on December 31, 1859. As a child he exhibited artistic proclivities that his parents—Octavio, a church organist, and Catherine, a bakery proprietor—eagerly cultivated. According to family legend, twelve-year-old Sylvester played so creatively at modeling with garden mud that his mother resolved to bring his talent to the attention of a sculptor. When a French sculptor arrived in 1872 to retrieve the wife and children he had left with the Poli family during the Franco-Prussian War, he agreed to bring the talented young Poli back with him to Paris for training. There Poli began his artistic career as an apprentice, learning first to model still life in clay, then moving to statuary and living models, and finally studying the art of wax sculpture.[3]

72

The circumstances of Poli's apprenticeship are significant not only for the skills he acquired, but also for the contested ideals of revolution and nationalism that characterized the era of his training. The end of the Franco-Prussian War that brought Poli's teacher through Lucca also rang with the short-lived revolutionary republicanism of the Paris Commune and the completed unification of Italy and Germany. These events carried forth the legacy of a Revolutionary era that had helped make wax sculpture a popular art that wove together realism, rebellion, and refinement. They also expressed the fervent nationalism that characterized not only many of the entertainments Poli produced during his career, but his public self-presentation as well.

The revolutionary tradition to which the Communards belonged had long before given birth to the nineteenth century's prototypical metropolitan wax museum, Madame Tussaud's. As Marie Grosholtz, the young Tussaud learned the art of wax modeling just as it was becoming increasingly fashionable among aristocratic eighteenth-century audiences. Her teacher was Christopher Curtius, a former physician turned wax sculptor and showman in Paris. As their trade developed, Curtius and Grosholtz moved from colored miniatures to life-size wax portraits of royalty and celebrities that they exhibited in museums at the Palais Royal and the Boulevard du Temple.[4] By 1789, their collection of wax statues and miniatures had expanded to include advocates of the people against the clergy and nobility—subjects whose cause Curtius supported. On July 12, in the wake of the king's attempt to fortify Paris with foreign troops and to dismiss the popular chief minister Jacques Necker, marching crowds descended on Curtius's museum to lay hold of their heroes' portraits. Curtius relinquished busts of Necker and the Duke of Orléans, which the marchers covered with crepe and carried through the streets. In the Place Louis XV (today's Place de la Concorde), German troops defending the Crown attacked the parading crowds, destroying the wax portraits and producing the first casualties of the French Revolution.[5]

Curtius's exhibits encouraged revolutionary uses of wax sculpture throughout the dramatic years that followed. In addition to featuring portraits of nobility and celebrities, Curtius had opened a *Caverne des Grands Voleurs* that appealed to eighteenth-century popular enthusiasm for public executions by exhibiting models of famous criminals and executioners, as well as gruesome "curiosities" and "relics." This proved an excellent venue for displaying effigies of enemies of the people, from the fall of the Bastille through the Terror. Meanwhile, the zeal with which the Jacobins preserved images of heroes and villains fostered a counterrevolution that also became part of the Tussaud museum's legacy to nineteenth-century entertainment. Because Curtius's duties as *Envoy Extraordinaire* for the National Convention necessitated long absences, Marie Grosholtz was obliged

73

to make casts from the guillotine's decapitated heads. A royalist at heart, she was further embittered against the Revolution by these morbid duties. After she inherited Curtius's business, and married and divorced the financially troubled civil engineer Francois Tussaud, she brought her hierarchical ideals along with her revolutionary relics to England in 1802.[6]

She was not alone in using wax sculpture to capitalize on Revolutionary-era enthusiasms. During this period wax figures moved from the realms of religious ritual, funeral parades, and fairground attractions into the arenas of metropolitan entertainment and scientific education. To a mix of established and fly-by-night eighteenth-century exhibits of noble likenesses and classical scenes, the age of revolution and enlightenment added wax sculptures adapted to fashions in private portraiture, the promotion of republican sentiments, and the spread of practical knowledge. Like the political ideals they helped to popularize, such exhibits regularly crossed national boundaries. In this vein, Tussaud had been preceded to England by the enterprising American Patience Wright. Wright had established a reputation for realistic portraiture in New York, and in 1772 seized an opportunity to have Benjamin Franklin introduce her to London society. In London, she executed portraits and historical groups for display at her residence and for shipment back to her sister's waxworks in Philadelphia. As typified waxwork exhibits of the period, Wright's enthusiasms embraced fashionable society as well as political ferment. Her outspoken support for American independence disrupted her friendly alliance with the king, and in later years she suggested to Thomas Jefferson a commemorative wax exhibit of the Peace of Versailles for a public building in the United States. Jefferson is not known to have replied, sharing, perhaps, his friend and political rival John Adams's expressed sense that waxworks were more valuable as tools for anatomical and natural education than as lifelike representations.[7]

Jefferson did contribute to one notable waxwork exhibit designed to promote enlightened education in his new nation. In the early nineteenth century he donated artifacts from the Lewis and Clark expedition to the museum that artist Charles Willson Peale had founded in Philadelphia to inform an American public of its Revolutionary and natural history. Peale, who apparently had learned waxwork techniques from Patience Wright's son or sister, integrated Jefferson's gifts into an exhibit featuring wax models of a variety of "racial types." These included native peoples of the Americas, the South Pacific, Siberia, China, and Africa, as well as a wax portrait of Meriwether Lewis wearing the buckskin costume he had received from Shoshone chief Cameahwaite. Intended to promote ideals of peace and harmony among diverse peoples, Peale's exhibit nevertheless endorsed a hierarchy of civilizations privileging the Anglo-Saxon. It attributed to Lewis a speech that enjoined the Shoshone to forswear war in imitation of the white men, who "will teach you many useful arts." Over time, this racial hierarchy took on increasingly sensational tones as Peale, desperate for a paying audience that Enlightenment ideals alone did not attract, tried to combine uplift with entertainment.[8]

Madame Tussaud's wax exhibits, established in London in 1835, became an influential model for this mixture. As in her traveling shows, Tussaud added the likenesses of noted criminals and celebrities to her London display of historical exhibits, stressing that all had been taken from life or portraits in faithfulness to rigorous standards of verisimilitude. Along with remnants of the Revolutionary-era guillotine, she used her collection of wax images cast from its victims as the basis for the famous Chamber of Horrors devoted to the exhibition of crime. As the century wore on, domestic criminals represented in the Chamber were joined by examples of imperial rebellion, such as the Indian warrior Nana Saib, described in the 1869 Tussaud catalog as a "monster" and "at heart a savage." With its themes of revolution, crime, and "barbarism," Tussaud's Chamber of Horrors provided a model for the sensational exhibits Sylvester Poli would help mount in the crypt of the Eden Musée and in his own exhibitions in America.[9]

Such themes were informed by the nationalist fervor that was at particularly high tide at the time Poli began his artistic apprenticeship. Poli traveled to Paris from an Italy brimming—in some quarters—with enthusiasm for its recently completed unification. In late 1870, Poli obliged such sentiments by interrupting his training to perform military duty for his newly unified nation. He served thirty-two months and earned the rank of sergeant, then hastened back to his suspended waxwork career rather than enlisting for another five years to earn higher military honors. Still, his brief stint as a soldier did not exhaust Poli's appetite for militaristic patriotism: his generous contributions to the Italian war effort during World War I would win for him the title of Chevalier of the Crown of Italy. That the path to those glories lay in the lucrative fields of art and entertainment did not mean that Poli abandoned nationalism with his uniform. Whether informed by Madame Tussaud's royalist leanings or by chauvinism regarding American democracy, nineteenth-century wax museum displays used celebrities representative of nation-states as building blocks for their hierarchies of civilization.[10]

Back in Paris, Poli found employment preparing a wax sculpture collection for the Musée Grévin, which opened on the boulevard Montmartre in 1882. Planned since 1867 by Albert Meyer, editor of the newspaper *Le Gaulois*, the

Grévin advertised itself as a new departure in wax exhibits. According to the museum's earliest catalogs, Tussaud's famous London institution was but an "industrial enterprise"; Paris's new venture had more artistic visions. Assisted by skilled artists, the Grévin offered representations that caught not only the traits but the character of their subjects through careful attention to every minute detail of attitude, bearing, and clothing. The name "Grévin" itself expressed the new museum's artistic aspirations and illuminated further its intended deviation from the practices of its London rival. Alfred Grévin was a popular artist of the illustrated papers, famous for his depictions of the Parisian *demi-monde*. This celebration of customs sported at the edge of Parisian respectability diverged from the Tussauds' advertised tradition of imparting moral lessons in wax. In citing Grévin, who became the first artistic director of the Musée, the new Parisian wax exhibit promised instead an evocation of *la mode parisienne*.[11]

Yet, for all this careful differentiation between the Grévin and Madame Tussaud's, the exhibits in the Parisian wax museum were remarkably similar to those its London counterpart had made famous. Displays of the Parisian *beau monde* complemented standard Tussaud features like the Chamber of Horrors (*Les Souterrains* at the Grévin), the celebrities of political life, and, increasingly, scenes of imperial adventure. Rather than expressing artistic novelty, the Grévin's rhetoric of national distinction articulated an international culture of metropolitan wax display. The language of this rhetoric was realism and its building blocks were the evolutionary cultural distinctions of class, race, nation, and "civilization." In the context of the wax museum, realism also meant minutely effected verisimilitude, whether the subjects be habitués of palaces, prisons, or boulevards. That this painstaking replication was itself the method of expressing national particularity was part of the museums' shared ethos. The Grévin catalog found national artistic superiority in representations of Parisian night life while Tussaud's insisted on the moral import of lifelike sculptures of royalty. But their definitions of national particularity drew on common measures of national superiority, including the identification and moral ostracism of the criminal, the evolutionary comparison of the "barbaric" and "civilized" societies, and the celebration of literary achievement and scientific prowess.

As he learned to represent these themes at the Grévin, Sylvester Poli became well versed in the dominant visual languages of popular realism. The museum's first displays spanned the range of popular realist representation in its French national version. *La vie parisienne* was elaborately presented with figures of noted ballet and theater celebrities like Rosita Mauri and Sarah Bernhardt and also in tableaux that featured the world of French culture and style. The *Salon des*

"We Gave Them Realism"

Célébrités Parisiennes placed Alfred Grévin amid a host of Parisian artistic lights, including Gounod, Zola, and the comic dramatists Samary and Daubray. In another tableau, *Un Salon Parisien*, mannequins offered a revue of the newest fashions. European political leaders and heads of state—those redoubtable public figures who fulfilled the museum's ambition to be a "visual newspaper"— were well represented in wax effigies of Jules Grevy, the French Chamber of Deputies, Bismarck, and a tableau of the coronation of the czar, among others. Equally as numerous as the cultural or political scenes were the statues and tableaux of imperial conquest, in which France was taking new interest just as the Musée Grévin opened. Imperial scenes in the museum's first collections depicted General Woolsey in Egypt and General Arabi, leader of the revolt against Khedive Tewfick—celebrities from an imperial arena where France was rapidly losing sway to England. Increasingly, the museum would focus on events and characters arising from France's renewed colonial designs in Tunisia, Algeria, West Africa, and Indochina. Early examples included a depiction of the death of Rivière, leader of the Tonkin expedition; a statue of Bou-Amena, who instigated a rebellion against the French in Algeria; and the scene of the Bey of Tunis signing over his domain to the protection of France.[12]

As cultural historian Vanessa Schwartz has observed, the Grévin's varied tableaux shared a unifying aesthetic that characterized the emerging style of popular realism more generally. Whether political, fashionable, or imperial, these scenes brought popular audiences in contact with images of people and places that had previously been unavailable to many viewers. They also rearranged the artistic hierarchies that had characterized museums as institutions of art and science since the era of the French and American Revolutions. Whereas the leaders of the First Republic had disdained Curtius's exhibits in favor of the state-sanctioned art displayed at the Louvre, and self-appointed American cultural authorities of the 1790s sought to integrate wax display into museums that emphasized edification, the metropolitan wax exhibits of the late nineteenth century dignified popular celebrity and visual entertainment as forms of art and education in their own right.[13]

Such institutions did not dispense with the aesthetics of hierarchy. Rather, by offering a wider accessibility to political elites, artistic celebrities, and imperial adventures, they invited popular audiences to participate in the cultural politics of hierarchy in new ways. Given the opportunity made available by the wax museum to appreciate, celebrate, and identify with the particular glories of French as opposed to English, or American as opposed to European culture, audiences whose tastes and enthusiasms had been excluded from the public sphere were now incorporated into it. Yet this popularization of national cultural hierarchies—as well as international hierarchies of civilization sharpened by an era of intensifying imperial rivalry—did not ensure their universal acceptance. Sylvester Poli's and Alexander Irvine's careers demonstrate the multiple perspectives on standards of cultural hierarchy addressed by a widening popular cultural sphere. This feature of Poli's realist aesthetic became increasingly prominent as he moved his artistic apprenticeship from France to America in 1881.

Poli jumped at the opportunity to go to America when the organizers of the Eden Musée recruited some of the Grévin's sculptors to begin preparing wax exhibits for their museum.[14] He had the added incentive of joining his brother, Joseph, who was trading in ornaments on Cherry Street and would help Sylvester transform sculpture into entrepreneurship. In the meantime, Poli and his fellow sculptors drew on the traditions and innovations in popular realism they had practiced at the Grévin to deliver an American mixture of realism and refinement. Through the realism of its exhibits, the museum's earliest catalog boasted, the Eden provided an excellent source of popular education. Children especially learned "more from plastic representations of events and persons than a book can teach." To stimulate such cultivation the Eden offered wax figures of "distinguished persons, rulers, artists, scientists from every country on the globe."[15]

The museum's organization magnified the hierarchical rankings implicit in such displays. Scenes such as "The Baptism of the Great Grandson of the Emperor William of Germany" and the "Lying in State of the Emperor Napoleon III" appeared in the entrance hall; lesser celebrities awaited in distant chambers. This arrangement ranked societies and individuals on an ascending scale of civilization. In the museum's early years, the most vivid manifestation of this hierarchy appeared in the Crypt. Here the Eden displayed devices for torture and execution and wax figures of famous criminals and crime victims—an exhibit that elaborated the tradition of Curtius's *Caverne des Grands Voleurs*. Supplemented by descriptions in the museum catalog, the Crypt provided graphic representations of the "savagery" that characterized the lowest rung on the hierarchy of civilization. In a scene depicting Native Americans, the catalog explained that "we see an unfortunate white man, captured by a band of savage Indians, who have tied him to a tree and are just on the point of tearing off his scalp. The squaw seems to revel in the agonies of the white man." The "ghastly scene" of a beheading in Morocco demonstrated what the Eden catalog described as a "brutal form of executing the death penalty," which "exists today, fortunately, only among the barbarous nations." Its presence in Morocco proved that nation's rulers and inhabitants, "despite their preposterous pretensions, are nothing but barbarians of the worst kind." Russia's punitive practices also belied seemingly civilized achievements. In explanation of the display of the knout, "a terrible whip of leather thongs interwoven with wire," the museum catalog opined that

> Russia has been allowed to enter the rank of civilized nations and contains a large class of society which, in refinement and culture, can rival with the best people of the most civilized countries of the world. Yet, withal, it retains many relics of Asiatic barbarism, which make it utterly unworthy of the place it pretends to hold. The use of the knout . . . is one of these tokens of barbarous origin.

In a gesture of evenhandedness, the museum also depicted Anglo-Americans who exercised uncivilized forms of justice. The catalog description of a wax lynch mob admitted that "this brutal mode of administering punishment is, even today, not infrequent in remote rural districts, where the confidence in the power of the law is not as firmly established as in the more civilized parts of the union." As against these examples of brutality, the museum offered the guillotine and later the electric chair as humane forms of execution.[16]

A hierarchical scheme so subtle as to distinguish the relative refinement of different forms of execution might be expected to rank individuals as well as societies on its scale of barbarism and civilization. The Eden Musée did not disappoint on this score. In the Crypt, a wax figure of President James Garfield's assassin, Charles Guiteau, presented an "apelike, repulsive countenance" that the catalog bid the viewer to compare to the "noble" visage of the martyred president exhibited in the cell opposite. David Livingstone and Henry Stanley provided further examples of nobility and refinement, their relative superiority emphasized by the savagery of the cannibalistic black men depicted in a neighboring display. From the earliest years of the Eden, such rankings of individuals along a hierarchy of civilization were apparent in museum exhibits outside the Crypt as well. The museum's wax model of the Mahdi awaited "the inevitable fate of cruelty and treachery" to overtake him, while nearby the likeness of General Gordon represented the lesson that "there are higher objects in life than those which are actuated by selfishness and sordid craving for earthly riches." A scene depicting the death of Napoleon-Eugene-Louis, Prince Imperial of France, who had sought military glory in the English military expedition against the Zulus of southern Africa, emphasized a similar distinction through "the exquisite skill" with which the artists had modeled "the brutal expression in the attitude and features of the attacking savages." Throughout the museum the upper reaches of the hierarchy of civilization were represented by the likenesses of individual artists, inventors, royalty, and statesmen known for illustrious contributions to European and American culture.[17] Later exhibits conceived this hierarchy more chauvinistically in scenes such as "America Enlightening the World," which substituted American imperial grandeur for the splendor of European royalty.[18]

For all its certainty about the distinction between civilization and savagery, however, the Eden also gestured at disagreements over the glory and condemnation its exhibits bestowed. The museum's first collection included an elaborate display entitled "The Rulers of the World," which featured the monarchs of England, Italy, Spain, Turkey, and Germany; the prince of Wales; the emperors of Germany, China, Austria, and Russia; the presidents of the United States and France; the pope; and, at the margins of the exhibit, Bismarck, Gladstone, and Gambetta. This gamut of figures was sure to please a range of national feelings. But other exhibits attested to national sensibilities that "The Rulers of the World" failed to entertain. Nearby stood a group of figures representing "Irish Patriots and Agitators," including Daniel O'Connell, Michael Davitt, Charles Parnell, Isaac Butt, and Robert Emmett.[19] The Eden Musée's exhibit of Irish patriots accommodated patrons whose Old World national sympathies might oppose their homeland's rulers, and acknowledged the conflicting loyalties that could color the way audiences might interpret the hierarchy of civilization pictured in its collection. Fidelity to the American chauvinism that increasingly dominated this hierarchy was mediated, in many cases, by ties to European or Asian homelands. At the same time, many an immigrant identified not with his or her erstwhile rulers but with ties to local or nationalist solidarities at odds with their purposes. Such preferences left room for alternative readings of wax exhibits and the historical personages that they depicted.

Elaborating such ambiguities, the Eden paid ambivalent homage to the Revolutionary heritage that had helped enhance the popularity of modern wax exhibits. The museum's first catalog included an entry expressly censuring the Paris Commune that had ended in defeat shortly before Poli commenced his Paris training. Concerning the wax figure of Victor Hugo—honored as "the greatest living poet and novelist of France" by being placed at the center of the museum's "Literary and Artistic Group"—the catalog claimed that "His actions during the commune were actually dangerous for a country which he loves with an overflowing soul. Victor Hugo's dream of government is an ideal which can never be realized in this world, where men's actions are ruled by selfishness and greed."[20] This depiction of Hugo wavered between reverence for his cultural prominence and anxiety about the alternative interpretations patrons might bring to the exhibit.

A counterpoint between reverence and whimsy permeated the Eden Musée to give further expression to the diverse tastes the museum tried to satisfy. The museum encouraged reverence through a number of devices. The catalog declared the museum "a Temple of Art"; to fulfill such descriptions, designers surrounded the museum's displays with sumptuous architectural flourishes modeled on the ornate Grévin, while sculptors fabricated scenes depicting artistic masterpieces and religious subjects.[21] The building itself, rendered in "the picturesque style of the Modern French Renaissance," provided "an ornament to the street—indeed, to the whole city." Inside the building, patrons had access not only to chambers filled with exhibits of current and historical events, but also a lavish winter garden complete with tropical plants, handsome mirrors, and an orchestra performing in the afternoon and evening. Around the winter garden stood decorative figures fashioned by the museum's sculptors. Some of these, like the scene depicting a young girl and child in a swing, expressed the more insouciant phases of the sculptors' creativity; others, like figures of "A Parisian Huntress" and "The Pierette," mimicked the Parisian themes emphasized at the Grévin; still others, like "The Temptation of Saint Anthony," borrowed from religion to capture a mood of aesthetic gravity. The Eden's artists rendered religious themes more elaborately still in The Sacred Chamber, where six tableaux represented scenes from the life of Christ, whose mission the catalog honored as "the most powerful factor in the public and private life of civilized nations."[22] But the museum also featured whimsical wax groups depicting scenes of daily life neither dignified nor vilified by their association with the collection's more somber hierarchical themes. These groups often portrayed the city's varied population, including a "loving young couple" enjoying an outing, a newsboy "with whose keen impudent face we have all become familiar with in our travels through the streets of New York," a visiting rural couple "refreshing themselves with a pinch of snuff," and a "colored couple sitting at a table enjoying a rest after touring the Eden Musée."[23]

As he fashioned exhibits to express these competing themes at the Eden, Poli equipped himself well for a career in popular entertainment. Military and artistic service in Europe had schooled him in languages of nationalism, empire, and cultural hierarchy that were shared across the lines of national prejudice that late-nineteenth-century wax museums helped to foster. Like Irvine, Poli found this training appealing to prospective employers in America. The Eden's organizers happily imitated the Grévin's extravagant architectural embellishments to impress decorum on their audiences and accepted copies of Grévin exhibits reproduced by their imported sculptors. But they also shaped such vestiges of continental cultural hierarchy to American tastes, engaging American conflicts about cultural hierarchy in the process. In some cases this resulted in displays designed to appeal to a cultural chauvinism most Anglo-American audiences might be expected to share, as when Native Americans were depicted as savages or Anglo-American culture compared favorably to European customs. But increasingly the museum featured celebrities and scenes whose significance for the hierarchy of civilization was in some dispute, such as the Haymarket anarchist figures Poli used to establish himself as an independent entrepreneur. As he developed his enterprises off the proceeds of such exhibits, Poli's success depended on his ability to appeal both to fascination with the social and cultural conflicts they addressed and to the more reverent themes in which he had trained as a wax sculptor.

As a staff sculptor at the Eden, Sylvester Poli was already looking out for the entrepreneurial opportunities that had attracted him to America in the first place. By 1884 he appeared in the New York City directory as the proprietor, along with his brother, of an ornaments business on Houston Street. In the next two years this establishment, "Joseph Poli & Bro.," turned to "figures" and then to "statues." Meanwhile, Sylvester had acquired an assistant in the person of his young wife, Rosa, whom he met at a christening party while employed at the Eden. Born Rosa Leverone in Genoa, she had come to America with her family at the age of ten. At sixteen she fell in love with the twenty-seven-year-old Poli, and they were married on August 25, 1885, in St. Anthony's Church. Then Poli set about making his young bride a student of his waxwork techniques which, by her own later account, she was eager to learn. She must have practiced in Philadelphia, where they moved soon after their wedding to begin preparing the opening collection for a new metropolitan wax museum, the Egyptian. Here too Poli maintained a sideline in figures or "show forms," now with a business bearing his own name. His sculptures at the Egyptian met a fiery end when, two days after the museum's December 1886 opening, some wax figures fell onto a gas flame and set the museum and an adjoining theater ablaze—a common hazard in the entertainment world. But by then Poli had moved on. Still keen to expand his personal enterprises, he grabbed at the chance to travel to Chicago to make figures of the Haymarket anarchists for the Eden. Rosa, who had become adept at needling hairs into wax models, was able to help her husband prepare the traveling exhibitions from which he began to gather capital for his own entertainment ventures.[24]

The Making of a Theatrical Entrepreneur

The Haymarket incident that gave Poli his first big break in independent showmanship was well suited to the popular realist aesthetic he had been developing since arriving in America. The event galvanized public opinion against widely demonized enemies of "civilization," thus lending itself to the cultural hierarchies Poli had been popularizing for the Eden. But, as Poli's exhibits demonstrated, images of the Haymarket convicts could call up more sympathetic responses as well, though such appeals were largely overwhelmed by garish specters of the convicts' alleged barbarity. Poli's representation of the anarchists epitomized the careful maneuvering of established hierarchies and their critics that characterized the theatrical enterprises he built from the proceeds of his Haymarket displays.

The bomb that exploded on May 4, 1886, at a workingmen's rally in Chicago's Haymarket square, killed at least one policeman and sparked outrage and anti-radical hysteria nationwide. Soon afterward, eight anarchist leaders were rounded up and accused of a "conspiracy" that had resulted in the policeman's murder. Lasting from June 21 until August 20, their trial unfolded in an atmosphere of rank hostility to the defendants and their political beliefs. Observers were alive to the theatrical possibilities of the case from the beginning: the vituperative *Chicago Tribune* printed a letter from an enterprising theater manager who offered to hang the eight prisoners one by one in his theater, as part of a play. Meanwhile, the bomb thrower was never identified, and the prosecution could not prove that writings or speeches of the accused had inspired anyone to throw a bomb. Nevertheless, seven of them were sentenced to death and the eighth to fifteen years in prison.[25] Not long after the conviction, Sylvester Poli was on the scene and secured permission to model from life four of the anarchists awaiting their executions in the Cook County Jail—the three others he sculpted from photographs. He produced two sets of wax anarchists. One he sent back to the Eden Musée, which began exhibiting the group in October 1886. The second set served Poli as the nucleus of a storefront exhibit that he mounted for several months in Chicago before putting it in a traveling show that earned him enough money to start his own career as a theatrical entrepreneur.[26]

Of the two anarchist groups Poli produced in Chicago, the one exhibited at the Eden Musée can be most accurately described. The display, entitled "The Chicago Anarchists," was illustrated in the museum's catalog with a line drawing accompanied by a half-page description of this "wonderful and most realistic group." The drawing showed the seven condemned men peacefully assembled at the office of their newspaper, the *Arbeiter-Zeitung*. Five figures are sitting or standing around a table in the office, identified in the accompanying catalog entry by name and, in some cases, nationality and trade. Albert Parsons, described as "an American by birth and a journalist by profession, who was said to be the life and soul of the Anarchist movement in Chicago," is seated at one end of the table correcting a proof-sheet for the paper. Louis Lingg, "a German, by trade a carpenter," stands next to Parsons. Michael Schwab, "also a German, and one of the editors of the *Arbeiter-Zeitung*," Samuel Fielden, "an English teamster," and George Engel, "a painter," are also seated around the table. To the left of the table, August Spies hands copy to aproned printer Adolph Fischer, who stands before a typecase. Dimly illuminated by oil lamps on the table and wall, the men are apparently engaged in work or conversation.[27] As supplemented by portions of the catalog's commentary, the scene depicts a close community, internally bound by ideals, work, and (partially) nationality, preoccupied with its own brand of fraternity. This community appears to possess its own terms of self-respect, terms that mediate relations with those outside its cultural bonds.

However, peaceful fraternity was not all that the Eden catalog description of "The Chicago Anarchists" implied. According to part of its catalog entry, the scene represented "the interior of the office of the Chicago *Arbeiter Zeitung*, where the seven men met who were found guilty of having instigated and taken part in the riots which occurred at the Haymarket, in Chicago, on the evening of May 4, 1886, in which several policemen lost their lives and many were wounded."[28] By identifying the scene as an office where the anarchists "met," and then immediately asserting their guilt, the description suggested that the accused men actually convened to plan the violence. Such a meeting—a gathering of German anarchists at which the Haymarket rally was planned—was described at the trial. However, it occurred not in a newspaper office but in a saloon, was attended by only two of the accused, and did not involve any discussion of violent actions planned for the rally.[29] By implying that the anarchists met at the newspaper to instigate a riot, the Eden Musée added a dimension of horror to the figures in the exhibit. This aspect of the anarchist display echoed representations of anarchists in the press, which routinely pictured them as wild-

3. In the 1880s and 1890s, the Eden Musée's catalogs pictured Poli's wax figures of the Haymarket anarchists assembled at the offices of their Chicago newspaper, the *Arbeiter Zeitung*. Drawing, Eden Musée catalog, December 1903, p. 31, Billy Rose Theatre Collection, New York Public Library for the Performing Arts. Photograph credit: Copy by Robert D. Rubic.

eyed barbarians.[30] In the process, it invoked a rhetoric of cultural hierarchy that competed with the autonomous working-class fraternity suggested in the attitudes of the wax anarchist models.

The available descriptions of Poli's traveling wax anarchists compound this ambiguity. For this display, Poli copied a backdrop from an exhibit in the Eden Musée's Crypt—"The History of a Crime."[31] At the Eden, this display had featured four sequential scenes depicting a murder, the arrest of the murderer in the brothel where he has spent his evil wages, the trial at which he is sentenced to death by a "stern and stolid" judge, and the murderer's last moments as the executioner awaits him. According to the museum's catalog, these scenes illustrated "the maxim that punishment follows the footsteps of crime," a message that encouraged little doubt regarding questions of guilt or judicial procedure.

No documents remain to establish whether Poli employed the scenery from this exhibit to the same rhetorical effect for his traveling anarchist display. In the obituaries that emanated from a lifetime of self-promotion, however, Poli's traveling wax anarchist show was identified as the nucleus of the Chamber of Horrors he installed in his earliest amusement ventures. Thus identified with murder at the Eden and displayed in the context of crime in Poli's traveling show, Poli's wax anarchists were located far down the hierarchy of civilization he had learned to portray in his apprenticeship as a sculptor. At least, this would seem to be the interpretation recommended by the context of the late-nineteenth-century wax museum.[32]

Yet the stories Poli himself circulated about his anarchist exhibit suggest that they also appealed to sympathies more favorable to their subjects. To enhance the realism of the exhibits, Poli claimed, he obtained clothing that the anarchists had worn from the condemned men's families. Such donations would hardly have been forthcoming (nor, if merely alleged, believable) had the exhibit itself not accommodated sympathy with as well as condemnation of its subjects. Another Poli anecdote maintained that his traveling anarchist display provoked profound emotional responses from those closest to the Haymarket convicts' plight. According to an account published in 1906, one of the anarchists' wives was so impressed with the veracity of the exhibit that she fell before it, calling madly for her husband.[33] This was a response more in keeping with the evocations of community among the anarchists in the Eden exhibit than with hints at their alleged mendacity. Implicated in the Eden Musée's hierarchy of civilization while representing the autonomous pleasures of an enclosed community, the two wax anarchist groups expressed equivocations between hierarchy and autonomy shared by many turn-of-the-century popular amusements, and thus offered a fitting foundation for Poli's entry into the field.

On the proceeds of his wax anarchist exhibits in Chicago and on the road, Sylvester Poli began his first experiments with theatrical formulas that elaborated the cultural equivocation reflected in his Haymarket display. In 1889 Poli went into partnership with a showman named Robinson and helped assemble The Robinson and Company Dime Museum in Toronto. This venture occupied a three-story building with a wax museum on the third floor, curios and freaks on the second, and a variety show on the first. In addition to their Toronto museum, Robinson and Poli mounted summer resort museums in Buffalo, Charlotte Beach, and Staten Island, New York. The Staten Island establishment, Poli Brothers' Eden Musée, was among the first theaters Poli named for himself, and also reflected his connection to the entertainment methods of his old employers. But, like other enterprises of their kind, these museums also borrowed entertainment formulas that went back to P. T. Barnum's American Museum of the 1840s, with its curio halls and polite drama. By the 1870s and 1880s such institutions had lost their polite patina and, as dime museums and variety houses, acquired a reputation for licentious ribaldry. During the same period, however, several entertainers and entrepreneurs, including the better-known Tony Pastor and B. F. Keith as well as Poli and Robinson, began refashioning the variety show into vaudeville by advertising decent acts to decorous audiences.[34]

In his early entertainment ventures, Poli expanded upon theatrical innovations that Pastor and Keith had pioneered. Tony Pastor was a New York showman with a special affection for songs about the Civil War, the city streets, and the nobility of hard-working men as compared to more comfortable classes—themes echoed in the more sympathetic resonances of Poli's anarchist displays. From 1865 to 1908, Pastor managed a series of New York theaters that featured shows emphasizing such motifs. He gradually moved these establishments northward in pursuit of audiences that would mix the boisterous crowds of the Lower East Side's concert saloons with the feminine and family shopping traffic farther uptown. To lure this combination of patrons, Pastor dissociated his shows from the consumption of liquor and offered presents of hams and coal to the family trade.

Meanwhile, B. F. Keith and his former circus associate Edward F. Albee experimented with many theatrical forms, finally arriving at a respectable "continuous performance" of variety acts in the 1880s. The "continuous" show repeated a sequence of variety acts several times over the course of a day and became a staple of vaudeville format until the emergence of "big time" vaudeville with its two shows a day. By attracting audiences to a house full of patrons, Keith's "continuous" policy gave the appearance that his Boston theater was already immensely successful. An aura of respectability ensured that these audiences included men, women, and families. Keith and Albee enforced their shows' genteel refinement by posting notices that commanded performers to delete profanity and ribaldry from their acts and by inviting a Sunday school dignitary to judge propriety at rehearsals. Printed cards handed out by theater employees enjoined audience members to refrain from foot stomping, conversation, and cigar smoking. Motivated by the same impulse toward "refinement" that influenced the design of the Eden Musée, Keith constructed ostentatiously ornamental theaters that further magnified the decorum he tried to associate with his enterprises. Keith and Albee soon replicated their Boston success in other Eastern cities and eventually consolidated their holdings into a vaudeville monopoly.[35]

They could not expand in every direction at once, however, and during the 1890s they left plenty of room for Sylvester Poli to improvise on their methods. In 1891 Poli dissolved the partnership with Robinson and started his own combination wax museum and theater in Troy, New York. This enterprise took Poli closer to Alexander Irvine's turf: like many of the theaters that emerged and disappeared in the late nineteenth century, the Poli theater in Troy was a remodeled church. This interchange of edifices gave material shape to a spirited rivalry between churches and theaters that offered vaudeville managers further motivations to tout the "refinement" of their enterprises. Churches in the late nineteenth century despaired of their weakening hold on men, who seemed especially susceptible to the allure of theatrical amusements, while theatrical managers were anxious to enhance their profits by making their theaters attractive to women, who were associated with the pious rounds of the church. This tug of war remained a central feature of the commonalities between Irvine's and Poli's careers, fostering the theatrical techniques Irvine imported into the church and the wholesome family entertainment Poli tried to introduce into the theater. Poli retained his predilection for former churches as he pursued his career from New York to Connecticut following the dissolution of his short-lived Troy theater. His first full-fledged New Haven vaudeville theater occupied St. Mary's Hall, a former Catholic church whose congregation had fled the bustle of downtown for more patrician quarters.[36]

But Poli did not establish his theater in the former St. Mary's until a year after he and Rosa had chosen New Haven as a permanent home for their theatrical ambitions and their growing family. Arriving in New Haven with their two children in 1892, the Polis first set up shop in a small museum in the Hoadley building on Crown Street, at the nexus of the city's manufacturing and retail traffic. To the south, east, and north lay New Haven's great hardware, rubber, and corset factories; to the north and west were the city's shopping district, the New Haven Green, and Yale University. A number of theaters vied for the dimes and dollars of amusement seekers passing through this city center. The Hyperion offered symphony concerts and legitimate theater at prices ranging from twenty-five cents to a dollar and fifty cents a seat. At the Grand Opera House an evening's entertainment starring "Dutch" comedian Gus Williams or "Irish" character actor Dan McCarthy cost from ten to fifty cents. Meanwhile, in the New Haven Family Opera House, popular comedies and melodramas were staged for prices ranging from ten to thirty cents.[37]

Several dime museums also competed for New Haven's amusement trade, offering some exhibits that enhanced the reputations such institutions had for promoting salacious fun. In January 1892, in addition to its usual fare of itinerant comics, singers, ventriloquists, and magicians, Bell's Church Street Dime Museum boasted of its expensive and beautiful illusion, "Aphrodite the Queen of the Air, or Venus Rising from the Sea," featuring "a beautiful young lady floating in space without support over an ocean scene, assuming graceful attitudes and positions with grace and ease." Bell's followed this up in July with "Paris by Gaslight, or Satan's Beautiful Victims," exhibited "for gentlemen only." But by the opening of the new theater season in September 1892, Bell's had disappeared, leaving an exhibition space available to the newly arrived Poli. Installing a theater, waxwork display, and curio hall, on October 24, 1892, Sylvester Poli opened the Bell's premises as "Poli's Eden Musée Theater," admission price ten cents.[38]

In arranging his Musée, Poli skillfully mixed the traditions of the dime museum and variety hall with the emerging theatrical conventions of the vaudeville house. His shrewd improvisations mingled the realism and refinement he had learned at the Grévin and Eden with the popular specialty acts he was able to lure from vaudeville theaters in New York and Boston for short stints in New Haven. The New Haven Eden Musée offered Poli's waxworks in a Chamber of Horrors featuring such scenes of barbarism as "The Cannibal Feast" and "A Scalping Scene," while variety sketch artists, monologuists, minstrels, acrobats, and magicians played in the adjoining theater. The titillating "Aphrodite" and "Satan's Beautiful Victims" faded from memory as the young manager followed the example set by Pastor, Keith, and Albee. He courted the feminine and family trade with Friday afternoon souvenirs, including "a magnificent handmade oil painting" for lady patrons.[39] Poli also carefully policed his reputation for morality and refinement. When a local newspaper reported that a Poli performer had been arrested in New Haven after a violent spree, the indignant manager quickly corrected the error and won free advertisement for his upright management policies in the process. Press announcements insisted that

> Manager Poli does not employ artists of a type capable of such reckless performances. He does not believe in making his vaudeville stage a panderer to depraved taste, and those whom he bills are obliged by the proprietor to act like ladies and gentlemen, if they do not of their own accord. . . . It has been [Mr. Poli's] effort to maintain a place of innocent amusement to which ladies and children may resort freely without escort. The immense success of his musee, which is daily crowded to the doors, shows how well he has succeeded in living up to his original plan.[40]

The emphasis on Poli's success was merited: within months he needed larger quarters. In 1893 he moved across the street to the old St. Mary's Hall and started Poli's Wonderland.

In his new theater, Poli struggled at first to keep his polite family audiences. After its career as a church ended in 1878, the building had acquired a reputation as a rowdy beer garden and variety house. But clever showmanship prevailed. Poli succeeded with a combination of freak-style acts like Ella Ewing, the seven-foot-tall "Missouri Giantess" who would stride through the audience holding aloft a five dollar bill that patrons could try to snatch, and "chic" acts like the Spanish Tortajada Entertainers, who offered mandolin solos, singing, and dancing representative of life in Spain, and had been delighting visitors at New York's Eden Musée. By the summer of 1894 Poli had won such a loyal following that he engaged the architectural firm of J. B. McElfatrick & Son to enlarge and redecorate his theater. Like the popular acts he continued to lure to New Haven to work for rock-bottom wages between runs in New York or Boston, Poli's remodeled theater placed him within the mainstream of the vaudeville form. In addition to concert halls and variety theaters in the South and West, McElfatrick had designed lavish theaters for B. F. Keith and for New York theatrical innovator Oscar Hammerstein. European decorative splendor was his specialty, which he provided to his clients in a profusion that colleagues deemed tawdry. He gave Poli what he had given Keith and Hammerstein: a playhouse festooned with ornate decorative trappings similar to those at the Eden Musée.[41]

The expanded, refurbished Wonderland that Poli opened on September 3, 1894, provided the seed for the vaudeville empire that he built on the East Coast over the next twenty years. Like Boston and New York showmen who drew on the same architectural and theatrical formulas, Poli molded vaudeville out of two interwoven cultural hierarchies. He continued to cultivate the hierarchy of civilization he had helped depict at the Eden Musée in New York. McElfatrick's decorative flourishes provided a popularized version of the artistic refinement the Eden had advertised, while projected slides and film clips of European royalty and, eventually, American imperial expansion celebrated the symbols of civilization that the Eden sought to popularize. At the same time, Poli played host to a constant stream of blackface, Irish, and "Dutch" (i.e., German) caricatures presented in sketches and songs that enacted a hierarchy of American immigrant groups. Drawn from parodies (and, sometimes, self-parodies) of the cultural traditions of black slaves and immigrant workers, these acts provided audiences with a sense of superiority over caricatured groups. But they also acknowledged alternative, autonomous values that such groups wielded against the hierarchical pretensions of self-appointed cultural elites.

Hierarchy, Autonomy, and Realism at Poli's Wonderland Theatre

With their interplay of cultural hierarchy and its discontents, Poli's early vaude-ville shows in New Haven reveal dynamics of vaudeville entertainment that remain largely unexplored. Several cultural histories of the late nineteenth cen-tury have cast vaudeville as a key terrain on which hierarchical "refinement" began to colonize the more bawdy frontiers of fun. Focusing on the efforts of vaudeville managers to bring audience and performer ribaldry under control, cultural historians have seen vaudeville as a crucial site for the transformation of American popular culture into a vehicle of cultural discipline for the masses.[42] While Poli's vaudeville programs are not completely inconsistent with this nar-rative, they complicate it. In particular, they demonstrate the multiple perspec-tives on urban life that vaudeville addressed.[43] The interpretation offered here looks to one of the qualities that Poli himself often invoked to describe acts in his shows—realism—in order to conceptualize the broader aesthetic this mul-tiplicity amounted to. Though Poli often used "realism" in a superficial sense to mean mimesis, his advertisements and audiences suggest that he and his patrons understood vaudeville's "realism" as a more complex phenomenon.

In mid-November 1894, about two months after the grand opening of his refur-bished Wonderland Theatre, Sylvester Poli ran an advertisement that testified to his mastery of the vaudeville form and represented the breadth of material included in his shows. "Shows may come and shows may go," the manager pro-claimed, "but Poli's Wonderland goes on forever. The continuous performance does the business. Persons seeking a short respite from work or business can run in, spend an hour, and witness an entertainment furnished by the leading artists in the variety profession." Having drawn attention to the fact that the "continu-ous" policy accommodated the schedules of working people and businessmen alike, Poli's ad proceeded to enumerate a bill of acts certain to appeal to a varied audience. For the week of November 15, 1894, Poli's Wonderland featured one acrobatic act, six musical acts, and two comedy sketches. Five of the singing and talking acts featured comic caricatures inherited from earlier nineteenth-century popular theatrical forms. Three of these caricatures were Irish: Essie Graham and Polly Holmes each celebrated the "ould sod" in song, while Gilmore and Leonard gave a comic Irish sketch. Grace Leith and Burt Hodgkiss gave a "rube" sketch with a "true to life" portrayal of rural Yankee ways. Carroll and Hinds provided the indispensable blackface musical act. The show also featured Ed Parker's topical songs, Billy Carter's banjo music and gags, and the exotic-sound-ing but obscure musical artist "Mlle. Theo."[44]

This combination of artists was typical of the fare that Poli offered his Wonderland patrons throughout the 1890s. The regularities in his programs were dictated in part by the emerging formula of vaudeville itself. Managers like Poli tried to choose acts they could combine into bills that stimulated audience interest according to a predictable pattern. Each bill consisted of eight or nine acts, at least one or two of which were "dumb" or nonvocal acts that would excite an arriving audience or gratify an already satisfied audience getting ready to leave. Among the talking and singing acts, managers selected some simple, pleasing turns—like little Essie Graham with her Irish songs or Billy Carter with his banjo and gags—that would settle and prepare the audience for the show's biggest stars without outshining them. Other acts were chosen to build momentum for the main attractions on the bill; often comedy sketches like Gilmore and Leonard or typical blackface musical routines performed this function. The main attractions themselves—"name" acts Leith and Hodgkiss who called themselves the "Belle of 76" and the "Rube of Showegan," or Polly Holmes, "the Irish Duchess"— usually appeared in the spots just before intermission and second-before-closing. They were the comedy sensations for which audience expectations had been carefully whetted throughout each half of the program.[45]

Like other vaudeville managers, Poli not only had to select acts that built smoothly to a pleasing crest of amusement in each half of the program; he also had to arrange them in an order that would allow full-stage sets to be changed while other acts were in progress. He therefore had to make sure that several acts in each show could play in front of the first curtain—or, in theatrical terminology, "in one"—so that acts using the entire stage could be prepared behind them. Finally, vaudeville managers had to fulfill audience expectations not only for momentum but for variety.[46] For this requirement, Poli could draw from a large pool of experienced actors well-trained in the ethnic caricatures of nineteenth-century popular theater, where blackface minstrelsy, Irish acts, and "Dutch" characterizations had been entertaining audiences since before the Civil War. He picked acts that would present varied programs weaving the traditions of ethnic mimicry with the themes of turn-of-the-century urban industrial life emerging from vaudeville itself.

Acrobatic and other "dumb" acts filled about a quarter of the space on Poli's bills.[47] Presented as audience members were still taking their seats or rising to leave, dumb acts displayed vaudeville skills that could come across without speech or song. Besides acrobatic feats, these acts included trick cycling, boxing, slapstick, juggling, and exhibitions of trained animals. Beyond their usefulness in opening and closing the shows, dumb acts added an important dimension of disciplined polish to vaudeville entertainment. To actress Ethel Barrymore, who returned regularly to vaudeville for the money and the theatrical discipline it offered, the practiced grace of the trapeze artist created a mood that made vaudeville work distinctively challenging:

> The vaudeville public is an exacting one and nothing must ever be slurred for them—perfect in the afternoon and perfect at night, over and over again for weeks and weeks. For instance, the slack-wire artist who does somersaults, swaying out over the audience, has to land on the wire or he's dead. The audience takes his perfection for granted, and if you follow him, you've got to be as good in your job as he is in his, or you might as well be dead. The audience are so used to perfection that they are tough.[48]

With her insight into the significance of the acrobat's self-control, Barrymore offered an interpretation of vaudeville amplified in more recent analyses that stress the resonance between vaudeville timing and the pace of urban industrial life.[49] The acrobatic acts offered at Poli's Wonderland in the 1890s emphasized this resonance by choosing titles like "New York Sidewalk Pastimes" or, in the case of one act set in a Chinese laundry, "Fun in a Wash House."[50] Just as the "continuous performance" policy catered to the increasingly compartmentalized leisure afforded by urban work, the acts themselves emphasized the speed and discipline to which workers and businessmen adapted as they negotiated the demands of the shop floor and the city streets.

Jugglers who moved into the field of talking acts helped spread the dumb acts' theme of urban bustle to the rest of the vaudeville show. W. C. Fields was the most famous of these; during the 1890s his like was represented in Poli's programs by Charles T. Aldrich, who went from juggling to character comedy, singing, and protean or "quick-change" roles.[51] Many such talking acts translated the agility of the dumb act into verbal form by cultivating a witty repartee understood by vaudeville actors and audiences as urban savvy. Poli advertised this skill as "lively talking" and identified acts that featured it as courses in clever urbanity. He noted in one case that a male comic "springs a lot of new sayings that are certain to become bywords before many days in New Haven." This urban milieu also appeared in the titles of the sketches that made up about one-third of Poli's talking and musical acts, including "At the Club," "In the Poolroom," "The Newsboy's Courtship," "The Flat Next Door," and "The Lamp Inspector." Through such acts, vaudeville helped sustain the self-satisfied street panache with which urban swells defied visions of cultural hierarchy institutionalized in more elite cultural monuments.[52]

The urban sensibility touted in Poli's shows extended to guarded experimentations with proprieties regarding women and marriage. Such experimentation had to be guarded in order to comply at least superficially with Poli's claim that his "family" shows could generate fun "without resorting to questionable methods."[53] In practice, Poli tended to call attention to racier elements in his programs by insisting that suggestive acts were not really obscene. In the case of comic singer Bonnie Thornton, Poli's newspaper notices distinguished with considerable nicety between the risqué and the objectionable:

> There is none in all the long list of vaudeville artists that the American stage has produced who can sing with the peculiar chic that characterizes Miss Thornton, and there is unquestionably none who could render the risqué songs that she essays with the charm and delicacy which have no trace of offensive suggestion in the minds of the most modest listener[s]. In skirting the border line of social wickedness and weakness, touching deftly some of the peccadilloes that prevail in all ranks of life, Miss Thornton shows that rare ability of touch and sentiment, and withal that artistic delicacy that amount to positive genius. . . .
>
> Certainly, if another were to sing songs that Miss Thornton does, they might be regarded as prohibitive to good taste in an assemblage where modesty is enshrined as a virtue, and yet when sung by Miss Thornton the same verses might be rendered in the parlors of the most orthodox worshipers of straight lace.[54]

Between their defensive assertions of rectitude, such advertisements effectively broadcast an opportunity for both women and men to explore the boundaries of sexual explicitness. Poli's advertisements for other singers publicized similar explorations: Kitty Mitchell, while singing of a simple Omaha maid drifting into the boisterous Midway of the 1893 Chicago Columbia Exposition, conveyed "by sly winks and naughty kicks the racy sentiments of the lines."[55] By mixing a nostalgia for innocence with an appreciation for intrigues that innocents missed, Poli's "risqué" singers cultivated a tension between sentimental moralism and playful seduction.

Vaudeville performers augmented this tension through their cynicism about the pieties of marriage. At least one in six of the comedy sketches appearing on Poli's stage during the 1890s focused explicitly on marriage; of these over half bore titles betraying irreverence for sentimentalities associated with wedlock. In January 1896 the comedy team Flynn and Walker came to New Haven with a sketch, entitled "Her Other Husband," about a man married to a widow who compares him unfavorably to her former husband. When he appears disguised as her departed mate, she becomes even more unhappy, demonstrating a popular image of wives as perennial malcontents. In November 1896, Filson and Errol appeared with the comedy skit "Women vs. Men," which portrayed the domestic troubles of a couple who are "married but not mated."[56] Sketch artists were not the only vaudeville performers to portray marriage in a dubious light. One of the comedy song and dance acts appearing at Poli's in the 1890s featured a confirmed bachelor who believed "that women were not good looking if they were good and were not good if they were good looking."[57] Such barbs contributed to a evolving philosophy of sensuous urbanity that later permeated the vaudeville show as a whole.

Throughout the 1890s, however, the metropolitan pace and sophistication of the dumb act or the risqué ditty had to compete with favorite sentimental songs of the decade. Sentimentality dominated the song and dance turns that made up nearly three-quarters of the musical fare in Poli's shows of this period. Over half these song and dance acts included sentimental songs as some part of their material, often mixed with comedy songs or even with the risqué offerings of singers like Bonnie Thornton. Her act included the new hit "Down in Poverty Row" by the African-American ballad writer Gus Davis, whose songs sympathized with people for whom urban life meant want and hunger rather than brisk material success, as well as those who clung nostalgically to values that more irreverent acts often mocked. Emma Carus, another popular singer appearing at the Wonderland, included Davis's tearjerker "The Baggage Car Ahead" in her 1890s repertoire. This song described the impatience of a group of travelers sharing a railroad car with several children who call plaintively for their mother; the song ended with the complainers comforting the children after hearing their father explain that the mother lay in a coffin "in the baggage car ahead."[58] Like many other songs of its type, "The Baggage Car Ahead" contrasted the callousness of anonymous urbanity with themes of family-centered love. Such songs articulated an ambivalence about the morals and materialism of urban life that reverberated throughout Poli's shows, complicating the rituals of city living these shows helped to inculcate.

Few expressed this ambivalence more poignantly than Paul Dresser, who was at the pinnacle of his songwriting career during the first years of Poli's Wonderland Theatre. Dresser used the income from his songs to fund a flashy, diamond-studded, brothel-based existence that awed his younger brother, Theodore Dreiser. In several literary portraits, Dreiser sketched the tension between Paul's love of urban freedom and abundance and his acute sensitivity to the appeals of those shunned, despoiled, or left behind by the pursuit of urban pleasure.[59]

This sensitivity made its way to Poli's stage — in addition to Davis's ballads, for example, Wonderland star Emma Carus sang Dresser hits like "Take a Seat, Old Lady." The song told of an old woman chased from a comfortable seat in a hotel lobby but welcomed to a chair by a newsboy operating a stand nearby. Grateful for the chair and the inevitable reminder of her own lost son, the old woman disappears, later to die and leave her thousands to the newsboy.[60] With its comparison between the hospitality shown by the humble and the haughtiness displayed by the elegant, the song hinted at urban class divisions that became important themes in Alexander Irvine's New Haven evangelism.

While sentimental songs expressed ambivalence about the urban sophistication celebrated elsewhere in Poli's shows, the character types enacted by performers who sang these songs reflected other dimensions of urban adversity and conflict. Vaudeville performers of the 1890s used racial and ethnic stereotypes in a wide variety of acts. Singers like Carus mixed "negro dialect" songs with sentimental favorites. Other musical teams specialized in blackface or Irish characterizations, and some singers gave a medley of ethnic types, including Irish, black, "Dutch," and, occasionally, Jewish (in the early 1900s Carus would adopt such a medley and call herself a "dialect cocktail"). Over half of the song and dance acts appearing on Poli's stage employed some kind of character typing (over a third of the musical acts, among which song and dance acts were the predominant category, did), and between one-third and one-half of all Poli's monologue, skit, and sketch acts featured character types.[61]

Performers specializing in character acting perpetuated the hierarchy of ethnic types that had dominated American popular theater throughout the late nineteenth century, but they also used their characterizations to poke fun at current local and national cultural hierarchies. Inherited from popular theatrical traditions prominent since before the Civil War, blackface and Irish characterizations remained the most prevalent stereotypes. The naive "rube" outwitted by the clever city-dweller was another nineteenth-century theatrical trope that showed up frequently in vaudeville. But vaudeville shows of the 1890s also gave rise to characterizations freshly inspired by the social distinctions of turn-of-the-century urban life, such as the "eccentric" tramp who offered a down-at-the-heels philosophy. In addition to articulating diverse perspectives on the pace and enthusiasms of city life, these characterizations contributed to and criticized themes of cultural hierarchy implicit throughout Poli's programs.

As they had in previous forms of popular theater, especially in the minstrel show, blackface performers brought a particularly ruthless ingenuity to their commentaries on cultural hierarchy. Blackface vaudevillians were overwhelmingly concentrated in the category of comic song and dance, thus perpetuating the racist minstrel view of the people they caricatured as childlike and unsophisticated. This theatrical commonplace gave rise to the use of burnt cork as a comic mask that facilitated ridicule of the high and mighty, a theatrical distancing device itself descended from the minstrel show. Ridiculed for their position at the bottom of vaudeville's ethnic hierarchy yet dimly recognized as architects of a distinctive community, the caricatured African Americans in Poli's shows provided a peculiarly complicated form of social criticism. Traditionally a satirist of cultural pretension, the blackface speech-maker became a familiar thorn in the side of local cultural and political potentates.

Famous blackface monologuists like Hugh Dougherty and Lew Dockstader took care to learn the local issues that vexed New Havenites before they appeared at the Wonderland, and used their knowledge to contrive stump speeches that, in the old tradition, belittled lowly blacks and powerful whites at the same time. For his March 1895 performances, according to Poli's advertisements, Dougherty successfully identified the questions that most interested New Haven, including municipal reform, law and order, the consolidation of New Haven's town and city governments, and women's rights. As Poli's notices put it, "to hear Dougherty devise town and city consolidation is to know less of it than before, which is about the result of all attempts of local orators to enlighten the public on the subject."[62] In short, Dougherty parodied efforts of local political leaders to advise ordinary citizens in the organization of their civic life. Appearing two months later, blackface performer Lew Dockstader took up such topics as the summer dust nuisance, a local sprinkling ordinance, and the problems of trolley crowding in the city.[63] With their characteristic malapropisms, such speeches confirmed the derogatory images of simple-minded blacks depicted in minstrel song acts while suggesting to suitably skeptical audiences that local political and social lights who tried to solve city problems might themselves lack some of the worldliness and sophistication to which they pretended.

Like Dockstader's and Dougherty's stump speeches, Irish monologues also took on topics of local and national significance. As announced by one Poli advertisement in the June 13, 1896 number of the *New Haven Union*, Irish comedian Pat Reilly showed he was "abreast of the times" with a "very funny story with regard to the A.P.A." By taking aim at the xenophobic American Protectionist Association, Reilly turned his wit on a target of spokesmen for New Haven's working-class and ethnic communities. Other Irish monologuists honored the peculiar values of the Irish working class in different terms. John Kernell, the "Irish Counselor," emphasized his experience as a boilermaker and wove "heart to heart talks" reminiscent of J. W. Kelly, whose well-known performances as the "Rolling Mill Man" had earlier popularized a style of ethnic- and class-specific wisdom that remained dear to both performers and audiences.[64]

But, unlike the parodied erudition of the minstrel stump speaker, the commentary of the Irish monologuist gained credence from a host of sympathetic comic representations of Irish culture and Irish-American life. In vaudeville shows of the 1890s, blackface characters were largely confined to the role of musical jesters. Even in those roles their skills were credited to the art of blackface entertainers rather than the African Americans they caricatured.[65] In the case of Irish acts, however, praise for the performer included a celebration of specifically ethnic and often working-class traditions and pastimes. Poli praised singers Polly Holmes and Nellie Waters for the "real Gaelic" they combined with their stage-Irish dialect songs. He also applauded the "lads from Donegal," Morton and Mack, for featuring fine bagpipe music and Irish national dances.[66] Comedy skits of Irish-American life sustained the celebratory attitude toward Irish pastimes cultivated in Poli's advertisements for Irish musical acts. James and Fanny Donovan, who appeared at Poli's in April 1896, were widely applauded as the "King and Queen of Irish Comedy" and praised for getting "as far as possible from baboon-faced Irish characters."[67] Even acts that satirized Irish characters could generate sympathy for Irishness. In May 1894 Tom Nawn presented a skit about a mean Irishman with two daughters that inspired this poem for Poli's press notices:

Comedy's King all hail to thee
Before thy throne we come and see
At the quaint antics laugh with glee
Cares free, forelorn
Forgetting "Father Time" we sit
And listen to thy Irish wit
And roar at some well chosen hit
Oh Thomas Nawn!
Long mayest thou live and as thy part
Hold Nature up with wondrous art
And shed thy sunshine o'er each heart
To trouble born.
If he is best who changes tears
And morbid gloom to laughs and cheers
Then thou art blest beyond the years
Oh Thomas Nawn.[68]

Such eulogizing cultivated a respect for Irish wit and wisdom that reinforced the peculiar perspective that Irish monologuists offered on topics of the day.

But while Poli's shows inspired good will for theatrical evocations of Irish community, they also placed Irish characterizations within a hierarchy differentiating the ridiculous, the lowly, and the refined. In advertising the multidialect monologue of comedian George Graham, Poli gave expression both to the barbs that character actors aimed at hierarchical pretension and to the hierarchies they nevertheless upheld. On one hand, Graham received praise for uniting on stage the urban communities that remained divided from one another in the city. As the advertisement told it, "A political Moses who blew into New Haven a few years ago invented an elaborate scheme for bridging the chasm between Hillhouse Avenue and Oak Street," between, that is, New Haven's most imposing mansions and most crowded tenements. The notice continued:

> He didn't succeed, of course, and is still toiling at his bridge. George [Graham], however, who is doing an eccentric monologue specialty at Poli's Wonderland theater, has succeeded in doing in comedy what the Mugwump Moses failed to do in politics. Mr. Graham, in fact, has done more, for he has brought together East Street and Howard Avenue as well, and joined Jocelyn Square and Westville.

After commending Graham for bringing Elm City dwellers from different classes and ethnic neighborhoods laughingly together, however, Poli's advertisement went on to applaud Graham further for his clever portrayal of the divisions between them:

> When he relates the experiences of a gang of hoodlums who have been "saved" at a Salvation Army meeting, using the various dialects peculiar to each of the different types of character illustrated, the most sedate spectator in the audience goes into convulsions of laughter.[69]

With its clash between evangelical enforcers of hierarchical refinement and those they tried to refine, Graham's Salvation Army sketch poked fun at a cultural confrontation many New Haven residents would find familiar. As Chapter 3 will show, evangelical institutions organized to uplift New Haven's working class had found themselves at odds with the plebeian evangelical style of those to whom they ministered. While Poli evidently delighted in seeing sedate refiners break their solemnity to laugh at such clashes, his description of the objects of uplift as "hoodlums" betrayed some allegiance to the hierarchical standards of refinement itself.

Poli reinforced this allegiance through the ornamental splendor of his theaters and by including an occasional "pretentious" or "gold brick" act that illustrated the upper stations of the vaudeville hierarchy. The "very finished singer"
Gertrude Mansfield appeared at Poli's in October 1896 offering classical selections like the jewel song from Gounod's *Faust* along with popular songs like
"Comin' Thro' the Rye." In February 1897, the Four Donazettis, veterans of
European grand opera, arrived at Poli's with selections "generally more pretentious than is common to vaudeville entertainment."[70] Such acts reflected the
same high cultural polish assumed by the dramatic actors who began to venture
into vaudeville stage from legitimate theater in the 1890s.[71] Some of these pioneering "dramatic" vaudeville performers also made their way to Poli's Wonderland. Presented without the singing, joking, and knockabout antics that punctuated vaudeville character sketches, they won advertisement praise for touches
of "pathos and serious acting." In his notice for Sidney Drew's 1896 playlet "In
Clover," for example, Poli particularly admired the "quiet, satirical, high-toned
comedy" that the Drews brought from the legitimate stage.[72] In effect, Poli flat-
tered both himself and his audience for their appreciation of the genteel. The
audience's appreciation was no doubt augmented by their knowledge that the
same "popular" prices that admitted them to see the Drews also bought them
the character acts and acrobats not available in New Haven's more exclusive and
expensive legitimate playhouses.

Though Poli boasted proudly about his tonier acts, his managerial aim was
not finally to force hierarchical artistic standards on his audience. Poli's appeal
lay in a vivid mixture of art, comedy, and realism. He emphasized the significance of realism, in particular, by attributing this quality to a wide variety of the
character acts his programs featured. He applauded Tom Nawn's Irish-American
sketch for being "true to life," as were the comic rubes caricatured by sketch
artists like Burt Hodgkiss and the Cotrells.[73] Despite such avowals of mimetic
accuracy, however, this was not the core of Poli's realism, as he and his audiences
knew. Character actors aimed not at mimesis but at caricature, which they
shaped and softened with varying degrees of sympathy for the subjects of their
sketches. Performers whom Poli had trouble categorizing illustrated the repre-
sentational vagaries of character acts. At the beginning of Johnny Ray's week-
long billing in May 1896, Poli detected in his act "less of the air of the shamrock
than of the eccentric," yet by the end of the week he claimed that it would be
impossible "to imagine a more thoroughly finished Irish comedian than Johnny
Ray."[74] Eventually, some turn-of-the-century vaudeville audiences demanded, and
others tolerated, more favorable depictions of groups who had been the main

subjects of stage caricature in the nineteenth century, demonstrating their recognition that ethnic caricatures were changeable theatrical conventions.

Instead of mimetic accuracy, Poli's vaudeville realism lay in the process through which actors and audiences negotiated vaudeville's cultural hierarchies and their alternatives. As in the tortured narratives that literary realists like Howells, Crane, and Dreiser constructed around the figure of the theater, the realism offered in Poli's actual theater was less an achievement than a pursuit. For Poli's vaudeville patrons, the pursuit was facilitated by the fact that he honored the mastery of artistic genius, the importance of the lowly and quotidian, as well as the authority of the real, without succumbing to bewilderment about the competing cultural standards implied by such diverse loyalties. Whereas literary realists found their own authority tremulously at stake as they addressed relations among art, realism, and social difference, Poli was at once more brash in his claims to realism and less anxious about contradictory appeals that might compromise such claims. The different conclusions about the nature and legitimacy of cultural hierarchy that diverse social groups could draw from a vaudeville show were advantageous to theatrical managers. This diversity of appeal filled theaters with patrons from various class and ethnic backgrounds. This is not to say that popular showmen ignored pretensions to status or failed to cater to the particular cultural tastes they attributed to disparate groups within their audiences. It is to say that they did not consider appeals to such varying tastes as indicators of their success or failure as realists. Realism was part of their product, while the measure of success or failure lay in the size of audience that product attracted.

By experimenting with changing juxtapositions of cultural hierarchy and class autonomy in their pursuit of this kind of success, vaudeville managers like Poli produced useful narrative resources for an evangelical project like Alexander Irvine's. Irvine found in the themes and techniques of popular theatrical culture a liberating twist to the hierarchical assumptions sustained by the religious institutions for which he labored. Rather than jettisoning hierarchy—a solution Irvine himself never considered—vaudeville suggested that hierarchical cultural schemes contained their own critiques. These critiques were to be found in the self-conceptions of those who found value in stations below the upper reaches of the hierarchy. Moreover, as they delivered their counter-hierarchical messages, some vaudeville artists addressed social issues that Irvine was taking up in his developing ministry. Alongside their impersonations of ethnic character types, the comedians appearing on Poli's stage poked fun at reformers like Reverend Parkhurst, who figured in Irvine's evangelical career.[75] In addition, the very emphasis on ethnic identity central to vaudeville's self-reflexive criticism of social hierarchy contributed to the class-conscious and sentimental terms in which Irvine revised his own identity in the course of his mission to American workers.

In the fall of 1896, Sylvester Poli introduced a fresh vaudeville novelty that provided another link between his programs and Irvine's missionary practice: the motion picture. Here again verisimilitude was an important element of the realism Poli claimed for his features; but the relation of cinematic content to wider cultural conflicts also played an important role in the realistic appeal of the movies. As Poli explained in his advertisement for the Lumiere Cinematographe:

> It is perhaps known to the public generally . . . that the cinematograph is the latest scientific invention for the display of moving pictures. . . . The faithfulness to life of the objects presented is absolute, every motion of the animals and men shown being perfectly true to life. One of the pictures which Mr. Poli has selected depicts incidents in the war that is raging in Cuba, showing an engagement between the Spanish troops and the insurgents. . . . In these views every motion of the troops is shown so to the observer it appears not like a panorama, but like the actual thing itself.[76]

The moving picture seemed to offer a means to scrutinize "actual" things minutely. As Poli's use of the motion picture soon demonstrated, however, the aura of scientific fact he and others attributed to the screen image was no solvent for the disputed hierarchies displayed on his stage. The "ingenious invention" of moving pictures ultimately magnified both the cultural hierarchies Poli's entertainments proposed and the conditions that provoked criticism of those hierarchies. Moreover, Poli's early films focused audience attention on the very hierarchical concepts that Alexander Irvine would contest through his evangelical use of the projected image.

The projected screen image had long been popular not only as entertainment but as a method of evangelism and reform. Since the seventeenth century the magic lantern had been the tool of itinerant lecturers and magicians, who often engineered ingenious combinations of painted slides and multiple projectors to create frightening "Phantasmagorias" filled with ghosts and spirits.[77] In the eighteenth and early nineteenth centuries projected images aided revolutionary and nationalistic enthusiasms by providing spectacular outdoor illuminations for triumphal parades and celebrations. Throughout the nineteenth century painted slides "illuminated" hymns and Bible stories for evangelical displays such as Alexander Irvine enjoyed as a boy and employed as a missionary. But, with the advent of photographic slides in the mid-nineteenth century, the magic lantern came down to earth. Middle-class entertainments like the Stoddard lectures presented travelogues of distant continents, while reformers like Jacob Riis seized on the projected photograph to probe visually the social divisions of urban industrial life. Meanwhile, vaudeville performers used the stereopticon to produce both spectacular visual effects and touching portraits of daily life. The Miller Brothers, who appeared at Poli's Wonderland in 1894, used three stereopticons to produce a stunning image of a man-of-war being blown up. The singing act of Maxwell and Simpson, which appeared repeatedly at Poli's throughout the 1890s, exploited the magic lantern to add visual diversion and local color to their musical performance. Their "fire song" was a particular favorite at the Wonderland: while Maxwell gave a musical tribute to the bravery of firemen, Simpson projected pictures of scenes described in the song as well as beloved images of New Haven's own fire chief and fire marshal.[78]

The use of the moving picture as a vaudeville act followed formulas already established by stereopticon exhibits. As Poli's initial advertisement of the Lumiere Cinematographe attests, war scenes and military maneuvers remained favored themes of early motion pictures. Such images made for captivating spectacles. As Poli's newspaper descriptions of Lumiere's films noted, "The last picture, 'Charge of the Seventh French Cavalry,' is one of dashing grandeur. The disciplined riders and horses bear down at full tilt toward the spectators. . . . When it was over, the spellbound spectators were silent a few seconds and then broke into universal applause."[79] In addition to military views, Lumiere Brothers provided scenes of daily life. A film of a train arriving at a French station captured on screen the urban rhythms celebrated by vaudeville's acrobats. "The beholder would think that the train is real and is rushing straight for the orchestra circle," explained Poli's advertisement. "When the train stops, out [step] the passengers and there is a rush of those men and women that want to get aboard and they're all in such a hurry, just like the Americans."[80] According to Poli, the famous clip *M. Lumiere's Employees Coming Home From Work* was especially popular because "of the familiarity of the scene depicted. . . . It is just what one witnesses every evening at the gates of a large factory, the toilers hurrying home in various ways, on bicycles, in street cars and on foot. The effect is very realistic, and no picture in the whole collection shown was received with more enthusiasm than this one."[81] Impressed with the reception of such quotidian views, Poli concluded that New Haven audiences would respond even more enthusiastically to motion pictures of their own daily lives.

Little more than a month after the Cinematographe left the Wonderland, Poli engaged the Biograph, manufactured in America by a former employee of

4. Poli's Wonderland Theatre program, week of January 4, 1897,
illustrates how Poli advertised the theater as both "popular" ("the people's
popular playhouse") and "respectable" ("strictly a family resort"). This program
also demonstrates Poli's efforts to use new techniques of visual realism to appeal
directly to local interests. Program courtesy Sanders Theatre Collection,
Special Collections, The University of Michigan Library.

Thomas Edison. Biograph exhibitors made their shows especially appealing by the extensive use of what film historian Robert Allen has called the "local actuality" film.[82] One of the collaborators in the Biograph company, William Dickson, traveled to New Haven to produce some of the earliest American "actualities" shown in vaudeville theaters.[83] As Poli's own advertisements boasted:

> If it were for nothing but the local views alone the biograph could easily lay claim to unapproachable superiority, for these views cannot be equalled in interest, beauty, and realism by any views of foreign scenes and manufacture. The Trinity Church view, the Orange street sleighing picture, and the comedy views arranged and taken under Manager Poli's special direction, all disclosing persons who are well known in the community, stand beyond any possibility of competition from foreign views.[84]

The Trinity Church view portrayed one of the stately churches that occupied New Haven's Green as the congregation was filing out after a Sunday morning service. Another Biograph film featured the local firefighting celebrities that Maxwell and Simpson had praised turning out in a response to an alarm. For the pleasure of local factory workers Poli provided an Elm City version of the Lumiere factory clip, noting that "[t]he Winchester Armory employees have also found much pleasure in singling out individuals from the group that issues from the factory gates at the noon hour, and this picture has proved very popular with them."[85] In short, Biograph "local actualities" allowed New Haven audiences to study the habits of the full range of their own social hierarchy.

Yet, however popular the local actuality film became, its appeal as a vaudeville specialty remained limited. Though eager for representations of local scenes, vaudeville audiences also expected variety—the precise quality that the local actuality film could not provide. Since its fascination was local it could not be circulated in exchange for new views, as could films that featured visual excitement or splendor. But neither could it be shown again and again in the same city after its novelty had worn off. Local vaudeville managers like Poli could ill afford to continue producing new actualities that would interest only small, geographically bounded audiences. Thus, in the wake of the "local actualities" exhibited in the winter of 1896–97, the Biograph waned in popularity as exhibitors and theater managers sought more sustainable ways to exploit it. By 1898 they had found two popular solutions to their problem: the Passion Play at Oberammergau and the events of the Spanish-American War.

Poli secured Thomas Edison's motion picture version of the Passion Play just after his former employers at the Eden Musée ended their successful exhibition of the films. His presentation of the Passion Play films echoed the civilized refinement that characterized the sacred exhibits he had helped mount at the Eden. For his week-long exhibition of the Passion Play in March 1898, Poli suspended his usual variety format to create a mood of reverence and decorum "meeting the approval of the best church people." Instead of the usual tumblers and slack-wire artists, Poli provided stereopticon views of "semi-sacred subjects" while the audience was coming and going. He permitted no passing to or from the theater during the presentation of the films and their accompanying lecture. The result, according to Poli's newspaper announcements, was a spectacle attractive both to Sunday school children and the adult public "who admire religious art and know the history of the play." Best of all, patrons could enjoy the exhibit's "vivid and realistic" depiction of "the great incidents of the life of the Savior" at "the small price of admission which is the regular tariff at the Wonderland." This provision of religious education as economical entertainment reproduced in Poli's theater the plebeian mixture of pleasure and piety that Alexander Irvine would begin exploiting to evangelical ends in New Haven only a few months later. It was a mixture with which some New Haven workers were quite familiar, and over which they repeatedly clashed with church officials who disdained combinations of religion and showmanship. Poli's careful creation of a reverential atmosphere for the Passion Play appeased a religious elite who regarded their own devotions as superior to more informal, working-class religious observances.[86]

Even the Passion Play failed to generate the enthusiasm for motion pictures that the Spanish-American War aroused. As Poli's advertisements for the Cinematographe demonstrated, the hostilities brewing in Cuba provided apt material for the vaudeville films even before the United States became a party to the conflict. Once American soldiers joined the conflict, its suitability as a vaudeville film exhibit expanded. Shots of Yale men going to war could serve as "local actualities" without losing their patriotic appeal outside New Haven. In addition, the war produced a plethora of exciting spectacles of military men and machines in motion, including cruising torpedo boats, charging United States cavalry men, and retreating Spanish troops. War films also provided exotic foreign scenes in Cuba and the Philippines, which had new significance to American audiences whose husbands, sons, and brothers were speeding off to fight in such places. Poli managed to exploit these war sensations from May through October 1898, punctuating the continuous stream of war images with theatrical celebrations of events such as Dewey's victory in Manila, in honor of which he festooned the Wonderland with "patriotic garb."[87]

"We Gave Them Realism"

The end of the Spanish-American War did not extinguish cinematic interest in America's new military glory. The ongoing fight between Americans and Filipinos did not offer quite the spectacle that the Spanish-American hostilities had provided, in part because the Filipino conflict was more brutal than heroic. But in October 1899 there was the triumphant return of Admiral Dewey to record. Poli advertised his employment of several camera operators to capture celebrations of Dewey's arrival in New York and Washington. The pictures showed the naval parade mounted in Dewey's honor, Dewey's ship, *The Olympia*, the triumphal Dewey arch erected on Broadway, as well as "several views in which Admiral Dewey is seen, a particularly fine view, the presentation of the $10,000 sword in Washington, showing the admiral in full uniform."[88]

In his cinematic tribute to Dewey, Poli recapitulated the themes of patriotic cultural hierarchy that had come to dominate the displays at the Eden Musée over the course of the 1890s. He echoed the celebration of Dewey's return recently mounted at the Eden, which involved a restructuring of the museum's exhibits that prepared the way for its especially chauvinistic 1903 display "America Enlightening the World." Even New Haven newspapers took note of the way the Eden was "outdoing itself during Dewey's triumphal stay in New York." The museum's sculptors prepared elaborate groups portraying Army and Navy units and scenes from the Spanish-American War for the occasion. The most important addition to the new exhibition was Dewey himself, attired in the full military dress of an admiral, surrounded by flags and banners, and occupying the most prominent place in the Musée. All other groups were arranged to pay him homage.[89] By reproducing locally this image of Dewey as the lord of an American-dominated hierarchy of civilization, Poli provided his audiences with a version of cultural hierarchy that departed somewhat from his earlier vaudeville fare. Throughout the 1890s, as we have seen, Poli offered vaudeville programs that depicted American social relations as an arrangement of hierarchically stratified groups. But these shows also gave voice to ethnic- and class-specific values that poked fun at hierarchical pretensions. The Dewey films offered a hierarchy in which Americans could share nationalistic supremacy in militaristic terms — a reassertion, and Americanization, of the hierarchy of civilization that had been popularized in wax museums since the 1870s.

In the wake of the Dewey celebrations, Alexander Irvine began a New Haven crusade that expressly challenged the ideals of cultural superiority that rendered the admiral heroic. Irvine used some of the same theatrical techniques that Poli exploited in his celebration of Dewey. He even endorsed some of the hierarchical cultural standards that Poli's shows upheld. Irvine's goal, however, was to make the cultural discourses that defined such standards more widely accessible without demeaning groups who had previously been excluded from them or relying on nationalism or militarism to enhance their appeal. Part II examines how Irvine pursued this goal by drawing on the themes and methods of popular realism, and on how such methods addressed conflicts among his religious followers as well as Poli's entertainment audiences.

CLASS CONFLICT AND THE MEANING OF CULTURE
Negotiating Hierarchy in New Haven

CHAPTER THREE

"THE TITHE TO MOLOCH"
Religion and the Cultural Politics of Class

IN THE SPRING OF 1900, shortly after Poli's cinematic celebration of Admiral
Dewey's return, Alexander Irvine delivered an antiwar sermon at the New
Haven YMCA. Taking America's recent hostilities with Spain as an object lesson, he described war as a moral holiday from Christian living that rulers enjoyed
while their subordinates paid the price. Irvine found the basis for a Christian
opposition to war in Christ's declaration to Pilate, "If my Kingdom were of this
world, then would my servants fight." The ruled, he concluded, must follow eternal authority, forsake their worldly leaders, and demand peace. Irvine predicted
that:

> Out of the dense forests of ignorance and prejudice we are going back to
> Christ. When the federated labor unions, the great army of toilers, shall cease
> their faction fights and unite on a bond of common weal, when they cease
> to be humbugged and led blindfolded to the polls by the always patriotic
> politicians, when they see—really see—that militarism enslaves them, that
> they pay tithes to Moloch in rivers of blood, fountains of tears and in cold
> cash, when they see this, they will sweep, by the power of the silent ballot,
> the war gods from thrones and offices and demand peace.[1]

Delivered over a year into Irvine's tenure as religious director for the New Haven
Y, this was the first public flourish of an identification with trade union culture
that would decisively shape his mission in the Elm City and reorient the cultural
politics of his American career.

According to Irvine's account, responses to his antiwar sermon divided along
class lines. After three daily newspapers printed the sermon, the city's trade
unionists applauded Irvine's confidence in their moral leadership. They showed
their appreciation by subscribing money to print the sermon as a pamphlet entitled "The Tithe to Moloch." Wealthy YMCA supporters, on the other hand, kept

the Association's telephone ringing for days in their eagerness to use Irvine's unorthodox pacifism as an excuse to withhold donations from the YMCA building fund.[2] These reactions expressed ongoing conflicts over the significance of religious observance. As he engaged these divisions during his eight years in New Haven, Irvine transformed his mission in ways that reveal how evangelism, popular entertainment, and class politics intersected in the expanding public sphere he shared with Sylvester Poli.

In order to illuminate the cultural conflicts that shaped that sphere, Part II examines the way Irvine and Poli appealed and responded to audiences in New Haven. In these relations, Irvine and Poli continued to draw on a global repertoire of cultural narratives taken from evangelicalism, imperialism, nationalism, class politics, and popular culture. But they refashioned these narratives in response to a welter of claims from local groups who saw their own stakes in the cultural themes on which the two men traded. Among their local allies and detractors were religious leaders, trade unionists, ethnic associations, and women's organizations, who not only saw themselves featured within the cultural hierarchies Irvine and Poli pondered, but also advanced conflicting commentaries on those hierarchies. Irvine's and Poli's involvement in these local rivalries demonstrates how the public sphere was shaped, as it were, from the bottom up.

Chapter 4 shows how New Haven trade unionists taught Irvine new assessments of the cultural hierarchies he had gleaned from his evangelical and military education. As he tried to devise a mission equal to the democratic vision they recommended, Irvine reformulated not only his training in Christian uplift, but also the way he wielded the theatrical techniques he borrowed from Sylvester Poli's world. Chapter 5 elaborates that world by situating Poli's entrepreneurial and civic career in the context of New Haven's urban rivalries. As his enterprises grew, Poli pursued cultural authority by negotiating competing definitions of cultivation advanced by ethnic communities and local elites, who were all objects of vaudeville humor. Over time, however, vaudeville's emerging corporate structure altered the way that Poli's shows addressed New Haven's ethnic class and gender rivalries, complicating the cultural authority Poli had constructed out of theatrical management.

The present chapter sets the local stage for Chapters 4 and 5 by describing controversies over religion, entertainment, and the cultural politics of class and ethnicity that had shaped the cultural landscape in which Irvine and Poli began their New Haven careers. It examines how working-class audiences that both men courted had laid claim to ideals of Christian justice and pious self-improvement. In the process, workers came in conflict with the city's most prominent religious spokesmen, national celebrities in their own right who were trying to chart a course of Protestant liberalization relevant to an era of industrial unrest. Class contests over religious uplift were not restricted to theological and sociological issues, however. They extended to questions of how religious practice might include amusements and address the interplay of cultural hierarchy and autonomy already developing in Poli's entertainment world. The YMCA, where Irvine was first employed in New Haven and where he gave his antiwar sermon, was in important respects the product of such controversies. Considered as part of this history of conflict, the sermon helps illuminate many themes that New Haven's audiences for popular religion and theater already shared with the broader currents of public culture Irvine and Poli had been sampling.

Workers, Religion, and New Haven Liberal Protestantism

Trade unions offered the most important organizational expression of the working-class approach to evangelical uplift that Alexander Irvine developed in New Haven. Their Christian philosophy and their conflicts with local religious elites thus provide apt points of departure into the patterns of working-class Christianity that he encountered there. While they were important organizational touchstones for class conflict over piety, however, trade unions drew on wider networks of religious practice that their members shared with workers outside their organizational ranks and with co-religionists from diverse class and ethnic backgrounds. Laborite Christianity also bridged political divides between trade unions and other forms of labor activism that competed with them. While trade unionist religion significantly shaped working-class Christianity in debates with New Haven's most prominent Protestant luminaries, a multiplicity of working-class religious orientations contributed to the "trade union gospel" that Irvine adopted in the Elm City.[3]

By the time Irvine arrived in New Haven, trade unions had established themselves as an important presence in the city's social and political life. Their shifting and often fractured movements had long supported the ideals of self-improvement and Christianity that Irvine preached. The city's earliest unions, such as the Mechanics' Society of New Haven, organized in 1811, were devoted primarily to a tradition of self-improvement similar to the one Irvine had imbibed in his years as scarecrow, stable boy, coal miner, and marine. New Haven labor activists had held to this tradition throughout the nineteenth century. A State Labor Convention hosted by the city in 1867 committed a newly formed Workingmen's Union of Connecticut "to maintain the honor and dignity of labor, to elevate the laborer, secure to him a fair share of the produce of his toil," and secure his "moral, intellectual, and physical improvement." The economic depression that began in 1873 decimated many of the New Haven union locals who pursued this vision, however. Though it carried forward the traditions of self-improvement and political activism that previous unions had pursued, the trade union movement that Irvine encountered in the 1890s and early 1900s was made up largely of unions that had either formed or reorganized after the economic crisis of the 1870s.[4]

The central body of this movement, the Trades Council of New Haven, celebrated its eighteen-year existence by publishing its own *Illustrated History* in 1899. The *Illustrated History* recounted how, during the 1880s, strong New Haven locals such as the cigarmakers, tailors, and typographers had worked to establish a federated body of trade unionists to educate working men in unionist principles and to support economic and political struggles in which union members engaged. The model of union organization these Council affiliates pursued paralleled the craft-oriented labor movement that the AFL was constructing nationally. They sought to protect the relatively high wages and organizational autonomy that skilled craftsmen enjoyed, often through rules limiting the employment of unskilled children, women, and recent immigrants at lower wages. But the history of the Council and its affiliates also included efforts to spread the benefits of organization to unskilled operatives such as the women employed at New Haven's rubber and corset factories. During the mid-1880s, the Trades Council's craft unions had worked in common cause with Knights of Labor assemblies that included skilled and unskilled workers, including one assembly of female workers. As in other industrial towns, the high point of this broad-ranging organization occurred in 1886, when New Haven workers, skilled and unskilled, men and women, craft unionists and Knights of Labor, participated in an unprecedented twenty-one recorded strikes—quadruple the average annual number of recorded strikes over the previous five years.[5]

Such expansive solidarity did not last. During the 1890s, the Trades Council and its affiliates consolidated their leadership among New Haven workers and focused more exclusively on craft-based organization. The city's labor movement boasted over fifty craft unions by the turn of the century, including unions that had founded the Council, other well-established locals representing bakers, the building trades, and the iron molders, and new unions in previously unorganized industries, such as retail clerks, hotel and restaurant employees, electrical workers, and hack drivers. Despite this consolidation of trade union power, there remained a number of labor spokesmen who questioned the Trades Council's craft orientation. The Knights of Labor, who had organized workers by industry rather than craft, invoked the parochial interests of the multiplying trade unions to explain their own demise.[6] The Socialist Labor Party (SLP) advocated a program of primarily political action supported by the unions of the Socialist Trade and Labor Alliance. The SLP had set up this Alliance to rival the AFL, whose leaders they regarded as "Labor Fakirs" controlling trade unions in the interests of capitalists. The Social Democrats, principally German cigarmakers, tried to join existing trade unions and move them toward political action in what eventually became the Socialist Party.[7]

In New Haven as elsewhere, Christianity provided a language through which craft unionists, labor reformers, and Socialists reached across these divisions to voice shared objections to the workings of industrial capitalism. To articulate the philosophy of labor in their *Illustrated History*, the New Haven Trades Council chose George McNeill, a seasoned labor reformer whose powerful and eloquent expression of trade unionism's Christian character had developed over several decades. His essay in the *Illustrated History* emphasized the class-specific meaning that Christian teaching held for workers. When laborers repeated the prayer "Give us this day our daily bread," he explained, they insisted not only on daily bread for the future, but bread for this day, now. As importantly, McNeill interpreted Christ's mission in terms that promised to bridge divides within the labor movement. McNeill taught that Jesus combined the visions of idealists "who promised future rewards and blessings" and the strategies of the practical reformer "who promised immediate relief or remedy." When the Gospel recorded that "the common people heard him gladly," McNeill reasoned, it paid tribute to this unifying tendency in Christ's teaching.[8]

McNeill's Gospel interpretations were well suited to turn-of-the century New Haven, where Christian themes sounded throughout a fractious labor movement. In an essay from the Trades Council's *Illustrated History* on "The Dignity of Labor," for example, the Reverend Austin Dowling insisted that "Christians may never forget that Jesus was known as the Carpenter's Son and we have no reason to think that He did not share the labors of Joseph." Even the SLP's contribution to the *Illustrated History*, an essay by George Mansfield entitled "The Power of Capital: Suggestions on How to Fight the Octopus," endorsed religious ethics. According to Mansfield, the SLP's political program recognized that all property was "bequeathed by God to man," and that "among the human race there are no preferred creditors." In an essay on the eight-hour day, Edwin C. Pierce offered a version of laborite Christianity that emphasized the ungodliness of the existing economic order. According to Pierce, "the social civilization that condemns every third man in it to be below the average in the nourishment God prepared for him, did not come from above; it came from below; and, the sooner it goes down the better."[9]

Not only did Christian philosophy span New Haven labor's political divides; it also united workers across lines of religious difference. While many of its published spokesmen were Protestant, the Trades Council's *Illustrated History* also reflected the prominence of Irish Catholics within New Haven's working class. Of thirteen union locals whose history and leadership were featured, over one-third (five) included first- or second-generation Irish immigrants among their listed officials. At the turn of the century, Irish-led unions were among the largest locals in the city, including the bricklayers, building laborers, and iron molders. Irish trade union leaders also provided links between unions and other important arenas of working-class religious experience. Joseph J. Reilly, a president of the typographers in the mid-1880s and secretary of the union from 1892 to 1908, took an active part in the Catholic temperance movement, serving as president of the St. Aloysius T.A.B. Society in the early 1890s.[10]

Despite the predominance of Irish officers among New Haven's locals, it was Protestant rather than Catholic clergy whose views stimulated the most comment and criticism within the city's labor movement. This preoccupation with the problems of Protestant teaching may have reflected a sense that the Catholic hierarchy was more sympathetic than the Protestant clergy to the strains of economic life that unionists sought to redress—a situation that paralleled the fellow feeling between priests and plebeian parishioners in Irvine's mid-Victorian Ireland. This sympathy did not extend to all philosophies of labor activism: in his 1891 encyclical, *De Rerum Novarum,* Pope Leo XIII explicitly censured socialism and upheld the sanctity of private property. But the encyclical also endorsed the trade union aims of shorter hours and wages that would sustain "reasonable and frugal comfort." Compared to the economic pronouncements made by Protestant clergy with whom New Haven's union spokesmen sparred, such statements suggested a modicum of sensitivity to the day-to-day struggles of working people. At the local level the Catholic clergy expressed their concern, if not support, for these struggles by lending parish buildings to union meetings, mediating in strikes, and helping working-class parishioners find jobs.[11]

That Catholicism seemed more congenial to labor philosophies than Protestantism did not prevent New Haven's Catholic parishes from generating conflict with spokesmen for labor causes or among the wider communities such spokesmen claimed to represent. This was especially the case within the Italian colony that claimed Sylvester Poli as one of its own. The colony's proud nationalists and radicals had little use for an institution that had repudiated the political legitimacy of their recently unified homeland. In the early twentieth century, Pericle Calza and Giovanni Lombardi—the editors of the left-leaning Italian-language paper, *Il Corriere del Connecticut*—scorned both the Vatican and the leadership of St. Michael's, New Haven's largest Italian Catholic church. The animosity was mutual: like Catholic clergy elsewhere in America, Reverend Merenghino of St. Michael's was severely critical of his socialist countrymen. Merenghino attacked *Il Corriere* for immorality and took the editors to court for libel. The conflict stirred animosity among the Italian faithful, some of whom sent statements to the English-language press rebuking Lombardi, Calza, and their sometime comrade Pasquale Cobianchi for political and religious treachery. For Italian immigrants inclined to side with the Church in such conflicts, a feeling of jealous protection was enhanced by the chilly reception they received in the more firmly established Irish-American Catholic parishes. The pastor of the predominantly Irish-American St. Patrick's Church, for example, stated in the midst of a Sunday Mass that Italian worshipers should contribute money at each Mass in the Irish-American custom or, preferably, attend their own church.[12]

Conflicts divided Italian Catholic parishes as well. After Reverend Merenghino moved to the newly established Italian-American St. Anthony's in 1903, many parishioners resented the unfamiliar cleric, Reverend Moretti, who upstaged popular assistant pastor Father Ricci in acquiring Merenghino's former post. Dissension became more vigorous after Reverend Moretti died under suspicious circumstances and was replaced by Reverend Oresto Lucia. In 1905, Lucia reportedly received anonymous communications casting aspersions on his connection with the Scalabrinian mission, which was founded in Italy in 1887 to train Italian clerics for service in Italian immigrant parishes. The dissatisfaction rose in part from Lucia's support of his music director in replacing soloists of the Italian-American church choir with trained, non-Italian singers. The Italian choir quit the church as a body to protest the insult to their musical abilities and the musical director's employment of his own pupils in a new choir. Whether stimulated by intraethnic group politics or interethnic rivalry, such cultural conflicts persistently divided New Haven's Catholic churches, complicating what moral sustenance they provided to their working-class parishioners.[13]

New Haven's older Irish-American Catholic churches reported less controversy than the rapidly expanding Italian churches at the turn of the century. But this did not mean that Irish Catholics were unambiguously loyal to their religious institutions. Devotional activity often appealed to male, working-class Irish-

Catholics as a way of identifying with a familiar Irish-Catholic culture associated as much with family and neighborhood as with the sacred teachings of the Church. This approach to parish activities put the Church in competition with other sources of camaraderie and entertainment. The diary left by one young Irish-Catholic worker, Michael Campbell, provides apt illustrations of this competition. The range of Catholic, Protestant, and secular enthusiasms that Campbell combined illustrates the wider web of religious meanings available to New Haven workers both within and outside the trade union movement.

Born in Ireland in 1860, Campbell emigrated to New Haven as a child. In adolescence, encouraged by his devoutly Catholic mother, he lent some of his leisure time to church affairs. At eighteen he was elected assistant librarian of the St. Francis Christian Doctrine and Library Association. Three years later Father Mulholland of St. Francis Church persuaded him to assist at a fundraising fair. Campbell described these duties enthusiastically, but also suggested that he often found church activities less enticing than their alternatives. Admitting he had had a good time at the church fair, Campbell added this was "something I did not look for as I had not the slightest idea of going until I was sent for the night before it commenced." Meanwhile, Campbell attended Mass and Confession sporadically, struggling to fit church attendance into a busy round of work, gymnasium practice, music lessons, and theatrical outings. He also mixed his halfhearted Catholic devotions with a curiosity about Protestant evangelism. He took particular interest in Dwight Moody's New Haven meetings of 1878. He described the revival Tabernacle in detail, attended services, and purchased souvenir photographs of Moody and Sankey.[14] But his was no conversion. Like Alexander Irvine's interdenominational experimentation in Antrim, Campbell's experiments in revivalism show how religious observances contributed to a varied round of entertainment, self-improvement, and devotion.

Campbell's adventures in piety also demonstrate some of the contours of plebeian religious practice as they developed outside the boundaries of trade unionist religious culture. Campbell was set on a program of self-improvement that led to promotion within J. B. Sargent's hardware factory, where he began working in the packing room in 1870 and eventually became inside contractor of a blacksmith's shop. He sought such favor by mixing his evangelical enjoyments with visits to the New Haven gymnasium, where J. B.'s brother, Henry Sargent, had recommended him for membership. While Michael Campbell mixed pleasure and piety to further individual self-advancement, however, his history also illustrates the rationale behind the alternative theme of solidarity that trade unionists wove into this mixture. He courted a local industrial elite that felt lit-

tle loyalty toward him. In promoting Campbell to the position of inside contractor, Sargent acquired an associate likely to cooperate in supplying him
information about the production process that he could use to undercut the contractors' authority throughout the factory. As Sargent pursued this objective,
Campbell's position became increasingly precarious. He resigned his position
as the only remaining contractor at Sargent's in 1907, claiming he had only a limited future at the company.[15]

Campbell might have seen the divisions between his interests and the Sar-
gents' concerns long before. At the age of twenty he had scribbled into his diary
his uncertainty about continuing at the New Haven gym, and his fear that he
would "disoblige" Henry Sargent if he quit. Campbell's reasons for giving up the
gym illuminate the circumstances separating him from the gymnasium's largely
Protestant, middle-class membership:

> I like it very much but I think it is not calculated to strengthen a person who
> has to work hard six (6) days of the week and study and read all he can to
> benefit himself both Intellectually and Financially, therefore, I am think-
> ing of giving it up. . . . I have no doubt that there is nothing better or more
> manly than exercise in a "Gym" provided the person who does it does but
> very little work during the day, or if they are robust and never read or study
> just contenting themselves with the exercise in such cases as that I think it
> would be beneficial.[16]

As the following chapter will recount, many Irish and Italian workers at Sargent's
substituted trade union solidarity for the individual success Campbell saw as the
goal of self-improvement.

As Campbell sought to rise independently through a workplace hierarchy,
many of his working-class co-religionists were already using pious self-improvement and religious fraternity to more collective ends. As the example of typographers' secretary Joseph Reilly suggests, loyal trade unionist Catholics often
identified more closely with Catholic temperance organizations that promoted
programs of self-discipline and self-improvement than with the Church itself.[17]
In many respects, such activities encouraged Irish-Catholics to embrace the self-
improvement traditions celebrated in American Protestant culture.[18] But
Catholic temperance rituals departed from Protestant temperance programs in
important ways. Rather than simply eradicating the social institutions like the
saloon, which Protestants saw as dangerous outposts of an autonomous working-
class culture, Catholics surrounded the temperance pledge with a set of alternative communal activities. Abstinence then involved not simply rejecting impi-

ous fellowship for individual uplift, but embracing alternate forms of sociability, including the soirees and literary activities that brought young Michael Campbell into Catholic temperance circles. While the delicate balance of self-improvement and social commitment involved in this temperance strategy might yield a career of individualistic success-seeking in a case like Campbell's, it also contributed to the collective self-help that active trade unionists cultivated.[19]

Indeed, the religious statements endorsed by the New Haven labor movement often echoed the Catholic temperance combination of self-improvement and communal fellowship. In applying Christian thought to explain labor exploitation, New Haven's labor movement suggested that a genuinely Christian economic order would encourage the development of individual capacities expressed in honest labor and shaped by social organizations modeled on the trade union. In his essay on the philosophy of the labor movement, George McNeill argued that the collective development of individual aptitude through steady work was part of a providential plan. The "higher inner organizations, religious, fraternal, and economic," wrote McNeill, "are growths from the root of human hunger for the attainment of the higher happiness." McNeill saw all social organization as an outgrowth of the development of hunger into desire:

> The labor movement is born of hunger; hunger for food, for shelter, for warmth, clothing and pleasure. The hunger provokes activities and the possession of the desired objects. The congregation of men develops other appetites and desires, increasing in number and quantity, each satisfaction awakening an aspiration for the possession of the opportunities and enjoyments of a higher manhood.

In this vision, the labor movement and true religion both directed hunger toward the cultivation of "higher manhood." Each interpreted in terms of the other demanded an economic system in which all men could develop their highest aspirations, rather than one in which the refinement of appetite was restricted to a grasping few.[20]

In affirming the connection between individual development and collective rhetoric, New Haven laborites expressed the crux of their conflict with institutionalized Protestantism. The emphasis on individual improvement that characterized local Protestant preaching did not in itself draw fire from the labor movement. As their endorsement of George McNeill's philosophy attested, New Haven labor activists reverently embraced self-improvement as a value. But they decried Protestant failures to interpret Christ's message as a call to a collective solidarity in service of such aims. They objected further to Protestants' refusal to identify the severities of wage labor as obstacles to individual moral cultivation and to the condescending gestures toward the "lower classes" made by local Protestant clergy.

The *New Haven Union*, a pro-labor penny daily founded in 1871 by former New York typographer Alexander Troup, often voiced these complaints.[21] Troup used his editorial page to point out that the cultural ideals generally shared by pious Protestants glossed over common economic concerns of working people, complaining that "We prate religion, we indulge in morbid sentimentalism over 'happy homes,' we spread ourselves in eagle flights of oratory over our American institutions and the liberty and equality we enjoy under the law, while at the same time we are manufacturing paupers to an extent which places it among our leading industries."[22] He singled out for special scrutiny the nationally known liberal Congregationalists, Newman Smyth and Theodore Thornton Munger, who preached in the stately Center and United Churches standing side by side on the New Haven Green. Smyth and Munger had come to epitomize what local labor activists found lacking in Protestant efforts to engage working-class concerns. Troup took Smyth to task in 1894 for a speech in which the minister had described city government as a "business problem" for which it was necessary to find "honest men, who have no jobs to put through, nor any sons or brothers or uncles or cousins fresh from Ireland or anywhere else to give a place." Objecting to Smyth's slur against a local Irish-American population that comprised a considerable proportion of New Haven's working-class and labor movement, Troup noted that "Dr. Smyth may be a gentleman of culture and ability but he is either training his mind in a narrow groove or letting his tongue run loose."[23] In 1901, Munger caught the barb of Troup's editorial pen for statements that minimized the economic hardships of workers:

The Reverend Dr. T.T. Munger is of the opinion that never before were the necessaries of life so cheap, nor the sense of contentment among the people so profound. These benefits, he thinks, are the fruits of prevailing commercial conditions in which the trusts play a prominent part. . . . It is unkind to disturb Dr. Munger's confidence, but we find his testimony contradicted by that of Dun's Review. . . . Dun finds that cost of the necessaries of life has increased 40 per cent within the last year, while wages have increased but 10 per cent. . . . The contentment which Dr. Munger alleges to have observed exists only in his imagination. The people are not contented and will not be while the results of their labor are divided so disproportionately between them and the trusts.[24]

Such statements by eminent local Protestants provided important targets not only for Troup, but also for the wider local labor movement whose opposing factions agreed that Christianity provided a basis for criticism of American industry.

These laborite complaints highlighted the class boundaries of Smyth's and Munger's own widely acclaimed theological liberalism. Both had criticized New England Congregationalism—and American Protestantism generally—for becoming too narrow and exclusive. They were nationally recognized for revisions in Calvinist theology, known as the New Theology, which effectively extended the bounty of divine grace and forgiveness to a wider community of believers. With regard to salvation, the New Theology emphasized the promise and mysteries of God's forgiveness rather than his wrath, and did not rule out the possibility that forgiveness might be granted beyond the grave. This theological extension of salvation paralleled the practical extensions of church membership and parish work that both Munger and Smyth advocated.

Ever since his first pastorate in the late 1850s, Munger had struggled against the elements of Congregationalism that had transformed Christian fellowship into local nests of quarrelsome theological bigots and worship into a meager statement of theology. He thought that congregations should revise their covenants to excise exclusive clauses such as the demand that members pledge total abstinence from alcohol. At the United Church in New Haven, Munger recommended the abolition of credal tests of membership altogether. Meanwhile, from the pulpit, he advocated a municipal rather than narrowly congregational or denominational church. Even the workers whose spokesmen occasionally called into question his grasp of current economic conditions were included in Munger's vision of an expanded church. At the time of Irvine's arrival in New Haven, the United Church had begun to devote evening services to topics such as "Some Aspects of the Labor Problem" in order to enlarge its mission.[25]

Smyth's status as a nationally recognized spokesman of the New Theology followed in part from a controversy he stirred in 1883 at Andover Seminary. He was denied a chair in systematic theology at Andover because of his reservations about the doctrine that eternal punishment was assured for those who failed to convert to Christianity in this life. Like Munger, Smyth found such doctrines unnecessarily exclusive in their allocation of grace. Moreover, like Henry Drummond, Alexander Irvine's mentor of the 1880s, Smyth saw in scientific exploration the possibility of a continuity between material and spiritual phenomena. This insight helped bolster Smyth's belief in the continuity of Christian forgiveness across the divide of human mortality. He also drew from the "higher criticism" that interpreted biblical texts as historical documents, challenging the inerrancy that evangelicals like Moody and the Plymouth Brethren claimed for the Bible. As he explained in his most famous work, *Old Faiths in New Light*, the "higher criticism" supported his conviction that divine inspiration was always given in terms appropriate to the specificities of time and place. He believed that the late nineteenth century required Christian inspiration appropriate to its own intellectual currents and social problems and tried to oblige by seeking out trade unionists and inviting them to attend his services.[26]

For all their expansive theological innovations and inclusive pastoral strategies, however, neither Smyth nor Munger saw labor organizations as appropriate foundations for liberal revisions of religious practice. Instead, both ministers periodically erupted in diatribes against trade unions. Munger had taken public aim at the economic theories implicit in trade union activity long before coming to New Haven. In 1872, he published a series of articles in *The Congregationalist* on the significance of the textile mill strikes in Lawrence, Massachusetts, where he was preaching at the time. He ended the series with a pair of articles on "The Futility of Strikes" and "The Futility of Labor Unions." In these two pieces, Munger rejected the "logic of the day" according to which workers contended that "our employer last year cleared twenty thousand dollars while we barely cleared our living: the profits came from our skill and his luck." According to Munger, this logic obscured complex economic laws to which employers were even more subservient than workingmen. Munger ignored trade unionist claims that it was the employer's power to control working conditions that provoked workers to collective action for shorter hours or higher wages. He was much more worried about labor's collective organizations gaining the power to compel employers or other workers to accede to wage and hour demands. Before joining a union, he counseled, a man should consider carefully how much liberty he was willing to part with and whether he would be willing to put his own skill and energy on a level with another's stupidity and indolence. Munger admitted that the willingness of workingmen to "forego the exercise of their profoundest convictions as Americans" testified to the intensity with which they dreaded the tyranny of capital. But it was labor union solidarity and not combinations of capital that most antagonized Munger's notion of individual freedom.[27]

Munger's labor essays of 1872 paralleled the views that Newman Smyth published and proclaimed throughout his New Haven ministry. Smyth made his first pulpit proclamations on industrial questions in 1885 with a series of three sermons that followed from discussions with the city's trade unionists and Socialists. In these sermons, later published in the *Andover Review*, Smyth counseled tolerance to both laborers and businessmen. The terms in which he offered this counsel, however, betrayed his negative view of labor agitators. The indiscriminate condemnation of labor organizations by manufacturers, Smyth warned, only threatened to "add fuel to human passions which it is not for the well-being of any of us to have inflamed." The inclination of workingmen to denounce the powers that be, on the other hand, exemplified the "easy hypocrisy of intemperate speech." Smyth supported trade unions so long as they augmented self-help among workingmen as individuals, but worried about their tendency to exceed this charge and operate as "instruments of tyranny" creating "labor monopolies." He insisted that Christians could not tolerate unionist regulations that sacrificed the principle of personal liberty, a principle that "the Christian pulpit will assert with no uncertain sound." Smyth placed his greatest hope for improved industrial relations in the common interests that men found beyond the workplace, finally offering the church as the most promising source of shared interests that might overcome animosities arising in economic affairs. Smyth's grave concern over the moral threats posed by labor unions would characterize his approach to industrial conflict throughout his pastorate at Center Church.[28]

In their aversion to trade union organization as a foundation for social reform, Smyth and Munger recapitulated the evangelical message that Irvine had heard from Henry Drummond. Salvation, Drummond had insisted, required a course of individual self-improvement that could be stymied by a life of manual labor. Not collective organization among those who toiled, but the pursuit of a career that would reduce the individual's toil in favor of opportunities to study and pray was what Drummond recommended. The parallel between Drummond's views on labor and those preached by Smyth and Munger was hardly fortuitous. Both Smyth and Munger shared the vision of divinely inspired natural progress that characterized Drummond's worldview. Munger had written a sympathetic criticism of Drummond's attempts to reconcile religion and evolutionary science, while Smyth sought in Yale's laboratories the same continuum of the natural and the spiritual that informed Drummond's theology.[29] Smyth and Munger, it is true, thought that the natural progress revealed by science compelled Christians to involve themselves more deeply in social conflicts than Drummond, who argued that Christianity should "take away the earth," recommended. Yet Smyth and Munger shared with Drummond a primary interest in the development of an individualistic, personal faith.

As the most prominent theological rivals of the local unions with whom Irvine would ally in New Haven, Munger and Smyth proved to be important figures in the public debates over religious culture that reshaped his mission there. In the process, they provoked Irvine to rethink his earliest evangelical training. As Irvine moved away from the individualistic program of uplift outlined in Drummond's theology, he also developed his early combinations of evangelism and entertainment into an alternative style of preaching that had its own precedents in New Haven. The New Haven YMCA that hired him as religious director in 1898 was the product of decades of contest between Christian workingmen and Protestant elites over the form that working-class evangelism should take, and the role entertainment should play in it.

The YMCA and Cultural Class Conflict

Born of evangelical doubts about the propriety of mixing piety and amusement, the New Haven YMCA became an important local testing ground for such mixtures. A group of local ministers formed the organization in 1857 as an offshoot from the Young Men's Institute, which promoted mental and spiritual self-improvement. Worried that the worldly diversions tolerated at the Institute tempted evangelical recruits away from religious devotion, the YMCA founders helped fuel an ongoing debate over the relation between pious self-improvement and popular cultural conviviality.[30] Hosting the first Connecticut State YMCA convention in 1867, New Haven clergymen argued fiercely over the use of games and entertainments to entice young men from saloons into YMCA meeting rooms. A Reverend Bacon proclaimed sternly that he had not heard of "a fiddling Christ, a dancing Christ, a Christ driving horses tandem." He insisted that amusements like chess constituted unchristian compromises with such wickedness, detracting from the message that "life is not a vain amusement or a song, it is the exordium and prelude to eternity." But not all of Bacon's colleagues shared his view of evangelistic work. A Reverend Clark of New Haven objected that Bacon's perspective was blind to the duty of YMCA workers to cultivate sympathy for the working poor. Proponents of Clark's view would eventually lead the New Haven YMCA into experiments in entertainment that provided a springboard for Irvine's combinations of hierarchical culture and popular amusement. Still, the sterner piety that Bacon expressed remained a decisive influence. This tendency was especially strong during the 1860s and 1870s, when the New Haven YMCA focused almost exclusively on the evangelism of praise services, prayer meetings, and devotional exercises.[31]

While the city YMCA preoccupied itself with pious soul saving, there was an outpost of New Haven Y activity that anticipated the forms of evangelism that Alexander Irvine would develop in the early twentieth century. This outpost, the New Haven Railroad YMCA, grew out of a small band of skilled workers on the New York, New Haven, and Hartford Railroad who came together to pray in churches and homes in the wake of the New Haven Moody–Sankey revival of 1878. This was a period in which the American YMCA was making special efforts to evangelize railroad men, hoping to quell the labor unrest that sparked the widespread, violent uprising of railroad workers in 1877.[32] However, the development of New Haven's early Railroad Y shows that the evangelical motivations of these workers, which arose from the same influences that inspired Irvine's religious epiphany in Antrim, could run athwart the purposes of those who sought to use evangelism to close the gap between employers and wage-earners.

No want of evangelical fervor among railway workers themselves accounted for these tensions. Members of the small band of railroad men who began meeting in the summer of 1878 carefully scrutinized their own souls and served as close custodians of one another's spiritual well-being. Gathered together one night in the home of John B. Sanner, a brass molder, the praying railroad men tried fervently to bring their host to Christ. As Secretary Charles A. Danforth, a depot draughtsman, noted:

> he [Sanner], in response to [an] urgent general invitation by [H. E. Squires, a switchman] rose asking for prayers. Then ensued a wonderful wrestling with God. Dorman groaned continually, as did others, and it was difficult to know who was leading. Munson created a smile when a person spoke of God's mercy: "*Just* like the Lord!"[33]

Danforth, who was among the more conventionally pious of the group, observed repeatedly that prayer meetings piqued the interest of fellow workers who had previously shown little concern for their spiritual condition. He reported after another meeting that "Allen S. Ostrander is not unwilling to talk about his soul, tho' he is the last one I wanted to approach. God help him."[34]

However, committed as they were to guarding their own and one another's souls, many railway men were reluctant to entrust this task to leaders from outside their own ranks. National leaders of the Railroad YMCA movement visited New Haven repeatedly between 1878 and 1880 to organize a Railroad YMCA among the praying railway men. But during the 1870s and 1880s members of this new organization remained divided over the matter of identifying themselves as a YMCA branch. While tolerating occasional services directed by officials of the city YMCA, some railroad workers jealously insisted on advertising their prayer meetings as "under the charge of railway men."[35] The men who ran the meetings had a more easygoing attitude toward integrating religious practice and popular amusement than the YMCA leaders did, and objected to insinuations by Protestant evangelical uplifters that the pastimes of railway workers rendered them immoral. One occasional prayer meeting leader, a brakeman named Morrell, drew directly on mid-nineteenth-century popular theater in styling himself the "Bowery Boy" of the religious fellowship. Another worker named Jim complained when a Mrs. Phelps, who attended prayer meetings to speak on temperance, implied that "all engineers were drunkards."[36] As the evangelical engineers, firemen, and brakemen who had led the meetings began to run their own reading room in the early 1880s, the forces motivating their jealous assertions of autonomy became increasingly apparent.

Under the supervision of a retired conductor, John Fullerton, the reading room provided a space where the railway men's prayer meeting could expand to include, in Secretary Danforth's words, "many a face . . . which would not appear in a church."[37] It opened in September 1880 under the auspices of the railway men's praying group at a building conveniently equidistant from New Haven's two railway depots. The reading room soon boasted a brisk spiritual trade.[38] Eager to consolidate this success, Danforth and other leaders among the praying railroad men paid a visit to George H. Watrous, president of the Consolidated Road, to request material support for the maintenance of the room. In May 1881 the company agreed to contribute three hundred dollars a year, but stipulated that the city YMCA should provide leadership for the railway men's activities. Some of the railway men resented this caveat. They rejected the designation of the reading room as a branch of the YMCA and the transfer of administrative responsibility for the room to a YMCA secretary.

This rebellion brought into the open intersecting class, ethnic, and religious conflicts that complicated the YMCA's overtures to working men. A special meeting of the railroad men's praying group in June 1881 focused on the appearance of a sign outside the reading room identifying it as the "Railroad Branch YMCA." The discussion revealed the contested meanings that the praying railroad men attached to their collective spiritual activity. William Fisher, a railroad engineer who had been the leader of the earliest railway men's prayer meetings in 1878, objected to the YMCA designation on the ground that YMCA management made the room so cold, stiff, and formal that railroad men did not feel at home there. If "YMCA" were wiped away from the sign, Fisher contended, the room would be full of attendants and subscribers. Conductor H. S. Beers added that the YMCA affiliation alienated Catholics; he claimed to know "Irish boys clean and decent who did their work well" who would not come into the room because of the YMCA designation. While he was not a Christian "as some would define it . . . a good Catholic is better than a poor Methodist," Beers asserted. Taken together, Fisher's and Beers's complaints reveal a conviction that the evangelical methods approved by their employers and the Y thwarted the railway men's own informal, unsectarian spiritual fellowship. Beers went further and associated the railway men's spiritual autonomy with their pride as skilled working men: if the railroad company trusted them to run its trains, he insisted, it could trust them to run a "Gospel Shop." For other praying railway workers, however, association with the YMCA was valued precisely because it signaled a Christian agenda respected outside the ranks of the railway men. According to Henry Squires, also a leader of the early prayer meetings, the YMCA sign should stay on the reading room door lest the railway men lose the good opinion of "Christian friends" if it came off.[39] With this concern, Squires expressed a hierarchical vision of Christian fellowship that Irvine was pursuing at the same time, through his respect for Henry Drummond and his demeanor as a marine. The debate over the YMCA sign thus gave voice to conflicts over cultural hierarchy in evangelical practice that Irvine would revisit at the New Haven YMCA.

Disputes over the leadership of the railroad men's reading room demonstrate how divisive these cultural conflicts could be. Shortly after the YMCA sign was removed, conflict erupted over the question of retaining John Fullerton, the retired conductor who had been in charge of the reading room since its inception. The arrival of George Butterfield, a YMCA secretary hired by the room's managing committee, threatened Fullerton's position. Butterfield was a former New Haven brakeman who had been associated with an informal local railway men's reading room during the late 1870s. Since then he had spent several months directing the work of a railroad men's reading room in Indianapolis under the guidance of pioneer Railroad Y secretary George W. Cobb. In the YMCA's eyes, Butterfield's efforts in Indianapolis qualified him to take over the management of New Haven's reading room. But, among railway men themselves, Butterfield's past as a railway worker did not make up for the indignity of having Fullerton replaced with a younger man whose alleged superiority derived from an organization many of them held in suspicion. Insult was added to injury when newspaper announcements heralding Butterfield's arrival commented that "with only a janitor in charge" the work of the reading room had not been developing as hoped.[40] Within two weeks of Butterfield's installation at the old reading room, a competing room opened with Fullerton in charge. Its managing committee included some of the central advocates of the policy of autonomy from the YMCA and its advertisements emphasized that it was "managed entirely by railroad men."[41]

Within a year of this split, evangelical railroad workers and their employers attempted to reorganize the Railroad Y under a new management that included representatives of both reading rooms. This reorganization failed to resuscitate the old Railroad Y reading room, where attendance continued to drop so much that meetings were no longer publicly advertised after July 1882.[42] But the new Railroad Y did anticipate the institution where Irvine later negotiated conflicts between cultural hierarchy and cultural autonomy in New Haven. During the 1890s, both the city and the Railroad YMCAs instituted multifaceted programs of evangelism, education, and recreation under the management of New Haven's business and railroad leaders. These programs incorporated the informal combinations of recreation and worship that advocates of working-class autonomy among the praying railroad men had tried to achieve by distancing themselves from the YMCA of the 1870s and 1880s. For the Railroad Y of the 1890s, the Consolidated Road provided a building with facilities not only for reading and prayer, but for bathing, gymnasium exercise, and entertainments such as a minstrel show staged by railway workers.[43] In the 1890s, the city YMCA also combined popular theatrical forms and spiritual uplift in its program of praise services, lectures, and classes. By incorporating a working-class synthesis of worship and entertainment, however, the city YMCA did not avert the conflicts it had previously provoked by resisting this synthesis. Instead, as Irvine's experience reveals, the YMCA played host to conflicting interpretations of the themes and strategies its workers used to evangelize, enrich, and entertain. Central among these were methods of popular realism that Sylvester Poli deployed in his theater.

Popular Realism, "The Tithe to Moloch," and Cultural Hierarchy

From the 1870s into the period of Alexander Irvine's New Haven mission, Protestant churches and institutions of evangelical outreach like the YMCA experimented with methods of visual realism as means of popularizing their ministries. Irvine had witnessed early versions of such work in Antrim, where his childhood religious yearnings were stimulated by a magic lantern lecture on *Pilgrim's Progress*. In adulthood he remembered this experience as having offered more benefit "than all the sermons I ever heard," most of which were "a pious bore . . . preached in a language we did not understand" and concerning "themes utterly beyond our ken."[44] Early uses of magic lantern technology found contemporary support from British evangelist and publicist W. T. Stead, who in 1890 called for a "Magic Lantern Mission" in his *Review of Reviews*. Stead recognized the ways the magic lantern could appeal to the long-standing predilection of poor families like the Irvines to use the church as a source of aesthetic enrichment. "Even down to our time," insisted Stead, "Voltaire's saying remains true, that in Catholic countries the parish is the poor man's opera-house. It is also his Madame Tussaud's, his collection of statuary, and his school of architecture. In olden times it was also his theatre."[45] Stead reviled the grim piety that caused Protestant churches to shrink from using the church as a picture gallery or a concert room.

Like the wax sculptures, lantern slides, and films that Sylvester Poli offered, the magic lantern mission described by Stead aimed to democratize the established cultural hierarchies of high art and religion and to provide a new, more accessible aesthetic based on popular realism. Stead urged magic lantern evangelists to fill their shows with great art treasures that had previously depicted biblical themes only to the rich. Few in England or America had ever been inspired by Raphael or Millet, Stead pointed out. But with the use of photography and the perfected lantern slide painting, "art will be democratized, and the masses in town and country familiarized with the choicest fruit of the artistic genius of mankind." Stead regretted that this was not the purpose for which urban evangelists generally used the lantern. They tended to see it as an entertainment that drew the unchurched into the mission or sanctuary, rather than as a feature of the evangelical service itself. But even as an entertainment, the mission lantern had much to offer, as it transformed into an inviting theatrical display the pastimes and adventures that boys like Irvine had once enjoyed only through story papers, temperance tracts, and military service. Stead listed slide shows in use among the city missions, Sunday schools, and temperance missions of England that included *"Pilgrim's Progress," "Buy Your Own Cherries!," "Principal Events in the Life of the Queen," "Egypt and the Holy Land," "Zulu War," "General Gordon," "Soudan War,"* and *"Peril and Adventure in Central Africa,"* among many others.[46]

Often these shows located distant lands in a hierarchy that offered spectators a sense of supremacy associated with imperial power or Christian conversion. A slide list from a Church Missionary Society program on the Niger district illustrates the Christian hierarchy at work:

Map of Intertropical Africa. Map of Niger Country. Slave Catching. Slave Gang. Slave Dhow. Boy. Woman. Bishop Crowther. Bishop Crowther's Pastors and Teachers. . . . Worshipping the Moon. Ifa. Bishop Crowther and Idols.[47]

Just as the wax exhibits arranged by Poli for the Eden Musée advertised the superiority of civilization over barbarism, this use of visual realism tended as much to advertise the superiority of Bishop Crowther as to illuminate the Niger Country. But as in Poli's popular cultural sphere, there remained room for divergent interpretations and uses. Irvine's deployment of realist methods in the context of New Haven's religious class conflicts indicated the social sources of such opposition, and some of the forms that it took.

During his first years in New Haven Irvine followed a magic lantern format that had been practiced by more conventional New Haven evangelists throughout the 1890s. In 1894, the YMCA had featured the Reverend George H. Filian's stereopticon lectures on "Mohammedan and Christianity"; in early 1898 the Salvation Army offered magic lantern services on "The Stations of the Cross" and "The Life of Christ." Irvine's Sunday afternoon men's meetings in the Grand Opera House held to this tradition by using stereopticon presentations on *Pilgrim's Progress* and *Ben Hur*. In addition, Irvine incorporated Stead's more visionary ideas of magic lantern mission work by projecting a reproduction of Jean-François Millet's *The Angelus* and interpreting it with the aid of Edwin Markham's poem about the painting.[48] Irvine found in Markham's description of God's cultural tastes a confirmation of his own developing working-class gospel:

He is more pleased by some sweet human use
Than by the learned book of the recluse;
Sweeter are comrade kindnesses to Him
Than the high harpings of the seraphim;
. . . .
More than the hallelujahs of the choirs
Or hushed adorings at the altar fires
Is a loaf well kneaded or a room swept clean
With a light-heart love that finds no labor mean.[49]

Irvine pursued this theme in sermons accompanying some of his more conventional stereopticon displays, including a talk on "Christ's Contribution to the Labor Problem" that followed a magic lantern exhibit on *Pilgrim's Progress* in 1899. As he had in Omaha, Irvine also experimented with stereopticon exposés of poverty, entitled "Christianity and Social Wreckage."[50]

Irvine used these presentations primarily to stimulate individual working men to embark on projects of spiritual and intellectual self-improvement that would relieve the individual pains of poverty. He expanded on this message in unillustrated sermons on the theme of Christianity and labor. In a sermon on "work and wages," Irvine dwelt at length on the significance of Christ's vocation as a carpenter. But he did not yet echo the conviction recorded in the New Haven Trades Council's *Illustrated History* that Christ's carpentry linked him with the collective efforts of working-class self-improvement. Irvine's "work and wages" sermon suggested that Christ's example recommended a more individual model of self-improvement:

> He wrote no book upon labor problems, made no speeches upon the sins of capital or the shortcomings of labor. He was a carpenter! That is His contribution, long years of uncomplaining manual toil, unnoticed and almost unknown. . . . Here is the perfect gentleman, the ideal man cut out of the pattern of God, and a tradesman! To the labor of the bench thirty years and to the Messiahship three years.

The Messiah's message to workingmen, as Irvine elaborated it, was a call "to do something besides earning a living" while youth still afforded the power to pursue such opportunities. The sermon ended with an enumeration of great works accomplished by artistic masters such as Mozart and Michelangelo just before death. Irvine urged workers to reach beyond their laboring lives to seize the cultural privileges his magic lantern shows offered, before early death or a wasted life set such privileges forever beyond their reach.[51]

But, as many of his illustrated sermons demonstrated, Irvine was also ambivalent about such cultural privileges. His antiwar sermon served to clarify this ambivalence. It drew on themes of popular realism to address the class conflicts through which cultural hierarchies were fought out in New Haven. Some of the most publicized portions of the sermon expressly censured celebrations of military heroism such as Poli had offered with his movie reels of the Dewey parade only months before. The *Evening Leader* headed its report of the sermon with the boldface statement: "CALLS DEWEY COWARD: Says the Fight at Manila was Unfair."[52] As this headline emphasized, Irvine treated triumphs for which Dewey was usually applauded not as heroism but as international bullying. For Irvine, the rout at Manila Bay was comparable to a fight between a trained pugilist and a consumptive:

> The crowd applauds the victor. . . . He is feted, decorated and triumphal arches are erected. He is paraded before the public. Meantime the con-

sumptive is expected to respect him and come to terms, any terms, the victor proposes. This is a true picture of the engagement at Manila Bay. It was wood against iron, tugs against armored cruisers, brains and wealth against ignorance and poverty.[53]

Irvine remarked on the long history of attempts to justify such aggression in the name of Christian teaching, noting that contemporary proselytizers drew on the self-righteous preachments offered by militarists of the past. As evidence, he offered "The Soldiers' Pocket Bible," printed by Oliver Cromwell in the seventeenth century for the edification of the troops sent to crush the rebel Irish Confederates. This pamphlet, he claimed, had been resurrected by the American Tract Society for the spiritual instruction of soldiers during the Spanish war. It abounded in Old Testament avowals of hatred that canceled out its sparse references to the New Testament message of love. Irvine pointed to the fruits of such teaching: the Irish, he emphasized, retained into the twentieth century an implacable hatred for the name of Cromwell. "How much 'benevolent assimilation,'" Irvine went on to ask, "will it take to wipe out the stains and horror of our 'criminal aggression' in the Philippine Islands?" Seeing that the spirit and results of Dewey's heroism stimulated not love but hatred, Irvine concluded, Christians should be more sickened than cheered by the spectacle of the Dewey parade.

While Irvine decried the plight of Filipinos subjugated by Testament-toting Americans, however, he was also capable of offering a stereopticon exhibit of the journey "From Savagery to Civilization by way of the Cross in Hawaii."[54] In this respect, he straddled ongoing social conflicts over portrayals of "civilization" and its "savage" alternatives. He shared with New Haven's elite Protestant clergy and with the labor organizations who often opposed them a hierarchical vision of civilization that echoed Poli's wax exhibits and vaudeville shows.

New Haven's leading liberal clergymen deployed the hierarchy of civilization to celebrate America's imperial destiny in terms only slightly more tempered than Sylvester Poli's. Theodore Thornton Munger greeted the news of Dewey's victory at Manila Bay with a vision of America's civilizing mission. Though chary of the dangers of militarism that Irvine lamented two years later, Munger was prepared to risk them in order to gain the relative benefits he attributed to America's influence in Cuba and the Philippines. The alternative was to allow America's new conquests to fall into the hands of powers far below the United States in the hierarchy of civilization. Unless "we retain them and civilize them," Munger warned, Americans might "suffer those in the east to fall back into such hands as may be strongest—Russia or Japan or Germany." Though he confessed that no mortal could yet decide what America should do, Munger speculated knowingly on the designs of Providence. "Perhaps a higher service lies before us than freeing Cuba," he mused. "Perhaps we are called to civilize her, and to Americanize her. It may be that our battleships are victorious in the farthest east for a higher end than to break the power of Spain. It may be in the divine plan that the force carried there shall be more than our guns."[55]

In the years that followed, Munger defined in greater detail the civilizing force associated with imperialism. By 1901, when controversy over the war against the Filipinos had diminished, Munger was elaborating a scheme of global social evolution powered principally by commerce. In a lecture on "Some probable changes in the 20th Century," he pronounced that "wheresoever anything is bought or sold, there will the railway or steamship go, whether the natives and tribes like it or not." Human qualms about this process had to yield to Munger's growing certainty about its Providential necessity. To the question "Will this be right?" Munger answered: "It will be done. Is it well? It is well that a barbarian nation as well as a boy go to school, and there are truant laws out for both." Savage societies would join this forward rush of commercial civilization or fall before it, depending on their level of "vitality" to "respond to the civilization thrust upon them." Those with sufficient vitality would rise through trade, those without it would forfeit "self respective" habits to the temptations of commercial civilization and undergo a rapid, vice-ridden decline.[56]

In linking the hierarchy of civilization to a complacent optimism about the development of American economic life, Munger departed from the vision of U.S. imperialism embraced by the New Haven labor movement. Since the earliest hostilities of the Spanish-American War, organizations and spokesmen that New Haven trade unionists supported had criticized American militarism and imperial designs. The journal of the Connecticut State Federation of Labor repeatedly questioned the honor and motives of American military activity in Cuba and the Philippines. When the explosion of the *Maine* in February 1898 excited battle-eager newspapermen and legislators to frenzied calls for war with Spain, *The Craftsman* warned that these military designs promised to enslave U.S. workers to the monopolistic interests that would benefit from such a war. "A gigantic . . . and cunningly-devised scheme is being worked ostensibly to place the United States in the front rank as a naval and military power," *The Craftsman* noted. But, "[t]he real reason is that the capitalists will have the whole thing and, when any workingmen dare to ask for the living wage . . . they will be shot down like dogs in the streets."[57] When, ten months later, the Treaty of Paris promised to deliver the Philippine Islands into U.S. possession, *The Craftsman* entered the lists against annexation. As U.S. military forces proceeded to crush the Filipino resistance to American rule in early 1899, *The Craftsman* was reduced to exposing and lamenting the brutality with which the war in the Philippines was waged.[58]

Meanwhile, the man that the New Haven Trades Council had chosen to voice "The Philosophy of the Labor Movement" in their *Illustrated History* was also lending his efforts to the struggle against U.S. imperialism in the Philippines. On the platform of the founding meeting of the Anti-Imperialist League, George McNeill linked the increasingly imperialistic cast of President McKinley's foreign policy with the growth of monopoly that was "devouring enterprise" at home.[59] In other contributions to trade unionist anti-imperialism, McNeill reiterated the time-honored relation between working people and the Christian teaching that Irvine insisted was so implacably opposed to the military feats through which empires were acquired. At a high point in trade unionist opposition to the treaty ceding the Philippines to the United States, the AFL's paper featured a poem by McNeill parodying Rudyard Kipling's widely echoed statement of "The White Man's Burden." Like many parodies of Kipling circulating at the time, McNeill's "The Poor Man's Burden" countered nearly verse for verse Kipling's description of the thankless efforts made by colonial governments to civilize their ungrateful subjects. McNeill insisted that it was not, as in Kipling's poem, the imperialists who served, but "the serfs of every land," not Kipling's "new-caught sullen peoples" who gained, but instead the "rich and grand." McNeill took special care to counter the lines in which Kipling identified imperialists as God's begrudged ambassadors:

Take up the White Man's burden—
    Ye dare not stoop to less—
Nor call too loud on Freedom
    To cloke your weariness.
By all ye will or whisper
    By all ye leave or do
The silent sullen peoples
    Shall weigh your God and you.

In McNeill's version, it was the Poor Man who advanced a Providential plan:

Pile on the Poor Man's Burden—
    The day of reckoning's near—
He will call aloud on Freedom,
    And Freedom's God shall hear.

He will try you in the balance;
  He will deal out justice true:
For the Poor Man with his burden
  Weighs more with God than you.[60]

McNeill's poem stated the distinction between labor's vision of an evolutionary hierarchy of civilization and that coined by Kipling and echoed by Munger. For McNeill and other unionists, labor's struggles for working-class dignity advanced a society along the ladder of civilization far more effectively than the imperialist's bid for supremacy or the capitalist's pursuit of profit.

But labor's hierarchy of civilization could also be every bit as derogatory and racist as that described by Munger. In the course of his anti-imperialist agitation, AFL president Samuel Gompers authored some especially egregious examples of evolutionary racism. Gompers emphasized that the AFL's primary objection to expansion lay in the prevalence of contract labor and other forms of highly exploitative toil in the lands the United States proposed to annex. However, Gompers also complained that U.S. possession of Hawaii or the Philippines would degrade American citizens by linking them with "barbaric" peoples. Decrying the transformation of the Spanish-American conflict from a war of liberation into a war of imperial expansion, Gompers editorialized:

> Already do we see promises solemnly made to the people of the whole civilized world that our war has been undertaken with but one definite noble and humanitarian purpose flung to the winds. It is common to hear the declaration that whenever through the necessity of war, we may plant our flag, even though temporary, it will never be taken down, thus implying that the Chinese, the half-breeds and semi-barbaric people of the Phillipine [sic] Islands, are to be admitted as part of these United States.[61]

Such views meshed better with Alexander Irvine's talks on savagery and civilization in Hawaii than they did with his antiwar sermon. As importantly, they show why the labor movement that would help inspire Irvine to revise intertwined hierarchies of civilization and race also became an arena in which he struggled against those hierarchies.[62]

In New Haven, Irvine began to reevaluate hierarchical cultural ideals as both working people's organizations and elite religious institutions deployed them. New Haven's heritage of religious debate across class lines contributed significantly to his mission by providing him with allies and rivals who actively debated the narratives of hierarchy, self-improvement, evangelism, and entertainment he had begun to rethink in the course of his transatlantic journey. The New Haven labor movement would be an especially important catalyst, first by encouraging Irvine to reexamine the Protestant ideals of individual self-improvement he still shared with Smyth and Munger, and later by provoking him to assail the ethnic and racial boundaries that characterized Gompers's style of trade unionism. In the process, Irvine experimented further with the interplay of cultural autonomy and hierarchy visible in Poli's vaudeville shows, and became increasingly cunning in his deployment of the popular realist methods Poli used to depict that hierarchy.

Chapter Four

"SOCIAL EVANGELISM, ITS DANGERS AND DIFFICULTIES"

Pastor Irvine and the Public Sphere

WHILE PREPARING HIS ANTIWAR SERMON, Alexander Irvine was also busy formulating a Sunday evening church service designed especially for working-class worshipers. Shortly after his arrival in New Haven, a YMCA executive board member called him to fill the empty pulpit at the Second Congregational Church of Fair Haven. A suburb located east of New Haven, Fair Haven bordered some of the city's most densely populated working-class neighborhoods. To attract their inhabitants to his Sunday evening service, Irvine began to refine the plebeian mixture of religion and recreation that characterized his YMCA meetings.[1] He combined theatrical techniques with innovations in parish organization and forays into labor politics. In the process, he brought the church into the thick of New Haven's religious class conflicts. Participants in the city's old YMCA battles joined the working-class committees Irvine formed at the church, and Irvine became a familiar figure in the industrial and political struggles mounted by local trade unions. Such alliances antagonized middle-class church leaders and their associates throughout the local Protestant elite. Hounded out of the Fair Haven church by their hostility, Irvine eventually shifted the institutional base of his gospel of work to a nondenominational People's Church.

This chapter follows the development of what Irvine called his "gospel of work" as he engaged class conflicts within the Fair Haven church, within the People's Church, and within New Haven's city politics and industrial life between 1900 and 1907.[2] These conflicts are crucial to understanding the way in which he transformed his evangelical message and methods. Though Irvine was trying to combine evangelism and theatrical entertainment from his first services for the Fair Haven church, his early experiments held to many of the hierarchical cultural ideals he still shared with established evangelical institutions like the YMCA. The alliances he forged with New Haven unionists through church, political, and trade union organizations taught him new ways to address and rearrange these hierarchies. His changing cultural perspective derived from commentaries on the hierarchies of public life that trade unionists had generated in the course of repeated clashes with employers and civic elites. In local political skirmishes and economic battles, his laborite allies regularly answered challenges to their cultural attainments and asserted their own cultural standards. By entering such struggles side by side with trade unionists, Irvine learned ways to reformulate narratives of cultivation and aspiration that had shaped his evangelical career. In the process, he turned the popular theatrical methods he borrowed from Poli's entertainment realm to the task of conveying the contested character of cultural hierarchy. The result was a practical model of an expanded public sphere in which working people drew on popular culture to address issues that economic and cultural elites regarded as their own domain.

While sparked by local issues, the cultural conflicts Irvine entered in New Haven also engaged wider oppositions. Irvine gave vivid expression to these broader themes when he participated in local disputes over the anthracite coal strike of 1902. This national labor crisis generated widespread discussion of the public's role in industrial struggles, a discussion to which the New Haven clergy contributed. Irvine contributed to this debate by making use of his developing theatrical techniques to rebuke nationally renowned local clerics who continued to exclude the concerns of organized labor from a Christian public sphere. In the process, he consolidated his gospel of work. This gospel became the program for his People's Church, which served to institutionalize the public discourse his labor struggles had inculcated. But while the People's Church demonstrated the possibilities of a more democratic public sphere forged at the nexus of evangelism, entertainment, and class politics, it also revealed the limitations that Irvine's labor education bequeathed to such a venture. Not only did opposition from employers and civic elites impede the church's development; so did the exclusionary politics of gender, ethnicity, and race that Irvine still shared with the trade unionists who had helped reshape his mission. These difficulties in "social evangelism" would continue to perplex Irvine as he took the lessons of his New Haven mission to national audiences.

Sunday Evening Evangelism

At first, Irvine's pastoral activities at the Second Congregational Church of Fair Haven betrayed little of the class conflict that would shape his local mission. He was in many ways an unexceptional Elm City minister, busily making use of resources that local clergymen considered their due. He joined the New Haven

Congregational Club, where prominent pastors and worshipers such as Theodore Thornton Munger, Newman Smyth, and Connecticut Supreme Court Judge (and later Governor) Simeon Baldwin met to discuss social issues.[3] He entered Yale Divinity School, enrolling in courses on Hebrew, New Testament Greek, and archaeology.[4] With the exception of his antiwar sermon, even the social and political activism Irvine initiated in the first years of his Fair Haven pastorate suited elite cultural prejudices. In the summer of 1899, he established a flower mission to interest middle-class youth in the living conditions of nearby tenement-dwellers. The mission quickly expanded into a social settlement. To sustain this institution, Irvine sought the support of Reverend Anson Phelps Stokes, secretary of Yale University, and Henry W. Farnam, an economics professor at Yale and prominent member of Newman Smyth's church. By early 1901 these men had formed an advisory council for the new institution, christened Lowell House, with Farnam as chairman, Irvine as secretary, and a membership drawn mainly from the ranks of Yale officials, professors, and professors' wives. Irvine also joined university and church leaders in a campaign for a municipal bathhouse.[5]

Irvine's first evening services at the Fair Haven church reflected this social intercourse. Many of these services focused on artistic and cultural practices familiar to Yale scholars and church elites, which Irvine tried to make more accessible to working-class worshipers. During the winter of 1901–2 he offered Sunday evening sermons on images of the Christ child in art as well as on paintings by Joseph Turner and Holman Hunt. He also lectured for several weeks on the life and art of nineteenth-century French realist painter Jean-François Millet and presented sermons on William Morris tapestries hanging at Oxford and on English poet Thomas Gray.[6]

But Irvine's increasingly popular Sunday evening ministry also cultivated specifically working-class interests. Irvine did not shrink from publicizing his stereopticon sermons for their entertainment value as well as their inspirational qualities. He played up the plebeian combination of recreation and religion that linked the traditions of his parents' cobbler's shop to the working-class evangelical style of the early New Haven Railroad YMCA. As his church reports proclaimed:

> This service, as carried on for several years, has been peculiarly a people's service. The audiences are probably the largest gatherings in any of the New Haven churches. They have had an evangelistic tone. They have been illustrated usually. The special attraction—I use the word advisedly, for the design was to "attract"—and the free pew system adopted at the second service has

had the effect of bringing hundreds of people out who had not been in a church for years and of bringing into our church membership scores of men, women and children.

Irvine recalled later that "very good people of the community" viewed the Sunday evening service as a "show" that represented a terrible "come-down" in church work. But he was not deliberately trying to appeal to lowbrow tastes, whatever well-heeled Protestants might think. He wanted to address working-class concerns as other local Protestant churches did not.[7]

To fulfill these aims, Irvine interpreted artworks in light of their relevance to working-class lives. His sermons on Turner and Hunt were part of a series on religion and labor in art, and his lectures on Jean-François Millet emphasized the dignity of labor.[8] Millet's paintings of French peasants at work provided Irvine with particularly rich images for the connection between labor and spiritual life. The revolutions of 1848 had inspired Millet to fashion heroic yet unidealized images of rural laborers in the *The Sower* and *The Man with the Hoe*. Other Millet paintings, such as *The Angelus* and *The Gleaners*, evoked a divine harmony that inhered in the life of the soil. With the help of photography and the magic lantern, Irvine linked these themes to the complexities of visual realism that his ministry shared with Sylvester Poli's amusement ventures.[9]

Irvine organized his Millet sermons around a set of photographs that documented the connections between Millet's paintings and the conditions of peasant life with almost pedantic literalism. He had taken these photographs during the summer of 1901 when, after a visit to Antrim to see his dying father, he traveled through France to record scenes of Millet's life and work.[10] Several of the photographs displayed peasants posed in scenes paralleling famous Millet paintings such as *The Man with the Hoe*; others recorded the landscapes in which Millet set such sanctified visions of peasant life as *The Angelus* or *The Church at Grenville*. In the scrapbook he kept of these photographs, Irvine positioned his posed reconstructions of Millet paintings next to reproductions of the works with which they shared formal arrangement or scenic content. Throughout this collection, his apparent aim was to establish compelling links between the transcendent religious themes of Millet's paintings and the prosaic lives of the rural working-class subjects the artist had painted. The heroism and sanctity of labor depicted in *The Man with the Hoe* and *The Angelus* were not just allegorical, Irvine's photographs seemed to say. Here was a real agricultural worker with a hoe, the real field where Millet's praying peasants met. Heroism and sanctity were tangible qualities that could affect the world of the present. Of course, Irvine had constructed his peasant photographs in ways that shaped the "reality" he claimed for these images. But all uses of visual realism did so—Irvine happened to manipulate its methods quite shrewdly.

Rather than imposing artistic refinements on chaotic working-class conditions, as in reformist uses of visual realism like Jacob Riis's famous lectures on tenement life, Irvine suggested that art should draw on and celebrate the moral claims of the "other half." He used Millet to demonstrate a continuum between working-class lives and the cultural hierarchies that informed fine art and religious uplift. His sermons focused on both the "deep religious atmosphere" of Millet's paintings and their portrayal of "the struggle of man with the forces of nature." According to Irvine's advertisements for his sermons, Millet's own life bespoke a connection between working lives and religious transcendence. "A peasant born and a peasant died," Irvine wrote, Millet "reminds one of the characters of the Old Testament."[11] Irvine's photographs of Millet-like peasants took the connection between manual labor and transcendence beyond Millet's painterly vision, presenting it as a fact of life visible in the likenesses of living laborers. Of course, Irvine believed that workers had to struggle for such transcendence: he saw cultural uplift as a personal goal and a collective project, not a birthright. But whereas for reformers like Riis such struggles advanced along a hierarchy supplied by middle-class moral distinctions, the hierarchy Irvine presented was immanent within workers' own daily lives.[12] This became a crucial distinction as Irvine linked religion, culture, and politics in his New Haven mission.

The connection between manual labor and artistic transcendence that Irvine evoked in his Millet sermons also played on the reflexive cultural hierarchy produced in Poli's popular cultural realm. Poli's vaudeville shows constantly questioned their own implied hierarchies from a variety of perspectives. Poli indicated his own preferred outlook, which celebrated "civilized" northern and Anglo-American cultural practices to the detriment of "barbaric" southern and non-European ones. However, in vaudeville this arrangement competed with alternative formulations. Vaudeville caricatures expressed rivalries in which the hierarchy among ethnic groups coexisted uneasily with proud displays of ethnic chauvinism. Moreover, the hierarchy of civilization lent itself to contested uses, as Irvine showed by taking issue with militarism while drawing on the idea of cultural hierarchy celebrated in Poli's exhibitions of military pomp. In his Millet sermons, Irvine addressed such contests by presenting artistic masterpieces as simultaneously attractive, in different ways, to well-heeled Protestants as well as unchurched workers. While deriding Irvine's visual imagery as "showy," mid-

5. Alexander Irvine (*center, front*) posing piously with the deacons of Pilgrim Church, Fair Haven, outside the church, around 1900. To poke fun at the hierarchical solemnity of this shot, Irvine placed the photograph in a scrapbook over the title "Pillars and Caterpillars," which only aggravated his differences with the deacons. Photo from Alexander Irvine, "From the Bottom Up: VII, Life Among 'The Squatters,'" *The World's Work* 19, no. 3 (1910): 12456; anecdote, Alexander Irvine, *A Fighting Parson: The Autobiography of Alexander Irvine* (Boston: Little, Brown, 1930), 63.

dle-class Congregationalists could still see his stereopticon lectures as means of drawing working-class parishioners along a cultural hierarchy for which their own cultural sensibilities were the upper stations. At the same time, by using photographs of French peasants to mimic Millet's paintings, Irvine invited workers to see Millet's message as emanating from the dignity of manual labor.

As Irvine developed his ministry to New Haven workers, he would find these messages increasingly incompatible. Once allied with organized labor, he would adopt working-class formulations of cultural hierarchy that scandalized local elites. But Irvine's direct links to trade unions were slow to develop; they remained limited to trade unionist acclaim for his antiwar sermon during the first years of his Sunday evening evangelism. In the meantime, however, he was attracting workers to his Sunday evening service (which had a congregation of seven hundred by mid-1900) and forming working-class committees and clubs within his church.[13] Together, these allies constituted a base of increasingly organized working-class support for his developing mission.

The committee Irvine established to help run his Sunday evening services provided a core of working-class support. Its proletarian cast departed sharply from the Fair Haven church's governing body, the Society's Committee. Only professionals, proprietors, and managers served on the Society's Committee. Its chairman was attorney William P. Niles, a prominent local Republican and corporation counsel for the borough of Fair Haven East. Other members owned or directed manufacturing and mercantile establishments in New Haven.[14] In contrast, the sixteen-member Sunday Evening Service Committee had only one member who owned or managed a business. Four were white-collar employees—two clerks, one salesman for the National Biscuit Company, and a collector. The majority of the committee, ten members, worked in the skilled trades that contributed the bulk of New Haven's labor movement. Five were employed by the railroad and express companies whose workers had formulated a proletarian evangelical movement twenty-five years earlier, including Franklin Page, an engineer who had been active in the New Haven Railroad YMCA in the 1880s. The committee also included a marine engineer, a machinist, a mechanic, an employee of the New Haven Carriage Company, and an electrotyper.[15]

The personal and occupational affiliations of Irvine's Sunday Evening Service Committee linked his evangelism to wider circles of working-class religiosity and politics. Through Franklin Page and his fellow railway workers, Irvine's ministry drew on previous flowerings of working-class evangelism in the city. Skilled tradesmen like Forrest Kelsey, the electrotyper, or Walter Chaffee, the carriage worker, belonged to an especially loyal group who followed Irvine as he engaged the class politics of New Haven's religious culture more directly. Through trades whose union organizations came to support Irvine, these men also provided links between Irvine's religious mission and the unionists who may have attended his services but never served on his church committees or joined his parishes.

While Irvine's Sunday Evening Service Committee was exclusively male, he did not ignore women in developing structures of working-class church participation. His early parish innovations included the Gaius Guild, formed in 1902. Irvine intended this organization to provide "a point of contact" for "the many women who are members of our church and at the same time strangers to the church members." He was especially concerned about the class divisions that he and others recognized as the main fractures in religious sociability. The leadership of the Gaius Guild suggests that it did appeal to working-class women: its president and treasurer, Mrs. Scarlett and Mrs. Pollard, were among the new members taken into the church during 1902, most of whom were workers and wives of workers attracted by Irvine's evening service. The guild's secretary, Mrs. Mallory, was the wife of an oysterman.[16]

Though the activities of the guild went unrecorded, its leadership illuminates the complicated gender dynamics of Irvine's developing ministry. Directed to working-class men and concerned with masculine themes, Irvine's preaching clearly attracted women as well. Yet Irvine was slow to articulate views about women's work, political concerns, or social relations. In New Haven, his few public references to women associated them with family concerns that he regarded as distractions from more crucial public business. Reflecting on the work of Lowell House to a reporter in 1904, Irvine observed that settlements only touched women and children, and could not affect "the great social problems of the community."[17] Irvine may well have regarded the Gaius Guild, with its provision for "social intercourse and spiritual help" among women, as a relatively insignificant addition to parish activities.[18] But Mrs. Scarlett, Mrs. Mallory, and Mrs. Pollard no doubt evaluated their participation more positively than he did. Women also made up a significant portion of the largest organizational base of working-class support Irvine built within his Fair Haven church: the members drawn by his Sunday evening evangelism. Of the sixty-nine new members Irvine reported for 1902, thirty-four were women. Twenty of these can be identified in the city directory by their own occupation or that of a husband or father. Only two were related to men of the managerial class who dominated the lay leadership of the church. Three were wage-earners and another fifteen were the wives or daughters of wage-earners. Together with the twenty identifiably working-class men who joined the church in 1902, these women helped make up a working-class phalanx of support for Irvine within the Fair Haven church.

As for the male recruits to Irvine's working-class congregation, they not only provided support within the parish, but also linked Irvine's evangelical following with the union and political alliances he soon began to develop outside the church. Several of the new working-class members Irvine brought into the church in 1902 worked in occupations organized by unions that helped shape Irvine's political activism.[19] Their occupations linked his evangelical activities and his growing political activism in late 1902. This link became vitally important in shaping both the rhetoric and the class relations of Irvine's ministry. Those who provided Irvine's most loyal following within the church would have had less opportunity to demonstrate their support if his own growing political activism had not alienated the church's middle-class leadership. Irvine's political activities provoked him to proclaim from the pulpit his own allegiance to the solidarities cultivated in working-class organizations. He forged his alliance with Elm City trade unionists and altered the rhetoric of his evangelism through two interconnected battles. The first was a trade union political movement that grew out of a campaign to municipalize the local water plant and developed into an electoral crusade. The second was a strike waged by the Sargent factory's predominantly Italian-American metal workers.

Political Alliances and Evangelical Defiance

The Cultural Lessons of Workingmen's Politics

Alexander Irvine arrived in New Haven just in time to form the political alliances that transformed his ministry. When he moved to the city in 1898, local trade unions were entering a five-year period of renewed growth and political activism. During this period, the craft unions that formed the backbone of the New Haven labor movement increased dramatically in size, number, and solidarity, both locally and nationally. In 1900, the state Bureau of Labor Statistics listed thirty-three separate union locals for New Haven, in addition to the Trades Council and the Building Trades Council. By 1903 this number had tripled.[20] As their numbers increased, local craft unionists took growing interest in adding independent political action to a tactical arsenal that consisted primarily of strikes and boycotts. By drawing Irvine into their political activities and their shop floor battles, they reshaped his mission. They forced him to choose between the claims of rival constituencies within his church and the community—between laborites and Congregational Club members, to begin with. Irvine irritated his elite parishioners as he embraced the values espoused by working-class organizations and integrated these values into his evening services.

The water campaign that Irvine joined in 1901 brought together New Haven trade unionists and a movement of disgruntled taxpayers, who jointly proposed either to reform the existing city water contract or to municipalize the water plant.[21] Speaking at a public hearing before the Water Committee of the New Haven Court of Common Council in December 1901, Irvine satisfied both constituencies. According to his autobiographical account, "I asked the committee to hold the balance level. 'We tax a banana vendor a few dollars a year for the use of the streets,' I said, 'then why should a rich corporation be given an infinitely larger use of them for nothing?'" This formulation echoed the sentiments of a leaflet on the water issues that the taxpayers' movement had distributed. One of the taxpayer's spokesmen, optical works foreman William Trueman, had sent a leaflet to Irvine with the postscript, "I wonder if A. F. Irvine will be there and speak for the people?"[22] But Irvine's participation in the water crusade also answered a general challenge issued by the Trades Council to the city's clergy at large. When the Trades Council thanked Irvine for his activism in an open letter to the press, their acknowledgment proclaimed the common religious spirit that linked his municipal stand to their own trade unionist Christianity. They interpreted actions such as Irvine's as support for the city's working people in their capacities not only as taxpayers, but also as producers of wealth. "We believe that the product should belong to the producer as against the whole world," the unionists explained:

> We believe that when some man gets something for nothing some other men must produce something and get nothing in return. We know that if a share in the New Haven Water company has a par value of $50, and yet sold for $118, that some man somewhere had to slave by the sweat of his brow to make up the difference of $68. . . . Can you blame us for not supporting an institution that is so clearly opposed to justice, humanity, and brotherhood?[23]

Such arguments linked the struggle for municipal ownership to the working-class Christianity that was shared across disparate positions on labor organizing and labor politics. To fail to support their rights against the water company, the Trades Council maintained, was to contradict God's will and the teachings of Christ.

With this logic, the Council drew Irvine into a developing working-class political movement that sharpened the cultural class allegiances implied in his own mission. The unionists pointed out a distinction between, on one hand, the unchristian upper-class privileges sought by the water company and its allies and, on the other, the cultural accoutrements that Irvine tried to establish as working-class birthrights. Irvine's stand on the water question dissociated him from elite privilege, in the Trades Council's view. In contrast, the clergymen who had failed to support labor's cause in the water campaign showed that they stood with the "professors, bankers, lawyers and so-called cultured element." They departed from the position taken by "the man of Galilee." "He worked for the poor," the Trades Council admonished. "You are on the side of the rich. He had no place to lay his head. You have elegant furnishings."[24] These words recalled cultural and material class divisions that Irvine had encountered from childhood. But the

Trades Council took a position within these divisions different from the one that Irvine had cultivated in his journey of self-education, and still proposed in his Sunday evening services. For the Trades Council, an elegant material standard of living amounted to "so-called" culture. Unionists set such elite equipment apart from the forms of religious and intellectual self-development that they endorsed.

As Irvine incorporated this concept of culture into his own mission, he infuriated elite parishioners who already took exception to his water campaign advocacy. Irvine's plea for municipal ownership raised the ire of shareholders in the water company who were also prominent church members and provoked his first serious dispute with the church's lay leadership. One church leader, Irvine recalled, came to warn him that former pastors had been "called of God" to other posts for lesser slights.[25] Parish elites contented themselves with this warning for the time being, since they could view Irvine's water campaign agitation as a potentially passing enthusiasm. In February 1902 the water company and city officials signed a new contract that disregarded nearly all of the municipal ownership advocates' complaints.[26] But Irvine soon found ways to intensify the rancor he had excited during the water campaign.

Laborite political ambitions gave him scant rest from controversy. Spurred to political action though the water issue, New Haven unionists took further political courage from the recent successes of working-class mayoral candidates in nearby cities. The new mayor in the city of Ansonia was Stephen Charters, a carpenter arrested under Connecticut's antilabor conspiracy law for his role in a 1901 machinists' strike. According to the *New Haven Union*, Charters's victory was a triumph not only for workingmen's electoral politics, but for cultural values that elevated laborite solidarity above the sanctities of "so-called" culture. Though he made no claim to collegiate education and occasionally said "I done" instead of "I did," the *Union* observed, Charters had done much to overturn what he perceived as a widespread "disregard . . . of what the man who works with his hands thinks and believes should be done," in part by appointing a majority of union men to local civic posts. On the same day Charters won office in Ansonia, Bridgeport voters promoted factory stoker Denis Mulvihill from alderman to mayor.[27] Meanwhile, trade unionists in Hartford were busy forming a political organization called the Economic League, which they used to champion the president of the State Federation of Labor, Ignatius Sullivan, as the Democratic mayoral candidate in their city.

New Haven trade unionists wanted to contribute to this laborite political crusade, but they were too weak within local Democratic circles and too alienated from regular Party politics to pursue an electoral strategy from inside the Party machine.[28] Rather than running labor men as regular Party candidates in the 1902 local election—as laborites in Ansonia, Bridgeport, and Hartford had done—they endorsed Republicans, Democrats, and Socialists who were union men or sympathetic to labor causes. In exchange for such endorsement they demanded that candidates pledge "to support labor matters and to support the reference of such matters as questions of the [public utility] franchises etc. back to the people for the referendum." Echoing the recent water campaign, this strategy had encouraging results. Ten of the twelve candidates that the Trades Council endorsed were elected. One of labor's endorsees, Democratic aldermanic candidate Cornelius Conway, won the largest vote in the election. Emboldened by their local victories and by the growing political presence of labor in the state, New Haven labor leaders joined with reformers like William Trueman and supporters like Irvine to form a New Haven branch of the Economic League.[29]

Within three months of its formation, however, New Haven's League fell to bickering over cultural class divisions. League president Andrew Kelly, a locomotive fireman, complained that, though trade unionists had founded the organization, lawyers and real estate brokers had taken over. The Trades Council's recording secretary, molder Philip Daly, seconded Kelly's point, and elaborated on how professionals deployed cultural and educational privileges in order to exclude trade unionists from League discussions. As Daly put it:

> I am aware of the fact that I am uncouth and not possessed of as glib a tongue as might be, but I do know that things are not as they ought to be. Every time a trades unionist stands on the floor to state his views the gentlemen of the law try to crowd him out by calling questions of order. This thing must be stopped. Many of the men from my ranks can express their opinion intelligently enough if you give them a few minutes time. It has apparently been the aim of the lawyers to drown them out. They have succeeded so far, and I recommend to every workingman who is a member to get up and say what he has to say in spite of the lawyers here or elsewhere.[30]

In his complaint about snobbery among "gentlemen of the law," Daly raised a sensitive issue for Irvine's mission. For Irvine, one of the primary values of working-class solidarity lay in the claims workers could make on the sublime satisfactions of learning and cultural self-improvement. From the perspective of his laborite allies, the hocus pocus of cultural refinement was a technique local dignitaries used to deny the legitimacy of working-class demands.

Within the Economic League, Irvine managed to plead for cross-class unity while maintaining alliances with frustrated labor men by calling on religious ideals that unionists had often shared across lines of political debate. Though skeptical of the ways politicians used cultural capacities that Irvine recommended in his ministry, League unionists spoke this skepticism in religious terms. For example, when Andrew Kelly resigned his position as League president in protest against the organization's lawyers and "spoils politicians," he declared that "I will never be a candidate for any office. . . . I took an oath upon a Bible, before an altar, kneeling on my knees, that I would be faithful to the union that I represent, and I will never abandon the work of watching over it to descend to the level of a politician."[31] Kelly's declaration drew on the long tradition of working-class religiosity that had knit together Protestants and Catholics in the New Haven Railroad YMCA of the 1870s and provided a rallying point across ethnic and political lines in the Trades Council. Family connections augmented Kelly's union ties to the network of fraternal and self-help associations that institutionalized this working-class faith. His brother, John J. Kelly, was prominent in the Connecticut Catholic Abstinence circles also frequented by Economic Leaguer Joseph Reilly. These ties linked Andrew Kelly's reverent attitude toward union leadership to the plebeian pieties that constituted Alexander Irvine's broadest appeal to the religious traditions of New Haven workers.[32]

As he addressed ongoing divisions within the Economic League, Irvine honed the political terms of this religious appeal. Trade unionist League members continued to suspect the self-promotional aims of career politicians. By fall, labor leaders such as Kelly and Daly were backing a new Labor-Economic ticket for the approaching state election. The new ticket substituted union men for the Economic League endorsements that labor leaders found objectionable. After months of negotiating with the party candidates to elicit support for the League's platform and slots on the Democratic ticket for League members like Joseph Reilly, the Economic League was reluctant to abandon this support shortly before the election for labor candidates who shunned regular party politics altogether.[33] As a member of the League's executive committee, Irvine tried to steer a course loyal to both the League's reformist coalition and the labor movement.

Irvine focused primarily on the campaign of the incumbent Republican Judge of Probate, Livingston Warner Cleaveland. He spearheaded Economic League support for Cleaveland's race against a Gold Democrat whose candidacy most League leaders opposed out of fierce loyalty to William Jennings Bryan. In his publicity for Cleaveland, however, Irvine was careful to include not only endorsements from stalwart Bryan Democrats but also those of labor men who had recently questioned local Party orthodoxy. In preparing Cleaveland campaign leaflets, Irvine placed letters from champions of the Labor-Economic ticket like Andrew Kelly above a letter from a Bryanite Economic League leader who was skeptical of labor's third-party efforts. By incorporating both wings of the Economic League into his campaign for Cleaveland, Irvine reproduced in his political activism the ambiguous appeals to working-class autonomy and cultural hierarchy that characterized his early religious mission in New Haven. Cleaveland's ties to the Connecticut YMCA and the New Haven Congregational Club resonated with Irvine's hierarchical vision of self-improvement. Meanwhile, Irvine's gestures toward the Labor-Economic ticket demonstrated his growing alliance with trade unionists and their cultural standards—the doctrines, as Kelly's endorsement of Cleaveland put it, of "charity and justice at all times to the poor."[34] The effect of this compromise was to pull Irvine further into the laborite alliances that would transform the cultural politics of his mission.

The Sargent Strike and the Politics of Class and Culture

As he deepened the labor alliances his political activities had produced, Irvine continued to aggravate the class rifts opening in his parish. He provoked renewed annoyance among his elite parishioners by lending his voice to the cause of Italian metal workers on strike against the Sargent hardware factory. Irvine's participation in the strike was an extension of his involvement in the Economic League, whose Philip Daly was a key spokesman for the Sargent workers. But the strike also complicated the labor alliances Irvine had solidified through the Economic League by giving expression to intraclass ethnic conflicts that would eventually confound his gospel of work. For the time being, however, the strike drove him to embrace working-class institutions as the organizational base of his mission.

Inside contractor Michael Campbell precipitated the Sargent strike by dismissing two Italian metal workers from his blacksmithing shop on June 4, 1902. By noon seven hundred members of the Italian-American polishers', buffers' and brass workers' union had quit work in protest. The strike spread rapidly throughout the plant, with 1,400 workers joining by June 6. Their demands extended beyond the grievances of the fired men to include the public posting of rates for each kind of piecework in the factory. This demand transformed the strike into a struggle against the system of inside contracting, which allocated authority over production, personnel, and wage rates to contractors like Campbell who managed shops within the factory. The twenty-six contractors had long kept piece rates secret in order to enhance their control over production arrangements and thereby improve their competitive positions in bidding on the jobs available at Sargent's.

Factory owner J. B. Sargent was not entirely pleased with the production arrangements that contractors contrived. To minimize their authority, he had attempted for years to discover and regularize piece rates in the various shops. He eagerly promoted contractors like Campbell who aided this scheme. Meanwhile, he employed increasing numbers of unskilled Italian laborers whose loyalty he courted with condescending paternalism. When Campbell caused a disturbance by dismissing two of these workers, Sargent's initial reaction was to address the workers' grievances over the contractor's head. Protesting that he had not been advised of the strikers' concerns, Sargent called a conference with Campbell and American, Irish-American, and Italian-American union leaders. He then magnanimously announced that all strikers would be reinstated and the price lists for piecework duly posted.[35]

But metal workers soon discovered that Sargent's efforts to minimize the inside contractors' authority did little to advance their desires for greater control over production. Sargent wanted to unlock the secret of piece rates in order to submit the production process to his own time and cost controls. He decided that he could best achieve this goal by attaching to each tray of work a slip indicating the price and recording the time spent on the task. This system did not give workers the shared knowledge of piece rates they had demanded, and within a week of the settlement there was talk of another strike. On July 7 Italian union leaders met briefly with Sargent to discuss their grievances. When talk yielded nothing, Irish- and Italian-American unionists quit the factory en masse, nearly two thousand strong.

Their new demands precluded a superficial, paternalistic agreement of the kind that had interrupted the strike in June. In addition to the publication of piece rates and reinstatement of workers discharged during previous disagreements, the strikers now wanted rates set by shop committees of workmen and managers, a 25 percent raise for the predominantly Italian day laborers, and a union shop. J. B. Sargent recognized these demands as nothing less than a bid for shop floor control. He refused to consider wage increases and rejected the posting of piece rates, preferring his system of individual slips. Of the demand for a union shop, he stated loftily that it was "so absurd that I hardly need say that it was refused. Our men cannot hope to dictate as to whom we shall hire and they make a big mistake in trying to do so."[36]

Initially the strikers' determination matched Sargent's resolve. The solidarity that fueled their confidence was long-standing and broad-ranging. The metal workers had been organizing for a year, and drew support from the political initiatives that labor had been making in that period, including the formation of the Economic League. The League's Philip Daly was fourth vice president of their international union and spoke strongly for their cause.[37] But trade unions and laborite political organizations were not the only sources of the Sargent workers' solidarity. About 75 percent of the strikers came from New Haven's Italian-American community. A network of Italian-American organizations encouraged unionized Italians to stand firm in their demands. Their efforts to organize had been aided by countrymen who, though employed elsewhere, committed themselves to the union as they did to other ethnic organizations. Editors of the Italian weekly *Il Corriere del Connecticut* boosted the Italian section of the metal workers' union before the strike, and sneered at J. B. Sargent's posturing as "Papa degli italiani." Socially prominent Italian-Americans also urged Sargent workers to stand firm and assert their dignity not only as workers but as Italians. Supported by ethnic, political, and trade union organization, the striking metal workers stood solid for two weeks in the face of Sargent's intransigence.[38]

When Sargent rejected even their compromise conditions, the strikers agreed to have Alexander Irvine attempt to mediate the dispute. On July 26, Irvine discussed the strike with Sargent for over three hours, but failed to secure any concessions. After his interview with Sargent, Irvine made a statement to the *New Haven Union* interpreting the strike in terms that recalled the sermon that first brought him to the attention of the Trades Council. He spoke of the strike as "a death grapple between a large corporation and a large force of laboring men":

> On one side there is an immense stock of goods to do business with, unlimited credit in the business world, and on the other hand, the daily wage and in a majority of cases a pittance, a bare living. It is like the battle of Manila bay—a fight between iron and wood.

Irvine also hailed the strikers' ethnic and union solidarity:

> The fact that 1,500 men, mostly Italians, have been on strike for three weeks and there had been no disturbance, no intimidation, no boycotting, speaks volumes for the laboring class of the Italian colony. This has been a real test of the character of these men. . . . [The strike] is a battle of intelligence and trained business capacity against a class of laborers whose only hope seems to be in a perfect organization. The next result of this strike as far as trade unionism is concerned will be a demonstration of the absolute need of united effort among workingmen.[39]

While Irvine tried to make the strike a lesson in widespread labor unity, however, the Sargent strike also illustrated a web of conflicts among New Haven workers who shared his religious vision.

At its inception, the strike had demonstrated the divisive meanings that different workers attached to the plebeian blend of pleasure and piety elaborated in Irvine's ministry. Michael Campbell, who precipitated the strike, shared in this plebeian tradition through visits to Dwight Moody's revival tent and attendance at Catholic temperance soirees. Alternatives to Campbell's individualistic version of such traditions were also well established. Members of the praying band of railroad men who struggled in the 1880s to keep their organization independent of the New Haven YMCA might have advised Campbell to embrace their working-class fraternity of self-improvement. By 1902 Alexander Irvine was the most vocal advocate of such fraternity in New Haven, as local trade unionists acknowledged by recognizing him as a legitimate spokesman for the Sargent strikers who defied Campbell. However, the strike also illustrated intraclass divisions that confounded any unified gospel Irvine might try to weave out of such plebeian religious traditions.

A week after Irvine celebrated the merits of ethnic and trade union solidarity in his public statement on the strike, officials of the metal workers' union began to craft a settlement that divided the concerns of organized labor from those of the Italian community. The workers won a nondiscrimination clause for union members, grievance procedures to protect workers from contractors, and new raises for polishers and buffers. President E. J. Lynch of the International Metal Workers' Union claimed a victory for the workers, but voices in the Italian colony disagreed. The editors of *Il Corriere del Connecticut* blustered that union leaders had deceived Italian workers. Indeed, the settlement abandoned the raises earlier requested for the predominantly Italian day laborers and, as *Il Corriere* reported for weeks afterwards, many Italian workers attempting to return to the factory found their jobs filled by strikebreakers. Ultimately, only skilled craft workers won anything from the strike, while the laborers were worse off than before. The strike thus demonstrated a narrow interpretation of craft union interests that Irvine would come to challenge as he identified himself more closely with organized labor.[40]

For the time being, the Sargent strike deepened the alliance between Irvine and New Haven trade unionists by aggravating differences between the minister and elite members of his parish. Irked by Irvine's participation in the water controversy, lay leaders of Pilgrim Church—which had changed its name from the Second Congregational Church of Fair Haven in March 1902—were horrified at Irvine's public statement in behalf of striking metal workers. During the week of his intervention at Sargent's, Irvine added insult to injury by socializing with William Jennings Bryan and New Haven Silver Democrat Philo Bennett. Though somewhat contradictory in themselves, each of these alliances was an affront to the Pilgrim grandees: combined, they sparked outrage within the church's governing clique. According to Irvine's account, church leaders soon informed him of their "disgust."

Culture, Politics, and the Pulpit

In September, when his wealthier communicants returned from their summer vacations, Irvine reminded them from the pulpit that he obeyed a higher authority. Referring to Bryan's visit and the Sargent strike, Irvine avowed that he acknowledged no master save God, and that he did right to heed calls to assist the poor. The sermon, which made front-page news, was no momentary rebuke. It signaled a substantial revision of the compromise between individual uplift and collective self-help that had characterized Irvine's ministry in the church. The nature of this revision became more apparent as Irvine resumed his Sunday evening services in November.[41]

In these sermons, Irvine began to take class divisions and the material interests of the poor as points of theological departure. Rather than offering religious teaching primarily as a source of high-cultural enrichment, as he had in previous Sunday evening discourses, Irvine publicized biblical criticism of the material inequalities against which his trade unionist allies were organized. Such minor prophets as Micah, complained Irvine, had "too much to say about justice and square dealing to be popular" among the clergy of industrial America. While the much-cited Isaiah was busy satirizing the city fashions and ecclesiastical corruption, Micah struck out against "the selfishness of the land grabber, who had squeezed out the peasant and robbed him of his heritage." Micah also inspired the ancient oppressed with the vision of a new leader and a new social order, of which he foretold: "This man shall be our peace. Swords shall be beaten into ploughshare[s] and every man shall get under his own vine and fig tree." According to Irvine, the leaders of American Protestantism had reneged on this promise so that:

> This most democratic of all leaders seems now to be the exclusive property of the rich and to be managed by machines with pretensions to divinity. He is fenced in by creeds and clothes and purchase[d] pews—this man whose ancestor was a shepherd and who was himself a carpenter, who selected honest fishermen to found a commonwealth, this man whom the common people heard gladly.

Such statements incorporated the religious creed of the New Haven Trades Council into Irvine's religious mission. No longer did he offer the refinements of the churched elite as improvements that religion offered to workers. Instead, like the Trades Council, he classed these refinements in the category of "so-called culture," dishonest pretensions designed to exclude plain and honest people. Against "churches, colleges and institutions of philanthropy . . . supported by ill gotten gains" and "clergy . . . prostrate before the charm of a big endowment" Irvine posed Micah's creed for a democratic religion of workers: do justly, love mercy, and walk humbly with thy God.[42]

Irvine still advocated cultural self-development and tried to acquaint his evening congregation with artistic genius. His evening services still accompanied hymns with radiantly illustrated stereopticon slides and focused on the pleasures of art and literature. But his new sermons suggested that just as religion had to be rescued from the hypocrisies of church leaders, so culture had to be rescued from the prejudices of the overly refined. One illustrated sermon vigorously defended Henryk Sienkiewicz's *Quo Vadis* against critics who branded it licentious. Irvine recommended the book as an excellent representation of Roman life that illuminated the circumstances under which early Christians preached and lived their doctrines.[43]

Irvine made especially vivid use of the magic lantern to distinguish his new approach to religion and culture from that of the local Protestant elite. On December 7, 1902, the day he announced to morning worshipers his intention to resign as pastor of Pilgrim Church, his evening topic was "What Is the Matter with the Churches?" Irvine illustrated his remarks by showing the slide of a cross surrounded by a fence. According to the *New Haven Union*'s account: "He explained that he took this photograph in Normandy and that this cross, which some wealthy land owner had so carefully kept apart, was typical of the church today where Christianity is 'fenced in,' as he said." Irvine then presented a slide of Christ and the fishermen, and explained that until the churches were open to all classes the cross would remain "fenced in." Irvine went on to offer contemporary evidence of the churches' failure to welcome workers and address their concerns. He referred to sermons given by Congregationalist ministers who celebrated scabs and described manual workers in derogatory terms. These sermons, he maintained, articulated the position of churches within industrial relations:

> The church is too much operated on a gold basis. Men are put on church and philanthropic boards, whose sole qualification is that they have money.

The few workingmen who are now in the churches managed by wealth are relegated to back seats. There is no democracy; no leveling on the basis of manhood or religion.

Irvine ended with advice to both workingmen and men of wealth who would change these conditions and unfence the cross. Workingmen, he admonished, must support ministers who seek democracy, and "as you stand shoulder to shoulder in unions, for a fair share of the wealth you create, and for a higher standard of living, . . . neglect not the assembling of yourselves together for the worship of God and the cultivation of those mental and moral qualities which differentiate man from the beasts of the field." The rich, Irvine insisted, must cease to behave as if they had a corner on cultivation, a "monopoly on God." "See to it that the church of the carpenter is not barred to the men of this and kindred crafts."[44]

The local Building Trades Council swiftly commended Irvine for his critique of hypocrites who corrupted a carpenter's religion. "[T]here are few Preachers of the Gospel," the Council stated, "who have the unswerving integrity to adhere strictly to the teachings of the Bible." They thanked him for "fearlessly stating the workingmen's side of the case," and, with the hope that he might not "thereby sustain any great material loss," took the liberty "to subscribe ourselfs your Friends."[45] The Building Trades Council recognized, in short, that Irvine had successfully incorporated trade unionist claims on cultural hierarchy into his evangelical project. Public recognition of his cultural and political alliances with trade unionists, in turn, propelled Irvine and his allies into new struggles that went beyond local conflicts. As 1902 turned into 1903, controversy over the massive strike recently conducted in the nation's anthracite coal fields engaged Irvine in a debate about the nature of working-class participation in the public sphere.

The Anthracite Coal Strike, the Public Sphere, and Cultural Class Conflict

The strike that gripped Pennsylvania's anthracite coal fields from May to October 1902 engaged on a national scale many of the interconnections between class conflict and religious culture that Irvine had recently been addressing in New Haven. The union that waged the strike, the United Mine Workers (UMW), was putting into practice ideals that Irvine had recommended to the Elm City labor movement. Organized along industrial rather than craft lines, the UMW reached across the boundaries of skill, race, and ethnicity that many trade unions erected as exclusionary barriers. Moreover, anthracite coal itself was a product in demand across a wide public, as it provided the basic source of heat for much of the nation. The prospect of a winter coal shortage stirred many observers to consider anew the relation of the public to industrial conflicts. President Theodore Roosevelt gave tangible expression to this public dimension of the strike by threatening to send federal troops to run the mines and break the siege in coal-strapped cities. His threat convinced the recalcitrant coal operators to settle the strike through arbitration by a federally appointed coal commission. Even before this settlement, however, the strike had stimulated commentary on the public's interest in the wage and hour demands made by the miners.[46]

Ministers saw their arena of public discourse as especially relevant to the issues raised by the anthracite strike. Clerical fascination with the strike was assured when Henry Demarest Lloyd publicized a letter sent by George Baer, president of the Philadelphia and Reading Railway Company, in reply to a clergyman's appeal for a fair and timely settlement. Baer insisted that "the rights and interests of the laboring man will be protected and cared for—not by the labor agitators, but by the Christian men to whom God has given control of the property rights of the country."[47] But Baer's audacious claim to divine right was not the only feature of the strike that attracted the attention of preachers.

The UMW's leader, John Mitchell, had institutional ties that suggested to many ministers a promising new overture to workers. Mitchell was a charter member of the National Civic Federation (NCF), an organization that treated industrial disputes not as conflicts but as misunderstandings amenable to friendly negotiations among capitalists, workers, and the general public. In the course of the coal strike, Mitchell had demonstrated his loyalty to these principles by cooperating with NCF leaders to prevent a sympathetic strike among miners of bituminous coal—a strike many UMW members had originally supported. Along with Mitchell's original opposition to the anthracite strike itself, this cooperation won him considerable applause as a "conservative" and "gentlemanly" labor leader, the kind Protestant ministers felt safe endorsing. It also helped that the NCF, which strongly encouraged Mitchell's conservatism, included many Protestant clergymen and editors on its advisory councils.[48] Protestant ministers saw in the NCF a path to rapprochement with union leaders at a time when workers' alienation from the church was a topic of widespread clerical concern.[49] Through the NCF and figures like Mitchell, they hoped, trade unionists might be included in a public sphere governed by the cultural hierarchies they approved.

Local clerical commentary on the anthracite strike offered Irvine a sterling opportunity to publicize his laborite critique of these hierarchies. Throughout the fall of 1902, New Haven ministers echoed the philosophy of their NCF brethren by using the coal strike to illustrate sermons on unselfishness. If capital and labor would but recognize their mutual interests, they suggested, unselfishness would blossom as a social virtue. This general rubric could accommodate a range of attitudes toward the coal operators, the miners, and the "public." Reverend Eugene W. Stone of the Grand Avenue Baptist Church swung his sermon decisively toward the strikers by calling on the public to endure sacrifices in the interest of workers too often maligned for lawless qualities that characterized capitalists just as much. Reverend T. B. Wilson of the Ferry Street Congregational Church also expressed hope for a union victory, but moderated his support by exhorting laborers not to see all capitalists as greedy and by calling for a "higher type of capitalists and laborers" aware of their common interests. Reverend Alexander Burns Chalmers of the Grand Avenue Congregational Church saw both unions and trusts as examples of modern, organized selfishness. "If only the principle of brotherhood which we see manifested between laborers and laborers and capitalists and capitalists could be extended until we could have a union of capitalists and laborers each recognizing a friend and not a foe in the other," he instructed, "then this warfare would cease." He added, however, that it was unfair to single out Mitchell for criticism, since labor in combination had as much right to a representative as combined capital. Reverend Eben C. Sage of the First Baptist Church recommended to both coal barons and miners the biblical grace of yielding to recognize others' rights. Finally, Reverend Henry Baker, pastor of the First M. E. Church, praised the halting efforts at mediation President Roosevelt was beginning to arrange in early October, while criticizing the operators for their lack of public concern and Mitchell for being a "dramatical demigod holding too great a position." Whatever their particular view of the strike, all of these ministers believed miners and coal operators would do well to examine their interests in the light of biblical teaching on unselfishness.[50]

In contrast to those who took the coal strike as a text on public goodwill, a few New Haven ministers turned it into a lesson in the incompatibility between union loyalty and sacred morality. Newman Smyth was the most prominent of these. In denouncing the threats that the striking miners posed to American ideals of individualism and patriotism, Smyth reiterated the anti-union views he had preached since the 1880s. He identified miners' attacks on nonunion men as dangerous threats to "the right of a man before God to free labor." This diatribe was one of the objects of Irvine's criticism in the sermon that the Building Trades' Council had applauded. In a solemn warning that Irvine quoted, Smyth had recommended to his parishioners that they fight threats to free labor in their own homes and neighborhoods. "It would be better," intoned Smyth,

> that the additions to our homes we plan should remain unbuilt, our homes unpainted, our city, if need be, left for nights without light, we ourselves put to much inconvenience, or our profits diminished, rather than that we should consent to any denial or abridgment of this right of a man before the Most High to do with his might whatsoever work which his hands find to do.[51]

Irvine found this a telling statement of the church's narrow sympathies. As represented in Smyth's exhortations, Irvine insisted, the church stood for a class "that profits from the abuses of our industrial life"; neither miners nor any other manual worker would find refuge there.[52]

Having rebuked Smyth, Irvine took to the pulpit in mid-December 1902 to offer an alternative vision of the miners' struggle. More than any other New Haven minister, Irvine praised the UMW and its leader, whom he regarded as a genius as well as a gentleman. This estimation of Mitchell echoed local trade unionist views as to which side in the anthracite strike upheld "civilized" cultural ideals. In October, Elm Lodge No. 420 of the machinists' union, having raised a hundred dollars to support the striking miners, had adopted a resolution to accompany the money denouncing "the attitude taken by the [coal] operators as being ungentlemanly, unAmerican and unreasonable." Elaborating on the claim that it was the miners and their leader who had civilized ideals at heart, Irvine quoted from a letter Mitchell had written to him illustrating the benefits of organization, including not only higher wages and lower hours but "less intemperance, a higher standard of citizenship and . . . opportunities for intellectual and moral and physical improvement." Mitchell's letter also explained how professional strikebreakers were brought in to work the mines. Irvine used these points to counter the charges of coercion that Smyth and others leveled against the union. He thus enhanced his developing alliance with local craft unionists who shared his support of Mitchell and his disdain for scabs.[53]

But Irvine was not content with definitions of the public restricted to union leaders, coal barons, and presidential intervention. He also made the miners' everyday conditions part of public religious discourse on the strike. To do so, he asked for assistance from one of Newman Smyth's more prominent parishioners, Yale political economy professor Henry Farnam. Farnam and his students had studied conditions in the anthracite region, and Farnam had visited the area and taken photographs of mining towns to illustrate his own lectures on the conflict.[54] Acquainted with Farnam through the Congregational Club and the advisory council of the Lowell Settlement House, Irvine secured permission to borrow the professor's slides for his sermon. However, he used these slides to illustrate an opinion of the strike opposed by Farnam, whose own lectures emphasized the impossibility of raising the miners' wages.[55]

During his sermon, Irvine alternated Farnam's slides of miners' cabins and company towns with images of peasant huts in the Zambesi valley of south-central Africa as well as photographs of Fifth Avenue mansions owned by coal magnates. His commentary on the contrasts between these images transformed the visual rhetoric of cultural uplift and civilization that his earlier stereopticon sermons had shared with the perspectives of Farnam and Smyth. As deployed in missionary magic lantern exhibits, popular theater, and free market Congregationalism, this rhetoric ranked societies in an ascending hierarchy from barbarism to civilization that offered audiences a ladder of individual self-improvement. Irvine rearranged this hierarchy by voicing an aesthetic preference for African peasants' huts over the American miners' dwellings and pointing to the riches of Fifth Avenue as the source of the miners' misery. To clinch this point, Irvine called on workers to use their own collective concepts of self-improvement to transform that institution that was supposed to stand for cultural hierarchy in its most beneficent guise. "I am prepared to advise that men who work with their hands go into the church of God," he stated, "and create in it that which is its greatest lack: democracy of religion."[56]

Amply covered in the New Haven press, Irvine's coal strike sermon provoked an epistolary exchange with Farnam that expressed their very different readings of visual realism and cultural hierarchy. Farnam wished to know whether Irvine had mentioned his name in the course of the sermon. If so, he warned, "I shall feel called upon to express publicly my strong dissension from some of the statements which . . . you made and which my pictures were apparently intended to prove." He added that he had been reluctant to lend Irvine the slides and admonished further that "nothing could be more inopportune at a season of the year which is associated with peace and good-will than the publication of remarks intended to embitter people's feelings."[57]

In his reply, Irvine stated his own understanding of the way he had wielded visual realism in the public debate over the coal strike. At the conclusion of his letter, Irvine denied interpreting Farnam's slides. If his use of the slides had buttressed views opposed to Farnam's, he insisted, it was not his fault but "merely because the monotonous procession of shacks and houses dissolving into one another without a word of explanation was more eloquent than speech." As other parts of his letter showed, however, Irvine was not completely committed to this belief in the projected photograph as uninterpreted realism. He also told Farnam that the photographs themselves had proved "nothing" to him, that he had drawn the message they illustrated from his own adolescent experiences as a miner in Scotland. He protested further that only intimate acquaintance with such a life could produce an accurate explication of the conditions the slides depicted. "You could not photograph odors, atmosphere, or language," Irvine told Farnam. "A lantern slide may show a company store, but it could not tell the story of the 'bob-tail check.'" Irvine implied that while the absence of beauty in the slides of the miners' huts suggested the story he told, he could render it as "real life" only through his own knowledge of hardship.[58]

In explaining his use of Farnam's slides, Irvine demonstrated a shrewd recognition of the ambiguity inherent in all uses of visual realism. The claim to objective truth that he made in his letter to Farnam constituted the lingua franca for visual realist display: the connecting belief that allowed exhibitors and audiences to look to realism to confirm diverse perspectives. Yet Irvine also acknowledged that positions on cultural hierarchy and autonomy that informed such perspectives were matters of social relation and historical experience. What African huts, miners' shacks, and New York mansions showed were variations in material life, not stories about civilization or barbarism. Such stories could be, and were, told about the images that Irvine used. But, debated across the discourses of Protestant liberalism, trade union activism, and popular realism, these narratives depicted competing visions of the cultural hierarchies they invoked, as Irvine's letters to Farnam attested. For Irvine to address this conflict explicitly was to position himself anew in the broad currents of religion and recreation within which visual realism was deployed—currents he had been traveling since childhood. More immediately, it was to take a decisive stand in New Haven's religious class conflicts.[59]

New Haven trade unionists rapidly signaled their appreciation of Irvine's sermon on the anthracite strike. A month after the sermon, the carriage makers' union wrote to Irvine requesting permission to name him as their first honorary member. On February 18, 1903, Irvine was inducted into the union "in view of the gallant and fearless stand he has taken in favor of organized labor." Commenting on the event, the "Union Labor" column of the *Evening Leader* noted that New Haven organized labor believed Irvine had sacrificed his position at Pilgrim Church to help them.[60] In early March the painters' and paperhangers' union followed the carriage workers' lead in conferring honorary membership on the laborite cleric. Building on these alliances, Irvine initiated extensive plans to stage a large parade of New Haven labor in John Mitchell's honor. He traveled to Philadelphia to arrange the visit with Mitchell, chaired a Trades Council delegation in charge of preparations, and signed the delegation's invitation. Repeated postponements by Mitchell, who was preoccupied with his role as witness before the president's commission on the coal strike, dampened enthusiasm for the plan, which apparently was abandoned. But, in pursuing it, Irvine had secured his place in New Haven trade union circles.[61]

As these ties grew stronger, local trade unionists entered into a dispute with Newman Smyth which confirmed that Irvine's arguments with New Haven's leading Congregationalist minister expressed a wider cross-class debate. Smyth provoked the dispute with a speech given before the New Haven Chamber of Commerce that described union recognition as a Faustian bargain: eager to speed production, the harried employer might acquiesce, but "in gaining the present world he may lose his own future industrial salvation." As in his earlier labor sermons, Smyth focused on the threat to individual merit that such a bargain entailed.[62] The speech infuriated the Trades Council, which published a retort in another open letter to the press. The Council decried Smyth's description of striking unionists exhibiting pistols to the wives of scabbing shopmates, claiming that Smyth implied these were organized labor's customary methods. They objected further to Smyth's characteristic emphasis on the "monopoly of labor" rather than monopolies of wealth as the source of injustice. Echoing Irvine's recent sermons, they reminded Smyth that views such as his turned workingmen from the church, "so they are almost driven to loathe the shadow of the steeple." These complaints, along with the claim that Smyth's arrogance was equaled only by his "stupendous lack of knowledge of that subject which you essayed to teach," drew further fire from Smyth. He protested that the Trades Council had misunderstood the spirit of his address, and offered to appear before them to discuss the questions at issue. The Trades Council accepted, and set up a debate between the minister and boot and shoe workers' organizer Frank Sieverman.[63]

The February 26 debate, which Irvine attended, recapitulated and embellished themes he had been emphasizing from the pulpit. After a nod of approval to conservative labor leaders and to the brotherly sacrifices that trade unions encouraged, Smyth devoted his talk to his characteristic warnings about the coercive nature of trade unionism. He also complained about the ways unionists used analogies between strikes and warfare to justify the "tyrannies" he decried. Smyth's view of the relations between strikes and modern militarism directly opposed the view Irvine had presented in his antiwar sermon. Whereas Irvine had equated the brutality of warfare with the brutality of capital's tactics during strikes, Smyth believed the "civilized" warfare entailed standards of conduct that strikers transgressed. Like Irvine, Sieverman replied that Smyth's notion of civility reflected the comfort and insularity of his social position. From his comfortable position, Sieverman explained, Smyth could not appreciate the wrongs that unionists battled. In an intriguing twist, Sieverman went beyond detailing the difficulties of "big burly men" to consider how women workers "who have to make certain concessions to dame fashion" were also ill-served by principles of political economy that determined wages by "the so-called rights of the individual."[64] Though hardly a challenge to standard gender categories prevalent among trade unionists, Sieverman's comments at least acknowledged the significance to women workers of cultural concerns with fashion and self-display, concerns that were becoming increasingly visible in workers' leisure pastimes such as vaudeville. As he continued to develop the cultural perspectives he had forged in alliance with New Haven trade unionists, Irvine would struggle to integrate such concerns into his own notion of working-class "civilization."

In the meantime, the controversies that linked Irvine's ministry to ongoing public debates between New Haven workers and clerics came full circle when Smyth became involved in the division within Irvine's parish. This split had widened throughout the months following Irvine's coal strike sermon. The Ecclesiastical Society of Pilgrim Church aggravated it by pleading inability to pay more than four-fifths of the minister's customary two-thousand-dollar annual salary for 1902. The missing four hundred dollars, Irvine believed, was his punishment for speaking against the water company's interests. Pilgrim's lay leaders became even more exasperated when Irvine questioned the legality of their governance and started a movement to rewrite the Ecclesiastical Society's bylaws. A working-class phalanx loyal to Irvine attempted to gain entrance into the Society, giving up only when Irvine's plans for a People's Church offered a more promising way to follow his call for "democracy in religion." But these supporters did try to even the score by calling a Council of Churches to resolve the question of Irvine's salary.[65]

The conduct of the Church Council dramatized the local class divisions that Irvine's ministry had engaged. Headed by Newman Smyth, the Council met once. It took no action because Pilgrim's Ecclesiastical Society disputed the Council's legality and refused to submit any papers regarding Irvine's pay. Despite Smyth's repeated promises to reconvene, the Council held no further meetings.

Irvine insisted that Smyth's negligence in the matter was the work of Morris Tyler, president of the Southern New England Telephone Company. A lay member of the Church Council, Tyler opposed Irvine because the minister had criticized the telephone company for "disfiguring the streets with ugly cross-bars that looked like gibbets." Whatever its source, the Council's inaction revealed that Irvine had stirred up currents of religious class conflict that extended well beyond his parish.[66]

In his farewell sermon at Pilgrim Church on April 27, 1903, Irvine boldly defined the lines of religious class conflict he had engaged in New Haven. He pointed out that he had expanded the church's ministry among children and among working people, who added over sixty new members to the church at its recent Golden Jubilee. But, he noted, since the new members brought no money to the church, they were unappreciated by the church officers. The officers focused instead on their pastor's political and industrial activism, which contradicted their idea of a church. Their idea, Irvine charged, was to come once a week and hear something to soothe their nerves:

> They say they pay for it and they will have what they pay for. The preacher is their "hired man." He may be brainy, but not too brainy—social, but not too social—religious, but not too religious. He must trim his sails to suit every breeze of the community; his mental qualities must be acceptable to the contemporary ancestors by whom he is surrounded, or he does not fit.

Forthwith, Irvine organized a new church according to a very different idea.[67]

The People's Church and the Difficulties of Social Evangelism

The People's Church of New Haven represented both the apotheosis and the collapse of Irvine's Elm City efforts to combine evangelism, trade unionism, and popular realism. In its original aims, its early membership, and its practical program, the new church successfully fused Irvine's message of spiritual uplift with the working-class solidarity he had learned from his local labor allies. Here, at last, Irvine could elaborate the plebeian mixture of religion and recreation within an organization that respected working people. While the People's Church fulfilled Irvine's purposes, however, its constituency was only precariously united by the principles he embraced. From its second year, the church's following fractured along several fault lines. The narrowed agenda that the local labor movement adopted in a period of renewed employer antagonism supplied one source of division. The growing socialist movement that engaged Irvine's sympathies was another. Additional complications arose out of Irvine's approach to the gender politics of his mission. As the fate of the People's Church demonstrated, these trials posed deep contradictions for Irvine's revisions of Protestant theology and practice, and more broadly for his effort to conjoin class politics, evangelism, and entertainment in the public sphere.

The opening service of the People's Church, held on May 10, 1903, articulated its early promise. Irvine's widely published sermon for the day explicitly tied the spiritual concerns of the church to the work-a-day preoccupations of labor. Irvine argued for a religion of common speech, touched with the spirit of modern times in order to address mechanics and artisans building a city in partnership with God. The church he proposed for this constituency would abandon abstract propositions in theology for a religious project in which "those weary of the day's cares could find a moment's rest in contemplation of a higher life possible for all, though attained by few." In short, as Irvine declared, the "gospel of work" would have a large place in his ministry:

> The whole scheme will be to give every man and woman a career in religion; a creed of labor to be worked at every day; to give the lie to the old age-worn fiction that one thing is sacred and another secular; to puncture the bubble of assumed sanctity and shatter the castle of professional goodness, to correlate the subtle currents of the heart and mind with the deftness of the hand and the honesty of labor with purity of heart.[68]

In pursuit of this gospel, Irvine offered a practical program combining religious education with social change on a number of fronts. A public service committee was to organize worship services in readily accessible theaters, halls, and vacant lots. For religious instruction there would be Bible classes, lecture courses, a pleasant hour for children, and a publishing department to distribute sermons and addresses. Social questions would be addressed in the holdings of a sociological library and the meetings of a study club focusing on the works and deeds of Jefferson, Lincoln, Henry George, and William Morris. A separate committee would agitate political issues by taking up such questions as the municipalization of the city's utilities.[69]

While the People's Church did not realize all of these heady plans, it did offer worship services as well as educational and recreational activities embodying its original program. Held for the first few meetings at the downtown Hyperion Theater and then at a former Congregational church, services regularly emphasized both religious reverence and the demands of working-class solidarity. Irvine often focused on Bible lessons and the rudiments of Christian living, offering such sermons as "A Refuge in God," "What's the Use of Praying?," "Man's Circuitous Journey From the City of Death to the City of Life," "The Life of Christ," and "Jesus as a Man of Prayer."[70] But he supplemented the "career in religion" these sermons recommended with lessons on local and national industrial issues. Before a sermon on "The Master Passion," he commented on strikes underway in New Haven. He championed the cause of the striking teamsters, "the most underpaid workmen in the city," whose bosses had refused arbitration. But he also rebuked striking bakers for rejecting arbitration. Regarding the bakers' strike, Irvine even ventured that "I don't think trades unionism is the solution of the present problems, but they're simply a step toward progress."[71] Irvine thus demonstrated his commitment to the clerical role he had assigned himself in the People's Church. Determined to be no one's "hired man," he had promised that

> the leader of this community will be a publicist as well as a preacher; he will not ask for any privilege for himself or his children that he will not seek to secure for all on equal terms, but when the Almighty sends him a message whether it be for a labor union or a corporation he will take counsel of no man and will be responsible only to God.[72]

Still, during the church's first year, Irvine usually supported views with which most trade unionists would agree.[73]

In addition to focusing on workplace issues, Irvine made the People's Church a showcase for his strategic mixture of pleasure and piety. The use of a theater for the church's first meeting was one sign of this popular cultural bent, and echoed Sylvester Poli's establishment of theaters in former churches. Also, the stereopticon became a constant feature of worship in the new parish. Themes of cultural uplift persisted from Irvine's earlier preaching, but his stereopticon practice also indulged delight in the common pleasure of the visual. In this respect Irvine's services paralleled uses of the magic lantern in the local vaudeville houses. Irvine offered fare similar to that available at Poli's, such as a discourse on the "Psychology of the Passion Play" illustrated with sixty stereopticon views. Other magic lantern sermons included illustrated renditions of the religious best-sellers *Ben Hur* (with colored slides) and *In His Steps, or What Would Jesus Do?* Irvine also offered a slide tour of his own travels as a marine in Egypt and Palestine.[74]

Irvine augmented the plebeian appeal of the church by trying to replicate the mixture of denominations that had characterized the Railroad Men's Reading Room of the 1880s and the cobbler's shop entertainments and church populations of mid-Victorian Antrim. The first meeting of the People's Church was led by a rabbi, two Unitarian ministers, Irvine himself, and one of his less notorious Congregationalist colleagues. In its social service programs, the church also drew on the Irish Catholic population that still dominated the city's working class. One of Irvine's pet projects, the Bennett Boys' Club, appealed to adolescent factory workers who lived in the Irish-American Cedar Hill neighborhood. Irvine supervised these youths in baseball, gymnastics, and debates of such civic questions as municipalization of the gas plant. To ensure community harmony, Irvine assured Father Kennedy of nearby St. Francis Roman Catholic Church that the club would not aim to transform Catholics into Protestants. This subordination of credal differences to the combination of pleasure, piety, and social responsibility increased Irvine's popularity within an ethnically and religiously divided working class and a labor movement that included many Irish-American leaders and members.[75]

Irvine enhanced his popularity further by distinguishing between the elements of cultural uplift he wove into the People's Church and the cultural varnish flaunted by the educated elite and prominent corporate leaders. Returning to a familiar theme in October 1903, Irvine responded to Yale President Arthur Hadley's recently published view that the Spanish-American War had helped heal the wounds of the Civil War. Complaining that Hadley was bound to be taken seriously "as the head of a great institution," Irvine offered a pungent rebuke. Hadley, he stated, "believes that the only way to overcome hatred of thirty years standing was to knock the daylight out of others. This is rot." The judgment summed up Irvine's attitude toward many a well-funded rhetorical flourish used to cover comfortable complacency. At a Lincoln Day banquet in 1904, he reminded civic leaders that applauding the revered dead without carrying on their work was a "cheap, nasty pretense of patriotism," and directed them to work for the freedom of industrial toilers. During a sermon on Hugo's *Les Miserables,* he took a swipe at industrialists who set up religious or educational institutions to legitimate their profits. Scoffing at criticism that dismissed Hugo's novel by claiming that poverty was not unwholesome or new, Irvine speculated that the critic probably worked in "one of these Methodist theological seminaries, put up and sustained by railroad magnates, or perhaps in John D. Rockefeller's university in Chicago." To such literati, Irvine continued, "poverty is perfectly delightful." Irvine preferred to mix the cultivation offered by Hugo and Tolstoy with the concerns he found among his working-class constituency. This, he proclaimed, was the way of Christ himself: "He was always get-at-able . . . He was especially the friend of the poor and oppressed. One cannot imagine Jesus as the hired preacher of a pudding headed clique of religious bigots."[76]

Irvine and members of his church found numerous ways to practice the civic duty they associated with true religion. As foretold in the original plans for the People's Church, Irvine and one of his most active and devoted officers, Edgar M. Camp, appeared at a city hearing on municipal ownership of the gas company. Their activism expressed Irvine's ideal of the citizen priest, who "relieves suffering, removes unhealthy conditions, fights corruption wherever he sees it and builds the city of God." This was an ideal Irvine saw little pursued in Yale's "charmed circle of academic caste," where "great men who have been teaching the world how to live" neither knew nor were known in New Haven. The cultivation practiced at the People's Church demanded a different approach: "Let the teachers of Aesthetics make a municipal crusade on Chapel Street," proclaimed Irvine, as he decried the hideous signs and ugly wires on New Haven's main thoroughfare.[77] The People's Church also took up social and political questions that extended beyond the city's boundaries. Irvine preached and lectured on the Russian-Japanese War, the French Revolution, and Mazzini as a prophet of democracy. The church's social clubs debated municipal questions and such national issues as immigration restriction. The church also expressed its broad political vision by inviting William Jennings Bryan to speak under its auspices in 1904. Bryan, whose path had crossed Irvine's several times already, reiterated much of the philosophy that guided Irvine's mission. Calling his speech "The Value of an Ideal," Bryan used personal anecdotes, references to Tolstoy, pleas for religion, and criticisms of political corruption to recommend the virtues of service to others and the protection of their rights.[78]

The original membership and leadership of the People's Church registered its initial success among New Haven workers. Irvine's plans for the new church attracted a contingent of worshipers who petitioned to transfer their membership from Pilgrim Church. Providing the only available list of People's Church members, whom newspaper reports numbered between two hundred and three hundred during its first year, these thirty-eight petitioners were primarily worshipers who had joined Pilgrim Church during Irvine's tenure. Twenty-seven had joined Pilgrim Church during 1902. Twenty-four can be identified as wage-workers or their wives or family members. These early People's Church members included two of the new parish's seven officers, a group drawn at first almost exclusively from ranks of mechanics and factory operatives. The new church's treasurer for 1904 was William H. Pollard, a Winchester Repeating Arms factory employee who had joined Pilgrim from another church in 1902. The People's Church trustees for 1904 included Forrest Kelsey, the electrotyper who had served on Irvine's Sunday Evening Service Committee since 1901. Other working-class officers of the People's Church in 1904 were newer recruits to Irvine's mission, such as Winchester draftsman Edgar Camp, who served as the church's clerk, as well as trustees William Floyd, a painter, and Wells Post, a railroad signal foreman. The two additional officers of the church were J. Leroy Dean, a carpenter who owned his own cabinet-making shop, and George Sanford, a businessman who served as chairman of the board of trustees.[79]

While the People's Church flourished, Irvine's popularity among trade unionists also grew. Within a week of the church's first service Irvine was elected honorary member of the striking teamsters' union, having already appeared before the strikers' executive committee to offer assistance in arranging arbitration with recalcitrant team owners. In the next year and a half Irvine also became an honorary member of the Pilgrim Lodge No. 48 of the International Association of Car Workers, as well as a temporary member and chaplain of the trolleymen's union. As a member of Local 281 of the Amalgamated Association of Street and Electric Railway Employees, he joined union leaders in urging restraint on strike-prone trolleymen in August 1904. Finally, in October 1905, Irvine was elected an honorary member of the New Haven Trades Council.[80]

For all his popularity with trade unionists, however, Irvine's church was disintegrating by the middle of 1905. Unable to secure its own meeting place, the church resorted to a Universalist parish for Sunday evening services. But, according to his own account, Irvine's church work generated little money, and one week all that was available had to be used to feed his family, so rent to the Universalists went unpaid. When the Universalist trustees balked, the People's Church was left to meet on the grounds of a small farm on the outskirts of the city, where Irvine had been trying to eke out a living since the previous October. Midway through the summer of 1905 the meetings ceased altogether. Thus, when the Trades Council elected Irvine to honorary membership, he had neither a pittance nor a pulpit. A week after his election, Irvine received a fifty-dollar donation from the Council, and used it to pay his rent.[81]

The difficult pass through which New Haven trade unionists were maneuvering by 1905 provided one source of the trouble that plagued the People's Church. The local labor movement had reached the peak of its turn-of-the-century strength in 1902, when its members had helped shape Irvine's mixture of religion and labor politics. Soon after, it was struggling to maintain a waning vitality. New Haven unionists faced the same concerted backlash that employers directed at organized labor throughout the country. This backlash temporarily subdued some of Irvine's closest trade union allies while fracturing his working-class constituency.

The teamsters' union whose cause Irvine had championed at the People's

Church in May 1903 was one of the first casualties. The teamsters held out for over a month against legal harassment by their bosses and scabbing by imported strikebreakers and Yale students. Some teamsters even managed to win concessions from their employers. In early June, however, nineteen strikers, including some of the city's leading labor organizers, were arrested on charges of conspiracy under Connecticut's anti-union law against boycotts. By the end of the month the remaining strikers returned to work, and in January 1904 nine of the arrested leaders were brought to trial, found guilty of conspiracy, and sentenced to three months in jail.[82] Upon beginning his jail term the following October, organizer and one-time Economic League leader Philip Daly summed up the significance of the teamsters' defeat in a statement that belied his earlier admission to being "uncouth":

> We are all just a lot of weak vessels at present, being broken. They say it is conspiracy now. In later years when people begin to understand the movements more than they do now, they will not call them conspiracies. . . . There is . . . as much of a conspiracy to break up labor formations as there is alleged to be conspiracy on our part. We are like martyrs.[83]

The teamsters' martyrdom was one of several troubling portents that provoked organized labor to revise its industrial and political strategy in New Haven. Local unionists had been exuberantly strike-prone in the first years of the twentieth century, waging sixteen strikes in 1902 and eleven in 1903. In 1904, however, the number of strikes in New Haven dropped by almost half, to six, and remained at the same level in 1905, when only seven strikes were waged. Two unions that elected Irvine to honorary membership—the trolleymen and the railroad car workers—came close to striking in 1904 but accepted compromises rather than risking the teamsters' fate. Workers who did strike could expect even less solidarity among different sectors of the labor movement than had characterized the Sargent conflict of 1902. A week after launching a strike against building contractors in May 1905, hod carriers returned to work with a compromise settlement reached under the threat that union bricklayers would soon begin accepting materials from scab laborers. Building tradesmen no doubt thought their own worries competed in importance with the hod carriers' concerns. Their strong locals and Building Trades Council had stimulated contractors to form a Master Builders' Exchange to provide mutual help in the event of strikes. Such signs of employer initiative against unions also affected labor's political strategies. Whereas in 1902 New Haven unionists had experimented with independent labor tickets and reform coalitions advocating expansive changes in local politics and municipal government, by 1905 they were preoccupied with defensive campaigns seeking to revise the antiboycott law used against the teamsters and to forestall bills that would impose new restraints on union conduct. At the same time, they abandoned independent politics for a coalition with prominent Bryan Democrats.[84]

Under such conditions, union members had less support to spare for an organization like Irvine's church, which treated their cause as one of many alternative visions of social salvation. While he had forged his gospel of work through alliances with organized labor, Irvine advertised his church as a source of individual careers in religion for all comers, regardless of class, industrial, or political affiliation. The socially ecumenical character of the People's Church — whose men's group, according to one report, brought together "the leading socialists and the leading single taxers of the city working in the same committee [with] . . . some of the most ardent republicans among working men" — became more difficult for trade unionists to champion as they sought solutions for their declining industrial influence. Though they might extend aid in Irvine's hour of need, they could not sustain his faltering mission. Hard-pressed unionists looked for allies who were more reliably focused on their own immediate concerns.[85]

Meanwhile, Irvine became disenchanted with the narrow vision of a labor movement under siege. By 1905, he saw the ideal of union solidarity increasingly perverted by a preoccupation with the wage and security concerns of a small segment of skilled workers who often ignored the needs of laborers like the Italian metal workers at Sargent's factory. To redirect the message New Haven trade unionists had pushed him to refine, Irvine turned to socialism as the collective embodiment of a more expansive solidarity.[86] As a theory and a social ideal, socialism was not new to Irvine. While connected with the YMCA, he had befriended two students of socialist theory: painter and YMCA art teacher Max Dellfant, who moved in with the Irvine family, and Edward Gertsch, an oyster-worker turned street railway employee who joined Irvine's church. Later, as the leader of a men's group at the Lowell Settlement House, Irvine had reported enthusiastically to Henry Farnam about a paper on socialism given by a mill worker. Irvine came to the attention of the local Socialist Party when he appeared before a September 1903 city hearing on the question of municipalizing the gas plant. The Socialists invited him to give an address on public ownership of the gas works, and his comments generated a hot exchange. Irvine inveighed against working-class apathy in municipal matters and instructed the Socialists that half

a loaf was better than none. Cigarmaker Frederick Grubbe countered by arguing socialism was the only remedy for the corporate evils of the day and advocating a class war of ballots to bring in the new order. Grubbe's arguments struck
a chord: after the interchange, Irvine's theoretical interest in socialism took political shape. By May 1904, he was giving court testimony on behalf of socialist orator Sol Fieldman. In October 1904, Irvine presided at a local rally featuring
socialist presidential candidate Eugene Debs. The following year, Irvine became
state secretary of the Socialist Party.[87]

Irvine's socialist connections weakened his religious mission further by setting
him at odds with former allies while generating new alliances uncongenial to
his evangelical purposes. Not all trade unionists objected: Grubbe was an active
member of the Trades Council, where he probably helped push through the
honorary membership, sympathy, and financial assistance awarded to Irvine in
the difficult days of late 1905. In the Socialist Party, however, Irvine made common cause with men who had ridiculed his earlier political enthusiasms, like
the Economic League. He also found himself working athwart the current political purposes of former League leaders. William Trueman, labor's erstwhile herald in the aldermanic chambers and Irvine's ally in the water affair, had turned
to the waning Populist Party and the single tax. The single taxers, Irvine recalled,
quit his church "in a bunch" after he declared himself a Socialist. While it alienated old allies, Irvine's Socialist Party activism brought no new recruits to the
People's Church either, since the predominantly German Socialists were
staunchly atheistic. Indeed, Irvine won socialist office over the objection of some
Party members who took exception to his Christian preachings. Still, Irvine
remained convinced that his new comrades had a faith he could not find elsewhere. In old age he related that "the red label was costly, but my mind had now
something akin to the Gospel to fight and suffer for."[88]

Supporters undaunted by Irvine's politics found participation in the People's
Church foreclosed by the antagonism his socialist leanings aroused among the
New Haven elite. In at least one case, Irvine believed that association with his
ministry cost a church member's job. After the Winchester company summarily
fired Edgar Camp, Mrs. Camp encountered the wife of one of the rifle factory's
directors, for whom she had once served as a nurse. The trustee's wife promised
to look into Camp's fate. As quoted by Irvine, her explanation of Camp's dismissal was that "He belongs to Irvine's church—and Irvine is an anarchist."
Antagonism aimed directly at Irvine weakened his church still further. Irvine
reported that the Congregationalist ministerial association dropped him from its

ranks and the rabbi who had participated in the opening services of the People's Church rebuked him for letting "the labor gang use you as a sucker." When he attempted to raise money by working for a bookbinder, he related, a Yale medical school professor informed Irvine's employer that he would lose lucrative Yale contracts by employing the minister. Its constituency fragmented and its minister nearly starved out, the People's Church was by 1905 primarily a collection of sympathetic friends.[89]

As workingmen and reformers dropped away from Irvine's church, there remained one group whose continued allegiance he might have solicited. Women had always made up a considerable portion of Irvine's working-class religious recruits. Roughly half of the new members drawn into Pilgrim Church during 1902 were women, as were twenty-one of the thirty-eight Pilgrim members who petitioned to join the People's Church in 1903. However, like many ministers of the day who viewed the preponderance of women in Protestant congregations as a "crisis" of feminized religion, Irvine focused his missionary efforts primarily on men. He shared this missionary masculinity with a broad spectrum of turn-of-the-century preachers, from liberal Protestants to more conservative revivalists like Billy Sunday.[90] Irvine's version of what historians have called "muscular Christianity" involved belittling what he saw as female concerns, delivering histrionic declarations regarding his own manliness, and describing women primarily as victims of the social wrongs he protested.[91] He declared his wish for a mission that went beyond women and children to touch "great social problems" during the prosperous first year of the People's Church. Irvine elaborated this gendered vision of his mission when an anonymous letter to the editor of the *New Haven Register* chastised him for attending an aldermanic meeting on street signs. In reply, Irvine cast his political activities as proof against the limited masculinity he believed his antagonist associated with the clergy. "You seem to object to my views," he replied, "not because they are erroneous or misleading but because you have catalogued me with a third sex—you have fixed me up in your mind with a nice, wee, white tie and you have set me away off with a small group of select set apart men. I am not that kind, brother. I am a socialist."[92]

When Irvine relaxed his vigilance against clerical effeminacy to attend to women as sermon topics or audiences, he tended to smother their lives in a melodramatic pall of poor conditions and consumer desires. A favorite topic was Hugo's Fantine, the destitute working woman whose maternal devotion drives her to prostitution and death in *Les Miserables*. "Society is simply buying a slave for misery," Irvine preached. "A soul is offered for a bit of bread. That is the story of Fantine." Fantine, he continued, was a "social butterfly" subsumed by her material needs and society's frivolously licentious desires. Irvine did not attribute much more moral volition to women whose cares involved managing a household rather than selling sexual favors. Hosting the Lowell Settlement House Mothers' Club at his farm in September 1905, he explained to his guests why they had to send their children to work instead of to school. Poverty and their husbands' low wages figured prominently in his account. These were crucial conditions, to be sure, but Irvine ignored the measures that women themselves undertook to deal with them. He focused on his own youthful struggles and on the conditions that boys like him experienced in the Pennsylvania coal mines. The peculiar concerns of growing numbers of women wage-earners went unspoken, as did any hint that women themselves saw connections between, on one hand, the trivialized household duties and preoccupations with fashion to which Irvine relegated them and, on the other, the great social questions that he manfully addressed. Irvine's idea of women remained in many ways as limited as that of the trade union movement he was growing away from. Though spokesmen such as Frank Sieverman might occasionally invoke the concerns of women workers in debates with union foes like Newman Smyth, for many union leaders women remained symbols of the happy domesticity that a successful labor movement would ensure. They could be but helpmeets to this movement within the home, and courted moral degradation outside of it.[93]

During his last years in New Haven, Irvine did begin to enlarge his estimation of women's public importance. He invited members of the mainly female laundry workers' union to his home, and subsequently described their struggles in a column he edited for the *Evening Leader.* Irvine also expressed compassion for women who worked outside the home in the memorial he penned for a volume of poetry by Genevieve Hale Whitlock. The sister of People's Church clerk Clifford Whitlock, Genevieve had embarked on a career in journalism after her father's death left the family in straitened circumstances. Her concern for workers like the striking Italian-Americans at Sargent's brought her to Irvine's attention, and he admired her devotion to Christian service. Besides her social compassion and political sympathies—according to his account, she declared herself a Christian Socialist shortly before her death in 1903—Irvine eulogized Genevieve Whitlock's devotion to her work. Noting that she might have enjoyed the social round pursued by other talented middle-class girls, or stooped to fashionable journalistic sensationalism, Irvine wrote that "she chose a pathway all her own. To do her own work—to be herself."[94]

Later, contact with socialist debates about women's place in a public sphere would encourage Irvine to develop these ideas into more explicitly feminist views. For the time being, he wrestled with gender questions in his own domestic circle, where conditions complicated the ideas about women he expressed publicly. As Irvine represented it, his marriage to Maude Hazen Irvine involved both intellectual camaraderie and constant strife over the life the two would lead. The daughter of a distinguished lawyer and politician in Iowa, raised on a cultural diet of literary and musical training, Maude was willing to share her husband's artistic and religious interests but little inclined to deprive herself or her children in the name of social conscience. She was active in the social life of the Fair Haven church, the work of Lowell Settlement House, and the women's auxiliary of the YMCA. She even joined Irvine's experiments with New Thought when his gospel of work crossed other spiritual paths leading away from the well-beaten Protestant trail. But her enthusiasm paled as social marginality led to poverty on an unremunerative farm. In October 1905, Maude defiantly rented the family a stately house near the center of the city while arguing with her husband to surrender his struggles in behalf of the New Haven poor. This tug of war continued through their remaining years together, as Maude urged settled, urban creature comforts against Alexander's penchant for adventures in communal and rural living. The battle became a model, perhaps a crucible, for new views of women that Irvine developed in the wake of his New Haven mission. As this mission drew to a close, however, such domestic strife was one of many pressures that left him suspended between comforts that obscured social sympathies among the elite, and narrow definitions of need that constrained the sympathies of workingmen.[95]

Beginning in December 1905, Irvine expressed his discouragement in a weekly column he edited briefly for the *New Haven Evening Leader*. Entitled "Union Labor News and Views," the column reported on the local labor movement and urged New Haven workingmen to support labor struggles around the country. It also advertised activities of the Socialist local, which Irvine was using as a new base for the combination of religious education, entertainment, and working-class solidarity he had forged at the People's Church. The *Evening Leader* column regularly publicized illustrated lectures offered under socialist auspices to illuminate social and economic questions. However, it also registered Irvine's sense that his efforts to resolve tensions between self-improvement and class distinction had left him stranded between unappreciative constituencies.

In his column, Irvine lashed out at pretensions flaunted in the city's Protestant churches and also bemoaned the limited ambitions of New Haven workers. Newman Smyth came in for one of Irvine's barbs by recommending a new "church of powerful love." Irvine rejoined that such churches were plentiful all over the city, but their love was inadequate. "It is too fat, sleek, and contented," he claimed. "It is gouty for lack of exercise. . . . Let it out among the people! Direct it against the various forms of oppression now masquerading in forms of law."[96] A few months later Irvine published his own suggestions for a new type of church service. Having surveyed bulletins from several local parishes, he complained that the choir was the "whole show," complete with intermezzos that were unlikely attractions for workingmen. As an alternative, Irvine proposed an order of service that registered his impatience with both churchgoing and laboring classes:

Hymn—God Save the People
Prayer—For the recovery of civic virtue and the Opening of the Eyes of the Blind Workers
Collection—For the wronged in Russia and the railroaded in Idaho
Notices—of meetings for workers
Sermon—the relation of "surplus value" to the present decadent condition of religion
Benediction[97]

Clearly, in disparaging church refinements, Irvine did not absolve workers of blame for the absence of a socially meaningful religious vision. As he tried to articulate such a vision outside the church, he despaired of a wide working-class hearing. Advertising a play about Russian Jewish life, Irvine doubted that it would awaken American "peasant workers" to the sufferings of their fellows abroad. He feared that a canvas of local workers would reveal "the overwhelming popularity of low class vaudeville over the blood and tears of a plundered peasantry."[98]

Such reproaches reflected the turning point at which Irvine's mission had arrived. Spurned by New Haven's conventional clergy, whose refined accoutrements he associated with feminine domestic comforts his wife missed at home, Irvine was by January 1906 more cynical about the confining, aristocratic nature of hierarchical culture than he had ever been, or would be again. Through his socialist activism he thought he could see new causes that would supply the breadth of vision he had previously sought in art and religion. In his contributions to the *Evening Leader* Irvine praised the recently formed Industrial Workers of the World (IWW) and published Cleveland Socialist and trade unionist Max Hayes's criticisms of Samuel Gompers, little comprehending that the IWW and Hayes held opposing positions in conflicts over trade unionism that were beginning to divide the national Socialist Party. To Irvine at this time, smarting over the desertion of trade unionists from his mission, both the IWW and Hayes represented attractive alternatives to the labor alliances that had helped him formulate his gospel of work, but had ultimately proved too confining.[99] Yet, despite his disappointments, Irvine did not abandon the message of self-development through working-class solidarity that New Haven trade unionists had pushed him to refine. As he moved beyond New Haven's local conflicts, he reformulated the laborite cultural perspective he had forged there into a series of public self-representations that addressed broader, national currents of socialist politics and popular entertainment.

As Irvine wove the lessons of his New Haven mission into tales of proletarian self-discovery, he continued to ponder many of the cultural conundrums this mission had posed. In experimenting with narrative formulas for representing the subjective cultural significance of class, he confronted more directly the intersection of class and ethnic identities that had hindered widespread trade union solidarity in New Haven. In his efforts to reinterpret his evangelical aspirations in light of his American labor and socialist education, he also repeatedly revised the masculine cast of his mission as well as his relation to the women who—as partners, converts, or fellow travelers—had influenced his religious, cultural, and activist ideals.

As it happened, such issues of ethnicity and gender were dimensions of New Haven cultural debate that Sylvester Poli engaged much more directly than Irvine. By virtue of his own cultural ambitions, the claims made on his leadership by diverse audiences, and changes within the vaudeville industry, Poli became involved in delicate negotiations of ethnic and gender identity among his New Haven audiences. The following chapter examines Poli's approach to these issues in order to illuminate dynamics of class, gender, and ethnicity that would become increasingly important to Irvine's career. It also charts changes in Poli's shows that followed from his involvement in the corporate reorganization of the vaudeville industry in the early twentieth century. These changes posed new wrinkles in the representation of ethnicity and gender that would shape both men's cultural politics in the public sphere.

Chapter Five

"MR. POLI IS THE BIG CHIEF!"

The Theatrical Manager, His Audiences, and the Vaudeville Industry

A S ALEXANDER IRVINE REACHED THE NADIR of his New Haven mission, Sylvester Poli was savoring success as the city's premier theatrical entrepreneur. Poli's enterprises had grown since the 1890s. He had enlarged and refurbished his original theater a second time in 1903, and in 1905 opened a new theater connected to the imposing office building he had erected across the street from the Wonderland. "Poli's New Theatre," later known as "Poli's Palace," was a glittering jewel—a gift to the city that had helped the manager establish himself in the vaudeville world. Decorated with imported Italian marble, studded with seventeen hundred incandescent lights, trimmed with two thousand dollars' worth of gold leaf, the new theater could accommodate twenty-five thousand patrons weekly.

As he courted favor with these patrons, Poli maneuvered among varied local constituencies who expressed competing visions of the cultural hierarchies addressed in his shows. He appealed to these diverse views both as an entrepreneur trying to satisfy the multiple tastes and prejudices of a mass audience and as an aspiring cultural authority trying to secure a prominent place in New Haven society. As Poli navigated among Yankee cultural elites, working-class audiences, and ethnic communities, he provided a trail of connections between the content of vaudeville shows and the local social relations and cultural debates that rendered such content meaningful. Poli's negotiation of these complex webs of cultural rivalry reveals resonances between the popular realism in his vaudeville shows and the cultural debates at issue among the audiences he shared with Irvine.

6. Poli's Theatre, Church Street, New Haven, completed in 1905, served as the headquarters for Poli's East Coast circuit. Photo courtesy of the Whitney Library of the New Haven Colony Historical Society.

7. Poli's Theatre in New Haven was elegant inside and out,
offering patrons the splendor of ornate architecture at popular prices.
Photo from "S.Z. Poli's Theatrical Enterprises."

Meanwhile, changing conditions in the vaudeville industry compromised Poli's efforts to blend entertainment entrepreneurship and local authority into cultural leadership. Forced in 1906 to join B. F. Keith's growing booking syndicate, the United Booking Offices of America (UBO), Poli became associated with Keith's corporate version of vaudeville's cultural hierarchies. The UBO connection propelled Poli toward cultural standards of genteel refinement with which vaudeville has often been identified. However, "refinement" was an ambiguous and contested ideal, in vaudeville as well as in the wider public sphere of which it was a part. At the turn of the century, "refinement" referred to exclusive standards of cultivation that distinguished the genteel from the vulgar, but it also conjured up a hackneyed Victorian prissiness that invited ridicule and thus raised questions about who had the authority to define cultural standards themselves. Poli had long appealed to such doubts through a popular realism that embraced the multiple perspectives from which his audiences approached questions of cultural hierarchy. When the UBO encouraged him to wield refinement as a more rigid standard of feminine propriety, Poli came to cast cultural authority in terms less attuned to his varied audience, though perhaps more in line with his own cultural aspirations. At the same time, the UBO's economies of scale contributed to changes in vaudeville content that undermined the narrowed standard of "refinement" the syndicate cultivated as a corporate cultural standard. As he tried to accommodate shifting constellations of vaudeville fare, industry relations, and audience enthusiasms during the UBO era, Poli struggled with gendered twists to the conundrums of cultural hierarchy that Irvine would also confront as he transformed his mission into popular culture.

Negotiating the New Haven Audience

The competing cultural standards featured in Poli's early vaudeville shows were well suited to his diverse New Haven audiences. By 1900, the city's 30,802 foreign-born residents accounted for 28.5 percent of its total population as reported in the census. Recent immigrants from Poli's native Italy had contributed most markedly to the growth in New Haven's immigrant population since 1890; growth in the Italian population accounted for 44 percent (3,386) of the difference (7,808) between figures for the city's foreign-born population in 1890 and 1900. Russian Jews contributed another 26 percent (2,033) of this difference, with Germans running a close third by contributing about 25 percent (1,941) of the change. Though they were no longer among the fastest-growing immigrant groups in town, the Irish still predominated among the city's foreign-born. In 1900 there were nearly twice as many Irish-born New Haven residents (10,491) as Italians (5,262), the next largest group. These immigrants settled into closely packed tenements and transformed the neighborhoods of Grand Avenue/ Wooster Square and "the Hill" into arenas of sometimes spirited ethnic rivalry. At the intersection of these neighborhoods sat Poli's theater, providing shows that stimulated and assuaged such divisions with their ethnic caricatures and self-reflexive commentary on hierarchical cultural ideals.[1]

As Poli sought patrons for his shows as well as social standing in New Haven, he maneuvered among competing cultural ideals traded within and between local ethnic groups. He concerned himself chiefly with three of these groups. As an Italian immigrant, he received requests for aid from the growing number of Italian-American organizations devoted to self-help and the cultivation of Italian cultural identity. At the same time, Poli sought affiliations with New Haven's Irish, especially through associations that offered him occasions to demonstrate Catholic devotion or to flaunt elegant tastes. Craving recognition as a patron of civic refinement and culture on par with the city's traditional Yankee bourgeoisie, whom he rivaled in wealth, Poli also accepted invitations to serve on civic improvement or charity committees overseen by New Haven's Protestant elite. Poli's social trajectory among these organizations highlights some of the ways ethnicity complicated the class divisions over self-improvement delineated by Irvine's New Haven career.

While Poli's social maneuvers dealt primarily with white ethnic and Yankee groups he attended to most consistently as audiences and peers, there were important racial dimensions to his interconnected theatrical and civic careers. Poli treated African-American patrons differently than white ethnic groups, in ways that amplified the derogatory cast of African-American caricatures on his vaudeville stage. His advertisements for singer Maud Huth in 1895 are revealing in this regard. Though Maud Huth and her husband, Billy Clifford, performed several ethnic and racial caricatures, Huth was known in the 1890s primarily as a "negro dialect singer." Poli advertised the team as a musical act offering "plantation melodies" and emphasized Huth's artistic skill in rendering an act so "Ethiopianly perfect" that the audience felt "transposed back to a Southern homestead before the War." By the middle of her week-long billing in New Haven, Poli was claiming that the most entertaining feature of Huth's act lay in the responses her singing elicited from black theater patrons. He noted that on Wednesday night an "individual whose face was blacker than the traditional ebony lost his head completely in the realistic singing . . . and he began shouting hallelujahs at such a rate that the theatre attendants had some trouble quieting him." Subsequent advertisements implied that Huth's act provided an opportunity for white audiences to laugh at the behavior of their black neighbors, asking:

> Is it kindness or cruelty to the colored population? That's the question Manager Poli is asking himself these days as he sees colored individuals losing their heads in the excitement and shouting hallelujahs at every performance to the hymns and camp meeting refrains sung by Miss Huth. . . . There is not a performance given where some dusky visitor doesn't start to shout, and last night two of them got going in a way almost to break up the singers on the stage.

Only at the end of the week did Poli dimly register that the cruelty of his showmanship might lie in the crude stereotype his advertisements attributed to black patrons. His notice for Huth's last appearance identified one of the "colored shouters" in his theater as the deacon of a local black church and noted that it was "no less creditable to his religious feeling that he should 'get the spirit' when hearing Miss Huth . . . sing." Hardly recompense for previous denigrations of local African Americans, this scant gesture toward the black community's own religious practices at least recognized the existence of venues where African Americans were not objects of ridicule.[2]

Poli's ads for Maud Huth illustrate how, while questioning some prevalent hierarchies, vaudeville enforced certain social distinctions quite insistently. Popular stage depictions of African Americans offered white workers, in particular, a potent stake in racism. Such images of African Americans, like the minstrel caricatures they evoked, established a racial line above which white ethnic workers could confidently position themselves.[3] At the same time, the Huth incident provides a vague outline of African Americans' own relations to Poli and his shows. By acknowledging, however faintly, the existence of autonomous black community organizations, Poli admitted the possibility of African-American perspectives that challenged the ridicule of disdainful whites. Of course, this perspective was dimly drawn in Poli's portrayals of his black patrons, whose capacity to question local and national social hierarchies on their own behalf he barely acknowledged. The boundaries he drew between African-American and white participation in the popular public sphere become more apparent when his treatment of black patrons is compared to his more careful flattery of white ethnic groups.

Poli expended special care on his relations with New Haven Italian-Americans and their ethnic institutions. He established his earliest theatrical ventures just as the Italian community who would claim his success as their own was beginning thirty years of rapid growth. In 1900 there were nearly three times as many Italian immigrants living in New Haven as there had been in 1890 (5,262 as opposed to 1,876); by 1920, the number had nearly tripled again, to 15,084. Unlike Poli—whose artisan parents could afford to provide the education their son would need for an artistic career deemed appropriate to his central Italian background—the majority of Italian immigrants who arrived in New Haven after 1890 were illiterate peasants from the peninsula's impoverished southern provinces. Life in crowded hillside villages had helped prepare them for the cramped conditions of the tenements, where careful economy paid off in money saved at La Banca Italiana. A history of exploitative rulers—among whom many southern Italians counted the armies of their own recently unified nation—had cultivated a strategic balance between deference and distrust in their relations with elites. With respect to religious authority this balance tipped toward contempt. Southern Italian immigrants defined religion in terms relatively independent of the Catholic Church, a prerogative they had long asserted in the face of an Italian clergy they regarded as self-serving and parasitic. Finding themselves ridiculed and marginalized among New Haven's Irish-American Catholics, they sought associates from their own villages with whom they celebrated local saints who evoked both religious and nostalgic sentiments.[4]

The familiar economies and pastimes that Italian immigrants tried to adapt to their new environment were viewed by the keepers of New Haven's cultural hierarchy as barbaric practices in need of reform. Lowell House, the social settlement Alexander Irvine had founded, became a key venue for such reform efforts. As he outlined the aims of the settlement, Lowell House Association President Henry Farnam gestured toward the need for "different types of the city population . . . to know and understand each other," but also spoke of trying to "absorb" an "alien race." Lowell House workers noted with distress the Italian immigrants' lack of facility in English and asked what they could do "with this mass of untrained humanity with so little material?" Headworker Dr. Julia Teele struggled daily against what she considered primitive, "old world" ideas: "Their fear of fresh air, and of water, their vague ideas of privacy, their love of crowding [which] can only be overcome by example, seeing how other people live." She worried, too, that with the Catholic Church losing hold and no other taking its place, Italian immigrants were "in danger of becoming irreligious." "We feel that our work among the Italians is of very great importance," she summed up in one report. "Our city has at least 15,000 of them at present, and upon their assimilation and civilization depends in large degree our future as a city."[5]

Such assessments of New Haven's Italian "problem" overlooked myriad efforts that Italian-Americans undertook to train fellow immigrants to cultural priorities formulated and contested in their own community. Like immigrants throughout the United States, New Haven Italians organized many associations of self-help and uplift. Paul Russo, an early immigrant who served as court interpreter and became the colony's most prominent lawyer and property owner, spearheaded New Haven's first Italian benefit society, *Fratellanza*. In addition to providing material aid, *Fratellanza* undertook projects aimed at the civic expression of ethnic pride, such as the statue of Columbus they erected in New Haven's Wooster Square Park in 1892. Following the formation of *Fratellanza*, Italian-American organizations devoted to mutual aid and cultural improvement multiplied rapidly, supplying ample voice for alternatives to Lowell House's cultural hierarchy.[6] Among these institutions, societies or *circolos* named for patriotic figures competed with clubs named after the local towns and saints. Their titles reflected the contested symbols of culture and civilization celebrated in the Italian colony. Mutual aid societies named after the heroes of Italian national unification included a Giuseppe Garibaldi Society formed in 1885, the *Circolo Cesare Battista* begun in 1887, and the *Circolo Vittorio Emmanuelle II* founded in 1905. Other organizations honored Italian scientific and cultural achievements: *Floia Gioia*, a mutual aid organization founded in 1894, was named after the Italian inventor of the first modern compass, and *Circolo Gabriele D'Annunzio* a social and mutual aid club founded in 1908, took the name of Italy's flamboyant modern nationalist poet. As immigration from southern Italy swelled the colony, the names of new mutual benefit societies expressed loyalties of a more local character.[7]

Such divided loyalties complicated Poli's negotiation of cultural leadership, especially when dramatic troupes sponsored by different ethnic societies looked to him for support. These productions mixed a wide range of material: opera, historical and contemporary Italian drama, sketches based on the *Commedia d'ell Arte* character Pulcinella, and dramas based on the adventures of current Italian and Italian-American celebrities like the Calabrian bandit Musolino. Various organizations offered such spectacles. One of the earliest, *Circolo San Carlino*, organized in 1897 by Angela Mazzarella of Caserta, had the aim "of keeping alive the Italian dramatic art in this land of adoption, by instructing its members and eventually their progenies, so that amid the turmoils and feverish activities of daily tasks there would be a ray of sunshine by attending a production of Italian dramas, performed by local talents in local theatres."[8] The proceeds from such events bought the group its own Grand Avenue theater, complete with reading and billiard rooms. Receipts also went to southern Italy to benefit the victims of the Calabrian earthquake of 1905 and the Vesuvius eruption of 1906. *Circolo del Sannio*, organized a month after *San Carlino* by marble worker Domenico D'Andrea and other natives of the Sannio section of Benevento, also supported its own theater and gave benefits for the needy and for such projects as an Italian-American kindergarten. *Del Sannio* distinguished itself theatrically by stipulating an interest in "serious" drama and music, undertaking Shakespeare and opera along with farces and *Commedia dell'Arte* scenarios.[9] Other New Haven Italian societies devoted primarily to mutual aid, such as *Circolo Vittorio Emmanuelle II*, formed dramatic sections to raise money for various causes. Poli's willingness to lend his theatrical facilities to such Italian-American theatrical efforts featured prominently in the chronicles of the Italian colony's development.[10]

Yet Poli's negotiations with local Italian dramatists also involved careful maneuvers around rival visions of ethnic culture. The diverse renditions of the popular Pulcinella, the *Commedia dell'Arte*'s mocking servant and generous clown, offer one way to measure the delicacy of Poli's position. Pulcinella showed up in a variety of Italian-American theatrical presentations. *Circolos* committed primarily to serious drama, such as the *Circolo Filodrammatico Dante Alighieri*, used Pulcinella to close their performances on a lighthearted note. Other dramatic clubs spiced the combination of light and serious drama with attacks on the clergy: *Il Circolo Follia* mixed Vincenzo Monti's classical drama *Aristodemo* with the burlesque song *"Il Chierico"* (presented along with a speech on the significance of the glorious anniversary of Rome's incorporation into the Kingdom of Italy) and a locally written Pulcinella skit.[11] *Circolo San Carlino* presented more purely comic evenings combining humorous sketches about working-class characters with Pulcinella skits featuring popular local Italian trade unionist Vincenzo Esposito, advertised as "l'unico e solo che sulle scene italiane di New Haven, si sia meritato il titolo di artista comico" ("the one and only on the New Haven Italian scene who merits the title of comic artist").[12] Dramatic companies organized to support specific community or political issues also featured Pulcinella, as in the 1903 presentation of *Le Metamortosi di Pulcinella*, starring local Italian socialist G. Volpicelli, which was staged in order to benefit a local Italian accused of murder.[13] Socialists presented Pulcinella under their own auspices as well: dramatic presentations by *La Sezione Socialista Italiana* in April 1904 included a "semi-serious propaganda piece" called *L'egoismo, ovvero L'eroismo di Pulcinella* (Selfishness, or the heroism of Pulcinella).[14]

If so many competing class, religious, and ideological versions of Italian identity had not claimed Pulcinella, the famous *Commedia dell'Arte* clown might have seemed an ideal object for Poli's ethnic patronage. With his characteristic role of mocking the pretentious, Pulcinella epitomized the appealing features vaudeville shared with the *Commedia dell'Arte*, similarities that vaudeville aficionados noted admiringly.[15] But the social rivalries among the different organizations that staged Pulcinella productions in New Haven hampered Poli's association with the Neopolitan clown. While willing to bestow occasional favors on local Italian dramatists, Poli chose such opportunities carefully and stopped short of actually joining any of the theatrical societies that featured Pulcinella. Rather than identifying with a dramatic society that supported one of several contending Catholic parishes, represented loyalties of a single Italian locality, or championed the interests of a particular class of Italian-Americans, better to show interest in aiding any Italian dramatic effort and to occasionally bestow such tangible gifts as the bronze bell in the Italian colony's newest Catholic church.[16] This strategy protected Poli from the opposing invocations of Italian identity and culture that Italian-American dramatists served.

The shifting editorial policies of New Haven's largest Italian weekly, *Il Corriere del Connecticut*, further complicated Poli's efforts to negotiate the politics of ethnic identity. *Il Corriere* supported socialist and republican movements that denounced local priests. Poli maneuvered carefully around these associations, even while the paper celebrated him as "l'egregio uomo, nostro connazionale" ("the excellent man, our co-nationalist") and advertised his theater as "unico ritrovo di divertimento per gli italiani" ("the one and only entertainment for Italians").[17] He offered his theater to productions combining multiple allegiances, such as a production of *I Tre Moschettieri* organized to benefit relief efforts following the Vesuvius eruption of 1906 and sponsored jointly by *Il Corriere* and its two rivals, *L'Unione* and *L'Indipendente*.[18] Meanwhile, he temporarily stopped advertising in *Il Corriere* after 1903, when the paper's republican, anticlerical, and prosocialist leanings became increasingly strident. Interested in supporting Italian dramatic expression, in short, Poli positioned himself very carefully within the intraethnic debates over Italian-American cultural and social hierarchies. Eventually aligning himself with an elite version of unified Italian nationalism, he remained aloof from the fragmentary regional and political distinctions that divided many dramatic *circolos* and beneficial associations in the colony.

Rivalries within the Italian colony only partially accounted for Poli's careful negotiation of Italian-American claims on his celebrity. Too close an association with specific Italian institutions threatened to alienate not only parts of Poli's Italian audience but also the large community of Irish-American trade unionists and their socially prominent middle-class countrymen, who often scorned Italians as a group. Here another complicated web of intersecting class and ethnic identifications came into play. Conflict between New Haven's Irish and Italians was in part a specifically working-class affair, as when skilled Irish-American unionists prominent in the local labor movement protected their positions against unskilled Italians they were reluctant to organize. Even when Irish- and Italian-American wage-earners did unite, as in the 1902 Sargent strike, Irish-American union leaders were apt to compromise Italian aims. Such tensions amplified the exclusive character of Irish-inflected celebrations of working-class pride that Poli's vaudeville shows and advertisements frequently offered. In emphasizing attractions like John Kernell, the monologuing Irish boilermaker, or Tom Nawn, whose popular skits featured Irish construction workers, Poli played to an ethnically inscribed construction of class. Through this construction, Irish-American workers and their vaudeville caricaturists not only challenged the conceits of self-styled cultural betters; they also circled their cultural wagons against newly arrived immigrant workers. On St. Patrick's Day Poli eagerly propitiated these sentiments, bedecking his theater with shamrocks and green crepe to augment such public festivities as the Ancient Order of Hibernians (AOH) parade. The local AOH chapter was dominated by skilled workers, saloon keepers, and small businessmen, so in contributing to their festivities Poli saluted an artisan class often celebrated by "Irish" acts on stage. He thus reaffirmed a long-standing theatrical fusion of working-class conviviality and Irish-American ethnic pride.[19]

But hailing the celebrations of working-class Irish pride was no simple affair for a socially aspirant theatrical entrepreneur. Such celebrations were objects of interclass conflicts that Poli also had to negotiate carefully. The Knights of St. Patrick offered him one way of accommodating such divisions. Their main purpose was to observe St. Patrick's Day with a dress ball or dinner that they hoped would replace the traditionally boisterous Hibernian parade. Compared to the artisanal officers of the parading AOH, the professionals, proprietors, managers, and government officials who dominated the organizing committee for the Knights of St. Patrick ball attest to the social distinction this separate ritual was meant to acknowledge. The ball's rigorous dress code, demonstrated in detailed newspaper descriptions of women dressed in "black velvet over taffeta," "real Venetian lace," and "diamond ornaments," magnified this distinction further. Sylvester Poli and his diamond-bedecked wife, Rosa, showed up among the honored guests mentioned in such accounts, for Poli was an acclaimed member of the Knights. His appearance at their functions reproduced in his relations with New Haven Irish-Americans the divided appeal to hierarchical affectation and its convivial alternatives that his vaudeville advertisements expressed.[20]

Poli's efforts to blend ethnic identification with social distinction did not stop at fancy dress balls and sumptuous finery. He displayed a taste for more sober forms of ethnic cultural hierarchy by joining the Knights of Columbus. The Knights of Columbus originated in 1882 among a group of Irish-Catholic businessmen who joined with Father Michael J. McGivney, a curate at St. Mary's Catholic Church, to contrive a formula for combining Irish-Catholic devotion with the culture of nineteenth-century fraternalism. Since most fraternal orders used ritual oaths proscribed by the Church, this combination proved difficult to achieve. The Knights of Columbus satisfied competing ecclesiastical and lay interests by celebrating the dignity and community of Irish Catholic faith.[21]

With its mutual benefit arrangements and initiation rituals, the order claimed for Irish-American Catholicism a vision of manly self-improvement cultivated by hundreds of secular fraternal orders. As Mark Carnes has pointed out, fraternal rituals spoke explicitly to male concerns about the feminization of bourgeois culture in the late nineteenth century. They dramatized the initiate's navigation from a domestic and sentimental world of women to a working world of men. Similarly, the Knights of Columbus offered rites of passage into "Columbian Catholic Manhood." The order's fourth degree conferred the status of "an American Catholic Citizen" who combined American patriotic ideals with the self-proclaimed dignity of an oft-reviled religious group. The leadership of turn-of-the-century Knights of Columbus councils indicates the ethnic twist the organization gave to this version of Catholic self-improvement: officers of the eight councils listed in the 1904 New Haven City Directory all had Irish names. They interwove hierarchical themes of self-improvement with the camaraderie of ethnic community in a combination similar to that offered in Total Abstinence societies that attracted Irish-American workers like Irvine's political ally Joseph J. Reilly. Indeed, some Columbian lodges were themselves former temperance societies, and Total Abstinence men like Reilly found their way into the leadership of Knights of Columbus councils. Thus, when he joined the order's founding San Salvador Council, Sylvester Poli embraced a civic association that intertwined themes of cultural hierarchy and ethnicity bandied on his stages and among his audiences.[22]

In 1915 Poli joined the Sons of Italy, which celebrated Italian-American identity in much the same terms as the Knights of Columbus honored Irish Catholicism. Founded in 1905 by New York Italians concerned about the divisions within Italian-American communities, the Sons of Italy aimed to "unit[e] in a single family all the Italians scattered throughout the United States of America" and "keep alive in their heart and mind the cult of the Mother Country, by sharing its joys and sorrows, and contributing to the diffusion of the Italian tongue." Concerned more with specifically Italian traditions and culture than with the American patriotism cultivated in the Knights of Columbus, the Sons of Italy nevertheless followed the hierarchical conventions of American fraternal orders in its pageantry and structural organization. Through the Sons of Italy, Poli could wield Italian-American identity as a badge of cultural leadership while still evading expressions of Italian ethnicity associated with politics, religion, or region.[23]

Poli also used festivities celebrating milestones in his theatrical career to flaunt his social standing. Through these celebrations, he identified with the upper reaches of social hierarchies that local ethnic communities shared, rather than with any ethnic identity in particular. The guests at a lavish banquet celebrating the 1905 opening of Poli's Palace included only one representative from the Italian colony, Poli's personal physician Dr. William Verdi. The others were political and business leaders from other immigrant communities, including German-Jewish political boss J. B. Ullman, Irish-born police chief James Wrinn, and Reverend J. D. Coyle, the pastor of St. John's Roman Catholic Church (Poli's own church, which mixed American and Irish-American Catholics with Italian-American worshipers who preferred it to less sedate Italian Catholic churches). This list grew to include some of the Yankee elite at Poli's Theatrical Silver Jubilee banquet in 1913. Connecticut Governor Simeon Baldwin headed the executive committee for this event, which included newspaper owner Alexander Troup, known for his interest in the Italian colony, as well as attorney Paul Russo, Italian Consul Michael Riccio, and President Isaac Ullman of the Strouse-Adler corset company.[24]

By embracing cultural leadership through the dignity of ethnic fraternalism and the spectacle of theatrical success, Poli eventually made himself an easy choice for a Yankee elite seeking to integrate ethnic leadership into its own programs of hierarchical uplift. But New Haven's Anglo-American cultural leaders opened their ranks to ethnic groups only gradually and under pressure from those they considered "below" them. The first notice Elm City cultural elites paid to Poli appeared in the *Saturday Chronicle*, an upscale weekly founded in 1902 to cover New Haven "Society" and cultural events. Every week this paper carried photographs illustrating the architecture and decoration of one of New Haven's finest homes. A 1907 article on "Art at Mr. Poli's New Home" featured the vaudeville manager's Howe Street residence. Describing and illustrating the "Palace-like decorations in his magnificent residence," the article suggested that Poli's home echoed the standards of decorative splendor observed in his theaters.

By cataloguing Louis XV color schemes, Louis XVI furniture, and elegant stained glass windows, the *Saturday Chronicle* admitted Poli's material wealth to the ranks of its elite readership without endorsing the character or social position of the man himself.[25]

Later in 1907, Poli gained admission to the New Haven Civic Improvement Committee, which included such Elm City aristocrats as water company attorney George Watrous and Yale Secretary Anson Phelps Stokes Jr. But even this honor seemed a feeble recognition of Poli's local cultural authority. Poli's name was an afterthought, intended to appease Italian-American property-owners who refused to contribute to the committee's fund without Italian-American representation. In addition, the committee itself was something of a dead letter. It commissioned a lengthy report, drawn up by Frederick Law Olmsted Jr. and Cass Gilbert, which suggested improvements in streets and parks as well as advertising restrictions. But municipal authorities largely ignored the report's recommendations for comprehensive city planning. It would take another decade for Poli to make his way onto a civic board that effectively molded local programs of cultural improvement.[26]

Poli's real advance into the ranks of Yankee-dominated civic leadership came with his appointment to the executive committee of the Settlement League, which coordinated work at Lowell House and several other settlement projects in the 1920s. Here Poli served alongside dignitaries from other local ethnic communities, indicating a broad rapprochement between New Haven's Anglo-American cultural elite and ethnic leaders. Lowell House reports suggest that settlement leaders were not just seeking ethnic tokens. The self-improvement programs advanced by organizations like the Knights of Columbus and the Sons of Italy had convinced them of the value of ethnically inflected uplift. As the headworker at Lowell House explained in 1917:

> I have given the use of our library to the Dante Alighieri Society for their free evening school. The object of this society is to preserve among the Italians in this country the best of the ideals and culture of their native land. . . . It has seemed to me that we very often blunder in dealing with the Italians through not sufficiently understanding their national prejudices, and that it is valuable for us who are trying to give them new world ideals to co-operate with those who are trying to preserve for them the best of their national ones.[27]

By carefully managing his own ethnic identifications, Poli had smoothed the way for New Haven's Yankee elite to seek his assistance in such a program. After nearly three decades of careful negotiation, he had concocted an Italian-American version of hierarchical civility that reigning elites could recognize as akin and useful to their own.

That Poli courted and received the blessing of Yankee cultural elites does not mean, however, that his maneuvering among other local groups only served his social ambitions. Though Poli sought legitimacy from groups whose vision of civilized culture approached the hierarchical standards cultivated at the early Lowell House, in theatrical advertisement and urban association he also recognized that such standards were variously evaluated and constructed. Just as Poli's shows and advertisements spoke to the multiplicity of positions on cultural hierarchy he acknowledged among his audiences, his delicate response to the appeal of competing ethnic associations, intraethnic class divisions, and cross-ethnic urban rivalry rendered this acknowledgment in social terms. His entrepreneurial interests pressed such recognition, for his efforts to draw a mass audience required that he appeal to a diversity of tastes. But cultural authority outside the theater demanded such sensitivity too, as settlement leaders found when they tried to impress their vision of civilized culture on immigrant communities. Discovering that such communities inculcated alternative constructions of cultural accomplishment, Lowell House workers made common cause with leaders like Poli who had come to represent such alternatives. Even this concession could not exhaust conflict over cultural hierarchy, since the Italian cultural refinement recommended by a Dante Alighieri Society or the Sons of Italy still clashed with the village religious rites and traditions of southern Italian peasants. Such divisions fueled a continuous, multifaceted debate over the terms of cultural hierarchy, a debate to which vaudeville's interplay of high-toned culture and mocking ethnic caricatures had long spoken.

By engaging these debates, Poli's civic career illuminates further ethnic dimensions of the cultural class conflicts that had transformed Alexander Irvine's mission in New Haven. Irvine recognized ethnic boundaries to the trade union solidarity he had embraced as the new model for his gospel. He had also negotiated the ethnic and religious dimensions of working-class identity in his alliances with Irish-Catholic union leaders and his forays into the Irish-Catholic neighborhood from which he recruited members for the Bennett Boys Club. But, while he occasionally brandished his Irish brogue and fairy stories to entertain the audiences that Yale students tried to gather at their University Mission, Irvine seldom incorporated ethnic identity into the public overtures he made to New Haven workers.[28] As the enthusiasms and interests of Poli's audiences suggest, such identities were important elements in the cultural rivalry that mobilized public debates over cultural hierarchies Irvine tried to address. Both within the vaudeville shows from which Irvine borrowed missionary techniques and within the neighborhood and community institutions that occupied their audiences in other moments of daily life, ethnic identity was a vital focus for cultural politics contested across class lines. Irvine seized on this dimension of cultural class conflict only after he left New Haven, but in doing so continued to elaborate the thematic ties that linked his mission to Poli's shows, audiences, and civic ambitions.

In the meantime, while Poli negotiated competing cultural standards in his quest for entrepreneurial success and local social influence, the conditions of this quest changed around him. New juxtapositions of class, ethnicity, race, and gender fostered new social distinctions for vaudeville performers to exploit. And, after a giant booking syndicate absorbed his enterprises, Poli found himself reconstructing cultural hierarchy in response to new corporate imperatives. These changed conditions transformed the cultural standards Poli claimed for his shows as well as the cultural authority he wielded among the audiences to whom both he and Irvine tried to appeal.

The Keith–Poli War and Corporate Vaudeville

As construction began on his new theater in the spring of 1905, Sylvester Poli was preparing the ground for an East Coast theatrical empire. On April 6, the *New Haven Union* announced the formation of "S. Z. Poli's Theatrical Enterprises," a corporation with five million dollars in working capital that proposed to control a theatrical circuit covering all major towns in New England and to extend into New York as well. The circuit would include twenty or more theaters, Poli boasted, and would make him "the foremost vaudeville manager in the United States." Most important, he intended to keep his circuit wholly independent of B. F. Keith's Vaudeville Manager's Association (VMA) and its booking combine, the UBO.[29]

Poli's boastful corporate plans were not mere bluster. When he announced the formation of "S. Z. Poli's Theatrical Enterprises," he was already operating theaters in New Haven, Waterbury, Bridgeport, and Hartford, Connecticut, and in Springfield, Massachusetts. During 1905, in addition to proceeding with the new Poli's Theatre in New Haven, he acquired a sixth theater in Worcester, Massachusetts. This move proved especially provocative to Keith and his partner Edward Albee, who saw their booking monopoly in Massachusetts, Rhode Island, and New York threatened by Poli's plans to build a Northeastern circuit booked through the rival William Morris agency. Even though Poli often paid actors less than the Keith combine did, he offered vaudeville artists an attractive alternative to the conditions that Keith imposed. Because of the short jumps between his theaters, actors could easily tour Poli's circuit between lucrative bookings at New York houses that remained outside Keith's organization. Having already neutralized the White Rats, a fledgling actors' union that the VMA had inspired, Keith was determined that Poli should not foil his trust-building designs by constructing a competing circuit where actors could work. Keith attacked Poli's enterprises by trying to block plans for Poli's Worcester theater through the city's board of aldermen. He also tried to weaken Poli's existing operations by announcing plans to build theaters in other cities where Poli had vaudeville houses.[30]

Keith and Albee soon found themselves locked in a nationally publicized battle with the stubbornly independent Poli. Like many a martial venture in this age of imperial crusades for the civilized values that vaudeville ambivalently popularized, their business war provided good copy. A new vaudeville sheet, *Variety*, first appeared in December 1905, just as the Keith–Poli fracas was heating up. No friend of the Keith–Albee trust, *Variety* publisher Sime Silverman took pleasure in chronicling Poli's entrepreneurial sorties into the heart of VMA terrain. In January 1906, *Variety* covered Poli's announcement of plans to build theaters in Providence, Jersey City, Philadelphia, Baltimore, Buffalo, and Detroit. Such expansion, the paper noted, would enhance the vaudeville booking routes of the William Morris agency, which would soon be able to start an act in Baltimore, play through Philadelphia, Trenton, Newark, and Jersey City, run through the independent theaters operated by managers Percy Williams, William Hammerstein, and F. F. Proctor in New York City, and then work through New England. The next month brought news that Poli was expanding his circuit further by acquiring theatrical properties in Scranton and Wilkes-Barre, Pennsylvania. "There is no first-class circuit with this number of houses that can play the time with such short jumps," Silverman enthused. "It will be the means of saving much transportation and will make Mr. Poli a magnate of power and one to be figured with in any vaudeville dealings."[31] Alarmed, Keith and his VMA allies rushed to Altoona to secure another Pennsylvania theater for their organization. They also threatened actors who contracted to play at Poli's Worcester house with cancellation of all their Keith bookings.[32]

In addition to circuit-building and intimidation, Keith used public denunciation to try to bring Poli to terms. He charged that Poli had engaged in "dishonorable" business tactics by fabricating stories about Keith's exploration of theatri-

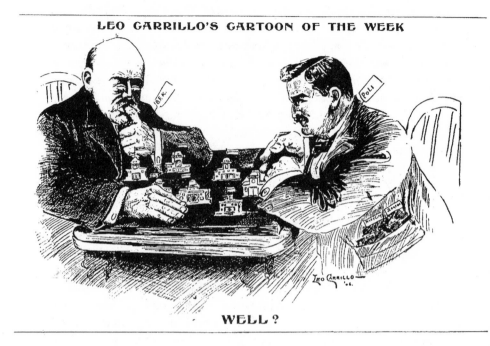

LEO CARRILLO'S CARTOON OF THE WEEK

WELL ?

8. *Variety*, vaudeville's weekly magazine, featured this cartoon picturing the war between B. F. Keith and S. Z. Poli as a game of chess played with theaters across New England and the Middle Atlantic states. Drawing from *Variety* March 24, 1906, p. 3. Photograph credit: Copy by Robert D. Rubic.

cal business opportunities on Poli territory. The Keith–Poli war was, according to Keith, "an obvious bit of showman's faking" designed to line Poli's pockets. Keith asserted that Poli had engaged in the mock entrepreneurial battle to advance a conspiracy hatched with other independent managers who wanted to undermine Keith's business. He added that Poli was not only dishonest but unoriginal, having borrowed theatrical designs from the elegant houses Albee conceived for the Keith–Albee company.

Responding to Keith's barbs in an interview for the *Morning Telegraph*, a sporting and theatrical daily, Poli expressed a serene confidence in his own entrepreneurial acumen. He dismissed Keith's allegations of unscrupulous entrepreneurial showmanship with a dignified confidence in the reputation he had carefully cultivated in New Haven and throughout his burgeoning circuit. "There is no capital I can gain from Mr. Keith in Hartford, or in Springfield, either," he vouched. "I am known in both cities for my record and I can stand on that." It was, in any case, Keith who had breached "the honor there should be among vaudeville managers" in a characteristic ploy to make "one more independent vaudeville manager bend the knee to his self-proclaimed autocracy." Poli dismissed Keith's charge of conspiracy as the panicked invective of a businessman bested by clever competitors. The conspirators Keith had named, according to Poli, all booked their houses through the William Morris agency, "which is offering more and better time to performers than the Keith booking agency is able to do." "Mr. Keith may flatter himself that his agency holds the key to the booking situation," Poli continued, "but he must receive many a bumping shock when he rouses from his dreams." As for claims that Poli had pilfered Albee's theatrical designs, the New Haven manager scoffed that "it will probably be cause for wonder to the long line of American architects and decorators that Mr. Albee, like Oliver Goldsmith's village schoolmaster, has a head so small that it carries all he knows."[33]

Eloquent remonstrances notwithstanding, Poli soon discovered that Keith did indeed hold the key to the booking situation. Keith effectively mixed chicanery and intimidation to secure the best acts for his own agency and to add the houses of independent managers like William Hammerstein and eventually Poli to the routes monopolized by his syndicate. He succeeded despite the fact that the terms he offered actors were only superficially favorable. The UBO charged actors a flat 5 percent booking fee and also deducted from their salaries a 5 percent agent's fee that was split between the UBO and the agent. This system was supposed to assure the agent of collecting his fee while preventing him from gouging the actor, but agents often collected additional fees to recompense themselves for the booking agency's cut. The "conveniences" that the Keith agency offered to actors were compromised in other ways as well. The growing number of houses booked through the Keith combine provided the actor with steady work, but the bookers often imposed awkward jumps between houses and subjected actors to constant surveillance in the form of weekly reports on their popularity and willingness to trim material deemed too ribald for vaudeville audiences. Keith and Albee overcame the actors' misgivings about this scheme by blacklisting performers who refused to follow the managers' dictates regarding what houses they could play or what material they could use. Though actors eventually revived the White Rats union as an AFL affiliate to try to beat this system, in 1906 they were divided, disorganized, and, as Keith successfully corralled more managers into the UBO, increasingly shy of the risks involved in signing with the few remaining independents.[34]

Stymied by his shrinking access to credit in cities where Keith threatened to build competing theaters and his growing need for vaudeville talent that Keith's syndicate monopolized, Poli finally relented in May 1906. He agreed to book his eight existing theaters exclusively through the UBO, in exchange for a pact in which he and Keith abandoned all rival ventures in cities where the other manager already owned a theater. Poli then turned his attention to expanding his collection of exquisite buildings, and convincing patrons that he remained lord of the New Haven-based vaudeville circuit that bore his name.[35] However, the shifting thematic emphases of his shows, along with his own changing managerial strategies, suggest that Poli's new role within corporate vaudeville posed complex challenges to the local cultural authority he was trying to cultivate. In the process, Poli struggled with cultural shifts that also affected Irvine's evolving mission.

Corporate Vaudeville's Cultural Hierarchies and the Politics of Feminine Display

In 1907 Poli and his staff produced a souvenir booklet that pictured the elegant façades and interiors of his theaters throughout New England and Pennsylvania. The booklet emphasized the personal attention Poli lavished on these enterprises and the pride of individual accomplishment he derived from them. "If there are successes," it proclaimed, Poli "has the credit; if success fails to wait upon effort, no one else bears the burden of blame. Mr. Poli is the big chief!" To reconcile this entrepreneurial bravado with his recent capitulation to the UBO, the manager described himself as a "leading spirit in the big booking combine known as 'The United Booking Offices of America'" and boasted that this association ensured that "there is not an act of any kind, nature or description playing vaudeville that is not within his reach."[36] The tension between entrepreneurial autonomy and corporate connections apparent in these public pronouncements gave apt expression to the shifting relations of entertainment management that Poli navigated after entering the UBO.

Though the UBO compromised his independence, Poli's profile as a domineering "chief" was in some ways enhanced by his new corporate alliances. Upon joining the UBO, Poli associated himself with a more rigid version of civilized refinement than he had previously cultivated. Keith and Albee were notorious for the prudish respectability of their "Sunday School Circuit." The UBO enhanced the scope of their power to police offensive acts and censure uncooperative performers—though standards varied from theater to theater, and shrewd actors took advantage of such inconsistencies.[37]

But, ironically, performances appearing at Poli's theater through the aegis of

9. The cover of Poli's promotional pamphlet of 1907,
"S.Z. Poli's Theatrical Enterprises," pictures the
proud impresario and his growing vaudeville circuit.
Pamphlet courtesy of Jeanne Poli.

the UBO also undermined these augmented claims to gentility. With the advent of the UBO, producers could mount increasingly lavish acts on the promise of weeks or years of uninterrupted booking. These acts celebrated an emerging ethic of showy consumerism and feminine display that departed from fastidious standards of taste such as those that Poli's shows of the 1890s had simultaneously cultivated and mocked. Indecorous daughters of the immigrant working class celebrated this ethic in their ragtime anthems. At the same time, the old ethnic caricatures that had poked fun at vaudeville's hierarchical values in the 1890s, while still visible, receded somewhat in the early twentieth century. Thus, while Poli's shows still gave lip service to a cultural hierarchy that placed artistic refinement and feminine purity at its summit while mocking that hierarchy from below, they also featured a competing hierarchy that celebrated material abundance and its opportunities for feminine display. Such shows reordered the cultural standards through which Poli appealed to diverse local audiences.

Many of these shifts derived from changed patterns of ethnic representation. Ethnic caricature itself remained a conspicuous mode of vaudeville entertainment, though its dominance declined. Through the first decade of the new century, ethnic caricature was a feature of between one-third and one-half of Poli's song and dance acts and talking acts. But the ethnic groups portrayed at Poli's theaters and the nature of their portrayal changed markedly from the 1890s. In the field of song and dance, where Irish and blackface caricatures had prevailed in the previous decade, identifiably Irish caricatures fell to about 4 percent of early-twentieth-century acts, while blackface or "negro dialect" singing by whites accounted for, at most, 15 percent of the song and dance routines. New song and dance caricatures were provided after 1900 by African-American performers, a group that had been absent from Poli's stage during the 1890s. In the field of talking acts, the dominance of the Irish diminished somewhat more slowly than among song and dance acts of the early twentieth century, falling from approximately 25 percent to approximately 16 percent of acts with identifiable themes. While Irish comics remained prevalent in the early 1900s, they moved to different forms of performance than they had dominated in the 1890s. Irish caricatures had been especially frequent subjects for sketch artists and monologuists of the 1890s, and still appeared in these categories after 1900. But they were increasingly concentrated among "playlets," the emergent vaudeville form that would engage Alexander Irvine's talents in 1913. As sketch artists, monologuists, and two-man teams, Irish caricaturists of the early twentieth century competed with a growing wave of comedians who mockingly portrayed more recently arrived immigrant groups, notably Jews and Asians.[38]

"Mr. Poli Is the Big Chief!"

This shifting pattern of ethnic representations recast the cultural hierarchy in which vaudeville shows of the 1890s had arranged caricatured ethnic types. Irish acts held most closely to the older hierarchical scheme. This was in part because performers representing Irish characters revised their material to conform to the standards of refinement that UBO entrepreneurs advertised for their shows. Irish caricaturists found incentives for such revisions in the angry rebukes Irish-American audiences directed at acts like "The Irish Servant Girls," a sketch presented by the popular Russell Brothers, who appeared repeatedly at Poli's in the years after 1900.[39] Described by critics as a "boisterous old style knockabout act," the Russells' sketch drew frequent criticisms from Irish-Americans around the country, who objected to its portrayal of two raucous Irish maids. To enforce such criticisms, the United Irish Societies of New York began to keep reports of productions that "brought the Celtic people into plain contempt." They sent a committee to demand that New York impresario Oscar Hammerstein cut the Russell Brothers' act from one of his 1907 bills. When Hammerstein refused, members of the Irish organization showed up at his theater armed with eggs and other missiles. After these weapons cut short the Russell act, a spokesman rose to assure the audience that while the Irish Societies did not aim to suppress all caricatures of their "race," they would continue to protest productions that put Irish women in contempt.[40]

To the undoubted delight of the Irish Societies men, the judge who dismissed the charges against them amplified their defense of refined womanhood. "My impression of the Russell show," the judge declared, "is very bad. The public should not encourage or patronize such plays. No man of blood, particularly Irish blood, could sit and listen to anyone who would thus disgrace the women of his race. I am satisfied from the testimony that this act was indecent, shocking and vulgar in the last degree."[41] The Russells themselves maintained that their act was thoroughly Irish in sentiment and that their critics were really representatives of the xenophobic American Protectionist Association. Other rumors insinuated that the entire conflict was a contrivance of dictatorial UBO managers who had long sought to compel the Russells to tone down their act.[42]

Whatever the source of the Russell imbroglio, such events carried weight. As acts appearing in Poli's shows revealed, vaudeville began to accord Irish women the dignity that managers attributed to femininity at large. Gracie Emmett's depiction of Irish womanhood in "Mrs. Murphy's Second Husband" became a favorite characterization of the period. Described as a "rollicking farce" in Poli's advertisements, Emmett's playlet demonstrated that unobjectionable feminine caricatures did not have to be staid. But Emmett also cultivated a reputation for campaigning to improve portrayals of the Irish by offering to coach actors whose representations were "unworthy."[43]

As ethnic caricaturists refined their depictions of Irish women, they also moved away from traditional caricatures of male working-class camaraderie. Actors who specialized in depicting convivial Irish-American workingmen observed that, as new ethnic groups had begun to take over the manual occupations with which their characters were associated, their street-smart stage concoctions were less recognizably appealing. Thomas Nawn, a New Haven favorite of the 1890s who was still trouping the Poli circuit in 1905, admitted in 1906 that he would soon have to abandon his classic rendition of the Irish-American worker. "The character no longer exists," Nawn told a reporter. "Bricks are hoisted by Italians and machinery now."[44] Nawn predicted that vaudeville would replace its traditional depictions of plebeian camaraderie with more refined dramas worthy of higher-priced legitimate playhouses. He was right in one respect: sketches of the comic caricature type for which he was famous increasingly gave way to new concoctions called "playlets." Developing out of the "refined" comedies that "legitimate" actors had brought to vaudeville in the 1890s, the playlet became a primary form of Irish-American vaudeville representation in the early twentieth century.

The "Irish act" in playlet form became the special repository for the wistful sentimentality that had once pervaded a larger proportion of vaudeville acts. Playlets like "Come Back to Erin" or "The Old Neighborhood" made the nostalgic loyalties that had saturated the sentimental song hits of the 1890s into defining characteristics of ethnic identity.[45] They echoed the more elaborate tributes to Irish nostalgia that appeared in contemporary musical comedies by Chauncey Olcott, whose 1910 hit "Mother Machree" provided a Celtic summation of late-nineteenth-century sentimental stage traditions. As "Mother Machree"'s chorus intoned:

> There's a spot in me heart which no colleen may own;
> There's a depth in me soul never sounded or known
> There's a place in my mem'ry, my life, that you fill,
> No other can take it, no one ever will.[46]

"Mother Machree" did homage to a version of Irish motherhood that was part of a complicated lineage of Irish-American theatrical representation. Its figure of immigrant mother love obscured the competing themes of romantic nostalgia, urban street smarts, and immigrant community solidarity that informed the image of the Irish on the American stage from the mid-nineteenth century.[47] But, while of comparatively recent coinage, "Mother Machree" was nevertheless a significant statement of ethnic identity. It would serve Alexander Irvine as a useful vehicle for his own construction of ethnicity as he devised new methods for popularizing his mission on his way to Poli's vaudeville stage. In the process, Irvine wrestled not only with the cultural implications of mother-love as a nostalgic symbol of ethnic self-construction, but also with the pleasures conjured up by less sentimentally rendered female images that were taking over Poli's shows.

Outside the Irish playlet, sentimentality was on the wane in the world of early-twentieth-century vaudeville. Poli's advertisements still touted performers who specialized in sentimental themes, such as Irish tenor Andrew Mack, whom Poli's notices congratulated for offering entertainment "free from vulgarity in any shape." But masters of the sentimental song like Paul Dresser, who celebrated in music the conventional moralities they had abandoned for high living, found their fortunes declining as fresh styles fostered a less apologetic urban revelry. As these newer styles came to dominate the vaudeville show, they helped popularize a consumerist imagery of cultural accomplishment with which Irvine contended as he incorporated the nostalgia-cloaked Irish mother into his public self-representations. The dominant feminine ideal of the emergent musical fashion was not a tearful rural mother but a brazen urban "mama"; its beat was not the simple 4/4 measure of the parlor ballad, but a syncopated rhythm called ragtime.

Ragtime was written and performed by African-American artists who helped transform cultural hierarchy in vaudeville. It mixed the jubilation of black spirituals—to which Poli had paid a back-handed tribute in advertisements for Maud Huth—with the percussive rhythm of African-American dance. It passed from itinerant pianists in honky tonks and saloons along the Mississippi and the Atlantic Seaboard to academically trained songwriters who sold songs to Tin Pan Alley publishers and novelty-hungry vaudeville singers. Ragtime lyricists enhanced the music's refreshing departure from cloyingly sweet ballad melodies by linking it to urban adventures that mothers in the old sentimental favorites had worried over and forgiven. Pioneer ragtime writers turned out songs entitled "I'm Livin' Easy (And cert'nly livin' high)," "Get Your Money's Worth," "Why Don't You Get A Lady of Your Own," "When It's All Goin' Out and Nothin' Comin' In," and "Why Adam Sinned"—also known, to clinch the point, as "Adam Never Had No Mammy."[48] But while such hits helped amplify an ethic of irreverent, urban flash and sophistication in vaudeville, black artists who authored them found their artistic opportunities constricted by established lines of demeaning blackface caricature.

Few of the black vaudeville artists who appeared on Poli's stages demonstrated this paradox more clearly than Ernest Hogan. Born Rufus Crowders in Bowling Green, Kentucky, Hogan got his start in show business touring with an African-American minstrel troupe in the 1880s, performing the same stereotypes that white men in blackface had popularized. During the 1890s he starred in the first all-black musical comedy, *Clorindy, The Origin of the Cake Walk*, by Paul Laurence Dunbar and Will Marion Cook. But Hogan's greatest fame came from authoring the first published ragtime hit, an 1896 number called "All Coons Look Alike to Me." The song proved both a tremendous commercial success and a perpetual embarrassment. Many African Americans resented Hogan's reiteration of an already prevalent slur, especially as the epithet he used in the title stuck to the style he had popularized. From the mid-1890s on, vaudeville publicists billed ragtime pieces as "coon songs."[49] This label grafted an old minstrel show tradition of ridiculing pseudo-sophisticated urban blacks onto the emergent musical formulas of ragtime, fashioning a virtual straitjacket for the black vaude-villians who appeared on their stages. Sylvester Poli did his part to enforce the prevailing stereotypes. He often listed black musical acts as "coon" specialties, and rarely advertised black singers in terms of talents that were not racially defined.[50]

Some black vaudeville entertainers tried to challenge such conventions. J. Rosamund Johnson and Robert Cole appeared on the vaudeville stage dressed in elegant tuxedos to perform a mixture of classical songs and the ragtime numbers they penned with writer James Weldon Johnson.[51] But such performers made little headway against racial discrimination in the theater. Though vaude-ville offered them greater access to big-name theaters than musical comedy, managerial agreements restricted black performers to one act per show and for-bade the billing of any black act as the "headliner," or star, of a show.[52] As a result, the performers who scored the greatest successes with ragtime hits penned by black songwriters were women who used the vaudeville stage to popularize a novel image of brazen feminine self-assurance.

Female vaudeville stars had featured ragtime songs since the 1890s, before black singers had appeared in vaudeville. In the early twentieth century, a number of female stars emerged who used these songs explicitly to contradict the modesty celebrated in overtures to feminine "taste" made by UBO managers. Some of these performers, like Jewish Sophie Tucker or Polish Gilda Gray, had roots in the new immigrant groups that had become the focus of vaudeville car-icature. Others, like Eva Tanguay, zestfully abandoned rural backgrounds older vaudeville stars had sentimentalized.[53] These were only the most renowned of their kind who appeared on Poli's New Haven stage. They defined a new ethos shared by a growing number of stars whose acts inspired advertising and program writers to emphasize looks, beauty, and magnetism, rather than feminine "refinement."[54] Collectively, these performers emphasized the riches and adventures available to ambitious urban women who would risk reputation and sentiment to acquire them.

Commercial ragtime music had highlighted feminine pluck from its inception. In the context of the song, the lyrics of Ernest Hogan's 1896 hit expressed the unsentimental calculations of a woman on the make. "All Coons Look Alike to Me" related the troubles of a man who has just been told. "I've found another beau, you see," his girlfriend explains in the chorus. "He spends his money free." This sense of feminine material aspiration and self-command remained a trademark of the female headliner in the twentieth century. Sophie Tucker, a Hartford kid who imbibed her lust for the good life at Poli's theater in that city and went on to tour Poli's circuit, came virtually to personify this message as she cultivated her image as "The Last of the Red Hot Mamas." Though she would echo the immigrant nostalgia of "Mother Machree" in her 1920s number "My Yiddishe Mama," Tucker had established her theatrical signature with the 1910 ragtime hit "Some of These Days," written by black artist Shelton Brooks. When "Some of These Days" told a wayward lover he would miss his "fat mama," the emotions it expressed were not the maternal solemnities of Olcott's ballad. Tucker sang self-consciously as a woman who wanted sex and material success and had learned the uses of ambition and the limits of sentimentality in both realms. With her theme song "I Don't Care," vaudeville singer Eva Tanguay evinced some of the same philosophy, declaring in the chorus that she didn't care "if I do get that mean and stony stare." In other favorite titles like "I Want Someone to Go Wild With Me," "It's All Been Done Before But Not the Way I Do It," and "Go As Far As You Like," Tanguay showed that not only did she not care about the stony stare, she positively courted it. This was a woman little concerned about fastidious taste.[55]

These defiant ragtime divas occupied a troublesome spot within vaudeville's cultural hierarchies. Their flagrant transgression of modesty and decorum could seem to reaffirm the hierarchy that vaudeville's ethnic caricatures had partially endorsed. Blackface caricature had always associated African-American and other "lowbrow" efforts at urban sophistication with gaudy display; the "coon song" transported this derogatory implication into the ragtime era. To the extent that black and immigrant ragtime acts reinforced this view, they amplified the hierarchy of civilization that Poli's entertainments had long popularized. By depicting ethnically and racially defined "lower orders" absorbed in sexual and material appetites, such acts also played into the imperial vision that New Haven audiences heard from ministers like Theodore Thornton Munger, who believed societies rose or fell along the hierarchy of civilization depending on their self-discipline in utilizing the material abundance made available by global commerce.

But vaudeville's ragtime ethos also encouraged an alternative interpretation of hedonism. The glittering sensuality embraced by a Tucker or a Tanguay conveyed the value they placed on material abundance, sexual adventure, and urban sophistication as ends in themselves, available to a mass audience, rather than as means toward or lessons about the value of genteel self-improvement. This ethos of impetuous feminine self-display produced new wrinkles in the increasingly visual culture that blossomed on all sorts of American stages with the growing commercialization of nineteenth-century theatrical practice. As Faye Dudden has observed, theatrical spectacles that showcased feminine beauty compromised women's capacity to use the theater as a doorway into the largely male province of public speech and its political and cultural debates, restricting them to much more vulnerable theatrical roles as sexual objects and props for material splendor. While not immune to these exploitative dangers, vaudeville's showy songstresses conveyed the meaning of sensual extravagance to audiences for whom the hierarchical terms of public debate were themselves often alienating and objectifying. These stars suggested that the métier of self-display provided alternative, more broadly accessible means to public distinction. They delineated a hierarchy built on the impressive charms that popular theater offered to those who would throw off artistic and moral niceties to flaunt their way across its spectrum of alluring possibilities.[56]

The vaudeville stage was hardly the most hedonistic theatrical arena where actors and audiences indulged this seductive ethos. Compared to the cabaret or the Broadway revue, vaudeville acts like Tucker's or Tanguay's were relatively restrained. Tucker and sometime vaudeville artist Gilda Gray reserved for cabaret acts performed for small, affluent audiences the sensuality that vaudeville managers prohibited. Unlike vaudeville's more democratic audience, the cabaret's elite clientele was more likely to view immigrant entertainers as alluring representatives of a "primitive" freedom from cultural refinements that elites found increasingly burdensome. Florenz Ziegfeld also contributed to this ethos by arranging expensively and revealingly attired chorus girls on lavish sets for the visual enjoyment of well-to-do patrons. Here, too, famous vaudeville stars like Nora Bayes or Eva Tanguay often presided over the extravagant proceedings.

Passing back and forth between vaudeville and these more expensive, luxurious, and libidinous entertainments, such stars dramatized the continuity among them. Poli and other UBO managers rallied their stringent codes of refinement to disrupt this continuity and draw a moral boundary around vaudeville. But the economies of scale that the UBO produced encouraged acts that tended to flout such boundaries.[57]

The UBO fostered the rapid expansion of a new type of billing—the ensemble act—which imported the appeals of the revue and the cabaret into the vaudeville show. Assembled by professional entertainment producers like Jesse Lasky, B. A. Rolfe, and George Homans, ensemble acts had as their common denominators beautiful women, glossy sets and costumes, and high budgets. The most elaborate and expensive of these acts appeared after 1906, when the ensemble form began to dominate the field of song and dance in vaudeville. Jesse Lasky, who claimed to have invented these extravaganzas on the model of European musical revue, was their acknowledged master.[58] He understood what tastes he was appealing to when he commented about a 1908 vaudeville hit that "'At the Country Club' . . . is a musical comedy of the most modern type. . . . Twenty-six unusually stylish and costly costumes are worn by four stunning show girls, and there are an equal number of hats of the most dazzling and modish creations."[59] Lasky and other "ensemble" producers amplified the theme of material indulgence by using settings associated with the purchase or conspicuous exhibition of dress goods. "At the Country Club" was an obvious example. In addition, "Hotel Laughland" and "The Leading Lady" were set in hotels frequented by entertainers and "In and Out of Society" was set in a department store. These settings provided the occasions for musical numbers that celebrated themes of shopping, self-adornment, and theatrical self-display, including "Won't You Buy?," "Hats," and "Parts I've Played." Other Lasky productions like "The Three Types: The Blonde, The Brunette and the Titian" showcased women themselves as attractive objects of display. Under the corporate conditions established in vaudeville by the UBO, such acts became virtually irresistible bookings. Their producers fronted money for actors, sets, and costumes on the strength of the long tours the UBO could guarantee. Producers then offered these showy productions at lower prices than managers had to pay for vaudeville's headliners or stars: between $750 and $1,500 a week as opposed to $2,500 or $3,000.[60]

Proliferating rapidly among "ensemble" acts, the seductions of wealth and women became dominant themes in Poli's promotion for a variety of vaudeville performers. In newspaper advertising Poli noted that "as is to be expected in anything put out by Jesse L. Lasky, "The Photo Shop" is costumed in a gorgeous and pretentious manner" and of another ensemble act that "it is a veritable dream of feminine grace and beauty." Poli considered a female performer's previous association with Lasky's productions a good advertisement for her later solo appearances. He also praised other acts for the physical charms that ensemble acts extolled. He advertised singers as "best looker" or "the handsomest as well as one of the most shapely women on the vaudeville stage." Thus the themes of the Lasky acts—"beautiful gowns, stylish millinery, and pretty girls," in the words of one contemporary critic—increasingly came to characterize Poli's shows.[61]

Poli did still publicly insist that performers observe "civilized" standards in his theater. He guaranteed such standards with the enhanced avowals of careful censorship that the UBO encouraged. Mae West was perhaps the most famous object of such purges, banished by Poli in 1912 for what newspapers called "that enchanting, seductive, sin-promising wriggle" (in an act that concluded with West wearing what some reviewers thought was a "nifty harem outfit"). A few years later, Poli also quibbled with the suggestively "primitive" costume worn by shimmy dancer Gilda Gray.[62] However, Poli's efforts to impose genteel standards of civility on such flashy female performers demonstrated managerial control only in a superficial sense. Poli could insist that Gray put on more clothes, but he had less control over the aura of feminine seduction and material indulgence that came to dominate his shows through the UBO's economies of scale. By advertising his surveillance of sexual indelicacies, Poli provided audiences with a shaky warranty of his allegiance to a standard of refinement that his own shows increasingly undermined.

At the same time, the new ethos of display celebrated in Poli's shows was subjected to the self-reflexive critique vaudeville had always provided for the cultural hierarchies it endorsed. During the UBO period that saw the rise of the ensemble act and the spread of its values across the vaudeville show, vaudeville sketches also pictured characters sunk in urban poverty or negotiating class differences that demonstrated inequalities in the distribution of material abundance. Sketches like "A Bowery Camille" or "An Idyll of the Slums" focused on the difficulties and peculiarities of those who lacked access to the dressy environments reproduced in ensemble acts. Other sketches—"The New Coachman," "Ticks and Chicks," "Minna from Minnesota"—featured urban working-class characters like office boys, typewriters, coachmen, and servants. Such acts suggested alternative perspectives on the splendor portrayed by vaudeville's more lavish performances. Their characters might evaluate beauty in terms of the toil that produced it or earned the price of admission to the arenas where it was displayed, rather than focusing on the elusive attractions of consumption itself.[63]

"Mr. Poli Is the Big Chief!"

Vaudeville shows also raised questions about their own values of consumption and self-display in some of the films that had become staples at theaters like Poli's by the early twentieth century. Like vaudeville itself, these films recommended a range of ambitions for both emulation and self-reflexive evaluation. In the tradition of the Passion Play films of the 1890s, some movies of the early silent era provided vaudeville with cinematic pieties representing the upper end of an older hierarchy of genteel culture and self-improvement. The filmed poses reproducing Millet's *The Angelus*, shown in Poli's theater in March 1903, was one such example. But most of the films that Poli advertised in this period featured humorous or dramatic vignettes of urban life. Films like Edwin Porter's *Life of an American Fireman* and other moving snapshots of daily life — *Life of a New York Policeman*, *Baby's First Outing*, *Picnic Hampers* — depicted quotidian adventures and pleasures familiar to ordinary theatergoers. These films extended the themes of local interest and everyday leisure that had served as a focus for visual realism from the days of Poli's work at the Eden Musée. They offered audiences the opportunity to identify with skills and communities that did not necessarily partake of vaudeville's more lavish displays.

In addition, new, narrative films used cinematic editing techniques to shift back and forth between different locations along a hierarchy of consumption. *The Kleptomaniac*, an Edwin S. Porter film that appeared in Poli's theater in April 1905, cut between the stories of a rich woman who steals luxury items from a department store and a poor woman who steals a loaf of bread to feed her hungry children. Portraying the treatment of the two women in court, the film showed that the wealthy woman was received with dignity and sympathetically dismissed, while the poor woman was humiliated by the police and summarily sentenced to jail. The implication that the wealthy lived in conditions not only materially but morally distinct from other classes left room for interpretations in which different stations along the hierarchy of consumption were not only culturally distinct but morally opposed. Alexander Irvine would try to elaborate this notion in print, vaudeville, and film as his mission drew him into Sylvester Poli's entertainment arena.[64]

Live sketches and films that questioned vaudeville's ethic of feminine and consumer display provided some continuity with the popular realism that characterized Poli's shows before his involvement in the UBO. In both eras, realism was largely the product of a variety format that appealed to a range of experiences of cultural hierarchy — whether that hierarchy celebrated gentility or display as its summit. Even so, the transformation in vaudeville's cultural hierarchy did challenge some of the ways Sylvester Poli had learned to wield popular realism and negotiate cultural authority. The relative decline of ethnic caricature and rivalry in vaudeville meant that UBO era shows curtailed the connections Poli could draw between his role as a theatrical manager and his pursuit of local cultural authority among diverse audiences. The new emphasis on feminine display also showcased female stars who abandoned the aura of civilization that vaudeville managers expected women to contribute to their theaters, however ambiguously they advertised women as performers.

Female audience members constituted one group for whom this shift might have introduced new horizons of cultural self-promotion. But their relation to Poli's twin quests for entrepreneurial success and cultural authority remains relatively obscure. Women were not prominent within most of the civic institutions where Poli courted public standing. However, the Lowell Settlement House—founded by Irvine and patronized by Poli as he succeeded in his quest for elite cultural authority—included a Mothers' Club that left behind some intriguing traces of the divergent perspectives from which women in New Haven made sense of the changing cultural standards promoted at their local vaudeville house.

Mrs. Delia Lyman Porter, wife of a Yale professor, organized the Lowell House Mothers' Club in 1900, drawing on the working-class neighborhoods around the settlement for members. Wives of clock, carriage, metal, and railway workers from Britain, Ireland, and Western Europe constituted the club's core membership.[65] These working-class women came together under Porter's leadership for a variety of recreational and educational activities. In addition to picnics and dances, their meetings featured instruction in artistic and musical appreciation offered by Porter and other middle-class women whom she invited to address the club. These instructional talks by Porter and her social peers offered civilizing refinement in terms remarkably analogous to the cultural hierarchy of Poli's early vaudeville shows.[66]

Porter aptly delineated such a hierarchy when she spoke on "making the best of what we have" for the benefit of the Mothers' Club's working-class members. Her discussion of this theme succinctly outlined a spectrum of ethnic communities ranked from the top down. To the king of England, she explained, a resident of New Haven's patrician Hillhouse Avenue might seem a small person, a fact that Mothers' Club members who envied mansion-dwellers should keep in mind. Furthermore, the Mothers' Club's working-class members were themselves more comfortable than the Italians huddled together in New Haven's most crowded tenements, and the Italians were better off than San Francisco's Chinese population. From this description of New Haven's status hierarchy it is not hard to see why Porter might approve of Poli's earliest vaudeville shows. Here

Porter summed up the hierarchy of ethnic and class groups these shows described. She even hinted at a tension between hierarchical values and their vaudeville alternatives by vacillating in her preference for royal refinement as opposed to working-class community. However, she insisted that the rich were a social asset whose culture and accomplishments benefited everyone.[67]

Middle-class speakers tried to demonstrate these benefits through programs that bestowed hierarchical cultural standards on the club's working-class members. However, working-class mothers did not necessarily accept the way such hierarchies were defined. The club's discussions of popular entertainment demonstrate such disagreements nicely. Mrs. Porter launched these discussions with a report on young female factory workers in New Haven that evaluated the amusements such workers enjoyed. According to the Club minutes, she observed that

> Girls in factories like to pass a pleasant evening by going to Poli's or the Bijou, where they have very good plays, the New Haven Opera House was not recommended as a good place. Music Hall was all right for some things, but not a place for a young girl to go every night, and cheap dances are awful for any girl and ought to be stopped.[68]

Porter rated Poli's vaudeville houses favorably as a safe amusement for young girls compared to more expensive theaters showing suggestive comedies or musical revues and especially to dance halls, which Lowell House leaders regarded as dens of sexual license. A month after her report, however, a working-class member of the Mothers' Club, Mrs. McManus, gave her own talk on local theaters and dances. By McManus's lights, there was only one local place of amusement—Germania Hall—not fit for young girls. She indicated a broad tolerance for varieties of amusement that Porter and other Lowell House leaders would have proscribed. While joining together to foster cultural refinements, in short, different classes of women involved in Lowell House's Mothers' Club divided over what amusement forms were sufficiently "refined" for working girls. Such divisions suggest that Poli's female audiences did not themselves agree on the narrowed standard of refinement, focused on feminine decency, which he cultivated in the UBO era.[69]

In other discussions, working-class Mothers' Club members indicated that they were more eager for education in adornment and display than for the training in gentility that their meetings usually provided. The high cultural offerings that middle-class women made available generated some piquant expressions of the working-class members' alternative ideals. Besides dispensing appreciation for such cultural achievements as fine art, classical music, and canonical literature, middle-class women offered short talks on their visits to living monuments of hierarchical culture. The club's working-class secretary set down appreciative reactions to these events in the club's minutes, but also recorded the working-class members' own suggestions regarding the programs of self-enhancement they would like. When Mrs. Tracy Peck described her meetings with the queen of Italy and the pope, the secretary noted that the talk was "interesting" but that the greater concern among club members had been for Mrs. Peck to return to talk on "How to trim bonnets." The comment suggests that these working-class women saw personal adornments as more appealing resources than the paintings, music, and hierarchical celebrities middle-class women promoted. For the hierarchical ideal of "civilized" refinement, they substituted the emergent values of self-display, choosing a form of self-improvement in keeping with the wide arena of entertainment they considered appropriate for their daughters.[70]

These different approaches to cultural hierarchy, entertainment, and display within the Lowell House Mothers' Club leave much to speculation. They suggest that women of various class and ethnic backgrounds picked and chose among competing cultural values, without telling much about the experiences that shaped such preferences. Poli's negotiation of cultural hierarchy in New Haven and in the vaudeville industry provides a useful set of contexts for interpreting the cultural alternatives these women disputed. For working-class members of the Mothers' Club, the flashy, self-revealing ebullience of Sophie Tucker, Eva Tanguay, Gilda Gray, or Mae West could understandably appear more satisfying than more conventionally hierarchical tastes such as those Mrs. Porter endorsed. The new, more transgressive vaudeville ethic of display challenged not only the authority of self-important settlement workers, but also the authority precariously wielded over female performers by Manager Poli himself. In this sense, the interest in adornment that working-class Mothers' Club members expressed illuminates the significance that popular audiences might attach to the emerging mass cultural styles and consumer aesthetics of the early twentieth century. Both contemporary observers and historical scholars have remarked on the growing popularity of such styles, often decrying the way developing culture industries encouraged women to invest in the pleasures and dangers of display. Considered in light of Poli's career as it unfolded nearby, the case of the Lowell House Mothers' Club offers a rare glimpse into the range of cultural alternatives against which particular women measured these pleasures. Given that Poli's negotiations of local cultural authority focused on institutions that offered limited voice to women like the working-class Mothers' Club members, they may well have seen their stake in cultural politics more effectively engaged by the new ethos of display.[71]

The changes Poli negotiated within the vaudeville industry and the conflicts he navigated among his local audience had important implications for the way Alexander Irvine reconstructed his mission on the way to the vaudeville stage. As Irvine sought new arenas to replace his fractured People's Church, he addressed more explicitly the politics of ethnicity and gender that confounded Poli. In the process, Irvine devised his own critique of the ethos of feminine display that characterized early-twentieth-century vaudeville. Like Poli, Irvine recognized in this ethos a challenge to ideals of feminine refinement he wished to uphold. However, Irvine tried to reconceptualize women's relation to the popular public sphere in ways that opposed both the dangers of self-display and the limitations of domestic propriety. He constructed this alternative through a series of autobiographical and journalistic narratives that provided him with a laboratory of literary self-discovery. Here Irvine could experiment with ethnicity and gender politics that had long characterized Poli's vaudeville shows and negotiations of local celebrity. Irvine's self-constructions suggest some of the ways that shifting popular representations of ethnicity and gender informed twentieth-century debates about cultural hierarchy.

PART III

HIERARCHY INTO AUTONOMY
Narrating Culture for a New Century

CHAPTER SIX

MAKING WORKING-CLASS NARRATIVE
"FROM THE BOTTOM UP"

Alexander Irvine, the Evolutionary Vernacular,
and the Socialist Bildungsroman

FROM 1906 TO 1913, Alexander Irvine traveled out of New Haven and back again on a surge of national celebrity. This fame derived in part from his successful retelling and retailing of his life in a series of popular narratives. Though only one of these ever reached the vaudeville stage, all of them participated in theatrics of class, race, ethnicity, and gender that vaudeville had helped popularize. As they implicated him ever more intricately in Poli's entertainment world, these narrative self-constructions also connected Irvine to a wider transformation in the understanding and representation of cultural difference. This transformation began to displace conceptions of difference that figured class, race, and gender in terms of hierarchically ranked inequalities determined by evolutionary mechanics with more relativistic, pluralistic visions of the varied cultures from which people seek value and meaning. It is usually studied within the history of academic philosophical and social scientific discourse. Chapters 6, 7, and 8 argue that Irvine's self-representational projects illuminate working-class and popular entertainment sources for the changing cultural evaluations this shift encompassed.

Irvine came to formulate this cultural transformation as the lesson of his own life story, but only after he had learned to narrate his life in popularly salable terms. This chapter examines the ambiguities of working-class identity that he discovered as he adapted popular languages of class distinction to the task of recounting his own cultural trajectory. Irvine originally picked up many of the basic formulas he would use in this endeavor from Jack London, whom he invited to lecture in New Haven under Socialist Party auspices in January 1906.

In a preface to his lecture, London narrated his own life as a struggle out of the social pit, through disillusionment with "civilized" society, and finally into a mature embrace of socialism. This socialist bildungsroman would ultimately serve Irvine as an outline for his own published autobiography.

But Irvine's apprenticeship in popular narrative involved more than a mere replication of London's model. London inspired Irvine to experiment with his own performances of proletarian selfhood as a means of constructing a popular working-class identity. Following London's example in these experiments, Irvine affected the dress and manner of a recently arrived immigrant laborer and traveled south to the coal mines, turpentine camps, and stockades of Alabama to investigate peonage. Then he worked these experiences into essays that revealed how his own process of working-class self-construction engaged broader trends in the representation of class. Since his investigation explored racial and ethnic divisions among southern workers, Irvine used them to formulate a working-class identity that highlighted complicated intersections of ethnic, race, and class distinctions, which he wove into popular autobiographical narratives for an expanding periodical press.

Periodical literature provided an important proving ground for Irvine's narrative experiments. By opening literary expression to subjects such as industrial work and immigrant life represented in a popular realist style of robust virility, the new mass magazines where Irvine published fostered public explorations of class differences. They featured what I call an "evolutionary vernacular" that cast such differences in terms of distinctions between "civilization" and more vigorous but brutal virtues that prevailed in the "social pit." Irvine used this language to construct a broadly appealing public self and give salable expression to the memories and experiences it embodied. As he deployed the evolutionary vernacular to narrate his life in a widening array of periodicals and public forums, however, he found that it served competing conceptions of cultural hierarchies with which he had wrestled throughout his career. Irvine's efforts to make narrative sense of his own life in popular evolutionary terms illustrate the contending interpretations to which these terms were subject in the early twentieth century.

Irvine serves especially well as a guide to the cultural politics of the evolutionary vernacular because, while using this language to construct his own narratives, he also continued to participate in political discussions about the nature of class distinction. He engaged in Socialist Party debates about the ethnic and gender boundaries for class solidarity he had begun to challenge in New Haven. He formulated these issues for wider audiences in church services and social forums that he directed at the Church of the Ascension in New York City. These activities connected his literary self-constructions to a broad public sphere. Within this sphere, heirs of the evangelical tradition that had shaped Irvine's own early aspirations contended with "scientific" Socialists who cast hierarchies of class, race, and gender in Darwinian evolutionary terms. The realm of popular entertainment helped inform such contests by providing widely accessible imagery for the racial and ethnic distinctions that complicated class politics during this period. As Irvine wove these diverse public constructions of class into his personal narratives, his combined efforts at authorship and agitation demonstrated a broad range of popular sources for the fluctuating terms of proletarian selfhood that shaped his increasingly public identity.

Jack London, Alexander Irvine, and the Evolutionary Vernacular

Irvine seized the opportunity to bring Jack London to New Haven when the attractive young Californian appeared on the East Coast in the course of a controversial national lecture tour. The renown of *The Call of the Wild, The Sea Wolf,* and London's Klondike tales was drawing avid audiences for his speeches. London told many of these crowds about working-class adversities under capitalism and how socialism promised to answer these woes. Such lectures helped raise funds for the Intercollegiate Socialist Society (ISS), a new organization of which London was president. A commercial chautauqua company sponsored the balance of his lectures, which focused on adventure and travel. However, the orations London used to stoke collegiate interest in socialism provoked revulsion among other audiences. Press and clergy denounced London's politics and library trustees banned his books, dog stories and all. To observers then and later, such reactions signaled a fissure between London's commercial successes and his socialist convictions, a gap that seemed to grow as he penned lucrative stories to fund extravagant travels and a lavish California ranch. Whether one viewed his politics as a rebellious accent to his vocation as a prosperous writer, or saw his popular fiction as detracting from a revolutionary nature, London's career seemed perilously suspended over a chasm between socialist ideals and the machine of popular culture.[1]

London's encounter with Alexander Irvine, and its aftermath in Irvine's career, puts this tension into new perspective. The two men met at a moment that each came to regard as a turning point, when socialist activism saved him from debilitating personal discouragement. At their first meeting, London had begun to narrate his socialist epiphany in terms that contrasted the vitality of proletarian solidarities with the enervation of bourgeois overrefinement. Such representations of class conflict were not unusual in popular culture: vaudeville had used plebeian revelry to puncture prissy refinement for over a decade. Irvine had already adapted some of these popular approaches to cultural hierarchy for use in his mission, but London showed how he could narrate his cultural politics in salable terms by translating his challenges to cultural hierarchy into fashionable Darwinian language. The model was only applicable, however, because both men's personal trajectories intertwined politics, popular culture, and personal faith. There were profound tensions in this cultural landscape, to be sure. Rather than opposing "politics" to "popular culture," these tensions grew out of debates that engaged popular representations of class, religion, ethnicity, race, and gender. The circumstances that brought them together in 1906, and the subsequent consequences of this meeting for Irvine's career, illustrate how both men drew on such debates to formulate their cultural politics and represent their ideals to popular audiences.

By 1906, as we have seen, Irvine was having trouble finding a public to sustain the working-class mission he had forged in New Haven. His People's Church had effectively dissolved, his relations with New Haven cultural elites had turned acrimonious, and his alliances with labor had collapsed. He remained state secretary of the Socialist Party, but even here he encountered resistance to his religious ideals from atheistic German comrades. In his isolation, Irvine tried to drum up student comrades at Yale. His following at the university was small, but he did help found "The University Federal Labor Union," a student organization devoted to supporting the trade union movement. When Irvine failed to find a church or hall available for London's lecture, he turned to a socialist student, Charles Field, who proposed to a Yale debating society that they sponsor the event. The officers agreed, though they fretted over the possibility that London might say something "socialistic." Irvine thereby gained access to Yale's ornate Woolsey Hall for an event that provided the inspiration he needed to restart his faltering mission.[2]

For his part, London came to Yale in a temper of uncharacteristically idealistic socialist conviction. Active in California's Socialist Labor Party since 1896, he had long considered socialism more a historical necessity than a humanitarian creed. As his dog stories attested, London was a convinced Darwinian and Spencerian who believed that his own life, his study of social relations, and his observation of late-nineteenth-century war and imperialism all warranted the doctrine of the survival of the fittest.[3] In their most distasteful form, these evolutionary views buttressed a virulent racism that some associates saw as inimical to London's socialist ideas. London replied to such criticism in 1899 that "Socialism is not an ideal system, devised by man for the happiness of a life; nor for the happiness of all men. . . . It is devised so as to give more strength to those certain kindred favored races so that they may survive and inherit the earth to the extinction of the lesser weaker races."[4] Such a cold-blooded evolutionary hierarchy was a far cry from the images of comradeship that London offered at Woolsey Hall, where he championed a socialism that "transcends race prejudice" and "knits men together as brothers." He later explained this change as the consequence of a "long sickness of pessimism" he had entered in 1903, and was still resolving early in 1906.[5]

London's writing career and personal life were both implicated in the "long sickness," which he identified as a consequence of having "read too much positive science and lived too much positive life."[6] When, after an adventurous youth and a frenzied education to prepare himself for writing, London had finally begun to publish stories, he saw his success as the reward for a steely repudiation of pretensions to art or culture. He had mastered the formulas of a hack writer for popular magazines, and held to them as the source of his livelihood. His marriage to Bess Maddern in 1900 issued from a similar disdain for lofty sentiments. London sought the companionship and steadying influence of a stable family life. But he declared to his wife that he was not in love, which he identified with natural sources of disorder like flood and fire.[7] However, London's convictions about the inefficiencies of love perished in his long sickness along with his belief that he could subordinate all ideals to material success. In 1903 he separated from Bess to pursue a passionate, enduring love affair with Charmian Kittredge, whose lust for adventure kept pace with his own. Their marriage in November 1905 added further controversy to London's lecture tour. Meanwhile, he embraced socialism as the one faith his Darwinian exertions had left unextinguished. As he explained later, "the PEOPLE saved me. By the PEOPLE was I handcuffed to life. There was still one fight left in me, and here was the thing for which to fight."[8]

This "salvation through socialism," as one biographer has styled it, reshaped London's socialist convictions in the direction of Irvine's gospel of work. From 1903 throughout his speaking tour, London repeatedly described his socialist beliefs in quasi-religious terms.[9] In his New Haven lecture, he allied himself with revolutionists who offered "service, unselfishness, sacrifice, martyrdom—the things that sting awake the imagination of the people, touching their hearts with a fervor that arises out of the impulse toward good and which is essentially religious in nature."[10] Such idealism was crucial to London's impact on Irvine, who could not easily have followed a socialist prophet who recommended a militaristic creed of racial superiority. The London of 1899 would have been anathema, celebrating as he did the first spoils of American imperialism as a blow for democracy. Irvine had denounced militarism, imperialism, and racial superiority in his sermons on the Spanish-American War and the coal strike, which subverted the popular hierarchies of civilization that London endorsed. London, for his part, never wholly abandoned his Darwinian views. As recently as 1904, after traveling to Japan and Korea to report on the Russo-Japanese War, London had spouted venom about the "yellow peril." Chided by socialist comrades, he reportedly rejoined, "I am first of all a white man and only then a Socialist!" Irvine claimed that they quarreled over such views in years to come. But at Yale London sounded the note of socialist brotherhood more loudly than that of evolutionary competition. This shift softened his hierarchical vision of progress into a narrative that proved useful to Irvine.[11]

On the stage of Woolsey Hall, London presented a short autobiographical account of his own search for men, women, and pursuits that were "clean, noble and alive," of his failure to find them in the university, and of his discovery of them among Socialists. This autobiographical prelude to his lecture on "The Coming Crisis" offered a socialist bildungsroman complete with youthful aspiration followed by cruel disillusionment, culminating in adult resolution of healthy political associations and faiths.[12] London began by describing his childhood in terms that encapsulated the perspective of someone at the base of the hierarchies Irvine had been learning to question. "I had no outlook," London quipped, "but what you might call an uplook":

> Above me towered the colossal edifice of society; and I thought that up there were beautiful clothes; men wore boiled shirts and women were beautifully gowned, and there were all good things to eat and plenty of them, so much for the flesh. I felt also that up there I would find things of the spirit, clean and noble living and deeds and ideals, and I resolved to climb up there.[13]

In the next phase of London's narrative, the ideal represented by his "betters" was wiped out by the rigors of body-breaking labor. He descended into what he vividly described as "charnel houses of civilization," where one saw "the men who had been worked out by society, the men who sold their muscles." The bitter agonies of this "abyss" sparked his determination to become a merchant of brain rather than muscle. London spoke of how the "parlor floor" of society then admitted him, revealing a deadening materialism where he had imagined only sweetness and light. Among the institutions on this plane of society, only the university struck him as being "clean and noble" enough to approximate his early ideals. But it was not sufficiently "alive." London ended his bildungsroman by assailing the university's lack of concern for "the people who are suffering, the people who are in want." He recommended socialism as the antidote that would reinvigorate intellectual institutions with a healthy respect for robust working-class virtues.[14]

London's bildungsroman narrative proved a useful model for Irvine in a number of ways. The bildungsroman genre itself had long harnessed the narrative of personal cultivation to questions about who defined culture in the public sphere. The bildungsroman appeared at the crux of late-eighteenth-century social ferment that produced a modern public sphere committed to broad-ranging debate among equals, but sharply bounded by lines of class and gender.[15] Its founding texts explored what the pietist project of *Bildung*, or self-development, might mean for an individual enmeshed in the expanding market for secular works that helped shape that sphere. In the most famously prototypical bildungsroman, Goethe's *Wilhelm Meister's Lehrjahre* [*Wilhelm Meister's Apprenticeship*], Wilhelm struggles through several youthful misadventures in meaning before arriving at the mature comprehension of his life produced for him by an aristocratic secret society. This resolution smacks of a pallid obedience to received cultural standards that mocks the more assertive self-constructions Wilhelm ventures early in the story. Yet Wilhelm's early efforts to narrate his own trajectory signal other risks located in the expanding realm of commercial culture. There, Wilhelm's narrative experiments prove capricious and inconclusive, for they are founded on the shifting sands of theatrical role playing and replications of published narratives that circulated in the literary market on which authors like Goethe increasingly relied.[16]

Whereas Goethe sentenced Wilhelm to an uninspiring retreat into what cultural historian Franco Moretti calls the "comfort of civilization," London and Irvine charted rather different paths through the ambiguities of commercial culture.[17] Venturing into the project of cultivation from outside the social boundaries of the classic public sphere, they seized on newly expanding arenas of periodical literature and popular theatricality. Here they found a cultural lode where they could stake a claim to working-class cultural legitimacy. These arenas were no less precarious than the market in representations where Wilhelm Meister failed to achieve narrative stability. Indeed, as Irvine would find when he moved from the popular press to vaudeville, they could dampen as well as augment the socialist ideals he tried to define and amplify through them. Still, for London and Irvine, commercial popular culture provided opportunities for a public refashioning of the standards of self and civilization to which the bildungsroman had long given voice.

As he emulated London within the popular literary market, Irvine also benefited from the strenuous language the Californian used in his autobiographical
address. London had established himself as an author by practicing this language
in virile tales written for a new crop of inexpensive mass magazines. These periodicals transformed the literary market previously dominated by genteel monthlies such as *Harper's* and the *Atlantic. Munsey's, McClure's,* and *Cosmopolitan*
had pioneered the new periodical form in the 1890s; by the turn of the century
Ainslee's, Metropolitan, and others joined them. An evolutionary vernacular
combining Spencerian vocabulary with hierarchically arranged racial categories
of civilization characterized much of the fare in these new journals. Such language contributed to the success of London's Klondike stories in *McClure's* in
1900–1901, as well as the tales that made Kipling a household name, Stephen
Crane's war reports from Cuba and South Africa, and a variety of other literary
explorations of the "submerged" and the "exotic."[18] As he followed London into
popular authorship, Irvine adopted the evolutionary vernacular to enhance his
literary popularity. Though he was often uncomfortable with its hierarchical
social gradations, they provided a popular formula for exploring the relation
between class distinctions and personal identity.

A changing tide in literary production enhanced the publishing opportunities available to writers who mastered the evolutionary vernacular. Editors of the
genteel monthlies had presided with remote, paternalistic repose over the public sphere that their periodicals helped to shape. From the well-upholstered
depths of the "Editor's Easy Chair" or "Editor's Study"—as William Dean
Howells entitled his editorial columns—they received unsolicited contributions
from amateur literary hopefuls. The genteel editors tried to shape these contributions into publications suited to the "gentle" readers they sought to edify—
even after a few, like Howells, began to demand "realism" as the morally appropriate fare for those readers. Editors of the popular magazines had different
expectations. Trained in metropolitan journalism, advertising, and commerce,
they disdained the "literary" style that the genteel editors favored. The popular
editors prized a vivid, accessible idiom that they deemed appropriate to fiction
and reportage that addressed contemporary realities. Rather than lounging in
easy chairs pondering prose, they actively surveyed the social landscape for story
"ideas" that they farmed out to promising writers.[19]

This managerial approach transformed the relations of periodical production,
which came to resemble those of a manufacturing corporation more than the
literary salons evoked by genteel editorial practices. The shift had important
implications for contributing writers. The periodical press became less inviting

to amateur contributions. But advance contracts—cleverly negotiated by writers such as London—meant that professional authors could more easily live by their pens.[20] Meanwhile, editorial eagerness for a more vivid "realism" that was associated with the rigors of Darwinian struggle, poverty, industrial work, or exotic difference opened literary careers to writers from a wider range of backgrounds.[21] This diversity provided for competing renditions of the virile, evolutionary language encouraged by the new editors. Many periodical managers and writers shaped this language into Progressive fables in which managerial experts improved social life by exerting order over the abysmal forces of the evolutionarily unfit.[22] But the evolutionary vernacular was open to alternative uses. By crafting it into narratives of emerging class consciousness, London and Irvine highlighted its significance as a popular mode for exploring their era's most acute cultural distinctions.

London's Yale bildungsroman illustrated the ambiguous character of the popular evolutionary style. By using terms such as "sordidness" and "wretchedness" to portray his early proletarian experiences and describing "charnel houses of civilization" where he found "inefficients" consigned by Social Darwinism to the wastes of human progress, London reproduced a conventional hierarchy that ranked what he called the "parlor" level of society "above" the rigors of working-class existence. However, in the denouement of his bildungsroman, he tempered such hierarchical sensibilities with his recent embrace of THE PEOPLE. Here London identified maturity with a socialist faith that valued vigorous working-class solidarities above the pallid virtues cherished by more comfortable classes. This aspect of his story played to a popular fascination with the "vitality" that the evolutionary vernacular associated with "lower" classes, "exotic" cultures, and nature in the "raw." Such appreciation for the vigor of working-class culture appealed to Irvine's imagination as he began to manipulate the evolutionary vernacular as a language of self-representation.[23]

London's impact on Irvine was both instantaneous and enduring. Immediately, the personal anecdotes London used to distinguish socialist vigor from elite decadence suggested a new tack for dealing with Irvine's New Haven detractors. In addition to decrying their degeneracy, Irvine began to assert his own mettle, starting in the *Evening Leader* column in which he reported London's Woolsey Hall appearance. "In the school filled with the sons of the high priests of capitalism," he wrote, "this young man of 30 who had played the game of life in many climes hit out straight from the shoulder." Below this report, Irvine emulated London by explaining how his socialism set him apart from the sexless ministers with "wee white ties." "I train with the exploited and the rejected and the disinherited," Irvine told his critics. "I am as bad as they are and as good."[24] This intertwining of class distinctions with issues of gender, race, and ethnicity proved to be important to the narrative experiments Irvine modeled on London's example.

Soon, Irvine began a series of adventures in authorship that revealed the enduring force of London's influence. Throughout the summer of 1906, he corresponded with London to report on his progress as a writer, to beg for literary guidance, and to solicit a recommendation to "some capitalistic literary concern" that would buy his wares. *Appleton's Magazine* offered Irvine seventy-five dollars for his first published story, "Two Social Pariahs," before any suggestions arrived from California. But the story shows that Irvine had already learned a great deal from London.[25] "Two Social Pariahs" is set in the bunkhouse haunts of Irvine's days as Bowery missionary. It recounts a tale told by a former lawyer whose career crumbled after he defended Jim Farren, the local degenerate in a Connecticut town. In Irvine's representation of the trial, the lawyer attributes Farren's notorious violence to his status as an outcast from society. In twenty-eight years, the lawyer explains, "the prisoner never had the touch of a kindly hand nor the sound of a tender word from a human soul. . . . Jim Farren is what this community made him by neglect."[26] In language and allegorical effect, this description of Farren closely parallels London's 1906 novel *White Fang*, which recounts the career of a dog born to the bestial laws of "EAT OR BE EATEN" but adopted into the world of men who set new laws for him by their behavior—laws of violent struggle through cruelty or laws of affectionate loyalty through kindness.[27] Similarly, Irvine limned Farren as the creature of a social abyss that reduced men to the level of muscled boors. The lawyer pleads for leniency by arguing that Farren could nevertheless respond to human kindness: Farren risked his life for the town sheriff, the one man who showed him compassion. Such behavior, the attorney claims, proves that Farren is not the "insensate brute . . . rotten to the very core" that the prosecutor describes. He wins his point and Faren gets two years rather than the maximum penalty of thirty years for his crime. But the story ends with the lawyer joining Farren as a "social pariah."[28]

Published in January 1907, "Two Social Pariahs" was an auspicious beginning for Irvine's career in commercial storytelling. Before it had even appeared, *Appleton's* offered him a new literary assignment—an undercover investigation of peonage in the lumber and turpentine camps of Alabama—that provided further opportunities to borrow from London's journalistic techniques. By experimenting with proletarian selfhood in the course of this investigation, Irvine began to forge the terms of his own socialist bildungsroman.

10. Posing with Jack London in New Haven (1906), Alexander Irvine (*right*) adopted the simultaneously relaxed and robust posture the California author had modeled on the lecture platform at Yale. Photo from Alexander Irvine, *From the Bottom Up: The Life Story of Alexander Irvine* (New York: Doubleday-Page, 1910).

"My Life in Peonage": Investigative Disguise and the Working-Class Self

Irvine conducted his peonage investigation from December 1906 to February 1907; "My Life in Peonage" appeared as a series of three articles in *Appleton's* the following summer. In these articles, Irvine vividly described the conditions in the camps of the Jackson Lumber Company of Lockhardt, Alabama, whose officials had recently been prosecuted under federal antipeonage statutes. These laws defined peonage as "causing compulsory service to be rendered by one man to another on the pretext of having him work out the amount of a debt, real or claimed." The trials exposed the customary violence of this system of forced labor, which was prevalent not only in the turpentine and lumber industries Irvine visited, but also on railways and farms in the South.[29] In his opening piece, "The Situation as I Found It," Irvine described his motives and methods for investigating these practices:

> The cry of "peonage" was in the air. Press dispatches from the South told of the coercion of men by whips and bloodhounds. It was said that a new slavery had arisen on the spot where the old had died. Arranged in a beard, a pair of overalls, and with a bright yellow bundle in my hand I went in quest of the facts. If slavery existed, the best way to find it was by being a slave—a wage slave.[30]

This kind of adventure was both a journey into a world of oppressed peons and an exercise in the widespread practice of journalistic investigation aimed at elucidating class difference.

Dressed up as a peon, Irvine joined a diverse group of investigators who crossed class and ethnic lines and reported their experiences. He was not the first to travel incognito through Florida and Alabama to study peonage in 1906. He had been preceded by a New York lawyer specializing in the concerns of East Side immigrants, Mary Grace Quackenbos, who later became an aide to Charles W. Russell, the assistant attorney general in charge of Justice Department campaigns against immigrant peonage.[31] Nor was Irvine's journey to the South his first experiment with undercover investigation: while ministering to the Bowery in the 1890s, he had briefly masqueraded as a laborer to tour the drinking establishments of his neighborhood to aid Reverend Charles Parkhurst's antivice campaign.[32] Throughout these decades, cross-class investigators served many other purposes besides the journalistic, moral, and legal ambitions that Irvine, Parkhurst, and Quackenbos pursued. Middle-class consumers probed the work environments where the goods they bought were produced. Housing reformers photographed "how the other half lives" to terrify middle-class audiences into tenement reform. Factory detectives sought the secrets of labor organization and working-class culture. Social scientists made academic careers as well as bureaucratic data out of ethnographic research on workers and "tramps." Together, these investigators made working-class impersonation a remarkably versatile genre.[33]

Especially when planning to narrate their experiences as literature, such investigators usually exchanged their customary selves for dramatically assumed identities. In adopting his "beard, overalls and a bright yellow bundle," Irvine followed examples set by Jack London as well as Stephen Crane, one of London's own early literary heroes. Both of these models, in turn, echoed practices of popular realism used in vaudeville caricature and based on long-established theatrical traditions. However distorted their creations, blackface "delineators" of African-American slave culture—as well as former minstrels like Edward Harrigan, who moved on to Irish and Italian characterizations in the 1870s—all claimed to have studied "authentic" models whom they tried to recreate through clothing, speech, and gesture.[34] Similarly, Crane's 1894 newspaper sketch, "An Experiment in Misery," had featured a youth bent on trying "rags and tatters . . . a couple of dimes, and hungry too, if possible" in order to "discover" the "point of view" of a tramp."[35] Jack London adopted a similar conceit in his 1903 exposé of the East End of London, *The People of the Abyss*. The book's opening chapter describes an "unending slum . . . filled with a new and different race of people" that London entered by donning the "well-worn . . . frayed . . . very dirty" clothes of "other and unimaginable men."[36] In these costumes, investigators felt equipped both to "blend in" and to "experience" the feelings of those who inhabited the social realms they visited.

Investigators used competing languages to portray such experiences. Brandishing the evolutionary vernacular he later applied to his bildungsroman narrative, London described the people of the East End "abyss" as "a welter of rags and filth, of all manner of loathsome skin diseases, open sores, bruises, grossness, indecency, leering monstrosities, and bestial faces." Crane opted for more aesthetic grotesqueries, as in his description of a "wretch who feels the touch of the imperturbable granite wheels, and who then cries with an impersonal eloquence, with a strength not from him, giving voice to the wail of a whole section, a class, a people." Investigators who authored academic and government treatises preferred to depict sagas of disease and disorderliness among the poor or to catalog outrages done to them by employers. These different languages for investigative accounts expressed competing purposes even as they articulated shared quandaries about the cultural hierarchies they explored.[37]

For some, including Irvine and his rivals, these stylistic differences indicated incompatible objectives. Russell and Quackenbos tried to suppress popular journalism on peonage because they believed such reports interfered with their legal cases. They were concerned about Irvine's series as well as an article by Richard Barry entitled "Slavery in the South Today," which appeared in *Cosmopolitan* in March 1907 and incited anger against Barry and Quackenbos for generating bad publicity about the region. To compound this rivalry, Quackenbos herself struggled for legitimacy among Justice Department officials who doubted her professionalism. They claimed that she fraternized improperly with journalists and even contracted to sell information from her own investigations to *McClure's*. To fund her earliest investigations into peonage, Quackenbos had accepted an advance from McClure, in exchange for refusal of her material. In addition, she had relied on Barry for information that had been denied to her by U.S. Attorney John M. Cheney. Curiously, she had also succeeded in gleaning information from the Lockhardt company by claiming to be a journalist from *McClure's*. This intriguing embellishment of her role apparently won the confidence of informants who were more suspicious of lawyers than of the popular press. Once she secured a position in the Justice Department, Quackenbos joined in its effort to protect legal information from sensational journalism. But she remained reticent about accusations that she had helped Irvine. Irvine eventually wove their association into a novel that highlighted Quackenbos's accomplishments as a female attorney, and thus commented on his own struggle with the cultural politics of gender. Meanwhile, in his peonage articles, Irvine retaliated against the attorneys' criticism of his methods by claiming that his impersonation of "a brother workingman" inspired peons to describe brutality in the lumber camps more truthfully than they would under oath.[38]

While disputatious, the diverse languages and procedures of cross-class investigation also overlapped, especially in their representation of working-class life as a distinctive social, cultural, and moral realm. Usually this realm ranked below the "civilization" with which disguised investigators identified themselves and their readers. But the practice of investigative disguise could be as ambiguous in this regard as the vaudeville shows whose ethnic caricatures it paralleled or the evolutionary vernacular its authors sometimes used to convey their discoveries.

Here again Jack London was a striking and influential model. In *The People of the Abyss*, London oscillated between expressions of distance and sympathy toward the laboring poor. Describing his transformation through disguise and his periodic retreats to the comforts of baths and bed linen, he emphasized his own familiarity with soft gray suits, light comfortable shoes, cleanliness, and white sheets. But he also addressed his readers as soft people whose remoteness from the slums fed a self-serving ignorance of miseries that produced their "civilization."[39] Some years later, London produced a fictional account of investigative disguise that pushed the genre's ambiguity even further. His 1909 story, "South of the Slot," described the transformation of Freddie Drummond, a sociologist known for his bourgeois refinement and "cold-storage" reserve. For several years, Drummond investigates San Francisco working-class life by masquerading as the wagon driver Bill Totts, a dues-paying member of the Longshoremen's Union "who could drink and smoke and slang and fight and be an all-around favorite." Drummond comes to savor his alter-ego until Totts becomes infatuated with Mary Condon—"a royal bodied woman, graceful and sinewy as a panther, with amazing black eyes that could fill with fire or laughter-love." To protect himself from this threat to his customary reserve, Drummond resolves to bury Totts by engaging himself to the primly inhibited Catherine Van Vorst. But Totts's virile appeal proves irrepressible. At the end of the story Drummond abandons his aristocratic fiancée to aid workers in a violent strike and disappears, arm in arm with Mary Condon, into Totts's working-class community.[40]

The working-class disguise Alexander Irvine adopted for his peonage articles encouraged him to internalize this popular imagery of wage-labor as a rugged struggle. Describing the labor he undertook as an undercover peon, Irvine explained,

I courted the danger points. I went where conditions were savage, where life was cheaper than lumber, where the physically fit survived. I came under the lash of a driver's tongue several times, but escaped the more painful experience of a peon. There were very good reasons for my escape. I looked like a man who when struck on one cheek turns the other fellow's. Besides, I could do more work than was required of me, and do it very well.[41]

This enactment of working-class virility turned out to share much of the equivocation that characterized Jack London's visit to the East End. While Irvine represented the working-class persona he had donned through disguise as vigorous and robust, he described the peons he met as men thoroughly worsted by the regimen that turpentine bosses administered according to "the law of beak and fang and claw—the law of forest and jungle."[42] Irvine drew this contrast especially sharply in his second article, "A Week with the 'Bull of the Woods,'" which recounted his own experiences working for the Jackson Lumber Company.

11. Alexander Irvine in "investigative disguise," posing as a Hungarian immigrant, bound for and working at a lumber camp in Alabama. Photos from Alexander Irvine, *From the Bottom Up: The Life Story of Alexander Irvine* (New York: Doubleday-Page, 1910).

Though he was arrayed as a laborer, "unkempt in appearance, and with a yellow bundle in my hand," Irvine claimed, his disguise could not completely camouflage the intimacy with refined culture that separated him from other peons. This distinction rendered him mysterious to laborers and bosses, who listened with intense interest as he told stories from Victor Hugo in a voice "that was not tuned either to the camp or to the clothes." These qualities did not interfere with the stupendous vitality that characterized Irvine's impersonation of a "brother workingman," but they made it difficult for him "to find things in common" with laborers who savored "distinctly theological" profanity and found recreation in heavy drink and smutty stories. The narrative momentum of "My Life in Peonage" developed out of Irvine's passion to pit his own vigor against the boss's brutality, a passion disappointed when the boss "tackled a weaker man." In this respect, "My Life in Peonage" followed London's managerial solution for the plight of poor workers in *The People of the Abyss*. Worked out between bosses and "superior" workingmen, such agendas proposed a reformed "civilization" in which the mass of laborers—those who had not self-consciously dressed for their parts—would have little cultural stake.[43]

Yet "My Life in Peonage" also betrayed Irvine's ambivalence about such visions of "civilization" and hinted at Tottsian preferences for proletarian solidarity. Modeled on the principles of collective self-improvement he had learned in New Haven, such visions also evinced a new interest in the ethnic and racial dimensions of proletarian camaraderie. Irvine described with special respect the sensibilities his fellow peons seemed to derive from communities defined by ethnicity, nationality, or race. He admired the "bright young Russian Jew," Herman Orminsky, "who having successfully eluded the terrors of Kishenev and the 'black hundred'" found himself virtually enslaved in an Alabama forest. Irvine empathized with Orminsky in finding the customs of American "civilization" uncompelling. "It is not wholly his fault," Irvine reflected, "if our democratic institutions have not as yet seriously impressed him. . . . He hopes to return to Russia some time where suffering has purpose. 'There,' he said in very broken English, 'when we suffer we suffer all together for liberty and freedom; but here we suffer bad punishment only for chust our belly stomach.'"[44] Irvine also appreciated the occasional Hungarian melody that entertained the white workers' boxcar dormitory. But his greatest sympathy went to the segregated African-American laborers, whose somber spirituals contributed a gravity and sweetness to the leisure moments of the laborers in the camp. Even the black workers' card games seemed to Irvine charged with an "intense excitement" that he found woefully absent among the inebriated revelers in his berth. He decided that "the most interesting place in the camp was the negro car."[45]

12. Irvine's photograph of the boxcars that served as segregated dormitories for peons at the camp of the Jackson Lumber Company in Lockhardt, Alabama, where he conducted his peonage investigation. Photo from Alexander Irvine, "My Life in Peonage: II. A Week with the 'Bull of the Woods,'" *Appleton's Magazine* 10, no. 1 (1907): 3.

In his peonage articles and afterward, Irvine followed these sympathies into complex negotiations of ethnic and racial differences that bedeviled the popular evolutionary vernacular he had learned from Jack London. In "My Life in Peonage" this negotiation took the form of repeated mockery of racial and ethnic hierarchies to which bosses and laborers subscribed. Irvine scoffed at the conceit of recently arrived immigrants from Southern and Eastern Europe, who grasped at racial superiority to deflect the brutality they endured in the peonage camp. Indulging the epithets used by his lumber camp peers, he noted that it was "amusing to hear the men who were held in the woods by fear talk of the 'nigger's' inferiority, in the face of the fact that the 'nigger' was doing the best work in the camp."[46] Irvine observed that immigrant peons won little status through such hierarchical gambits, since "there was a small class of Southern lumber jacks who talked of these 'superior' men as 'dagos' and 'sheenies.'" He attributed such racial and ethnic slurs to the degrading influence of the peonage system itself. His final article told the story of Arthur Buckley, an Italian-American tenement youth turned peon whose testimony of cruel treatment had figured in the trial of the Jackson Lumber Company managers. Irvine lamented that Buckley's "experience in the South as a slave at the wheel of labor gave him not the slightest hint of class consciousness." Instead, peonage's strongest effect on Buckley was "a race consciousness that at times is as bitter as anything found in Alabama." As Irvine explained:

> They called him a "Dago." He in turn calls the black man a "nigger." They told him to keep his place—the place of an inferior—of a slave. That is exactly what he learned to say of the colored man. Some bitter experiences that have left no bitterness, and a legacy of hatred, are the net results of his journey into that region where things are raw—where life means only labor and where labor and life are cheap.[47]

Throughout his peonage articles, Irvine identified such racial and ethnic denigration with the brutal regime that reduced the peons to the status of craven cowards. He implied that, if laborers could shed "crouching subservience" for the virile class consciousness enacted in his own disguise, their ethnic and racial jealousies would dissolve into class solidarity.[48]

Here Irvine engaged wider cultural politics of race. As James Barrett and David Roediger observe, early-twentieth-century "new" immigrants from Southern and Eastern Europe negotiated confusing racial categories on several fronts. On the job and in the trade unions that tried to regulate their access to it, as well as in their encounters with political parties and the state, immigrants found themselves "inbetween" an "American" whiteness to which they were encouraged to aspire and the maligned racial categories to which Asians and African Americans were often consigned. Peonage camps were not the only work sites where intricate negotiations of race took place; "new" immigrants in western mining towns as well as the industries of the East and Midwest encountered these racial conundrums as well.[49] These conflicts were enhanced both by employers' labor management policies—which Irvine blamed for racialized divisions among the peons—and by the exclusionary boundaries set by AFL-style unionism. Irvine, of course, had encountered these trade unionist versions of racial hierarchy before, especially in the 1902 Sargent strike, where "old immigrant" Irish-American unionists compromised the demands of "new immigrant" Italian laborers. As he made sense of ethnic and racial distinctions in his peonage articles and the proletarian self-representations they inspired, he rethought racial and ethnic conundrums that had already substantially influenced his approach to cultural hierarchy.

In the process, Irvine also navigated hierarchies of ethnicity and race that workers encountered in their leisure time. Here, popular Darwinian categories mingled with older hierarchies of "civilization," "barbarity," and "vulgarity" that theaters and museums had featured since the mid-nineteenth century. As enacted on the far-flung vaudeville circuits to which Sylvester Poli's enterprises were now attached, these hierarchies reinforced the distinctions Irvine saw at play in the peonage camps. "Coon songs" and ethnic caricatures pegged people as "inferior" or "uncivilized" as effectively as arguments about "backward" races or "fierce" peoples. Practitioners of investigative disguise like Irvine emphasized this continuity between entertainment and Darwinian thought when they borrowed tropes of theatrical caricature to probe class experiences that they expressed in terms of the evolutionary vernacular. But, as Poli's shows reveal, vaudeville's cultural hierarchies were unstable, encouraging invidious distinctions of class, race, and ethnicity while also using ribaldry to poke fun at the cultural pretensions of "civilization" itself. Irvine had seized on such ambiguities when he adapted theatrical methods of popular realism to reinterpret Protestant evangelical hierarchies. As he pondered the hierarchical schemes implied in the evolutionary vernacular, Irvine experimented with new combinations of entertainment and politics that redrew familiar lines among class, race, and ethnicity.

In later efforts to express what his Southern adventures had meant personally, Irvine would portray ethnic culture as a catalyst for class solidarity, rather than an obstacle to class consciousness. His peonage investigations encouraged this tendency by provoking him to enact ethnic sensibilities of his own. In order to venture South in the guise of a peon, he applied to New York agents who supplied recently arrived immigrants to lumber, turpentine, and railroad companies in Florida, Alabama, Georgia, and Mississippi. At first he drew anew on his Irish origins—which for twenty years he had only rarely invoked—to fashion an ethnic identity for the agents' edification. According to his *Appleton's* account, he changed to a more marketable Finnish character when he learned that the agents considered Irishmen too intractable for southern labor. Thereafter, Irvine continued to refashion ethnic identity—borrowed from people he met or elaborated out of an Irish past in which he saw new value—as a crucial dimension of the working-class self he was constructing. Since this ethnic rendition of working-class identity took its initial shape during his peonage investigation, Irvine continued to negotiate the meaning of racial division in subsequent narratives of ethnicized working-class life.[50]

Irvine's variations on these narratives are especially valuable for the way they illuminate the multilayered public sphere on which he drew. While the evolutionary vernacular offered him a popular language in which to imagine the contours of his own proletarian persona, Irvine found that the terms of this language were subject to wide-ranging debate. In New York, where he soon settled to write, Irvine situated himself in the midst of several overlapping venues where such debates took place and wove them into his popular self-representations.

Cultural Politics at The Church of the Ascension

Upon returning north from his peonage investigation in early 1907, Irvine penned stories fashioned on Jack London's example while he gradually shifted his base of operations from New Haven to New York. Lured by New York's role as the nation's literary center and by his work as part-time lecturer for the West 57th Street YMCA, Irvine had contemplated a permanent move even before heading to the South. The months he spent investigating peonage eased the shift, loosening the bonds of family life in New Haven and reinforcing his new vocation as a writer. Eventually, Maude and the couple's three children followed him to New York and set up house in Washington Heights. In the meantime, Irvine took shelter in a residence—the A Club at 3 Fifth Avenue—that connected him to New York's literary, political, and social activists. Inimical to his YMCA connections, which soon dissolved, these activist contacts brought Irvine into arenas of public debate where he could hone the proletarian persona he was constructing in the periodical press.[51]

Part communal residence and part debating society, the A Club's Fifth Avenue mansion provided a gathering place for intellectuals interested in many of the social issues with which Irvine was engaged. In addition to Irvine, Socialist Party members such as William English Walling, his wife Anna Strunsky Walling (a close friend of Jack London), Leroy Scott, and Robert Bruere lived at or frequented the club. It also drew Progressive writers sympathetic to socialist ideas, including Mary Heaton Vorse, Ernest Poole, and Walter Weyl. Authors William Dean Howells, Samuel Clemens, and Theodore Dreiser dropped in to partake of the club's discussions as well. Such contacts put Irvine in the thick of the intersecting networks of socialist politics, literary realism, and Progressive reform out of which he was reconstructing his mission. Irvine tried to extend these networks across racial lines by writing to W. E. B. Du Bois on behalf of the A Club, urging the Atlanta scholar to give an address at the club and exchange observations on race relations in the South. Though he does not seem to have received a reply, Irvine continued to draw on Du Bois's example as he contemplated the intersections of class and race. Meanwhile, the A Club introduced Irvine to wider forums for his current experiments in self-representation by introducing him to the prominent Episcopalian cleric Percy Stickney Grant.[52]

Grant preached at New York City's Church of the Ascension, where he was determined to make Christianity speak to working people. The Ascension Church had long been associated with the Knickerbocker elite, but when Grant arrived in 1893 it was rapidly going bankrupt as its traditional constituency moved to more fashionable uptown neighborhoods. To rebuild the church, Grant put its program on a social gospel basis. He abolished pew rents and began to address "the whole City of New York" with a simplified litany and sermons on social questions.[53] He expanded the Sunday afternoon service into a musical festival, and instituted a new "revivalistic" Sunday evening service to attract a socially varied audience. Seeking inspiration for his sermons in debates at the A Club, Grant came to appreciate Irvine's views on the responsibility of churches to working people. Though wary of organized religion, Irvine agreed to join in Grant's work in August 1907. He soon established himself as the leader of a packed Sunday evening service.[54]

In these services, Irvine integrated the themes he had emphasized in New Haven with questions raised by his recent literary experiments. He called for democratic access to material comfort and aesthetic cultivation, and continued to remind his working-class audience to demand cultural and spiritual improvements as well as material ones. But he also expressed the more militant attitude toward conventional cultural hierarchies that his Elm City experiences had instilled. This shift is particularly clear in the Ascension addresses he gave on his beloved Jean-François Millet. Rather than focusing on Millet's images, as he had early in his New Haven mission, Irvine told his New York congregation the story of the funeral of a French department store owner, H. A. Chauchard, which had been disrupted by disgusted Parisian proletarians. To Irvine, this outburst seemed a fitting comment on a man who had refused him access to Millet's *The Angelus*. As a piece of individual property secreted in the home of the arrogant Chauchard, according to Irvine, the Millet painting provided a lesson in the vast material and human riches guarded by men of wealth:

> I thought of human lives that were imprisoned, locked, barred, circumvented, by the system of which this great merchant prince of Paris was the flower and fruit. . . . I said, "This is not the path of glory; this is the track of a successful shopkeeper. And if a shopkeeper is great it is in spite of his shopkeeping, and not by virtue of it; for all the cunning and the shrewdness and the fierceness of the beast is produced in a man in modern shopkeeping."

This attack on Chauchard was typical of Irvine's Ascension sermons, which urged transformations of the "system" that prevented cultural cultivation from being widely accessible. He also resorted frequently to the evolutionary language of "fierceness" and "beasts" that this sermon displayed. Over the course of his Ascension sermons, however, Irvine used this language in ways that conveyed his ambivalence about social distinctions in the new, democratic culture he had in mind.[55]

In some sermons, Irvine used the evolutionary vernacular to picture men who could effect the cultural transformations he urged. He called for robust men willing to follow the biblical examples of the disciples and the historical examples of Marx and Mazzini. Such men were "fools for truth" who pushed the world "out of its lethargy, out of its sluggishness, out of its lazy satisfaction, to great heights of achievement, in art, in science, in industry, in literature." Contrary to conventional hierarchies, according to Irvine, "progress has always come by the fool, by the barbarian."[56] In this category, Irvine especially commended Abraham Lincoln and Eugene Debs. Lincoln was "cut out of the earth, with the tang and odor of it clinging to him"; people judged him "ungainly" and "not fit to go into polite society." But Lincoln's vigorous humanity permitted him to confront the challenging issues of slavery and the Union. Similarly, into the twentieth century's industrial battles came Debs, "just as tall, just as ungainly, just as homely, just as lacking in the erudition of his age as Lincoln was." Debs was "an embodiment of the passionate appeal of the poor, of the bitter cry from the abyss, with heart rending agonies from ten hundred thousand factories." Like Lincoln, Debs was the "barbarian" of his age, shocking contemporaries by announcing labor's claims on their sympathies, destined to be widely reviled until later generations recognized him as an agent of God.[57]

But while Irvine celebrated the "barbarian" vitality of Lincoln and Debs, he still revered cultural standards associated with "civilization." In one of several sermons on his experiences in the Sudan, Irvine recalled seeing

A long white line of half-civilized people, dressed in flowing garments, and turbans, and sandals, with obsolete guns . . . the war implements of generations that are dead. . . . They go through a prayer. Then they get up, and with the quotations from the Koran, and prayer in their hearts, and murmuring song in their lips, they go out to the certainty of the rising and the setting of the sun, as it appears to them, to put the invader from their home.

Clearly Irvine admired the courageous faith of his erstwhile foes. But he also applied "civilization" as a standard to which they did not measure up. Like other left-wing flourishes of the evolutionary vernacular, Irvine's Ascension speeches decried the brutality of imperial and industrial exploitation while evincing disdain for the weakness of the exploited.[58] In another sermon, Irvine described what he had seen in the desert as the result of "a whip wielded in Downing Street, London" being applied "to the black hides of the people of the Sudan." Here "whip" and "hides" compete as images of a "barbarity" far removed from the vigorous humanity Irvine associated with Lincoln and Debs. Nor were such racial lines limited to Irvine's descriptions of military clashes in foreign lands. He also excluded black Americans from the robust brotherhood in which he included himself, Lincoln, Debs, and others willing to smash "the shackles of social slavery." Trying to incite zeal for such causes in the twentieth century, Irvine proclaimed that his audiences must "do it for the white man, not the black."[59] In these passages, race became a boundary across which the class sympathies evoked by the evolutionary vernacular did not extend. Such racial boundaries became especially volatile elements of Irvine's public performances and literary self-representations over the next several years. During this period, Irvine's approach to race linked modes of expression he had borrowed from popular theater and London-esque journalism to socialist political contests over the boundaries of class solidarity.

At the time of Irvine's Ascension mission, these connections were just taking form, and were especially apparent in his references to socialist debates over immigration, racial difference, and gender. In a June 1910 sermon, Irvine decried the debate on immigration restriction and "Asiatic exclusion" that had taken place at the Socialist Party's recent National Congress in Chicago. Remarking that some of the Socialists wanted only to "take hold of those fellows who were sleek enough to earn a good day's wages like ourselves," Irvine expostulated, "Shame on any man, or any clique of men, or any country that draws a line on color, or quality! These foreign hordes that have been thrashed and oppressed and beaten, why should not they have bigger opportunity, if they are crushed at home? This country has been made by its foreign immigrants." He claimed to speak in the name of a Christ who stood for the brotherhood of man, meaning "a man that is black, and a man that is white, or brown, or yellow, or copper-colored." This was a more inclusive vision than some of Irvine's sermons describing Africans and African Americans. But Irvine's association of the "color line" with a "quality line" and references to "beaten" hordes compromised his avowal of equality.[60]

In this respect, Irvine shared in conundrums of race and immigration that delegates to the Party's national meetings were rehearsing. These questions first flared at the 1908 Socialist Party National Convention during discussion of a resolution on immigration. The resolution opposed the importation of contract labor as well as immigration subsidized or stimulated "by the capitalist class." Regarding the "racial differences" emphasized by western delegates who supported "Asiatic exclusion," however, the resolution judged the 1908 convention "incompetent to decide" and proposed a special committee to submit these questions to "scientific investigation." Irvine probably derived his distaste for the discussions that this proposal inspired in part from his friendship with Sol Fieldman, who was a New York delegate to the 1908 National Convention as well as a frequent visitor to the Ascension Church. A socialist orator whose freedom of speech Irvine had championed in New Haven, Fieldman spoke fervently against the 1908 resolution on immigration and in favor of a class solidarity that defied racial divisions:

> I do not care whether it is the yellow workingman or the black workingman or the white workingman, or the Irish or the German or the American workingman who rule this country so long as it is the working classes that rule it. That is the main proposition. . . . We are agreed that the workers of the world are equal; that there are no differences—or if there are, we ought to wipe them out and not encourage them.[61]

But Fieldman's comrades were not agreed on the equality he proposed. The resolution on immigration was approved, and a committee appointed to study the race question "scientifically."[62] The terms in which Fieldman articulated racial equality, however, did highlight racial categories that he and Irvine shared with Socialists of a more resolutely racist cast of mind. These racial categories, in turn, connected socialist debates to broader conflicts over the meaning of race.

As was the case with workers in the industries and unions they hoped to transform, Socialists wielded "race" divisions that were not clearly distinct from what later scholars have identified as the "ethnic" cultures of the white working class. Distinctions of "yellow," "black," and "white" slid into "Irish," "German," and "American" in Fieldman's statement, and "Greeks" and "Jews" in other orations. That some delegates, and the 1908 resolution itself, proposed to clarify these distinctions through science highlights how scientific discourses participated in a wider cultural politics of race distinction. The implacably racist Victor Berger of Wisconsin, attempting to put the discussion on a "scientific and materialistic basis," ventured to draw a sharper line between European immigrants, "who in the second generation . . . will become part of us," and Chinese and Japanese immigrants, who would "wipe out our civilization." But even Berger's comparatively definite racial distinctions were ambiguous. In his version, European immigrants were only *becoming* "the same as us": "they are of our own race and make-up, in a measure." This uncertain measure—the measure of "race"—was at issue not only among Socialists but in the wider public sphere in which they participated. For Irvine's self-constructions, the conflicts it incited were pivotally important, fueling dynamic transformations of racial and ethnic self-conception.[63]

For Irvine, as for many prominent as well as rank-and-file Socialists of the time, Party literature, newspapers, meetings, and organizations comprised a network of information and discussion that applied prevailing intellectual and cultural concepts to questions of cultural distinction between classes and within the working class. Party pronouncements on "race" and "ethnicity" drew from the virulent contemporary cocktail of Darwinian notions about the struggle for survival, Neo-Lamarckian notions of "race improvement" that linked evolution to aspirations toward "civilization," and fears of an impending "Teutonic race suicide" as backward races out-reproduced decadent whites. The authors of these pronouncements—particularly Ernest Untermann, chair of the Committee on Immigration and the Party's most ambitious theoretician of socialism as an evolutionary system—encased their racism in an encompassing scientific system borrowed chiefly from Herbert Spencer, for whom biology, society, and culture progressed together in an organic whole. But, as revealed in debates over the "Committee on Immigration" and its reports, this deployment of evolutionary thought was contested even among those who traded in the same confusing categories of "race" and "civilization" as Untermann and Berger. Eventually, socialist debates on "race" would fragment around issues of "constructivist" gradualism and "revolutionary" activism. Although these conflicts did not separate Socialists into neatly divided camps of evolutionary racists and democratic egalitarians, in cases like Irvine's they could provoke profound reassessments of the evolutionary terms in which race was formulated. But, during Irvine's Ascension years, these factional divisions were just emerging.[64]

Meanwhile, debates over immigration began to give new shape to some of Irvine's oldest cultural quandaries. Like Irvine, convention delegates who opposed evolutionary racism did so frequently in terms of a vision of the "brotherhood of man." Though dismissed by the likes of Untermann and Berger as expressions of unscientific, utopian sentimentality, these appeals to international brotherhood represented an important vein in socialist thought that drew on evangelical values that were part of Irvine's intellectual heritage as well. They articulated the ideals of rural and small-town Socialists in the West and Midwest, whose democratic notions of Christian morality had led them to socialist camp meetings and literature rather than the conservative creed of revivalists like Billy

Sunday. Delegate Joseph Cannon of Arizona applied this tradition when he declared in the 1910 National Socialist Congress debate on immigration, "in Arizona . . . [w]e have the Mexican peon escaping across the line. Am I going to send him back across the line? No; I am going to try to lift him as high as I am myself and perhaps higher. The Mexican peon is a convict. So was Jesus Christ; so was Eugene Debs." Delegate T. J. Morgan of Illinois applied it when he complained that august evolutionary theoreticians had garbled the issues at hand, accomplishing within socialism what theologians had brought to pass in religion: "The simple message of the carpenter and the fisherman was understood; the workmen took it; they received it gladly and then the intellectuals took up the message, and carried it along for nineteen hundred years, and who understands it now? No one understands it. . . . The simple, plain propositions have been buried in a mass of words. So it has been with the Socialist movement." Even Jack London echoed this evangelical legacy as he vacillated between religious brotherhood and racial supremacy as apt images for socialist aims. Such men struggled with a socialist variation of the tension between evolutionary thought and evangelcal heritage that confounded many who inhabited the nexus of religion, culture, and politics—including Fundamentalists, who rejected evolutionary science as blasphemy, as well as clergymen like Irvine, who tried to wrest Christian justice from the hierarchies of liberal Protestant evolutionary thought. Thus, socialist debates on immigration and race became new battlegrounds for an old, plebeian evangelical legacy that Irvine had been revising since before he had arrived in America. This legacy continued to color his reevaluations of the evolutionary vernacular as he penned successive stories about his own immigrant odyssey.[65]

Irvine's Ascension sermons also revised the way gender figured into the proletarian self-representations that he was beginning to figure in terms of ethnicity and race. Within the socialist debates in which he participated, gender was bound up with the same intellectual tendencies that influenced discussions of race and immigration. In "scientific" treatises like one that Joseph Cohen published in the *International Socialist Review* in 1909, woman appeared "nearer to the savage than man." Expressing the same hierarchy in evolutionary vernacular terms, popular socialist writers like London extolled vigorously masculine working-class heroes who demonstrated their superiority over excessively civilized middle-class maidens or courageous but unsophisticated working women.[66] In works like his peonage articles, of course, Irvine also quite happily identified himself as a socialist he-man little concerned with the feminine cares that he had disparaged throughout his mission.

During Irvine's years of his work at the Ascension Church, however, social-ist women began to challenge such contempt for their political demands and organizational capacities. They established a network of women's auxiliaries and ladies' branches that forced the Party to accommodate their concerns by insti-tuting a Woman's National Committee (WNC) in 1908. The WNC served as a base from which women waged an uphill battle to make their concerns part of the socialist program. While endorsed by the Second International in 1907, agi-tation for woman suffrage remained suspect in the eyes of many Socialists, who believed it diluted class solidarity with mystifying ideas of sex solidarity and attracted unwanted middle-class reformers to the Party. Attempts by socialist women to aid workingwomen in union building and strikes won wider support, but still met with resistance among craft unionists, who had long disdained women as rate-busting unskilled labor. Meanwhile, women who took on the task of theorizing feminism as a socialist project sometimes redeployed the very evo-lutionary notions that male unionists had used to dismiss them. This was espe-cially true of Charlotte Perkins Gilman, who sought to advance her "race" by liberating women from domestic drudgery and sexual slavery in order to facili-tate their full participation in "civilization." According to Gilman's evolutionary view, women had helped to fashion that civilization by domesticating the prim-itive "sex passion" that spurred men to racial progress.[67]

In his sermons at the Church of the Ascension, Irvine registered his own response to these socialist gender quandaries. A May 1908 sermon, "Equal Pay for Equal Work," proclaimed that teachers should be paid according to their posi-tions, not "because this teacher is a man, or this teacher is a woman." In a ser-mon on "Women and the Bourgeois Mind," he argued that it was a peculiar lim-itation of bourgeois culture in America that women were believed incapable of governing in politics or leading in professional and artistic life. Such beliefs lagged behind the economic forces driving thousands of working women into factories where their former domestic tasks of spinning and sewing were per-formed. Though many of these women might long for the "homes" to which the bourgeois mind confined them, Irvine insisted that it was time they ceased wait-ing on marriage to realize such goals. These declarations suggested that women's activism within the Party had begun to shift Irvine's approach to gender.[68]

But while Irvine urged women to exercise economic and political power out-side the conjugal bargain, the public role he conceived for them was still fash-ioned on a model of feminine domesticity. In his defense of the female teachers, he defined childhood education as labor to which a woman was peculiarly suited "by her instinct, by her training, by her ability." As for changing the "bourgeois mind," Irvine averred that "the dirt and graft that we are trying to sweep out of Albany and out of Washington will never be obliterated until the sovereign American women go up in their strength, in their purity, and in their power." By insisting on a domestic version of feminine aptitude, Irvine's vision fell short of a more complete equality in which both men and women bore the pride and responsibilities of material production and social reproduction within and outside the home. This equivocation over gender equality was in part a symptom of a wider transition in gender politics. New perspectives on relations between men and women were gradually emerging from various arenas of intellectual and domestic experimentation, including the A Club and other salons where young intelligentsia flouted conventional moralities and gender distinctions. But these adventures in urban living still raised more questions than they answered. As Nancy Cott has observed, they provided a break with the feminine moral logic of the late-nineteenth-century Woman Movement, but had yet to define the new logic of feminism that they heralded.[69] Irvine's approach to gender would be reshaped in part by the private anguish as well as the public debates these unsolved gender questions produced.

Irvine's sermons on women also illuminate the slippery character of the language of "civilization" and "savagery" he wielded. In one sermon, "The Murder of Mary Farmer," he enumerated his reasons for opposing the execution of a woman convicted of murder. He included the objection that Mary Farmer was a woman, but acknowledged that "a great many of my friends . . . say I am mistaken—advocates particularly of Woman's Suffrage." He maintained his gendered view of the execution nevertheless, because "most men who knew the tender love of a mother will feel as I feel . . . [that] a woman is a thing just a little more highly sensitized, just a little more refined, just a little more divine, than a man." This was, he said, an "instinct . . . call it divine, call it savage, call it whatever you please," alternatives which suggest that the suffrage advocates he had debated concurred in Gilman's view that sex distinctions were holdovers from "primitive" evolutionary stages. Irvine figured the relation between gender and civilization differently. For him, to impugn sex differences that allowed women to contribute "refinement" to "civilization" was no evolutionary advance, but an insult to "civilized" values themselves.[70]

As other sermons revealed, however, Irvine sometimes wondered whether he should apply the term "civilization" to the society he inhabited. He emphasized these questions in sermons responding to attacks on socialism by Theodore Roosevelt and Andrew Carnegie. Irvine was especially vexed that Roosevelt and Carnegie identified socialism as hostile to the domestic symbols of civilization he celebrated. Roosevelt, Irvine complained, pointed to examples of individual Socialists' marital perfidy as examples of "immorality" and "obscenity." Carnegie worried that socialism would destroy, as Irvine quoted him, "the foremost of civilization's triumph—the creation of the happy home—the product of man and woman, holily married." Without such a home, according to Carnegie, "to millions who possess it—the best of the race—life becomes unbearable." What Carnegie overlooked, Irvine insisted, was that to millions life was unbearable and uncivilized because of Carnegie's industrial achievements. Irvine cited the recently completed Pittsburgh Survey on conditions of homes and families around Carnegie's steel mills for evidence that the "civilization" Carnegie produced was not worth its price in human suffering, or worthy of the name. "Better no advance at all," Irvine concluded "than to advance over the dead bodies of thousands of men and women." He thought that Roosevelt also belied the "civilization" to which he pretended by smearing Socialists with sensational charges of immorality that might apply just as well to Republicans. Such charges exposed the flimsiness of Roosevelt's claim to being a "gentleman" who "wants to discuss public issues in a public way." In short, Irvine suggested that the society Socialists were trying to change was no "civilization" at all—and its political and industrial leaders no proper models of enlightened discourse in a public sphere.[71]

Altogether, Irvine's unconventional formulations of civilization, attacks on prominent political and industrial leaders, and open avowal of socialism made Ascension vestrymen uneasy. At the end of his third year at the parish, they refused to renew his position as lay reader. As Grant explained it, the financiers who sat on the vestry could no longer endure the calumny excited on Wall Street by news of Irvine's services. Irvine's ideas were only part of the problem. His position might have been more secure had he not agreed to oversee a series of community discussions on the issues raised by his sermons. These "after-meetings"—which Irvine and Grant later identified as the seeds of the "Church Forum" movement—drew attention from the press. In the process, they demonstrated the capriciousness of the ethnic and racial categories Irvine was pondering. While he tried to deploy these terms to call into question capitalist "civilization" and recommend socialism, other voices in the public sphere wielded them to deride American workers and their political allies.[72]

The Ascension after-meeting began as a social hour following Irvine's Sunday evening service. Irvine and Grant intended it as an opportunity for conversation among the cosmopolitan congregation these services had attracted. Participants who thought the refreshments interfered with lively give and take soon transformed the meetings. Sol Fieldman was the first to offer an address; his speech, according to Irvine, captured the inclusiveness that people came to expect from these events. "I have never been in a Christian church before," Fieldman declared. "I am the son of a rabbi, and a revolutionist; but I take my hat off to this church. Here you are interpreting life as I think Jesus, who was also a Jew and a revolutionist, would do it." Other participants made short addresses in the next few weeks. Then Grant and Irvine began inviting guests to give brief speeches followed by time-limited comments from the audience.[73]

Unnoticed by the daily press during its first six months, the after-meetings offered opportunities for candid exchanges between people accustomed to seeing one another represented as theatrical types or newspaper headlines. Madge Jenison, a sympathetic observer writing in the reformist periodical *The Outlook*, gave an eloquent catalog of the assemblage, worth quoting in full:

> These meetings are not for the workingman and the Socialist alone; there are all kinds of people. There are the graceful women at the back of the platform, in their plumed hats and delicate gowns, drooping upon the carved arms of the chancel chairs, silent and absorbed, seeing a strange world. There is the young workman in a sweater; gigantic, vital as an oak, and with the power to use the English tongue; the self-contained college professor whose poise comes out sharply in contrast with the little East Side hotheads who are shot to their feet with the intensity of their emotions, and can only lash about in a sea of words and hammer the unretaliating air like boys in an oratorical contest; and the gentle old saint who gets to his feet in sections, and offers for our consideration a few beautiful sentiments culled from the social philosophy of the fall of 1846. There is the young man who has given up law or medicine or art and left a happy home to hasten social progress by stoking a furnace or trimming the trees in Central Park—in deadly earnest, but somewhat outgeneraled by his new-found altruism. There is the trade-unionist who thinks that organized labor has spoken the last word in social evolution; the physician who believes that economics is the same thing as biology; the theosophist, preoccupied with the soul, and far distant from that great world of material misery which modern life has set itself to conquer.

To mediate conflicts among these groups, Grant and Irvine stood ready to apply antidotes of delicacy and laughter. According to Jenison, Irvine's affinity for methods borrowed from the popular stage was especially effective in diffusing discord. When discussions grew heated, she noted, Irvine would tell a story and raise spirits "with his big, open-handed gestures, his explosive Irish laughter, which is an olive branch and a comic opera and a philosophy in itself."[74]

Such melioratives were especially helpful in dealing with arguments that ensued following an aborted demonstration of the unemployed and subsequent bomb explosion at Union Square in March 1908. Some participants in the Ascension after-meeting were angry that the demonstration had incited sensational newspaper stories of anarchist conspiracies reminiscent of the Haymarket incident. They thought such publicity harmed the causes that Irvine's sermons espoused. Others stood firm in support of a demonstration that had been barred by the police. Because Irvine was able to speak to all groups regarding the issues of social justice raised by the event, Jenison observed, by the end of the meeting "Capitalists and Socialists agreed that free institutions can be preserved only by free speech."[75]

However, the publicity generated by the demonstration sorely tested the Ascension after-meeting as an arena for wide-ranging interchange. Not only did newspaper reports about the demonstration mention Irvine's presence; they also put him next to one of the event's chief speakers at the moment that police had charged to break up the crowd.[76] Irvine's part in the demonstration attracted new attention to his ecclesiastical experiments. The first newspaper reports on the Ascension after-meeting appeared a week after the Union Square incident. They covered a discussion marked by rancor over the presence of several critics of socialism planted, Irvine believed, by the National Civic Federation. A *Herald* reporter informed Irvine that newspapers had been tipped off about the expected debate. The *Herald*'s own reports of the forum were very derisive. They described the meeting as lacking a "serious tone" prior to the eruption of the antisocialist speakers. In subsequent weeks the *Herald* ridiculed the forum under headlines proclaiming "Dr. Irvine's Meeting Sees Good Nowhere." Instead of celebrating Irvine's theatrical style, as Jenison had, the newspaper borrowed from stage caricatures to enhance its disparagement of the Ascension meetings. Discussing the meetings' less "serious" aspects, the *Herald* reporter noted that one pro-socialist speaker had a "Weber-Fields Accent"—a description that associated him with one of the best known "Dutch" and "Hebrew" caricatures of the comedy stage.[77]

Such press accounts of the Ascension meetings only aggravated the discomfort of wealthy church members. They detracted from what Irvine and Grant both regarded as their finest achievement: the opportunity they provided for Socialists, workers, and conservative men of wealth to meet and talk across the barriers of ignorance and preconception that divided them. By reasserting the most derogatory terms in which class and ethnic divisions were popularly portrayed, newspaper accounts made their meetings vulnerable to widespread popular fears and prejudices. The specter of "fiery," "suspicious" naysayers monopolizing these discussions in stage dialect put wealthy vestrymen on the defensive regarding the radicalism and indecorousness permitted in the Ascension Church.

According to Irvine, many of Ascension's wealthy members sympathized with the actual aims of the after-meeting, as distinct from those the newspapers attributed to it. But they shrank before the derision of the press and the disgust it excited among their associates. Irvine's position at the church was the price of their squeamishness. Ending his tenure at the Church of the Ascension in June 1910, he sought alternative employment.[78]

By this point, Irvine was well equipped with contacts derived from his literary successes and socialist alliances. Well-wishers marked his departure from Ascension with a lavish banquet. In a series of speeches, prominent reformers and Socialists praised his work at the church and promised to support him in the future. Lincoln Steffens marveled that "the poor have had Christianity preached to them in a Christian church," and Florence Kelley enjoined Irvine's supporters to find him a fit place to labor, as "we are too many to allow him to take a back seat."[79] Not all Socialists were so sanguine about the lessons of the Ascension experiment. André Tridon editorialized in the *New York Call* that the church's leaders had justly fired Irvine for failing to represent their views. But even Tridon believed that, liberated from the position of "paid retainer of wealthy men and women," Irvine now had a chance to "regain his self-respect."[80] Eugene Debs soon provided the means for such rehabilitation by recommending that Irvine assume some of the far-flung speaking engagements that Debs could no longer pursue.[81]

If Irvine was an apt candidate to stand in for the "barbarian" Debs, it was in part because his recent autobiography had secured even greater circulation for his robust public persona than the Ascension meetings could offer. *From the Bottom Up: The Life Story of Alexander Irvine* was serialized in the periodical press and then published as a book during the last year of his Ascension work. It demonstrates that Irvine's investigative experiments and public flourishes of proletarian self-assertion had fostered a personal narrative of emergent class consciousness—a socialist bildungsroman of his own. But it also reveals the ominous contours that the racial and ethnic conundrums he had probed at the Ascension meetings and discussed with his comrades could take.

From the Bottom Up: Alexander Irvine's Socialist Bildungsroman

From the Bottom Up signaled Irvine's arrival as a spokesman for working-class culture within the public sphere of periodical literature. It was commissioned by Walter Hines Page, who was legendary for his energetic efforts to generate stories that would make Doubleday-Page's house journal, *The World's Work*, a popular, Progressive periodical. Having persuaded John D. Rockefeller to write his autobiography for the magazine, Page asked Irvine for a companion series to contrast with the financier's memoirs. Irvine produced a set of sketches that answered this requirement in content and style. Advertised as "a unique autobiography of a ditch-digger—soldier—miner—socialist—preacher," these articles seethed with the virile evolutionary vernacular Irvine had practiced for *Appleton's*.[82] Appearing in *The World's Work* from July 1909 to February 1910, when Doubleday-Page published it in expanded form as a book, the autobiography illuminates Irvine's struggles with the evolutionary style in which he had learned to cast his life story and his proletarian loyalties.

Irvine's embrace of the evolutionary vernacular was apparent from the beginning of the autobiography, where he depicted a childhood among hungry people who struggled for existence amidst limited resources. This struggle inhibited all ambitions toward refinement—as his mother's alcoholism and his father's beatings attested. Then a glorious sunset and the lines of a hymn inspired him to an "upward look"—a device reminiscent of London's youthful "uplook." Irvine portrayed this new perspective in images redolent of London's picture of the "parlor" level of society. His spiritual epiphany provoked a revelation that he was "in rags and dirty" and prompted novel exertions at cleanliness, grooming, and Bible study. Outfitted as a stable boy at Chaine's estate, he found fuel for his new aspirations in an improved wardrobe—"shoes well polished, starched linen, and a hard hat"—as well as in glimpses of the "inner world of beautiful things" his employers enjoyed. He resolved to seek "a life where people had time to think, and to live a clean, normal, human life."[83] But before finding a path out of "shameful" ignorance, the youth of *From the Bottom Up* descended into an industrial abyss. The coal pits of Scotland convinced him that wage labor was incompatible with a religious program of self-improvement. The Scottish mines that Irvine recounted contained "a writhing, squirming mass of blackened humanity struggling for a mere physical existence, a bare living." Such language paralleled the evolutionary idiom Jack London had used to portray the charnel houses of civilization that had terrified him into "brain work." Amidst this struggle, Irvine recalled, "the desire to learn to read and write returned to me with renewed intensity" and led him out of the pits into the Royal Marines.[84]

In recounting his military service, Irvine emphasized his eager use of educational resources and occasional contact with aristocratic officers, but also stressed his more vigorous adventures in the rough and tumble of military life. The story of his years as a marine began with an anecdote that neatly dramatized this conflict. With his attention focused initially on the training-depot classroom, Irvine

13. This frontispiece for *From the Bottom Up* (1910) shows Irvine at the peak of his oratorical and literary career, at the age of forty-seven. Photo from Alexander Irvine, *From the Bottom Up: The Life Story of Alexander Irvine* (New York: Doubleday-Page, 1910).

recalled, "it took a good deal of forcing to interest me in the handling of guns, bayonets, and swinging of clubs, vaulting of horses, and other gymnasium exercises." This dilatory attitude toward the "chief business" of a soldier won derision from officers and recruits. As noted in Chapter 1, it also inspired a drill sergeant to alter Irvine's ambitions by means of a thrashing in the gymnasium boxing ring. Duly stunned, Irvine bargained with a barrack-room mate for boxing lessons and hastened back to the gymnasium to repay his first assailant. His account of the match drew on the experiments in ethnic identity he had begun in his peonage articles to produce a virile Celtic rendition of the London-esque evolutionary vernacular:

> There is something fiendish in the Celtic nature, some beast in the blood, which, when aroused, is exceedingly helpful in matters of this kind. . . . There was a positive viciousness in my attack . . . it was the first time I had ever felt the beast in my blood, and I turned him loose. . . . [I]nside of thirty seconds, I had stretched my instructor on his back at my feet, and in absolute joyfulness and ecstasy of my soul, I yelled at the top of my voice: "Hurry up, ye blindtherin' spalpeen, till I knock yez down again!"

True to the genteel sensibilities he had aspired to in the military, Irvine represented this episode as a lapse. He emphasized how hard he had tried throughout this period to shed the marks of his humble origins—his ignorance and Irish brogue—in order to become a more effective witness for his religious convictions. Still, the vitality of the boxing match repeatedly resurfaced as a rebuke to overrefined emissaries of cultivation such as the Plymouth Brethren, who held in contempt his "red-blooded and jubilant" Irish nature.[85]

Irvine next shifted his story to America, where he encountered further oppositions between mannered gentility and robust proletarianism. He told of beginning as a Bowery missionary by making the rounds of lodging houses and saloons armed with a Bible and a contempt for the "pale, haggard" people there. But he soon changed his view. Irvine's account of the change both demonstrated his own ability to contend with the raw forces of a London-esque "social abyss" and illuminated his struggles with the cultural ambiguities at the heart of the evolutionary vernacular. As Irvine recalled, he focused his first missionary efforts on "Gar," "the toughest specimen of a man I ever saw," a man whose verbal and physical brutality made him an effective bouncer for a Mulberry Street lodging house. "There was a challenge in him," Irvine recalled, "which I at once accepted. . . . It was an intimation that he was master—that missionaries were somewhat feeble-minded and had to do with weak people. . . . I outlined a plan of campaign the major part of which was the capture of this primordial man."[86] To "capture" his "primordial man," Irvine explained, he had to survive "nauseating" visits to cheap restaurants and saloons and witness vicious attacks on bunkhouse denizens without betraying disgust. In the terms of the evolutionary vernacular, to win Gar's allegiance was to bridge the gulf between civilizing evangelical improvement and the more virile energies of the evolutionary social pit. But there remained some question as to what this success implied. From the perspective of his missionary employers, Gar's conversion demonstrated the superiority of Christian "gentleness and love" over the lower-class "brutality," a "graphic and striking" story that, Irvine admitted, he and other missionaries "exploited" among well-heeled congregations to support their work. Within the narrative of Irvine's bildungsroman, however, Gar's transformation attracted Bowery converts who pushed Irvine beyond his early program of individual "improvement." From this perspective, Irvine's success with Gar lay in the class solidarity that followed from his enactment of proletarian vitality.[87]

The fruits of this interpretive shift appear in Irvine's final chapter on his Bowery experiences. Here the proletarian circle to whom Gar introduced him offered a new perspective on missionary work. "After some years' experience in missions and mission churches," Irvine explained,

> I would find it very hard if I were a workingman living in a tenement not to be antagonistic to them; for, in large measure, such work is done on the assumption that people are poor and degraded through laxity in morals. The scheme of salvation is a salvation for the individual; social salvation is out of the question . . . and the reason is that [missions] are supported by . . . the very people who perpetuate the evils against which prophet, priest and pastor ought to cry out continually.

To the new "political economy" his converts taught him, Irvine recalled, he soon added a new theology gleaned from East Side street politics. "The East Side has a soul," he discovered, "but it is not an ecclesiastical soul! It is a soul that is alive—so much alive to the interest of the people that many times I felt ashamed of myself when I listened to the socialistic orators on the street corners and in the East Side halls." These memories inspired Totts-like effusions of proletarian allegiance. Irvine remembered the thrill of repudiating orthodox religious beliefs in order to say to himself, "Soul, if this multitude is doomed to hell, be brave; gird up your loins and go with them!"[88]

As he described his missions in the Midwest and New Haven, Irvine recounted how this enthusiasm for lively working-class camaraderie developed into mature socialism. He continued to flirt with what Jack London called society's "parlor floor" in these passages. He told of how he parlayed his association with New York's middle-class charity and vice crusades into an alliance with Midwestern progressives, and became intimate with New Haven notables who were national leaders in Progressive religious thought. But the call of proletarian solidarities prevailed. His descriptions of his life in Omaha's squatters' camp provided ample opportunity for the tales of combative virility. Returning from town one night with a banana in his pocket, Irvine recalled, he saw two figures emerge from deep shadows, and feared for his life. "I whipped the banana from my pocket," he continued, "and pointing it as one would a revolver I said—'Move a muscle, either of you, and I'll blow your brains out!'" Such rehearsals of working-class vitality prepared Irvine for the epiphanies of trade union alliance and socialist belief in New Haven. Socialism enlivened the virtues idealized in evangelical self-improvement with working-class vigor. "As I looked around . . . at the churches and the university," Irvine wrote of his new faith, "I could find nothing equal to the social passion of the socialists—it was a religion with them. True, they were limited in their expression of that passion, but they were live coals, all of them, and I was more at home in their meetings than in the churches." Jack London's visit to Yale capped Irvine's tale of spiritual homecoming by revealing how he could give his own forceful expression to socialist passion by borrowing the tools of popular literary culture.[89]

However, the final chapters of the autobiography registered misgivings about this culmination to Irvine's journey. These chapters portrayed his work at the Ascension Church, his recently purchased rural home on the Hudson, and his Christian socialist beliefs. While Irvine celebrated his Ascension mission as an opportunity to foster "a new attitude toward society as well as a change of the heart," he also complained that his socialist message found its warmest welcome among the richest people in the church, while the poorest sneered at socialism as "dividing up" and complained about the preponderance of Jews among the radicals. "The average laboring man is incapable of such conference," he explained, "for . . . it is only when he becomes a Socialist that he becomes an intelligent advocate of anything." Yet developments on his Peekskill farm suggested that socialist convictions did not unfailingly produce the amalgam of virtue and vitality on which he now staked his hopes. Though Irvine exulted that "Socialists are the only people who seem to have the Bible idea of work," those he invited to spend a summer camping on his land were more visionary than vigorous when it came to manual labor. "In a community where the communers have to chop the fire-wood," he philosophized, "canned salmon is a good standby."[90] But the tension between socialist ideals and proletarian vitality also challenged the integrity of his working-class persona. This was a challenge that he could answer only through an ongoing revision of his story, rather than in any single narrative—or culinary—reconciliation. These difficulties pointed to a problem common to bildungsroman narratives: how to blend the protagonist's adult identity into a wider community full of ongoing conflicts and new disappointments.

The chapter of *From the Bottom Up* devoted to Irvine's peonage investigation identified race as a central touchstone for these anxieties. Irvine's account of "My Experience as a Laborer in the Muscle Market of the South" served as a bridge from his narrative bildungsroman to a statement of the convictions his journey had produced. Like Irvine's peonage articles, this chapter opened with the costume change that signaled his participation in the genre of investigative disguise, with its promised glimpse of a proletarian viewpoint. Then Irvine recounted experiences left out of his *Appleton's* pieces, including a train journey to his first job in the South as a "mucker," or miner's helper, for the Tennessee Coal and Iron Company (TCI) near Bessemer, Alabama. Here the sympathy with African-American workers that fueled Irvine's disdain for racial slurs in "My Life in Peonage" gave way to a truculent haggling over the application of Jim Crow. Irvine recounted how, as the "leader" of a contingent of European laborers herded into a southbound Virginia railroad car marked "colored," he rose to inquire of a black porter whether Virginia had a law on "the separation of the races." Emphasizing the ambiguous racial status of the immigrants he accompanied, Irvine described the porter as grinning in response, "Dere sho' is boss— but you ain't no races. You is jest Dagoes, ain't you?" Placed on a second Jim Crow car in Georgia, Irvine tried again "to solve my race problem" by inquiring about segregation laws. This time a white porter confounded his racial identity by silently changing the car's "Colored" sign to "White." The muckers' camp where Irvine and his fellow laborers debarked brought his "race problem" into further relief. Lodged in unfinished buildings on a hill "where the blacks lived," pressed into labor in iron mines that rendered black and white alike "in color and condition," the muckers from the North quickly reached the lowest standing Irvine could imagine. Rather than rebuking immigrants who claimed superiority over black workers, Irvine now acquiesced in the view that equality with black laborers represented the meanest condition to which white laborers could fall. His interactions with African Americans in the southern chapters of his autobiography demonstrated the "superior" combination of respectability and vigor he embodied as an exemplary white worker.[91]

The "race problem" Irvine located on the railroad cars of his autobiography was not his alone. He shared in interconnected social and literary distinctions that were symptomatic of the ways that divisions between "black" and "white" were articulated in America at the turn of the century. The TCI mines that provided the southern scenes in *From the Bottom Up* witnessed an especially dramatic division between black and white workers in the years Irvine visited and wrote about them. They had been sites of repeated efforts to express working-class interests across racial lines. From the 1870s on, the Greenback-Labor movement, the Knights of Labor, and the United Mine Workers (UMW) had each defied the rising tide of racial segregation to agitate economic grievances that black and white workers shared.[92] Anti-union forces in the Birmingham mining region combated these initiatives by fanning fears of "social equality"—of interracial unions promoting integrated social interactions in which blacks might exert baleful "moral" influences on whites, especially white women. These efforts succeeded in all but eradicating the UMW from Alabama in 1908. Though "social equality" was only one weapon in the anti-union arsenal, it was an especially powerful one in a period when the progress of Jim Crow had already advanced to a crescendo of terror over the supposed moral dangers of race mixing. Irvine's autobiographical silence about the crumbling interracial culture of the UMW and his suggestion that industrial conditions fostered a frightening equality of social standing among black and white workers were surely products of this pervasive racial dread.[93]

Irvine's autobiography also participated in the ways these developments in race relations found expression in debates over the changing literary fashions that had shaped his writing career. As Kenneth Warren observes, in an era that saw the social and legal institutionalization of Jim Crow, it is intriguing that literary criticism should adopt the imagery of railway trains—highly visible sites of racial separation—to discuss the dangers of expanding the frontiers of literary discourse too far. Warren focuses on Henry James's propensity to equate the changing literary market with train travel in the era of Jim Crow. James pictured the new periodical press for which London and Irvine wrote as a "ponderously long" train that can only begin its journey with every seat occupied and therefore resorts to mannequins when there are not enough passengers. These "dummies,"

Warren notes, were not merely "false" figures on James's literary railroad; they were injuriously malevolent. James associated them with a proliferation of criticism that was "fatal as an infectious disease," polluting the sensitive organism of literature through "bad company" that caused it to lose heart. Such language, Warren suggests, echoed many defenses—as well as pale critiques—of Jim Crow legislation. Both focused on "the fear of suffering harmful effects from forced association with unworthy others." In this context, the analogy between letters and trains made literary culture the equivalent of a segregated conveyance. Rejecting even the ambiguous proletarian vitality that writers like Irvine and London injected into literary narratives of social difference, James tried to redefine true literature as a safe haven from the specter of "social equality" in the popular press.[94]

Irvine's Jim Crow car scenes betrayed similar fantasies of retreat. They showed that he had not completely abandoned the hierarchical aspirations that his bildungsroman described and criticized. Of course, Irvine was not James. By transposing his own prejudices into the popular cultural idiom he had learned from Jack London, he demonstrated an affinity for the "bad company" James could never bring himself to characterize fully in print. But in doing so, Irvine adopted a vernacular associated with the Darwinian racism that London never entirely abandoned. In some respects this was but a more visceral variation of James's genteel squeamishness about his literary associations. However, as Irvine continued to revise his self-representation in response to new political experiences, he rethought the relations among class, ethnicity, and race he was weaving into his life story. His revisions demonstrate intriguing links connecting the literary formulas he had mastered to popularize his life story, the political conflicts he continued to engage, and a wider set of intellectual shifts in the meaning of culture itself.

Race and ethnicity were not the only dimensions of class identity that Irvine revised as he wove together politics and popular culture. In the literary and theatrical self-constructions he produced after *From the Bottom Up*, Irvine also rethought the gender distinctions implicit in his depictions of working-class culture and values. In the autobiography, gender figured most prominently in the robust masculinity to which Irvine attributed his own triumph over the abyss— "the beast in my blood." But his almost total silence regarding his two wives and their domestic arrangements also spoke to gendered dimensions of the proletarian persona he had adopted. Though he dedicated the book to Maude, she had only a bit part in the narrative, and he completely omitted his first wife,

Nellie. On its face, this relegation of women to the margins of life simply reiterated constructions of gender that Irvine shared with the labor movement and the Socialist Party. But it also involved the negotiation of a private anguish, generated by Maude's advancing mental instability. Hard as he tried to cover this tragedy with a veil of domestic privacy, Irvine could not help reflecting on the implications it raised for the contours of his public image. As literary and political renown opened new opportunities to engage public debates on the cultural character of class distinction, he wove his quandaries about gender and race into new revisions of his proletarian persona. In the process, he drew even more substantially on Sylvester Poli's realm of entertainment, where public images of race and gender were also being reformulated.

CHAPTER SEVEN

FROM *THE MAGYAR* TO *MY LADY OF THE CHIMNEY CORNER*

Weaving Gender, Race, Ethnicity, and Working-Class Identity

IN THE YEARS FOLLOWING the publication of his autobiography, Alexander Irvine weathered a series of personal and public struggles that moved him to change the terms in which he cast his life story. The dissolution of his second marriage provoked him to rethink the gender politics of his literary persona. As Irvine revised how women figured into his story, he addressed dynamics of self-display that were coming to dominate images of women in vaudeville. He linked these gender revisions to his ongoing reformulations of race and ethnicity, which also combined politics with entertainment. The culmination of these reevaluations appeared in the memoir that became Irvine's most popular work, *My Lady of the Chimney Corner*. In this 1913 paean to Irish mother-love and plebeian camaraderie, Irvine sought resolution for America's cultural divisions in the wisdom of his own immigrant past.

While *My Lady* affectingly identified Irvine's adult convictions with the lowly Irish wisdom he had learned as a child, the urge to make this identification derived from his struggle to comprehend his trajectory through American cultural politics. As in the case of his previous literary adventures, this process of self-reconstruction reveals much about the public sphere in which Irvine was becoming an increasingly prominent figure. Most important for the history told here, *My Lady* reveals how much he owed his popular self-representation to the nexus of evangelicalism, entertainment, and class politics that had long shaped his mission and life. Read against the wider political struggles in which Irvine engaged as he began to imagine ethnic foundations for his class identity, the memoir suggests how these debates participated in wider transformations in the interpretation of cultural hierarchy and social distinction.

Private Tragedy and Public Self-Making

In 1910, Alexander Irvine's second marriage disintegrated into a tragedy profoundly disturbing to the notions of divine, civilizing "refinement" that he associated with wife- and motherhood. Maude Hazen Irvine experienced psychological agonies that are visible chiefly through her husband's published and unpublished memoirs. These chronicles suggest that the couple continued to differ over their domestic arrangements, with Maude preferring settled living to the adventures that Irvine courted. Irvine described her as happy with the home they had established in Washington Heights while he worked at the Ascension Church. She enjoyed the proximity of markets and cultural events, but Irvine had begun to hanker for rural life. As they moved their family from New York City to Irvine's Peekskill farm, "Happy Hollow," in 1910, Maude struggled with persistent domestic worries. She had a large household to manage, including her own children, sons from her husband's first marriage, artist Max Delfant and ex-con Joe Wiersky, both of whom Irvine had invited to join the family, and a rotating company of socialist squatters and tented transients. Her four children were still young: Robert, ten years, Anna, five years, Maurice (known as "Swanee"), four years, and Jack, one year. The last three were born in rapid succession during a trying period when the couple felt virtually friendless in New Haven and when Irvine was often absent. Irvine frequently repeated the grim story of Swanee's arrival in 1906: when Maude awakened him in the middle of the night to say the child would soon be born, the couple had only money enough to phone the doctor. A few days after, Irvine wrote to Maude's parents of his plans to move from New Haven to New York, and two months later he took off for his peonage investigation. No sooner had the family regrouped in New York than Jack was born; then, a year later, Irvine wanted to move to Peekskill. Contrary to Irvine's idyllic representation of the farm in *From the Bottom Up*, it provided no refuge for Maude. He neglected to mention her share in the life of Happy Hollow in part because it belied his portrayal of the farm as a place of physical and spiritual rest from the rigors of socialist *Bildung*.[1]

In the whirl of Irvine's travels and relocations, confronted by the hostility his beliefs engendered, Maude no doubt found the isolated care of her family and home a heavy burden. In the absence of her own reflections it is impossible to do more than speculate, but it is also difficult not to see the violence she began to express toward her family as, in part, a tragic attempt to relieve the tensions of a domestic environment for which she had great responsibility but little control. According to Irvine, Maude had been under a mental strain for several years when she first tried to drown her two youngest children in Washington Heights. She defended her action by claiming that God had told her he wanted the children with himself: a shrewd if painfully twisted reprisal against Irvine's own tendency to cloak his ambitions in divine purposes. Irvine hoped that the quiet farm would heal her. But there Maude resolved to poison the children and became enraged when Irvine did not help with this divinely commanded task. Bewildered and despairing, Irvine sought psychiatric advice and was told Maude's symptoms indicated advanced schizophrenia. He sent her to a mental asylum, and became the sole parent for his daughter and sons.[2]

These events did not greatly alter Irvine's abstracted attention to his family. Instead, the unraveling of his domestic ties seemed to provoke more avid efforts to construct and disseminate a compelling personal narrative. Dispersing his children to friends and relatives, Irvine sought new venues for the developing story of his life.[3] From 1910 to 1912 he used the platforms provided by socialist lecture circuits and political campaigns to continue reconstructing the working-class identity he had begun to develop in his literary works. He incorporated his disappointments with domestic life into narratives that romanticized domestic responsibilities Maude had found overwhelming. These stories suggest that Irvine never wholly grasped the pressures that had combined to crush her. Still, by bringing gender politics into his portrayals of proletarian solidarity, they testify to interpenetrations of "public" and "private" that his mission and his literary self-constructions had previously overlooked. As such, they gave voice to the ways that popular languages of class and gender spoke to shifting categories of "public" and "private" themselves.

As a traveling lecturer for commercial chautauqua companies, the ISS, and the *Appeal to Reason* in 1910 and 1911, Irvine began to weave the plot of self-definition and self-dramatization that he would use to address these questions in his most popular literature. The chautauqua circuits, where he had been lecturing since 1908, offered him a popular venue for illustrated orations, but these speeches occupied the least of his attention. They helped pay the bills so Irvine could offer his services at cut rate on socialist lecture circuits.[4]

Irvine's socialist lectures, and the organizations that sponsored them, elaborated cultural ideals that were central to his unfolding mission. The ISS was the brainchild of Upton Sinclair, who hoped the organization would encourage the study of socialism on university campuses. Jack London, its first president, was lecturing partially under its auspices when Irvine invited him to appear at Yale. Now Irvine used the ISS to spread his own combination of reverence and disdain for university training far beyond New Haven. In lectures on "The College Man and the World" or "The Socialist Spirit of English Literature," he urged college students to apply their cultural privileges to problems of industrial labor and urban life, in order to make these privileges meaningful to working people.[5]

In Irvine's estimation, the *Appeal to Reason* lecture circuit allowed him to address the audience he wanted to reach most of all. As he put it in the paper's columns: "The APPEAL speaks the language of the working class—it is shockingly plain. . . . Its function is to make Socialists."[6] Plain speaking and shrewd subscription drives had won the *Appeal* the widest circulation of any radical publication in early-twentieth-century America. Though the *Appeal* hired Party theoretician Untermann to give the paper a more "scientific" cast in 1903, its editor, Fred Warren, remained more concerned with exhortation than meticulous theorizing, and disinclined to devote many columns to arcane evolutionary systems or internecine factional battles. Consequently, the *Appeal* often drew fire from Party ideologues for pandering to readers who had yet to adopt the discipline of Party commitments and sophisticated materialist analyses. However, as some of these critics allowed, it was precisely by reaching this group that the *Appeal* swelled the Party's ranks. As right-wing socialist W. J. Ghent explained, "many of the most sober-minded leaders of the movement are men who got their first sight of Socialism in the *Appeal*'s columns. . . . This paper was their recruiting agent. . . . other forces whipped them into shape for more disciplined, orderly service."[7]

The *Appeal*'s project drew on cultural currents familiar to Irvine and congenial to his developing life story. His cultural trajectory paralleled those of the newspaper's founder, Julius A. Wayland, as well as its most popular lecture circuit speaker, Eugene Debs, and editor, Warren. All of these men had embraced evangelical ideals of individual self-improvement and success. In the 1890s, Wayland and Debs had turned briefly to the Populist Party to protest the obstacles that men of wealth placed before ordinary individuals inspired by such ideals; meanwhile, Warren had combined his interest in socialism with devoted service as superintendent of a Methodist Sunday school. Eventually, all of them became convinced that socialism provided the only effective means of confronting the impediments to working-class self-improvement. Their writings and lectures appealed to socialistically inclined working people throughout the Midwest and Southwest for whom lines of self-improvement, reform, and revolution were similarly intertwined. These were the rank-and-file faithful whose convention delegates wielded evangelical ideals of brotherhood against the Party's evolutionary theoreticians. While the *Appeal* entertained its own unsavory conundrums regarding "race" difference, such audiences provided Irvine with a forum in which he could reevaluate the racial terms of his bildungsroman.[8]

From September 1910 through June 1911, Irvine traveled from New York to California and back, telling the story of how he became a Socialist. Reporting on Irvine's earliest *Appeal* performances, Warren noted the evolutionary vigor with which the former minister related his experiences of the industrial order. As Irvine "tells the story of his struggles with the Beast of Capitalism," said Warren, "I have seen men and women grip their seats until it seemed the blood from their veins would leap out in protest against the barbarism of modern society." These audiences sat fascinated as Irvine "unfolded chapter after chapter from his own experience, each incident bringing out clear and distinct the class line that divides society into two hostile camps—the robbers and the robbed."[9] Other reports show how Irvine used evolutionary language in the service of the older evangelical tradition that he shared with many of the *Appeal*'s readers. These accounts depict socialist revivals that touched witnesses with personal appeals worthy of evangelicalism's most flamboyantly democratic heritage. In Everett, Washington,

> The crowd was drunk, emotionally intoxicated, and the glistening eyes and suffused faces meeting one's gaze in every direction told the story that the lips would probably deny, that of quickened heart beats and feelings strained to the breaking point. As an emotional spree it was well worth the price, even if it should bring forth no fruit. But I believe that today the mind of every non-Socialist present is like a well-plowed field, ready for the seed, class-conscious revolutionary Socialism, and it will not be the great Irishman's fault if the field is neglected and the crop will be weeds.[10]

This was precisely the kind of passion Dwight Moody had tried to banish from the revival tent. Irvine brought it back as he sought to turn the great evangelist's methods to different social ends than Moody had envisioned.

Three months after his Everett appearance, Irvine stirred an audience at Ann Arbor, Michigan, to similar ecstasies. According to one correspondent, Michigan Socialists had reacted coolly to advance announcements of Irvine's visit, doubting that any socialist orator could match Eugene Debs and wary of the "let-us-pray-brethren kind of Socialism" they expected of an ex-minister. But after Irvine's lecture, the same correspondent declared:

> We are penitent. We thought he was a minister—and he is. But such a minister! Driving with whip and spur like the very devil of righteousness, in fiery eloquence over the capitalist system, he leaves in his trail the wreckage of all

that is rotten and vicious. We expected a parlor Socialist, an oily man of God, full of words but empty of ideas. There came to us a man, with a message glowing and passionate, a message of the Co-operative Commonwealth. . . . His stinging rebuke to the unthinking, to the man who stands apart from the class struggle, must bring the blush of shame to the face of every coward thus inclined. His eloquent appeal to all to gather around the flag of Socialism is one that will inflame many a faltering spirit. . . . We were thrilled. The witty sallies, the vitriolic invective, the onward rush of sentence after sentence neatly turned, with words so nicely chosen, the thunderous eloquence dropping now and then to the commonest conversational tone—all these brought home to us as never before the message of Socialism.[11]

In addition to combining Irvine's evangelical zeal with the evolutionary vigor he had adopted to represent his class sympathies, these performances provided apt rehearsals for the theatrical arena from which Irvine had already drawn many methods and themes. As a comrade in Lansing reported, his "description of the way charity is misplaced in this country and its results was truly dramatic." Drawing on the narratives he had devised to popularize his struggles with cultural hierarchy, in short, Irvine fashioned himself into a stirring vehicle of socialist propaganda. By 1911 Socialists were calling him "a second Debs."[12]

As Irvine wove together these religious and popular cultural strands of self-presentation, socialist political associations challenged him to rethink the racial contours of the proletarian self he offered. Irvine's *Appeal* lectures deepened his socialist alliances in New York City and throughout the country in a period when Socialists were renegotiating their approach to the racial plight of African Americans. Maligned as inferior outcasts by the Party's outright racists, African Americans also had complaints against more sympathetic Socialists. Though Debs and others rejected racism, they often relegated explicit calls for African-American rights to a socialist future, when they believed the necessity for such demands would have largely disappeared. Black workers, they supposed, would benefit from the same economic and social transformations they demanded in the name of all workers. But as rank-and-file black Socialists as well as prominent African-American spokesmen like W. E. B. Du Bois observed, such expectations failed to challenge the racial exclusiveness of craft unions, the spread of legalized segregation throughout American society, or the general atmosphere of disdain generated by the categories of "race" that many Socialists deployed. By 1910, black Socialists had made little headway in persuading the Party to address these concerns. But they did have small successes, as when Irvine's New York local agreed to employ a paid black organizer for a brief period. For Irvine such skirmishes prompted a reevaluation of the racial categories he had deployed in *From the Bottom Up*.[13]

Irvine's involvement with the *Appeal* assured that the terms of this reevaluation would be contradictory, questioning but not completely overturning race distinctions associated with the evolutionary vernacular he wielded in oratory and literature. The *Appeal* was itself a study in socialist divisions over race. The paper often featured columns comparing the plight of wage-workers to that of chattel slaves, with a range of implications as to possible alliances between white and black workers in the present. Some *Appeal* writers seemed to concur with the Ascension sermons in which Irvine had excluded African Americans from the socialist cause. Pleading with wage-workers to embrace socialism in order to show that they were not "as ignorant of the real character of wage slavery as the blacks were ignorant about the character of chattel slavery," these writers treated slavery as an object lesson for the white working class. In other cases, the *Appeal* stood resolutely against racial exclusion in labor unions. One July 1909 article insisted that "race prejudice" was "brutal and antiquated," unworthy of the broader solidarities that Socialists cultivated. According to another article, all workers—including "Japanese and negroes and Mexican greasers"—"need to live the same as we do" and would pose no threat to "American" workers under socialism. As this distinction between "we Americans" and the "Japanese and negroes and Mexican greasers" betrayed, however, a resistance to "social equality" lurked behind the *Appeal*'s avowals of interracial equality in economic concerns.

The limits to racial brotherhood at the *Appeal* were underscored by Wayland's expressed belief that socialism would produce a voluntary segregation based on the preferences of black and white workers "for their own communities." Such appeals to community expressed a more general inclination—among popular intellectuals at the *Appeal*, Socialist Party theorists, as well as academic social scientists—to cloak racism in a beguiling appreciation of "cultural" differences which, according to turn-of-the-century Neo-Lamarckianism, could be inherited. This cultural approach to racial difference shaped the revision of proletarian selfhood that Irvine began working out in literary terms while he lectured for the *Appeal*. Irvine's self-constructions never wholly overcame Neo-Lamarckian cultural categories of "race." But they did work these categories into popular conceptions of cultural difference that began to point beyond the Lamarckian legacy.[14]

Irvine's alternatives to evolutionary notions of race derived in part from ethnic associations and self-representations he developed during his years as an

Appeal lecturer. Between 1910 and 1912 he affiliated with the Irish Socialist Federation, an organization that urged Irish-Americans to vote the Socialist ticket to support working-class demands in the United States and nationalist demands in Ireland. Building on the Irish self-representations he had begun to develop in his peonage investigation and at the Ascension Church, Irvine reproduced the Federation's message as an Irish twist to his proletarian narrative. On the *Appeal* circuit he sometimes prefaced his story by telling of the Irish famine of the 1840s, citing its harvest of death as an example of the exploitation of the working people he had fought all his life. According to one observer, audiences "alternately laughed and cried, as Irish humor would alternate with the pathos born of Irish suffering and nurtured by his struggles in America."[15] These flourishes of Irish identity elaborated Irvine's earlier flirtations with "Irish" disguises and made "Irishness" an integral part of his personality. As such, they also became intriguingly intertwined with Irvine's negotiation of racial distinction.

As many historians have observed, having been a despised "race" at home, Irish immigrants had found themselves maligned in American racial terms as well. They were popularly classed in the same racial category as African Americans in nineteenth-century epithets like "niggers turned inside out" for the Irish and "smoked Irishmen" for blacks. Irish responses to such racialization provided a kind of archetype for the immigrant struggle to achieve American whiteness. Many Irish-Americans joined the ranks of blackface minstrel actors who borrowed, distorted, and belittled what they believed their proximity to blacks had taught them about African-American culture. Others amplified these theatrical caricatures through physical assaults against blacks and abolitionists in the streets. As Irvine continued to embellish his own Irish self-representation, he would try to redirect this racial legacy toward a cross-racial cultural kinship of common oppression. His most popular expression of this vision, graced by a sainted Irish mother, gave a plebeian cast to the anguished plea against Irish-American racism made in 1843 by Daniel O'Connell, whose heroic visage had still appealed to Irish patriots in New York City wax exhibits at the beginning of Irvine's American career. "It was not in Ireland you learned this cruelty," O'Connell had admonished. "Your mothers were gentle, kind, and humane."[16]

But, while Irvine tried to reconcile Celtic sentiment with cross-racial sympathy, such sentiment was being pressed into service for competing versions of Irish-American identity. It had triumphed on the vaudeville stage in part because self-appointed Irish-American spokesmen objected to ribald sketches that seemed to bring Irish women into disgrace. While these objections derived from

sensibilities attributed to the Irish "race," enthusiasm for more "refined" celebrations of Irish identity was not universal. Among the Irish-American organizations Sylvester Poli patronized in New Haven, as elsewhere, it broke down
across class lines. In his own construction of ethnic identity, Irvine attended to
these intraethnic debates over cultural hierarchy as well as to the cultural categories that arranged Americans hierarchically by ethnic and racial group. What
is the more intriguing about his efforts to conceive Irish identity as an expression
of cross-racial plebeian camaraderie is the literary route he took to get to this ethnic self-construction. It was by imagining himself in fictional disguise as a Hungarian, one of the "new" immigrants, that Irvine first wrestled seriously with the
problems of ethnic cultural hierarchy and cross-racial class feeling. His vehicle
for this ethnic persona was a novel called *The Magyar*, which combined quandaries about race, ethnicity, and gender into an explosive emotional stew.

Rewriting Proletarian Identity in The Magyar

Written during Irvine's first year with the *Appeal to Reason*, *The Magyar* bore
marks of the cultural, personal, and political issues he was confronting at the
time. Though awkward, at best, as literature, the novel demonstrates how Irvine
made use of popular literary techniques to rethink social distinctions that confounded his home life and sparked debate in the public venues where he lectured. It portrayed complementary male and female modes of class loyalty by
recounting gender-specific adventures in social disguise and self-discovery that
crossed lines of class, ethnicity, and race.

The Magyar's two main characters—Stephen and Madeline Ruden—appear
at the beginning of the novel in a situation drawn from Alexander and Maude
Irvine's last years in New Haven. Stephen Ruden is a crusading minister who
preaches a gospel of work that alienates the elite leaders of his suburban parish
in "New Oxford." Condensing the high points of Irvine's New Haven mission,
Ruden moves rapidly from speaking out for workers at a City Hall meeting to
preaching socialism at the Alumni Hall of "Colonial University." In depicting
this latter event, Irvine borrowed from Jack London's Yale performance, but also
demonstrated the distance he had traveled from London. At Yale and in subsequent writing, London had portrayed socialism as arriving through a series of violent revolutionary upheavals. Ruden declares that "Socialism is neither cata-
clysmal, confiscatory nor iconoclastic. It does not work from the top down, but
from the bottom up. . . . To begin from the top is revolution. To work from the

bottom is evolution."[17] Here, Irvine had Ruden articulate a perspective on socialism central to the questions about working-class cultural values he was pondering through successive versions of his life story.

More than Irvine's previous autobiographical narratives, *The Magyar* attends not only to the intellectual substance of socialist agitation but also to its household consequences. The book's early chapters feature an ongoing quarrel between Stephen and Madeline. Madeline complains that Ruden alienates New Oxford's "best people" in the name of a questionable moral code reserved for "a privileged few whose wives and children pay the price with starved and naked bodies." Her protests comprise some of the most poignant concessions Irvine ever made to the burdens that domestic duties placed on women, burdens to which his own wife had succumbed. In *The Magyar*, Irvine began to weave these domestic issues into the cultural politics he was trying to sort out. In response to Madeline's reproaches, Ruden identifies women's domestic discontents with the luxury and self-display that women increasingly flaunted in popular culture. According to Ruden, Madeline has "the itch to be uncommon, to possess what others cannot possess, to do what others cannot do." Ruden's problem, Madeline retorts, is that "the blood of a foreign proletariat" runs through his veins. These statements provided creative twists to the conundrum of the "new" immigrants' capacity to achieve an "American" standard of living. Madeline rehearses contemporary evolutionary notions that racialized immigrant culture in order to express its distance from "American" culture. Ruden, on the other hand, identifies her tastes with craven luxuries that deviate from a robust proletarian respectability. The rest of the novel chronicles adventures that resolve this dispute by leading Ruden to the ethnic wellsprings of his working-class sympathies and prompting Madeline to renounce luxury in order to cleave to Ruden's socialist ideals.[18]

Separating after Ruden's socialist speech, Stephen and Madeline deposit their children with relatives and set out on journeys of self-discovery across class, racial, and ethnic boundaries. Traveling south to investigate peonage, Ruden traces Irvine's evolving assessment of the lines of class, ethnicity, and race he had crossed in his undercover travels. Again, race provides an especially delicate touchstone for identity. Many scenes in the *The Magyar* reproduce the invidious racial distinctions that permeated turn-of-the-century social thought and popular culture. *The Magyar* recapitulates the railroad car scenes in *From the Bottom Up*, with their complicity in Jim Crow. It also portrays Ruden brandishing London-esque "Saxon" vitality to defend helpless black men from the brutality of peonage bosses and prison officials. In these cases, Ruden only halfheartedly challenges the racial hierarchies he discovers in the South. In an altercation with a physician who refuses to care for a black convict suffering from a whipping, Ruden declares, "This isn't a question of race, doctor. If this was a horse or a dog or a pig, I would appeal for pity, for consideration!" When the doctor proceeds to kick the wounded black man, Ruden flies into the breach, exclaiming, "You cowardly cur! . . . you can beat an old man to death, but when you face a man, you play the baby and squeal for help." Such encounters merely demonstrate that Ruden's racist pity is more robust than southern racist viciousness.[19]

While it colluded in hierarchical racial categories, however, *The Magyar* also offered images of African Americans and their culture that figured "race" much differently. Irvine fashioned the novel's main African-American character—a gardener named William—out of his profound respect for W. E. B. Du Bois. William is a Harvard-trained Socialist who meets Ruden in a private convict stockade. Together they attempt to uplift black and white convict laborers culturally and to agitate for better conditions. Asked to explain his hopes for "your people," William explains to fellow Socialists the great debate between Booker T. Washington and Du Bois:

> One leader pointed the way to salvation through labor—the black man was to appeal to the white man through a well tilled field or a well built house. The other was more revolutionary—he spoke of rights and urged the black man to stand on his feet as a man, and a citizen. William . . . was an advocate of armed resistance . . . advancing rapidly to leadership himself, he was anxious to air his views.

Irvine's evolutionary vernacular clinches William's claims to equal citizenship by depicting the gardener triumphing in his own robust fistic battle with a brutal white "superior." William knocks his plantation-owner boss on his back "with a blow the crash of which could be heard a hundred yards away," then stands "erect and ready," gun in hand, declaring, "I'll rid the earth of a cowardly cur who doesn't possess the morals of a dog." But he tempers this rage from the abyss with sympathy for the collective African-American culture that is also prominent in the novel. In mine, prison, and stockade, William and other black laborers sing about liberty in a heavenly home, providing a "spiritual wind up" appreciated by black and white alike.[20]

Here, Irvine called on long-established traditions that defined white working-class identity and politics through ambiguous preoccupations with African-American culture. Except for William, Irvine's black characters speak in the cadences of the nineteenth-century blackface minstrel show that had provided the most visible institutionalization of these traditions, and bequeathed them to vaude-ville. "O, Massa Jesus, mend yo' licks an' squelch d' ol' debil in dese yere white folks!" one character entreats as she observes from depths of her lowly wisdom the petty quarrels of the self-proclaimed master race. Even William, who speaks standard English, gets in on the minstrel act Irvine concocts for his novel: the gardener is beloved for the "coon songs" he contributes to the uplifting enter-tainments he and Ruden provide for convict laborers.[21] Irvine's autobiographi-cal gloss on minstrel traditions shows how fused the two moments of cross-racial sympathy and racial ridicule had become in proletarian appropriations of the minstrel tradition.[22] As Ruden's adventures demonstrate, Irvine was especially interested in the positive images of African-American community evoked by his spiritualizing black characters. But his novel also shows how thoroughly this thread of association was wound around derogatory blackface caricature in white fantasies of class identity.

As a whole, *The Magyar* narrates a journey of self-discovery that helps Ruden locate the origins of his socialist faith in an ethnicity modeled on the more romanticized images of African-American culture Irvine depicts, and on wider, popular engagements with cultural hierarchy in which they participated. Ruden begins this personal quest while waiting at The Magyar Slovensky Hotel in New York to be transported south disguised as a peon. Here he befriends a Hungar-ian youth named Franz whose native tongue sounds vaguely familiar, "like the sounds of a life [Ruden] had lived before." It is particularly appropriate that Franz should bestir this memory, since the youth is a model of working-class self-respect who carries his certificates as a journeyman butcher and refuses to work accord-ing to lumber camp orders that do not match the terms of his written contract — to him, a sacred document. Ruden's efforts to defend Franz (accomplished, of course, "like an enraged panther") land the minister in the penitentiary and then in the stockade, where he meets William. During these episodes Ruden encoun-ters convicts whose stories lead him to the southern mill town of Arden, Alabama. Arden's working-class community revolves around Emrich Zapolya, a Hungarian immigrant from a noble line who is committed to working-class rev-olution. Ruden discovers that Zapolya is his long-lost father, whose combination of ancient nobility and contemporary revolutionism accounts for his son's pro-letarian sympathies. Zapolya's class consciousness is loyal to community values but respectful of higher learning, a combination Irvine struggled to reconcile in his own socialist creed.[23]

In depicting Ruden's cultural heritage, Irvine pondered his own cultural and religious ideals in light of intraethnic hierarchies of the kind Sylvester Poli negotiated in New Haven. Organized expression of "Magyar culture" often drew its imagery not from the customs of the immigrants' own predominantly peasant and working-class ancestors, but from the Magyar landed gentry, with their egret-feathered hats, braided coats, and fur-lined and gold-braided gala dress. Franz, the journeyman butcher, enacts this dimension of Magyar pride by arriving in America wearing "a black velvet jacket trimmed with silk," while the patriarchal Zapolya gives it a more subtle expression in the noble demeanor that inspires his nickname, "Baron." These hierarchical accents in Hungarian-American culture echoed conflicts over the representation of national sensibilities that erupted in other immigrant groups as well. Like the institutions that sought to uplift southern Italian immigrants to a national culture defined by northern Italians like Poli, Hungarian-American organizations often tried to conscript immigrants of diverse ethnic and social backgrounds into a shared culture imagined in terms of a noble Magyar past. But nationalist feeling was not the only motivation for such constructions. They also sustained immigrant pride in the face of nativist derision. Irvine captured this dimension of immigrant experience in *The Magyar,* as he had in his peonage articles, by repeating epithets like "sheenie" and "guineas" that American workers used to remind "new" immigrants of their "inbetween" racial status. Zapolya's quiet nobility represents, in part, a vision of ethnic identity that refuses such insults.[24]

Still, despite his filial affection, Ruden has some misgivings about the hierarchical prejudices implied in Zapolya's character. These misgivings challenge cultural concepts embedded in early-twentieth-century notions of race. The idea that Ruden could inherit his ideals from parents he had separated from in childhood derived from Neo-Lamarckian assumptions that acquired characteristics such as skills, beliefs, or cultural attainments could be passed from parents to offspring. Irvine invented a ludicrous illustration of this principle to "prove" that Ruden had really found his father: Ruden has the birthmark that Zapolya remembers on his first child, a patch on his thigh that was the exact color of some wax that had become fastened to his mother's leg. But *The Magyar* also confounds Neo-Lamarckian cultural notions about "backward" peoples acquiring "civilization" in the form of improvements their children would biologically inherit. While he respects his father's erudition, Ruden is not completely enamored of Zapolya's "aristocratic" bearing, especially when it tends toward a haughty vanguardism that sets itself above working people it claims to serve. Ruden feels greater cultural kinship with the mother he knows only from a daguerreotype and from Zapolya's descriptions of the abiding religious faith she maintained in the face of the indignities of immigrant life. Reinforcing this religious dimension of ethnic culture, Franz and Zapolya, for all their hierarchical posturing, find the most poignant tie to their language and culture in reading the *Meistershaflesbuch*, or Magyar New Testament. Thus, in Ruden's self-discovery, as in the immigrant audiences Irvine had shared with Poli, the cultural politics of ethnicity posed as many conundrums as it solved.[25]

Irvine partially addressed these problems by constructing a broader community of interracial socialism around the ethnic kinship that Ruden and Zapolya share. Many of the conversations in which the two men discover their relationship as well as their disagreements take place in the cottage of a mulatto writer named Nell Palmer. Nell's cottage is Ruden's first stop in Arden, where he originally comes to inform her of the death at the penitentiary of her childhood friend and sweetheart. The story of this interracial romance provides background for the contemporary cross-racial community that forms at the cottage among Ruden, Zapolya, Nell, and William, the socialist gardener. Here Irvine wrote against the grain of the education in hierarchical whiteness he had seen developing among European immigrant peons. While the proletarian sympathy that Ruden and Zapolya share thrives on ties of kin and culture—blood and language—it is but part of a wider camaraderie in which the cultural peculiarities of "ethnicity" and "race" enhance a common moral vision. This kind of cultural kinship is not a means of diminishing or excluding anyone on racial grounds. Instead, it provides the moral adhesive within which divergent visions of social transformation can be debated without shattering the community. In this respect, Nell's cottage is a microcosm of the wider socialist movement depicted in a mass meeting at the end of the novel, a movement that "has no race distinctions."[26]

As he elaborated on the significance of this camaraderie, Irvine pondered the politics of gender as well as race. The story of Madeline Ruden's adventures took up this strand of Irvine's narrative project. While her husband probes the ethnic roots and cross-racial ethics of his socialism, Madeline also assumes disguises that carry her across social lines. At first she is pampered at Wetumpka Mansion, the Alabama plantation owned by Congressman Llewellyn Oglethorpe. Oglethorpe dresses her in an expensive, seductive gown and shows her off at a Christmas ball, where she stimulates his own lusts and wins the admiration of the governor. Both men promise further extravagances, and access to political power, in return for Madeline's complicity in adultery and social injustice. These scenes serve as Irvine's moral indictment of the luxuries for which Madeline hankers.

Here Irvine again took issue with evocations of female display at the vaudeville show and other contemporary theatrical venues. He portrayed such display as the expression of the lascivious sexual debauchery enjoyed by a parasitic elite that lures women into its own moral turpitude. Madeline's extravagance involves little agency of her own, certainly not the self-conscious sexual assertiveness of a Sophie Tucker or an Eva Tanguay. Instead of playing knowingly with the passions she arouses, Madeline answers Oglethorpe's advances with breathless avowals that combine remorse about her methods with awe for the suitor she has attracted:

> My nerve's all right, it's my conscience that's out of joint! . . . I have longed to be in vital touch with men who are not dreamers, but actual powers. Men of success. Now here I am and yet I know you not. I am thrilled by the senses at times, and frightened by them as often as I am thrilled. You have never tried to find out whether I have a soul or a mind. . . . You are a worshipper of physical beauty—it is your god and your heaven!

Madeline imagines that she might use this worship to effect "reforms." But she finds that the theater of social distinction she has entered imposes its own calculations. Irvine did not entertain the possibility that—like vaudeville's divas—Madeline might fulfill herself through display. Lured by borrowed extravagance into Oglethorpe's materialist religion, the only moral agency available to her lies in renouncing his vulgar worship to commit herself to Ruden's socialist ideals.[27]

The handmaiden in this journey of redemption is Mabel Oglethorpe, Madeline's old school friend and Llewellyn Oglethorpe's wife. Mabel provides one of *The Magyar*'s most dramatic enactments of the renunciation required of women in Irvine's narrative of class identity. Tortured by the recognition that her husband's wealth feeds his lust for her friends and servants, Mabel seeks expiation in the teachings of a new convict laborer who has been preaching salvation and social change to the plantation's labor force. She and Madeline visit the shed where the laborer-prophet "Elijah" tells stories of Jean Valjean and other worker heroes, interspersed with the black laborers' stories and songs. Madeline nearly faints upon seeing that "Elijah" is really her estranged husband. But Mabel immediately embraces the working-class fellowship over which he presides, where white and black workers bring together their separate cultural traditions in mutual enjoyment. When Mabel's presence inhibits the expression of this fellowship, Ruden explains the social and cultural boundaries she has crossed. "It is kind of you to step over the line," he comments, "we are not ungrateful, but simply surprised."[28]

Mabel promptly demonstrates what her step entails. While her husband confers with President Roosevelt in Washington, she strikes the shackles from the convicts' legs and prevails upon William to draw up plans for a more enlightened management of the plantation. As final deliverance across the "line" to which Ruden refers, Mabel serves Oglethorpe with divorce papers that name as correspondent one of the black women who have endured his advances and borne him children. Through this legal action, Mabel defies the hierarchy of race by recognizing the black mother of Oglethorpe's children "as a woman—a human being, like myself."[29] This is the novel's most dramatic linkage of gender and race relations, intended to declare a racial equality of sexual persecution that lies at the heart of "bourgeois" marriage.

Madeline soon follows her friend over "the line." After encountering Ruden in the Oglethorpe shed, she travels to Arden, where she masquerades as a plain mill worker in order to understand the lives of the people her husband champions. By rejecting oppressive display to adopt a working-class disguise, Madeline gains admission to the circle of working-class solidarity that her husband's ethnic traditions represent. She, too, finds Nell and Zapolya and through them a dedication to socialism. Unlike Ruden, however, Madeline does not follow a path of self-discovery into this circle. She is admitted, instead, because she reconstitutes her domestic ties to Ruden, "one of the noblest souls that ever loved his kind . . . the man I bartered away for a round of pleasure with the inane Bourgeoisie."[30]

Irvine used this reconciliation to ponder what kind of domestic virtue was appropriate to the proletarian sympathies that *The Magyar* dramatized. Near the end of the novel, the main characters assemble to debate the political implications of love and marriage. Abandoned by Madeline, Ruden has fallen in love with a religious protégé, Ethel Ainsworth, who long since renounced her privileged background to embrace his Christian socialist vision. In the novel's move from North to South, Ethel enjoys her own adventure in disguise as a peonage investigator and legal counsel for the Justice Department, modeled on the real-life Mary Grace Quackenbos. Such an educated, independent New Woman brings to *The Magyar* Irvine's recent acknowledgment of feminist challenges to his own assumptions about gender distinctions. She also testifies to Irvine's belated recognition that domestic responsibilities alone could not fulfill women's ambitions to participate in the public sphere from which he gained so much pleasure. At the same time, Ruden's affection for Ethel expresses Irvine's unrealized desire for a marriage that might effortlessly combine social ideals and domestic arrangements, bridging the ragged divide between public and private. "I have thirsted for a fellowship that was evenly balanced—not a mere breeding arrangement, but a soul comradeship," Ruden tells Ethel early in the novel. "But the struggle to get bread and appear respectable is so absolutely engrossing, that there is no time to live, to laugh, to make a brighter world!" Here Irvine addressed Maude's private tragedy through a vision of hetero-social comradeship that went beyond his conventional visions of feminine domesticity.

Ultimately, however, *The Magyar* reasserts conventional domestic propriety, albeit in socialist terms. Ruden, Madeline, Ethel, and Zapolya jointly determine that the Rudens should stay together, though not because of any smug complicity in bourgeois gender prescriptions. "We are not cattle to be herded for the convenience of a decadent public," Madeline declares, and Ruden reflects that he knows of "no law of God or man to prevent me loving what and whomsoever I please." But they decide that to love for personal pleasure alone would be to deny the claims made on them by the larger socialist movement. Since the appearance of sexual impropriety might harm that movement, Stephen and Madeline reunite in "service and the joy of comradeship."[31]

The Magyar turned out to be much more successful as a narrative effort at resolving political and personal uncertainties than it was as a literary commodity. Unable to find a commercial press willing to publish it, Irvine resorted to the scheme that Upton Sinclair had tried when seeking a publisher for *The Jungle*—an *Appeal to Reason* advertisement soliciting subscriptions to subsidize a first edition. Irvine claimed in his advertisement that only the novel's positive portrayal of black characters and its uncompromising socialism prevented its publication by a major press.[32] But the book exhibits plenty of defects that might give a publisher pause. The narrative is hopelessly at odds with itself as it careens from London-esque flights of strenuous masculinity to maudlin dialect sketches of dying peons, from poignant depictions of everyday working-class life to romantic platitudes delivered by Irvine's emotionally overcharged protagonists. Of course, other turn-of-the-century protest novels that found commercial publishers and audiences were similarly uneven; a further difficulty with Irvine's book was that he borrowed many narrative devices from these models. For example, he explains Ethel's social fervor by furnishing her with a recent trip to the Chicago stockyards to investigate the sources of her father's wealth, a conceit lifted out of Jack London's 1908 revolutionary novel, *The Iron Heel*.[33] Such appropriations gave Irvine's novel a stale taste even when it recounted fresh adventures that he was quite capable of expressing vividly.

Yet, for all its failings as a novel, *The Magyar* does illuminate the construction of working-class identity in early-twentieth-century America by dramatizing Irvine's effort to comprehend the historical contours of his own personality. Though some of his more flatfooted literary appropriations served him ill in this project, the artifice of investigative disguise continued to provide a potent medium for self-discovery. Irvine's ongoing use of this device offers poignant testimony to its larger significance as a way of probing the investigator's own identity. Even where investigators focused on what they had learned about the communities they visited, the lines of class and ethnic difference they drew by means of costume, language, and description told much about how their investigations helped define their own social location. Irvine's case amplified this subjective dimension of investigative disguise. His investigative narratives continuously redefined what working-class origins and socialist politics meant personally.

The Magyar was an important milestone on this journey. By imagining, through Ruden's character, that proletarian compassion and socialist faith derive from ethnic traditions cherished in an interracial community, Irvine transformed his own experiments in investigative disguise into a narrative of self-discovery tailored to resolve some of his current political dilemmas. In the characters of Madeline, Nell, and Ethel, Irvine turned the disguise narrative to the task of reconciling himself to his personal domestic difficulties and to the feminist challenges with which socialist activism acquainted him. Whether because of political controversy or literary triteness, *The Magyar*'s marginality made this amalgam of selfhood and politics primarily a personal achievement. Still, within its narrative, Irvine had delineated new contours of a public self that redrew the lines of race, ethnicity, and class in terms of which he depicted working-class identity.

Irvine carried many components of this new formula from *The Magyar* into his more popular memoir of ethnic origins, *My Lady of the Chimney Corner*. There, Nell's comradely, interracial community of Socialists reappears as a festival of Irish plebeian camaraderie. Irvine's vision of domestic repose combined with social service is realized in the figure of his mother, Anna, a domestic angel who defends her home circle with the savvy of a clever barrister. And, once again, his characters derive their shape and verbal color from popular entertainments whose methods of disguise he had borrowed in his adventures of proletarian self-discovery. But while *The Magyar* set a cultural agenda for *My Lady*, it did not provoke Irvine to rewrite his story as a tale of Irish plebeian wisdom. That provocation came, again, from the arena of class politics.

Political Performances, Party Factionalism, and Socialist Faith

While Irvine was writing *The Magyar*, his nationwide popularity as a socialist lecturer led to new opportunities for agitation. In 1911, lawyer and former preacher Job Harriman was running for mayor on the socialist ticket in Los Angeles. He hoped to convert a promising coalition of trade unionists and Socialists into a stunning electoral victory for socialism. Ranged against him were some of the nation's most bitter opponents of unions and Socialists: *Los Angeles Times* proprietor Harrison Gray Otis and the Merchant and Manufacturers Association he had mobilized to keep his city free of union contracts. But Harriman had the support of one of the most powerful and politically effective trade unionist organizations in the country: the San Francisco Building Trades Council (BTC). The San Francisco BTC combined hardheaded defense of craft union prerogatives with visions of the just society that unionists might lead after the immediate goals of the closed shop, the eight-hour day, and a union pay scale were established. Its leaders hoped to extend to Los Angeles the working-class social vision that its president, P. H. McCarthy, had tried to cultivate during a term as San Francisco's mayor. On the strength of his lecture tour, Alexander Irvine was called in July 1911 to serve this cause as Harriman's campaign manager.[34]

Irvine's campaign duties allowed him to enlarge on a variety of previous missionary methods, but also aggravated political tensions within his mission. Drawing from his experience with trade unionist politics in New Haven, Irvine elaborated old arguments for municipal ownership and attached them to larger proposals for collective civic development, including the public improvement of a Los Angeles harbor that had long been ceded to private developers. He also drew on such familiar themes as the desirability of public baths, parks, and school buildings, and the democratic cultivation of civic culture. His propaganda efforts were enthusiastically reported by *The Citizen*, the official organ of the Los Angeles Central Labor Council, as well as the *California Social Democrat*, the newspaper of the Los Angeles Socialist local.[35] Eventually, Irvine's association with the alliance of trade unionists and Socialists represented by these two papers implicated him in socialist faction fights born of the rivalry between the AFL and the more militant and inclusive Industrial Workers of the World (IWW). For the brief period of the campaign itself, however, Irvine found among Socialists and trade unionists a unified constituency for his consolidation of Christian socialist self-dramatization.

In campaign speeches, Irvine combined arguments about the relevance of literature to working-class life with his more recent experiments in the dramatic uses of his own story. A series of talks on *Les Miserables* urged audiences to study Hugo's masterpiece both to enhance their literary repertoire and to understand economic and political struggles. In addition to drawing connections between Hugo's story and the social ills that Harriman's candidacy addressed, Irvine drew parallels between Hugo's characters and his own life experiences. Just as Hugo's bishop, M. Myriel, protected galley slave Jean Valjean from a thievery charge by claiming to have given Valjean the silverware the slave had actually stolen, Irvine explained, so he had taken the ex-convict, Joe Wiersky, into his own home and explained that all his paintings and books belonged to Joe. Similarly, the story of Fantine had a parallel in the plight of an impoverished Bowery mother whom Irvine had once defended from a landlord's lascivious advances.[36] By mixing Hugo's narrative and his own public self-constructions, Irvine elaborated his emulation of Jack London. Five years before, while stumping the nation for socialism, London had persuaded Irvine to turn his unremunerative mission into salable material for the popular press. Now enjoying his own national name as a magazine writer and socialist orator, Irvine offered his bildungsroman to illustrate a cultural creed that anchored literature in working-class concerns.

Irvine also used the Harriman campaign to augment his theatrical techniques, building on the reputation for "drama" that his *Appeal* lectures had established. "Irvine the inimitable," an *Appeal* correspondent called him soon after his arrival in Los Angeles, "he is a show by himself." The campaign allowed Irvine to expand the scope of his showmanship. Beginning in September 1910, he assisted in the operation of a socialist movie house in downtown Los Angeles. The first motion pictures shown in the theater were clips of a Los Angeles Labor Day parade and rally addressed by Job Harriman. A decade after the local actuality film had introduced vaudeville audiences to the novelty of motion pictures, Los Angeles Socialists had seized on the cinematic presentation of their own daily struggles as a method of political mobilization. While audiences flocked to see the Labor Day pictures, cinematographers were busy recording new views featuring striking metal trades workers and the activities at the Harriman campaign "storm center," where Irvine presided. Meanwhile, as commercial film producers had moved on to the production of narrative fiction films, the socialist movie house promised nothing less. According to the *California Social Democrat*, a series of filmed plays "by Alexander Irvine, the noted Socialist orator and campaign manager," was in preparation in September 1911. While audiences awaited these movies, Irvine provided a series of stereopticon talks, the Wage-Earners' Suffrage League mounted a stereopticon display portraying efforts on behalf of women's suffrage that were proceeding collaboratively with the socialist campaign, and slides of labels of various craft locals that supported the socialist electoral campaign were also flashed across the movie screen.[37]

Irvine's association with the socialist movie house allowed him to embellish his earlier uses of the screen image. In New Haven, he had used the stereopticon to rearrange hierarchies of civilization that workers, preachers, and theatrical entrepreneurs all deployed. In Los Angeles, Irvine sharpened his screen practice by participating in an ongoing struggle over the cinematic portrayal of class conflict. As Stephen Ross observes, "Labor and Capital" stories formed a recognized genre in silent film by 1910. To the dismay of Socialists and trade unionists, many of these films depicted labor leaders and union members as self-serving troublemakers who advanced a murderously criminal cause.[38] Such portrayals of union struggles angered Irvine's Los Angeles allies. In August 1911, the *California Social Democrat* carried a story urging workingmen not to patronize films that portrayed "lies about labor," murder films, war films, or "any of the horrors which it is in the interest of capitalism to make you like."[39] When Los Angeles Socialists opened their movie house a month later, they joined national efforts to counter the film industry's antilabor bias. Two of the earliest films generated by this counterattack focused on a labor drama that was integrally linked to the fate of the Harriman campaign: the trial of James B. and John J. McNamara for the October 1, 1910 bombing of Harrison Gray Otis's *Los Angeles Times*, which had killed twenty people.

The *Times* bombing had contributed to the political alliance of Los Angeles Socialists and trade unionists since the beginning of the Harriman campaign. Otis had immediately turned it into grist for his anti-union mill. He attributed the explosion to the unions with whom he was locked in a fierce battle over the open shop. Union leaders just as quickly denied responsibility for the bombing. When, in April 1911, John J. McNamara, secretary-treasurer of the International Association of Bridge and Structural Iron Workers (BSIW), and his brother, James B. McNamara, were arrested in Indianapolis for the bombing and summarily extradited to California, unionists and Socialists joined in their defense. Job Harriman conferred with the McNamaras while AFL leaders were arranging to retain Clarence Darrow to defend them in court; when Darrow arrived in Los Angeles, Harriman was among the lawyers engaged to assist him. Harriman's connection with the McNamara case enhanced his own popularity among striking metal workers. This communion of concern over the McNamara case helped solidify the political rapprochement between the Socialist Party and the Los Angeles Union Labor Political Club, who agreed on Harriman as their candidate.[40] Harriman's campaign found in the McNamaras' martyrdom an apt rhetorical weapon to use against the incumbent "Good Government" administration of Mayor George Alexander, who had commissioned the investigation that led to the brothers' arrest. Accordingly, campaign manager Irvine hailed the workers whose cause the McNamaras represented. "See the man who clambers aloft and swings the mighty steel beam in the modern structure," he lectured, "that man, my brothers, is fit to build the [new] Jerusalem!"[41] With these themes already prominent in their campaign, Irvine and his Los Angeles comrades were eager to screen pioneering pro-labor films that made the martyrdom of the McNamaras their central theme.

The first of these films, *A Martyr to His Cause*, appeared as the trial began. Produced by the AFL, *A Martyr to His Cause* followed John McNamara's career as a courageous iron worker and a stalwart union official and portrayed his arrest and extradition to California. From the jail cell where he was depicted at the end of the film, McNamara wrote a letter to "The Brotherhood of Organized Labor." Flashed on the screen, the letter assured viewers "That I am innocent of any infraction of the law in word or act needs no emphasis from me, for the truth is mighty and will prevail right speedily. . . . I am also confident that it is not asking too much of the public to suspend judgment in these matters until opportunity for a full and fair defense has been afforded."[42] While it provided a stirring call for a fair trial in the McNamara case, however, *A Martyr to His Cause* lacked the wider perspective of a later film about the trial, *From Dusk to Dawn*.

Though not completed until the McNamara trial and the Harriman campaign were over, *From Dusk to Dawn* resonated with the themes and imagery that linked the two events as object lessons in a socialist vision of justice. The film followed the struggles of two fictional characters—iron molder Dan Grayson and laundress Carla Wayne—who preach workplace safety to unresponsive bosses. Employer carelessness results in an explosion that kills Carla's brother, prompting Dan and Carla to more militant activities. They unionize their shops and undertake a socialist political campaign that wins Dan the California governor's chair. As he presented the saga of Dan and Carla, filmmaker Frank E. Wolfe used clips of Clarence Darrow, the McNamara jurymen, and Socialists involved in the Harriman campaign. He tried to redirect public concern over industrial violence toward the industrial dangers workers encountered on the job and socialist efforts to protect them. Wolfe envisioned *From Dusk to Dawn* as the first of many projects that would "take Socialism before the people of the world on a rising tide of movie popularity."[43] It was a vision aptly suited to Alexander Irvine's developing mission. In concert with Wolfe, Irvine might well have turned his early motion picture projects into a new version of the amalgam of evangelism, class consciousness, and entertainment realized in his stereopticon experiments ten years before.

Before Irvine could forge an alliance with Wolfe, however, the McNamara trial took a turn that destroyed the Harriman campaign. On December 1, 1911, four days before a runoff election between Harriman and Alexander, the McNamara brothers appeared in court to change their pleas to guilty.[44] This about-face resulted from a complicated plea bargain: the defendants agreed to plead guilty before the election, thus delivering a certain victory to Alexander, in exchange for a promise that their lives would be spared. The deal, from which Harriman had been excluded, worked to the mutual favor of the incumbent administration and Los Angeles businessmen who had opposed that administration's Progressive program until the Socialists' ominous success in the primary election. To Irvine, this collusion between the "Good Government" forces supposedly friendly to labor and self-proclaimed enemies of unionism demonstrated again the perfidy of comfortable reformers, long one of his pet lecture themes.[45]

What Irvine found especially exasperating was the seemingly willful self-delusion betrayed by his erstwhile supporter, muckraker Lincoln Steffens, who claimed credit for the deal. Steffens engineered the plea bargain to demonstrate his conviction that Los Angeles's labor strife could be alleviated if both sides adopted a Christian spirit of humility and forgiveness, accepted culpability for the violence their conflict had wrought, and sat down together to hear one another's complaints. He saw an opening when Darrow confessed to increasing pessimism about the outcome of the case. Steffens proposed that Darrow might still save the McNamaras' lives by pursuing his "Christian" strategy: get prominent Los Angeles businessmen to back a bargain whereby the McNamaras pled guilty but went free as a first step in a process of labor-capital reconciliation. Desperate to save the men he had undertaken to defend, Darrow agreed to let Steffens seek support for the plan among southern California business elites, who approved of the idea. They failed to persuade District Attorney John Fredericks to let the McNamaras go unpunished, but they managed to negotiate an agreement in which James McNamara, charged with actually planting the explosives, would get life imprisonment, and his brother John a shorter sentence. Getting the defendants to agree was more difficult. James McNamara preferred to hang rather than countenance a guilty plea from John, a union official whose conviction would disgrace the labor movement that had supported his defense and made him a cinematic martyr. James relented only under Darrow's insistence that no one must die, and with the provisos that John's sentence would be short, that no other suspects in the case would be prosecuted, and that a capital-labor conference would be called in accordance with Steffens' vision.[46]

Steffens then explained the principles behind the deal to the public. He related to reporters covering the trial how he had "determined that the gospel of Christ ought to be applied," and they trumpeted his assessment nationwide:

Los Angeles has done something which, if the people here and in the country at large will understand it aright, must put the ancient controversy between labor and capital on a new and clearer basis forever. This city had labor down; she could have reaped vengeance on its agents, and the leaders and (excepting Job Harriman) the attorneys of labor knew it. But the commanding men in this community didn't do that. They let labor up. And one reason why these capitalists did that was because they knew that they were also at fault. . . .

What the public here will think about it when all the facts are known; what the effect on the election may be, are interesting questions to be answered in the next two or three days. But the questions that I should like to leave on the national mind are just these:

What are we Americans going to do about conditions which are breeding healthy, good tempered boys like these McNamara boys who really believe, as they most sincerely do, they and a growing group of labor, that the only recourse they have for improving the conditions of the wage-worker is to use dynamite against property and life?

And is it possible for a group of employers, well meaning as these are whom we have dealt with in Los Angeles, to understand their employees' point of view, not to take it, mind you, but simply to comprehend it?[47]

As Irvine saw it, the outcome of the election was more than an "interesting question." It was the central factor motivating the businessmen whom Steffens thought he had brought to Christ.

Having worked tirelessly for four months to ensure Harriman's victory, Irvine resented being robbed of success by means of hollow pieties he had often heard from men of wealth who were eager to put him out of a job. What Steffens facilitated, Irvine commented acidly, was nothing more than a masquerade by privileged men who liked their self-interest trimmed in the gilt of a sham righteousness. In a 1912 pamphlet offering a postmortem on the election, Irvine observed:

that bunch of businessmen . . . saw one thing and one only in this Golden Rule business brought to their notice by Steffens, and that was that a plea of "Guilty" would disturb the social mind and bias it against labor. Most of these men . . . carry on a social brigandage against the interests of the working class, and in those conferences with Steffens they saw only a political advantage that could be gotten under the guise of religion.[48]

Irvine allowed that, in the glow of the businessmen's flattery, Steffens probably believed that they had taken up his plan in good faith. He reflected that Steffens "knows now they didn't." Indeed, Steffens admitted that subsequent events demonstrated the treachery of Alexander's business backers. None of the promises made to the McNamaras were kept: the ten-year sentence for John McNamara to which the brothers agreed was extended to fifteen; prosecution of other suspects in the case continued; wage-earners and their employers never convened to listen to one another's perspectives. It was but small consolation that this outcome vindicated Irvine's views about the religious hypocrisy of business elites. He had hoped to inspire a political victory that would demonstrate the hardier religious convictions of unionized workers and Socialists.[49]

Still, though the electoral support for Harriman dissipated in the wake of the McNamaras' guilty pleas, the local socialist circles that Irvine had attached himself to were still intact. Had he remained affiliated with them, Irvine might still have joined in Frank Wolfe's socialist movie plans, which did not yield their first big cinematic product until 1913. Irvine's access to such opportunities was enhanced when, in January 1912, his renown as Harriman's campaign manager carried him into the ranks of the Socialist Party's National Executive Committee (NEC). But, instead of securing his role in the party and its innovations in popular realism, Irvine's rise to national prominence rapidly fractured the ties he had forged during the campaign. As a national official, Irvine became embroiled in the party's intensifying factional battles, and ultimately parted from his California allies. In the process, he found further political fuel for the popular reformulations of class identity he had already begun to imagine in *The Magyar*.

Having joined the NEC along with Harriman, Irvine at first dutifully represented his "constructivist" views. Party "constructivists" propounded a program of gradual social evolution and working-class education that resembled evangelical uplift—the program Irvine had Ruden endorse in *The Magyar*. In the context of internecine socialist battles, this position pitted Irvine against Party "revolutionists," and most directly against William D. Haywood, the IWW national organizer who was also elected to the NEC in January 1912. Harriman and other constructivists reviled Haywood for his insistence that Socialists' dominant strategy should be direct action by industrial workers against their employers, rather than electoral victories. The McNamara case had steeled their hatred by highlighting the deathly violence that right-wing Socialists associated with sabotage, which Haywood deemed indispensable to the class struggle. Haywood exacerbated the tension by unabashedly expressing sympathy for the McNamaras, even after their admission of guilt, when many leaders and members of the AFL repudiated them.[50] Opining that "you can't see the class struggle through the spectacles of capitalist law" like that which condemned the McNamaras, Haywood added insult to injury with constructivist lawyers on the NEC like Morris Hillquit and Job Harriman, who already deplored the IWW leader's contempt for craft unions.[51]

Meanwhile, soon after his election to the NEC, Alexander Irvine had become an editor of the *California Social Democrat*. For several weeks in early 1912 he used the paper's columns to express his own version of the Harrimanite critique of Haywood. In March, the paper carried an Irvine speech on "Los Angeles Socialist Policy," which championed the Harriman campaign's alliance with trade unionists in explicit opposition to Haywood's rhetoric. Haywood, Irvine complained "has a permanent sneer for the intellectual and loses few opportunities of taking a whack at the trade unions. He spreads the sneer and distributes the clubs wherever he goes." Haywood's "impossibilist" insistence on revolutionary industrial unionism only interfered with the successful electoral coalitions that Harriman's constructivist strategies promised.[52] By April 1912, Irvine had a regular front-page column—"A Week in the World"—which he used to attack Haywood and the IWW for their leadership of the free speech fight then underway in San Diego. Trade unionists, Socialists, and the IWW had all joined in the fight against a San Diego ordinance restricting street speaking, and authorities were deploying jails, whips, clubs, and bullets to defeat them. In concert with Hillquit and Harriman, Irvine recommended a careful analysis as to whether the San Diego struggle was a battle "purely along IWW lines" and thus a battle that Socialists should leave the IWW to fight alone.[53]

Then, the following month, Irvine abruptly reversed himself. He devoted nearly half his May 18 column to praise for syndicalist strategies and to Haywood-like questions about the efficacy of political action. Now he declared that syndicalism was "a force that must be reckoned with":

> It works for an industrial revolution. It exists for the benefit of the working class. It has introduced a new method of strike. It puts working-class morality up against capitalist morality. It is fighting the class struggle instead of talking about it. It flouts the ballot probably because labor has acquired so little by that process.

To Socialists who repudiated syndicalism as anarchism that tainted the Party with criminal associations, Irvine responded that "we are fighting for an industrial revolution and not an expurgated edition of the present political democracy."[54] Two weeks later, he recounted the events that explained his change of heart.

In NEC meetings leading up to the Party's May convention in Indianapolis, Irvine had begun assessing William Haywood for himself. "In the meetings of the N.E.C.," Irvine reported, Haywood "was affable, considerate, and as bent on the real thing as any man on the committee. He is like a flame of fire on his specialty, but there is nothing small about him—maybe he is right and we are wrong—maybe it's the other way about, but after ten days of vital daily contact with him I learned to know that he typifies the revolution as mighty few men in our movement do." It was not that Irvine had abandoned his constructivist allies for the Party's revolutionary wing. He also wrote respectfully of Hillquit and Harriman, and still saw himself as an advocate of political action trying to develop a reasoned view of direct action. But he had decided that the rigid opposition to Haywood prevalent within the California Party leadership no longer appealed to him. Appointed to a NEC subcommittee charged with demonstrating how locals could use stereopticon slides and motion pictures to advance socialism, Irvine asked Haywood to deliver an illustrated address on the recent IWW-led Lawrence textile strike. Irvine reported back to California Socialists that Haywood "delivered one of the most powerful addresses I ever heard."[55]

The National Convention in Indianapolis gave further expression to the connections between Irvine's and Haywood's positions, especially as they related to the questions of class identity Irvine was exploring in literature. Attending as NEC members rather than official delegates, both Irvine and Haywood spoke sparingly on the convention floor. Irvine addressed the convention during a debate over the support that Socialists proposed to offer to the participants in San Diego's free speech fight. Intervening in a quarrel over whether to include the IWW among the organizations the convention pledged to defend, Irvine pleaded with delegates to cut to the chase and dig deep into their pockets for an immediate contribution to the combined forces in the San Diego crusade, the IWW included. Though it failed to win a second, Irvine's motion expressed his own changing assessment of the IWW. It also captured the spirit of unity between warring factions of the socialist and labor movements that echoed through the first days of the convention.

This spirit crested on the afternoon of May 16, when the convention discussed and approved the report of the Party's Committee on Labor Organizations. Crafted by Harriman in concert with a committee representing the Party's increasingly hostile factions, the report endorsed the principles of industrial unionism and urged all unions to organize unorganized workers regardless of trade, especially immigrants and the unskilled. But it also disavowed the Party's right or desire "to interfere in any controversies which may exist within the labor union movement over questions of form of organization or technical methods of action in the industrial struggle." Delegates hailed this as a triumph of statesmanship, which bridged the chasms that divided the Party.

The most heartfelt testimonial came from Haywood. Once the convention adopted the report, he declared:

> I can go to the working class, to the eight million women and children, to the four million black men, to the disfranchised white men. . . . I can urge them, and do it from the Socialist platform, to organize the only power that is left to them, their industrial power. . . . To my mind this is the greatest step that has ever been taken by the Socialist party of America. . . . I feel that I can shake hands with every delegate in this convention and say that we are a united working class.[56]

Resounding with concerns for how women, African Americans, and immigrants fit into the socialist cause — concerns *The Magyar* addressed — Haywood's speech articulated the inclusive vision of class solidarity Irvine was trying to work out. As the next day's debates revealed, however, many convention delegates objected to Haywood as the pilot in such a project.

The fellow-feeling generated by the Report on Labor Organizations dissolved into acrimony on May 17. Debates that day focused on an amendment to the Party constitution calling for the expulsion of "any member of the party who opposes political action or advocates crime, sabotage, or other methods of violence as a weapon of the working class." Directed against Haywood by the Party's constructivists, the amendment was assailed by several delegates for its assault on the previous day's harmony. But its supporters prevailed and the amendment was adopted.

Irvine regarded this as a blunder. In the *California Social Democrat*, he summed up the arguments in defense of the sabotage amendment as messages to the working class to "be law abiding men though the law crushes you to powder." Opponents of the amendment, Irvine believed, had recognized rightly that "the fight is not ours, it belongs to the men in industry," a position that echoed the unifying statement on Labor Organizations. Irvine's subsequent reflections on the divisions expressed in the sabotage amendment suggest that it was the dissolution of the Party that bothered him most. Though he had reassessed his constructivist allies' position on Haywood, what he wanted was a socialist public sphere where the alternative methods posed by constructivists and revolutionists could be openly discussed. This was very similar to the vision of the Party that his hero Eugene Debs held privately. But, in the absence of any leader willing or able to check the excesses of the constructivists (who later succeeded, with Debs's support, in recalling Haywood from the NEC) or of the revolutionists (who continued to brandish direct action in defiance of political strategies), it was a vision doomed to disappointment.[57]

For Irvine, the Party's disintegration was the more poignant in that it tore at the ethnic and racial concord his recent novel had envisioned. Haywood's speech on the Report on Labor Organizations was the only statement at the convention even to mention the concerns of African-American workers. The majority and minority reports of the Committee on Immigration might have generated further debates about "race" issues. But these came to the floor after the delegates had already spent their energies debating amendments to their constitution. The convention simply accepted both reports and charged the committee to continue its "scientific" investigations. Appearing as appendixes in the convention proceedings, however, the Immigration Committee reports, accompanied by a statement from Finnish-American committee member Leo Laukki, expressed important racial dimensions to the factional issues that had divided the convention.

The two reports on immigration testified to deepening socialist divisions over issues of "race." The majority report went further than its equivalent of 1910 in trying to dignify exclusive racial categories with the imprimatur of science. It unambiguously defined "race" distinctions as biological differences, identified racism as the product of a natural competition that Socialists could not hope to overcome, described "Asiatics" as "primitive" and "incompatible race elements" that American workers justly feared, and denounced ideals of international brotherhood as "sentimental formulas." The minority report curtly proposed that the convention support the resolution condemning restrictions on immigration based on national or racial grounds that had been passed at the 1907 International Socialist Congress at Stuttgart. These reports did not in themselves link the divisions that they expressed directly to the factionalism pitting constructivists against revolutionaries. Signatories to the minority report like John Spargo and majority report supporters like Victor Berger both supported a gradualist political program and Party alliances with the AFL. However, if socialist ideas about "race" did not necessarily correspond neatly with the Party's factional disputes, Laukki's statement revealed that it was not difficult to see them as intertwined.[58]

Laukki argued that efforts to protect American workers from competition with other "races" extended the exclusive policies of craft unions, who had always tried to shut out more workers than they admitted. "Isolated craftsmen have secluded themselves behind their big initiation fees. . . . May it only be said here that the idea of excluding the Asiatic laborers from America is the same idea and emanates before this convention from the garbage pile of outworn ideas of the A.F. of L." Laukki consigned constructivists to this same heap of "vote catchers" who pandered to AFL prejudices. He proposed a practical alternative designed to achieve in the Party an integration of cultural particularity and class unity similar to what Irvine had been trying to work out in literature. The Party, he insisted, must make meaningful efforts to include Asian immigrants in its ranks by appointing Asian organizers who could address these immigrants in their own languages and thus "help them to become acquainted with Socialist ideas," as it had in the case of European immigrant federations like his own. This vision resonated with Haywoodite criticisms of the Party's political strategies, Haywood's own statement of racial inclusion, and the IWW's recent successes in using foreign language organizers in the Lawrence textile strike. On all counts, Laukki's statement helped to amplify Haywood's appeal to a Socialist with Irvine's sympathies.[59]

Meanwhile, Irvine's growing affection for Haywood severed his socialist alliances in California. The California delegation had voted as a bloc in favor of the amendment on sabotage, and California Socialists and trade unionists were strong advocates of immigrant exclusion. After the convention, the *California Social Democrat* stopped listing him as an editor, and soon his column disappeared as well. Years later he described the disaffection as mutual and less sudden than his about-face on Haywood made it appear. Irvine claimed in retrospect that he had begun questioning Harriman's ideas before the election, when the candidate proved that he was primarily interested in parceling out the spoils of victory.[60] Whatever the origins of the split, it placed Irvine, once again, in a position of ideological and organizational limbo. He found this experience even more dispiriting than previous instances in which he had watched his alliances crumble around him. In New Haven and New York, socialist politics had offered new venues and audiences for his self-representations. Now, the most tangible embodiment of the public for his socialist bildungsroman had dissolved. He was still equipped with the narrative resources that Jack London had urged him to develop, but his own emerging doubts about the evolutionary language London had taught him were also reinforced by the debacle of the 1912 convention.

Fed up with socialist wrangling, Irvine sought the refuge of his Peekskill farm only to find that this, too, had disappeared, buried in a mountain of unpaid mortgage interest. He moved to Stamford, Connecticut, apparently as a guest on socialist millionaire J. G. Phelps Stokes's Connecticut estate. Here he turned back to writing, but no longer with the confident assurance that he could weave socialist convictions into popular evolutionary adventures. He hoped, rather, that out of the dissolution of his political ambitions he might craft a "working formula" for faith, where the "simple, unsophisticated soul . . . confronted with . . . a vast mass of conflicting opinions" would "find rest for her feet." An inspiration came, he recalled later, from a trip to the theater to see former blackface minstrel Chauncey Olcott perform "Mother Machree" in *Barry of Ballymore*, which moved him tremendously. His mother, he recalled, had also left him with a legacy yet unsounded, a wealth of simple sayings that amounted to a philosophy of life. Irvine sat down to record this philosophy in his most popular work, *My Lady of the Chimney Corner*. In the process he clothed his mother, Anna, in a faith that wove together the socialist battles he had recently witnessed, his questions about evolutionary cultural categories, popular theatrical methods on which he had often drawn, and widely shared themes of cultural hierarchy and working-class autonomy on which he had improvised throughout his American mission.[61]

Class and Ethnic Community in My Lady of the Chimney Corner

My Lady of the Chimney Corner marked an important turning point in Irvine's literary self-construction. Its characters had first appeared in a pair of stories he published in June 1911 and January 1912 in the most prestigious of the popular weekly magazines, *McClure's*.[62] These pieces demonstrated Irvine's continued viability in the literary market while introducing the Irish community around whom he would organize a new persona. But it was only when he developed these characters into the book-length memoir that appeared in 1913 that Irvine found ways to use them to resolve his political quandaries through a reformulation of his public self. The magazine pieces had emphasized the deficiencies of the social pit that characterized his earlier autobiographical self-constructions. In contrast, while *My Lady*'s characters are poor in the amenities that tantalized culturally ambitious youths like Irvine and London, they are mainly fonts of ethnic camaraderie and commonplace wisdom. As the central focus of *My Lady*, Irvine's mother Anna is the primary voice for its folksy morals, which draw on popular entertainment to address various contradictions within Irvine's ideals of Christian faith and socialist solidarity.

Anna's signature statement—"love is enough"—answers the false social distinctions expressed in the sectarian battles of Irvine's childhood. Anna first utters this motto at the beginning of the memoir as a challenge to the prejudices that drove her to abandon her hometown after the scandal of her Protestant-Catholic marriage. When asked by her new husband, Jamie, what they should do about religion, the once devoutly Catholic Anna responds that love is "bigger than colour of ribbon or creed of church . . . bigger than religion." Henceforth her religion will rest on two assurances: "One is love of God. He loves all His children and gets huffed at none. The other is that the love we have for each other is of the same warp and woof as His for us, and *love is enough*, Jamie." At the end of *My Lady*, Anna reiterates this connection between her love for Jamie and her disdain for credal divisions. This time she answers Alexander's adolescent, church-trained concern for the safety of her soul in a letter to the Holy Land, apparently quoted whole. "Don't worry about our souls," she admonishes, in response to the stern evangelical pieties he had recently embraced. "When we come one by one in the twilight of life, each of us, Jamie and I, will have our sheaves. They will be little sheaves, but we are little people. I want no glory here or hereafter that Jamie cannot share." Throughout the book, Anna elaborates her theology of love, with its mixture of kinship and divinity, in ways that address not only Antrim's religious battles, but many of the social and cultural divisions Irvine had encountered since he had left her corner.[63]

Prominent in Anna's gospel, nostalgic Irish identity is an important thread weaving together the strands of conflict the memoir addresses. The almost saccharine stage-Irish dialogue between Anna and her neighbors is one of the most striking (and, for some readers, nauseating) qualities of the book, and accents Irvine's long-established affinity for popular theatrical effects. Irvine's literary "Mother Machree" employs many of the cultural conventions that popular theater had invested in the image of Irish mother-love. Almost echoing the lines of the Olcott ballad that inspired it, the scene of Alexander's parting from Anna to sail for the New World expresses this kinship with particular transparency. In reply to Anna's worry that "Maybe ye'll get rich an' forget," he declares, "Yes, I shall be rich. I shall be a millionaire—a millionaire of love, but no one shall ever take your place, dear!" Of course, Irvine drew here on theatrical pieties that were not confined to stage portrayals of the Irish. Like the songs of Paul Dresser, in which wandering and fallen sons and daughters bathetically recall the affections of hard-working rural mothers, Irvine depicts Anna's wisdom as deeper in meaning for having once been forsaken. This was a stock image in sentimental culture, whatever its ethnic hue. Still, Irvine's liberal use of dialect stamped Anna's love as Irish in origin, associated with immigrant longings for a specific home. Though Anna articulates knowledge drawn from all of Irvine's far-flung experiences, her poignant expressions use a stagey Irish brogue that ties her ideals to a nostalgically rendered local context. She reminds neighbors that Christ's works "can be done in Antrim by any poor craither who's got th' Spirit." And, asked by her son to define her religion for him as he leaves for America, she quips "All in all, it's bein' kind an' lovin' kindness. *That* takes in God an' maan an' Pogue's Entry, an th' world."[64] Such sentimental colloquy meshed perfectly with the nostalgic sketches of Irish life that, by the time of *My Lady*, had come to dominate Hibernian caricature on the vaudeville stage.

But Irvine's stage-Irish sentimentality had significance beyond its theatrical resonances. It connected immigrant nostalgia to popular discourses of class, racial, and ethnic division he had lately been reevaluating. The ascendancy of the sentimental Irish on stage was partly the product of Irish-American efforts to dissociate their image from the "uncivilized" characteristics of groups they had come to regard as beneath them in America's racial hierarchy, as well as from insufficiently refined members of their own ethnic community. Irvine had evinced some of this racial superiority in his autobiography, but had since begun to rethink this hierarchy and revise the way he wielded ethnic culture within it. *My Lady of the Chimney Corner* continued this process by associating stage-Irish dialect with the plebeian camaraderie of the Irvine cabin—a gathering of convivial neighbors whose debates translate into Hibernian tones of the cross-racial comradeship of Nell's cottage in *The Magyar*. *My Lady*'s most vivid scenes take place around Anna's chimney corner, where neighbors surround a kettle of broth or a pot of "tay," swapping stories based on Celtic legends or trading gossip on the latest news concerning Antrim's working poor. These conversations reveal the texture of comradeship among Irish laborers whose wages afford little else to entertain them. As they share food, peat, and tobacco, retell stories of the Banshee and Leprechaun, and toss drained tea cups to read the fortunes revealed in their scattered leaves, they express their understanding of material need through a common folk culture. When Anna tosses Jamie's cup and sees "a wee bit of garden wi' a fence aroun' it," he ventures an interpretation shaped by the confines of a poor cobbler's cabin: "Wud that be Savage givin' us a bit of groun' next year t' raise pirtas?" Throughout, *My Lady* uses the common beat of a brogue on the tongue to articulate the common want of brogues for the feet.[65]

Imagining Irish ethnicity as a cultural fellowship of the working poor, Irvine depicted this culture as a unifying bond that permitted the expression of conflicting visions of camaraderie. With fortunes, stories, and maxims, Anna sets her listeners' sights on the possibilities of gradual change. In tea leaves she reads the day-to-day hopes of nineteenth-century Irish life: a bit of land to raise potatoes, or a letter from a relative removed to Scotland or America. The stories she trades with visitors and improvises on Celtic legend reveal a domain full of fairy agents of magical transformation: Leprechauns grant wishes, a Banshee signals coming death. A similar theme runs through Anna's religious and ethical philosophy. Celebrating the appearance of God at the end of every tether and the advantages of seeing and speaking about the good rather than the bad in people, her moral mottoes point to the small changes that her neighbors might effect in a world of slender resources. Anna relies primarily on the tools of imagination and attitude to produce these glosses on the possibilities of change. These are her levers for transforming want into comradeship. With optimism inspired by "wee people" who can alter the course of human fate, tea cup hieroglyphs that foretell the future, and a loving God who provides for the poor, Anna coaxes those around her chimney corner to think a little better of the lot they share.[66]

Throughout *My Lady*, Anna urges her vision of uplift against the alternative notion of fellowship offered by Willie Withero, the genial stonebreaker who drops in every Sunday for "tay" and a "crack" with the Irvines. Withero bases his version of fraternity on the inherent worth of work performed rather than attitudes about the worker or magical notions about a spirit world that might aid him or her. In fact, from Withero's perspective, such attitudes and notions interfere with true fellow-feeling. Against Anna's use of Celtic lore to raise courage and enhance good-will, Withero points out that fanciful ideas may damn as easily as praise, and obscure the intrinsic value of honest labor either way. He has firsthand experience with such misrepresentation, having gained a reputation for the uncanny capacity to "blink" a cow so she can give no milk. Withero has no patience for Anna's attempts to turn the superstitions of folk legend to friendly ends, as in the case of the beggar Hughie Thornton. When Hughie's reputed ability to "blink" a cow places him in danger of being stoned to death in an Antrim field, Anna turns the tables for him by spreading a rumor that the beggar is of an ancient line, wandering in search of the Holy Grail and recording the deeds of the poor as he goes. This manipulation of attitude draws gifts for Hughie from all but Withero, who will have no "palaver about an' oul throllop what niver earned salt t' 'is pirtas."[67]

For Willie, the substance of fellowship lies in mutual regard for the work that does earn salt. Willie rejects all compromises of this tangible comradeship, including the titular "Misther" condescendingly offered to Antrim laborers by their purported superiors ("only quality calls me 'Misther,' an' I don't like it—it doesn't fit an honest stonebreaker") as well as the imagined nobility lent by legend to enhance sympathy among the poor. As he explains to the newly married Anna and Jamie at the beginning of the book, he finds in an anthill an apt model of human fellowship:

What's this world but an ant-hill? . . . Jist a big ant-hill and we're ants begorra an' uncles, but instead ov workin' like these wee fellas do—help aych other an' shouldther aych other's burdens, an' build up th' town, an' forage fur fodder, begobs we cut aych other's throats over th' colour ov ribbon or th' kind ov a church we attind! Ugh, what balderdash! . . . Now mind ye, I'm not huffed at th' churches, aither Orange or Green, or th' praychers aither—tho 'pon m' sowl ivery time I luk at wan o' thim I think ov God as a first-class journeyman tailor! But I get more good switherin' over an ant-hill than whin wan o' thim wee praychers thry t' make me feel as miserable as th' divil!

Directed explicitly at sectarian religious rivalries, Withero's anthill sermon illustrates his implicit challenge to all notions that might dilute the alliances inherent in honest work.[68]

The debate between Anna and Withero recapitulates several different contests between cultural hierarchy and working-class autonomy that Irvine had negotiated in the American public sphere. Irvine's early missionary efforts had followed Anna's methods of inculcating faith and fellowship. Drawing on a complex heritage of evangelical self-improvement, his training in history, art, and literature, as well as the arts of storytelling he had enjoyed in his parents' home, Irvine tried to set the sights of his working-class flocks beyond their immediate privations. But, to his dismay, the institutions that employed him in this endeavor often conceived of themselves as possessing funds of sanctity to be sparingly distributed or carefully guarded. This view of spiritual values contradicted the teachings of what Irvine came to call the "gospel of work," a set of ideals embodied in the daily lives and occupations of his working-class audiences. The gospel of work elaborated the worth of laboring lives not for what they might become through the offices of others, but for the intrinsic worth of the work they performed. Moved to forge this alternative gospel as he entered the economic and political struggles waged by his working-class congregations, Irvine found that the gospel of work imposed its own limitations. Offended at the condescension and possessiveness of much middle-class piety and culture, proponents of the gospel of work sometimes scoffed at the spiritual, artistic, or literary disciplines claimed by the materially privileged. Withero's cynicism about superstitions and sectarian beliefs gives voice to such disdain, which Irvine could never wholly embrace.

Anna and Willie also speak to the factional battles that had torn Irvine's socialist faith. They both measure human worth by standards that honor the dignity of their own impoverished community, but they differ, as did Harriman and Haywood, over the appropriate strategy for cultivating these standards at large. Anna's strategy is one of patient and gradual education drawing on a wide variety of cultural resources, from fairy stories to Bible verses to commercial story papers. Withero articulates more class-specific ideals. Echoing Haywood, Withero even derives these ideals from manual labor itself. "A good day's stone breakin' 's my prayer," he tells the young Alexander.[69] As *My Lady* is primarily a celebration of Anna's philosophy, she gets the last word. But the common bonds of Irish identity that pervade the book provide cords of fellow-feeling that allow for the articulation of both strategies by weaving hierarchical ideals and autonomous standards, constructivism and revolutionism into a nostalgic web of ethnic culture.

The cloak of Irish mother-love that Irvine wove specifically for Anna spoke to the domestic crises and gender politics he had recently encountered. In the wake of Maude's breakdown and the dispersal of his children, Irvine could take solace in the nostalgic image of Anna as the center of a family harried by material want, yet united by the love she provided. At the same time, the idealized feminine character Irvine concocted for her expressed ambiguities in his pronouncements on the politics of gender. Irvine vacillated between urging women to new public prominence and defining their public roles in the moral terms of a feminine domestic sphere he had earlier deprecated. His recent efforts in Los Angeles revealed some of the perils of such ambivalence. During the Harriman campaign, Irvine helped rally socialist support for the cause of woman suffrage, but also extolled feminine purity and excoriated capitalism for forcing women out of the home into the workplace. In the final election, many women reportedly voted for "purity" by repudiating the socialist ticket as tainted with "an element of hoodlumism."[70] In contrast, Irvine's depiction of Anna in *My Lady* reassuringly reconciled domesticity and class consciousness. Submerged in her stage-Irish enclave—seeking "no glory" her husband cannot share—Anna personifies domesticity calibrated to the demands of class solidarity.[71]

But Anna is not merely an Irish angel on the hearth; she is also a capable spokeswoman for her working-class community. She is Madeline Ruden, Nell Palmer, and Ethel Ainsworth. Anna unambiguously renounces all of the snobbery that Madeline exhibited at the beginning of *The Magyar*, but she retains Madeline's fierce protection of her domestic circle. Though, like Nell, she spends much of her life brewing tea to wet the comradely debates entertained in this circle, she also uses some of Ethel's skills to defend its members against condescending intruders. When she delivers her sharp rebuke to the tract distributor for acting "like a petty sessions-magistrate" and making "my bhoy feel like a thief," Jamie compares her to a notorious contemporary barrister. The compliment suggests that Irvine saw Anna wielding within the domestic sphere skills that New Women of the early twentieth century were claiming as public rights.

Within the ethnic bonds of kin and culture he wove around her—his public sphere writ small—perhaps this prospect was not so threatening to Irvine's conflicted visions of manhood and womanhood.[72]

In a sense, the Anna of *My Lady* could combine public and domestic womanhood because she was as spiritual as she was historical—a Catholic Virgin Mother who renders religion kind and homely by mediating between God and man. This dimension of Anna's image in *My Lady* gave literary shape to Irvine's misgivings about having been fated to seek a democratic faith through Protestant means, when the Catholic Church often seemed more responsive to the working-class audiences his mission addressed. In the memoir, Anna fulfills Irvine's religious ideals by working miracles in her own alley and corner. As she explains to Withero, she has seen the Son of Man every day of her life: "I've more'n seen 'im. I've made tay fur 'im, an' broth on Sunday. I've mended 'is oul duds, washed 'is dhirty clothes, shuk 'is han', stroked 'is hair an' said kind words to 'im!" This rendition of the gospel injunction, "Whin ye do it t' wan o' these craithers ye do it t' me!" sums up practices of plebeian sainthood in which *My Lady* figured the abiding spiritual significance of Irvine's own cultural politics.[73]

Altogether, the vignettes of *My Lady of the Chimney Corner* offered a much rosier picture of Irvine's early experiences than he had provided in *From the Bottom Up*. There Anna had appeared as a "kind-hearted old mother" so addicted to drink that she could offer little more than bewildered enthusiasm to support her son's aspirations toward self-improvement. Though *My Lady* substantially revised this image, however, it still bore the marks of the experiments in self-representation that had produced the various versions of Irvine's autobiographical bildungsroman. Through these successive narratives, and the public debates over cultural standards and distinctions that shaped them, Irvine had crafted a substitute for Jack London's naturalist social pit. Where the social pit had been in previous renditions of his story, Irvine now put the ethnic community, whose combined social, personal, and religious meaning he had concocted as he sought his own identity in the genre of investigative disguise. But the bildungsroman narrative leading from poverty through self-improvement and disillusionment to a mature collective consciousness remained. In *My Lady*, the ethnic community's comradely wisdom constituted the collective sensibility to which the erring striver must return, after learning that what looked like more sophisticated creeds are not what they seem.

While *My Lady* helped resolve Irvine's uneasiness with socialist politics of race and ethnicity, however, it did not thereby provide a workable socialist vision of its own. *My Lady*'s depiction of ethnic bonds as the cultural sustenance of the working poor went beyond many contemporary socialist debates. As prefigured in the cross-racial camaraderie of *The Magyar*, *My Lady*'s Irish community recognized ethnic fellow-feeling as part of working-class culture without invoking exclusive, evolutionary levels of civilization. But, in the process, it also equated class solidarity with community boundaries that competed with the trade unionist and socialist ideals Irvine advocated. In the years and decades to come, ethnic fellow-feeling was often the breeding ground for working-class militancy in America. But appeals to ethnic "community" have also been deployed to oppose militancy as well as the cross-racial solidarity on which Irvine came to believe it should be based. As Sylvester Poli's New Haven maneuvers demonstrated, ethnic "community" was itself a contested ideal, marshaled to diverse ends of cultural improvement and class solidarity by rival groups within particular ethnic populations. It did not lend itself to a timeless vision of working-class unity standing independent of the kinds of publics and debates from which Irvine had forged *My Lady*. Moreover, the book itself could be read in the light of new debates and its author's reputation used to social ends rather different from those that inspired it, as Irvine would find in the 1920s.[74]

Whatever its strengths and weaknesses as a political vision, however, the device of locating adult convictions in childhood influences worked well for Irvine as a popular literary device. By the time of his death in 1941, *My Lady of the Chimney Corner* had appeared in several editions in the United States and Britain. Its readers often saw in the memoir a charming document of life among the Irish lowly and of abiding mother-love. Irvine encouraged such readings by subtitling the book "a story of love and poverty in Irish peasant life" and identifying it in a "Foreword" as "the torn manuscript of the most beautiful life I ever knew." "I have merely pieced and patched it together," he claimed, "and have not even changed or disguised the names of the little group of neighbours who lived with us, at 'the bottom of the world.'"[75] This declaration that *My Lady* accurately represented a plebeian world reclaimed through memory is not without foundation. Many of *My Lady*'s characters appear in documents such as the 1862 Valuation of Tenements, which listed the owners, occupants, lessors, and ratable worth of Antrim's lands and buildings. Read in this way—as in Chapter 1 of this book—Irvine's memoir gives voice and substance to lives that "official" documents often registered as mute entries.[76]

But as a narrative, a work of self-fashioning as much as recall, *My Lady* also reveals much more. It shows what Irvine had made of his trajectory—that it had provoked him to reconstruct proletarian affiliations in terms of a sentimental nostalgia for an ethnically conceived community. This *was* a kind of guise, though not a sense that renders the sentiment, the ethnicity, or the community any less "real" than Irvine claimed they were. These elements of Irvine's memoir constituted a new construction of the "real," shorn of evolutionary languages of racial inferiority, prefiguring a twentieth-century vision of pluralistic cultural difference. To conceive of this alternative, Irvine himself had undertaken many disguises, as he donned the costumes and the language of cultural distinction his contemporaries conceived through contending visions of hierarchy and autonomy. Like the popular theatrical realm that played such visions against one another and offered models for some of the self-representations through which Irvine evaluated them, the reality of these distinctions was the product of multiple perspectives on cultural difference—the product of a complex and dynamic popular public sphere.

As Irvine's most affecting statement of the connections among religion, theater, and class politics he had discovered in that sphere, *My Lady* occupies many historical registers at once. It looks back to reclaim the complex heritage of evangelical personalism that fueled his earliest ambitions, recapturing the thrill of conversion as an ineffable bond between sainted mother and anointed son. In ways that the next chapter addresses more fully, it looks forward to replace the evolutionary hierarchies that Irvine deployed as an author and propagandist with a popular version of cultural relativism. Finally, it draws liberally from its own contemporary public sphere—the networks of cultural debate and popular representation that Irvine had been combining for over a decade.

Insofar as *My Lady* elaborates theatrical themes in this sphere, it does so in sentimental terms that were being displaced in the realm of the popular stage itself. But Irvine was not one to remain out of touch with the wellsprings of his own public appeal, at least not yet. In 1913, he again revised his socialist bildungsroman by adapting his negotiations of hierarchy and autonomy, pleasure and piety, political and industrial action to themes more in keeping with popular theatrical fashions. In the process, he briefly became a vaudeville fashion himself.

CHAPTER EIGHT

TO "CHANGE THE FACE OF CIVILIZATION"
Religion, Popular Theater, and the Politics of Culture

IN 1913, ALEXANDER IRVINE was in New York City on a summer respite from a dispiriting job teaching literature and counseling students at the Culver Military Academy in Indiana. He did not object to shaping the minds and moral mettle of young men. His own preoccupations with educational self-improvement and masculine self-assertion had prepared him well for such duties. But he found the school's pretensions to rigid military discipline trying. In New York, he welcomed opportunities for more genial self-presentations as lecturer for the ISS and occasional guest preacher at evening church services. At St. Mark's Episcopal Church one evening, a theatrical manager—probably one of Sylvester Poli's UBO associates—witnessed Irvine's dramatic skill. "You held that crowd spellbound for an hour *without scenery*," Irvine remembered him exclaiming afterward. "I saw the choir girls stick their chewing gum under their chairs and stare at you with rapt attention." Irvine was not surprised. After years of practice in the pulpit and on the lecture circuit, he was accustomed to seeing audiences "paralyzed with astonishment," as one Michigan spectator had put it. The manager pressed his case. The spell Irvine cast in the church could carry his message to much larger numbers in vaudeville. He offered to have a playlet writer prepare a script if Irvine would agree to take the leading role. Irvine demurred—he wanted to deliver his message in a dramatic vehicle of his own devising. The manager was dubious—he preferred a writer more familiar with popular theatrical conventions. But, ten days later, Irvine presented his patron with a one-act drama, "The Rector of St. Jude's," that was cleverly attuned to current vaudeville trends. The manager determined to put it into production at once.[1]

In his vaudeville playlet, Irvine temporarily abandoned the themes of ethnic community that dominated *My Lady of the Chimney Corner*, but he addressed many of the cultural dilemmas for which his memoir had sought nostalgic resolution. "The Rector of St. Jude's" offered a dramatized sermon that linked religion and cultural refinement to industrial class conflict. As he toured the country with this act, Irvine reestablished connections among religious debate, working-class militancy, and entertainment that had long shaped his approach to questions of class and culture. He also highlighted links between the public identity he had forged in adulthood and the cultural contests that characterized Sylvester Poli's entertainment world. "The Rector of St. Jude's" thus provides an apt springboard for observations about the wider perspective on changes in American cultural politics that Irvine's and Poli's intersecting careers offer.

Vaudeville Playlets, Preacher-Thespians, and Cultural Politics

Irvine could easily compose a suitable vaudeville playlet because he was well versed in the themes that vaudeville addressed. While the ethnic and domestic sentimentality of his recent memoir were fading, though still visible, vaudeville motifs, his ongoing formulations of the gospel of work suited current vaudeville fashions. Several contemporary playlets celebrated the moral rectitude of urban workers. Though vaudeville writing guides warned authors away from playlets advocating "causes," there were also precedents for what critics called Irvine's "capital and labor" skit. The same labor paper that enthusiastically reported Irvine's campaign work in Los Angeles touted a playlet entitled "The Union Label" that featured a self-confident forelady—"a splendid type of the class-conscious worker," according to *The Citizen*—who rebuffed her boss's offer of gifts in exchange for sexual favors and joined the Garment Workers' local to win a union contract for her shop. Another contemporary playlet, "The Bishop's Candlesticks," drew from one of Irvine's favorite literary models for socialist propaganda, Victor Hugo's *Les Miserables*.[2]

As vaudeville playlets multiplied, they attracted many writers connected to Irvine's concerns outside the theater. In 1903, Sylvester Poli's New Haven theater featured "Her First Divorce Case," penned by Single Tax advocate and New Thought poet Ella Wheeler Wilcox, a friend of both Maude and Alexander Irvine. In Wilcox's playlet, an accomplished woman lawyer tries to reconcile a husband and wife who consult her separately about a divorce but still love one another. The playlet form also tempted English writer J. M. Barrie, who later befriended Irvine and whose mother-memoir, *Margaret Ogilvey*, was often compared to *My Lady of the Chimney Corner*. During the same years that Irvine toured with "The Rector of St. Jude's," Barrie's "The Twelve Pound Look," brought to vaudeville by its star, Ethel Barrymore, became a hit with audiences and critics. Barrymore played a sprightly, independent stenographer assigned the task of typing a speech for her ex-husband, a pompous, self-made man preparing to be knighted. The stenographer explains that, to escape her former spouse's condescending superiority, she had saved twelve pounds to buy a typewriter, learned to use it, and set off to make her own way in the world. Wilcox's and Barrie's playlets featured images of female independence that Irvine had explored in literature and that his own playlet ambiguously endorsed. Like *The Magyar*—as well as "The Twelve Pound Look" and "The Union Label"—"The Rector of St. Jude's" embellished the ideal of female independence with a moral twist, suggesting that women should reject any finery or cultural pretension that compromised social ideals.[3]

Irvine's vaudeville tour also echoed the efforts of other preachers who had turned to literature and the stage. The most famous of these was Thomas E. Dixon, the former Baptist minister who worked his novels of Reconstruction into a successful play that became the basis for D. W. Griffith's cinematic blockbuster of racist national regeneration, *The Birth of a Nation*. Vaudeville critics compared Irvine and Dixon, but did not elaborate on the cultural complexities the comparison entailed. The son of a struggling preacher in post–Civil War North Carolina, Dixon had turned to the ministry in the late 1880s after experimenting with acting, the law, and politics. By the early 1890s, he had attained a comfortable post as minister of the Twenty-Third Street Baptist Church. Moved to address the unchurched masses, Dixon anticipated several of the religious experiments that Irvine instituted a decade later in New Haven. He enlivened services with theatrical effects, repelled the "feminization" of Protestant religion by boldly addressing "public" questions of "masculine" interest, and even abandoned his denomination for a "Church of the People" when the strictures of more orthodox preaching became too confining. But Dixon rode such cultural currents in different directions than Irvine. Dixon's "People's Church" derived in part from a failed plan to build a large temple in downtown Manhattan that he had hatched with the support of John D. Rockefeller. And, contrary to Irvine's gospel of work, Dixon's sermons celebrated Dewey's victory at Manila, lionized Theodore Roosevelt, and castigated all visions of socialist collectivism as naive idealism laced with sexual indecency. Like Dwight Moody, Billy Sunday, and the New York City Mission and Tract Society, Dixon's religious vision stressed individual improvement within the prevailing social order, and drew little on the plebeian veins of evangelical ferment that Irvine tapped.[4]

Dixon's and Irvine's trajectories away from the pulpit into popular culture also provide illuminating comparisons. Both men published their first books through

the aegis of Walter Hines Page of Doubleday-Page. Dominated by Frank Doubleday's entrepreneurial spirit, this newcomer to the world of publishing treated
the book trade as a business aimed at a mass audience, just as mass magazine
publishers treated periodicals. Dixon caught the firm's attention as a likely seller
when he sent Page the first of his Reconstruction-era historical novels, *The Leopard's Spots*, in 1902. The phenomenal success of this novel and its 1905 sequel,
The Clansman, betrayed a popular taste for racial imagery with which Irvine
experimented to different ends. Dixon deployed his version of the evolutionary
vernacular to drive home his unyielding view that African Americans were ani-
malistic beasts and sexual predators who must be separated from whites before
they ruined feminine virtue and destroyed "Anglo Saxon" civilization. Like
Irvine, Dixon extolled manly vigor, but did not associate this quality with the
social pit or attribute it to black characters, as in *The Magyar*. Instead, Dixon
mixed his evolutionary racism with the tradition of historical romance associated
with Sir Walter Scott, a style that enjoyed a wave of popularity among audiences
fatigued with literary realism's grim social visions. Moreover, Dixon alternated
his Reconstruction novels with fictionalizations of his antisocialist views. Though
controversial, this mix made profits for his publisher and a fortune for Dixon,
who augmented his wealth with stage versions of his novels and the cinematic
triumph of *The Birth of a Nation*.[5]

Meanwhile, Irvine wondered why his one Doubleday-Page title, *From the Bottom Up*, was not more aggressively marketed. Though the memoir's racial politics came closer than any of Irvine's other works to Dixon's racist hierarchy, it
found virtue in social arenas that the firm's chiefs had deemed insufficiently "literary" in other cases. In 1900, Doubleday-Page had reluctantly published and
then failed to advertise *Sister Carrie*, which Doubleday regarded as immoral and
Page saw as filled with "unfortunate" characters. Moreover, while Irvine's treatment of the evolutionary vernacular sold stories, it did not produce the commercial bonanza that Dixon's less self-reflective formulas did. Unlike Dixon,
Irvine had little hope of transforming his literary successes into scripts for the
legitimate theater, where producers ventured greater financial risks and looked
for surer rewards than did agents for individual vaudeville acts. Vaudeville's traditions of cultural contest—and its professed, if erratic, standards of decency and
inoffensiveness—were more hospitable to Irvine's cultural queries.[6]

The vaudeville preacher/actor Edwards Davis prefigured Irvine's vaudeville
stint in ways that further illuminate the wider cultural politics he engaged on
stage. Formerly a minister in Oakland, California, Davis had abandoned the pulpit to present some of vaudeville's first dramatic playlets.[7] As Irvine prepared for

his vaudeville debut, Davis was touring vaudeville circuits with his poetic drama, "The Kingdom of Destiny." In the publicity for this popular poetic saga, Davis articulated ideals of cultural democracy and vigorous literature that were vital to Irvine's mission as well:

> Poetry, as the exclusive luxury of the elect few, has failed to be utilized for all that it is worth to the unelected many. I want a new poetry to be written that will have a punch in it for the masses—an uplift in it that will raise the many that are oppressed with discouragement into the height of mental exhilaration and social content. . . . What we need today in our new poetry is more thought, not more gush; a message from the heart of truth, not a message from a dewdrop in a dell; a challenge to damn petty deceits that may glorify our big ambitions.[8]

Through democratically available elegance, Davis believed, vaudeville theaters distributed big artistic ambitions to the masses. Since "that which is beautiful is not far from divine," he claimed, vaudeville could serve religious causes that elite churches, like elite poets, had forsaken.[9]

As he elaborated his theatrical perspective, however, Davis betrayed contradictions within vaudeville's "democracy" and the wider social relations that shaped it. Celebrating vaudeville magnates for lifting their entertainments above variety show "vulgarity," Davis identified them as benefactors who "have given as much to society as Carnegie, Rockefeller, and Vanderbilt." While such comparisons surely pleased vaudeville's corporate leaders, they obscured the more complex engagement with cultural conflicts over hierarchies of class and ethnicity that local vaudeville managers like Poli engaged. In equating vaudeville's cultural contributions with Carnegie's and Rockefeller's philanthropy, Davis also neglected the efforts to democratize culture that Irvine had found in working-class organizations. Davis's reflections on the intellectual level of theatrical audiences illustrated his disdain for the kinds of alliances out of which Irvine had crafted his own cultural politics. Davis's theatrical publicity quoted his observation that when theater failed to please audiences, "the fault is frequently with the mediocrity of the proletariat . . . the stupefied brains of the lazily content."[10] Of course, Irvine questioned working-class intellectual acumen too, but he also tried to meld cultural self-improvement with existing forms of working-class solidarity. As he ventured into vaudeville, Irvine infused Davis's "divinely inspired" struggle for democratic beauty with the gospel of work he had forged throughout his career. The result reproduced cultural debates that had long linked his mission to the vaudeville show.

"The Rector of St. Jude's" and Its Audiences

The plot of "The Rector of St. Jude's" drew on Irvine's struggles as a minister at New Haven's Pilgrim Church and New York's Church of the Ascension. Irvine evoked the class tensions he had encountered at these institutions by placing the playlet's title character, Dr. Gordon, in the midst of a strike being waged against one of his vestrymen. The curtain rose to reveal Dr. Gordon, played by Irvine, preparing for a service in his vestry. A telephone call notifies him that the daughter of one of the strikers—a former communicant at St. Jude's—has died after being shot by militiamen charged with protecting the vestryman's factory. The factory owner, Mr. Stuyvesant, enters at this point and demands Dr. Gordon's resignation from St. Jude's. His grounds for this demand present an exaggerated version of the complaints that Ascension vestrymen had lodged against Irvine: "the news has been flashed over every state of the union that the rector of St. Jude's is in sympathy with the rabble and scum of the city!"[11]

At this point Irvine embellished the romantic dimensions of his own story. Stuyvesant reveals that his consternation derives not only from Gordon's class loyalties but also from the rector's intimacy with his daughter, Marjory. He suggests that this relationship might continue if Gordon revises his social opinions. Both Gordon and Marjory, now arrived on the scene, assail Stuyvesant's willingness to reduce religion and fatherhood to a cash nexus. A debate ensues as to who most clearly grasps the links between religious morality and industrial relations. Stuyvesant contends that his employees, his daughter, and his church all benefit from his competence in business affairs. Marjory claims that it is really Stuyvesant who relies on his workers for his position, and declares her intention to renounce the benefits he provides unless he accedes to his employees' demands. Gordon rejects Stuyvesant's conception of God as a "cash register for capitalism" and demands his removal from St. Jude's. This argument proceeds in circles until Bill Taggert—the father of the girl slain by the militia—arrives to shift the terms of the debate.[12]

Taggert seeks to avenge his daughter's death by killing Stuyvesant, whom he sees as the embodiment of all the social conditions that oppress him. These include the existence of a militia empowered to kill his daughter, a church whose members dress in "glad rags made out of . . . sweated slaves," and a working class harried and hungered by men of wealth who—in Irvine's complaint about his own childhood—offer their employees less than they provide their horses and dogs. With Taggert's arrival, Gordon takes up the task of interpreting the workingman's anger to Stuyvesant while trying to redirect this anger into political action. Gordon explains that "the rebellion of hell" seething in the striker's breast is produced by the brutal instrument that Stuyvesant calls the law. But—in another of Irvine's narrative efforts to mediate between Haywood and Harriman—he also insists that it is not Stuyvesant as an individual but the system that produced him that Taggert must try to eliminate. The playlet ends with Gordon proclaiming:

> Our fight is to abolish the whip altogether! There shall be no slaves and no master. With violence you may make the streets run red and accomplish nothing. By the power of a great ideal and a combined working-class vote, you can change the face of civilization!!!"[13]

As in *My Lady of the Chimney Corner*, Irvine's playlet gave "constructivist" methods of idealistic gradualism preference over "revolutionist" direct action. Still, on stage as in his memoir, Irvine created a conversation that articulated both points of view. Instead of weaving bonds of ethnic sentimentality to contain this debate, "The Rector of St. Jude's" relied on vaudeville's tradition of cultural contest and repartee to provide a common public for divergent values.

Like Irvine's Irish memoir, "The Rector of St. Jude's" recapitulated conflicts that had shaped his mission for half a century. In the argument between Gordon and Stuyvesant, Irvine reproduced his conflicts with the lay leaders of the churches where he had preached his gospel of work. As Gordon explains to Stuyvesant, the two have opposed views of why the rector was hired at St. Jude's: "From your point of view, I was hired to be good, to keep quiet and cover your piracy with the cloak of religion. From my point of view I came to interpret God—to teach virtue, truth and kindness!"[14] With chicanery ranging from corruption of political officials to reliance on a violent militia to control his workers, Gordon goes on to point out, Stuyvesant has left the rector no choice but to side with Taggert and his fellows. This analysis summed up Irvine's discontent with the self-righteous positions taken on temporal issues by the Pilgrim Church leaders, the Ascension vestrymen, and the pious hypocrites of Los Angeles who had bartered the Golden Rule to defeat the Socialists. Like Irvine, Gordon not only endorses the strikers' material demands, but links them to Christian teachings that other church leaders only honor in the breach.

In addition to providing a romantic interest, Marjory Stuyvesant presents Irvine's characteristically confused vision of women's part in a gospel he defined in masculine terms. She declares to her father, "as for my friendship for Dr. Gordon, take that away and you take away my life!"[15] Generously interpreted, this proclamation refers as much to the Christian ideals Gordon expounds as to the man himself. Even so, Marjory's dependence on Gordon for access to these ideals severely limits the range of her own moral efficacy. Aside from endorsing Gordon's righteousness, Marjory suggests that the material abundance with which women were increasingly associated in the theater was tainted by the exploitative labor relations out of which their finery was produced. Even in articulating this position, she expresses a curtailed vision of her own agency. Upon hearing the news that Bill Taggert's daughter has died, Marjory wails, "Oh my God, and to think of it, a poor little slave who had nothing should die that I, an idler, might have more than I need." But the "more" she repents of enjoying consists of luxuries her father provides. There is no hint that other women of her class—notably the women of the National Consumer's League, whose president Florence Kelley had taken part in Irvine's Ascension services—organized themselves as shoppers who based consumer choices on analyses of labor conditions.[16] In "The Rector of St. Jude's," the choice of a man remained a woman's principal exercise of moral judgment. She might choose between dependence on a man who provided material comfort or self-sacrifice in service of a man's socialist calling—the very options that helped produce domestic tragedy in Irvine's life.

The debate between Taggert and Gordon poignantly records the central contradictions of Irvine's American mission. Taggert immediately puts Gordon on the defensive by attacking his association with a church run by a "respectable crook" like Stuyvesant. "And *you*," Taggert charges, pointing at Gordon, "you stand by a man like that and call this a house of God! Why, this isn't a church, it's a bucket shop where ye take chances on religion at so much a share."[17] Taggert's challenges prod Gordon to denounce laws that protect Stuyvesant's interest in property from Taggert's interest in life. But it is still Taggert who makes this argument most forcefully, even implicating Gordon in the laws the rector decries. "And part of *your* game," Taggert tells Gordon, "is to keep me quiet! Oh, it's legal for him to send the militia, to shoot us down like dogs, to kill us with their rotten sweatshops, filthy factories and tenements, but it's illegal for me to revolt—well—I'll show you!"[18] At his most compelling, Taggert suggests that Gordon's Christian ideals really derive from the moral perspectives of laborers like himself. He echoes Irvine's questions about the virtues of cultural achievements that in more optimistic moods he pressed workers to claim as their own. Taggert voices Irvine's suspicion that William Haywood was right to declare that "You can't see the class struggle through the stained glass windows of a cathedral." Or, as Irvine had Taggert put the same idea, "no more of your religious dope, Gordon."[19]

Irvine handled the disparity between Taggert's views and Gordon's final speech by exploiting the defining feature of the playlet form: its focus on a central character whose personality is revealed through the dramatic action.[20] Gordon's debates with the other characters articulate various perspectives on cultural hierarchy that expressed Irvine's own shifting ideals. Gordon's unity of character derived less from any definitive resolution of Irvine's cultural ambivalences than from a dramatization of his determination to address the relations between class and culture through a gospel of work. This structure left the play open to diverse audience interpretations, which are at least partially recoverable from the critical comment the playlet received.

Two issues were in particularly vivid dispute among Irvine's critics: his acting ability and the suitability to vaudeville of his playlet's "socialistic" message. His acting won tributes to his "exceptional ability" in the *Philadelphia Telegraph*, appreciation of his "earnestness" in the *Philadelphia North American* and the *Toledo Blade*, and observations by a *Syracuse Post Standard* reviewer that he had "a voice of good power and other superficial qualifications" backed by "a high pressure reservoir of energy." These favorable views of Irvine's thespian skills tended to coincide with sympathy, or at least toleration, for the play's politics. The *Philadelphia Telegraph*'s critic suggested that Irvine's excellent acting brought applause which indicated the audience's agreement with his views. In the case of critics who praised Irvine's acting in more subdued terms, his "earnestness" and "sincerity" appeared to make up for what he lacked in "stage experience." For these critics, Irvine's success lay in compensating for his theatrical limitations by lending authenticity to his playlet's drama. Whether they considered Irvine's message part of his artistry or a redeeming feature of a somewhat amateur performance, however, critics who applauded the act accepted its message as an appropriate component of a vaudeville show.[21]

In contrast, reviews that objected to Irvine's acting skill also usually impugned the message of his play. Commenting on a February 1914 performance, one critic remarked that "Mr. Irvine is reported to have left the ministry in order to deliver a 'message from the stage.' He should have learned his new medium before trying to develop a message in it. As it is, one gleans only some beneficent generalizations, which are all right no doubt, but are not given any force or point. The acting throughout is weak and stilted." In March, the *Chicago Tribune* noted that Irvine excited "sympathy if not . . . admiration," and observed cynically that audience members in the front rows who laughed at him were "capitalists, no doubt, writhing under the sting of his scourge." Such comments reveal a contempt for Irvine's playlet that derived in part from respect for artistic practice unsullied by class politics.[22] Combined with the comments of critics who appreciated

Irvine's theatrical efforts, they express vaudeville's long tradition of popular debate over cultural standards.

Whatever their perspectives within such debates, Irvine's vaudeville audiences were sufficiently enthusiastic about his performance to encourage him in temporary fantasies of a lifelong theatrical career. Throughout the early weeks of his vaudeville appearances, the novice actor announced brave plans for future plays. By the middle of 1914, however, Irvine's theatrical prospects had soured. Though his playlet was still a critical success and he continued to enjoy the fellowship of vaudeville performers, Irvine had tired of the intricacies of agents and booking that the business of vaudeville required. Such details entailed conflicts over fees and profits far removed from his social concerns. Moreover, in an unpublished manuscript on the "Vaudeville Audience" that he wrote after his tour, Irvine revealed that he was uncomfortable with vaudeville's increasing emphasis on rank sensuality, which seemed to detract from the "healthy laughter" he tried to promote. Losing patience with the business of vaudeville as well as its patrons, he returned to his teaching post at the military academy in the fall of 1914.[23]

Of all Irvine's vaudeville audiences, those in New Haven probably responded most warmly to the conflicts he addressed on stage. New Haven was an early stop on Irvine's vaudeville tour. He appeared at Sylvester Poli's small-time Bijou theater in the second week of his acting career, from October 20 to 25, 1913. At first, Poli booked Irvine for an experimental half-week engagement. According to the ever-magnanimous manager, patrons familiar with Irvine's past inundated him with pleas to extend the minister's booking so that the hundreds who had been turned away from early performances could see the former New Haven divine. Noting approvingly that "The Rector of St. Jude's" "has created more genuine discussion than any other vaudeville vehicle that has ever been presented in this city," Poli obliged by offering Irvine a second half-week in his theater.[24]

Theatrical attendance, conversation, and letters to Manager Poli were not the only ways New Haven audiences expressed interest in Irvine and his play. Members of the Bennett Club, the boys' organization Irvine had founded at the People's Church, presented him with a monogrammed gold chain on his first evening at the Bijou. Later in the week, eighteen electrotypers employed at the W. T. Barnum company on State Street paid tribute to Irvine's New Haven reputation in another way. After walking off their jobs in a bid for union recognition, Barnum's electrotypers appealed to Irvine to arbitrate the conflict with their superintendent, former minister James Grant. Grant and Irvine had a cordial chat, but the Barnum company remained an open shop. However, if the strike demonstrated Irvine's limitations as a union spokesman on the shop floor, it still signaled his cultural significance as labor's spokesman on the stage. In calling on Irvine to use his gospel of work to counter their supervisor's gospel of management, the Barnum electrotypers recognized that the ideals Irvine was expressing at Poli's were linked to their union struggles for solidarity and recognition.[25]

Irvine's vaudeville playlet finds its greatest historical significance in illuminating the relevance of these workaday struggles to the cultural conflicts of a public sphere that spanned religion and popular entertainment. By taking the vision of evangelical self-improvement he had revised in the midst of labor's economic and political struggles to the pulpit and the stage, Irvine demonstrated the important role played by working people in shaping debates that cultural elites considered their own province. As his career shows, working people contributed to these debates in a number of ways. They insisted on a mixture of pleasure and piety that shaped religious inspiration to the peculiar requirements of wage-earning lives, and embraced versions of the hierarchy of civilization that linked social progress to the collective ideals of the labor movement. In the process, Irvine and his working-class audiences proved that there was good reason for the anxieties that literary realists expressed about the authority of their renditions of cultural hierarchy and class autonomy. Questions of cultural hierarchy and autonomy were hotly contested in social conflicts that did not yield stable terms of cultural authority. As revealed in the tragedy of Irvine's private life and in the autobiographical projects through which he developed his message, such conflicts were pervasive and complex—mixing class, gender, race, and ethnicity into intricate conundrums that linked private and public, domestic and political life.

On his way through these conflicts, of course, Irvine had boldly asserted his own authority. "The Rector of St. Jude's" was his most public statement of this authority—and of the cultural terms in which he conceived it, the class loyalties that shaped it, and the battles through which he thought it had been earned. In tribute to his recognition that their struggles informed the cultural authority he enjoyed, New Haven unionists and Socialists interrupted Irvine's first performance of "The Rector of St. Jude's" in their city with a standing ovation.[26]

Alexander Irvine, Sylvester Poli, and the Making of Twentieth-Century Cultural Politics

Though Irvine may well have reached larger audiences with his vaudeville playlet than with any other single rendition of his life story or his religious and social philosophy, "The Rector of St. Jude's" enjoyed only fleeting fame. Like many vaudeville acts, it participated in transitory fashions that emerged out of the efforts of theatrical managers to offer novelty in a context that reconciled—or, more often, counterposed—hierarchical cultural standards and the perspectives of those who contested them. It is this wider theatrical context—and the broader cultural debates that vaudeville shows addressed over time—that makes this ephemeral culmination to Alexander Irvine's mixture of piety and pleasure important as cultural history. The same is true, on a larger scale, for Irvine's and Poli's careers, and for the fame they had achieved by the time their entangled trajectories combined to launch "The Rector of St. Jude's" into brief vaudeville success. This fame was also fleeting, though far more substantial than their relative obscurity in the late twentieth century would suggest. In their own time, Irvine and Poli were well known to enthusiastic, overlapping publics who debated cultural hierarchy and autonomy at the juncture of religion, popular culture, and class politics.

As guides to these publics and their cultural conflicts, Irvine and Poli illuminate transformations in the meaning of culture that historians more often locate within academic discourses of the period. Like leading pragmatic philosophers and professionalizing social scientists, Irvine followed a cultural odyssey that questioned conventional Protestant moral hierarchies in the light of intensifying class divisions and proliferating ethnic and racial distinctions, tried to address those questions through evolutionary accounts of cultural distinction, and then began to replace evolutionary cultural hierarchies with an appreciation of the multiple, varied cultures within which people find value and meaning. This transformation was no more complete for Irvine than for America's emerging academic experts. He derived shifting versions of culture from parishioners, trade unionists, Socialists, and theatrical audiences who were engaged in debates of their own. Poli's theatrical enterprises, along with the complex relations of patronage and authority he negotiated with his publics, illustrate the shifting contours of these debates as they informed popular entertainments. Together, Irvine's and Poli's careers trace a web of popular debates over the meaning of culture and civilization that provides an instructive counterpoint to the ways in which turn-of-the-century academic intellectuals reconceptualized these terms. This intellectual transformation includes complexities and variations documented by a rich historiography that I will not assess in depth in this conclusion. My purpose here is to sketch illustrative changes in intellectual concepts of civilization and culture for which the popular debates that Irvine and Poli engaged offer provocative analogies and contrasts.

William James and John Dewey are important in this context because their philosophical initiatives informed many other contemporary conceptualizations of culture. Moreover, their intellectual trajectories typified a broader movement from Protestant cultural superiority and evolutionary thinking toward more relativistic visions of culture. Sensitive to the blow that post-Darwinian naturalism dealt to nineteenth-century Protestantism's morally purposeful universe, James sought a place for an active, moral will in a world governed neither by a spiritual absolute nor by a monolithic evolutionary mechanism. Though his psychology grounded human consciousness in biological evolution and his philosophy derived truth from scientific inquiry, he argued consistently for individual agency rather than natural law as the warrant of truth. This activist approach to belief underlay James's extraordinary sympathy for the otherworldly experiences that people like the young Alexander Irvine knew as religion at its most profound, and also James's rudimentary notion of cultural relativism. James respected the belief in the worldly power of higher forces because he himself believed that meaningful truth lay in the practical consequences of ideas. In public addresses, James urged such empathy with seemingly alien beliefs on predominantly genteel, college-educated, liberal Protestant lecture audiences. He identified cultural intolerance, especially across class lines, with individual failure to appreciate another's meaningful engagement with distinctive ideals. At one point he even suggested that the wider revelation of "the inner joy and meaning of the laborer's existence" might await an Alexander Irvine: "some one born and bred and living as a laborer himself, but who, by grace of Heaven, shall also find a literary voice." But, characteristically, James imagined such cross-class cultural appreciation as a more individual exchange than the adult Irvine would have described it. James's general antipathy toward social movements would likely have prevented this otherwise broad-minded philosopher from confusing Jack London with the "grace of Heaven."[27]

John Dewey was inspired by James's psychology and pragmatism as he negotiated his own struggles with the meaning of moral ideals in a post-Darwinian world. But, more explicitly than James, Dewey applied these ideas to social questions about democratic culture. The social emphasis of Dewey's pragmatic philosophy was shaped in part by his early preoccupation with Hegelian idealism, which helped him shore up the Christian moral purposes of his youth against the assault of evolutionary science. Dewey soon followed James in abandoning the comforts of a Hegelian absolute to take his chances in an open-ended universe. But traces of Hegelian organicism remained in Dewey's ongoing inquiry into how the processes of individual inquiry on which pragmatism based its notion of truth—the efforts of a "doer, sufferer and enjoyer"—developed into a common democratic culture. Dewey envisioned democracy as a collective life that enhanced the capacity of individuals to test truth pragmatically and derived its shared ideals from such individual inquiry and self-development. He participated in a range of Progressive era reforms aimed at reconstructing American social institutions in this democratic vision. During the 1890s, Dewey joined avidly in Jane Addams's Hull House settlement and its efforts to bridge the gulf between middle-class Protestant civilization and the concerns of an increasingly immigrant working class. He pursued a similar project in education by advocating schools where students continuously reconstructed knowledge by using scientific inquiry to link received ideas to their own experiences. Children would be transformed in this process, but so would the accumulated wisdom Dewey thought educators too often regarded as a static, finished fund of culture.[28]

Such ideas had affinities with the efforts that Alexander Irvine and his working-class allies, as well as Sylvester Poli and his audiences, made to define the prerogatives of culture in their interests. But Progressive intellectuals who embraced Dewey's formulations of democratic culture often took them in directions far removed from the cultural debates that Irvine and Poli engaged. In *Twenty Years at Hull House*, for example, Jane Addams identified the settlement's "Labor Museum" as a project that effectively demonstrated Dewey's concept of education as "a continuing reconstruction of experience." The Labor Museum brought together women from a variety of immigrant backgrounds to display "traditional" weaving and spinning techniques, and related these techniques to the processes of industrial production in which the children of such immigrants labored. Addams hoped that such displays would "reconstruct" relations between immigrants and their Americanized children, who had little appreciation for the skills and traditions in which their parents had been raised. She claimed that, by illustrating different stages in an "orderly" industrial evolution that led to "our present form of factory production," the display "enabled even the most casual observer to see that there is no break in the orderly evolution if we look at history from the industrial standpoint; that industry develops similarly and peacefully year by year among workers of each nation." This "reconstruction of experience" identified industrial production with a peaceful development quite alien to the experiences of dislocation and contest that Irvine, his family, and many of his fellow immigrants encountered on both sides of the Atlantic. It obscured working-class experience rather than bringing new meanings out of a diversity of perspectives, as in Dewey's democratic vision. While this particular instance may be attributed in part to Addams's extreme antipathy to social conflict, it suggests some of the limitations to which Deweyan notions of democratic culture were prone in the Progressive era.[29]

Dewey also inspired thinkers who wanted to displace Protestant gentility from American culture more thoroughly than Jane Addams and her fellows in the settlement movement did. While settlement workers sought to reinvigorate Protestant culture through contact with immigrant working-class life, younger intellectuals like Randolph Bourne attempted to undermine the complacent superiority of Anglo-American Protestant pieties. Bourne and fellow cultural critics of the 1910s like Van Wyck Brooks chafed at hierarchical categories that stiffened cultural self-improvement into rote acceptance of sterile aesthetic conventions. Bourne complained that programs of education and uplift figured in these terms reduced aesthetic training to "learning about what is good" — "the jacking-up of one's appreciations a notch at a time until they have reached a certain standard level." Those who adopted such an approach to culture failed to develop spontaneous, emotional responses to art, merely maintaining rigid boundaries of "taste" that excluded most people not raised or inclined to appreciate the classics. Drawing liberally on John Dewey's ideas about schooling, Bourne argued that education should connect cultural ideals to practical experience, generating a varied conversation of taste accessible to scholars and working people. This recasting of American cultural ideals to appeal across class boundaries resonated with the criticisms of culture that Alexander Irvine learned from trade unionists in the same period. Indeed, Bourne derived his cultural critiques from some of the same public debates in which Irvine developed his ideas and self-representations. As a Columbia undergraduate, Bourne became active in the ISS for which Irvine was a popular lecturer. He also championed IWW struggles in the Progressive journals of opinion, where he published wide-ranging criticism of American politics and culture during the 1910s.[30]

In criticizing Anglo-American cultural hierarchies, however, Bourne enclosed his alternative definition of "legitimate" culture in boundaries that excluded many of the popular negotiations of cultural distinction in which Irvine and Poli participated. These boundaries are particularly apparent in the 1916 essay, "Transnational America," where Bourne applied his redefinition of culture to a concept of Americanism—the "melting pot"—which he believed overemphasized Anglo-American traditions. Rather than forging these traditions into rigid standards of Americanism with which to browbeat recent immigrants, Bourne argued, Americans should look on their diverse cultural traditions as the source of a new, more democratic form of national culture. In Deweyan fashion, Bourne envisioned this new Americanism developing out of a process of exchange and debate that would transform both the prejudices of the "Anglo-Saxon" native and the traditions of transplanted Italian or Jew. Bourne located the most fruitful instances of this transformation in American colleges. College liberated young Americans from "stale and familiar attitudes" by offering vital friendships with immigrants or their children, who had also had the "baser metal" of provincial or national prejudices burned away. Crucially, Bourne distinguished the emergence of college-trained cosmopolitanism from a more superficial assimilation occurring within popular culture. There, he complained, immigrants abandoned their native cultures for "the flotsam and jetsam of American life, the downward undertow of our civilization with its leering cheapness and falseness of taste and spiritual outlook, the absence of mind and sincere feeling which we see in our slovenly towns, our vapid moving pictures, our popular novels." At this level Americanization made for a "detritus of cultures" rather than the refined cosmopolitanism Bourne looked for. But to construe the problem this way was to nominate a new class of experts to legislate a novel standard of cultural "good." It also excluded from that standard, and its definition, the broad audiences assembled at Poli's vaudeville theaters, who were engaged in their own debates over cultural hierarchies.[31]

Bourne's description of a "Trans-national America" elaborated a concept of "cultural pluralism" that Horace Kallen was developing during the same period. Kallen's ideas are particularly suggestive of the ways in which popular debates that shaped Irvine's and Poli's careers related to contemporary intellectual trajectories. Brought to America at the age of five by his Silesian Jewish parents in 1887, the young Kallen abandoned the orthodox faith preached by his father, a rabbi, for what seemed the more compelling triumphs of American freedom. Then, at Harvard, he embraced the views of literary historian Barrett Wendell, who claimed that America's Puritan cultural foundations could be traced to the Hebraic tradition. "Re-Judaized" by Wendell, Kallen became convinced that "to be a Zionist was to be a good American." He generalized this conviction to other ethnic groups, arguing that immigrants served American democracy best by cleaving to their own cultural communities and traditions. His Harvard training encouraged him to conceive of his ethnic philosophy as a variant of William James's "pluralistic universe." But, in Kallen's vision, ethnic cultures were distinct units that were not reducible to the individuality characteristic in James's thought. Kallen imagined American democracy as a federation of ethnic collectivities from which people derived fundamental and unchangeable identities. Pointing to ethnic organizations and newspapers as expressions of this identity, he obscured the intraethnic conflicts that such institutions engaged, as Poli's relations with New Haven's Italian- and Irish-American communities demonstrated. Kallen's formulation of ethnicity as an "inner life" to which individuals were born also muddled the distinction that social scientists were beginning to draw between biology and culture as sources of "race" difference. This confusion gave

Kallen's vision of ethnic culture a timeless permanence that connected it to con-temporary biological hierarchies of "race" and set it at odds with the process of ethnic self-construction that characterized his own education. This trajectory provides an illuminating contrast with Irvine, who formulated ethnic identity by challenging the racial hierarchies of the evolutionary vernacular as he recon-structed Irish folk wisdom on the model of a cross-racial plebeian camaraderie.[32]

In the 1910s and 1920s, Kallen's cultural pluralism proved less compelling than assimilationist approaches to race and ethnicity that were gaining influence within the social sciences. While Kallen emphasized the maintenance of ethnic particularity, sociologists pictured interethnic and interracial interactions as processes leading toward the amalgamation of segregated communities into a common American culture. Chicago sociologist William Isaac Thomas's stud-ies of European immigrant experiences in America set the agenda for this schol-arship. Thomas's intellectual trajectory, and the refashioning of his approach by more scientistic scholars in the 1920s, illuminates parallels and contrasts between the social scientific study of ethnic and racial difference and the more popular debates in which Irvine and Poli engaged.

Like many social scientists of his era, Thomas at first assumed that evolution had produced innate, biological distinctions that accounted for observed differ-ences between ethnic and racial groups. In the early twentieth century, however, Thomas modified his views. Stimulated by the psychology of John Dewey and George Herbert Mead, which cast the mind as an active agent rather than a repository of instinct, he became interested in the way that socially constructed habits organized "attention," or the ability of an individual to "take note of the outside world and manipulate it." Anthropological reading and Thomas's own predilection for cultural sleuthing in Chicago's ethnic neighborhoods—and in saloons and brothels associated with the margins of conventional American cul-ture—reinforced his developing sense that cultural differences were too unsta-ble to be explained by the framework of evolutionary change. As in Irvine's pop-ular adventures in investigative disguise during the same period, Thomas's researches helped generate a revised vision of the significance of cultural dis-tinction. His classic texts on immigrant culture, *The Polish Peasant in Europe and America* and *Old World Traits Transplanted*, combined appreciation for immigrant cultural institutions with concern about the effects of "underdevel-oped" cultural influences on American civilization, a combination analogous to the mix of vitality and degradation attributed to the "social pit" in the literature of investigative disguise.[33]

As such ambivalence suggests, Thomas did not share Kallen's conservationist attitude toward immigrant tradition. Thomas saw social change as a sequence of social organization, disorganization, and reorganization within which he plotted peasant and immigrant cultural practices. This picture had no place for the inborn "traditions" that Kallen wanted ethnic communities to maintain. Thomas's appreciation for the importance of immigrant newspapers and associations derived instead from the way these institutions reorganized ethnic culture in the context of a diverse, modernizing society. This perspective on immigrant institutions was closer to the process of ethnic self-construction Irvine experienced in America than Kallen's vision of innate ethnic sensibilities was. While Irvine conceived a loyalty to Irish plebeian tradition, he generated this loyalty out of his engagement with American popular debate over class, race, and ethnicity (as did Kallen). He did tend to sentimentalize the collective meanings of ethnic identity more than Thomas, whose delight in industrial urban life brooked little nostalgia for the *Gemeinschaft* stage of peasant social "organization" implied in his theory of social change. But this is a distinction more of degree than of kind. Thomas's appreciation for ethnic institutions expressed his wider concern with the ways modern, urban individuals navigated diverse, changing cultural expectations. In scholarship and life, he extolled "marginal" people who took advantage of this variety rather than cleaving to particularistic community expectations. Though Irvine continued to elaborate his ethnic rendition of proletarian solidarity into the 1920s, he observed a similarly modern aesthetic in the shifting theatrics of self-representation through which he forged his adult identity, and the ease with which he moved between ethnic nostalgia and vaudeville bravado.[34]

Thomas's penchant for urban adventure also produced illuminating commentaries on cultural politics of gender with which both Irvine and Poli wrestled. His 1897 dissertation had traced gender distinctions to metabolic differences between active "katabolic" men and passive "anabolic" women. It echoed widely shared perceptions of gender dichotomy, including the evolutionary hierarchy that placed women closer to "animals" and "lower races" in the socialist press. By the 1900s, though, Thomas had come to trace differences between men and women, like differences between racial and ethnic groups, to habit, discrimination, and bigotry. He applied his new view to analyzing the plight of the very sort of woman vaudeville both featured and proscribed in the early twentieth century—"the so-called sporting woman . . . the gamester, adventuress, or criminal." Rather than identifying these social types with biological inferiority, as contemporary eugenicists did, Thomas described them as elaborations of gender-specific habits appropriate to earlier social orders. In industrial society, men had

taken over productive industries that had been women's responsibility in earlier economies, consigning women to a parasitic dependence, as feminists like
Charlotte Perkins Gilman also pointed out. If women then exaggerated the arts
of cunning and display in the direction of extravagance and sexual adventure,
Thomas suggested, this was an understandable effort to adapt to new circumstances habits they had been encouraged to develop.

Thomas identified such behavior specifically with women set adrift into a
whirl of urban excitement of the kind often celebrated in vaudeville. "To be completely lost sight of by all who have previously known her may . . . become an
object" for such a woman, Thomas argued, "the only means by which she can
without confusion accept more intense stimulations than are legitimate in the
humdrum life of a poor home." Sympathizing with the sporting-woman without
endorsing her behavior, he recommended vocational training in occupations
that would hold women's attention as the remedy for moral wandering. This suggestion prefigured Irvine's effort to rectify the moral distortions of self-display
through a gospel of work. But while Irvine continued to identify his gospel with
masculine socialist prophets, and vaudeville managers dithered over the propriety of the sporting-woman as vaudeville professional, Thomas encouraged
women's full, creative participation in the modern world of industrial work and
leisure.[35]

Though Thomas questioned cultural convention, he and his Chicago colleagues did not completely abandon cultural hierarchy in their studies of assimilation. While relinquishing biological notions of ethnic, racial, and gender inferiority, both Thomas and Robert Park, who led the sociology program at Chicago
after 1918, attributed distinct "temperaments" to diverse racial groups and measured these temperaments against the urbane, metropolitan standards they
favored. Unlike Poli's vaudeville shows and Irvine's gospel of work, the scholarship of Thomas, Park, and their students did not suggest that the cultural standards of modern, industrial civilization were subject to critique by groups
excluded from them. They lamented such exclusion, which they regarded as the
product of racial and ethnic prejudice, not biology or class exploitation. But
Chicago sociologists assumed an increasingly detached perspective of scholarly
observation in regard to the cycles of group interaction that, according to Park's
formulations, led toward cultural assimilation. Though, like Thomas, Park
encouraged students to "enter as fully as possible into the social worlds they studied," he did not mean that they should develop a sense of combative solidarity
with such communities. He distinguished between generalized, rationalized

"civilization" to which assimilated individuals adapted and more local cultures that they shared as "races or peoples," but rejected Horace Kallen's pluralist advocacy for ethnic "culture" against American "civilization." Within Park's rubric, social scientists observed the process by which members of specific ethnic and racial groups were individually assimilated into American society. They disdained the collective, and especially the class-specific critiques of American "civilization" that Irvine had engaged throughout his career.[36]

The distinction between civilization and culture developed somewhat different implications in anthropology, the scholarly discipline most closely associated with the development of a relativistic culture concept in American thought. American anthropology's shift from an evolutionary hierarchy of civilization to an appreciation for the integrity of multiple cultures was primarily the work of Franz Boas and his students. Like many of his social scientific peers, Boas began his career conceiving of culture as a singular measure of artistic achievement or intellectual capacity. But, reflecting on ethnographic fieldwork among the Eskimo and Kwakiutl during the 1880s, Boas noted that common beliefs appeared among groups of people otherwise culturally and linguistically distinct. He moved toward a conception of culture as a varied historical construct, developing through diffusions of meanings among different groups. Cultural distinction, in this view, was the result of varied historical experience rather than different stages of development along a single evolutionary hierarchy. It demanded the study of "total cultures," with particular emphasis on the way in which they incorporated and modified meanings borrowed from neighboring peoples. Still, Boas never wholly abandoned his liberal faith in such universalistic human values as scientific knowledge, human fellowship, and individual freedom for a purely pluralist view of culture. For Boas, other cultures offered external reference points from which to criticize his own civilization while retaining an abiding faith in an ideal of civilization common to humankind. As refined by Boas and his students from the 1890s into the 1920s, this double-edged concept of culture came closer than other current social scientific constructs to the local web of meanings that Alexander Irvine described in *My Lady of the Chimney Corner* and the Irish stories he later improvised out of its characters. Irvine, too, portrayed "culture" as a construct of stories and beliefs that traveled from locality to locality, where they were woven into the fabric of a whole way of life with its own moral integrity. While Irvine's Irish narratives criticized hierarchical cultural standards he had adopted in youth and questioned in adulthood, however, they also denounced the poverty and ignorance that had kept many of his Antrim neighbors from grasping the hierarchical ideals he had pursued. Like Boas, in short, Irvine applied a universalizing cultural hierarchy, while subjecting it to criticism from the perspective of autonomous cultural values.[37]

Irvine's popular self-constructions also resembled Boasian culture concepts in their ambiguous engagement with ideas about race. Boas used the egalitarian perspective on cultural variety he derived from ethnological work to counter both scientific and popular evolutionary racism in American thought. He began criticizing biological notions of racial inferiority in the 1890s, and in the early twentieth century he actively publicized African cultural accomplishments as evidence against racist ideas about American blacks. Irvine echoed such counterhierarchical thinking when he compared African villages favorably to American miners' cabins in his coal strike sermons and praised African-American spirituals in his peonage articles and socialist fiction. However, neither Boas nor Irvine abruptly abandoned evolutionary hierarchies in favor of racial equality. Boas continued to hope that physical anthropology would reveal biological truths about racial differences even while his culturalist arguments led him to expect that such distinctions owed more to discrimination than theorists of biological race distinctions admitted. Such vestigial biological notions of race were linked to the concept of civilization that Boas shared with social scientific contemporaries like Park and more popular thinkers like Irvine. Whatever their appreciation for cultural particularity, all of them associated human civilization with the culture and politics of Western societies, to which they thought America's ethnic and racial minorities should aspire. In this respect, evolutionary hierarchies remained the medium out of which both academic and popular discourses gradually distilled more relativistic notions of culture.[38]

While the value Boas saw in particular cultures remained in tension with the broader standards of civilization he championed throughout his career, he influenced anthropologists of the 1920s who did draw on cultural variety to criticize American "civilization" more explicitly. Such criticism brought Boasian anthropology closer to Irvine's cultural politics than the Chicago sociologists' scientific detachment came. It was implicit in Boas's approach to American racism, and more pronounced in the work of a group of anthropologists George Stocking has styled "ethnographic Apollonians," after Ruth Benedict's appreciation of Zuni culture for its minimization of both conflict and individual excess in favor of moderation, sobriety, and cooperation. Like Robert Redfield's ethnography of Tepoztlán, Mexico, and Margaret Mead's research in Samoa, Benedict's admiring evaluation of Pueblo life drew on the meanings of "primitive" culture "to pass judgment on the dominant traits of our own civilization," as Benedict later put it. Using ethnographic perspective as a fulcrum, Apollonian ethnography contributed to a wider critique of the materialism and superficiality of American "civilization" in the name of "genuine culture," a critique advanced by Boas-trained anthropologists such as Edward Sapir as well as literary intellectuals like Van Wyck Brooks, Harold Stearns, and H. L. Mencken. Boas's student Robert Lowie aimed a similar critique of civilized "superiority" at the outworn hierarchies of the evolutionary socialists in the 1910s. Such assaults on counterfeit civilization in the name of genuine culture echoed the trade unionist critique of "so-called culture" that Irvine had worked into his own appreciation for the cultural peculiarities of his Irish plebeian origins. But the trade unionist roots of Irvine's cultural politics also set him apart from the Apollonian ethnographers in important ways. The anthropologists tended to abstract their cultural comparisons from the global political economy in terms of which Irvine had long pictured the cultural distinctions of class, race, and ethnicity he negotiated throughout his career.[39]

However, Boas's broad influence also generated scholarship outside anthropology that did take account of class as a dimension of culture. From the 1920s on, Boasian anthropology inspired sociologists and historians to capture the everyday meanings of work and leisure within urban, industrial life. Tilting against the vogue of sociological positivism in the 1920s, Robert and Helen Lynd laid claim to the anthropological notion of culture as the organizing concept of *Middletown*, their effort to comprehend the indigenous, class-specific meanings of industrial change in Muncie, Indiana. *Middletown* and its anthropological antecedents in turn informed the "cultural approach to history" developed and publicized by Caroline Ware. Ware had already begun to fashion cultural history out of the experience of industrial labor in her 1931 work, *The Early New England Cotton Manufacture*. The Lynds' study served as a model for Ware's second book, *Greenwich Village 1920–1930: A Comment on American Civilization in the Post-War Years*, in which she transplanted her interest in working-class culture to New York City's ethnic neighborhoods. In 1940, Ware coordinated the American Historical Association's volume on *The Cultural Approach to History*, in which she included an essay on "Cultural Groups in the United States" that set forth the cultural experience of industrial workers as a pressing historical research agenda.

Ware's program for a study of "industrial culture" was a poignant plea for historians to address cultural concerns that had preoccupied Alexander Irvine since the beginning of the century:

The ethnic groups drawn to industrial cities have been the people in terms of whose lives this industrial culture has been taking shape. They are the industrial workers. . . . The emerging patterns of their lives, their attitudes, values, habits, are the patterns, attitudes, and habits of workers in an industrial society. . . . [T]he great bulk of urban new Americans are and always have been the factory workers, miners, bridge builders, pick-and-shovel men, and, more lately, white-collar workers. They are the readers of the mass "pulp" magazines and the sport pages; they are the rank and file in the mass unions. . . . It is these people rather than the frontiersmen who constitute the real historical background and heroic tradition of the mass of urban Americans.

Ware called for a history "from the bottom up" focused on the "non-dominant cultural groups of the industrial cities." Presaging the research program of a later generation of historians, she also echoed a popular experience of cultural history to which Irvine had earlier given voice. Not only had the title of his autobiography used the slogan that Ware and later historians would select for this project; as he continued to elaborate his story, Irvine acknowledged the methods required for the history Ware advocated. As he wrote in *The Souls of Poor Folk*—a 1921 sequel to *My Lady of the Chimney Corner* that offered further adventures of his Antrim characters—"the men who were great townsmen in my youth are unknown to fame. Their names are not found in the pages of history. They are enrolled in the musty records of the churches and in the faded, worm-eaten books of the tax gatherers—and some of them can be found only in the latter."[40]

Still, while Irvine's Irish narratives prefigured Ware's cultural history, their shared interests did not make Irvine's popular self-constructions part of the scholarly discourse to which Ware contributed. Drawing on the popular and political debates in which he had been immersed, Irvine rethought culture along lines analogous to those his scholarly contemporaries were devising. But he pursued these revisions at a juncture of popular religion, entertainment, and class politics that was becoming increasingly remote from the academic study of American culture during his and Poli's careers. Paradoxically, while Franz Boas came closer than many social scientists to the cultural politics Irvine concocted as he borrowed from Poli's entertainment realm, Boas's early career also aptly illustrates the growing separation between scholarly debates over culture and the more popular cultural contests that Irvine and Poli engaged.

Boas entered anthropology during its "museum age," and his early fieldwork contributed to displays shaped by some of the same museum traditions that informed Poli's waxworks. Both the metropolitan wax museums where Poli worked and the natural history museums that Boas assisted incorporated the contradictory appeals of entertainment and education that American museum practice had juggled since the Enlightenment age of Charles Willson Peale. Both types of museum also organized their exhibits according to evolutionary schemes that abandoned Enlightenment era ideals of human commonality in favor of a hierarchy of civilization dividing higher and lower races, nations, and individuals. From the 1890s on, Boas struggled against evolutionary classification in anthropological exhibits. He argued that displays should convey the historical integrity of whole cultures rather than evolutionary "stages" represented by specific inventions and artifacts. To effect this revision in exhibition practices, Boas used techniques that came quite close to Poli's wax artistry. To portray his vision of culture to a mass public, Boas assembled "life groups"—collections of wax, plaster, or papier-maché mannequins arranged to represent scenes from the daily life and rituals of "primitive" societies. Introduced to American ethnological exhibits at the Chicago World's Columbian Exposition of 1893, life groups offered some of the same pleasures of visual realism and dramatic effect that metropolitan waxworks like Madame Tussaud's, the Musée Grévin, and the Eden Musée provided in their comparisons of civilized culture and ferocious barbarism.

For Boas's purposes, however, the kinship between anthropological display techniques and commercial visual realism proved problematic. He did not want spectators to marvel at the achievement of realist effects in life groups, or get excited by their dramatic spectacle, as wax museums often urged. He insisted that museum displays suppress these features in favor of ethnographic observations elaborated in exhibits of artifacts surrounding the life groups. While he saw natural history museums as institutions serving both entertainment and scientific aims, he subordinated entertainment to the purposes of scholarly research. These priorities ultimately brought him in conflict with his employers at the American Museum of Natural History in New York City. Administrators became impatient with Boas's emphasis on fieldwork that did not directly fill gaps in existing exhibitions and on displays that challenged visitors to rethink prevalent hierarchies of civilization rather than categorizing anthropological exhibits in familiar evolutionary classifications. After this conflict provoked Boas's resignation from the American Museum in 1905, he came to see the research university as preferable to the public museum as an institutional base for his anthropological approach to culture.[41]

In contrast to Boas and the social sciences he helped shape, Poli's waxworks and vaudeville shows owed little to academic scholarship or rigorous scientific methods, though they often celebrated scientific discovery. Within the transatlantic traditions Poli began to master at the Grévin and Eden museums, popular realism undercut hierarchical concepts of culture by appealing to audience divisions over the standards and values such hierarchies upheld. Metropolitan wax museums of the late nineteenth century only faintly registered this critique. Appealing to nationalist cultural hierarchies and celebrities that they made visually accessible to an increasingly wide public, these institutions tried to suture the class and political divisions that had given birth to the modern wax museum as much as they tried to address the cultural divisions within their own audiences. But they did acknowledge divergent perspectives on the hierarchies they extolled by depicting competing nationalist loyalties and offering sensational "horrors" that, while distinguishing carefully between the barbarously criminal and genteelly civilized, also appealed to fascination and even sympathy with their subjects. This was the case with Poli's exhibits of the Haymarket anarchists, which applied the wax museums' ambivalent revolutionary heritage and visual realist techniques to the class conflicts of late-nineteenth-century America. These displays implied that the anarchists were guilty of heinous, savage crimes. But by showing the condemned men engaged in peaceful camaraderie and claiming to use the subjects' own clothes, they also acknowledged loyalties that might cast the anarchists' criticisms of American civilization in a more sympathetic light. Poli engaged such contested perspectives on "civilized" hierarchies even more strategically in managing the vaudeville theaters he launched on the proceeds of his traveling wax exhibits.

Poli's vaudeville shows and the wider debates they addressed helped transform popular concepts of culture. As this transformation developed in Poli's entertainments, however, it differed from both the scholarly inquiry of academic intellectuals and from the efforts to impose genteel standards that cultural historians have previously attributed to vaudeville impresarios. Like other vaudeville managers of his era, Poli tried to differentiate his shows from rowdier, lewder variety halls, burlesque theaters, and concert saloons, thus reinforcing a cultural hierarchy that equated civilization and "refinement." But, as Poli's early shows suggest, vaudeville also catered to alternative cultural orientations that mocked highbrow pretensions and parlor orthodoxy. As Poli's maneuvers among his New Haven patrons reveal, this was not a matter of wholesale opposition to "genteel" cultural standards from below. His diverse audiences advanced conflicting standards that they debated within particular class and ethnic communities and across class and ethnic lines. By offering a space where cross-class, multiethnic audiences came together to watch performances that spoke to diverse cultural values, Poli's vaudeville theaters appealed to these popular public debates over culture. His shows juxtaposed conventional hierarchies and their critiques in ways that proved useful to Alexander Irvine, who challenged the exclusive boundaries that hierarchical cultural standards implied. While Poli's own approach to cultural hierarchy was less overtly politicized than Irvine's, the popular realism of his vaudeville enterprises helped reshape the meaning of civilized "refinement" and the cultural authority associated with it. By posing "civilization" and "refinement" as contested terms, Poli gave his managerial and civic claims to cultural authority a broad scope. While he expressed a preference for relatively genteel values, he based his local authority on the competing standards advanced by various ethnic and class communities.

This clash of cultural values constituted a different approach to cultural distinction than American social scientists and cultural critics produced, though it addressed some of the issues they raised. It did not offer the scholarly understanding of cultural variety to which Boasian anthropology aspired. As entrepreneurs, Poli and other vaudeville managers sought to draw mass audiences from diverse communities that encompassed competing cultural standards. Beyond an unstable and ambivalently defined gentility, they recommended no general perspective on the cultural distinctions to which they appealed. But neither did Poli's entertainments produce the "detritus of cultures" that cosmopolitan culture critics like Randolph Bourne decried. Though Bourne failed to see in vaudeville caricatures the ironic interplay of cultures he envisioned for a "trans-national America," such acts registered popular contests over cultural standards with which Poli and his audiences were familiar. Poli's local audiences and associates did not experience these contests as conflicts between American standards and ethnic traditions, as cultural pluralists like Horace Kallen were wont to picture them. As Poli's maneuvers through New Haven society reveal, "ethnic" identity was itself contested across lines of class, regional origin, religious expression, and political ideology. Poli's success as a cultural authority in New Haven derived in part from his subtle negotiation of these multiple lines of cultural contest.

Meanwhile, however, Poli's cultural authority was confounded by shifting vaudeville fashions and changing corporate economies of the national entertainment industry. After 1900, African Americans gained a slightly larger presence in vaudeville shows; older immigrant groups witnessed the relative gentrification and receding dominance of their representations in vaudeville; and young women from new immigrant groups strutted across the stage brazenly throwing off the modesty of the parlor. Acts reflecting these changes did not lend themselves to the same appeals Poli had previously directed to local constituencies. At the same time, vaudeville managers tried to distinguish their shows from new types of theatrical competition, such as cabarets and musical revues. The themes of material indulgence and feminine self-display emphasized in vaudeville's emerging ensemble acts complicated this task. Forced into the corporate organization—the UBO—responsible for the economies of scale that made such acts attractive bookings, Poli was left to reconcile the narrowed standard of refinement promulgated by the UBO with the transgressions of that standard that UBO acts flaunted. Though the UBO helped consolidate vaudeville managers' collective control over performers (albeit imperfectly), Poli's career suggests that its effect on vaudeville managers' local cultural authority was ambiguous. The restriction of vaudeville's "refinement" to a caveat on feminine display diminished the connections Poli could draw between his role as vaudeville manager and his status as a local authority conversant with diverse cultural standards. From promoting a multifaceted refinement shaped by multiple constituencies, Poli came to enforce a more rigid standard focused especially on women, the group he and other vaudeville managers depended on most to ensure theatrical respectability.

The cultural disputes that Poli had previously engaged did not completely disappear from early-twentieth-century vaudeville or the popular cultural sphere of which it was a part. Working-class, immigrant women may well have felt that the new ethos of feminine self-expression and display expanded such debates to include their standards and tastes. Indeed, historians of popular culture and sexuality note that many forms of twentieth-century commercial culture incorporated working-class modes of sexuality that challenged "refined" moral standards. In his maneuvers through New Haven's social hierarchy, however, Poli had usually engaged challenges to conventional hierarchies as they were advanced through institutions founded and run by men. When vaudeville's flashy ensemble acts and strutting divas encouraged women to defy gentility in the name of their own pleasure, Poli sought new ways to categorize and control them. In this respect his negotiation of cultural authority paralleled the efforts of experts in other venues who were formulating new definitions of female "sexual delinquency" and "hypersexuality," or, in William Thomas's case, explaining the "sporting woman's" adventures as consequences of her exclusion from masculine arenas of public accomplishment. Like them, Poli was experimenting with new modes of cultural authority, rather than applying a firm, established standard of propriety. The social relations through which he negotiated this authority provide a purchase on popular, quotidian meanings of broader changes occurring in American culture.[42]

To "Change the Face of Civilization"

Even if Poli's enterprises did not provide the studied reconceptualization of civilization produced by contemporary academic scholars, they did offer a wide range of competing perspectives on that civilization. However, whether vaudeville thereby fostered critical debates over the changing shape of American culture—a public sphere in itself—remains questionable. "The Rector of St. Jude's" and other sketches of its era that reflected on working-class experience did carry vaudeville's critical self-reflexivity into the twentieth century. They addressed the cares of people for whom the pleasures of vaudeville's emerging hierarchy of self-display remained rare treats or remote fantasies. But when playlets like Irvine's appeared alongside acts that expressed vaudeville's indulgence of such fantasies, their social and cultural criticism may have been blunted even as they made such criticisms available to wide audiences. For as singers like Sophie Tucker strutted across the same stages where Irvine preached, they tempted audiences to cherish the very extravagances his playlet excoriated for exacting suffering in the form of wage labor.[43] To juxtapose Tucker and Irvine was not necessarily to foster a full-fledged debate between the different social and cultural perspectives they offered. To the extent that vaudeville managers like Poli combined such fare primarily to attract large audiences, they created a venue that entertained diverse views of America's changing culture without necessarily inspiring audiences to consider, collectively, the implications of that diversity.

In this sense, the power of Irvine's vaudeville playlet derived less from its vaudevillian venue than from the wider mission on which it drew. In the course of that mission, Irvine had long deployed popular realist techniques he shared with Poli's entertainment arena in order to engage broader social conflicts over the meaning of culture. His playlet broadcast the lessons he had learned from his involvement in New Haven's labor movements and in the debates he encountered in national Socialist Party circles. Irvine's career thus illustrates the importance of considering wider controversies to which entertainment spoke in the study of cultural politics and the conceptualization of the public sphere. The course of Irvine's trajectory reveals how working people who were also practicing Christians as well as theater audiences reconceived civilization and culture.

Like many of the intellectuals who pondered "civilization" within the academy, Irvine and his allies rethought "civilization" in the context of Protestant evangelical traditions. As Irvine encountered them, however, these traditions offered much more than the dry husk of conventional morals that college-trained idealists like Jane Addams or Randolph Bourne tried to revitalize or escape. From adolescence, Irvine knew evangelical faith as an uplifting claim on experiences of spiritual and intellectual cultivation that had seemed reserved for the "quality" who loomed above him in childhood. But he also found in this heritage a web of conundrums about the spiritual significance of industrial conflicts that shaped the working-class lives he thought it should inspire. While many late-nineteenth-century evangelical spokesmen deployed their traditions of self-improvement and otherworldly expectation to diffuse labor militancy, Irvine found allies who laid claim to the same traditions as challenges to pious apologies for industrial exploitation. He also drew on plebeian traditions of self-culture that mixed entertainment and religion to fit evangelical practice to the rhythms of working-class lives.

In this respect, Irvine's example invites reassessment of the relationship between commercial entertainment and Protestant practice in turn-of-the-century America. Scholars such as Jackson Lears and Susan Curtis have suggestively characterized Protestant appropriations of popular cultural techniques as pivotal moments in the transformation of American middle-class culture from individualistic Victorian piety to a new consumer order "based on immediate gratification, material comfort, and group orientation."[44] This reading of liberal Protestant and social gospel revisionism parallels the Habermasian understanding of early-twentieth-century transformations in a public sphere no longer ordered by conventional cultural hierarchies. As the classic bourgeois public sphere described by Habermas expanded, it was reshaped by bureaucratic media that offered "psychologically accessible" culture to passive audiences and thus attenuated public debate over cultural standards. As Irvine wielded commercial entertainment techniques, however, he helped broadcast a wide-ranging debate over hierarchies that popular culture both upheld and criticized. Like the wax museums where Poli began his career, Irvine's magic lantern sermons made hierarchical culture more accessible to audiences that had often been excluded from it. But like Poli's vaudeville shows, Irvine also invoked the alternatives posed to that culture by his working-class allies. Formulated in a variety of organizations—from praying groups to union halls to immigrant associations to socialist parties—these alternatives shared components of elite hierarchies, especially the widespread tendency to conflate Victorian "civilization" with evolutionary racial and ethnic distinctions. But they also subjected such hierarchies to critical reevaluations regarding their suitability as standards of cross-class aspiration and argument.

Irvine's most enduring contributions to this conversation bear witness to the ways that trade unionist and socialist battles informed both the religious aspirations to which he spoke and the entertainment forms on which he drew. His New Haven labor alliances imbued his evangelical visions of self-improvement with the distinction between elite "so-called culture" and the collective values of organized labor. Subsequently, Irvine continued to recommend that workers cultivate spiritual ideals and high culture. But he redefined such hierarchical values in light of the working-class solidarities and concerns he associated with the labor movement and the Socialist Party. In the process, he juxtaposed cultural hierarchy and autonomy in ways that depart intriguingly from the formulations offered by literary realists who pondered the same nexus of religion, popular theater, and class distinction that he negotiated. Irvine neither searched for nor despaired of finding a working-class autonomy uncontaminated by hierarchical ideals, as Stephen Crane did. Nor did he treat such ideals as illusory desires that scientific expertise could dispel with "real" explanations of class distinction. For Irvine, the evolutionary thought that Theodore Dreiser flaunted as scientific knowledge provided a language for debating and transforming cultural class distinctions, rather than promising to explain them once and for all. In this sense, Irvine's mission testifies to the culturally constructed, shifting significance of class distinctions in this era. But it also begs us to understand the cultural construction of class as it was shaped by class conflict. As it intersects Poli's career, it reveals how cultural constructions of class hierarchy and autonomy were themselves fought out at work, in politics, and in the everyday rivalries of civic life.

These conflicts continued to inform the autobiographical narratives that made the lessons of Irvine's mission nationally popular. It was here that Irvine most explicitly engaged the encounter between Protestant hierarchies of civilization and evolutionary thought. His literary narratives translated the evangelical aspirations he had revised in the midst of America's class conflicts into the evolutionary vernacular that many writers were using to make sense of their experience of class distinction. But this translation was not so much an abandonment of evangelical pieties in favor of evolutionary mechanics as an effort to make sense of the cultural politics of religion in popular terms. In this respect, Irvine's narrative self-constructions spoke to a range of audiences—for vaudeville shows as well as socialist lectures—who pondered and interrogated both religious and evolutionary hierarchies rather than choosing decisively between them. At the same time, Irvine's evolutionary renditions of cultural politics addressed hierarchies of ethnicity, race, and gender that fractured the class solidarities in terms of which he had reformulated "civilized" culture.

Irvine registered some of these fractures more effectively than others. Though feminist agitation did provoke revisions in his estimation of women's public and private accomplishments, he never completely relinquished the reverence for feminine domesticity his own marriages so tragically belied. In the case of ethnic and racial distinctions, Irvine's engagement with the evolutionary vernacular was more incisive. Some of his self-constructions evoked the evolutionary cultural politics of racial and ethnic exclusion that his labor allies shared with anti-labor theologians and vaudeville caricaturists. But Irvine's deployment of the evolutionary vernacular also revealed it to be a contested language through which intertwined cultural hierarchies of class, race, and ethnicity might be challenged and rethought. As in his reconceptualization of evangelical hierarchies, this project connected changing concepts of culture to the politics of class. His literary experiments with the evolutionary vernacular encouraged him to explore ethnic and racial "cultures" as repositories for the proletarian solidarities in terms of which he had reevaluated hierarchical notions of "civilization." But it was the crucible of socialist campaigning and Party debates that provoked Irvine to embrace his nostalgically rendered ethnic heritage as a cultural construct that effectively blended the democratic aspirations of plebeian evangelicalism with the stalwart solidarities of proletarian camaraderie.

The popularity of this rendition of working-class culture fluctuated in the decades that followed, as the public sphere that Irvine and Poli had helped shape changed around them. During World War I and after, Irvine and Poli pursued their careers in an era many historians associate with the triumph of mass culture over concerns such as ethnic identity, religious morals, or class solidarity. Their adventures after 1914 do not contradict this image of a transformed public sphere. But they complicate it in ways that suggest the ongoing, twentieth-century legacy of the cultural conflicts they had engaged on their way to national prominence.

Poli, Irvine, and the Public Sphere after 1914

The war years intensified the competing civic claims that Sylvester Poli negotiated as a local, regional, national, and international theatrical celebrity. The hostilities in Europe kindled fresh calls on Poli's Italian patriotism, inspiring him to join the Sons of Italy, a venue through which he and his wife, Rosa, could add to their long list of charitable activities by raising funds for the Italian Red Cross and other relief agencies working in their war-torn native land. To honor such philanthropy as well as Poli's prominence as an Italian-American success story, King Vittorio Emanuele III of Italy awarded the impresario the medal and title of Chevalier of the Crown of Italy in 1915. The Polis celebrated this honor at yet another lavish banquet organized and attended by a cross-section of New Haven's ethnic and Yankee elite, along with prominent citizens from other cities where Poli owned theaters. The theatrical manager spoke to this assemblage of his combined ethnic pride and American nationalism. Though he had whole-heartedly embraced the "fields of broader opportunity" he had found in the United States, Poli affirmed, his loyalty to America had not extinguished the "tender memories and cherished associations" that sustained his affection for Italy. He testified to the experience of many ethnic elites who used their American prestige to reconstruct ethnic identity in more sentimental and unifying terms than they had known it in the process of emigration, while reconciling such ethnic constructions to demands for American patriotism that reached a crescendo during the war.[45]

Echoes of ethnic pride persisted in Poli's theaters during the war years as well, contributing to shows that sustained vaudeville's plural traditions even at the height of its corporate consolidation. Poli's vaudeville programs, like others nationwide, were increasingly dominated by the feature films that eventually displaced vaudeville entirely. But the growing prominence of film did not immediately eclipse ethnic humor and camaraderie in his shows. Between 1915 and 1919 he screened a series of Italian films featuring the Italian dockworker, Ernesto Pagani, who won movie fame as matinee idol "Maciste." Originally cast as a slave in Gabriele D'Annunzio's feature *Cabiria*, Maciste went on to stardom as the "Italian Douglas Fairbanks" in films that showcased his athletic prowess. Eagerly advertised in both Italian- and English-language newspapers, Maciste shared bills with acts that continued other strains of nostalgic vaudeville ethnicity into the war years, such as Eugene Emmett, the "Chauncey Olcott of Vaudeville." Shortly after Emmett's 1919 appearance, Poli's Palace also played host to a local skirmish reminiscent of the class rivalries its traditions of ethnic caricature had once invoked. Hosting a performance by the 102nd Regimental Band, the theater became embroiled in a town-gown battle touched off over what some residents perceived as Yale students' snobbish disrespect for returning soldiers. Thus, even as feature films competed with variety acts for the attention of vaudeville audiences, those audiences still found their own competing identities addressed at Poli's.[46]

Still, these *were* echoes, muffled in the 1920s by new cultural forms that fed on vaudeville's traditions while dissipating its social variety. Vaudeville's skits and music lived on in radio, where they played to families and neighborhoods rather than the diverse audiences that attended the vaudeville house. Metropolitan audiences still assembled in palatial theaters downtown, but by the mid-1920s they were looking for feature films more often than vaudeville programs. Consolidated in Hollywood under the direction of a handful of corporations that rivaled the vaudeville trust and challenged anti-trust law, the movies offered an increasingly uniform celebration of the psychological and cultural releases provided by leisure and abundance. These fantasies of mass luxury were punctuated much less frequently than vaudeville by self-critical reflections on poverty or social conflict. The ethos of vaudeville's ensemble acts thus came to dominate entertainment, literally in the sense that Jesse Lasky's Feature Play Company produced the earliest work of Cecil B. DeMille, paving the way for DeMille's popular movie celebrations of lavish self-indulgence. This triumph of the hierarchy of display on screen left few resonances of civic rivalry for a local manager like Poli to adjudicate. He turned his attention to building and refurbishing theaters throughout his circuit to accommodate Hollywood's products.[47]

Meanwhile, Poli's dynastic plans for his theatrical circuit foundered on family tragedy and his own notions of gender-appropriate behavior. He had groomed his son, Edward, to take over in 1923, but Edward died suddenly in 1922. Of Poli's four daughters—Adelina, Juliette, Laurina, and Lillian—only the eldest, Adelina, ever participated actively in her father's enterprises. Their marginal roles in the family business appear to have derived at least partly from Poli's convictions about gender-appropriate behavior. While they were welcome with their friends as audience members seated decorously in the Poli family box, the backstage, business side of the house was generally off limits. "We were always to sit there like ladies and enjoy the show—we were never allowed to go back there like a bunch of fresh kids interfering with the performers," Juliette Poli Sheehan recalled later. The prospect of young women seeing actresses in tights also dismayed Poli, his granddaughter reported. In short, though Poli had negotiated fine lines between feminine propriety and transgressive performance that vaudeville comediennes regularly skirted, and envisioned his son doing so as well, he apparently harbored other ambitions for his daughters than to tangle professionally with those lines. They married comfortably—aristocratically in the case of Lillian, who became Marchesa Lippo Gerini of Florence, Italy—into the gracious domesticity and civic benevolence that Poli's wife, Rosa, had practiced since her days as his assistant in wax sculpture had ended. Villa Rosa—Poli's summer and, later, retirement estate at Woodmont, Connecticut—was his crowning tribute to this notion of womanhood.[48]

Without a male heir to take over his circuit, Poli's enthusiasm for theatrical management waned. But he had to dispose of his lavish theaters before he could turn to fishing and sculpting in sand at Woodmont. Though B. F. Keith had compromised his managerial autonomy, Poli remained proud of his theatrical circuit and determined to see it maintained intact. The fulfillment of this end involved several rounds of negotiation with new corporate titans in the film industry—organizations founded by immigrants like Poli who built vast enterprises on the nickels and dimes of working-class vaudeville and movie patrons. They met their match in the New Haven impresario. In 1928 Poli sold his circuit to William Fox's enterprises, but retained 76 percent interest in the properties through first mortgage bonds. William Fox set about fitting the Poli circuit for the sound-movie era, which he had helped pioneer with his "Movietone" sound-on-film process. In the imperial tradition of popular cultural entrepreneurship that vaudeville had inaugurated, he was also busily trying to topple rivals in order to enhance his own consolidation of movie production and distribution. This ambition sent Fox into financial difficulties after he tried to best Adolph Zukor by acquiring ex-vaudeville entrepreneur Marcus Loew's production enterprises and theaters. In the wake of Fox's debacle, Poli organized a new company to buy back his circuit in its entirety. In 1934 he sold this enterprise, Poli's New England Theatres, to Loew's Theaters. His theaters became Loew's-Poli's cinemas, and Poli relaxed into a consulting role. He did not get to enjoy it for long. He and Rosa celebrated their golden wedding anniversary, complete with presidential greetings, in 1935. Then, on May 31, 1937, after catching a cold that developed into pneumonia, he died suddenly of heart failure at Villa Rosa.[49]

By preserving his circuit, Poli ensured that Hollywood's massive culture industries did not wholly eclipse his own achievements. Nevertheless, his efforts to secure this end derived increasingly from shrewd negotiations with national entertainment concerns rather than from the way his shows addressed the more local rivalries that Irvine's playlet invoked. If Poli's post–World War I successes thus illustrate a corporate consolidation that overwhelmed the more vibrant popular public sphere he and Irvine had shared, however, Irvine's adventures during the same era reveal moments in which the debates they had engaged still stirred audiences who had moved on from the vaudeville show to the movie palace. After World War I, Irvine did find fewer and fewer lucrative venues for the mixture of entertainment, class politics, and evangelism he had hocked in the popular press and on the vaudeville stage in the early twentieth century. But he continued to adapt new methods to his missionary aims, attracting new audiences whose interest attested to the ongoing relevance of his mission and the cultural politics he had waged.

Like Poli, Irvine found World War I a spur for old sentiments of ethnic and national loyalty. Convinced that in the crisis of war he belonged with the working-class fighting men of the United Kingdom, Irvine went to Britain in the summer of 1916. The British YMCA sent him to speak at military camps throughout the British Isles in 1916 and 1917 and, in 1918 to the Western Front in France to encourage the fighting troops. With the German offensive of March 1918, the Y had to curtail its lecturers' activities, but Irvine had earned such acclaim among fighting men and such respect from their superiors that he was allowed to continue his tours through France until the end of the war. On the strength of this success, Lloyd George's government asked that he undertake a year-long mission to uplift Britain's "industrial army" as they made the transition to peace in 1919. Advertised as "The Uplift Man" and "The Sunshine Man," Irvine toured shop floors, variety halls, and cinemas throughout Britain, preaching patience, fair play, and a balance between spiritual and material reconstruction. He embroidered this message with testimonies to his solidarity with the working class, but his lectures also had a strong flavor of evangelical self-help, filtered through institutions like the Y that he had previously defied as well as wartime bureaucracies and the culture industries they commandeered. In this respect Irvine's mission to Britain during the war anticipated the more general dilution of the public sphere that critics like Habermas associate with the growth of culture industries and state bureaucracies. Rather than engaging popular debates over class prerogatives of culture, Irvine increasingly lent his voice to institutions that offered audiences more private comforts and satisfactions. Contrasted with erstwhile comrades like Eugene Debs, who went to prison for defying state efforts to curtail his participation in public debate, Irvine's wartime mission seems like docile acquiescence to forces that threatened to overwhelm the arenas where he had fought his most meaningful battles.[50]

Significantly, however, Irvine did not regard his wartime activities as compromises or defeats of the labor and socialist campaigns he had waged in the United States. On its face this may appear, at best, as self-delusion, especially in light of reminiscences that reveal his delight in the attention he attracted from MPs, aristocrats, and, in one case, the monarch.[51] But Irvine's conduct during and after the war often confirmed his interpretation of his actions. He took pains to emphasize that his morale-raising efforts were motivated by the camaraderie he felt with working-class fighting men. He substantiated these sentiments in several books: *God and Tommy Atkins* (1918) featured his lectures at military training camps in Britain and Ulster, where he pleaded with officers to respect the hopes and ideals of rank-and-file recruits; *The Carpenter and His Kingdom* (1922) interpreted the life of Christ for workingmen; *The Man from World's End* (1926) reproduced the anecdotes of life and love that working-class soldiers had exchanged in France. On his tour of postwar England, Irvine emphasized the nation's debt to workingmen and celebrated a government-sponsored industrial conference that endorsed many of the labor movement's principal aims. In 1921, he used his publicity networks to express a guarded sympathy with Irish rebels seeking the long-delayed implementation of Home Rule. In an article for the *London Evening News* based on a tour of Ireland in which he had tried to make contact with "Sinn Feiners and Unionists" as well as cadets of the Royal Irish Constabulary, Irvine affirmed that "behind all the violence, all the blunders, all the rebellion" of the IRA "there is the ideal of a race." Echoing the ethnic sensibilities he had affirmed in *My Lady of the Chimney Corner*, Irvine paid tribute to this ideal as a vision that "cannot be discounted . . . cannot be murdered."[52]

For Irvine, then, participation in a public sphere that was increasingly administered from above did not entail a complete retreat from his prewar cultural politics. He found novel venues for his mission, but continued to draw on class and ethnic sensibilities as he engaged new cultural political configurations. Such maneuvers could prove quite delicate, especially in the United States in the early 1920s, where wartime patriotism, postwar repression, and internal factionalism had decimated labor and socialist circles that remained more active in Britain. Under these circumstances, Irvine sought audiences and a livelihood in unlikely places for someone dedicated to proletarian causes. He lectured on health and success to Rotary Clubs and Chambers of Commerce, and went back to teaching and counseling at a private boys' school. These may seem the expedients of a charlatan to the professional heirs of those who watched from the academy cultural transformations that Irvine pursued in the popular public sphere. But on closer examination, Irvine's activities in the 1920s and 1930s reveal arenas where he could carry on, athwart new adversaries, the cultural politics that had shaped his mission before the war.[53]

Journalism provided one venue where Irvine contended with the changing contours of the public sphere. From his first visit back to the United States in 1920, Irvine privately cursed newspapers as "paid hirelings of the master class" and complained that they accepted advertising revenues for his lectures but did not report his message. Such laments reflected the process of commercialization and consolidation that journalism shared with other sectors of the public sphere. Still, throughout the 1920s Irvine often made part of his living by writing for the daily press on both sides of the Atlantic, and frequently injected his misgivings about the materialism of the 1920s and his own lingering class and ethnic solidarities into these projects. His *Evening News* piece on Ireland was one such instance, as was his interest in the German youth group, the *Wandervögel* (birds of passage), who rejected materialism and militarism for self-realization, and whom Irvine found "the most hopeful movement in Europe" when he toured

Germany to write a series of articles for a London newspaper in 1927. But Irvine's most sustained journalistic success was the column he published from October 1922 to March 1923 in William Randolph Hearst's *New York Journal*. This column featured anecdotes drawn from his life, embellished with timely morals and often accompanied by "Psalms of the Times"—poems in rhyming meter or blank verse on concerns of the day. Emphasizing the spiritual emptiness of a material age, the hypocrisy of business elites, and the dignity of labor, these pieces carried Hearst's reputation for populism into the 1920s (when the newspaper mogul was turning to congenial relations with business-friendly Republican presidents) and allowed Irvine to continue to draw on his own life to illustrate his gospel of work. The arrangement ended abruptly, however, when Irvine tried to negotiate a better position in the commercial markets that Hearst had mastered. Hoping to distribute his newspaper pieces more broadly, Irvine contracted with Cornelius Vanderbilt's newspaper syndicate, only to have the *Journal* drop him and the new syndicate neglect to place his pieces.[54]

Outwitted by commercial forces in journalism, Irvine found in New Thought circles another arena where his ideals jibed with prevailing cultural fashions. Here he did flirt with charlatanism, by hocking his ideas to Orlando Edgar Miller, a practitioner of psychology and mental healing who rose phoenix-like from an 1890s prison term for bank fraud to become an international figure in the New Thought movement. The two first met in London, where Miller ran the New Life Centre from 1910 until new legal wrangles prompted his return to the United States. Irvine remained a loyal supporter, claiming that Miller's ministrations maintained his failing health for the rigorous schedule of his lectures in France. During respites from his war work, Irvine spoke at Miller's London meetings, which prepared him for American collaborations after the war.

In these endeavors, Irvine found another popular venue slightly at odds with his own social sensibilities yet not completely antagonistic to them. Mixing nineteenth-century mental healing practices with the twentieth-century vogue of psychology and positive thinking, New Thought catered to middle-class desires for a moral philosophy that facilitated the enjoyment of material prosperity. Miller contributed to this ethos in lectures promising to teach "Scientific Salesmanship" and dispense the mental means to "promotion, power, fortune."[55] Yet, by advocating a shift from orthodox preoccupations with sin and redemption to the practical cultivation of spiritual health, New Thought also echoed Irvine's laborite gospel, with its demand for a democratic distribution of the means to religious self-realization. Irvine found he could even weave Debsian socialism into the lectures he contributed to the summer schools in applied psychology that Miller ran in Chicago and San Francisco in the early 1920s. The mixture resonated powerfully for at least one audience member, Frances Blanche Quinlivan, a Chicago office clerk who rushed home from one of Irvine's psychology lessons to write to the still-incarcerated Debs, pledging her vote and praising the "red headed, raw boned Irishman" who had championed Debs's martyrdom on the lecture platform.[56]

Relocated to San Francisco by 1923, Miller offered Irvine a position editing and writing his journal, the *Psychological Review of Reviews*, and assisting in the productions of his film syndicate. In the journal, Irvine interwove the themes of class and ethnic identity that characterized his earlier successes in the popular press with the psychological and unconscious forces that fascinated many progressive intellectuals in the 1920s.[57] Even more enticing, perhaps, Miller's film syndicate, Rellimeo ("Better Pictures with a Psychological Punch"), offered Irvine a new opportunity to collaborate in the production of movies intended as alternatives to mainstream cinematic fare. Irvine contributed the story for *The Bowery Bishop*, one of the two films Rellimeo produced. Elaborated out of Irvine's missionary experiences and London-esque style, *The Bowery Bishop* featured a robust protagonist in a series of crises involving accusations of seduction, gang warfare, moral vindication, and domestic reconciliation. While it is difficult to see how it was different from, much less better than, other films of the era that focused on similar sensational themes, *The Bowery Bishop* did put on screen the missionary persona Irvine had developed before the war, and whetted his appetite for cinematic immortality. After 1924, however, he pursued this hope in cultural waters beyond the harbor Miller provided. For, while Miller welcomed Irvine's socialist ideals, he was eager to exploit all the advertising devices of commercial culture to realize them. When his questionable scruples drew Irvine too far into the commercial ethos of the 1920s, Irvine abandoned the healer for freelance lecturing, preaching, and writing.[58]

Irvine's scant fortunes in these pursuits suggest that, while his mixture of evangelism, entertainment, and class politics still found audiences, his public was reduced since the 1910s. While venues like Hearst's and Miller's involved compromises with commercial imperatives that Irvine had found constraining since his days in vaudeville, he was hard pressed to make a living outside of them. The old audiences of Socialists and trade unionists he had mobilized before the war were decimated by factionalism, postwar antiradicalism, and the emergence of the Communist Party. New narratives and performances of sexual self-revelation prevailed in magazines, the popular press, and the movies. On his own, Irvine found few buyers for his old formula of proletarian vitality. To secure audiences for his written and oral self-representations, he depended increasingly on his nostalgia value as a wartime morale raiser, an evangelical success story, and a sentimental Irishman. Along with his war reminiscences, he published articles and two more books about the chimney corner characters—*The Souls of Poor Folk* (a title that paid homage to W. E. B. Du Bois and the cultural politics of race out of which Irvine had forged his Irish characters) and *Anna's Wishing Chair*. A second autobiography, which he entitled *A Celtic Pilgrimage* but his publisher called *A Fighting Parson*, sold poorly at the beginning of the Depression. By then, Irvine was working as a counselor for a private boys' school in Santa Barbara and making repeated visits to the United Kingdom to lecture in venues—the YMCA and temperance crusades—reminiscent of his mission before trade union activism had inspired his gospel of work. These activities generated support for memorials to the vision of plebeian Irish camaraderie his books had popularized. Such memorials included a headstone engraved with the motto "love is enough" for his parents, and, eventually, a museum established at the Irvine cabin in Pogue's Entry. They were touching tributes, but must have felt like meager outposts from a public sphere that had little room left for Irvine's ideals of class solidarity and cultural democracy.[59]

Still, the transformations in public culture that Irvine witnessed in the 1920s were no more permanent than the public sphere he had occupied before the war. Corporate consolidations in the culture industry reshaped that sphere, but so, too, did new initiatives in labor militancy in the 1930s. Though an ailing septuagenarian by this time, Irvine was quick to find alliances that breathed new cultural life into his socialist sensibilities. In 1929 he had already visited the Soviet Union—the model of social reorganization for the left of the 1930s—though illness prevented him from touring there. In 1932 he moved to Los Angeles and organized "The Church of the Kingdom" as a "challenge to modern materialism," opposed to the "fundamentalism and medievalism" that had absorbed much of his plebeian evangelical heritage. Publicity for the church described Irvine as a "champion of the working class," a title he confirmed by lending his support to union battles of immigrant farmworkers in the Imperial Valley. Enlisted by the American Civil Liberties Union to speak in support of farmworkers' rights and against the violent tactics of the anti-union "Associated Farmers," Irvine was kidnapped by vigilantes in Calexico, California, wounded, and left in the desert. Galvanized for further battle, he supported the CIO and the blossoming of proletarian themes in the public sphere throughout the rest of the decade.[60] His enthusiasm affected his Northern Irish evangelism as well: after a 1934 speech in Belfast's Labour Hall endorsing labor unions and socialism, Irvine was no longer welcome among the more conventional evangelical Protestants who had been sponsoring his visits. He gladly shed what he had come to feel a false position, even rejecting an offer to secure him a civil pension from the government of Northern Ireland lest he compromise his freedom to speak for "fair play for the working classes . . . the dominating activity of my life." Back in California, where he scraped by in graceful poverty and worsening health, Irvine sustained his "paramount interest in social progress" by supporting labor martyrs like Harry Bridges and Tom Mooney. Once again, class conflict inspired him to affirm a gospel of work that resonated with wider cultural transformations.[61]

At the end of his life, Irvine hoped he might once again follow this gospel into the spotlight of commercial culture, this time by selling *My Lady of the Chimney Corner* to the film industry. He claimed to have come close to a movie deal in the late 1920s, only to back off when he learned that the studio planned to caricature his Irish vignettes. In 1939 he thought he saw more promising possibilities. From his Hollywood home Irvine followed the political battles that surrounded the filming of John Steinbeck's *The Grapes of Wrath*, which he predicted would be "the most radical picture ever produced here." But he thought *My Lady of the Chimney Corner* would be an even more effective vehicle for the cinematic depiction of "hunger and discomfort" since the characters in his book had "humor," "the buoyancy of the Celtic temperament" and "spiritual uplift," as he wrote in a film prospectus. His expectations may have been exaggerated, but they were not utterly unfounded. The Popular Front culture of the 1930s, nourished by the renewal of labor activism, had helped create spaces in the Hollywood culture industry for proletarian sagas like *The Grapes of Wrath*. *My Lady's* vision of working-class ethnicity in some ways hewed closer than Steinbeck's novel to Popular Front concerns with the intersection of ethnic, racial, and class distinctions, while maintaining the ethos of militant motherhood that characterized the gender politics of much Popular Front culture.[62] However, Irvine died quietly on March 15, 1941, without seeing a film version of *My Lady* or, as his prospectus had self-confidently suggested, of "the spectacular and extraordinary story" of its author's life.[63]

Instead, Irvine left behind the legacy contained in his memoirs of Antrim life, his autobiographies, and the scattered documents by which cultural historians might trace his trajectory. His conviction that the cultural politics of *My Lady* remained compelling even in a changed public sphere provides a fitting commentary on the kind of history his story helps us reconstruct, and its relation to recent formulations of "cultural studies" across many disciplines. As it intersected Poli's entertainment world, Irvine's career broadens our view of a shift that led

14. Alexander Irvine (*right*) with Tom Mooney, the San Francisco trade unionist who had been convicted of murder, on flimsy evidence, in connection with a bomb that exploded along the route of a 1916 Preparedness Day Parade. They posed together shortly after Mooney's pardon and release from prison in 1939. Photo courtesy of Alexander Irvine, Santa Barbara, California.

from questions about Protestant cultural hierarchies and evolutionary racial distinctions to questions about the multiple cultures that render lives meaningful—questions that have persisted through further transformations in the public sphere after his death. In the process, Irvine's and Poli's intersecting stories provide something of a prehistory for more recent reassessments of the cultural industries in which they struggled. Like many contributors to the project of cultural studies, Irvine and Poli identified commercial entertainment as an arena of cultural production that they could shape even while they found their participation constrained by its developing corporate institutions. As they formulated conceptions of culture out of such encounters, they demonstrated the relevance of their own popular debates to scholarly discourses about culture, thus eliding categories of high and popular culture—as well as "authentic" and "commercial" culture—that more recent cultural studies scholars have questioned in provocative ways. The shifting narratives of working-class identity that Irvine forged out of his own engagement in these debates, in turn, anticipated the interrogation of class in relation to social categories of race, ethnicity, and gender that has also informed cultural studies scholarship. By no means, however, did Irvine, Poli, or their contemporaries bequeath these questions—or the insights into cultural politics derived from them—intact to later generations. As Michael Denning has observed of the cultural analyses generated out of the Popular Front—the arena of Irvine's own final cultural political crusades—such insights must be repeatedly reclaimed and reconstructed as they and their authors are obscured by new cultural political battles.[64]

In offering such a reconstruction, this book has drawn on Irvine's and Poli's trajectories to contribute its own perspective on the historical study of cultural politics. It has emphasized how the competing ideas about cultural hierarchy, group autonomy, and cultural pluralism Irvine and Poli engaged were shaped by class conflicts, the political debates they generated, and the self-reflexive cultural hierarchies of the popular cultural arena. As they engaged the juncture of popular culture and class politics, both men's trajectories remind us that class distinctions, the social conflicts they generated, and the meanings woven around them had important intellectual implications for the meaning of culture. Historical subfields that separate parties to class conflict and audiences for popular culture from the trajectory of American intellectual history too easily neglect these implications. Such divisions are understandable in light of developments in Irvine's and Poli's own era, when academic professionalization and depoliticized "scientism" became institutionalized characteristics of scholarly work. However, Irvine's and Poli's stories compel us to look beyond these scholarly divi-

339

sions in recounting the struggles and insights that gave rise to the terms of cultural debate that outlasted them and their public sphere, and persisted into our own. They show that class politics and popular culture were crucial sites where concepts of class distinction changed, along with conceptions of ethnicity, race, and gender that complicated and often disrupted the cultural politics of class.

This is not to say that the cultural constructions debated in the arenas that Irvine, Poli, or their audiences inhabited were superior to those emerging from the academy or from other sectors of the public sphere that transformed around them. From the era of Irvine's and Poli's public sphere into the late twentieth century, within academic scholarship as well as more popular debates, pluralist visions of culture have never decisively displaced evolutionary hierarchies of race and class. Celebrations of ethnic cultural distinction such as Irvine generated in his Irish stories have sometimes strayed into essentialist identity politics that muddle the complex intersection of material, cultural, and social relations he tried to articulate. Meanwhile, some self-proclaimed advocates of "working-class" interests have continued to construe these as purely material questions, neglecting the intersecting distinctions of ethnicity, race, and gender through which Irvine, Poli, and their audiences made sense of class distinctions. To include the cultural conflicts illuminated by Irvine's and Poli's stories in the history of these ongoing debates does not solve the problems they pose. But it does help identify more accurately the wellsprings of our own cultural concepts and political predicaments. Perhaps it may also inspire some of us to recapture the imaginative and political will that Irvine and many of his allies demonstrated as they addressed the nexus of class and culture.

APPENDIX A

VAUDEVILLE ACTS AT POLI'S NEW HAVEN THEATERS: PART I, 1894–1899

My discussion of vaudeville shows appearing at Poli's theater in the 1890s draws on a sample of vaudeville acts that appeared in Poli's advertisements between January 1894 and December 1899. I chose 1894 because it was the year Poli employed J. B. McElfatrick to redesign his theater, bringing it architecturally into the "mainstream" of American vaudeville associated with B. F. Keith. The sample runs for six years, making it comparable to the samples described in Appendixes B and C. I assembled the sample by selecting at random one week from each calendar month in which Poli presented vaudeville in his New Haven theater, usually January to June and September to December. For each week chosen, I noted the advertisements for Poli's that appeared in at least one of three New Haven newspapers: the *Union*, the *Journal Courier*, or the *Register*. In the case of the sample for 1894–1899, this selection process yielded 492 acts, or 8.2 acts per week studied.

Often, Poli's advertisements listed only the names of performers in identifying an act. I added to this information by consulting the archives at the New York Public Library of the Performing Arts and several secondary sources.[1] I was thus able to categorize at least roughly 352, or 71%, of the original 1890s sample of 492 acts. My discussion of the relative predominance of various types of acts draws on calculations made with these 352 acts, which broke down into the following broad categories:

Appendix A

Table A1
Vaudeville Acts at Poli's, by Type

Category	# of Acts	% of Nondumb Acts	% of Total
Dumb acts: freaks, circus, cycle,slapstick, acrobat, juggling, animal	86	0	25
Musical: dance, song and dance high culture song, musical novelty	116	44	33
Talking: sketch, skit, monologue	117	44	33
Film: stereopticon, illustrated song, early motion picture	18	6	5
Magic/conjurer	7	2.5	2
Ventriloquist	4	1.5	1
Puppets	2	1	0.5
Other: gramophone, rapid drawing	2	1	0.5
Total	352	100	100

Within major categories of musical and talking acts, I calculated thematic subcategories of specialty acts. Here percentages overlap, since one song-and-dance or sketch act may feature character acting, sentimentality, and themes of city life. The calculations for subcategorizations were made against two totals—that of the subcategory itself (e.g., song-and-dance acts that have sentimental themes) and that of the acts within the subcategory with identifiable themes. The first percentage reflects a conservative estimate of the type's prevalence within the subcategory, the second percentage counts only those acts for which a specific theme could be identified. Presumably, if more themes could be identified, these acts would be distributed roughly according to the "identifiable theme" percentages.

Table A2
Vaudeville Acts at Poli's, by Theme

Subcategory and % of Category	Type	Type as % of Subcategory	Type as % of Identifiable Theme in Subcategory
Musical Acts			
Dance (12) 10%			
Song and Dance (79) 70%			
Identifiable Theme = 62	Blackface (25)	32	40
	Irish (10)	13	16
	Sentimental (43)	54	69
	Character (46)	58	74
	City Life (6)	8	10
	High Culture (3)	4	5
Musical Novelty (25) 20%			
Talking acts			
Sketch (77) 65%			
Identifiable Theme = 56	Irish (12)	16	21
	Character (19)	25	34
	City Life (17)	22	39
	Marriage (9)	12	16
Monologue (10) 9%			
Identifiable Theme = 5	Irish (2)	20	40
	Blackface (2)	20	40
	Character (3)	30	60
	City Life (4)	40	80
Other: Two-Act, Impersonation, Parody, Juvenile, Misc. Comedy (32) 26%			
Talking Act			
Identifiable Theme = 72			
	Irish (18)		25
	Character (36)		50
	City Life (20)		27
	Yankee/Rube (8)		11
	Tramp (6)		8

APPENDIX B

VAUDEVILLE ACTS AT POLI'S NEW HAVEN THEATERS: PART II, 1902–1907

Appendix B is made up of 453 total vaudeville acts appearing at Poli's theater from 1902 through 1907. 437 could be identified by category, and broke down into the categories and thematic subcategories enumerated in Tables B1 and B2.

Table B1

Vaudeville Acts at Poli's, by Type

Category	# of Acts	% of Nondumb Acts	% of Total
Dumb acts: freaks, circus, cycle, slapstick, acrobat, juggling, animal	86	0	20
Musical: dance, song and dance, high culture song, musical novelty	148	42	34
Talking: sketch, skit, monologue	147	42	34
Film: stereopticon, illustrated song, early motion picture	45	13	10
Magic/conjurer	3	1	0.5
Ventriloquist	4	1	1
Other	4	1	0.5
Total	437	100	100

Table B2

Vaudeville Acts at Poli's, by Theme

Subcategory and % of Category	Type	Type as % of Subcategory	Type as % of Identifiable Theme in Subcategory
Musical Acts			
Dance (14) 9%			
Song and Dance (113) 75%			
Identifiable Theme = 71	Black (16)	14	35
	Blackface (10)	9	12
	Irish (3)	2	4
	Character (37)	32	50
	City Life (4)	3	6
	High Culture (4)	4	6
	Ensemble (8)	7	11
Musical Novelty (23) 16%			
Talking Acts			
Sketch (78) 53%			
Identifiable Theme = 33	Irish (5)	6	16
	Character (18)	25	34
	City Life (10)	13	33
	Marriage (7)	9	23
	Social Class (17)	22	56
	Stage Life and Fashion (3)	6	10
Playlet (23) 16%			
Identifiable Theme = 9	Irish (4)	17	44
	Marriage (5)	22	55
	Class (4)	17	44
Monologue (12) 8%			
Identifiable Theme = 5	Irish (1)	10	20
	Blackface (1)	10	20
	Hebrew (2)	20	40
	Marriage (1)	10	20

Continued on next page

Table B2—*Continued*

Subcategory and % of Category	Type	Type as % of Subcategory	Type as % of Identifiable Theme in Subcategory
Other: Two-Act, Impersonation, Parody, Juvenile, Misc. Comedy (32) 23%			
Talking Act Identifiable Theme = 65			
	Irish (10)		16
	Hebrew (8)		13
	Marriage (11)		18
	Character (38)		58
	Stage Life and Fashion (3)		5

VAUDEVILLE ACTS AT POLI'S NEW HAVEN THEATERS: PART III, 1908–1913

Appendix C is made up of 384 total vaudeville acts appearing at Poli's theater from 1908 through 1913. 366 could be identified by category, and broke down into the categories and thematic subcategories enumerated in Tables C1 and C2.

Table C1
Vaudeville Acts at Poli's, by Type

Category	# of Acts	% of Nondumb Acts	% of Total
Dumb acts: freaks, circus, cycle, slapstick, acrobat, juggling, animal	59	0	16
Musical: dance, song and dance, high culture song, musical novelty	142	46	39
Talking: sketch, skit, monologue	108	35	30
Film: stereopticon, illustrated song, early motion picture	39	13	10.5
Magic/conjurer	6	2	1.5
Ventriloquist	2	7	0.5
Other	10	3.3	2.5
Total	366	100	100

Appendix C

Table C2
Vaudeville Acts at Poli's, by Theme

Subcategory and % of Category	Type	Type as % of Subcategory	Type as % of Identifiable Theme in Subcategory
Musical Acts			
Dance (13) 9%			
Song and Dance (115) 81%			
Identifiable Theme = 88	Black (5)	4	6
	Blackface (10)	1	11
	Irish (3)	3	3
	Character (30)	26	34
	City Life (4)	3	8
	High Culture (7)	6	8
	Ensemble (26)	23	30
Musical Novelty (14) 10%			
Talking Acts			
Sketch (54) 50%			
Identifiable Theme = 23	Irish (1)	2	4
	Character (5)	9	22
	City Life (6)	11	26
	Social Class (1)	2	4
	Stage Life and Fashion (7)	13	30
Playlet (217) 15%			
Identifiable Theme = 8	City Life (5)	29	63
	Marriage (2)	12	25
	Stage Life and Fashion (1)	6	13
Monologue (7) 7%			
Other: Two-Act, Impersonation, Parody, Juvenile, Misc. Comedy (30) 28%			

Continued on next page

Table C2—*Continued*

Subcategory and % of Category	Type	Type as % of Subcategory	Type as % of Identifiable Theme in Subcategory
Talking Act Identifiable Theme = 51			
	Irish (3)		6
	Hebrew (6)		12
	Marriage (4)		8
	Character (21)		41
	Stage Life (11)		22
	Western (2)		4
	Rube (4)		8
	Blackface (1)		2
	Black (2)		4
	Asian (1)		2
	Italian (1)		2

Note

1. Douglas Gilbert, *American Vaudeville, Its Life and Times* (New York: McGraw-Hill, 1940); Joe Laurie, *Vaudeville: From the Honky-tonks to the Palace* (New York: Henry Holt, 1953); and Albert McLean, *American Vaudeville as Ritual* (Lexington: University of Kentucky Press, 1965).

ABBREVIATIONS USED IN NOTES

AGDC Arnold Guyot Dana Collection, New Haven Colony Historical
Society

AIC Alexander Irvine Collection, privately assembled by Anna Irvine Buck
and Anna Giarretto, now located at the Huntington Library,
San Marino, California

AIPABC Alexander Irvine Papers, Antrim Borough Council

APSP Anson Phelps Stokes Papers, Yale MS Group 299, Manuscripts and
Archives, Sterling Memorial Library, Yale University

AR *The Appeal to Reason*

BRTC Billy Rose Theatre Collection, New York Public Library for the
Performing Arts

CSD *California Social Democrat*

CTC Crawford Theatre Collection, Manuscripts and Archives, Sterling
Memorial Library, Yale University

FFP Farnam Family Papers, MS Group 203, Manuscripts and Archives,
Sterling Memorial Library, Yale University

ICC *Il Corriere del Connecticut*

JLC Jack London Collection, Huntington Library, San Marino,
California

LHMCR Lowell House Mothers' Club Records, 1900–44, MS 33, New Haven
Colony Historical Society

LWCP Livingston Warner Clevealand Papers, MS B-13, New Haven Colony
Historical Society

MFCD Michael F. Campbell Diaries, Diaries (Miscellaneous) Collection,
MS Group 181, Manuscripts and Archives, Sterling Memorial
Library, Yale University

NECR New England Church Records, Record Group 48, Manuscripts and
Archives, Yale Divinity School Library

Abbreviations Used in Notes

NHEL *New Haven Evening Leader*
NHJC *New Haven Journal Courier*
NHU *New Haven Union*
NHR *New Haven Register*
PCEHP Peoples of Connecticut Ethnic Heritage Project, WPA Writers'
Project, Historical Manuscripts and Archives, University of
Connecticut, Storrs
PROK Public Record Office, Kew
PRONI Public Record Office of Northern Ireland
RYMCA New Haven Railroad YMCA Collection, MSS B-18, Supplement C,
Box I, New Haven Colony Historical Society

NOTES

Introduction: Piety, Pleasure, and the Public Sphere: Cultural Politics and the Problem of Realism

1. This picture is drawn from a vast literature on American religious history that contains far more nuance and dissension than I can represent here. For pieces of the trajectory I describe, see Martin Marty, *Pilgrims in Their Own Land: 500 Years of Religion in America* (Boston: Little, Brown, 1984), 62–66, 75–78; John Butler, *Awash in a Sea of Faith* (Cambridge, Mass.: Harvard University Press, 1990); Rhys Isaac, *The Transformation of Virginia: Community, Religion, and Authority, 1740–1790* (Chapel Hill: University of North Carolina Press, 1982); Nathan O. Hatch, *The Democratization of American Christianity* (New Haven, Conn.: Yale University Press, 1989); Susan Juster, *Disorderly Women: Sexual Politics and Evangelicalism in Revolutionary New England* (Ithaca, N.Y.: Cornell University Press, 1994); T. J. Jackson Lears, *No Place of Grace: Anti-Modernism and the Transformation of American Culture, 1880–1920* (New York: Pantheon, 1981); Susan Curtis, *A Consuming Faith: The Social Gospel and Modern American Culture* (Baltimore: Johns Hopkins University Press, 1991); John Kasson, *Rudeness and Civility: Manners in Nineteenth-Century America* (New York: Hill & Wang, 1990).

2. See Jürgen Habermas, *The Structural Transformation of the Public Sphere: An Inquiry into a Category of Bourgeois Society* (Cambridge, Mass.: MIT, 1989); Terry Eagleton, *The Function of Criticism* (London: Verso, 1984); Peter Uwe Hohendahl, *The Institution of Criticism* (Ithaca, N.Y.: Cornell University Press, 1982). For applications to American history, see Michael Schudson, "Was There Ever a Public Sphere? If So, When? Reflections on the American Case," and Mary P. Ryan, "Gender and Public Access: Women's Politics in Nineteenth-Century America," in *Habermas and the Public Sphere*, ed. Craig Calhoun (Cambridge, Mass.: MIT, 1992); Mary P. Ryan, *Women in Public: Between Banners and Ballots, 1825–1880* (Baltimore: Johns Hopkins University Press, 1990); Miriam Hansen, *Babel and Babylon: Spectatorship in American Silent Film* (Cambridge, Mass.: Harvard University Press, 1991); Phillip Ethington, *The Public City: The Political Construction of Urban Life in San Francisco, 1850–1900* (Cambridge: Cambridge University Press, 1994), though note that Ethington's conception of the public sphere counterposes politics to material conflict much more diametrically than the approach advanced here.

3. Though not derived from them, this use of the notion of trajectory is somewhat analogous to recent studies of transcultural observations made by anthropologists as well as by migrant members of the societies they observed. Here, too, cultural concepts are seen to be under construction as "Western" scholars and their anthropological "subjects" cross the boundaries that distinguish specific nations and cultures. For suggestive examples, see James Clifford, *The Predicament of Culture: Twentieth Century Ethnography, Literature and Art* (Cambridge, Mass.: Harvard University Press, 1988); and idem, "Traveling Cultures," in *Cultural Studies*, ed. Lawrence Grossberg, Cary Nelson, and Paula Treichler (New York: Routledge, 1992).

4. Alexander Irvine, *From the Bottom Up: The Life Story of Alexander Irvine* (New York: Doubleday, 1910); idem, *My Lady of the Chimney Corner* (London: Ernest Benn, 1913).

5. These debates are discussed in more detail below; see note 16.

6. For other recent scholarship stressing the significance of narrative for class as well as gender distinctions, see Judith Walkowitz, *City of Dreadful Delight: Narratives of Sexual Danger in Late-Victorian London* (Chicago: University of Chicago Press, 1992); Patrick Joyce, *Democratic Subjects: The Self and the Social in Nineteenth-Century England* (Cambridge: Cambridge University Press, 1994); Regenia Gagnier, *Subjectivities: The History of Self-Representation in Britain, 1832–1920* (Oxford: Oxford University Press, 1991); Carolyn Steedman, *The Radical Soldier's Tale: John Pearman, 1819–1908* (London: Routledge, 1988); Regina Kunzel, "Pulp Fictions and Problem Girls: Reading and Rewriting Single Pregnancy in the Postwar United States," *American Historical Review* 100, no. 5 (1995): 1465–87; Sean McCann, "A Roughneck Reaching for Higher Things: The Vagaries of Pulp Populism," *Radical History Review* 61 (Winter 1995): 4–34; Ann Fabian, "Making a Commodity Out of Truth: Speculations on the Career of Bernarr Macfadden," *American Literary History* 5 (Spring 1993): 51–76; Mari Jo Buhle and Paul Buhle, "The New Labor History at the Cultural Crossroads," *Journal of American History* 75, no. 1 (1988): 151–57. On working-class autobiography, see also Mary Jo Maynes, *Taking the Hard Road: Life Course in French and German Workers' Autobiographies in the Era of Industrialization* (Chapel Hill: University of North Carolina Press, 1995); and David Vincent, *Bread, Knowledge and Freedom: A Study of Nineteenth-Century Working Class Autobiography* (London: Europa, 1981). On the analysis of autobiography in general I have been helped by Roy Pascal, *Design and Truth in Autobiography* (London: Routledge & Kegan Paul, 1960); James Olney, *Metaphors of Self: The Meaning of Autobiography* (Princeton, N.J.: Princeton University Press, 1972); and Philippe Lejeune, *On Autobiography* (Minneapolis: Uiversity of Minnesota Press, 1989).

7. The Bibliographical Essay, sec. II.B, discusses these issues in detail.

8. For a discussion of this literature, see Bibliographical Essay, sec. II.B.

9. Hatch, *Democratization of American Christianity*; Richard Cawardine, *Trans-Atlantic Revivalism: Popular Evangelicalism in Britain and America, 1790–1865* (Westport, Conn.: Greenwood, 1978); Jama Lazerow, *Religion and the Working Class in Antebellum America* (Washington, D.C.: Smithsonian Institution, 1995); Juster, *Disorderly Women*.

10. For the "therapeutic" interpretation, see especially T. J. Jackson Lears, "From Salvation to Self-Realization: Advertising and the Therapeutic Roots of the Consumer Culture, 1880–1930," in *The Culture of Consumption: Critical Essays in American His-*

tory, 1880–1980, ed. Richard Wightman Fox and T. J. Jackson Lears (New York: Pantheon, 1983); idem, *No Place of Grace*; for the longer view, see R. Laurence Moore, *Selling God: American Religion in the Marketplace of Culture* (New York: Oxford, 1994). For further literature on popular religion and popular culture, see Bibliographical Essay, sec. II.B.

11. Moore, *Selling God*, 188–203.

12. See especially Lawrence Levine, *Highbrow/Lowbrow: The Emergence of Cultural Hierarchy in America* (Cambridge, Mass.: Harvard University Press, 1988); Kasson, *Rudeness and Civility*; Robert C. Allen, *Horrible Prettiness: Burlesque and American Culture* (Chapel Hill: University of North Carolina Press, 1991).

13. For historiographical literature on vaudeville, see Bibliographical Essay, sec. II.E.

14. Each part of the sample runs for six years (1894–99, 1902–7, 1908–13) and is comprised of acts publicized during one week chosen randomly from each month that Poli presented vaudeville acts. The appendix to this book summarizes these categories. I have constructed the narrative of shifting cultural hierarchies and constructions of refinement I will discuss by comparing the shifting categories of acts revealed in this three-part sample.

15. On cultural studies conceived in these terms, see especially Stuart Hall, "Cultural Studies: Two Paradigms," in *Culture/Power/History: A Reader in Contemporary Social Theory*, ed. Nicholas B. Dirks, Geoff Eley, and Sherry B. Ortner (Princeton, N.J.: Princeton University Press, 1994); Patrick Brantlinger, *Crusoe's Footprints: Cultural Studies in Britain and America* (New York: Routledge, 1990), 95–101; George Lipsitz, *Time Passages: Collective Memory and American Popular Culture* (Minneapolis: University of Minnesota Press, 1990). The reading of Gramsci used here is indebted to Raymond Williams, especially *Marxism and Literature* (Oxford: Oxford University Press, 1977), 108–14. On the uses of "hegemony" in American history, see T. J. Jackson Lears, "The Concept of Cultural Hegemony: Problems and Possibilities," *American Historical Review* 90, no. 3 (1985): 567–93.

16. This brand of cultural studies is represented especially by John Fisk. See, for example, *Reading the Popular* (Boston: Unwin Hyman, 1989). It receives a cogent critique along lines similar to mine in Mike Budd, Robert M. Entman, and Clay Steinman, "The Affirmative Character of U.S. Cultural Studies," *Critical Studies in Mass Communication* 7 (June 1990): 169–84; for a sampling of the range of cultural studies methods and concerns, see Grossberg, Nelson, and Treichler, eds., *Cultural Studies*. Among historians of the United States, Robin D. G. Kelley has advanced a most provocative model of culture as an arena of African-American resistance in "'We Are Not What We Seem': Rethinking Black Working-Class Opposition in the Jim Crow South," *Journal of American History* 80, no. 1 (1993). For the significance of such cultural definitions of politics for the redefinition of political history, see Mark Leff, "Revisioning U.S. Political History," *American Historical Review* 100, no. 3 (1995): 829–53. For a recent example of cultural studies that combines culture and politics, see Michael Denning, *The Cultural Front: The Laboring of American Culture in the Twentieth Century* (New York: Verso, 1996).

17. The debates over social-historical and cultural-historical approaches to class are laid out with particular clarity in a series of articles and responses published in the journals *Past and Present* and *Social History*. See Lawrence Stone, "Notes: History and Post-Modernism," *Past and Present* 131 (May 1991): 217–18; Patrick Joyce, "History and Post-

Modernism I," *Past and Present* 133 (November 1991): 204–9; Catriona Kelly, "History and Post-Modernism II," *Past and Present* 133 (November 1991): 209–13; Stone, "History and Post-Modernism III," *Past and Present* 135 (May 1992): 189–94; Gabrielle Spiegel, "History and Postmodernism IV," *Past and Present* 135 (May 1992): 194–208; David Mayfield and Susan Thorne, "Social History and Its Discontents: Gareth Stedman Jones and the Politics of Language," *Social History* 17, no. 2 (1992): 165–88; Jon Lawrence and Miles Taylor, "The Poverty of Protest: Gareth Stedman Jones and the Politics of Language—A Reply," *Social History* 18, no. 1 (1993): 1–15; Joyce, "The Imaginary Discontents of Social History: A Note of Response to Mayfield and Thorne, and Lawrence and Taylor," *Social History* 18, no. 1 (1993): 81–85; Mayfield and Thorne, "Reply to 'The Poverty of Protest' and 'The Imaginary Discontents,'" *Social History* 18, no. 2 (1993): 219–33; Joyce, "The End of Social History?" *Social History* 20, no. 1 (1995): 73–91; Geoff Eley and Keith Nield, "Starting Over: The Present, the Post-Modern, and the Moment of Social History," *Social History* 20, no. 3 (1995): 355–64; Joyce, "The End of Social History? A Brief Reply to Eley and Nield," *Social History* 21, no. 1 (1996): 96–98; Marc W. Steinberg, "Culturally Speaking: Finding a Commons between Post-Structuralism and the Thompsonian Perspective," *Social History* 21, no. 2 (1996): 193–214; Dror Wahrman, "The New Political History: A Review Essay," *Social History* 21, no. 3 (1996): 343–54. For further expositions of the different positions in this debate and their antecedents, see E. P. Thompson, *The Making of the English Working Class* (New York: Pantheon, 1963); Gareth Stedman-Jones, *Languages of Class: Studies in English Working Class History, 1832–1982* (Cambridge: Cambridge University Press, 1983); Patrick Joyce, *Visions of the People: Industrial England and the Question of Class, 1840–1914* (Cambridge: Cambridge University Press, 1991); idem, *Democratic Subjects*; Joan Wallach Scott, "The Evidence of Experience," *Critical Inquiry* 17 (Summer 1991): 773–97; Bryan Palmer, *Descent into Discourse: The Reification of Language and the Writing of Social History* (Philadelphia: Temple University Press, 1990); Gabrielle Spiegel, "History, Historicism, and the Social Logic of the Text in the Middle Ages," *Speculum* 65 (January 1990): 59–86; Lynn Hunt, ed., *The New Cultural History* (Berkeley: University of California Press, 1989); Patrick Joyce, ed., *Class* (Oxford: Oxford University Press, 1995).

18. William Dean Howells, *The Editors' Study* (Troy, N.Y.: Whitston, 1983), 95–96 (September 1887); Amy Kaplan, *The Social Construction of American Realism* (Chicago: University of Chicago Press, 1988), 17, 21–23.

19. Howells, *Editor's Study*, 30–31, 329 (July 1886).

20. William Dean Howells, *Annie Kilburn*, in *Novels, 1886–1888* (New York: The Library of America, 1978), 643–45, 649–50, 668–72, 680–84, 764–65, 772–74, 818, 860–63.

21. William Dean Howells, *A Hazard of New Fortunes* (New York: New American Library, 1965), 55–67, 241, 365–69, 431.

22. For readings of Crane and Dreiser as working-class realism, see F. O. Mathiessen, *Theodore Dreiser* (New York: William Sloane Associates, 1951), 73–87; Alfred Kazin, "Theodore Dreiser: His Education and Ours," in *The Stature of Theodore Dreiser*, ed. A. Kazin and C. Shapiro (Bloomington: Indiana University Press, 1955), 158; Larzer Ziff, *The American 1890s* (New York: Viking, 1966), 341. For more recent readings of Crane and Dreiser as focusing on speculative transformations of the self, see Amy Kaplan, "Naturalism with a Difference," *American Quarterly* 40 (December 1988): 582–89; and *The*

Social Construction of American Realism, 7–8; Walter Benn Michaels, "*Sister Carrie's* Popular Economy," *Critical Inquiry* 7 (Winter 1980): 373–90; Philip Fisher, "Acting, Reading Fortune's Wheel: *Sister Carrie* and the Life History of Objects," in *American Realism: New Essays*, ed. Eric Sundquist (Baltimore: Johns Hopkins University Press), 259–77.

23. R. W. Stallman, *Stephen Crane: A Biography* (New York: George Braziller, 1968), 26–30; Reverend J. T. Crane, *Popular Amusements* (Cincinnati: Hitchcock & Walden, 1869).

24. Ferenc M. Szasz and Ralph F. Bogardus, "The Camera and the American Social Conscience: The Documentary Photography of Jacob A Riis," *New York History* 55, no. 4 (1974): 202–3, 215, 221; Peter Bacon Hales, *Silver Cities: The Photography of American Urbanization, 1839–1915* (Philadelphia: Temple University Press, 1984), 192–98; Jacob A. Riis, *How the Other Half Lives* (New York: Dover, 1971), 1, 41, 115, 121–22, 192; Stephen Crane, *Maggie: A Girl of the Streets*, in *The Portable Stephen Crane*, ed. J. Katz (New York: Penguin, 1969), 20.

25. On Crane's contrasting languages in *Maggie*, see Donald B. Gibson, *The Fiction of Stephen Crane* (Carbondale: Southern Illinois University Press, 1968), 26–34, excerpted in *Maggie: A Girl of the Streets*, ed. Thomas A. Gullason (New York: Norton, 1979); Arno Karlen, "The Craft of Stephen Crane," *Georgia Review* 28 (Fall 1974): 473–77; and more recently, June Howard, *Form and History in American Literary Naturalism* (Chapel Hill: University of North Carolina Press, 1985), 104–5; and Michael Davitt Bell, *The Problem of American Realism: Studies in the Cultural History of a Literary Idea* (Chicago: University of Chicago Press, 1993), 136–41.

26. Crane, *Maggie*, 3, 24; Charles Rosen and Henri Zerner, *Romanticism and Realism* (New York: Viking, 1984), 155, 161.

27. Crane, *Maggie*, 39–65, 72.

28. Ibid., 61.

29. Theodore Dreiser, *Sister Carrie* (New York: New American Library, 1961), 11–18, 42–43, 54, 108.

30. Ibid., 74–75, 140, 180–81, 462–63; Dreiser, *Dawn* (New York: Horace Liveright, 1931), 25, 348–49, 360; idem, *Newspaper Days* (New York: Beekman, 1974), 478.

31. Dreiser, *Sister Carrie*, 92–93.

32. For historians who stress the autonomy of working-class culture, see Roy Rosenzweig, *Eight Hours for What We Will* (Cambridge: Cambridge University Press, 1983); and Kathy Peiss, *Cheap Amusements: Working Women and Leisure in Turn-of-the-Century New York* (Philadelphia: Temple University Press, 1986); for historians who stress cultural hierarchy, see Levine, *Highbrow/Lowbrow*; and Kasson, *Rudeness and Civility*.

33. On realist authors and this transformation in the literary public sphere, see especially Kaplan, *The Social Construction of American Realism*, passim; and Bell, *The Problem of American Realism*, passim.

34. Habermas, *Structural Transformation*, 36, 164–66.

35. On Habermas's approach to religion, see Craig Calhoun, "Introduction: Habermas and the Public Sphere," and David Zaret, "Religion, Science, and Printing in the Public Spheres in Seventeenth-Century England," in *Habermas and the Public Sphere*, ed. Calhoun, 35–36, 212–35; on the significance of evangelical religion to American public

debate, see especially Mary Ryan, "Gender and Public Access: Women's Politics in Nineteenth-Century America," in *Habermas and the Public Sphere*, ed. Calhoun, 259–88; and Hatch, *Democratization of American Religion*.

36. On "counterpublics" and their significance in the eighteenth, nineteenth, and twentieth centuries, see Nancy Fraser, "Rethinking the Public Sphere: A Contribution to the Critique of Actually Existing Democracy," Ryan, "Gender and Public Access," and Geoff Eley, "Nations, Publics, and Political Cultures: Placing Habermas in the Nineteenth Century," in *Habermas and the Public Sphere*, ed. Calhoun, 109–42, 259–339; Ryan, *Women in Public*; Oskar Negt and Alexander Kluge, *Public Sphere and Experience: Towards an Analysis of the Bourgeois and Proletarian Public Sphere*, trans. P. Labanyi, J. O. Daniel, and A. Oksiloff (Minneapolis: University of Minnesota Press, 1993); Evelyn Brooks Higginbotham, *Righteous Discontent: The Women's Movement in the Black Baptist Church, 1880–1920* (Cambridge, Mass.: Harvard University Press, 1993); The Black Public Sphere Collective, *The Black Public Sphere: A Public Culture Book* (Chicago: University of Chicago Press, 1995).

Chapter One: "A Celtic Pilgrimage": Culture, Class, and Evangelism in Alexander Irvine's Global Apprenticeship

1. *Celtic Pilgrimage* is the title Irvine would have preferred for his second autobiography, published in 1930 as *A Fighting Parson* (Boston: Little, Brown, 1930).

2. Alexander Irvine, *From the Bottom Up: The Life Story of Alexander Irvine* (New York: Doubleday-Page, 1910), 4; idem, *My Lady of the Chimney Corner* (London: Ernest Benn, 1913), 46–47.

3. Irvine, *My Lady*, 45; idem, *The Chimney Corner Revisited* (Belfast: Appletree, 1984), 60–62, 66; idem, *The Souls of Poor Folk* (Belfast: Appletree, 1981), 33; idem, *From the Bottom Up*, 4. The description of the Irvines' relation to wealthier members of Antrim society as a "cash nexus" is Irvine's.

4. Irvine, *My Lady*, 3. The number of shoemakers in County Antrim fell from 1,366 to 853 during this period. Shoemakers in Antrim town numbered between three and seven throughout the final three decades of the century, depending on the source consulted. Registrar General, *Census of Ireland, 1871* (Dublin, 1872), pt. 1, vol. 2, 73; Registrar General, *Census of Ireland, 1901* (Dublin, 1902), pt. 1, vol. 3, n. 1, 80.

5. Richard Griffith, *General Valuation of Rateable Property in Ireland: Union of Antrim* (Dublin: Alexander Thom, 1862), 109; *Annual Revision Lists, Antrim 1877–1884* VAL12B/1/1C, PRONI; *Slater's Directory of Ireland* (1870), 7; *Provincial Directory: Belfast and the Province of Ulster* (Belfast, 1870), 33; Alastair Smith, *The Story of Antrim* (Antrim: Antrim Borough Council, 1984), 67.

6. Anna and Jamie Irvine had twelve children in all, eight of whom survived to adulthood. Alexander was their ninth child. Irvine, *From the Bottom Up*, 3; idem, *My Lady*, 49–51, 56–58; idem, *Chimney Corner Revisited*, 94–108; idem, *Souls of Poor Folk*, 122; E. J. Hobsbawm, *Industry and Empire: The Making of Modern English Society* (New York: Pantheon, 1968), 2:136; Nathan Wilson Todd, "A Social and Economic Study of Part of South County Antrim in the Second Half of the Nineteenth Century" (master's thesis, Queen's University, Belfast, 1975), 58.

7. Irvine, *Fighting Parson*, 14–15; idem, *From the Bottom Up*, 9–10, quote from p. 3;

Kerby A. Miller, *Emigrants and Exiles: Ireland and the Irish Exodus to North America* (New York: Oxford University Press, 1985), 152–60, 371–72.

8. Alan John Megahy, "The Irish Protestant Churches and Social and Political Issues, 1870–1914" (Ph.D. diss., Queen's University, Belfast, 1969), 39–40, 52; Todd, "A Social and Economic Study," 254.

9. Smyth, *Story of Antrim*, 35–46; Michael Davitt, *The Fall of Feudalism in Ireland* (New York: Harper & Brothers 1904), 21, 74, 116ff.; Miller, *Emigrants and Exiles*, 184, 336ff.; Lawrence J. McCaffrey, *The Irish Diaspora in America* (Bloomington: Indiana University Press, 1976), passim; Eric Foner, "Class, Ethnicity, and Radicalism in the Gilded Age: The Land League and Irish America," *Marxist Perspectives* 1 (Summer 1978): 6–55; David Scobey, "Boycotting the Politics Factory: Labor Radicalism and the City Mayoral Election of 1884," *Radical History Review* 28–30 (1984): 280–325.

10. In the 1870s America was the most popular but not the only destination for emigrants from County Antrim. Scotland held the greatest attraction within the British Isles. Emigration to America reached a low point in 1877, when only some 15.6 percent went to America, 40.9 percent to Scotland, and 35.4 percent to England and Wales. Todd, "A Social and Economic Study," 230–33.

11. Miller, *Emigrants and Exiles*, 40–41, 51–52; Irvine, *Chimney Corner Revisited*, 7–8, 66–69; idem, *Souls of Poor Folk*, 43; idem, *My Lady*, 82, 94.

12. Irvine, *Souls of Poor Folk*, 26.

13. Irvine, *My Lady*, 1–21, 96; idem, *Souls of Poor Folk*, 18, 40, 144–45.

14. H. O'Loughlin to Poor Law Commissioners, Dublin, January 24, 1868, as copied into the Minute Book of the Board of Guardians for Antrim Union, PRONI BG1/A/17, 28–29.

15. Reverend Maurice H. Fitzgerald Collis, B.D., Vicar of Antrim, "Antrim Parish Church," UJA 2nd ser., vol. 3 (1897): 30–39, 90–98, photocopy in local history files, Greystone Library, Antrim, Ireland.

16. Kenneth Stanley Inglis, *Churches and the Working Classes in Victorian England* (London: Routledge & Kegan Paul, 1963), 121; Miller, *Emigrants and Exiles*, 420–21, 463–64; McCaffrey, *Irish Diaspora*, 53, 75–76; Irvine, *Souls of Poor Folk*, 16–17, 33–34, 143, 144, 212; idem, *From the Bottom Up*, 293.

17. Irvine, *Souls of Poor Folk*, 33, 212; Todd, "A Social and Economic Study," 254; John Richard Brown McMinn, "The Reverend James Brown Armour and Liberal Politics in North Antrim, 1869–1914" (Ph.D. diss., Queen's University, Belfast, 1979), 147, 154.

18. Irvine, *Souls of Poor Folk*, 36–37; idem, *Chimney Corner Revisited*, 124; Henry Patterson, *Class Conflict and Sectarianism: The Protestant Working Class and the Belfast Labour Movement, 1868–1920* (Belfast: Blackstaff, 1980), xviii, 1–6; Peter Gibbon, *The Origins of Ulster Unionism: The Formation of Popular Protestant Politics and Ideology in Nineteenth Century Ireland* (Manchester: Manchester University Press, 1975), 99–102.

19. Todd, "A Social and Economic Study," 151–62.

20. Ibid., 251; Megahy, "The Irish Protestant Churches," 21–24.

21. Irvine, *Souls of Poor Folk*, 16, 33–34; see also idem, *From the Bottom Up*, 8–9.

22. Irvine, *Souls of Poor Folk*, 145.

23. Ibid., 24–27; idem, *Chimney Corner Revisited*, 40.

24. Irvine, *My Lady*, 192; idem, *Souls of Poor Folk*, 143, 145; Smyth, *Story of Antrim*, 64–65.

25. Irvine, *Souls of Poor Folk*, 16–17; idem, *Fighting Parson*, 7–8; idem, *From the Bottom Up*, 11–12; Smyth, *Story of Antrim*, 89.

26. Irvine, *Fighting Parson*, 9–11; idem, *From the Bottom Up*, 16–17; idem, *My Lady*, 185.

27. Irvine, *My Lady*, 186–87; idem, *From the Bottom Up*, 15–16, 18, 293; idem, *Fighting Parson*, 9, 15–16.

28. Irvine, *My Lady*, 188.

29. Ibid., 185, 189.

30. James L. Findlay Jr., *Dwight L. Moody: American Evangelist, 1837–1899* (Chicago: University of Chicago Press, 1969), 164–65; William G. McLoughlin Jr., *Modern Revivalism: Charles Grandison Finney to Billy Graham* (New York: Ronald, 1959), 196–97; George M. Marsden, *Fundamentalism and American Culture: The Shaping of Twentieth Century Evangelicalism, 1870–1925* (New York: Oxford University Press, 1980), 34; George Adam Smith, *The Life of Henry Drummond* (London: Hodder & Stoughton, 1899), 72–76.

31. Richard Cawardine, *Trans-Atlantic Revivalism: Popular Evangelicalism in Britain and America, 1790–1865* (Westport, Conn.: Greenwood, 1978), passim; Reverend William Gibson, *The Year of Grace: A History of the Ulster Revival of 1859* (Edinburgh: Andrew Eliot, 1860), esp. 38, 118; Nathan O. Hatch, *The Democratization of American Christianity* (New Haven, Conn.: Yale University Press, 1989), chs. 1–6; Susan Juster, *Disorderly Women: Sexual Politics and Evangelicalism in Revolutionary New England* (Ithaca, N.Y.: Cornell University Press, 1994), ch. 1.

32. McLoughlin, *Modern Revivalism*, 244–45; Findlay, *Dwight L. Moody*, 220–23.

33. For a discussion of scholarship on evangelical Protestantism as a culture of bourgeois social control, see Bibliographical Essay, sec. II.B. On Moody's criticism of working-class radicalism, see McLoughlin, *Modern Revivalism*, 255, 269–73; Findlay, *Dwight L. Moody*, 278, 323–28; James Gilbert, *Perfect Cities: Chicago's Utopias of 1893* (Chicago: University of Chicago Press, 1991), 179–81; Myron Raymond Chartier, "The Social Views of Dwight L. Moody and Their Relation to the Workingman of 1860–1900," *Fort Hays Studies, New Series, History Series* 6 (August 1969): 17–25, 65–66.

34. Irvine, *From the Bottom Up*, 19; idem, *Fighting Parson*, 16; David G. Browne, *Hugh Hanna: Protestant Champion and Warrior Against Romanism and Republicanism* (Belfast, 1972); Finlay Holmes, *Henry Cooke* (Belfast: Christian Journals Limited, 1981), 190; Hugh Hanna, *The Right To Property: Being Notes In Refutation of the Land Theories of Mr. Henry George* (Belfast: Wm. Strain & Sons, 1885).

35. J. A. Jackson, *The Irish in Britain* (London: Routledge & Kegan Paul, 1963), 10, 87; Fred Reid, *Keir Hardie: The Making of a Socialist* (London: Croom Helm, 1978), 33; Hobsbawm, *Industry and Empire*, 2:263–64.

36. Irvine, *From the Bottom Up*, 21–22; idem, *Fighting Parson*, 17; Smith, *Life of Henry Drummond*, 124, Hobsbawm, *Industry and Empire*, 2:263–64.

37. Drummond, *Natural Law in the Spiritual World* (New York: A. L. Burt, n.d.), 73. On Drummond's relation to Moody, see George Adam Smith, *The Life of Henry Drummond*, 63, 72–76, 420–21; McLoughlin, *American Revivalism*, 275; Findlay, *Dwight L. Moody*, 411–12; Henry Drummond, *Dwight L. Moody: Impressions and Facts* (New York: McClure, Phillips, 1900).

38. Henry Drummond, "The Programme of Christianity," in *Essays and Addresses* (New York: James Pott, 1904), 36–37, 44.

39. Fred Reid, "Keir Hardie's Conversion to Socialism," in *Essays in Labour History, 1886–1923*, ed. A. Briggs and J. Saville (London: Macmillan, 1971), 17–46; Reid, *Keir Hardie*, 38–41, 61–62, 72–99; Irvine, *From the Bottom Up*; Chartier, "The Social Views of Dwight L. Moody," 55–56.

40. Herbert Gutman, "Protestantism and the American Labor Movement: The Christian Spirit in the Gilded Age," *American Historical Review* 72, no. 1 (1966): 75–100; Stephen Yeo, "A NEW LIFE: The Religion of Socialism in Britain, 1883–1896," *History Workshop* 4 (Autumn 1977): 5–56.

41. Michael Lewis, *The Navy of Britain: A Historical Portrait* (London: George Allen & Unwin, 1948), 318–20; idem, *The Navy in Transition, 1814–1864: A Social History* (London: Hodder & Stoughton, 1965), 150; Eugene L. Rasor, *Reform in the Royal Navy* (Hamden, Conn.: Archon, 1976), 15, 35–37, 105; Irvine, *From the Bottom Up*, 21, 24, 41; idem, *Fighting Parson*, 20, 27–28, 34.

42. Dinah Maria Mulock (Mrs. Craik), *John Halifax, Gentleman* (New York: E. P. Dutton, 1916), 15; Irvine, *From the Bottom Up*, 32; idem, *Fighting Parson*, 22–23.

43. Irvine, *From the Bottom Up*, 34–36.

44. Ibid., 42; Service Register, Alexander Irvine, No. 2467, ADM 159/4, PO RMLI Service Registers, 1947 to 2548, PROK; F. Roy Coad, *A History of the Brethren Movement* (Exeter: Paternoster, 1968), passim; Ernest R. Sandeen, *The Roots of Fundamentalism: British and American Millenarianism, 1800–1930* (Chicago: University of Chicago Press, 1970), 29–41, 60–70, 75–76; McLoughlin, *Modern Revivalism*, 257–58; Findlay, *Dwight L. Moody*, 125–27, 250–51, 260–61, 406; Chartier, "The Social Views of Dwight L. Moody," 33; George Marsden, *Fundamentalism and American Culture*, 46, 54.

45. Irvine, *From the Bottom Up*, 40–42; idem, *Fighting Parson*, 26–27.

46. Irvine, *From the Bottom Up*, 45–50; idem, *Fighting Parson*, 32.

47. Alexander Irvine, *Three Days in the Holy Land*, ms. in possession of Alexander Irvine, Santa Barbara, Calif.

48. Ibid.

49. Ibid.

50. Irvine, *From the Bottom Up*, 54, 63–64; idem, *Fighting Parson*, 33; RMLI Service Register, Alexander Irvine; Charles Chenevix Trench, *The Road to Khartoum: A Life of General Charles Gordon* (New York: Norton, 1978), chs. 15–18; Thomas Pakenham, *The Scramble for Africa, 1876–1912* (New York: Random House, 1991), ch. 13; Robin Hallett, *Africa Since 1875, A Modern History* (Ann Arbor: University of Michigan Press, 1974), 94, 98.

51. Irvine, *From the Bottom Up*, 63–64; idem, *Fighting Parson*, 32–33; P. M. Holt, *The Mahdist State in the Sudan, 1881–1898* (Oxford: Clarendon, 1970), 1–104; A. B. Theobald, *The Mahdiya* (London: Longmans, Green, 1951), 27–121.

52. Irvine, *From the Bottom Up*, 70.

53. Rudyard Kipling, "Fuzzy-Wuzzy," in *Rudyard Kipling's Verse: Definitive Edition* (New York: Doubleday, Doran, 1940), 398–99; Carolyn Steedman, *The Radical Soldier's Tale: John Pearman, 1819–1908* (London: Routledge, 1988), 37–51.

54. Irvine, *From the Bottom Up*, 80; Steedman, *Radical Soldier's Tale*, 37–51.

55. Service Register, Alexander Irvine; Irvine, *From the Bottom Up*, 77–81; idem, *Fighting Parson*, 34–35; *Syracuse Post Standard*, May 12, 1914.

56. Alastair Smyth, interview, Antrim, Northern Ireland, October 28, 1987; Mrs. Anna Irvine Buck, interview, December 27, 1987; Service Register, Alexander Irvine; Certified Copy of Entry of Marriage, Alexander Irvine and Nellie Skeens, General Register Office, London; Irvine, *From the Bottom Up*, 59.

57. Certified Copy of an Entry of Birth, Ellen Mary Skeens, August 13, 1868, General Record Office, London; Certified Copy of an Entry of Birth, William Henry Irvine, May 13, 1887, General Record Office, London; Certified Copy of Entry of Birth, Gordon Francis Irvine, August 23, 1888, General Register Office, London; Certified Copy of Entry of Birth, Alexander Fitzgerald Irvine, September 20, 1891, General Register Office, London; Verne Linderman, "Bill Irvine Finds Pleasure in Helping Others," clipping, *Santa Barbara News Press*, February 1962, in possession of Alexander Irvine, Santa Barbara, Calif.

58. Irvine, *From the Bottom Up*, 82–88; idem, *Fighting Parson*, 36–39.

59. Irvine, *From the Bottom Up*, 84–87, 89; idem, *Fighting Parson*, 35, 39; NHR: December 13, 1903.

60. Carroll Smith Rosenberg, *Religion and the Rise of the American City: The New York City Mission Movement, 1812–1870* (Ithaca, N.Y.: Cornell University Press, 1971), 70–96, 187–99; Kenneth D. Miller and Ethel Prince Miller, *The People Are the City: 150 Years of Social and Religious Concern in New York City* (New York: Macmillan, 1962), 67, 112ff.; Irvine, *From the Bottom Up*, 90–91.

61. On moral categories applied to petitioners for missionary aid, see Christine Stansell, *City of Women: Sex and Class in New York, 1789–1860* (Urbana: University of Illinois Press, 1987), ch. 4.

62. Alexander Irvine, "Report of Work Among the Lodging Houses," *Work in New York, being the Sixty Fifth Annual Report of the New York City Mission and Tract Society* (New York: New York City Mission and Tract Society, 1891), 138.

63. E. L. Godkin, "Introductory," in *The Triumph of Reform: A History of the Great Political Revolution, November Sixth, Eighteen Hundred and Ninety-Four* (New York: Souvenir, 1895); Irvine, *From the Bottom Up*, 91–92, 147–49, 162; idem, *Fighting Parson*, 44–45; Reverend Charles H. Parkhurst, *Our Fight With Tammany* (New York: Charles Scribner's Sons, 1895), passim; Walter S. Murray, "Rev. C.H. Parkhurst, D.D. — A Character Sketch," *Our Day: The Altruistic Review* 14 (January–June 1895): 287–304; M. R. Werner, "Dr. Parkhurst's Crusade," in *It Happened in New York* (New York: Coward-McCann, 1957), 36–116; Timothy Gilfoyle, *City of Eros: New York City, Prostitution, and the Commercialization of Sex, 1790–1920* (New York: W. W. Norton, 1992), 298–306.

64. Alexander F. Irvine, "Work Among Homeless Lodgers," *Work in New York, being the Sixty-Sixth Annual Report of the New York City Mission and Tract Society* (New York: New York City Mission and Tract Society, 1892), 152–53.

65. On working-class traditions of evangelical self-improvement, see Jama Lazerow, *Religion and the Working Class in Antebellum America* (Washington, D.C.: Smithsonian Institution, 1995); and Theresa Murphy, *Ten Hours Labor: Religion, Reform and Gender in Early New England* (Ithaca, N.Y.: Cornell University Press, 1992).

66. Irvine, *From the Bottom Up*, 96–104, 156–57; idem, *Fighting Parson*, 41; the suggestion of cooperative work projects was also a part of Irvine's report on "Work Among Homeless Lodgers" in *Work in New York*, 152.

67. *New York* Herald, November 19, 1893, 3rd section, 14.

68. *Work in New York*, 11–12, 152; Irvine, *From the Bottom Up*, 146; idem, *Fighting Parson*, 43, 45.

69. *University Settlement Society Bulletin*, no. 2, December 1892, 8. For scholarly literature on the settlement movement, see Bibliographical Essay, sec. II.B.

70. *University Settlement Society Bulletin*, no. 2, 29–34; *University Settlement Society. Report of the Year's Work*, December 1895, 8–11, 32; Irvine, *From the Bottom Up*, 146; William D. P. Bliss, ed., *The Encyclopedia of Social Reform* (New York: Funk & Wagnalls, 1897), 657, 1283.

71. Irvine, *From the Bottom Up*, 159.

72. Norma Fain Pratt, *Morris Hillquit: A Political History of an American Jewish Socialist* (Westport, Conn.: Greenwood, 1979), 16; Nora Levin, *While Messiah Tarried: Jewish Socialist Movements, 1871–1917* (New York: Schocken, 1977), 79–81, 119–22, 142–46; Irving Howe, *World of Our Fathers* (New York: Harcourt, Brace, Jovanovich, 1976), 460–85; Hutchins Hapgood, *The Spirit of the Ghetto* (Cambridge, Mass.: Belknap Press at Harvard University Press, 1987), 113–87.

73. Verne Linderman, "Bill Irvine Finds Pleasure in Helping Others"; Irvine, *From the Bottom Up*, 170; idem, *Fighting Parson*, 47–48, 274–75; idem, *My Cathedral: A Vision of Friendship* (Belfast: Quota, 1945), 37–39.

74. *Omaha World Herald*: June 14, 1894, 1; July 6, 1894, 1; March 12, 1896, 1. Howard Quint, *The Forging of American Socialism* (Indianapolis: Bobbs-Merrill, 1953), ch. 7.

75. Irvine expressed growing disenchantment with churches as denominational and financial institutions, which found expression in such sermons as "Denominationalism: Its Birthplace and Author," "Jesus in the Homes of the Poor," and "God and Mammon." *Omaha World Herald*: November 10, 1894, 2; November 17, 1894, 4; November 24, 1894, 2; March 9, 1895, 8.

76. *Omaha World Herald*: May 27, 1894, 13; July 15, 1894, 6; October 13, 1894, 2; November 10, 1894, 2; November 17, 1894, 4; November 24, 1894, 2; January 5, 1895, 8; January 18, 1985, 8; September 22, 1895, 2; October 6, 1895, 7. Irvine, *From the Bottom Up*, 166–74; idem, *Fighting Parson*, 49–50.

77. *Omaha World* Herald: November 24, 1895, 2. Irvine, *From the Bottom Up*, 172; George D. Herron, *The Christian Society* (Chicago: Revell, 1894), 80; Henry F. May, *Protestant Churches and Industrial America* (New York: Harper & Brothers, 1949), 256.

78. William G. McLoughlin Jr., *Billy Sunday Was His Real Name* (Chicago: University of Chicago Press, 1955), 23–28, 98, 100, 118–22, 139–40, 155–58, 161–63, 175; idem, *Modern Revivalism*, 399, 400, 407–8, 411–13, 426–27, 432–33; Lyle W. Dorsett, *Billy Sunday and the Redemption of Urban America* (Grand Rapids: Eerdmans, 1991) 67–69, 112, 147; Betty A. DeBerg, *Ungodly Women: Gender and the First Wave of American Fundamentalism* (Minneapolis: Fortress, 1990), 88–91, 96–98, 147. On scholarly debate over the interpretation of proto-Fundamentalism, see Bibliographical Essay, sec. II.B.

79. Irvine, *From the Bottom Up*, 183; idem, *Fighting Parson*, 52–53; Alexander Irvine Scrapbook, AIC.

80. Sources on Irvine's second wife and attitude toward relationships with women include Alastair Smyth, interview, Antrim, Northern Ireland, October 28, 1987; Mrs. Anna Irvine Buck, interview, December 27, 1987; Alexander Irvine, "Little Pilgrims of the Dawn," MS, AIC; idem, "The Choice of a Wife," MS, AIC; idem, *My Cathedral*, 37–38.

Chapter Two: "We Gave Them Realism": Sylvester Poli's Theatrical World

1. *Catalogue of the Eden Musée*, April 7, 1884, Beinecke Rare Book Library, Yale University; *Eden Musée Catalogue*, February 1887, March 1889, BRTC; George C. D. Odell, *Annals of the New York Stage* (New York: Columbia University Press, 1940), 12:336.

2. Hugh Leamy, "Waxing Rich," *Colliers*, July 7, 1928, 52.

3. Donald C. King, "S. Z. Poli, From Wax to Riches," *Marquee* 2, no. 2 (1979): 11; E. Robert Stevenson, ed., *Connecticut History Makers* (Waterbury, Conn., 1930), 2:198; interview, Jeanne Poli, September 21, 1990.

4. Madame Tussaud, *Memoirs of France* (London: Saunders & Otley, 1838), 4–8; John Theodore Tussaud, *The Romance of Madame Tussaud's* (New York: George H. Doran, 1920), 56–69.

5. Madame Tussaud, *Memoirs of France*, 85–90; John Tussaud, *Romance of Madame Tussaud's*, 82–86; George Rudé, *The French Revolution* (London: Weidenfeld & Nicolson, 1988), 53; Pauline Chapman, *Madame Tussaud's Chamber of Horrors: Two Hundred Years of Crime* (London: Constable, 1984), 2–3, 8–11.

6. Madame Tussaud, *Memoirs of France*, 21–73; John Tussaud, *Romance of Madame Tussaud's*, 87, 89–91, 95–96; Chapman, *Madame Tussaud's*, 4–8, 11–21.

7. Charles Coleman Sellers, *Patience Wright: American Artist and Spy in George IIIs' London* (Middletown, Conn.: Wesleyan University Press, 1976), 35–45, 119–20; Richard D. Altick, *The Shows of London* (Cambridge, Mass.: Harvard University Press, 1978), 50–56.

8. According to David Brigham, a visitor to Peale's in 1819 criticized the "racial" display, saying it was in disrepair and glorified violence against Native Americans rather than reflecting racial harmony as Peale had intended. See David Brigham, *Public Culture in the Early Republic: Peale's Museum and Its Audience* (Washington, D.C.: Smithsonian Institute, 1995), 60; Charles Coleman Sellers, *Mr. Peale's Museum: Charles Willson Peale and the First Popular Museum of Natural Science and Art* (New York: W. W. Norton, 1980), 30, 93–94; idem, *Charles Willson Peale* (New York: Scribner's Sons, 1969), 324, 344–45; *The Selected Papers of Charles Willson Peale and His Family*, vol. 2, pt. 2 (New Haven, Conn.: Yale University Press, 1988), 765–66, 1037, 1051, 1055–57.

9. John Tussaud, *Romance of Madame Tussaud's*, 98–119, 298–99; Altick, *Shows of London*, 333–38; *Madame Tussaud & Sons Catalogue* (London: G. Cole, 1869), 36–39.

10. King, "S. Z. Poli," 11; ICC: August 21, 1915, 2; November 27, 1915, 1. NHR: November 24, 1915, 24.

11. *Catalogue-Almanach du Musée Grevin*, 1883, 1st edition, 3–7, Bibliotheque Nationale, Paris; Statuts, Musée Grevin (Documents administratifs), Bibliotheque Nationale, Paris; *Dictionaire de Biographie Française* (Paris: Librarie Letouzey et Ané, 1985), 16:1199.

12. *Catalogue-Almanach du Musée Grévin*, 1883, 1st edition, 9–25.

13. Vanessa Schwartz, "Museums and Mass Spectacle: The Musée Grévin as a Monument to Modern Life," *French Historical Studies* 19, no. 1 (1995): 7–26; idem, "Cinematic Spectatorship before the Apparatus: The Public Taste for Reality in *Fin-de-Siècle* Paris," in *Cinema and the Invention of Modern Life*, ed. Leo Charney and Vanessa R. Schwartz (Berkeley: University of California Press, 1995), 297–319; Carol Duncan, "Art Museums and the Ritual of Citizenship," in *Exhibiting Cultures: The Poetics and Politics*

of Museum Display, ed. Ivan Karp and Steven D. Lavine (Washington, D.C.: Smithsonian Institution, 1991), 88–103.

14. King, "S. Z. Poli," 11; Jeanne Poli, September 21, 1990; Antonio Cannelli, *La Colonia Italiana di New Haven, Connecticut*, (New Haven, Conn.: A. Cannelli, 1921), 214–17; translated by V. Rocca, PCEHP; Charles Musser, *Before the Nickelodeon: Edwin S. Porter and the Edison Manufacturing Company* (Berkeley: University of California Press, 1991), 116–17.

15. *Catalogue of the Eden Musée*, April 7, 1884, 1.

16. Ibid., April 7, 1884, 28–29; *Eden Musée Catalogue*, March 1893, 41.

17. *Catalogue of the Eden Musée*, April 7, 1884, 2–5, 21ff., 28–30, 35ff.; *Eden Musée Catalogue*, February 1887, 41–45.

18. *Catalogue of the Eden Musée*, April 7, 1884, 1–16.

19. Ibid., 16–17.

20. Ibid., 21.

21. Ibid., 1.

22. Ibid., 31ff.

23. Ibid., 17, 35ff.

24. *Trow's New York City Directory* (hereafter *Trow's*) (New York: The Trow City Directory Co., 1884), 97:1340; *Trow's*, vol. 97 (1885), 1396; *Trow's*, vol. 99 (1886), 1526; *Gopsill's Philadelphia City Directory* (Philadelphia: James Gopsill's Sons, 1887), 1364; King, "S. Z. Poli," 11; *Philadelphia Inquirer*: December 27 1886, 5; December 28, 1886, 1.

25. Paul Avrich, *The Haymarket Tragedy* (Princeton, N.J.: Princeton University Press, 1984), xi, 260–79.

26. Odell, *Annals of the New York Stage* (1942), 12:337; *Eden Musée Catalogue*, February 1887; see also Leamy, "Waxing Rich," and King, "S. Z. Poli," 11–12, though these authors' dates for the anarchist exhibit are questionable.

27. *Eden Musée Catalogue*, March 1893, 37, BRTC.

28. Ibid.

29. Avrich, *Haymarket Tragedy*, 191–93; David DeLeon, *The American as Anarchist: Reflections on Indigenous Radicalism* (Baltimore: Johns Hopkins University Press, 1978).

30. Carl Smith, *Urban Disorder and the Shape of Belief: The Great Chicago Fire, The Haymarket Bomb, and the Model Town of Pullman* (Chicago: University of Chicago Press, 1995), 150–51; Franklin Rosemont, "A Bomb-Toting, Long-Haired, Wild-Eyed Fiend: The Image of the Anarchist in Popular Culture," in *Haymarket Scrapbook*, ed. D. Roediger and F. Rosemont (Chicago: Charles H. Kerr, 1986), 202–12.

31. The Eden, the Grévin, and Tussaud's all used some version of the "History of a Crime" display. *Catalogue-Almanach du Musée Grevin*, 1883, 1st edition, 41ff.; *Madame Tussaud's Exhibition Guide* (London: Madame Tussauds, 1892), 60ff.; *Catalogue of the Eden Musée*, April 7, 1884, 29–30.

32. King, "S. Z. Poli," 12; *Catalogue of the Eden Musée*, April 7, 1884, 29–30; "Rites Today for S. Z. Poli," *New York American*, June 2, 1937, clipping, S. Z. Poli File, BRTC.

33. King, "S. Z. Poli," 12; NHEL: November 19, 1906, 13.

34. S. Z. Poli File, BRTC; Neil Harris, *Humbug: The Art of P.T. Barnum* (Chicago, 1973); King, "S. Z. Poli," 12; Leamy, "Waxing Rich," 52; Book 95, AGDC; Odell, *Annals of the New York Stage*, 15:269.

35. Robert Snyder, *The Voice of the City*, 14–35, 84; Myron Matlaw, "Tony the Trouper:

Pastor's Early Years," *Theatre Annual* 24 (1968): 72–90; Gilbert, *American Vaudeville*, 103–10; B. F. Keith, "The Vogue of Vaudeville," in *American Vaudeville as Seen by its Contemporaries*, ed. Charles Stein (New York: Da Capo, 1984), 15–20.

36. King, "S. Z. Poli," 12; Book 95, 3, 8–9, AGDC.

37. NHU: January 2, 1892, 3; January 4, 1893, 5, March 6, 1893, 8.

38. NHJC: January 7, 1892, 3; March 16, 1892, 3. NHU: January 6, 1892, 4; February 22, 1892, 4; February 23, 1892, 4; February 29, 1892, 4; April 11, 1892, 4; April 25, 1892, 4; April 27, 1892, 4; May 3, 1892, 8; July 2, 1892, 4; October 22, 1892, 8; January 4, 1893, 5. Book 95, 9, 18, 27, AGDC.

39. NHU: October 22, 1892, 8; January 16, 1893, 8; January 17, 1893, 8; January 19, 1893, 8.

40. NHU: February 24, 1893, 8.

41. Reel 95, 8–9, AGDC; NHJC: January 1, 1894, 2. NHU: January 4, 1893, 5; January 6, 1894, 6; April 16, 1894, 6; September 9, 1894, 5. Joe Laurie Jr., *Vaudeville: From the Honky-tonks to the Palace* (New York: Henry Holt, 1953), 395–96; William H. Birkmire, *The Planning and Construction of American Theatres* (New York: John Wiley & Sons, 1901), 41, 45, 48–49; obituary, J. B. McElfatrick, *The American Architect and Building News* 89, no. 1590 (1906): 198.

42. Lawrence Levine, *Highbrow/Lowbrow: The Emergence of Cultural Hierarchy in America* (Cambridge, Mass.: Harvard University Press, 1988), 195–97; John F. Kasson, *Rudeness and Civility: Manners in Nineteenth-Century America* (New York: Hill & Wang, 1990), 247–51.

43. Snyder, *Voice of the City*, quote, xiv. For a discussion of scholarly literature on vaudeville, see Bibliographical Essay, sec. II.E.

44. NHU: November 14, 1894, 6; November 16, 1894, 6; November 17, 1894, 6.

45. Marian Spitzer, "The Mechanics of Vaudeville," and George Gottlieb, "Psychology of the American Vaudeville Show from the Manager's Point of View," in *American Vaudeville*, ed. Stein, 167–81; Frederick Edward Snyder, "American Vaudeville — Theatre in a Package: The Origins of Mass Entertainment" (Ph.D. diss., Yale University, 1970); R. Snyder, *Voice of the City*, 66–67.

46. Spitzer, "The Mechanics of Vaudeville," 173–76.

47. The acts discussed in aggregate and in detail throughout the rest of this section are part of a sample of Wonderland Theater acts of the 1890s selected from newspaper advertisements for Poli's shows. The selection process and quantitative breakdown of this sample of acts are discussed in Appendix A.

48. Quoted in "Two Great Ladies of the Theatre Play Vaudeville," Stein, ed., *American Vaudeville*, 90.

49. Gunther Barth, *City People: The Rise of Modern City Culture in Nineteenth-Century America* (New York: Oxford University Press, 1980), 224–25.

50. NHU: January 15, 1895, 6. NHJC: February 7, 1898, 2. The link between acrobatic acts and urbanity should not be overstated; other such acts were entitled "Fun on the Farm" and "Three Rubes" (which depicted a husking bee). NHU: June 5, 1894, 6; December 15, 1894, 6.

51. NHU: April 13, 1893, 8; November 22, 1896, 10. Laurie, *Vaudeville*, 22, 96; program, ·

"The Rival Lovers," December 29, 1888, clipping, *Moving Picture World*, September 4, 1915, BRTC.

52. NHU: January 15, 1895, 6; September 8, 1896, 8; December 9, 1896, 8; February 12, 1897, 8; December 7, 1897, 8; December 11, 1899, 10. Buckley, "To the Opera House: Culture and Society in New York City, 1820–1860" (Ph.D. diss., State University of New York and Stony Brook, 1984).

53. NHU: January 11, 1899, 6.

54. NHU: January 13, 1896, 8; January 14, 1896, 8.

55. NHU: April 7, 1897, 8; April 8, 1897, 8; January 11, 1899, 6. For descriptions of the Midway, see John F. Kasson, *Amusing the Million: Coney Island at the Turn of the Century* (New York: Hill & Wang, 1978), 23–26; Robert Rydell, *All the World's a Fair: Visions of Empire at American International Expositions, 1876–1916* (Chicago: University of Chicago Press, 1984), 38–71; James Gilbert, *Perfect Cities: Chicago's Utopias of 1893* (Chicago: University of Chicago Press, 1991), 75–130.

56. Other sketches on the vicissitudes of marriage were *The Alimony Club, Divorces While You Wait*, and *One Wife Too Many*. NHU: January 15, 1896, 8; November 17, 1896, 8; April 6, 1897, 8; February 7, 1899, 10; May 22, 1899, 8.

57. NHJC: April 6, 1898, 2. Clipping, *New York Telegraph*, September 25, 1906, BRTC.

58. NHU: January 16, 1896, 8; June 10, 1896, 8. Clipping, *New York* Review, September 3, 1910, Robinson Locke Collection, series 2, V. 30, 24, BRTC; Marks, *They All Sang*, 81–82.

59. See Theodore Dreiser, "My Brother Paul," in *Twelve Men* (New York: Boni & Liveright, 1919); idem, "Whence a Song," in *The Color of a Great City* (New York: Boni & Liveright, 1923), 142–60; idem, "Concerning the Author of These Songs," in *The Songs of Paul Dresser* (New York: Boni & Liveright, 1927), v–x.

60. Clipping, *New York* Review, September 3, 1910, Robinson Locke Collection, BRTC; "Take a Seat, Old Lady," in *The Songs of Paul Dresser*, 4–7.

61. See Appendix A.

62. NHU: March 5, 1895, 6; March 6, 1895, 6. For literature on the blackface minstrel tradition, see Bibliographical Essay, sec. II.D.

63. NHU: May 7, 1895, 6; May 8, 1895, 6.

64. NHU: June 8, 1896, 8; June 13, 1896, 8; September 30, 1899, 8; January 5, 1903, 8. Clipping, "Exit John Kernell from Life's Stage," *Philadelphia Public Ledger*, December 20, 1903, BRTC. On Kelly, see *Irish Songs, Jokes, Reminiscences and Monologues* (Chicago: Will Rossiter, 1902), BRTC; Edwin Marks, *They All Sang*, 131.

65. See, for example, the ad for Kasten, Duey & Kasten, who could do a cakewalk "that few genuine negroes could duplicate." NHU: April 8, 1896, 8.

66. NHU: November 14, 1894, 6; September 4, 1895, 6; February 13, 1896, 8; May 19, 1897, 8.

67. NHU: April 20, 1896, 8. Robinson Locke Collection of Dramatic Scrapbooks, series 2, vol. 128, 97: clipping, no source, December 20, 1902, clipping, *Toledo Blade*, December 16, 1920, BRTC.

68. NHU: May 2, 1894, 6.

69. NHU: January 17, 1896, 8.

70. NHU: October 14, 1896, 8; February 9, 1897, 8.

71. Gilbert, *American Vaudeville*, 156; Laurie, *Vaudeville*, 50, 403–6. For description of these as "gold brick acts," see Nasaw, *Going Out: The Rise and Fall of Public Amusements* (New York: Basic, 1993), 28.

72. In 1896 Sidney Drew and his wife gave a playlet called *In Clover* depicting the tribulations of a wedded couple whose marriage turns frosty, and Hugh Stanton came in 1899 with *For Reform*, a gentle spoof of socially minded clubwomen. Other visitors to the Wonderland from the legitimate stage were Anna Bonnard and Albert Deltwyn, who provided "artistic comedy acting" in their sketch "My Wife's Portrait." Gilbert, *American Vaudeville*, 156; NHU: April 20, 1896, 8; April 21, 1896, 8; September 30, 1899, 8.

73. NHU: May 1, 1894, 6; May 3, 1894, 6; November 16, 1894, 6; June 13, 1895, 6; June 15, 1895, 6.

74. NHU: May 12, 1896, 8; May 15, 1896, 8.

75. NHU: December 4, 1894, 6; December 18, 1895, 8.

76. NHU: September 10, 1896, 8.

77. "Travels in the Limelight: Projections of the World Through the Magic Lantern," exhibition review, *The Magic Lantern Bulletin* 18, no. 1 (1988): 9–12; X. Theodore Barber, "Phantasmagorical Wonders: The Magic Lantern Ghost Show in Nineteenth-Century America," *The Magic Lantern Gazette* 2, no. 1 (1990): 9–21; on early screen practice, see also Charles Musser, *The Emergence of Cinema: The American Screen to 1907* (New York: Charles Scribner's Sons, 1990).

78. Ibid., 29–30, 39–40; NHJC: January 7, 1892, 3. NHU: April 21, 1896, 8; October 12, 1897, 8.

79. NHU: September 15, 1896, 8.

80. Ibid.

81. NHU: September 22, 1896, 8.

82. Robert C. Allen, "Vaudeville and Film, 1895–1915: A Study in Media Interaction" (Ph.D. diss., University of Iowa, 1977), 101–3, 129.

83. Musser, *The Emergence of Cinema*, 145–55.

84. NHU: January 7, 1897, 8.

85. NHU: December 11, 1896, 8.

86. NHJC: March 7, 1898, 6; March 10, 1898, 3; March 12, 1898, 2. On Passion Play films, see Musser, *Before the Nickelodeon*, 121–25; idem, *The Emergence of Cinema*, 212–18; on religious censorship of the films, see Charles Musser, "Passions and the Passion Play: Theater, Film and Religion in America, 1880–1900," in *Movie Censorship and American Culture*, ed. F. G. Couvares (Washington, D.C.: Smithsonian Institute, 1996), 43–72. The Passion Play was not Poli's only attempt to win favor with New Haven church people through the use of motion pictures. In March 1899 he offered his theater for an exhibition of the Biograph pictures of Pope Leo XIII, to benefit the city's Catholic churches. NHU: March 16, 1899, 10.

87. NHJC: May 2, 1898, 3; May 3, 1898, 2; May 2, 1898, 7. NHU: September 5, 1898, 8; October 3, 1898, 8. For the popularity of the Spanish-American War as film subject, see also Musser, *The Emergence of Cinema*, 241–60; Allen, "Vaudeville and Film," 134–40.

88. NHU: September 27, 1899, 10; October 2, 1899, 7. NHJC: October 17, 1899, 3.

89. NHU: September 14, 1899, 5. Musser, *Before the Nickelodeon*, 132–33.

Chapter Three: "The Tithe to Moloch": Religion and the Cultural Politics of Class

1. Alexander Irvine, "The Tithe to Moloch," pamphlet, Box 300, Folder 3609, FFP.

2. Alexander Irvine, *From the Bottom Up: The Life Story of Alexander Irvine* (New York: Doubleday, Page, 1910), 187. For Irvine's sermon, see NHEL: May 7, 1900, 11. NHJC: May 7, 1900, 2. NHU: May 7, 1900, 10. For reprint, see Irvine, "The Tithe to Moloch."

3. See Kenneth Fones-Wolf, *Trade-Union Gospel: Christianity and Labor in Industrial Philadelphia* (Philadelphia: Temple University Press, 1989).

4. NHU: February 24, 1867, 4; Connecticut State Bureau of Labor Statistics, *Annual Report, 1901–1902* (Meriden, Conn.: Journal Publishing, 1902), 331, 347; Marta Mortet, "A Brief History of the Connecticut Labor Movement" (Storrs: Labor Education Center, University of Connecticut, 1982), 12–13; David Montgomery, *Beyond Equality: Labor and the Radical Republicans, 1862–1872* (Urbana: University of Illinois Press, 1967), 296–302.

5. Trades Council of New Haven, *Illustrated History of the New Haven Trades Council and Affiliated Unions* (New Haven, Conn.: Trades Council of New Haven, 1899), 111–13; Connecticut Bureau of Labor Statistics, *Annual Report, 1886* (Meriden: Journal Publishing, 1886), 416.

6. Connecticut State Bureau of Labor Statistics, *Annual Report 1901–1902*, 347, 435ff.

7. Ibid.; John W. McConnell, *The Evolution of Social Classes* (Washington, D.C.: American Council on Public Affairs, 1942), 161; Howard H. Quint, *The Forging of American Socialism* (Indianapolis: Bobbs-Merrill, 1953), 51–60; "The Socialist Trade and Labor Alliance versus the 'Pure and Simple' Trade Union: A Debate held at the Grand Opera House, New Haven, Conn., November 25, 1900 between Daniel De Leon . . . and Job Harriman" (New York: New York Labor News Company, 1900).

8. Herbert Gutman, "Protestantism and the American Labor Movement: The Christian Spirit in the Gilded Age," *American Historical Review* 72, no. 1 (1966): 75–100; Trades Council, *Illustrated History*, 211, 213.

9. Ibid., 160, 178, 196–97.

10. All of these unions reported memberships of two hundred or more in early 1903. Trades Council, *Illustrated History*, 229–67; NHEL: March 10, 1903, 12.

11. MFCD, vol. 22, May 1, 1880; NHU: September 1, 1903, 8; Aaron Abell, *American Catholicism and Social Action: A Search for Social Justice, 1865–1950* (Garden City, N.Y.: Hanover House, 1960).

12. ICC: July 25, 1903. NHU: July 6, 1904, 1; December 30, 1903, 9; January 23, 1905, 10.

13. NHU: November 1, 1904, 1; January 28, 1905, 5. Rudolph Vecoli, "Prelates and Peasants: Italian Immigrants and the Catholic Church," *Journal of Social History* 2, no. 3 (1969): 217–68; on Scalabrinian missions generally, see Peter R. D'Agostino, "The Scalabrini Fathers, The Italian Emigrant Church, and Ethnic Nationalism in America," *Religion and American Culture* 7, no. 1 (1997): 121–59; on mismanagement and corruption that limited Scalabrinian expansion in Connecticut, see Dolores Ann Liptak, *European Immigrants and the Catholic Church in Connecticut, 1870–1920* (New York: Center for Migration Studies, 1987), 37–42, 96–101.

14. MFCD, vol. 21: November 25, 1877; March 10, 11, April 3, 14, 18, 23, 25, November 13, 1878; vol. 22: November 17, 20, 24, 26; December 25, 31, 1879; January 8, 17, 21, Feb-

ruary 3, 11, 17, 18, 19, 23, 25, 26, 1880; January 15, 19, February 16, 18, 19, 23, March 2, 1881; Karin Frankel, "Work and Ethnicity in the Gilded Age: The Diary of Michael Campbell," senior essay, History Department, Yale University, April 1982.

15. Jonathan H. Gillette, "Inside Contracting at the Sargent Hardware Company," *Theory and Society* 17, no. 2 (1988): 159–77; Karin Frankel, "Work and Ethnicity."

16. MFCD, vol. 21: March 11, 1878; December 31, 1879.

17. The Trade's Council's *Illustrated History* emphasized Reilly's work in Catholic total abstinence societies, but did not specify an institutional religious affiliation for Reilly or any other local labor leader, whether Catholic, Protestant, or Jewish. Trades Council, *Illustrated History,* 259, 229–67.

18. Ibid.; Jay Dolan, *Catholic Revivalism: The American Experience, 1830–1900* (Notre Dame, Ind.: University of Notre Dame Press, 1978), 161–63.

19. Roy Rosenzweig, *Eight Hours for What We Will: Workers and Leisure in an Industrial City, 1870–1920* (Cambridge: Cambridge University Press, 1983), 102–8; Barbara Epstein, *The Politics of Domesticity: Women, Evangelism, and Temperance in Nineteenth-Century America* (Middletown, Conn.: Wesleyan University Press, 1981).

20. Trades Council, *Illustrated History,* 161, 209–10.

21. Alexander Troup arrived in New Haven from New York in 1871, in the midst of a printers' strike against the *New Haven Journal-Courier*. The striking printers were eager to work on a new paper that would be the organ of a local workingmen's party. Troup's background as architect of the political program of the National Labor Union in the 1860s suited him for this project. In July 1871 he launched the *Union* to win the electoral support of politically wary craft unionists. His efforts garnered a growing readership for the *Union*, but the independent workingmen's political movement foundered. Subsequently, Troup attempted an unsuccessful alliance with state Democratic forces, and ran athwart unionists when he criticized the union apprenticeship program. But, while Troup and the Trades Council differed over political questions, on religious matters they agreed. William John Niven Jr., "The Time of the Whirlwind: A Study of the Political, Social and Economic History of Connecticut, 1861 to 1875" (Ph.D. diss., Columbia, 1954), 518–36; Montgomery, *Beyond Equality,* 183.

22. NHU: September 12, 1891, 4.

23. NHU: October 22, 1894, 2, 4.

24. NHU: December 9, 1901, 4.

25. Benjamin Bacon, *Theodore Thornton Munger: New England Minister* (New Haven, Conn.: Yale University Press, 1913), 123, 195, 283; NHJC: March 19, 1898, 7.

26. Newman Smyth, *Recollections and Reflections* (New York: Charles Scribner's Sons, 1926), 104–5, 126–43, 151; see also idem, *Old Faiths in New Light* (New York: Charles Scribner's Sons, 1879); Cynthia Eagle Russett, *Darwin in America: The Intellectual Response, 1867–1912* (San Francisco: W. H. Freeman, 1976), 37–38, 42.

27. Reverend T. T. Munger, "The Futility of Strikes," *The Congregationalist* 24, no. 27 (1872): 1; "The Futility of Trades Unions," *The Congregationalist* 24, no. 28 (1872): 1.

28. Newman Smyth, "Claims of Labor," *Andover Review* 3 (April 1885): 303, 307–8, 310–11; idem, "Use and Abuse of Capital," *Andover Review* 3 (May 1885): 426–36; idem, "Social Helps," *Andover Review* 3 (June 1885): 512–19.

29. Theodore T. Munger, "Henry Drummond," *The Homiletic Review* 4, no. 3 (1906):

169–73; *The Homiletic Review* 4, no. 4 (1906): 252–57; Smyth, *Recollections and Reflections.*

30. William Miller, *The History of the State YMCA of Connecticut* (New Haven, Conn.: Eastern, 1951), 16–18.

31. Ibid., 23–53.

32. Folder A, notes from *New Haven Palladium,* August 2, 1880, Folder C, Amos B. Hulen, "The Rise and Fall of the First Railroad YMCA in New Haven, 1878–1886," 3–6, RYMCA. For an account of the organization of Railroad YMCAs and their negotiation of wide-ranging conflicts with railroad workers over entertainment and labor-management relations, see Thomas Winter, "Contested Spaces: The YMCA and Workingmen on the Railroads, 1877–1917," in *Men and Women Adrift: The YMCA and the YWCA in the City, 1859–1980,* ed. Nina Mjagkij and Mary Spratt (New York: New York University Press, 1997), 65–85.

33. Folder F, Records, Railroad Branch YMCA, prayer meeting August 21, 1878, RYMCA. Newton G. Dorman was a tallyman for the railroad—Folder C, Hulen, p. 6, RYMCA. *New Haven City Directory* (New Haven: Price & Lee, 1878), 213.

34. Folder F, prayer meeting, August 14, 1878, RYMCA. Danforth also commented that "Fletcher said he began to understand why all should pray for him and his family. *He's coming round all right I guess. I pray." See also notes for July 31, 1878: "Three young men were present who were not Christians who appeared impressed but not decided."*

35. *Folder C, Hulen, 7–8, 18, abridged Railroad Y Records, 47–48, 64–67, Secretary's Report, March 16, 1879, April 11, 1881, July 19, 1881. Folder F, meeting notes, August 28, 1878, September 21, 1878, RYMCA.*

36. *Folder C, Hulen, 7, abridged Railroad Y Records, 60, 64, RYMCA. While the complaint about Mrs. Phelps reflected wider tensions between the individualistic self-help of Protestant temperance movements and the mutuality of working-class culture, it should also be noted that Mrs. Phelps may have expressed a frustration with the household consequences of male drinking that was widespread among female temperance advocates. See Epstein,* The Politics of Domesticity.

37. Folder C, 52, Secretary's Report, September 20, 1880, RYMCA.

38. Fullerton reported 1,258 visitors during January 1881, and by April of that year a monthly patronage of 1,798, 1,100 of them railroad men. Folder A, notes from *New Haven Palladium,* February 7, 1881, May 16, 1881, Folder C, Hulen, 11–12, RYMCA.

39. Folder C, abridged Railroad Y Records, 65–66, June 17, 1881, RYMCA.

40. Folder A, notes from *New Haven Palladium,* August 20, 1881, Folder C, Hulen, 12–13, Folder C, abridged Railroad Y Records, 67, July 30, 1881, RYMCA.

41. Folder A, notes from *New Haven Palladium,* August 20, 1881, Folder C, Hulen, 12–13, Folder C, abridged Railroad Y Records, 67, July 30, 1881, RYMCA. William Fischer presided over the managing committee of the new room. Some who advocated the railway men's autonomy stayed with the old reading room, notably Beers. He may have been motivated by his membership in the male quartet that sang at the reading room services.

42. Average daily attendance at the reading room during the next year dropped to thirty-five, down from approximately fifty before the split. Folder C, Hulen, 15–6, RYMCA; *New Haven City Directory* (New Haven: Price & Lee, 1886), 184, 926.

43. Miller, *The History of the State YMCA of Connecticut,* 69–72; Folder C, Hulen, 20–21, RYMCA; *Railroad News* (1901): 91–92.

44. Alexander Irvine, *The Souls of Poor Folk* (Belfast: Appletree, 1981), 27.
45. W. T. Stead, "The Magic Lantern Mission," *Review of Reviews* 1, no. 12 (1890): 562.
46. Ibid., 564–65.
47. Ibid.
48. NHU: October 16, 1894; November 10, 1894, 3; December 3, 1898, 3; December 16, 1899, 10; January 12, 1901, 10.
49. Alexander Irvine, "The Lesson of The Angelus," in *The Master and the Chisel* (New Haven: The People's Church, 1904).
50. NHU: November 12, 1898, 10.
51. NHU: June 18, 1900, 3.
52. NHEL: May 7, 1900, 11.
53. Irvine, "The Tithe to Moloch."
54. NHJC: February 20, 1900, 9.
55. NHR: May 9, 1898, 5.
56. NHU: January 21, 1901, 10; Paul A. Carter, *The Spiritual Crisis of the Gilded Age* (Dekalb: Northern Illinois University Press, 1971).
57. *The Craftsman*: April 1898, 87, quoted in Philip S. Foner, *History of the Labor Movement in the United States* (New York: International Publishers, 1964), 2:410.
58. *The Craftsman*, December 1898, 3–5; May 1899, 17.
59. Daniel B. Schirmer, *Republic or Empire: American Resistance to the Philippine War* (Cambridge, Mass.: Schenkman, 1972), 79; Foner, *History of the Labor Movement in the United States*, 2:422.
60. *The American Federationist* 6, no. 1 (1899): 9. On the multiple parodies of Kipling circulating among American anti-imperialists at this time, see Painter, *Standing at Armegeddon*, 153–66; and Richard E. Welch Jr., *Response to Imperialism: The United States and the Philippine-American War, 1899–1902* (Chapel Hill: University of North Carolina Press, 1979), 126.
61. *The American Federationist* 5, no. 5 (1898): 93.
62. A hierarchy of savagery and civilization also appeared in McNeill's "The Philosophy of the Labor Movement." But McNeill measured "civilization" in terms of social relations rather than race. "Examined by the light of all past history," McNeill declared, "individualism as a factor in the progress of civilization is a failure. . . . Enlightened civilization is dependent upon the right direction of the aspirations, wants, and demands of the many." Trades Council, *Illustrated History*, 212–13.

Chapter Four: "Social Evangelism, Its Dangers and Difficulties": Pastor Irvine and the Public Sphere

1. NHJC: February 3, 1900, 9; March 24, 1900, 9; March 31, 1900, 9. NHEL: April 14, 1900, 15; May, 12, 1900, 13.
2. The chapter title is one Irvine gave to his years in Omaha, New Haven, and the South in the brochure for a series of lectures of the 1930s entitled "Fishing for Men in Many Waters: A Series of Six Consecutive Evening Addresses, for the quickening of the spiritual life." AIC.

3. New Haven Congregational Club Announcement, LWCP; letter from A. F. Irvine to A. P. Stokes, October 4, 1900, Box 194, Folder 439, ASPS.

4. Alexander Irvine, *From the Bottom Up: The Life Story of Alexander Irvine* (New York: Doubleday-Page, 1910), 188; *Yale University Catalogue, 1901–1902* (New Haven, Conn.: Tuttle Moorhouse, Taylor, 1902), 630. Though Irvine claimed that he completed a full course at the Yale Divinity School, Yale lists him as a junior for both academic years 1901–2 and 1902–3, after which his name disappears.

5. Anson Phelps Stokes, *The Early History of Lowell House* (New Haven, Conn.: Farnam-Neighborhood House, 1946), 4–8, 11–14, 25–29; Anson Phelps Stokes to Alexander Irvine, May 20, 1940, Box III, Folder 1907, ASPS; clipping, NHU: October 30, 1900, Scrapbook, 1899–1901, LWCP; Irvine, *From the Bottom Up*, 192.

6. "Attempt great things for God in the Winter of 1901–1902," pamphlet (Fair Haven, Conn.: Pilgrim Congregational Church), Box 12, NECR.

7. *Bulletin*, Pilgrim Church, January 1903, Alexander Irvine Scrapbook, ca. 1902–8, AIC; Irvine, *From the Bottom Up*, 189–90.

8. He also devoted a sermon to the work of painter George Frederick Watts as a "prophet of labor." "Attempt great things for God . . . "

9. On Millet and nineteenth-century French realist painting, see Linda Nochlin, *Realism* (Harmondsworth: Penguin, 1971); Gerald Needham, *Nineteenth Century Realist Art* (New York: Harper & Row, 1988); Gabriel Weisberg, *The Realist Tradition: French Painting and Drawing, 1830–1900* (Cleveland: Cleveland Museum of Art; Bloomington: dist. by Indiana University Press, 1980).

10. Irvine Photo Album, AIPABC. The album also includes shots of Coventry, apparently intended to illustrate Irvine's sermon entitled "Footprints of John Davenport in Coventry and London," and scenes of Oxford probably used for sermons on Ruskin and Morris, all of which were given in the fall and winter of 1901–2. Cf. "Attempt great things for God . . . "

11. NHJC: November 2, 1901, 6.

12. Maren Stange, "Jacob Riis and Urban Visual Culture: The Lantern Slide Exhibition as Entertainment and Ideology," *Journal of Urban History* 15 (May 1989): 292–93.

13. NHJC: March 31, 1900, 9.

14. The Society's Committee included Charles Keeler, assistant secretary and treasurer of the H. B. Ives Company, a New Haven hardware manufacturer; George M. Baldwin, vice president of The New Haven Saw Mill; Marcus Hemingway, co-proprietor of the Connecticut Adamant Plaster Company; Richard G. Davis, owner of a grain milling establishment; Charles E. Bray, stove dealer; and Willet A. Hemingway, manager at the W. S. Robinson Company, a manufacturer of kegs, pails, and tubs. "Attempt great things for God . . . "; NHU: March 22, 1905, 10; *Greater New Haven Directory* (New Haven, Conn.: Price & Lee, 1902).

15. *Bulletin*, Pilgrim Church, 2; *Greater New Haven Directory* (New Haven, Conn.: Price & Lee, 1902), 112, 451, 483, 505, 544, 635; *Greater New Haven Directory* (New Haven, Conn.: Price & Lee, 1904), 584; NHEL: May 2, 1903, 1; NHU: April 5, 1902, 1.

16. Irvine remembered in an autobiography that it had been impossible to mix the working-class attendants at the evening service and the middle-class congregation who

paid pew rents for the morning service. *Evening Leader* columnist William J. O'Brien praised Irvine for ministering to working people in a city where the churches were "to an unusual and unnatural extent provincial and exclusive" with regard to working-class worshipers. *Bulletin*, Pilgrim Church, 2, 4; Alexander Irvine, *Fighting Parson* (Boston: Little, Brown, 1930), 57. NHJC: May 11, 1903, 3. NHEL: May 17, 1903, 9.

17. This comment belied Irvine's own concern for children, an interest that he pursued by devoting a midweek afternoon to the conduct of a children's service. Clipping, NHR: April 24, 1904, Item P, Scrapbook, 1903–4, LWCP; Irvine, *From the Bottom Up*, 190.

18. *Bulletin*, Pilgrim Church, 4.

19. Two of these members were carriage workers whose union was the first to elect Irvine to honorary membership. Irvine's church following also included three men whose trades were affiliated with the Building Trades Council, the first body of organized workingmen in New Haven to endorse one of his sermons for the Fair Haven church. The painters', paperhangers', and decorators' union also named Irvine to honorary membership. "Attempt great things for God . . . "; *Greater New Haven Directory* (New Haven, Conn.: Price & Lee, 1902).

20. 1900 was the first year the Bureau published a directory of labor organizations by city. Connecticut State Bureau of Labor Statistics, *Annual Report*, 1899–1900, 233–34; 1902–3, 369–71.

21. This was not the labor movement's first effort to municipalize the water plant; they had supported an earlier effort in 1881. Trades Council of New Haven, *Illustrated History of the New Haven Trades Council and Affiliated Unions* (New Haven, Conn.: Trades Council of New Haven, 1899), 112; National Civic Federation, *Municipal and Private Ownership of Public Utilities* (New York: NCF, 1907), 124–28; Frederick M. Heath, "Politics and Steady Habits: Issues and Elections in Connecticut, 1894–1914" (Ph.D. diss., Columbia University, 1965), 230–40, 273–75.

22. W. Trueman, "Notice to Taxpayers," New Haven, December 9, 1901, Alexander Irvine Scrapbook, ca. 1902–8, AIC; NHU: December 14, 1901, 6; Irvine, *From the Bottom Up*, 207–8.

23. NHU: January 7, 1902, 8.

24. Ibid.

25. Water company shareholders in the church included Charles Hemmingway and his son Arthur, the company's assistant treasurer. According to Irvine's account, several of these men skipped the church's annual meeting to attend the public hearing on the water question. Irvine, *From the Bottom Up*, 207–8; Second Congregational Church of Fair Haven, Membership List, Box 12, NECR; *New Haven Directory*, 1902, 290.

26. National Civic Federation, *Municipal and Private Operation of Public Utilities*, 130–32; NHU: February 6, 1902, 2; February 12, 1902, 1, 10.

27. NHU: March 15, 1902, 1; April 4, 1902, 1; December 8, 1901, 7; Heath, "Politics and Steady Habits," 204–7; Alfred F. Howe, "Connecticut's Labor Mayors," *The Independent* 55, no. 2 (May 1903): 1259–64.

28. New Haven unionists were wary of local party politics in part because their movement had gained little from previous alliances with Democratic or Republican politicians. William John Niven Jr., "The Time of the Whirlwind: A Study of the Political, Social and

Economic History of Connecticut, 1861 to 1875" (Ph.D. diss., Columbia, 1954), 523–38; Michael E. McGerr, *The Decline of Popular Politics: The American North, 1865–1928* (New York: Oxford University Press, 1986).

29. NHU: April 5, 1902, 2; April 15, 1902, 1. Heath, "Politics and Steady Habits," 204–7; Howe, "Connecticut's Labor Mayors," 1259.

30. NHEL: July 17, 1902, 10.

31. NHU: July 24, 1902, 2.

32. NHU: February 19, 1904, 14.

33. NHU: October 20, 1902, 1; October 23, 1902, 4; October 26, 1902, 1; October 30, 1902, 2.

34. Col. N. G. Osborn, ed., *Men of Mark in Connecticut* (Hartford, Conn.: William R. Goodspeed, 1910), 5:434; "Letter from Alexander F. Irvine, Pastor of Pilgrim Congregational Church of New Haven, and a Member of the Executive Committee of the Economic League Endorsing Judge Cleaveland for Governor," and "Judge Cleaveland and the Economic League," leaflets, Box II, Folder L, LWCP. Cleaveland was briefly a contender for the Republican nomination for governor in September 1902.

35. The conference included Campbell, Philip Daly, officers O'Brien, Sullivan, and McDermott of Metal Polishers and Buffers Local 25, a union of Irish-American metal workers, and President Pietro Iaccarino of Local 205, the Italian metal workers' union. NHU: June 4, 1902, 1; June 5, 1902, 1; June 6, 1902, 1; June 7, 1902, 5. Jonathan H. Gillette, "Inside Contracting at the Sargent Hardware Company," *Theory and Society* 17, no. 2 (1988): 159–77.

36. NHU: June 13, 1902, 1; June 30, 1902, 8; July 7, 1902, 8; July 8, 1902, 1. Gillette, "Inside Contracting," 165–66, 172–73.

37. State Economic League activists, including John J. O'Neill, a Connecticut organizer for the AFL, also aided the strike effort. Gillette, "Inside Contracting," 170; NHU: May 24, 1901, 3; July 15, 1902, 2.

38. One of the first New Haven industrialists to employ Italian workers, Sargent tried to cultivate gratitude and loyalty among the city's Italian immigrants through charitable activity rendered both inside and outside the factory. He set up cooperative coal buying for his workers and had ties to the Lowell Settlement House established near the Wooster Square neighborhood where many of his Italian employees lived (Sargent's daughters Ellen and Elizabeth both worked briefly as volunteers at the settlement house). Of the 1,750 workers who went out on the first day of the strike, according to the *New Haven Union*, 550 were in the Italian Local 205 of the Buffers, Polishers and Allied Metal Trades Union, 200 in Local 25, an American (and Irish-American) local of the same union, and a thousand were predominantly Italian unskilled laborers in Federal Union 205. Italian colony luminary Paul Russo, an attorney, joined Italian trade unionists in assuring the metal workers that their demands were just. Gillette, "Inside Contracting," 168, 174; "Lowell House: A New Haven Social Settlement," 1902 leaflet, Box 194, Folder 442, ASPS; "Lowell House: A New Haven Social Settlement," promotional leaflet, 1900, Lowell House Mailing List, 1903, Box 300, Folder 3609, Box 261, Folder 1, FFP. ICC: March 8, 1902; April 26, 1902; May 3, 1902; June 7, 1902; August 9, 1902. NHEL: July 21, 1902, 10.

39. NHU: July 26, 1902, 1.

40. Gillette, "Inside Contracting," 174–75.

41. Irvine, *From the Bottom Up*, 208–10; NHU: September 15, 1902, 1.

42. NHU: November 1, 1902, 6; November 29, 1902, 6; December 22, 1902, 5. Micah 4:3–4 and 6:8.

43. NHU: November 10, 1902, 5.

44. NHU: December 8, 1902, 7; clipping, "A Reply to Rev. Dr. Smyth Given by Rev. Mr. Irvine," n.d., Alexander Irvine Scrapbook, ca. 1902–8, AIC.

45. Letter from P. F. Smith, secretary, Building Trades Council of New Haven, to Alexander Irvine, December 13, 1902, Alexander Irvine Scrapbook, ca. 1902–8, AIC.

46. Nell Irvin Painter, *Standing at Armageddon: The United States, 1877–1919* (New York: Norton, 1987), 180–86; Donald L. Miller and Richard Sharpless, *The Kingdom of Coal: Work, Enterprise and Ethnic Communities in the Mine Fields* (Philadelphia: University of Pennsylvania Press, 1985), 242–83; Philip S. Foner, *History of the Labor Movement in the United States* (New York: International Publishers, 1964), 3:86–102; Robert J. Cornell, "The Anthracite Coal Strike of 1902" (Ph.D. diss., Catholic University of America, 1957); *Report to the President on the Anthracite Coal Strike* (Washington, D.C.: Government Printing Office, 1902).

47. Foner, *History of the Labor Movement in the United States* 3:96.

48. 23 in 1901. David Montgomery, *The Fall of the House of Labor: The Workplace, the State, and American Labor Activism, 1865–1925* (Cambridge: Cambridge University Press, 1987), 303–4; Foner, *History of the Labor Movement*, 3:63, 86–98.

49. See Ken Fones-Wolf, *Trade Union Gospel: Christianity and Labor in Industrial Philadelphia* (Philadelphia: Temple University Press, 1989).

50. NHU: September 1, 1902, 10; September 22, 1902, 5; October 6, 1902, 6; October 13, 1902, 5. NHJC: September 1, 1902, 3; September 22, 1902, 2.

51. Smyth's determination to protect individualism and patriotism from the assaults of unionism was echoed by Reverend L. R. Streeter of New Haven's Pearl Street Methodist Episcopal Church, who attacked the UMW as coercive and un-American in its attempts to prevent scab labor from working the mines, and counseled workingmen unhappy with their wages to be content and trust in a Providential plan. NHU: October 13, 1902, 5; November 17, 1902, 1, 2; November 24, 1902, 5.

52. NHU: November 24, 1902, 5; December 8, 1902, 7. "A Reply to Rev. Dr. Smyth. . . ."

53. In endorsing Mitchell, however, Irvine also embraced a spokesman of the narrow craft interests that soon bedeviled his labor alliances in New Haven and led him to view trade union leaders with increasing wariness. By 1907, far from extolling NCF-oriented unionists like Mitchell or Gompers, Irvine would use his position as YMCA factory missionary to urge organization on employees of New York's Interborough Rapid Transit Company, whose owner, August Belmont, presided over the NCF. NHU: October 15, 1902, 9. NHJC: December 15, 1902, 9. Irvine, *From the Bottom Up*, 248–49. Irvine's reference to Mitchell as a gentleman and a genius can be found in a clipping entitled "Lessons of the Coal Strike: The Views of an Optimist Whose Heart is Warm," by Alex. F. Irvine, n.d., Alexander Irvine Scrapbook, ca. 1902–8, AIC.

54. One of Farnam's students was Peter Roberts, who served as a minister in the anthracite region in order to research his *Anthracite Coal Communities: A Study of the Demography, the Social, Educational and Moral Life of the Anthracite Regions* (New York: Macmillan, 1904). An earlier volume, *The Anthracite Coal Industry: A Study of the Economic Conditions and Relations of the Co-operative Forces in the Development of the*

Anthracite Coal Industry of Pennsylvania (New York: Macmillan, 1901), provided both Farnam and Irvine with background on the coal strike. Peter Roberts to H. W. Farnam, December 23, 1904, December 30, 1904, H. W. Farnam to Peter Roberts, December 29, 1904, FFP.

55. Letters from Alexander Irvine to Prof. Henry Farnam, December 9, 1902, December 15, 1902, Box 261, Folder 3358, FFP; Henry Farnam, "Lecture on Anthracite Coal Strike of 1902," Box 234, Folder 3144, FFP.

56. NHJC: December 15, 1901, 9.

57. Henry W. Farnam to Reverend A. F. Irvine, December 15, 1902, FFP.

58. Irvine to Farnam, December 15, 1902, FFP.

59. Henry Farnam had his own way of indicating Irvine's alienation from the New Haven elite: whereas letters he wrote to Irvine regarding Lowell House always began "My dear Mr. Irvine," the letters concerning the controversy over the slides began curtly "Dear Sir." In contrast, Newman Smyth continued cordial relations with Irvine throughout their disputes. Attending a reception in honor of Irvine's fortieth birthday in 1903, Smyth announced, "I count Mr. Irvine among my friends . . . and am here, like the rest of you, to wish him many happy returns of the day." FFP; NHR: January 21, 1903.

60. The *Leader* had first appeared in 1892 to boom the Republican ticket. By catering to ethnic communities and union news, it attracted a popular readership and a series of politically diverse columnists. The only paper in New Haven to carry the printers' union label, the *Leader* was honored by the Trades Council for "aiding the cause of organized labor by printing complete and fair reports of all affairs in which labor has a vital interest." See Trades Council, *Illustrated History*, 219; NHEL: January 11, 1903, 3; May 17, 1903, 9. On Irvine's induction into the carriage maker's union, see letter from Louis F. Maire, secretary, Carriage and Wagon Workers International Union, Local Union 32, to Reverend Alexander F. Irvine, January 20, 1903, and Carriage and Wagon Workers International Union of N. A. Traveling Card, Alexander Irvine Scrapbook, ca. 1902–8, AIC; NHEL: February 19, 1903, 12.

61. Irvine, *From the Bottom Up*, 213–15; NHEL: January 11, 1903, 3; January 16, 1903, 14; February 3, 1903, 10; March 4, 1903, 12; March 10, 1903, 12; March 31, 1903, 12; April 13, 1903, 12. Irvine's and the Trades Council's emphasis on Mitchell's "gentlemanliness" was only partly a tribute to the "conservative" qualities that made the UMW president attractive to the NCF. Within local cultural conflicts, insistence on the contrast between Mitchell's "gentlemanly manner" and the boorish stubbornness of the coal barons reiterated the Trades Council's point that their claim on culture was genuine, while that of the pretentious, "so-called cultured element" was sham.

62. NHR: January 15, 1903, 5. NHEL: January 15, 1903, 1, 3.

63. NHU: January 17, 1903, 3. NHEL: January 18, 1903, 1; January 19, 1903, 10; February 22, 1903, 5; February 25, 1903, 10.

64. NHEL: February 27, 1903, 1, 3, 5.

65. NHU: December 13, 1902, 2. NHEL: March 25, 1903, 11; April 24, 1903, 1; April 25, 1903, 4; April 27, 1903, 5. Irvine, *From the Bottom Up*, 211; *Bulletin*, Pilgrim Church, 4.

66. NHEL: April 25, 1903; May 21, 1903. Irvine, *From the Bottom Up*, 211–12.

67. NHEL: April 27, 1903, 5. Irvine, *From the Bottom Up*, 220–23.

68. NHEL: May 11, 1903, 2.

69. NHEL: May 10, 1903, 4; May 11, 1903, 2.

70. NHU: May 15, 1903, 6; June 6, 1903, 6; February 27, 1904, 5; March 19, 1904, 2; April 16, 1904, 7.

71. NHU: May 25, 1903, 3.

72. NHU: May 11, 1903, 10.

73. NHU: May 30, 1903, 6; June 1, 1903, 5.

74. NHU: February 20, 1904, 10; March 5, 1904, 2; April 9, 1904, 7; June 4, 1904, 2.

75. The Bennett Boys Club was named after Philo S. Bennett—the New Haven merchant and Silver Democrat who was the main financial support for the People's Church until his death three months after its establishment. NHU: May 11, 1903, 10; October 21, 1903, 9; November 13, 1903, 13. Book 25, 18, AGDC. Irvine, *From the Bottom Up*, 223–26.

76. NHU: October 12, 1903, 2; December 28, 1903, 1; April 11, 1904, 7. Clipping, "Irvine on Lincoln," NHEL: February 13, 1904, in Item M, LWCP.

77. NHU: September 18, 1903, 2; Irvine, *The Master and the Chisel* (New Haven, Conn.: The People's Church, 1904), 46–49.

78. NHU: November 10, 1903, 10; January 12, 1904, 5; March 28, 1904, 3; April 19, 1904, 2; April 23, 1904, 6; December 6, 1904, 14; April 22, 1905, 8.

79. NHEL: May 2, 1903, 1; clipping, NHR: April 24, 1904 in Item P, LWCP; *Bulletin*, Pilgrim Church, 2; *Greater New Haven Directory* (New Haven, Conn.: Price & Lee, 1902), 28, 42, 51, 107, 112, 125, 248, 343, 380, 421, 476, 505, 603. The *Leader* listed forty-three members of Pilgrim who had petitioned to join the People's Church; the list included Irvine, his wife Maude, and three sons from his first marriage, all of whom have been excluded from this summary. Some of the working-class members who joined Pilgrim under Irvine's aegis apparently shifted to the People's Church without bothering to petition directly to the Pilgrim deacons—People's Church clerk William Pollard was one of these.

80. Along with Dennis Fitzgerald of the local's executive board, Irvine persuaded disgruntled conductors to accept concessions short of their original aims rather than strike for higher overtime rates and recognition of their union. NHU: May 15, 1903, 1; August 2, 1904, 2; August 8, 1904, 2. NHEL: May 18, 1903, 12. Certificate of Membership, International Association of Car Workers, July 17, 1904, Alexander Irvine Scrapbook, ca. 1902–8, AIC; letter to Irvine from John E. Hague, Recording Secretary, New Haven Trades Council, October 5, 1905, Alexander Irvine Scrapbook, ca. 1902–8, AIC.

81. NHU: December 6, 1904, 14; June 3, 1905, 8. Irvine, *From the Bottom Up*, 242.

82. NHU: May 11, 1903, 1; May 15, 1903, 10; May 16, 1903, May 20, 1903, 1; May 26, 1903, 1; May 28, 1903, 1; June 3, 1903, 1; June 4, 1903, 8; June 5, 1903, 1; June 30, 1903, 2; January 21, 1904, 1; February 12, 1904, 1.

83. NHU: October 11, 1904, 1.

84. NHU: November 18, 1902, 6; March 10, 1905, 7; March 11, 1905, 9; March 11, 1905, 9; March 22, 1905, 1, 11–12; March 28, 1905, 7; April 5, 1905, 1; April 11, 1905, 3; April 13, 1905, 1; April 15, 1905, 6; May 1, 1905, 1; May 3, 1905, 1; May 6, 1905, 1; May 8, 1905, 1. Connecticut State Bureau of Labor Statistics, *Reports* (Meriden: Journals Publishing Company), 1901–2, 512–21; 1902–3, 402–11; 1903–4, 406–9; 1904–5, 106–9.

85. Clipping, NHR: April 24, 1904, Item P, Scrapbook, 1903–4, LWCP. As Ken Fones-Wolf has shown, in the early twentieth century some trade unionists closed ranks with

Protestant ministers who offered unions legitimacy in exchange for moderation. Irvine, however, never devoted himself to the particular craft privileges that moderate unionism upheld. Fones-Wolf, *Trade Union Gospel*, 155–65.

86. Irvine, *From the Bottom Up*, 233–35; idem, *Fighting Parson*, 70.

87. NHU: October 15, 1903, 2; May 23, 1904, 1; October 27, 1904, 5. *Bulletin*, Pilgrim Church, 2; NHEL: May 2, 1903, 1; New Haven Colony Historical Society, *Max Dellfant: Catalogue* (New Haven, Conn.: NHCHS, 1975); Alexander Irvine to H. W. Farnam, n.d. (ca. March 1902), Box 261, Folder 3358, FFP; Irvine, *Fighting Parson*, 70.

88. NHU: June 27, 1903, 2; October 27, 1904; 5, April 11, 1905, 3. NHEL: April 17, 1903, 1; April 19, 1903, 8. Irvine, *From the Bottom Up*, 230, 233–34; idem, *Fighting Parson*, 70.

89. Its officers included treasurer Max Dellfant, the artist who resided with Irvine, and clerk Clifford Whitlock, a bookseller who was the son of reformers. The church's sole trustee and only wage-earning officer was a tinner named Joseph Stannard. NHU: January 18, 1905, 10; Irvine, *From the Bottom Up*, 231–32, 237–38; idem, *Fighting Parson*, 66.

90. Gail Bederman, "'The Women Have Had Charge of the Church Work Long Enough': The Men and Religion Forward Movement of 1911–1912 and the Masculinization of Middle-Class Protestantism," *American Quarterly* 41, no. 3 (1989): 432–65.

91. Paul A. Carter, *The Spiritual Crisis of the Gilded Age* (Dekalb: Northern Illinois University Press, 1971), 70, 87; William E. Winn, "*Tom Brown's School Days* and the Development of 'Muscular Christianity,'" *Church History* 29 (March 1960): 64–73.

92. NHEL: January 28, 1905.

93. NHU: December 28, 1903, 1; Minutes, 1905–8, September 12, 1905, LHMCR; on labor movement views of women, see *The Union Label, Its History and Aims* (Washington, D.C.: American Federation of Labor, n.d.), 2–3; Alice Kessler-Harris, "Where Are the Organized Women Workers?" in *A Heritage of Her Own: Toward a New Social History of American Women*, ed. Nancy F. Cott and Elizabeth Pleck (New York: Simon & Schuster, 1979), 343–66; Ruth Milkman, "Organizing the Sexual Division of Labor: Historical Perspectives on 'Women's Work' and the American Labor Movement," *Socialist Review* 10, no. 1 (1980): 95–150; Meredith Tax, *The Rising of the Women: Feminist Solidarity and Class Conflict, 1880–1917* (New York: Monthly Review Press, 1980); Nancy Shrom Dye, *As Equals and as Sisters: Feminism, Unionism, and the Women's Trade Union League of New York* (Columbia: University of Missouri Press, 1980).

94. Visitors List, Reception to Laundry Workers, November 20, 1905, Alexander Irvine Scrapbook, ca. 1902–8, AIC; NHEL: December 3, 1905, 8; Alex. F. Irvine, "Memorial," in Genevieve Hale Whitlock, *Poems* (New Haven, Conn.: Clifford E. H. Whitlock, 1906), vii–xii. Thanks to Reverdy Whitlock for a copy of this volume.

95. The conflicts between Alexander and Maude are pieced together from a variety of representations Irvine made of his home life, for domestic life took up but a small space in his autobiographies, and Maude Irvine herself left no known document of the experience. The most extensive representation of their differences is in Irvine's semiautobiographical novel *The Magyar: A Story of the Social Revolution* (Girard, Kans.: The Socialist Publishing Company, 1911), discussed in ch. 7. The Irvines' marital troubles are also described in the unpublished manuscript "Little Pilgrims of the Dawn," AIC.

96. NHEL: December 3, 1905, 8.

97. NHEL: March 4, 1906, 10.

98. NHEL: December 3, 1905, 8.

99. NHEL: December 17, 1905, 24.

Chapter Five: "Mr. Poli Is the Big Chief!": The Theatrical Manager, His Audiences, and the Vaudeville Industry

1. "New Haven Ethnography: Census of New Haven Population, 1870–1930," Box 67:175:3, PCEHP; as an example of ethnic rivalry, see news story in NHU: August 12, 1902, 1: "Trouble, Trouble, Trouble: Four Races in an Oak Street Row."

2. NHU: June 10, 1895, 6; June 11, 1895, 6; June 13, 1895, 6; June 14, 1895, 6; June 15, 1895, 6.

3. See David Roediger, *The Wages of Whiteness: Race and the Making of the American Working Class* (London: Verso, 1991); Eric Lott, *Love and Theft: Blackface Minstrelsy and the American Working Class* (New York: Oxford University Press, 1993); David Nasaw, *Going Out: The Rise and Fall of Public Amusements* (New York: Basic, 1993), ch. 5.

4. Phyllis Williams, *South Italian Folkways in Europe and America* (New Haven, Conn.: Yale University Press, 1938); Ralph Vecoli, "Prelates and Peasants: Italian Immigrants and the Catholic Church," *Journal of Social History* 2, no. 3 (1969): 217–68; Robert Anthony Orsi, *The Madonna of 115th Street: Faith and Community in Italian Harlem, 1880–1950* (New Haven, Conn.: Yale University Press, 1985).

5. *Report of the Third Annual Meeting of the Lowell House Association* (New Haven, Conn.: Lowell House, 1904), 10–11, 20–21; *Report of the Fourth Annual Meeting of the Lowell House Association* (New Haven, Conn.: Lowell House, 1905), 14; *Report of the Fifth Annual Meeting of the Lowell House Association* (New Haven, Conn.: Lowell House, 1906), 19.

6. "The Fratellanza Oldest Italian Society Here," NHR: August 13, 1922, 7.

7. "Italians of New Haven," V. Racca MS, Box 57:256:5a, PCEHP; Louis Petruccelli, "New Haven Society Named for Great Italian Scientist," NHR: September 17, 1922, 5; Louis Petruccelli, "San Carlino and Sannio Clubs Keeping Culture of Native Land Alive Among Countrymen of this City," NHR: May 21, 1922, 8.

8. Petruccelli, "San Carlino and Sannio Clubs," NHR: May 21, 1922, 8.

9. Petruccelli, "San Carlino and Sannio Clubs"; M. Earle, "New Haven Drama Tournament Groups," and C. P. Butts, "The Organized Life of the Italians of New Haven," MSS, PCEHP; Emelise Aleandri and Maxine Schwartz Seller, "Italian-American Theatre," in *Ethnic Theatre in the United States*, ed. Maxine Schwartz Seller (Westport, Conn.: Greenwood, 1983), 237–76.

10. Antonio Cannelli, *La Colonia Italiana di New Haven* (New Haven, Conn.: A. Cannelli, 1921), 217, from notes by V. Racca, Box 57, Folder 156:5a, PCEHP.

11. ICC: September 6, 1902.

12. In May 1902, for example, *San Carlino* offered a comic sketch entitled *Un Chiodo Nella Serratura* involving a real estate clerk and railroad engineer as central characters, followed by Esposito enacting the Pulcinella mask in *Il Furioso All'Isola Di San Domingo*. The following year *San Carlino* offered the Neopolitan sketch *Ammore Muorto* and Esposito as Pulcinella in *E Tre Scartellate*. ICC: May 3, 1902; November 21, 1903.

13. ICC: May 2, 1903; August 29, 1903.

14. ICC: April 16, 1904.

15. Vadim Uraneff, "*Commedia Dell'Arte* and American Vaudeville," *Theatre Arts Magazine* 7 (October 1923): 321–28.

16. NHU: November 1, 1904; Poli also hosted one of the Musolino dramas as a church benefit in 1902. ICC: June 28, 1902.

17. ICC: April 27, 1901; September 7, 1901; July 25, 1903; October 29, 1904.

18. ICC: June 9, 1906.

19. For the working-class nature of the Ancient Order of Hibernians, see *New Haven City Directory* (New Haven, Conn.: Price & Lee, 1902, 1904).

20. NHU: February 10, 1902. This was a version of Catholic respectability open to working-class Catholics as well. As judged by officials listed in the *New Haven Directory*, individual lodges were usually composed of primarily working-class or primarily middle-class membership.

21. Christopher J. Kauffman, *Faith and Fraternalism: The History of the Knights of Columbus, 1882–1982* (New York: Harper & Row, 1982), 1–17.

22. Reilly served as an officer of the predominantly working-class Elm City Knights of Columbus council. Mark Carnes, *Secret Ritual and Manhood in Victorian America* (New Haven, Conn.: Yale University Press, 1989), passim; Kauffman, *Faith and Fraternalism*, 33, 139; *New Haven City Directory*, 1904, 872.

23. "Order Sons of Italy," Box 156: 1b; Cannelli, *La Colonia Italiana of New Haven*, 298, V. Racca Notes, People's of Connecticut Ethnic Heritage.

24. NHJC: November 21, 1905, 3; "The S. Z. Poli Silver Jubilee," S. Z. Poli File, BRTC; Nicholas M. Kliment, "*Padrone* of the People: The Life and Times of Vaudeville Mogul S.Z. Poli (1859–1937)," unpublished senior essay, History Department, Yale University, 1985. On New Haven's various Catholic churches, see John W. McConnell, *The Evolution of Social Classes* (Washington, D.C.: American Council on Public Affairs, 1942), 83–84.

25. *Saturday Chronicle*, May 4, 1907, 9.

26. Cass Gilbert and Frederick Law Olmsted, *Report of the New Haven Civic Improvement Commission* (New Haven, Conn.: New Haven Civic Improvement Committee, 1910); *Saturday Chronicle*, August 10, 1907, 2; Rollin G. Osterweiss, *Three Centuries of New Haven* (New Haven, Conn.: Yale University Press, 1953), 391–92.

27. "Our Settlements: What They Do and Why You Should Support Them," Promotional Leaflet, Series II, Box 300, Folder 3610, FFP; *Report of the Sixteenth Annual Meeting of the Lowell House Association* (New Haven, Conn.: Lowell House Association, 1917), 17.

28. James Reynolds, Samuel H. Fisher, and Henry B. Wright, eds., *Two Centuries of Christian Activity at Yale* (New York: G. P. Putnam's Sons, 1901), 274.

29. NHU: April 6, 1905, 2.

30. Donald C. King, "S. Z. Poli, From Wax to Riches," *Marquee* 2 (1979): 12–13.

31. *Variety*: January 13, 1906, 2; February 3, 1906, 2.

32. *Variety*: January 13, 1906, 2; February 10, 1906, 2.

33. Clipping, *Morning Telegraph*, April 22, 1906, S. Z. Poli File, BRTC.

34. Robert Snyder, *The Voice of the City: Vaudeville and Popular Culture in New York* (New York: Oxford University Press, 1989), 68–73.

35. Poli abandoned plans to build in Providence, Jersey City, Philadelphia, Baltimore, Buffalo, and Detroit. He retained theaters in New Haven, Waterbury, Hartford, Bridgeport, Springfield, Scranton, and Wilkes-Barre. He soon added another vaudeville theater in Meriden, Connecticut, and also ran stock companies in the former Wonderland, now called the Bijou, and in a second Waterbury theater. In 1912 Poli converted the Bijou into a "small time" vaudeville house playing five acts and several motion pictures. It was in this theater that Irvine would make one of his first vaudeville appearances. King, "S. Z. Poli," 13; *New York Telegraph,* May 17, 1906, S. Z. Poli File, BRTC.

36. *S. Z. Poli's Theatrical Enterprises,* promotional brochure (New Haven, Conn.: Poli's Theatrical Enterprises, 1907; reprint Notre Dame: Theatrical Historical Society, 1978); NHJC: October 10, 1907, 3.

37. Snyder, *The Voice of the City,* 141–45; see also M. Alison Kibler, "The Keith Vaudeville Circuit, 1890–1920: Gender, Sexuality and the Cultural Hierarchy" (Ph.D. diss, University of Iowa, 1994).

38. For distributions of vaudeville act types between 1902 and 1908, see Appendix B.

39. NHU: February 11, 1902, 12; November 18, 1902.

40. Clipping, *New York Telegraph,* January 25, 1907, Russell Brothers File, BRTC.

41. Clipping, *New York Telegraph,* April 16, 1907, Russell Brothers File, BRTC.

42. Clippings, *New York Telegraph,* January 25, 1907; February 3, 1907, Russell Brothers File, BRTC.

43. NHU: March 11, 1902, 10; clipping, *Cleveland Plain Dealer* December 12, 1909, Gracie Emmet File, BRTC..

44. NHJC: September 11, 1905, 2; clipping, *Morning Telegraph,* February 4, 1906, Thomas Nawn File, BRTC.

45. NHU: October 19, 1903. NHJC: December 10, 1906, 8; January 16, 1912, 7. Paul Dresser, *The Songs of Paul Dresser* (New York: Boni & Liveright, 1927); Nicholas E. Tawa, *The Way to Tin Pan Alley: American Popular Song, 1866–1910* (New York: Scribner, 1990), 159.

46. Daniel Blum, *A Pictorial History of the American Theatre, 1860–1976* (New York: Crown, 1977), 123; Mark Slobin, *Tenement Songs: The Popular Music of the Jewish Immigrants* (Urbana: University of Illinois Press, 1982), 60.

47. See Laurence Hutton, *Curiosities of the American Stage* (New York: Harper & Brothers, 1891; reprint, New York: Johnson Reprint Corporation, 1968), 47–53; Maureen Murphy, "Irish-American Theatre," in *Ethnic Theatre in the United States,* ed. Seller, 223–24; Richard M. Dorson, "Mose the Far-Famed and World Renowned," *American Literature* 15 (November 1943): 288–300; E. J. Kahn, *The Merry Partners: The Age and Stage of Harrigan and Hart* (New York: Random House, 1955).

48. James Weldon Johnson, *Black Manhattan* (New York: Atheneum, 1968), 111–16; Eileen Southern, *The Music of Black Americans: A History* (New York: W. W. Norton, 1971), 313–14; Isaac Goldberg, *Tin Pan Alley: A Chronicle of American Popular Music* (New York: Frederick Ungar, 1961), 155–61; Tawa, *Way to Tin Pan Alley,* 181–93; Snyder, *Voice of the City,* 135–36.

49. Tom Fletcher, *One Hundred Years of the Negro in Show Business* (New York: Da Capo, 1984), 135–43; clipping, "This Week with the Player Folk," n.d., Ernest Hogan File, Robinson Locke Collection, BRTC.

50. NHU: September 18, 1903, 10; October 14, 1903, 8. There remains some uncertainty about the distinction between "coon songs" and ragtime: Tawa notes that while some musicians saw ragtime replacing the "coon song" of the 1890s, others continued to use "coon song" to refer to lyrics of especially derogatory, pseudodialect songs, and used "rag" to refer to the new music. Poli's ads made little distinction between the two terms. Fletcher, *One Hundred Years*, 135, 143, 235; Tawa, *Way to Tin Pan Alley*, 186–87.

51. James Weldon Johnson, *Along This Way* (New York: Viking, 1933), 187–88.

52. Fletcher, *One Hundred Years*, 235; Snyder, *Voice of the City*, 44.

53. Sophie Tucker, *Some of These Days* (Garden City, N.Y.: Doubleday, 1945); Snyder, *Voice of the City*, 54–56; Slobin, *Tenement Songs*, 202–5; Lewis Erenberg, *Steppin' Out: New York Nightlife and the Transformation of American Culture, 1890–1930* (Chicago: University of Chicago Press, 1981), 187. For appearances of these artists at Poli's, see NHU: November 2, 1913, 2; Poli program, February 17, 1909, CTC.

54. After 1908 female advertisements for song and dance acts often referred to women's appearance and figures: The ABCD girls were "four of the best lookers with song and dance"; Miss Linden Beckwith was "The Magnetic Mistress of Melody"; Billie Seaton was "one of the handsomest as well as one of the most shapely women on the vaudeville stage." NHJC: January 6, 1908, 4; May 7, 1910, 5. Poli's handbill, April 22, 1912, CTC.

55. Goldberg, *Tin Pan Alley*, 256; Slobin, *Tenement Songs*, 202–5; Erenberg, *Steppin' Out*, 176–202; Snyder, *Voice of the City*, 150; Douglas Gilbert, *American Vaudeville, Its Life and Times* (New York: Whittlesey House, 1940), 328.

56. Faye E. Dudden, *Women in the American Theatre: Actresses and Audiences, 1790–1870* (New Haven, Conn.: Yale University Press, 1994). The opportunities and dangers of women on the nineteenth-century stage are also illuminated in Tracy C. Davis, *Actresses as Working Women: Their Social Identity in Victorian Culture* (London and New York: Routledge, 1991). On various meanings of the "New Woman," see Kathy Peiss, "Making Faces: The Cosmetics Industry and the Cultural Construction of Gender, 1890–1930," *Genders* 7 (Spring 1990): 143–69. Also see Bibliographical Essay, sec. II.E.

57. Of course American theatrical entertainments had played on the appeal of beautiful women, lavish costumes, and opulent sets before the early twentieth century. Burlesque shows had focused attention on female bodies since the 1870s, as Robert Allen points out. But burlesque quickly became associated with "lowbrow" tastes rather than the heterogeneous audiences to which vaudeville appealed, and indeed became one of the risque entertainments from which vaudeville entrepreneurs of the 1890s tried to dissociate their entertainments through a judicious wielding of "refinement" (though my reading of this standard is different than Allen's). In the 1890s, feminine pulchritude and sartorial extravagance were also central to the appeal of the sensationally popular Lillian Russell, who rose from Tony Pastor's to more lucrative and high-priced roles in comic opera. But her rise meant that Russell played to a more homogeneous middle- and upper-middle-class audience than vaudeville attracted. Russell's own forays into variety and vaudeville in the 1890s and 1900s were carefully orchestrated to maintain the higher theatrical status she sought; in later years she took pains to dissociate herself from theatrical displays that might be deemed salacious (e.g., the wearing of tights) and gained notoriety for advocating limits on immigration from the eastern and southern European countries that gave vaudeville and cabaret their stars. The 1890s also saw the beginnings of

the revue-style theatrical display that Ziegfeld would perfect in the next decade, which combined titillations associated with "low-class" entertainments with the opulence previously restricted to the wealthy. It was this combination that began to proliferate in Poli's acts and advertisements and changed the way he dealt with "refinement." Vaudeville's industry journal *Variety* frequently noted the competition that cabaret posed for vaudeville. See "Cabaret's Real Opposition to Regular Vaudeville," *Variety* 26, no. 3 (1912): 9; I. B. Pulaski "Origin of the Cabaret," *Variety* 29, no. 3 (1912): 51. For scholarship on theatrical feminine display, see Bibliographical Essay, sec. II.E.

58. Lasky gave institutional expression to the kinship between his vaudeville productions and cabaret when he used his vaudeville profits to open a nightclub called the Folies Bergere in 1912. The enterprise quickly folded, but helped inspire restauranteurs who employed vaudeville stars to host successful cabaret entertainments on a more intimate basis. NHJC: March 28, 1905; Jesse Lasky, *I Blow My Own Horn* (Garden City, N.Y.: Doubleday, 1957); Erenberg, *Steppin' Out*, 75, 122; Pulaski, "Origin of the Cabaret."

59. Clipping, *Pittsburgh Gazette*, November 1, 1908, Jesse Lasky file, BRTC.

60. Hartley Davis, "In Vaudeville," *Everybody's* 13 (August 1905): 231–40.

61. In the program notes for ensemble acts, Poli listed not only actresses and actors but also scenery specialists, costume and millinery designers, and shoe manufacturers, highlighting their opulent artistry as central to the acts' appeal. The billing and ads for these acts emphasized the splendors of sets and costumes. Poli programs: May 11, 1908; September 21, 1908; May 24, 1909; May 15, 1911; September 18, 1911, CTF. NHJC: January 6, 1908; May 13, 1908; May 7, 1910; October 8, 1910. NHU: November 3, 1913. For shifting emphases of shows, see the appendix to this book.

62. Mae West, *Goodness Had Nothing To Do With It* (Englewood Cliffs, N.J.: Prentice-Hall, 1959), 41–43; *Variety* 27, no. 7 (1912): 16; "Closing of Poli Theater Stirs Memories of Great Stage Era," NHR: December 6, 1959, 16; Erenberg, *Steppin' Out*, photograph of Gray's costume. For a contrasting analysis of West in vaudeville, see Allen, *Horrible Prettiness*, 274–75.

63. NHU: March 11, 1902, 10; May 27, 1903, 6; November 11, 1902, 12; December 17, 1903, 8. NHJC: November 4, 1907, 5.

64. NHJC: March 18, 1903, 7; May 30, 1905, 5; April 17, 1905, 3; September 7, 1907, 3; October 8, 1907, 5. NHU: February 2, 1903, 10. Descriptions of *The Kleptomaniac* are from Kay Sloan, *The Loud Silents: Origins of the Social Problem Film* (Urbana: University of Illinois Press, 1988), 18; Kemp Niver, *The First Twenty Years: A Segment of Film History* (Los Angeles: Locare Research Group, 1968), 85.

65. A second club was formed specifically for Italian-American mothers, many of whom did not speak English and whose community was reviled by more established immigrant groups. Though its discussions would undoubtedly offer further insight into the cross-class and -ethnic cultural negotiations among New Haven's women, the Italian Mothers' Club did not leave the rich archive of minutes available for the club discussed in this paper. It is discussed ably by Margo Schlanger, "'A Lively Lot of Women Who Intend to Make Themselves of Use in This World': The Mothers' Clubs of Lowell House, 1900–1920," unpublished Yale senior essay in the author's possession.

66. Letter from Frank C. Porter to Anson Phelps Stokes, July 30, 1941, ASPS; Minutes, 1900–1902, LHMCR.

67. "Members of Mothers Club, November 1901–November 1902," LHMCR.

68. Minutes, 1905–8, June 5, 1906, LHMCR.

69. Minutes, 1905–8, July 17, 1906, LHMCR.

70. Minutes, 1902–3, LHMCR.

71. On the relation between mass culture and popular style, see Kathy Peiss, *Cheap Amusements: Working Women and Leisure in New York City at the Turn of the Century* (Philadelphia: Temple University Press, 1986); and Peiss, "Making Faces," as well as Jane Gaines and Charlotte Herzog, eds., *Fabrications: Costume and the Female Body* (New York and London: Routledge, 1990).

Chapter Six: Making Working-Class Narrative "From the Bottom Up": Alexander Irvine, the Evolutionary Vernacular, and the Socialist Bildungsroman

1. For descriptions of the tour, see Joan London, *Jack London and His Times* (New York: Doubleday, Doran, 1939); Philip S. Foner, "Jack London: American Rebel," in *Jack London: American Rebel*, ed. Philip S. Foner (New York: Citadel, 1947), 3–130; Joan Hedrick, *Solitary Comrade: Jack London and His Work* (Chapel Hill: North Carolina University Press, 1982); Mark E. Zamen, *Standing Room Only: Jack London's Controversial Career as a Public Speaker* (New York: P. Lang, 1990).

2. Alexander Irvine, *From the Bottom Up: The Life Story of Alexander Irvine* (New York: Doubleday-Page, 1910), 250–55; *Jack London at Yale* (color xerox of scrapbook prepared by Alexander Irvine and Max Dellfant to commemorate London's lecture at Woolsey Hall, January 25, 1906), Beinecke Library, Yale University (hereafter *Jack London*: Scrapbook); *Jack London at Yale*, ed. State Secretary of the Socialist Party of Connecticut (Westwood, Mass.: Ariel Press, for Connecticut State Committee of the Socialist Party, 1906), 3–10.

3. Carolyn Johnston, *Jack London—An American Radical?* (Westport, Conn.: Greenwood, 1984), 45, 51–53; London, *Jack London and His Times*, 125–36.

4. London to Cloudesley Johns, December 12, 1899, quoted in Johnston, *Jack London*, 48; London, *Jack London and His Times*, 212–13.

5. Jack London, "Revolution," in *Novels and Social Writings* (New York: The Library of America, 1982), 1148.

6. Jack London, *John Barleycorn*, in *Novels and Social Writings*, 1065–66.

7. London, *Jack London*, 197–200, 222–23; the quote is from Jack London and Anna Strunsky, *The Kempton-Wace Letters* (New York: Macmillan, 1903), published anonymously; on London's loveless first marriage, see also Johnston, *Jack London*, 71–74.

8. London, *John Barleycorn*, 1066.

9. Jack London, "How I Became a Socialist," in *Novels and Social Writings*, 1117.

10. Ibid.; London, "Revolution," 1149, 1162. This was the most infamous speech of London's lecture tour, which he repeated in several cities.

11. London was more equivocal about his racial views than many biographers have recognized. Throughout his career, he treated race as an immutable boundary that defined a "civilization" he criticized but felt bound to uphold. But he was capable of moving portrayals of imperial exploitation or revolutionary valor that crossed racial lines in their sym-

pathies. His racism is most virulently expressed in his letters to Cloudesley Johns in Jack London, *The Letters of Jack London*, ed. Earle Labor, Robert C. Leitz III, and I. Milo Shepard (Stanford, Calif.: Stanford University Press, 1988), 81–93. For suggestions of cross-racial sympathy, see "The Chinago," "Mauki," and "The Mexican," in Jack London, *Novels and Stories* (New York: The Library of America, 1982), 834–48, 868–82, 920–44. The quote is from London, *Jack London and His Times*, 166–67, 284. The tension between Irvine and London on the relative merits of scientific materialism and idealism are recorded in "A Letter to Jack London," which Irvine wrote on hearing of London's death in 1916, AIC, and in "A Causerie in Shadowland," in Alexander Irvine, *Anna's Wishing Chair and Other Chimney Corner Stories* (Belfast: Quota, 1937).

12. London's Yale bildungsroman served as the outline for several later literary works. Two months later, he published roughly the same story in *Cosmopolitan Magazine* under the title "What Life Means to Me"; in his 1909 novel, *Martin Eden*, he twisted it into the tragic saga of a life missing the adult resolution that socialism offered. Jack London, "Revolution," 1147–65; "What Life Means to Me," *Cosmopolitan Magazine* 40 (March 1906): 526–30; *Martin Eden* (New York: Macmillan, 1909); *Yale Alumni Weekly*, January 31, 1906, cited in *Jack London at Yale*, 15–16.

13. *Jack London at Yale*, 15–16.

14. Ibid.

15. See Nancy Fraser, "Rethinking the Public Sphere," and Geoff Eley, "Nations, Publics, and Political Cultures," in *Habermas and the Public Sphere*, ed. Craig Calhoun (Cambridge, Mass.: MIT, 1992), 109–42, 288–39; Joan Landes, *Women and the Public Sphere in the Age of the French Revolution* (Ithaca, N.Y.: Cornell University Press, 1988); Mary Ryan, *Women in Public: Between Banners and Ballots, 1825–1880* (Baltimore: Johns Hopkins University Press, 1990).

16. Todd Kontje, *Private Lives in the Public Sphere: The German Bildungsroman as Metafiction* (University Park: Pennsylvania State University Press, 1992) and *The German Bildungsroman: History of a National Genre* (Columbia, S.C.: Camden House, 1993).

17. Franco Moretti, *The Way of the World: The Bildungsroman in European Culture* (London: Verso, 1987).

18. Luther Mott, *A History of American Magazines* (Cambridge, Mass.: Harvard University Press, 1957), 48–50, 483–93, 590–602; Richard Lingeman, *Theodore Dreiser: At the Gates of the City, 1871–1907* (New York: G. P. Putnam's Sons, 1986), 193; Christopher P. Wilson, *The Labor of Words: Literary Professionalism in Progressive America* (Athens: University of Georgia Press, 1985), chs. 2 and 4; Matthew Schneirov, *The Dream of a New Social Order: Popular Magazines in America, 1893–1914* (New York: Columbia University Press, 1994). For a contrasting account emphasizing consumption and romance more than the evolutionary vernacular discussed here, see Richard Ohmann, *Selling Culture: Magazines, Markets, and Class at the Turn of the Century* (London: Verso, 1996). In efforts to emulate the new periodicals, magazines like *Harper's* and the *Atlantic* also published work like London's.

19. Wilson, *Labor of Words*, chs. 2 and 4; Schneirov, *Dream of a New Social Order*, ch. 4.

20. Jack London's preoccupation with literary contracts is best gleaned from his voluminous correspondence with editors, contained in London, *Letters*, esp. 547ff.

21. Wilson, *Labor of Words*, ch. 2; Schneirov, *Dream of a New Social Order*, chs. 4, 6, 7.

22. Schneirov, *Dream of a New Social Order*, esp. ch. 6.

23. See Jack London, *John Barleycorn*, 1065–66; Johnston, *Jack London*, 45, 51–53; London, *Jack London*, 125–36, 166–67.

24. NHEL: January 28, 1905.

25. Alexander Irvine to Jack London, JL 8248, June 30, 1906, JL 8249, July 17, 1906, Box 222, JLC; letter from D. Appleton Company to Alexander Irvine, October 24, 1906, AIC; Irvine, *From the Bottom Up*, 256.

26. Alexander Irvine, "Two Social Pariahs," *Appleton's Magazine* 10, no. 7 (1907): 118–21.

27. Jack London, *White Fang* (New York: Macmillan, 1906).

28. Irvine, "Two Social Pariahs."

29. U.S. Department of Justice, *Report On Peonage*, by Charles W. Russell, Assistant Attorney General (Washington, D.C.: Government Printing Office, 1906), 3.

30. Alexander Irvine, "My Life in Peonage: The Situation as I Found It," *Appleton's Magazine* 9, no. 6 (1907): 643. Irvine may have responded to newspaper stories generated when Florida resident Emma Stirling wrote to the president to request federal investigation of peonage in her state. Department of Justice, *Report On Peonage*; Pete Daniel, *The Shadow of Slavery: Peonage in the South, 1901–1969* (Urbana: University of Illinois Press, 1972); Jonathan Wiener, *Social Origins of the New South: Alabama 1860–1885* (Baton Rouge: Louisiana State University Press, 1978); William Cohen, *At Freedom's Edge: Black Mobility and the Southern White Quest for Racial Control* (Baton Rouge: Louisiana State University Press, 1991).

31. Department of Justice, *Report On Peonage*, 20–21; Daniel, *Shadow of Slavery*, 83–84.

32. Irvine, *From the Bottom Up*, 148.

33. See, for example, Jacob Riis, *How the Other Half Lives* (New York: C. Scribner's Sons, 1890); Mrs. John and Marie Van Vorst, *The Woman Who Toils* (New York: Doubleday-Page, 1903); Whiting Williams, *What's on the Workers' Mind, by One Who Put on Overalls to Find Out* (New York: C. Scribner's Sons, 1920). These are examples of a vast literature in social exploration during this period. For scholarly literature on the genre, see Bibliographical Essay, sec. II.D.

34. Eric Lott, *Love and Theft: Blackface Minstrelsy and the American Working Class* (New York: Oxford University Press, 1993), 40–55; Robert Toll, *Blacking Up: The Minstrel Show in Nineteenth Century America* (New York: Oxford University Press, 1974), 27–51; E. J. Kahn, *The Merry Partners: The Age and Stage of Harrigan and Hart* (New York: Random House, 1955), esp. 49–53.

35. Stephen Crane, "An Experiment in Misery," in *The Portable Stephen Crane*, ed. Joseph Katz (Middlesex and New York: Penguin, 1969), 154.

36. Jack London, *The People of the Abyss* (New York: Macmillan, 1903; reprint New York: Lawrence Hill, 1995), 7, 10, 12. On the trope of imperial adventure, see Bibliographical Essay, sec. II.D.

37. London, *People of the Abyss*, 62, 96, 284; Crane, "An Experiment in Misery," 157, 160; on academic and governmental style, see Department of Justice, *Report On Peonage*; the reports on "floating laborers" produced by the U.S. Commission on Industrial Relations investigator Peter Speek, cited in Toby Higbie, "Crossing Boundaries: Tramp

Ethnographers and Narratives of Class in Progressive Era America," *Social Science History* 21, no. 4 (1997): 559–92; and the most renowned of the academic observers of working-class life, Walter Wyckoff, *The Workers: an Experiment in Reality* (New York: C. Scribner's Sons, 1898). London was contemptuous of Wyckoff's representation of tramps, and preferred the investigative reports published by Josiah Flynt, a tramp turned journalist. See London, *Letters*, 191–93, 259–60; Josiah Flynt, *Tramping with Tramps* (New York: Century, 1899).

38. Richard Barry, "Slavery in the South Today," *Cosmopolitan* 42 (March 1907): 481–91; Daniel, *Shadow of Slavery*, 101–2; Department of Justice, *Report On Peonage*, 21; letters from Special Agent A. J. Hoyt to U.S. Attorney John M. Cheney, from Cheney to Attorney General Charles J. Bonaparte, and from Quackenbos to Bonaparte, Case File 50–162, Section 3 in United States Department of Justice, Peonage Files, 1901–45 (microfilm edition), ed. Pete Daniel; Irvine, "My Life in Peonage: I—The Situation as I Found It," 653.

39. London, *People of the Abyss*, 12–13, 75–77, 136–37.

40. London, "South of the Slot," in *Jack London: American Rebel*, ed. Foner, 258–72. The distinction between Van Vorst and Condon was a subtle comment on the practice of cross-class investigation as practiced by the Van Vorst sisters in *The Woman Who Toils*.

41. Irvine, "My Life in Peonage: The Situation," 643–44.

42. Ibid., 647.

43. Alexander Irvine, "My Life in Peonage: A Week with the 'Bull of the Woods,'" *Appleton's Magazine* 10, no. 1 (1907), quotes from pp. 5, 10, 12.

44. Irvine, "My Life in Peonage: The Situation," 649–50.

45. Irvine, "My Life in Peonage: A Week . . . ," 9, 12, 13.

46. Ibid., 9.

47. Alexander Irvine, "My Life in Peonage: The Kidnapping of 'Punk,'" *Appleton's Magazine* 10, no. 2 (1907): 197.

48. Irvine in this sense anticipated some of the enthusiasm for cross-racial organizing among timber workers that would appear a few years later in the timber fields of Louisiana and Texas, led by the IWW-affiliated Brotherhood of Timber Workers. See George T. Morgan, "No Compromise—No Recognition: John Henry Kirby, the Southern Lumber Operators' Association, and Unionism in the Piney Woods, 1906–1916," *Labor History* 10 (Spring 1969): 193–204; James Green, "The Brotherhood of Timber Workers, 1910–1913: A Radical Response to Industrial Capitalism in the Southern USA," *Past and Present* 60 (August 1973): 161–200; James Fickle, "Race, Class and Radicalism: The Wobblies in the Southern Lumber Industry, 1900–1916," in *At the Point of Production: The Local History of the I.W.W.*, ed. J. R. Colin (Westport, Conn.: Greenwood, 1981); David Roediger, "Gaining a Hearing for Black-White Unity: Covington Hall and the Complexities of Race, Gender and Class," in *Towards the Abolition of Whiteness* (London: Verso, 1994), 127–80.

49. James R. Barrett and David Roediger, "Inbetween Peoples: Race, Nationality and the 'New Immigrant' Working Class," *Journal of American Ethnic History* 16, no. 3 (1997): 819–949. For further literature on working-class experiences and constructions of race in this period, see Bibliographic Essay, sec. II.D.

50. Kenneth W. Warren, *Black and White Strangers: Race and American Literary Realism* (Chicago: University of Chicago Press, 1993).

51. Irvine's contemplated move to New York is discussed in a September 1906 letter to his wife's family reporting the birth of the couple's third child. Interview, Mrs. Anna Irvine Buck, December 27, 1987. See also "Little Children of the Dawn," unpublished MS on the Irvines' years in New York, AIC; Irvine, *From the Bottom Up*, 274.

52. Mary Heaton Vorse, *A Footnote to Folly* (New York: Farrar & Rinehart, 1935), 32–34; Albert Parry, *Garrets & Pretenders: A History of Bohemianism in America* (New York: Freide, 1933), 267; Mari Jo Buhle, *Women and American Socialism, 1870–1920* (Urbana: University of Illinois Press, 1983), 258; "Rev. Dr. Grant Tells His Own Story," *New York Evening Post*, February 1, 1923, 1, 4; letters from Irvine to Du Bois, n.d. (ca. 1907), *The Papers of W. E. B. Du Bois* (Sanford, N.C.: Microfilming Corporation of America, 1980). Thanks to George Shepperson for calling these to my attention.

53. Grant had developed his concern for working-class Christianity during a seven-year mission to weavers and spinners in Fall River, Massachusetts. "Rev. Dr. Grant Tells His Own Story," clipping, *New York Evening Post*, February 1, 1923, 4, AIPABC.

54. Ibid.; Madge C. Jenison, "The Church and the Social Unrest," *The Outlook* 5, no. 79 (1908): 112; Irvine, *From the Bottom Up*, 274–75.

55. "A Shopkeeper's Last Advertisement: Sermon by Rev. Alexander Irvine At the Church of the Ascension . . . June 13, 1909," MS, AIC. During his 1901 trip to France, Irvine obtained a letter from the U.S. ambassador to Chauchard requesting permission for him to view *The Angelus*, Scrapbook, AIC.

56. "Ancient and Modern Fools: Address by Rev. Alexander Irvine at Church of the Ascension . . . April 18, 1909, at 8 p.m.," MS, AIC.

57. "A Modern Prophet of the Poor: Address of Rev. Alexander Irvine Delivered At Church of the Ascension . . . January 30th, 1910," "Lincoln and Debs: Address delivered by Rev. Alexander Irvine at Church of the Ascension . . . February 3, 1910," MSS, AIC.

58. "International War Exhibit: Address of Rev. Alexander Irvine, Church of the Ascension . . . January 17, 1909," MS, AIC. The passage quoted ended with the Soudanese massacred by British "fighting cylinders" in "the machinery of war."

59. "On Strike Against God: Address delivered by Rev. Alexander Irvine at Church of the Ascension . . .January 16, 1910," MS, AIC; "Lincoln and Debs."

60. "Jesus and Battleships: Sermon by Rev. Alexander Irvine at Church of the Ascension . . . June 5, 1910," MS, AIC.

61. *Proceedings of the National Convention of the Socialist Party* (Chicago: Socialist Party, 1908), 119.

62. See Mark Pittenger, *American Socialists and Evolutionary Thought, 1870–1920* (Madison: University of Wisconsin Press, 1993).

63. *Proceedings . . .* , 107, 111–12, 115.

64. Pittenger, *American Socialists*, 128–45, 168–79.

65. *Proceedings of the First National Congress of the Socialist Party of the United States* (Chicago: Socialist Party, 1910), 125–26, 138–39, 143.

66. Joseph Cohen, "Socialist Sociology," *International Socialist Review* 9 (May 1909): 875; Jack London, *Martin Eden* (New York: Macmillan, 1909); London, "South of the Slot."

67. See Buhle, *Women and American Socialism*, chs. 3–7; Meredith Tax, *The Rising of the Women: Feminist Solidarity and Class Conflict, 1880–1917* (New York: Monthly Review Press, 1980), chs. 6–7; *Proceedings* 1908, 300–306 (a discussion of the report of the

first Woman's Committee which shows that socialist women could be every bit as dismissive of "women's issues" as socialist men); Gail Bederman, *Manliness and Civilization: A Cultural History of Gender and Race in the United States, 1880–1917* (Chicago: University of Chicago Press, 1995), ch. 4; Pittenger, *American Socialists*, 186–97.

68. "Equal Pay for Equal Work: Address Delivered by Rev. Alexander Irvine at Church of the Ascension . . . May 16, 1908," MS, AIC; "Women and the Bourgeois Mind: Address Delivered by Rev. Alexander Irvine at Church of the Ascension . . . March 20, 1910," MS, AIC; "The Murder of Mary Farmer: Address Delivered by Alexander Irvine at Church of the Ascension . . . March 28, 1909," MS, AIC.

69. "Equal Pay"; "Women and the Bourgeois Mind"; Nancy F. Cott, *The Grounding of Modern Feminism* (New Haven, Conn.: Yale University Press, 1987), ch. 1.

70. "The Murder of Mary Farmer."

71. Alexander Irvine, fragment of sermon on Carnegie, Church of the Ascension, n.d.; "Mr. Roosevelt's Attack on Socialism," sermon, n.d., AIC.

72. Irvine was granted the title of "lay reader" during his first year at the Ascension by a license from Episcopalian Diocese of New York, Irvine Scrapbook, AIC; on the claim of having originated the "Church Forum," see Irvine, *Fighting Parson*, ch. 6 and "Rev. Dr. Grant Tells His Own Story."

73. "Rev. Dr. Grant Tells His Own Story"; Jension, "The Church and the Social Unrest," 112; Announcement for Church of Ascension Sunday Evening Service and After-Meeting, *New York Call*, March 12, 1910; Irvine, *From the Bottom Up*, 274–77; idem, *A Fighting Parson* (Boston: Little, Brown, 1930), 81–82.

74. Jenison, "The Church and the Social Unrest," 113–14.

75. Ibid.; *New York Herald*, March 29, 1908, 1, 4.

76. *New York Times*, March 29, 1908, 2–3; *New York Herald*, March 29, 1908, 1.

77. *New York Herald*: April 6, 1908, 5; April 27, 1908, 6.

78. Irvine, *Fighting Parson*, 83–86; "Rev. Dr. Grant Tells His Own Story"; *New York Herald*, June 25, 1910, 5; *New York Call*, June 25, 1910, 2.

79. *New York Call*, June 25, 1910, 2.

80. "Can Socialism and Christianity Be Reconciled?" (review of *From the Bottom Up*, quoting Tridon's criticism), *Current Literature* 49 (August 1910): 176–78.

81. Eugene V. Debs to George D. Brewer, June 26 and July 7, 1910, in *Letters of Eugene V. Debs*, ed. J. R. Constantine (Urbana: University of Illinois Press, 1990), 1:364–66.

82. For Page's legend, see Isaac F. Marcosson, *Adventures in Interviewing* (New York: Dodd, Mead, 1931), ch. 2; Wilson, *Labor of Words*, 54–55; for advertisement of Irvine's story, see *The World's Work* 18, no. 3 (1909): cover; Irvine, *Fighting Parson*, 94.

83. Alexander Irvine, "From the Bottom Up: Boyhood in Ireland," *The World's Work* 18, no. 3 (1909): 11790, 11793–97; idem, *From the Bottom Up*, 11–14, 15–21.

84. Irvine, "From the Bottom Up: Boyhood in Ireland," 11797–98; idem, *From the Bottom Up*, 18–23.

85. Irvine, "From the Bottom Up: Training for the British Navy," "From the Bottom Up: Life On Board a British Man-of-War," "From the Bottom Up: The Gordon Relief Expedition," *The World's Work* 18, nos. 4 , 5, 6 (1909): 11948–12029, 12033–37; 12126–27; idem, *From the Bottom Up*, 24–51.

86. Irvine, *From the Bottom Up*, 106.

87. Irvine, "From the Bottom Up: The Battered Hulks of the Bowery," *The World's Work* 19, no. 2 (1909): 12365–68; idem, *From the Bottom Up*, 105–9.

88. Irvine, *From the Bottom Up*, 156–59.

89. Ibid., chs. 13, 14, 16, 17, 19, quotes from pp. 173 and 234.

90. Ibid., chs. 21, 22, quotes from pp. 277, 280, 283, 289, 300.

91. Ibid., 256–58, 265.

92. See Paul B. Worthman, "Black Workers and Labor Unions in Birmingham, Alabama, 1897–1904," *Labor History* 10 (Summer 1969): 375–407; Daniel Letwin, "Interracial Unionism, Gender and 'Social Equality' in the Alabama Coalfields, 1878–1908," *Journal of Southern History* 61, no. 3 (1995): 519–54; as well as Herbert Gutman, "The Negro and the United Mine Workers of America," *Work Culture and Society in Industrializing America*, 121–208; on the expansion of Jim Crow, see C. Vann Woodward, *The Strange Career of Jim Crow* (New York: Oxford University Press, 1955); Joel Williamson, *The Crucible of Race* (New York: Oxford University Press, 1984), ch. 7.

93. Letwin, "Interracial Unionism," 551–53.

94. Warren, *Black and White Strangers*, 106–8.

Chapter Seven: From The Magyar *to* My Lady of the Chimney Corner: Weaving Gender, Race, Ethnicity, and Working-Class Identity

1. Alexander Irvine, *From the Bottom Up: The Life Story of Alexander Irvine* (New York: Doubleday-Page, 1910), 245; idem, *A Fighting Parson* (Boston: Little, Brown, 1930), 72–73.

2. Irvine, *From the Bottom Up*, 245; idem, *Fighting Parson*, 72–73, 94–95; idem, "Little Pilgrims of the Dawn," MS, AIC; interview, Mrs. Anna Irvine Buck, December 27, 1987; interview, Alastair Smyth, October 28, 1987.

3. During Irvine's years as a socialist publicist and vaudeville actor, his children lived in a variety of households spread from coast to coast. While Irvine traveled for the *Appeal*, his daughter was cared for in Hartford. Newspaper reports of their participation in socialist cultural activities, along with memories provided by Irvine's daughter, place Robert, Anna, and Swanee in Los Angeles at the time of the Harriman campaign. They apparently stayed on with the Stevens family, socialist friends of Irvine's in Los Angeles, after their father left the city, but later joined him at the military academy where he began teaching in 1912. The children moved later to a household of family friends in Kentucky. Interview, Mrs. Anna Irvine Buck, December 27, 1987; *The Citizen*, April 19, 1912, 16.

4. "Alexander Irvine, Lecturer," Notice from Wm. B. Feakins, 317 W. 56th St. New York, "A Bureau for Speakers and Singers with a Message," Scrapbook, AIC; AR: November 15, 1910, 1; December 10, 1910, 2.

5. Students who had helped Irvine arrange London's Woolsey Hall address used the event to try to organize an ISS chapter, a project they hoped Irvine would assist. But in 1906 Irvine had other adventures in store. A Yale ISS chapter that formed in 1912 still reaped the whirlwind of Irvine's earlier activities: Woolsey Hall remained closed to student-sponsored events for a decade after London's lecture. *Bulletin of the Intercollegiate Socialist Society*: December 1, 1908; April 1, 1909; October–November 1910; Decem-

ber–January 1910–11; February–March 1911; November–December 1912. Intercollegiate Socialist Society Executive Committee Minutes: September 15, 1911; April 8, 1912. Letter from Chas. M. Field to G. H. Strobell, November 7, 1905; letter from Morgan Thomas Riley, secretary-treasurer pro-tem, Yale Chapter ISS, to M. R. Holbrook, Sec. ISS, March 4, 1906. All found in Intercollegiate Socialist Society Records, Collection XII, Socialist Collections at the Tamiment Library, Microfilm edition, Reels 27 & 28.

6. Alexander Irvine, "The Power of the Appeal," AR: January 21, 1911, 2.

7. In 1902 the *Appeal*'s circulation of 150,000 was the fourth highest of any weekly in the country; it grew to 500,000 by the paper's peak in 1912. John Graham, ed., "*Yours for the Revolution*": *The Appeal to Reason, 1895–1922* (Lincoln: University of Nebraska Press, 1990), 1–16; W. J. Ghent, "The Appeal and Its Influence," *The Survey* 26 (April 1911): 27–28; see also Paul Buhle, "The Appeal to Reason, Girard Kansas, 1895–1917 . . . ," in *The American Radical Press, 1880–1960*, ed. Joseph R. Conlin (Westport, Conn.: Greenwood, 1974), 1:50–59.

8. Graham, "*Yours for the Revolution*," 7; Ghent, "The Appeal and Its Influence"; J. A. Wayland, *Leaves of Life* (Girard, Kans.: Appeal to Reason, 1912); Nick Salvatore, *Eugene V. Debs: Citizen and Socialist* (Urbana: University of Illinois, 1982).

9. AR: September 17, 1910, 1.

10. AR: March 11, 1911, 4.

11. AR: May 27, 1911, 3.

12. AR: November 12, 1910, 1; December 12, 1910, 4; March 18, 1911, 4; May 27, 1911, 3.

13. Philip Foner, *American Socialism and Black Americans* (Westport, Conn.: Greenwood, 1977), 207–18; David Roediger, "Gaining a Hearing for Black-White Unity" in *Towards the Abolition of Whiteness* (London: Verso, 1994), 139–48.

14. AR: April 17, 1909, 7; June 12, 1909, 2; July 3, 1909, 2; July 24, 1909, 2; October 29, 1910, 1; Foner, *American Socialism and Black Americans*, 108; Graham, "*Yours for the Revolution*," 52–53; for literature on Neo-Lamarckianism applied in early-twentieth-century American social thought, see Bibliographical Essay, sec. II.C.

15. AR: November 12, 1910, 1; November 26, 1910, 2; *The Citizen*, August 19, 1911, 8.

16. Eric Lott, *Love and Theft: Blackface Minstrelsy and the American Working Class* (New York: Oxford University Press, 1993), 35, 95–96; David Roediger, *The Wages of Whiteness* (London: Verso, 1991), 150–56; Noel Ignatiev, *How the Irish Became White* (New York: Routledge, 1995), ch. 2, O'Connell quote from p. 29.

17. Alexander Irvine, *The Magyar: A Story of the Social Revolution* (Girard, Kans.: The Socialist Publishing Company, 1911), 11–42, quote from p. 38.

18. Ibid., 1–8.

19. Ibid., 58, 103–4.

20. Ibid., 71, 187, 191, 198, 199, 232–33.

21. Ibid., 162, 167, 171.

22. For scholarly debate on these two moments, see Bibliographical Essay, sec. II.D.

23. Irvine, *The Magyar*, 55–81, 214–28.

24. Julianna Puskás, *From Hungary to the United States (1880–1914)* (Budapest: Akadémiai Kiadó, 1982), 169–89, 205; Irvine, *The Magyar* 51, 56, 214, 217.

25. Ibid., 55–57, 61–81, 214–28.

26. Ibid., 212–13, 223–34, 258.

27. Ibid., 124–34, 148.

28. Ibid., 155–69, quote from p. 168.

29. Ibid., 159, 188.

30. Ibid., 240–57, quote from pp. 255–56.

31. Ibid., 240–77, quotes from pp. 47–48, 269, 277.

32. Sinclair managed to place *The Jungle* with Doubleday-Page before his private "sustainer's edition" appeared. Upton Sinclair, *American Outpost* (New York: Farrar, Rhinehart, 1932), 162–64; Leon Harris, *Upton Sinclair: American Rebel* (New York: Crowell, 1975), 80–81. For Irvine's ad, see *Appeal to Reason*, March 11, 1911, 2. *The Magyar* appeared with the imprint of "The Socialist Publishing Company" in Girard, Kansas, the *Appeal's* headquarters.

33. Also, the central intrigue of the second half of the book, in which a middle-class woman embraces working-class causes by cleaving to her Hungarian socialist husband, echoes the main narrative of Charlotte Teller's 1907 novel *The Cage*. Jack London, *The Iron Heel* (New York: Macmillan, 1908); Charlotte Teller, *The Cage* (New York: D. Appleton, 1907); Walter Rideout, *The Radical Novel in the United States, 1900–1954* (Cambridge, Mass.: Harvard University Press, 1956), chs. 1–3.

34. Grace Heilman Stimson, *Rise of the Labor Movement in Los Angeles* (Berkeley: University of California Press, 1955), 340–41; Michael Kazin, *Barons of Labor: The San Francisco Building Trades and Union Power in The Progressive Era* (Urbana: University of Illinois Press, 1987), 67–73, 185–208.

35. For reports of Irvine's speeches on the socialist platform in these papers, see CSD: September 2, 1911, 5; *The Citizen*, July 28, 1911, 2; October 13, 1911, 3; October 20, 1911, 8. Irvine also outlined his own arguments for the socialist platform in a pamphlet written after the campaign, *Revolution in Los Angeles* (Los Angeles: Socialist Party, 1912).

36. *The Citizen*: August 11, 1911, 7; August 26, 1911, 8. CSD: August 5, 1911, 4.

37. CSD: September 9, 1911, 5; September 16, 1911, 5. *The Citizen*, September 22, 1911, 14.

38. Examples include *The Blacksmith's Strike* (1907), *The Strikers* (1909), *The Right to Labor* (1910), *The Strike* (1912), and *The Strike at the Centipede Mine* (1915), Stephen J. Ross, "Cinema and Class Conflict: Labor, Capital, the State, and American Silent Film," in *Resisting Images: Essays on Cinema and History*, ed. Robert Sklar and Charles Musser (Philadelphia: Temple University Press, 1990), 71.

39. CSD: August 5, 1911, 1.

40. Stimson, *Rise of the Labor Movement in Los Angeles*, 362, 392, 398–99.

41. CSD: August 5, 1911, 4.

42. Philip Foner, "A Martyr to His Cause: The Scenario of the First Labor Film in the United States," *Labor History* 24 (Winter 1983): 111.

43. Ross, "Cinema and Class Conflict," 79–80; *The Western Comrade*, July 1913; *The Citizen*, September 1, 1911, 14.

44. Stimson, *Rise of the Labor Movement in Los Angeles*, 401–7.

45. Irvine, *Revolution in Los Angeles*, 72–75.

46. Lincoln Steffens, *The Autobiography of Lincoln Steffens* (New York: Harcourt, Brace & World, 1931), 666–83.

47. *Los Angeles Express*, December 2, 1911, quoted in Irvine, *Revolution in Los Angeles*, 65, 73–74.

48. Ibid., 75.

49. Steffens, *Autobiography*, 670–89; Irvine, *Revolution in Los Angeles*, 62; Stimson, *Rise of the Labor Movement in Los Angeles*, 405–23.

50. For the contrasting positions, see William Haywood, "Socialism the Hope of the Working Class," *International Socialist Review* 12 (February 1912): 461–71; Samuel Gompers, "Gompers Speaks for Labor: The Organized Assault Against the Rights and the Leaders of the American Workingman," *McClure's* 38 (February 1912): 371–76.

51. Haywood, "Socialism the Hope of the Working Class," 464; Ira Kipnis, *The American Socialist Movement, 1897–1912* (New York: Columbia University Press, 1952), 370–420.

52. Irvine failed to note that in 1904 right-wing Colorado Socialists were busy denouncing Party members who joined Haywood's Western Federation of Miners and, moreover, had accepted paid workers in both the Democratic and the Republican Parties into the Denver socialist local. CSD: March 9, 1912, 2; Kipnis, *American Socialist Movement*, 180–81.

53. Irvine's alliance with Harriman and Hillquit was more than rhetorical—he had recently toured with them to raise money to cover the Los Angeles campaign debt. CSD: April 20, 1912, 1.

54. CSD: May 18, 1912, 1.

55. CSD: June 1, 1912, 1.

56. *Proceedings of the National Convention of the Socialist Party, 1912* (Chicago: Socialist Party, 1912), 72, 99–100, 195.

57. *Proceedings, 1912*; "The National Socialist Convention of 1912," *International Socialist Review* 12 (June 1912): 826–27; Kipnis, *American Socialist Movement*, 403–16; Salvatore, *Eugene Debs*, 251–58.

58. On the scholarly debates over the significance of race to intraparty politics, see Bibliographical Essay, sec. II.C.

59. *Proceedings, 1912*, 211–13; Salvatore, *Eugene Debs*, 130; Melvin Dubofsky, *We Shall Be All: A History of the Industrial Workers of the World* (Urbana: University of Illinois Press, 1988), 227–35.

60. Irvine, *Fighting Parson*, 99–102.

61. Ibid., 102–6; "Continuity for My Lady of the Chimney Corner," interview with Irvine and dramatization of *My Lady of the Chimney Corner*, broadcast from Station KNX,, Los Angeles, March 6, 1935, MS, AIC; letter from Elizabeth Robins to Alexander Irvine, December 23, 1912, addressed to Happy Hollow Farm, Peekskill, N.Y., forwarded to 1414 Douglas Los Angeles, 912 Creighton, Ohmer Park, Dayton, Ohio, Stamford, Conn., c/o J. G. Phelps Stokes, AIC.

62. Alexander Irvine, "In the Glow of a Peat Fire," *McClure's* 37, no. 2 (1911): 203–9; idem, "My Lady of the Chimney Corner," *McClure's* 38, no. 3 (1912): 345–50. On *McClure's* stature among the popular periodicals, see Matthew Schneirov, *The Dream of a New Social Order: Popular Magazines in America, 1893–1914* (New York: Columbia University Press, 1994), 80.

63. Alexander Irvine, *My Lady of the Chimney Corner* (London: Ernest Benn, 1913), 19, 191–92.

64. Ibid., 221.

65. Ibid., 228, 89.

66. Ibid., 88–89, 148, 199, 132ff. For Anna's storytelling capacities, see also Irvine's later volumes, *The Souls of Poor Folk* (London: W. Collins & Sons, 1921; reprint Belfast: Appletree, 1981) and *Anna's Wishing Chair* (Belfast: Quota, 1937).

67. Withero accords Jamie the status of "the dacent maan" about Antrim for agreeing that rumors about him are the product of "bletherin' fools." Irvine, *My Lady*, 92–93, 139.

68. Ibid., 13–16.

69. Ibid., 177.

70. CSD: September 2, 1911, 4. *The Citizen*: August 26, 1911; October 13, 1911; December 1, 1911, 1. Sara Bard Field Erghott, copy to the *Journal*, Portland, Oreg., November 2, 1911, Charles Erskine Scott Wood Collection, Box 89, Folder 1, Huntington Library, San Marino; Irvine, *Revolution in Los Angeles*, 48–50.

71. Irvine, *My Lady*, 192.

72. Ibid., 87.

73. Ibid., 204–5.

74. On the contested uses of "ethnic community" for radical and antiradical ends in the 1920s and 1930s, see Lizabeth Cohen, *Making a New Deal: Industrial Workers in Chicago, 1919–1939* (Cambridge: Cambridge University Press, 1990); Gary Gerstle, *Working-Class Americanism: The Politics of Labor in a Textile City* (Cambridge: Cambridge University Press, 1989); Ewa Morawska, *For Bread with Butter: The Life-Worlds of East-Central Europeans in Johnstown, Pennsylvania, 1890–1940* (Cambridge: Cambridge University Press, 1985); David Montgomery, "Labor and the Political Leadership of New Deal America," *International Review of Social History* 39 (December 1994): 335–60; Michael Denning, *The Cultural Front: The Laboring of American Culture in the Twentieth Century* (London: Verso, 1996).

75. Irvine, *My Lady*, "Foreword." For interpretations of Irvine's book stressing its recreation of Antrim, see L. A. M. Priestly-McCracken, "Dr. Alexander Irvine," *Great Thoughts* 8, Tenth Series (November 1929): 51–52; Alastair J. Smyth, "Introduction," to *My Lady of the Chimney Corner* (Belfast: Appletree, 1980).

76. Richard Griffith, *General Valuation on Rateable Property in Ireland: Union of Antrim* (Dublin: Alexander Thom, 1862), 109–19.

Chapter Eight: To "Change the Face of Civilization": Religion, Popular Theater, and the Politics of Culture

1. Alexander Irvine, *A Fighting Parson* (Boston: Little, Brown, 1930), 116–18, describes Irvine's experience at the Culver Academy, but places it after his acting episode; contemporary newspaper reports of his vaudeville appearance reveal that he had already begun teaching at Culver prior to going on the stage. See clippings, *New York Evening Mail*, November 15, 1913, and *New York Sun*, October 23, 1913, Robinson Locke Collection, Envelope 803, BRTC.

2. Hartley Davis, "Tabloid Drama," *Everybody's* (October 1909): 249–58; *The Citizen*, September 15, 1911, 14; Brett Page, *Writing for Vaudeville* (Springfield, Mass.: The Home Correspondence School, 1915), 168; *Variety*, November 21, 1913, 16.

3. NHU: January 25, 1903, 8; October 19, 1913, 23. Interview, Mrs. Anna Irvine Buck, December 27, 1987; Alexander Irvine, *The Chimney Corner Revisited* (Belfast: Appletree,

1984), 89, claims Wilcox's poem "One of Us Two" was inspired by his description of his parents; idem, "J. M. Barrie: A Radio Talk," April 25, 1934, (KFAC), AIC; Irvine noted his August 6, 1920 meeting with Barrie in his diary, AIPABC. Caroline Caffin, *Vaudeville* (New York: Mitchell Kennerley, 1914), 122–24.

4. Raymond A. Cook, *Fire from the Flint: The Amazing Careers of Thomas Dixon* (Winston-Salem: John F. Blair, 1968), chs. 2–4; Lary May, *Screening Out the Past: The Birth of Mass Culture and the Motion Picture Industry* (Chicago: University of Chicago Press, 1980), 80; for comparisons of Irvine with Dixon and Edwards Davis, see clipping, *Chicago Tribune*, March 6, 1914, Irvine File, BRTC.

5. Thomas Dixon, *The Leopard's Spots* (New York: Doubleday-Page, 1903); Cook, *Fire from the Flint*, 107–12, 135–50; Raymond A. Cook, *Thomas Dixon* (New York: Twayne, 1974), 64–74, 80–83; Richard Lingeman, *Theodore Dreiser: At the Gates of the City, 1871–1907* (New York: G. P. Putnam's Sons, 1986), 282–83.

6. Alexander Irvine, *From the Bottom Up* (London: Eveleigh & Nash, 1914), 7–8. The story of *Sister Carrie* at Doubleday-Page is told in Lingeman, *Theodore Dreiser*, ch. 32.

7. Clipping, *Times Magazine*, March 13, 1910, Robinson Locke Collection of Dramatic Scrapbooks, ser. 2, v. 113, 107; clipping, *New York Mirror*, April 2, 1910, Robinson Locke Collection of Dramatic Scrapbooks, ser. 2, v. 117, 101, BRTC.

8. Clipping, *Cincinnati Tribune*, April 19, 1913, Robinson Locke Collection of Dramatic Scrapbooks, ser. 2, v. 117, 109, BRTC.

9. Clipping, "Edwards Davis on Vaudeville," August 21, 1910, Robinson Locke Collection of Dramatic Scrapbooks, ser. 2, v. 117, 99, BRTC; clipping, no source, September 25, 1910, Robinson Locke Collection of Dramatic Scrapbooks, ser. 2, v. 117, 100, BRTC.

10. Clipping, "Edwards Davis on Vaudeville," *Dramatic Mirror*, October 9, 1909, 96, Robinson Locke Collection of Dramatic Scrapbooks, ser. 2, v. 117, 96, 99, BRTC.

11. Alexander Irvine, "The Rector of St. Jude's" MS, AIC, 1–3.

12. Ibid., 6–11.

13. Ibid., 11–18.

14. Ibid., 8.

15. Ibid., 5.

16. Ibid.; Kathryn Kish Sklar, "Introduction," *Autobiography of Florence Kelley* (reprint, Chicago: Charles H. Kerr, 1986), 14; Kathryn Kish Sklar, *Florence Kelley and the Nation's Work* (New Haven, Conn.: Yale University Press, 1995); Jacqueline Dirks, "Working Under Cover: The National Consumer League's Reform Narratives," paper delivered at the Berkshire Conference on Women's History, Rutgers University, June 10, 1990.

17. Irvine, "The Rector of St. Jude's," 13.

18. Ibid., 14.

19. Haywood, "Socialism the Hope of the Working Class," 464; Irvine, "The Rector of St. Jude's," 14.

20. Page, *Writing for Vaudeville*, 154–56.

21. Clippings: *Philadelphia Telegraph*, November 25, 1913; *Toledo Blade*, February 26, 1914, *Syracuse Post-Standard*, May 5, 1914; all from Alexander Irvine File, BRTC.

22. Clippings: unidentified *Journal*, February 10, 1914; *Chicago Tribune*, March 6, 1914, Alexander Irvine File, BRTC.

23. Irvine, *The Fighting Parson*, 114–15; idem, "The Vaudeville Audience," unpublished MS, AIC. Clippings: *Toledo Times*, February 21, 1914; *Syracuse Post-Standard*, May 5, 1914, Robinson Locke Collection, Envelope 803, BRTC. One agent had turned Irvine's playlet loose in February 1914, claiming he could not get money for the playlet, but Irvine stayed on the road for several months. *Variety*, February 15, 1914, 3.

24. NHU: October 23, 1913, 3.

25. NHR: October 21, 1913, 9; October 25, 1913, 1. *New Haven Times-Leader*: October 23, 1913, 3, 8; October 24, 1913, 1. NHU: October 19, 1913, 23; October 23, 1913, 3.

26. NHR: October 21, 1913, 1.

27. William James, "On a Certain Blindness in Human Beings," and "What Makes Life Significant," in *The Writings of William James*, ed. John J. McDermott (Chicago: University of Chicago Press, 1977), 629–60, quote from p. 650; William James, *The Varieties of Religious Experience* (New York: Longmans, Green, 1928), 485–527; Bruce Kuklick, *The Rise of American Philosophy: Cambridge, Massachusetts, 1860–1930* (New Haven, Conn.: Yale University Press, 1977), chs. 9, 14, 16.

28. Robert Westbrook, *John Dewey and American Democracy* (Ithaca, N.Y.: Cornell University Press, 1991), chs. 1–4, quote from p. 126.

29. Jane Addams, *Twenty Years at Hull House* (New York: New American Library, 1960), 172–73; on Addams's antipathy for conflict, see Westbrook, *Dewey*, 80–81.

30. Randolph Bourne, "The Cult of the Best," "The Democratic School," "Class and School," "What Is Exploitation?" in *The Radical Will: Randolph Bourne, Selected Writings, 1911–1918*, ed. Olaf Hansen (New York: Urizen, 1977), 193–97, 203–11, 285–89, quote from p. 193; Hansen, "Introduction: Affinity and Ambivalence," *Radical Will*, 28; Casey Nelson Blake, *Beloved Community: The Cultural Criticism of Randolph Bourne, Van Wyck Brooks, Waldo Frank, and Lewis Mumford* (Chapel Hill: University of North Carolina Press, 1990), passim.

31. Randolph Bourne, "Trans-national America," in *Radical Will*, ed. Hansen, 248–64, quotes from pp. 255, 259; for a contrasting interpretation, see Blake, *Beloved Community*, 114–21.

32. John Higham, *Send These To Me: Jews and Other Immigrants in Urban America* (New York: Atheneum, 1975), 203–9; Werner Sollars, "A Critique of Pure Pluralism," in *Reconstructing American Literary History*, ed. S. Bercovitch (Cambridge, Mass.: Harvard University Press, 1986), 250–79; Westbrook, *John Dewey*, 212–14; Horace Kallen, *Culture and Democracy in the United States: Studies in the Group Psychology of American Peoples* (New York: Boni & Liveright, 1924).

33. William I. Thomas and Florian Znaniecki, *The Polish Peasant in Europe and America*, ed. and abridged Eli Zaretsky (Urbana: University of Illinois Press, 1984); Herbert A. Miller and Robert E. Park, *Old World Traits Transplanted* (New York: Harper, 1921)—this book was written by Thomas but published under Miller's and Park's names after Thomas's dismissal from Chicago in the wake of a moral scandal; Dorothy Ross, *The Origins of American Social Science* (Cambridge: Cambridge University Press, 1991), 307–10, 347–57; Stow Persons, *Ethnic Studies at Chicago, 1905–45* (Chicago: University of Illinois Press, 1987), chs. 3, 6.

34. Ibid.; Eli Zaretsky, "Editor's Introduction," Thomas and Znaniecki, *The Polish Peasant*.

35. William I. Thomas, "The Adventitious Character of Woman," *American Journal of Sociology* 12 (January 1906): 32–44, quote from p. 42; idem, "The Mind of Woman and the Lower Races," *American Journal of Sociology* 12 (January 1907): 435–69; Rosalind Rosenberg, *Beyond Separate Spheres: Intellectual Roots of Modern Feminism* (New Haven, Conn.: Yale University Press, 1982), 120–31; Adolph Reed Jr., "DuBois's 'Double Consciousness': Race and Gender in Progressive Era American Thought," *Studies in American Political Development* 6 (Spring 1992): 128–29. Thomas and Irvine echoed Thorstein Veblen's effort to counter conspicuous consumption with the instinct of workmanship.

36. This orientation reflected Park's background as press agent for Booker T. Washington's Tuskeegee Institute, and also the growing vogue of scientific objectivity that came to dominate social science in the 1920s. Fred H. Matthews, *Quest for an American Sociology: Robert E. Park and the Chicago School* (Montreal: McGill-Queen's University Press, 1977), 61–82, 160–78; Persons, *Ethnic Studies*, chs. 4, 5; Eli Zaretsky, "Editor's Introduction," in Thomas and Znaniecki, *The Polish Peasant*.

37. George Stocking, "Franz Boas and the Culture Concept," in *Race, Culture and Evolution* (New York: The Free Press, 1968), 195–231; idem, "Anthropology as *Kulturkampf*: Science and Politics in the Career of Franz Boas," in *The Ethnographer's Magic* (Madison: University of Wisconsin Press, 1992), 92–113.

38. Ibid., 101; Marshall Hyatt, "Franz Boas and the Struggle for Black Equality: The Dynamics of Ethnicity," *Perspectives in American History*, New Series, 2 (1985): 269–95.

39. George W. Stocking Jr., "The Ethnographic Sensibility of the 1920s and the Dualism of the Anthropological Tradition," in *The Ethnographer's Magic*, 276–341; idem, "Anthropology as *Kulturkampf*," 110; George E. Marcus and Michael M. J. Fischer, *Anthropology as Cultural Critique: An Experimental Moment in the Human Sciences* (Chicago: University of Chicago Press, 1986); Mark Pittenger, *American Socialists and Evolutionary Thought, 1870–1920* (Madison: University of Wisconsin Press), 233–38.

40. Robert and Helen Lynd, *Middletown: A Study in Modern American Culture* (New York: Harcourt, Brace, 1919); Richard Wightman Fox, "Epitaph for Middletown: Robert S. Lynd and the Analysis of Consumer Culture," in *The Culture of Consumption: Critical Essays in American History, 1880–1980*, ed. Richard Wightman Fox and T. J. Jackson Lears (New York: Pantheon, 1983), 143–73; Ross, *Origins of American Social Science*, 441–42; Caroline F. Ware, *The Early New England Cotton Manufacture* (Boston and New York: Houghton Mifflin, 1931); idem, *Greenwich Village 1920–1930: A Comment on American Civilization in the Post War Years* (Boston and New York: Houghton Mifflin, 1935); idem, "Cultural Groups in the United States," in Caroline Ware, ed., *The Cultural Approach to History* (New York: Columbia University Press, 1940), 72–73; Ellen Fitzpatrick, "Caroline F. Ware and the Cultural Approach to History," *American Quarterly* 43, no. 2 (1991): 173–97; Alexander Irvine, *The Souls of Poor Folk* (Belfast: Appletree, 1981), 28.

41. Ira Jacknis, "Franz Boas and Exhibits: On the Limitations of the Museum Method of Anthropology," in *Objects and Others: Essays on Museums and Material Culture*, ed. George W. Stocking Jr. (Madison: University of Wisconsin Press, 1985), 75–111; Curtis Hinsley, *Savages and Scientists: The Smithsonian Institution and the Development of American Anthropology, 1846–1910* (Washington, D.C.: Smithsonian Institution, 1981); George W. Stocking Jr., "Ideas and Institutions in American Anthropology: Thoughts Toward a History of the Interwar Years" and "Philanthropoids and Vanishing Cultures:

Rockefeller Funding and the End of the Museum Era in Anglo-American Anthropology," in *The Ethnographer's Magic*, 114–211. With its mixing of scientific and "exotic" representations of primitive culture, the Chicago World's Columbian Exhibition helped provoke Boas's doubts about "public" anthropology as early as the 1890s; see Curtis Hinsley, "The World as Marketplace: Commodification of the Exotic at the World's Columbian Exposition, Chicago, 1893," in *Exhibiting Cultures: The Poetics and Politics of Museum Display*, ed. Ivan Karp and Steven D. Lavine (Washington, D.C.: Smithsonian Institution, 1990), 344–65. On the origins of wax "life groups" in nineteenth-century Scandinavian folk museums, see Mark B. Sandburg, "Effigy and Narrative: Looking into the Nineteenth-Century Folk Museum," in *Cinema and the Invention of Modern Life*, ed. Leo Charney and Vanessa R. Schwartz (Berkeley: University of California Press, 1995), 320–61.

42. M. Alison Kibler, "The Keith Vaudeville Circuit, 1890–1920: Gender, Sexuality, and the Cultural Hierarchy" (Ph.D. diss., University of Iowa, 1994), ch. 1; Kathy Peiss, "Commercial Leisure and the 'Woman Question,'" in *For Fun and Profit: The Transformation of Leisure into Consumption*, ed. R. Butsch (Philadelphia: Temple University Press), 105–17; idem, *Cheap Amusements: Working Women and Leisure in Turn-of-the-Century New York* (Philadelphia: Temple University Press, 1986); Elizabeth Lunbeck, "'A New Generation of Women': Progressive Psychiatrists and the Hypersexual Female," *Feminist Studies* 13 (Fall 1987): 513–44; Joanne J. Meyerowitz, *Women Adrift: Independent Wage Earners in Chicago, 1880–1930* (Chicago: University of Chicago Press, 1988); Regina Kunzel, *Fallen Women, Problem Girls: Unmarried Mothers and the Professionalization of Social Work, 1890–1945* (New Haven, Conn.: Yale University Press, 1993), ch. 2.

43. Irvine and Tucker appeared on the same vaudeville bill in Toledo. Clipping, *Toledo News Blade*, February 24, 1914, Robinson Locke Collection, Envelope 803, BRTC.

44. Susan Curtis, *A Consuming Faith: The Social Gospel and Modern American Culture* (Baltimore: Johns Hopkins University Press, 1991), 228–79, quote from p. 277; T. J. Jackson Lears, "From Salvation to Self-Realization: Advertising and the Therapeutic Roots of Consumer Culture, 1880–1930," in *The Culture of Consumption: Critical Essays in American History*, ed. Fox and Lears, 3–38.

45. Antonio Cannelli, *La Colonia Italiana di New Haven* (New Haven, Conn.: A. Cannelli, 1921), 298, from notes by V. Racca, Box 57, Folder 156:5a, PCEHP. ICC: May 1, 1915, 1; October 23, 1915, 2; November 27, 1915, 1–2. NHR: November 24, 1915, 24. On the wider significance of such constructions of ethnicity by Italian-American elites considered in the context of "inventions" of ethnicity among American immigrant groups more generally, see Kathleen Neils Conzen et al., "The Invention of Ethnicity: A Perspective from the U.S.A.," *Journal of American Ethnic History* 12, no. 1 (1992): 3–41.

46. Clippings: *Spokesman*, April 24, 1916; "Pagani in Class by Himself in Comedy of War," *Cleveland Plain Dealer*, January 19, 1918; "Maciste Shows How Italians Are Fighting," *Los Angeles Examiner*, June 25, 1918, all from Maciste File, BRTC. ICC: October 3, 1914, 4; November 20, 1915, 2; March 8, 1919, 2; March 15, 1919, 7. NHJC: March 10, 1919, 6. Rollin G. Osterweis, *Three Centuries of New Haven* (New Haven, Conn.: Yale University Press, 1953), 408.

47. For vaudeville managers trying to curtail performer radio appearances, see *Variety*, April 16, 1924, 4; on family and neighborhood context of radio and its working-class over-

tones, see Lizabeth Cohen, *Making a New Deal: Industrial Workers in Chicago, 1919–1939* (Cambridge: Cambridge University Press, 1990), ch. 3; on film in the 1920s, see Lary May, *Screening out the Past: The Birth of Mass Culture and the Motion Picture Industry* (Chicago: University of Chicago Press, 1980), chs. 5–8; Robert Sklar, *Movie Made America: A Cultural History of American Movies* (New York: Vintage, 1975), chs. 5, 6, 10; Peter Roffman and Jim Purdy, *The Hollywood Social Problem Film* (Bloomington: Indiana University Press, 1981), 9–11. On Poli's theater building, see Donald C. King, "S. Z. Poli, From Wax to Riches," *Marquee* 2, no. 2 (1979): 15–16.

48. Ibid., 16; "Closing of Poli Theater Stirs Memories of Great Stage Era," NHR: December 6, 1959, 6; "Sylvester Z. Poli—Humanitarian . . . Theatrical Pioneer . . . one of New Haven's most distinguished citizens," five-page typed ms, n.d., NHCHS; interview, Jeanne Poli, September 21, 1990; clipping, "Polis Celebrate 50th Wedding Anniversary," *New York Herald Tribune*, August 26, 1935, Sylvester Zeffarino Poli Clipping File, BRTC.

49. King, "S. Z. Poli," 16–17; "Closing of Poli Theater"; "Polis Celebrate 50th Wedding Anniversary"; Sklar, *Movie-Made America*, 165–66; Douglas Gomery, *The Hollywood Studio System* (New York: St. Martin's, 1986), 51–85; Osterweis, *Three Centuries*, 416.

50. *Y.M.: The British Empire Y.M.C.A. Weekly* 2, no. 99 (1916): 1, AIPABC; Alexander Irvine, WWI Scrapbook, AIPABC; Young Men's Christian Association, *A Short Record of the Educational Work of the YMCA with the British Armies in France* (Letchworth, Herts.: Garden City, 1919), 8, 37, 41–42; Alexander Irvine, Post-WWI Scrapbook, AIC; Irvine, *Fighting Parson*, 122–96; Nick Salvatore, *Eugene V. Debs: Citizen and Socialist* (Urbana: University of Illinois Press, 1982), 293–96.

51. See Irvine, *Fighting Parson* 180–83, 194, 202–3; idem, *A Yankee with the Soldiers of the King* (New York: E. P. Dutton, 1923). Irvine, 1918 diary, AIPABC.

52. Alexander Irvine, *God and Tommy Atkins* (London: Hutchinson, 1918); idem, *The Man from World's End and Other Stories of Lovers and Fighting Men* (London: T. Fisher Unwin, 1926); idem, *The Carpenter and His Kingdom* (London: Evans Bros., 1921); idem, "Behind the Veil in Ireland," *London Evening News*, May 19, 1921, 1, 5; idem, *Fighting Parson*, 197–200; Irvine Post-WWI Scrapbook, AIC.

53. The charge of "charlatanism" is one I have heard Irvine subjected to repeatedly when I have recounted his postwar fate to other cultural historians; I tend to regard it as a signal of the difficulty academics of the expanded university system in the post–World War II era have in comprehending the struggles for audience and livelihood of those who engaged cultural politics in other arenas and other times. For Irvine's postwar activities generally, see Irvine, *Fighting Parson*, 205ff.; Irvine diaries for 1920 and 1927 and Irvine Scrapbooks, 1925 and 1934, AIPABC.

54. Irvine, diaries for 1920 and 1927; Irvine, "The German Youth Movement," MS, AIC; Scrapbook of Irvine's *New York Journal* columns, AIPABC; Irvine, *Fighting Parson*, 208–11, 230–32; W. A. Swanberg, *Citizen Hearst: A Biography of William Randolph Hearst* (New York: Charles Scribner's Sons, 1961), 323–406; Frank Luther Mott, *American Journalism: A History, 1690–1960* (New York: Macmillan, 1962), 635–50.

55. Even Irvine was not immune; during his years with Miller he collaborated on a pamphlet that explained how to apply psychological insights to produce "Better Bank Advertising" (New York: Irvine & Fyscher, 1923), AIPABC.

56. Irvine, *Fighting Parson*, 163–64; Horatio W. Dresser, *A History of the New Thought Movement* (New York: Thomas Y. Crowell, 1919), 263–64. *Rocky Mountain News*: May 24, 1896; December 15, 1896; December 17, 1896; December 19, 1896; December 22, 1896; December 24, 1896; December 29, 1896; January 31, 1897. *Mastery* (New Thought Journal edited by O. E. Miller, 1914–15); Irvine, 1920 diary, AIPABC. *San Francisco Chronicle*: March 2, 1923; March 24, 1923; March 31, 1923. Walter Bromberg, *Psychiatry Between the Wars, 1918–1945: A Recollection* (Westport, Conn.: Greenwood, 1982), ch. 1; Ferenc M. Szasz, "'New Thought' and the American West," *Journal of the West* 23 (January 1984): 83–90; letter from Frances Blanche Quinlivan to Eugene V. Debs, Eugene V. Debs Collection, Cunningham Library, Indiana State University.

57. For example, his story, "The Soul of a Slav," depicted the brutal conditions that immigrant workers confronted in the United States, but focused primarily on their psychological consequences for a Russian-American steelworker driven to murder and then inspired to psychological rebirth on death row. *Psychological Review of Reviews* (November 1923): 11–14, 20–23, 29, AIC.

58. Before *The Bowery Bishop*, Rellimeo (O. E. Miller backwards, a pseudonym Miller often used) produced *Pagan Passions*, a film that embellished sexual scandal with racial ambiguity in a script that took characters from the Malay Peninsula to China to the United States. Reflecting Miller's flirtation with racial thought and eugenics, this plot suggests further reasons why his enterprises offered Irvine tenuous respite. *San Francisco Chronicle*: February 10, 1923; March 3, 1923; July 7, 1923; December 2, 1923. *Psychological Review of Reviews* (November 1923), (January 1924), (March 1924), AIC; Patricia Long Hanson, ed., *The American Film Institute Catalog of Motion Pictures Produced in the United States*, v. F2 (New York: Bowker, 1971), 79, 583; Irvine, *Fighting Parson*, 211–12.

59. Irvine, *Fighting Parson*; idem, "The Bog-Queen's Flittin'," *Good Housekeeping* 57 (December 1913): 786–92; idem, "The Coming of the Lamp," *Atlantic Monthly* 146 (September 1930): 388–93; idem, *The Souls of Poor Folk* (London: W. Collins & Sons, 1921); idem, *Anna's Wishing Chair and Other Chimney Corner Stories* (Belfast: Appletree, 1937).

60. Order of Service, October 8, 1933, The Church of the Kingdom and clipping, "Creedless Worship," no source, n.d., both in scrapbook of Mrs. Anna Irvine Buck, in possession of Mrs. Anna Giarretto; Alexander Irvine, "Terrorism in California," AIC. On the organizing drive among farmworkers to which Irvine contributed, see Carey McWilliams, *Factories in the Field: The Story of Migratory Farm Labor in California* (Boston: Little, Brown, 1939), 224–26; Cletus Daniel, *Bitter Harvest: A History of California Farm Workers, 1870–1941* (Ithaca, N.Y.: Cornell University Press, 1981), 227–29; Dorothy Ray Healey and Maurice Isserman, *California Red: A Life in the American Communist Party* (Urbana: University of Illinois Press, 1990), ch. 3; Camille Guerin-Gonzales, *Mexican Workers and American Dreams* (New Brunswick, N.J.: Rutgers University Press, 1994), 122–23. For Irvine's support for union initiatives in the 1930s, see his unpublished letters to John L. Lewis and Harry Bridges, AIC.

61. "Dr. Irvine and Socialism: Why He Supports the Movement," clipping, Belfast, n.d, Irvine Papers in possession of Alastair Smyth, Antrim, Northern Ireland. The Belfast episode is recounted in John Hewitt, "Alec of the Chimney Corner," in *Ancestral Voices: The Selected Prose of John Hewitt*, ed. T. Clyde (Belfast: Blackstaff, 1987), 38–47. Alexander Irvine to Herbert Ireland, May 20, 1937, D. 2398, PRONI. A little over a year before

his death, Irvine confirmed his abiding faith in social progress to his daughter-in-law, Virginia, Alexander Irvine to Virginia Irvine, December 29, 1939, AIC. For his support for Bridges and Mooney, see unpublished letter to Bridges, AIC and photograph of Irvine and Mooney after Mooney's release from prison, Alexander Irvine, Santa Barbara.

62. Alexander Irvine, "My Lady of the Chimney Corner: A Story of Love and Poverty in Irish Peasant Life, Synopsis," MS, AIC; "Meetings with Famous Men: Dr. A. Irvine's Novel May be Filmed," clipping, no source, n.d., ca. 1935, copy sent by Mrs. Anna Irvine Buck, 1987; letter from Alexander Irvine to Anna Irvine Buck, December 21, 1939; Alexander Irvine to Virginia Irvine, December 29, 1939, AIC. On the Popular Front cultural context in relation to Steinbeck's novel and the film based on it, see Richard H. Pells, *Radical Visions and American Dreams: Culture and Social Thought in the Depression Years* (New York: Harper & Row, 1973); William Stott, *Documentary Expression and Thirties America* (New York: Oxford University Press, 1973); and especially Michael Denning, *The Cultural Front: The Laboring of American Culture in the Twentieth Century* (London: Verso, 1996). On the maternalist themes of Popular Front culture, Paula Rabinowitz, *Labor and Desire: Women's Revolutionary Fiction in Depression America* (Chapel Hill: University of North Carolina Press, 1991); and Barbara Melosh, *Engendering Culture: Manhood and Womanhood in New Deal Public Art and Theater* (Washington, D.C.: Smithsonian Institution, 1991).

63. Irvine, "My Lady of the Chimney Corner: A Story of Love and Poverty in Irish Peasant Life, Synopsis," MS, AIC.

64. Denning, *The Cultural Front*, 424–25. The cultural studies approaches summarized are developed in a proliferating and varied scholarship, some of which has informed my approach and some of which I take issue with, as described in the Introduction. For useful discussions of the particular dimensions of cultural studies scholarship I name here, for which Irvine's and Poli's trajectories provide a prehistory, see especially the introductions to Lawrence Grossberg, Cary Nelson, and Paula Treichler, *Cultural Studies* (New York: Routledge, 1992); and Michael Schudson and Chandra Mukerji, *Rethinking Popular Culture: Contemporary Perspectives in Cultural Studies* (Berkeley: University of California Press, 1991).

BIBLIOGRAPHICAL ESSAY

This book crosses several historical subfields, and is informed by research in a range of archives, published primary sources, and scholarly literatures that do not conventionally fall into the same bibliographies. I have confined myself here to key primary sources on my central figures and their alliances, and secondary literatures relevant to historiographical debates that this book engages directly. Theoretical and methodological literature may be found in the notes to the Introduction, and references to the wide scope of documents and secondary works that served primarily as background are cited in notes where appropriate.

I *Primary Sources*

The reconstruction of Alexander Irvine's life and career involved most importantly the assembling of an archive from materials that had been scattered among his descendants after his death. Irvine's daughter, Mrs. Anna Irvine Buck, of San Francisco, and his granddaughter, Anna Giarretto, graciously collected the bulk of these family materials for me, and made them available in Mrs. Buck's home between December 1987 and June 1995. The resulting archive included scrapbooks assembled by Irvine documenting his activities in New Haven in the early twentieth century and in Britain during World War I; manuscripts of his sermons at the Church of the Ascension; a copy of his vaudeville playlet; numerous manuscripts for published as well as unpublished journalistic and literary works dating from the 1920s and 1930s; copies of the *Psychological Review of Reviews*; and personal correspondence. Discussions with Mrs. Buck during my research trips to her house also provided insight into her father's life. Following Mrs. Buck's death in November 1994, Mrs. Giarretto asked me to assist her in finding a repository for this archive, favoring the Huntington Library, where Mrs. Buck had hoped to see the materials deposited. In 1996 most of them were given to the Huntington Library, where as of this writing they await archival organization. Once available, they will complement the library's other holdings relevant to Alexander Irvine and his socialist circle in the early twentieth century, notably the Jack London Collection, which includes several letters from Irvine.

Alexander Irvine of Santa Barbara, California, the grandson of the Alexander Irvine in this book, made available another small private collection of Irvine documents. This collection includes the memoir *Three Days in the Holy Land*, recounting Irvine's tour of the Holy Land in 1884 and many helpful newspaper clippings.

Several important Irvine collections are also available in Northern Ireland. The Antrim Borough Council keeps a rich collection of materials that Alexander Irvine originally donated at the time that his childhood home, Pogue's Entry, was made into a public museum, supplemented in the 1950s by his son, Robert. These include diaries from 1918, 1920, and 1927; scrapbooks documenting Irvine's mission to the Midwest in the 1890s and New Haven in the early twentieth century; scrapbooks documenting his lecturing activities during and after World War I; a scrapbook of his *New York Journal* columns from the early 1920s; and numerous unpublished manuscripts documenting his efforts to maintain his literary career in the changed cultural climate of the 1920s and 1930s. The offices of advocate William Swann of Antrim also hold Irvine diaries from 1916, 1917, and 1938. I was assisted in finding my way through these documents by Alastair Smyth of Antrim, who also made available sources on Alexander Irvine that he held privately. The Public Record Office of Northern Ireland (PRONI) in Belfast has a collection of correspondence between Irvine and his Northern Irish patrons of the 1920s and 1930s and several letters relating to the opening of Pogue's Entry as a public museum. The PRONI also holds several archival sources illuminating the context of Irvine's childhood in Antrim, including correspondence between Father Henry O'Loughlin and the Poor Law Commissioners as well as the 1862 General Valuation for Antrim. I also used a number of local sources, such as directories and local histories, available in the Greystone Library in Antrim.

The Public Record Office at Kew holds Alexander Irvine's service record in the Navy, along with a number of other naval records relating to Irvine's years as a marine.

Several manuscript collections devoted to the papers of individuals and organizations with whom Irvine allied were invaluable for piecing together his institutional and political trajectory in the United States. In the Manuscripts and Archives division of Yale University Library, the Farnam Family Papers, the Anson Phelps Stokes Papers, and the Diaries (Miscellaneous) Collection were very useful, as were the microform editions of the Intercollegiate Socialist Society Records, the W. E. B. Du Bois papers, and the U.S. Department of Justice, Peonage Files for 1901–45. The New England Church Records at Yale Divinity Library provided essential documents on Pilgrim Church in Fair Haven. The New Haven Colony Historical Society holds the Livingston Warner Cleaveland Papers, the Lowell House Mothers' Club Records, the New Haven Railroad YMCA Collection, and the Arnold Guyot Dana Collection, all of which were helpful in reconstructing the social and cultural context of Irvine's mission in New Haven. In addition to the Jack London Collection, the Charles Erskine Scott Wood Collection at the Huntington Library helped me trace Irvine's activities in Los Angeles. The published letters of early-twentieth-century Socialists who influenced Irvine were also helpful, including Jack London, *The Letters of Jack London*, ed. Earle Labor, Robert C. Leitz III, and I. Milo Shepard (Stanford, Calif.: Stanford University Press, 1988); and Eugene V. Debs, *Letters of Eugene V. Debs*, ed. J. R. Constantine (Urbana: University of Illinois Press, 1990).

Published organizational records relevant to Irvine's life include annual reports and bulletins of the New York City Mission and Tract Society (published as *Work in New York*), the University Settlement Society, and the Lowell House Settlement. The Trades Council of New Haven's *Illustrated History of the Trades Council of New Haven and Affiliated Unions* (New Haven, Conn.: Trades Council of New Haven, 1899) was indispensable. Journalistic organs of the trade unionist institutions with which Irvine became involved included the *Workmen's Advocate*, the journal of the Trades Council of New Haven and the Socialist Labor Party during the 1880s; *The Craftsman*, the organ of the Connecticut State Federation of Labor; *The American Federationist*, the organ of the American Federation of Labor; *The Citizen*, the official organ of the Los Angeles Central Labor Council; and *The California Social Democrat*, the newspaper of the Los Angeles Socialist local. *International Socialist Review* reflected intellectual trends and conflicts in the Party, while the *Appeal to Reason* spoke to a wider rank-and-file audience and documented Irvine's lectures for that audience. The records of the Socialist Party's national meetings in the early twentieth century were also useful, especially *Proceedings of the National Convention of the Socialist Party* (Chicago: Socialist Party, 1908); *Proceedings of the First National Congress of the Socialist Party of the United States* (Chicago: Socialist Party, 1910); and *Proceedings of the National Convention of the Socialist Party* (Chicago: Socialist Party, 1912).

Irvine's own published writings are of course essential sources of information about his life, though they generally need corroboration in the sources listed above. His two autobiographies are *From the Bottom Up: The Life Story of Alexander Irvine* (New York: Doubleday-Page, 1910) and *A Fighting Parson: The Autobiography of Alexander Irvine* (Boston: Little, Brown, 1930). The "chimney corner" stories that relate his early life in Antrim are collected in *My Lady of the Chimney Corner* (New York: Century, 1913; and London: Ernest Benn, 1913; reprinted Belfast: Appletree, 1980); *The Souls of Poor Folk* (London: W. Collins & Sons, 1921; reprinted Belfast: Appletree, 1981); and *Anna's Wishing Chair and Other Chimney Corner Stories* (Belfast: Quota, 1937; reprinted as *The Chimney Corner Revisited* Belfast: Appletree, 1984). Other important works are *The Carpenter and His Kingdom* (London: Evans Bros., 1921); *God and Tommy Atkins* (London: Hutchinson, 1918); *Jack London at Yale* (Westwood, Mass.: Ariel Press, for Connecticut State

Committee of the Socialist Party, 1906); *The Magyar: A Story of the Social Revolution* (Girard, Kans.: The Socialist Publishing Company, 1911); *The Man from World's End and Other Stories of Lovers and Fighting Men* (London: T. Fisher Unwin, 1926); *The Master and the Chisel* (New Haven, Conn.: The People's Church, 1904); *My Cathedral: A Vision of Friendship* (Belfast: Quota, 1945); *Revolution in Los Angeles* (Los Angeles: Socialist Party, 1912); *A Yankee with the Soldiers of the King* (New York: E. P. Dutton, 1923).

For the life of S. Z. Poli, I was primarily interested in his transatlantic and U.S. trajectories, his enterprises and social interactions in New Haven, and the fate of his shows and enterprises in the corporate era of vaudeville, and pieced these stories out of a range of sources. Catalogs and administrative records of the *Musée Grevin* in Paris, where Poli worked as a wax sculptor early in his career, were available at the Bibliotheque Nationale in Paris. Catalogs for the *Eden Musée* were available at The Beinecke Rare Book Library at Yale University and the Billy Rose Theatre Collection of the New York Public Library of the Performing Arts. I supplemented these with catalogs of the archetypal wax museum of the nineteenth century, *Madame Tussaud's*, available at the British Library. Poli's progress in the United States was also traceable through documents in the Arnold Guyot Dana Collection at the New Haven Colony Historical Society as well as city directories for New York, Philadelphia, and New Haven.

Regarding Poli's vaudeville enterprises and social career in New Haven, his granddaughter, Jeanne Poli, supplied me with information and, through a Yale undergraduate, Nicholas Kliment, who had also been working on Poli's life, documents such as the souvenir pamphlet *S. Z. Poli's Theatrical Enterprises*. Two archives were indispensable for documenting the changing fare at Poli's vaudeville theaters: the Crawford Theatre Collection at Sterling Memorial Library, Yale University; and the Billy Rose Theatre Collection at the New York Public Library of the Performing Arts (which includes clipping files on both Poli and Irvine). Poli's relations with New Haven's various ethnic groups, especially its Italian colony, were illuminated by the People's of Connecticut Ethnic Heritage Project, WPA Writer's Project papers, housed in the Historical Manuscript and Archives division at the University of Connecticut, Storrs.

The relations among Poli's New Haven theaters, his circuit, and the vaudeville industry are illuminated by a number of published primary sources. The vaudeville industry weekly, *Variety*, was indispensable for documenting these relations. M. B. Leavitt's *Fifty Years in Theatrical Management* (New York: Broadway, 1910) was a valuable source for changes in the popular theatrical industry from the late nineteenth into the early twentieth centuries.

The wider context of the vaudeville industry in which Poli worked is illuminated by a number of contemporary sources that publicized the spirit of the shows and the inner workings of the industry. Several of these articles are available in a collection edited by Charles Stein, *American Vaudeville as Seen by its Contemporaries* (New York: Da Capo, 1984). Also extremely useful are William H. Birkmire, *The Planning and Construction of American Theatres* (New York: John Wiley & Sons, 1901); Caroline Caffin, *Vaudeville* (New York: Mitchell Kennerley, 1914); Hartley Davis's essays "In Vaudeville," *Everybody's* 13 (August 1905): 231–40 and "Tabloid Drama," *Everybody's* (October 1909): 249–58; Brett Page, *Writing for Vaudeville* (Springfield: The Home Correspondence School, 1915); Laurence Hutton, *Curiosities of the American Stage* (New York: Harper & Brothers, 1891; reprint, New York: Johnson Reprint Corporation, 1968). Two books by contemporary participants in and observers of vaudeville are Joe Laurie Jr., *Vaudeville: From the Honky-Tonks to the Palace* (New York: Henry Holt, 1953); and Douglas Gilbert, *American Vaudeville: Its Life and Times* (New York: McGraw-Hill, 1940). Autobiographies of some of the stars who appeared at Poli's are also useful, including Jesse Lasky, *I Blow My Own Horn* (Garden City, N.Y.: Doubleday, 1957); Sophie Tucker, *Some of These Days* (Garden City, N.Y.: Doubleday, 1945); Mae West, *Goodness Had Nothing To Do With It* (Englewood Cliffs, N.J.: Prentice-Hall, 1959).

Finally, newspapers were crucial for mapping the intersection of worship, entertainment, and politics that connected Irvine's and Poli's careers. Daily papers consulted for this project included the *New Haven Evening Leader*, the *New Haven Journal Courier*, the *New Haven Register*, the *New Haven Union*, the *New York Herald*, the *New York Times*, the *Omaha World Herald*, the *Philadelphia Inquirer*, and the Italian-language *Il Corriere del Connecticut*, as well as scores of papers from which clippings were taken that ended up in the scrapbooks of the Billy Rose Theatre Collection, the Arnold Guyot Dana Scrapbook Collection, and the Alexander Irvine Collection.

II Secondary Sources

A. Alexander Irvine and Sylvester Poli

There is little secondary literature available on the lives of Alexander Irvine or Sylvester Poli, but a few sketches of their careers helped provide points of departure for this project. In Irvine's case this scholarship derives primarily from his continued popularity in Northern Ireland, where his childhood home in the town of Antrim remains a museum. R. S. J. H. McKelvey's *The Chimney Corner* (Belfast: Northern Whig, 1967) provides a short introduction to the museum and Irvine's life and writings. Information on Irvine and the nineteenth-century context of his childhood is also available in Alastair Smyth, *The Story of Antrim* (Antrim: Antrim Borough Council, 1984), and Smyth has also provided informative introductions to new editions of Alexander Irvine's "chimney corner" books, *My Lady of the Chimney Corner* (Belfast: Appletree, 1980), 9–15; *The Souls of Poor Folk* (Belfast: Appletree, 1981), 9–13; and *The Chimney Corner Revisited* (Belfast: Appletree,

1984), 4–6. A short piece by Northern Ireland's regional poet, John Hewitt, gives a delightful account of Irvine's charm and charisma at the end of his life, "Alec of the Chimney Corner," in *Ancestral Voices: The Selected Prose of John Hewitt*, ed. Tom Clyde (Belfast: Blackstaff, 1987), 38–47. Alexander Irvine was also one of the subjects treated by George Shepperson in his Alan Graham Memorial Lecture "North America and Northern Ireland: Some Literary Linkages," given at the 37th Annual Conference of the British Association for American Studies, Queen's University, Belfast, 1992. In addition, Gillian O'Rourke of Antrim has written a 1994 dissertation on Irvine for her teaching degree at Stranmillis College, Belfast.

Sylvester Poli's career is chronicled in two journal articles: Hugh Leamy, "Waxing Rich," *Colliers* (July 7, 1928): 10, 52–53, was written during his life and is partially based on interviews; Donald C. King, "S. Z . Poli, From Wax to Riches," *Marquee* 2, no. 2 (1979): 11–18, is based on family interviews and archival sources. They are useful guides to his life but need corroboration from independent sources. Shorter accounts of Poli's life are available in E. Robert Stevenson, ed., *Connecticut History Makers* (Waterbury, Conn.: American-Republican, 1930), 2:198–200, and Antonio Cannelli, *La Colonia Italiana di New Haven* (New Haven, Conn.: A. Cannelli, 1921), 214–17. An unpublished, 1985 senior essay written for the Yale History Department—Nicholas M. Kliment, *"Padrone* of the People: The Life and Times of Vaudeville Mogul S. Z. Poli, (1959–1937)"—was also useful.

The dissertation on which this book was based, Kathryn J. Oberdeck, "Labor's Vicar and the Variety Show: Popular Religion, Popular Theatre, and Cultural Class Conflict in Turn-of-the-Century America" (Ph.D. diss., Yale University, 1991), also contains some additional contextual material on Irvine's and Poli's careers.

B. *Religion and the Working Class*

Existing scholarship on class and religion, especially Protestantism, in industrial America has provided both excellent background and considerable scholarly provocation for this work. For the period on which this book focuses, the social gospel has dominated scholarship on the relation between Protestantism and industrial labor. The classic social gospel scholarship such as Charles Howard Hopkins, *The Rise of the Social Gospel in American Protestantism, 1865–1915* (New Haven, Conn.: Yale University Press, 1940); Aaron Ignatius Abell, *The Urban Impact on American Protestantism, 1867–1900* (Cambridge, Mass.: Harvard University Press, 1943); Henry F. May, *Protestant Churches in Industrial America* (New York: Harper, 1949); and Paul A. Carter, *The Spiritual Crisis of the Gilded Age* (Dekalb: Northern Illinois University Press, 1971), noted both the multiplicity of social gospel rhetoric and its distance from working-class critiques of the church. See also Liston Pope, *Millhands and Preachers: A Study of Gastonia* (New Haven, Conn.: Yale University Press, 1942). Jacob Dorn, "The Social Gospel and Socialism: A Comparison of the Thought of Francis Greenwood Peabody, Washington

Gladden, and Walter Rauschenbusch," *Church History* 62 (March 1993): 82–100, also illuminates tensions between social gospel approaches to labor questions and the perspectives of workers and Socialists.

However, much recent work has focused on the consolidation of social gospel aims within denominational institutions or the ways that social gospel practices facilitated a middle-class cultural passage from the Protestant work ethic to secular consumerism. The work of T. J. Jackson Lears was especially influential in shaping this interpretation, especially *No Place of Grace: Anti-Modernism and the Transformation of American Culture, 1880–1920* (New York: Pantheon, 1981) and "From Salvation to Self-Realization: Advertising and the Therapeutic Roots of Consumer Culture," in *The Culture of Consumption: Critical Essays in American History, 1880–1980*, ed. Richard Wightman Fox and T. J. Jackson Lears (New York: Pantheon, 1983), 3–38. See also Richard Wightman Fox, "The Culture of Liberal Protestant Progressivism, 1875–1925," *Journal of Interdisciplinary History* 23 (Winter 1993): 639–60. This perspective has been applied to study of the social gospel in Susan Curtis, *A Consuming Faith: The Social Gospel and Modern American Culture* (Baltimore: Johns Hopkins University Press, 1991); and Donald K. Gorrell, *The Age of Social Responsibility: The Social Gospel in the Progressive Era, 1900–1920* (Macon, Ga.: Mercer University Press, 1988). While this is certainly an important dimension of the changing culture of Protestant practice at the turn of the century, and one with which Alexander Irvine engaged, I found it insufficient for understanding the meanings attributed to Protestant piety by working-class worshipers during this period.

It has fallen to labor historians studying religion and trade unionism in specific cities to examine how workers received social gospel overtures and incorporated them into the agendas of working-class institutions. Such work takes up the challenge posed by Herbert Gutman, "Protestantism and the American Labor Movement," *American Historical Review* 72 (October 1966): 75–100 for social historians to devote more attention to Protestant themes in American working-class culture and politics and to the distinction between working-class criticisms of religion and the more familiar, middle-class social gospel. With the recent exceptions of Ken Fones-Wolf's "Religion and Trade Union Politics in the United States, 1880–1920," *International Labor and Working-Class History* 34 (Fall 1988), 39–55, and *Trade Union Gospel: Christianity and Labor in Industrial Philadelphia, 1866–1915* (Philadelphia: Temple University Press, 1989); Donald E. Winters Jr., *The Soul of the Wobblies: the I.W.W., Religion, and American Culture in the Progressive Era, 1905–1917* (Westport, Conn.: Greenwood, 1985); and Clark D. Halker, *For Democracy, Workers and God: Labor Song-Poems and Labor Protest, 1865–95* (Urbana: University of Illinois Press, 1991), American historians have largely neglected this field, unlike British historians, who have long debated the role of Protestant piety in working-class popular culture and politics. See Eric Hobsbawm, *Primitive Rebels*

(Manchester: Manchester University Press, 1959); E. P. Thompson, *The Making of the English Working Class* (New York: Vintage, 1963); Kenneth Stanley Inglis, *Churches and the Working Classes in Victorian England* (London: Routledge & Kegan Paul, 1963); Hugh McLeod, *Class and Religion in the Late Victorian City* (London: Croom Helm, 1974); Brian Harrison, *Peaceable Kingdom: Stability and Change in Modern Britain* (Oxford: Clarendon, 1982); see also the useful essays in Robert Stroch, ed., *Popular Culture and Custom in Nineteenth-Century England* (London: Croom Helm, 1982), especially John Rule, "Methodism, Popular Beliefs and Village Culture in Cornwall, 1800–1850," pp. 48–70; and David Hempton and Myrtle Hill, *Evangelical Protestantism in Ulster Society, 1740–1890* (London: Routledge, 1992).

For America, attention to the importance of religious belief in the organization of working-class daily life remains largely the province of historians of immigrant, and especially Catholic communities, whose main emphasis is often on the autonomous values that set ethnic communities off from dominant political and cultural hierarchies. See the work of Jay Dolan, *The Immigrant Church* (Baltimore: Johns Hopkins University Press, 1975); Robert Orsi, *The Madonna of 115th Street: Faith and Community in Italian Harlem, 1880–1950* (New Haven, Conn.: Yale University Press, 1985); Roy Rosenzweig, *Eight Hours for What We Will: Workers and Leisure in An Industrial City, 1870–1920* (Cambridge: Cambridge University Press, 1983); and the collection Dolores Liptak, ed., *The Church of Many Cultures: Selected Historical Essays on Ethnic American Catholicism* (New York: Garland, 1988). Historians of ethnic-Catholicism have also charted the considerable tension between claims on ethnic and religious solidarity among Catholic immigrants. These concerns are addressed in Rudolph Vecoli, "Prelates and Peasants: Italian Immigrants and the Catholic Church," *Journal of Social History* 2, no. 3 (1969): 217–68, and, with regard to both Catholic and Protestant immigrants, in John Bodnar, *The Transplanted: A History of Immigrants in Urban America* (Bloomington: Indiana University Press, 1985), ch. 5. These are all important dimensions of working-class religious experience that have informed this study as well. But they also leave open questions addressed in this book about how intracommunity struggles were linked politically and ideologically with questions such as cultural hierarchy that pervaded public discourse.

The pieties peculiar to industrial era workers have been obscured in the historiographical literature in part because the nineteenth-century traditions on which many workers drew have long been associated with a middle-class culture of "social control" inimical to working-class interests. The most pointed interpretations of evangelical Protestantism as a culture of bourgeois social control distinct from artisanal culture or interests are Paul E. Johnson, *A Shopkeeper's Millennium: Society and Revivals in Rochester, New York, 1815–1837* (New York: Hill & Wang, 1978); Bruce Laurie, *Working People of Philadelphia, 1800–1850* (Philadelphia: Temple

University Press, 1980); and Sean Wilentz, *Chants Democratic: New York City and the Rise of the American Working Class* (New York: Oxford University Press, 1984). On the significance of social control as an urban middle-class culture, see Paul Boyer, *Urban Masses and Moral Order in America, 1820–1920* (Cambridge, Mass.: Harvard University Press, 1978). William R. Sutton, "Tied to the Whipping Post: New Labor History and Evangelical Artisans in the Early Republic," *Labor History* 36, no. 2 (1995): 251–79, offers a penetrating critique of this interpretation in relation to the scholarly worldviews that have obscured the significance of religion within American labor and social history. A variety of recent work has begun to recognize the centrality of evangelical ideals to working-class culture and agitation in the nineteenth century. See especially Theresa Murphy, *Ten Hours Labor: Religion, Reform, and Gender in Early New England* (Ithaca, N.Y.: Cornell University Press, 1992); Jama Lazerow, *Religion and the Working Class in Antebellum America* (Washington, D.C.: Smithsonian Institution, 1995); and several dissertations: Mark Shantz, "Piety in Providence: The Class Dimensions of Religious Experience in Providence, Rhode Island, 1790–1860" (Ph.D. diss., Emory University, 1991); Gregory Kaster, "'We will not be slaves to avarice': The American Labor Jeremiad, 1837–1877" (Ph.D. diss., Boston University, 1990); and William R. Sutton, "'To Grind the Faces of the Poor': Journeymen for Jesus in Jacksonian Baltimore" (Ph.D. diss., University of Illinois, 1993).

This work contributes to a wider literature that has reevaluated the transatlantic, nineteenth-century tradition of evangelical Protestantism in terms of plebeian strains of democracy contributed by a variety of groups—such as women and African Americans as well as workers—who saw in this tradition an invitation to democratic worship and salvation. From this literature I have found especially helpful Richard Cawardine, *Trans-Atlantic Revivalism: Popular Evangelicalism in Britain and America, 1790–1865* (Westport, Conn.: Greenwood, 1978); Nathan O. Hatch, *The Democratization of American Christianity* (New Haven, Conn.: Yale University Press, 1989); Susan Juster, *Disorderly Women: Sexual Politics and Evangelicalism in Revolutionary New England* (Ithaca, N.Y.: Cornell University Press, 1994); and Rhys Isaac, *The Transformation of Virginia: Community, Religion, and Authority, 1740–1790* (Chapel Hill: University of North Carolina Press, 1982).

Settlement houses represent important arenas in which historians have traced the affinity between Protestantism and middle-class agendas into the late nineteenth and early twentieth centuries. Pioneering work such as Allen F. Davis, *Spearheads for Reform: The Social Settlements and the Progressive Movement, 1890–1914* (New York: Oxford University Press, 1967) somewhat uncritically interpreted settlement work as an expression of Progressive era efforts to expand culture and democracy to the oppressed and disadvantaged, though what settlement leaders such as Jane Addams self-consciously understood as the "subjective" motivations for such work were already under scrutiny in Christopher Lasch, *The New*

Bibliographical Essay

Radicalism in America, 1889–1963: The Intellectual as a Social Type (New York: Vintage, 1965), chs. 1 and 2. More recently scholars of the settlement movement have been more critical of settlement workers' attempts to shape immigrant working-class culture in the image of their own cultural traditions. See especially in this vein Rivka Lissak, *Pluralism and Progressives: Hull House and the New Immigrants, 1890–1919* (Chicago: University of Chicago Press, 1989); Paul McBride, *Culture Clash—Immigrants and Reformers, 1880–1920* (San Francisco: R & E Research Associates, 1975); Howard Jacob Karger, *The Sentinels of Order: A Study of Social Control and the Minneapolis Settlement House Movement, 1915–1950* (Lanham, Md.: University Press of America, 1987); and Elisabeth Lasch-Quinn, *Black Neighbors: Race and the Limits of Reform in the American Settlement House Movement, 1890–1945* (Chapel Hill: University of North Carolina Press, 1993). While this scholarship attends usefully to a cultural and, often, political divide between settlement workers and their clients that Irvine also observed, however, its emphasis on "social control" has at times obscured the efforts of many settlement workers to revise and reform their own cultural and religious trditions even as they tried to "uplift" immigrant workers. It is this double agenda that made settlement workers part of the larger project of interrogating the cultural meaning of class distinction to which Alexander Irvine also contributed.

While liberal Protestantism at the turn of the century revised the strictures of evangelical piety for an urban middle-class constituency seeking leisure and psychological release, in many historical accounts it is proto-Fundamentalist religion that became the repository of a sterner evangelical piety unleavened by modern scientific knowledge or entertainment. Historical interpretations that have cast Fundamentalists as rural, backward-looking, and antiscientific include Ray Ginger, *Six Days or Forever?: Tennessee vs. John Thomas Scopes* (Boston: Beacon, 1958); and Richard Hofstadter, *Anti-Intellectualism in American Life* (New York: Knopf, 1963). An early revision that complicated this view was Lawrence Levine's study of the later years of William Jennings Bryan, who carried the mantle of Populism into his final religious battle on the side of Fundamentalist biblical inerrancy against scientific modernity at the Scopes trial: *Defender of the Faith: William Jennings Bryan: The Last Decade 1915–1925* (London: Oxford University Press, 1965). The past three decades have seen an accumulation of scholarship on Fundamentalists and their religious antecedents that continues to complicate the picture of how they saw the evangelical tradition in relation to such "modern" cultural trends as Darwinian science and secular, urban entertainment. This scholarship has been especially useful for interpreting a career like Irvine's, as it engaged and reinterpreted proto-Fundamentalist movements like Dwight Moody's revivals and the Plymouth Brethren, demonstrating the way in which these movements shared in wider shifts in worship, entertainment, and social thought even as they criticized these transformations. See especially Ernest Sandeen, *The Roots of Fundamen-*

talism: British and American Millenarianism, 1800–1930 (Chicago: University of Chicago Press, 1970); George M. Marsden, *Fundamentalism and American Culture: The Shaping of Twentieth-Century Evangelicalism, 1870–1925* (Nw York: Oxford University Press, 1980); volumes 1 and 2 of *The Fundamentalism Project* edited by Martin E. Marty and R. Scott Appleby (Chicago: University of Chicago Press, 1991, 1993); and Betty A. DeBerg, *Ungodly Women: Gender and the First Wave of American Fundamentalism* (Minneapolis: Fortress, 1990). The ambiguous character of late-nineteenth-century revival movements that contributed to twentieth-century Fundamentalism is important to understanding this complex legacy, and is usefully traced in James L. Findlay Jr., *Dwight Moody: American Evangelist, 1837–1899* (Chicago: University of Chicago Press, 1969); William G. McLoughlin Jr., *Modern Revivalism: Charles Grandison Finney to Billy Graham* (New York: Ronald, 1959); and James Gilbert, *Perfect Cities: Chicago's Utopias of 1993* (Chicago: University of Chicago Press, 1991).

The plebeian religious practices explored here are part of a wider and variously defined category of "popular religion," often connected to popular culture, that has received increasing scholarly attention. For examples in U.S. history, see Marshall William Fishwick, *Great Awakenings: Popular Religion and Popular Culture* (New York: Havorth, 1995); Colleen McDaniel, *Material Christianity: Religion and Popular Culture in America* (New Haven, Conn.: Yale University Press, 1995); R. Laurence Moore, *Selling God: American Religion in the Marketplace of Culture* (New York: Oxford University Press, 1994); Peter W. Williams, *Popular Religion in America: Symbolic Changes and the Modernization Process in Historical Perspective* (Urbana: University of Illinois Press, 1989); David D. Hall, *Worlds of Wonder, Days of Judgement: Popular Religious Belief in Early New England* (New York: Knopf, 1989).

C. Socialist Strategy, Evolutionary Thought, and the Politics of Race and Gender

The Socialist Party became the primary arena in which Alexander Irvine tried to sort out intersecting distinctions of class, ethnicity, race, and gender that complicated his vision of evangelical uplift. The socialist cultural and political contests in which he engaged have themselves been the focus of considerable debate among historians of the pre–World War I Party. The most useful recent treatment of evolutionary thought and its implications for race and ethnicity in socialist politics is Mark Pittenger, *American Socialists and Evolutionary Thought* (Madison: University of Wisconsin Press, 1993). Scholars differ on the extent to which socialist views on race divided along party factional lines. Pittenger points out that "revolutionists," notably Jack London, also subscribed to Darwinian racial hierarchies. For an alternative view that sees socialist factionalism more clearly aligned with alternative views of race, see Ira Kipnis, *The American Socialist Movement, 1897–1912* (New York: Columbia University Press, 1952). Pittenger notes that one prominent contemporary Socialist—William English Walling—read the situation as Kipnis did. Leo Laukki, discussed in Chapter 7, seems to be another. Readings of Socialist Party politics that accord less decisive importance to battles between constructive and revolutionary Socialists than Kipnis does include James Weinstein, *The Decline of Socialism in America, 1912–1925* (New Brunswick, N.J.: Rutgers University Press, 1967), ch. 1; and Nick Salvatore, *Eugene V. Debs: Citizen and Socialist* (Urbana: University of Illinois Press, 1982), which is also an excellent reading of the evangelical roots of the socialist sensibility Debs shared with Alexander Irvine. Further exploration of this tradition is available in Howard Quint, *The Forging of American Socialism* (Indianapolis: Bobbs-Merrill, 1953); James R. Green, *Grass-Roots Socialism: Radical Movements in the Southwest, 1895–1943* (Baton Rouge: Louisiana Stae University Press, 1978); Mari Jo Buhle, *Women and American Socialism, 1870–1920* (Urbana: University of Illinois Press, 1981); Donald Critchlow, ed., *Socialism in the Heartland: The Midwestern Experience, Nineteen Hundred to Nineteen Twenty-Five* (South Bend, Ind.: University of Notre Dame Press, 1986); Elliott Shore, *Talkin' Socialism: J. A. Wayland and the Role of the Press in American Radicalism, 1890–1912* (Lawrence: University Press of Kansas, 1988); and the Introduction to John Graham, ed., *"Yours for the Revolution": The Appeal to Reason, 1895–1922* (Lincoln: University of Nebraska Press, 1990). The "reformist" or "constructivist" wing of the Party is also treated in Norma Fain Pratt, *Morris Hillquit: A Political History of an American Jewish Socialist* (Westport, Conn.: Greenwood, 1979); Sally Miller, *Victor Berger and the Promise of Constructive Socialism, 1910–1920* (Westport, Conn.: Greenwood, 1973); and Richard W. Fox, "The Paradox of 'Progressive' Socialism: The Case of Morris Hillquit, 1901–1914," *American Quarterly* 26 (May 1974): 127–40. On intersecting debates over race, ethnicity, and gender in the Socialist Party, see Sally M. Miller, *Race, Ethnicity and Gender in Early Twentieth-Century American Socialism* (New York: Garland, 1996).

The wider intellectual and popular cultures of evolutionary thought and Social Darwinism in which socialist thinkers and activists participated are addressed from very different perspectives in Richard Hofstadter, *Social Darwinism in American Thought* (Boston: Beacon, 1955); and Robert Bannister, *Social Darwinism: Science and Myth in Anglo-American Social Thought* (Philadelphia: Temple University Press, 1979). Though, unlike Hofstadter, Bannister sees Social Darwinism as a foil constructed by Progressives, both tend to ignore the internal debates over the meaning of evolution and race within the Socialist Party. The Lamarckian tradition on which many socialist thinkers drew is treated in Pittenger, *American Socialists and Evolutionary Thought, 1870–1920*; George Stocking, *Race, Culture, and Evolution: Essays in the History of Anthropology* (New York: The Free Press, 1968); and Adolph Reed Jr., "Du Bois's 'Double Consciousness': Race and Gender in Progressive Era American Thought," *Studies in American Political Development* 6 (Spring 1992): 93–139. Reed's article is included in his *W. E. B. Du Bois and Amer-*

ican Political Thought: Fabianism and the Color Line (New York: Oxford University Press, 1997), which also usefully orients Du Bois in relation to twentieth-century American socialism. Among other useful sources on Du Bois in this context are David L. Lewis, *W. E. B. Du Bois—A Biography of Race, 1868–1919* (New York: H. Holt, 1993); and Thomas C. Holt, "The Political Uses of Alienation: W. E. B. Du Bois on Politics, Race and Culture, 1903–1940," *American Quarterly* 42, no. 2 (1990): 301–23. For African Americans in the Party, see also Philip Foner, *American Socialism and Black Americans* (Westport, Conn.: Greenwood, 1977).

The activism and debates over gender that Irvine engaged in the Socialist Party are addressed in Mary Jo Buhle, *Women and American Socialism, 1870–1920;* Meredith Tax, *The Rising of the Women: Feminist Solidarity and Class Conflict, 1880–1917* (New York: Monthly Review Press, 1980); Delores Hayden, *The Grand Domestic Revolution: A History of Feminist Designs for American Homes, Neighborhoods, and Cities* (Cambridge, Mass.: MIT, 1983) and, with respect to Charlotte Perkins Gilman's evolutionary thought in particular, Gail Bederman, *Manliness and Civilization: A Cultural History of Gender and Race in the United States, 1880–1917* (Chicago: University of Chicago Press, 1995), ch. 4.

D. *Popular Discourses of Class, Ethnic, and Racial Hierarchy*

The debates over evolution and race that Irvine engaged in the Socialist Party drew on broad currents of popular culture that encompassed Sylvester Poli's theatrical realm. These popular discourses on race and ethnicity, and their significance for conceptions of class, are subjects of a growing literature. A particularly useful example that highlights the ambiguity of racial categories in the work relations, labor politics, and popular culture encountered by "new immigrants" like those Irvine wrote of in *The Magyar* is James Barrett and David Roediger, "In Between Peoples: Race, Nationality and the 'New Immigrant' Working Class," *Journal of American Ethnic History* 16, no. 3 (1997): 819–949. Their perspective builds on a literature on the construction of racial categories, not all of which is as nuanced about the racial ambiguities they describe, including Thomas F. Gossett, *Race: The History of an Idea in America* (Dallas: Southern Methodist University Press, 1963); Gloria Marshall, "Racial Classification, Popular and Scientific," in *The Racial Economy of Science*, ed. Sandra Harding (Bloomington: Indiana University Press, 1993); Thomas G. Dyer, *Theodore Roosevelt and the Idea of Race* (Baton Rouge: Louisiana State University Press, 1980); and Barbara Fields, "Slavery, Race and Ideology in the United States of America," *New Left Review* 181 (May–June 1990), 95–118. On constructions of race and ethnicity in the labor movement, see also Gwendolyn Mink, *Old Labor and New Immigrants in American Political Development* (Ithaca, N.Y.: Cornell University Press, 1986); and Gunther Peck, "Padrones and Protest: 'Old' Radicals and 'New' Immigrants in Bingham, Utah, 1905–1912," *Western Historical Quarterly* (May 1993), 157–78.

Recent literature on the significance of race for constructions of working-class class identity that take place across the boundaries of labor politics and popular culture has been especially valuable for the story told here. See especially David Roediger, *The Wages of Whiteness: Race and the Making of the American Working Class* (London: Verso, 1991); idem, "Gaining a Hearing for Black-White Unity: Covington Hall and the Complexities of Race, Gender and Class," in *Towards the Abolition of Whiteness: Essays on Race, Politics and Working-Class History* (London: Verso, 1994); Alexander Saxton, *The Rise and Fall of the White Republic: Class Politics and Mass Culture in Nineteenth-Century America* (London: Verso, 1991); Noel Ignatiev, *How the Irish Became White* (New York: Routledge, 1995); and Eric Lott, *Love and Theft: Blackface Minstrelsy and the American Working Class* (New York: Oxford University Press, 1993). Roediger, Saxton, and Lott are especially significant for their discussions of blackface minstrelsy as an arena for working-class identity formation. All stress links between minstrelsy and antebellum working-class politics in ways that offer models for the construction of "cultural politics" developed here. However, they depict these links in divergent ways. Lott emphasizes how minstrel actors invested the "black culture" they performed with attractive associations of popular rowdiness and nostalgic community that appealed to white working-class grievances against a new industrial order even as they offered African Americans as racial scapegoats for workers' declining status. In contrast, Roediger insists that the profoundly racist character of blackface performance defeated all overtones of cross-racial sympathy. My own interpretation suggests how these two moments of blackface intertwined by the era of Irvine's and Poli's careers. Earlier work on blackface minstrelsy that has influenced my interpretation of blackface in vaudeville includes Robert C. Toll, *Blacking Up: The Minstrel Show in Nineteenth-Century America* (New York: Oxford University Press, 1974); and Carl Wittke, *Tambo and Bones: A History of the American Minstrel Stage* (Durham, N.C.: Duke University Press, 1930).

The popular and academic literature of cross-class investigation to which I attribute the "evolutionary vernacular" has also drawn growing scholarly attention. See especially Mark Pittenger, "A World of Difference: Constructing the 'Underclass' in Progressive America," *American Quarterly* 49, no. 1 (1997): 26–65; Toby Higbie, "Crossing Boundaries: Tramp Ethnographers and Narratives of Class in Progressive Era America," *Social Science History* 21, no. 4 (1997): 559–92; Jacqueline Dirks, "Righteous Goods: Women's Production, Reform Publicity, and the National Consumers' League, 1890–1920" (Ph.D. diss., Yale University, 1996), ch. 4; Alan Trachtenberg, "Experiments in Another Country: Stephen Crane's City Sketches," in *American Realism: New Essays*, ed. E. J. Sundquist (Baltimore: Johns Hopkins University Press, 1982), 138–54. On the trope of imperial adventure—the discovery of "dark" places—conceived in Darwinian terms which London and Irvine shared with many British investigators of the working-class, see Regenia Gagnier, *Subjectivities: A History of Self-Representation in Britain, 1832–1920* (New York: Oxford University Press, 1991), 118ff.; Peter Keating, ed., *Into Unknown England, 1866–1913* (Manchester: Manchester University Press, 1976); Micaela di Leonardo, "Foreword," to Jack London, *People of the Abyss* (New York: Macmillan, 1903; reprint New York: Lawrence Hill, 1995).

E. *Vaudeville*

Scholarship on vaudeville has acknowledged the contested cultural values vaudeville expressed but attended little to the relations among specific audiences, local entrepreneurs, and corporate structures that shaped these contests. Although in "Under Worlds and Underdogs: Big Tim Sullivan and Metropolitan Politics in New York, 1889–1913," *Journal of American History* 78 (September 1991): 536–58, Daniel Czitrom has examined the relation between popular amusement and popular city politics in New York, historians of popular theater and urban life have often diminished the counterpoint of diverse and even opposing cultural values expressed in vaudeville. Until recently, Albert F. McLean Jr.'s *American Vaudeville as Ritual* (Lexington: University of Kentucky Press, 1965) stood alone as a book-length scholarly examination of vaudeville. Deftly researched, McLean's book is encumbered by a reading of vaudeville as the expression of a shared "Myth of Success" that takes little account of the multiple and conflicting vantage points from which urban life was represented by vaudeville actors. It also slights the 1890s as an important formative period for vaudeville, treating the decade instead as an anomalous period in which archaic themes like ethnicity, class, and sentimentality were gradually shed in favor of shared urban values. Since contemporary chroniclers of vaudeville such as Joe Laurie, *Vaudeville: From the Honky-tonks to the Palace* (New York: Henry Holt, 1953) or Douglas Gilbert, *American Vaudeville: Its Life and Times* (New York: McGraw-Hill, 1940) have looked to the 1890s as the era of some of vaudeville's greatest talents, teleological interpretations that seek the emergence of an "essential" vaudeville after the 1890s would seem to beg closer scrutiny. More recent scholarly treatments of vaudeville have paid greater attention to the conflicts within vaudeville representations of city life. Though Gunther Barth's chapter on vaudeville in *City People: The Ris of Modern City Culture in Nineteenth-Century America* (New York: Oxford University Press, 1980) describes vaudeville's appeal for a rather undifferentiated group he calls "city people," he does attend to the class and ethnic differences within city life that vaudeville acts portrayed. Robert Snyder's study of vaudeville, *The Voice of the City: Vaudeville and Popular Culture in New York* (New York: Oxford University Press, 1989), dispenses entirely with the idea of vaudeville as the expression of a common city experience, recognizing instead that "vaudeville had . . . as many voices as the city where it thrived." But Snyder's excellent study does not venture many interpretations of what this new multiplicity amounted to, and still treats "refinement" itself as a relatively uncontested value, as does Robert Allen's very different but also illuminating reading of vaudeville in *Horrible Prettiness: Burlesque and American Culture* (Chapel Hill: University of North Carolina Press, 1991), 178–93. In contrast, this book charts the multivalent and mutable nature of the "refinement" associated with vaudeville, seeks the peculiar aesthetic of vaudeville in the "realism" that managers like Poli claimed for it, and finds its meanings in its resonance with wider public debates over culture. Recent research by Richard Canedo on managers' reports sent to the headquarters of the B. F. Keith circuit also documents the variety of audience preferences across vaudeville theaters in many American cities. See Richard Canedo, "From Parquet to Gallery: American Vaudeville's Appeal to Diverse Audiences," paper presented at the 1994 annual meeting of the American Studies Association.

Cultural historians interested in wider shifts in American culture have also focused on vaudeville as an important arena in which hierarchical standards of refinement and taste were imposed on more participatory, plebeian traditions of theatrical amusement. See David Nasaw, *Going Out: The Rise and Fall of Public Amusements* (New York: Basic, 1993); Lawrence Levine, *Highbrow/Lowbrow: The Emergence of Cultural Hierarchy in America* (Cambridge, Mass.: Harvard University Press, 1988), 195–97; and John F. Kasson, *Rudeness & Civility: Manners in Nineteenth Century America* (New York: Hill & Wang, 1990), 247–51. This book has profited from all of these analyses, while complicating them by addressing the ongoing conflicts over hierarchical standards that vaudeville expressed and its audiences engaged.

Amusements like vaudeville also figure in the work of historians who have identified popular culture as an arena in which working-class men and women sustained autonomous cultural values at the turn of the century, such as Roy Rosenzweig, *Eight Hours for What We Will: Workers and Leisure in an Industrial City, 1870–1920* (Cambridge: Cambridge University Press, 1983); Frank Couvares, *The Remaking of Pittsburgh: Class and Culture in an Industrializing City, 1870–1920* (Albany: State University of New York Press, 1984); and Kathy Peiss, *Cheap Amusements: Working Women and Leisure in Turn-of-the-Century New York* (Philadelphia: Temple University Press, 1986). I have found these accounts very valuable, but depart from their general suggestion that the new mass cultural industries of vaudeville and film decisively breached working-class autonomy, redefining the distinctions between middle-class and working-class culture. I see a more protracted history of contest and negotiation between working-class and middle-class uses of autonomy and hierarchy as cultural concepts.

The account of the rise of a hierarchy of feminine display on the vaudeville stage builds on considerable scholarship about women in the theater. This scholarship has tended to focus on burlesque's more ribald feminine display or the tonier exhibitions of Lillian Russell in the 1890s and the Ziegfeld Follies and cabarets of the early twentieth century. On these phenomena, see Allen, *Horrible Prettiness*; Faye E. Dudden, *Women in the American Theatre: Actresses and Audiences, 1790–1870* (New Haven, Conn.: Yale University Press, 1994); Parker Morell, *Lillian Russell: The Era of Plush* (Garden City, N.Y.: Garden City, 1943); John Burke, *Duet in Diamonds: The Flamboyant Saga of Lillian Russell and Diamond Jim Brady in America's Gilded Age* (New York: Putnam, 1972); Charles Higham, *Ziegfeld* (Chicago: Regnery, 1972); and Lewis Erenberg, *Steppin' Out: New York Nightlife and the Transformation of American Culture, 1890–1930* (Chicago: University of Chicago Press, 1981). For discussions of women's role in vaudeville, see Shirley Staples, *Male-Female Comedy Teams in American Vaudeville, 1865–1932* (Ann Arbor: UMI Research Press, 1984); and M. Alison Kibler, "The Keith-Vaudeville Circuit, 1890–1920: Gender, Sexuality, and the Cultural Hierarchy" (Ph.D. diss., University of Iowa, 1994).

The relationship between vaudeville and film, at Poli's theaters and elsewhere, is usefully addressed in Robert C. Allen, "Vaudeville and Film, 1895–1915: A Study in Media Interaction" (Ph.D. diss., University of Iowa, 1977); and Charles Musser, *The Emergence of Cinema: The American Screen to 1907* (New York: Charles Scribner's Sons, 1990).

Like other scholarship on vaudeville, this book has profited from a wealth of research on theatrical forms from which vaudeville drew much of its material. In addition to the literature on minstrelsy cited above, I have benefited especially from David Grimsted, *Melodrama Unveiled: American Theater and Culture, 1800–1850* (Chicago: University of Chicago Press, 1968); Neil Harris, *Humbug: The Art of P. T. Barnum* (Chicago: University of Chicago Press, 1968); Peter Buckley, "To the Opera House: Culture and Society in New York City, 1820–1860" (Ph.D. diss., State University of New York at Stony Brook, 1984); Bruce A. McConachie, *Melodramatic Formations: American Theatre and Society, 1820–1870* (Iowa City: University of Iowa Press, 1992); George C. D. Odell, *Annals of the New York Stage* (New York: Columbia University Press, 1940); Richard M. Dorson, "Mose the Far-Famed and World Renowned," *American Literature* 15 (November 1943): 288–300; Maxine Schwartz Seller, ed., *Ethnic Theatre in the United States* (Westport, Conn.: Greenwood, 1983); E. J. Kahn, *The Merry Partners: The Age and Stage of Harrigan and Hart* (New York: Random House, 1955); Edward Marks, *They All Sang: From Tony Pastor to Rudy Valée* (New York: Viking, 1935); Isaac Goldberg, *Tin Pan Alley: A Chronicle of American Popular Music* (New York: Frederick Ungar, 1961); Nicholas E. Tawa, *The Way to Tin Pan Alley: American Popular Song, 1866–1910* (New York: Scribner, 1990); Mark Slobin, *Tenement Songs: The Popular Music of the Jewish Immigrants* (Urbana: University of Illinois Press, 1982); Tom Fletcher, *One Hundred Years of the Negro in Show Business* (New York: Da Capo, 1984);

Myron Matlaw, "Tony the Trouper: Pastor's Early Years," *Theatre Annual* 24 (1968): 72–90; G. C. Duggan, *The Stage Irishman: A History of the Irish Play and Stage Characters from the Earliest Times* (Dublin: Talbor, 1937).

F. *Popular Realism*

The formulation of popular realism developed here is largely my own construction, based on comparisons of the realism practiced in Irvine's and Poli's popular cultural arenas and the practices of literary realism described in the Introduction. But it is informed by a range of scholarship on realist art and literature in America, the history of screen practice, and the history of popular museums in which Poli participated as a wax sculptor. On American literary realism and the wider popular discourses with which it competed I have found especially useful Amy Kaplan, *The Social Construction of American Realism* (Chicago: University of Chicago Press, 1988); Michael Davitt Bell, *The Problem of American Realism: Studies in the Cultural History of a Literary Idea* (Chicago: University of Chicago Press, 1993); June Howard, *Form and History in American Literary Naturalism* (Chapel Hill: University of North Carolina Press, 1985); and David E. Shi, *Facing Facts: Realism in American Thought and Culture, 1850–1920* (New York: Oxford University Press, 1995). On screen practice and the "visual realism" I have learned from Peter Bacon Hales, *Silver Cities: The Photography of American Urbanization, 1839–1915* (Philadelphia: Temple University Press, 1984); Maren Stange, "Jacob Riis and Urban Visual Culture: The Lantern Slide Exhibition as Entertainment and Ideology," *Journal of Urban History* 15 (May 1989): 292–93; *The Magic Lantern Bulletin*; and Musser, *The Emergence of Cinema*. On popular museums and the culture of exhibitions as they contributed to the cultural and evolutionary hierarchies that popular realism addressed, see Harris, *Humbug*; Leo Charney and Vanessa R. Schwartz, eds., *Cinema and the Invention of Modern Life* (Berkeley: University of California Press, 1995); Ivan Karp and Steven D. Lavine, eds., *Exhibiting Cultures: The Poetics and Politics of Museum Display* (Washington, D.C.: Smithsonian Istitution, 1991); and Robert Rydell, *All the World's a Fair* (Chicago: University of Chicago Press, 1987).

INDEX

Index

Catholic Church (*continued*)
  cans, 116, 185–87; and S. Poli, 188, 191; and
  trade unionism, 116
Cawardine, Richard, 8
Chamber of Horrors: in Madame Tussaud's,
  75, 76; in S. Poli's Eden Musée Theater, 89
Character acting, 96, 343, 345, 346, 348, 349
Chautauqua circuits, 260
Christianity: "muscular," 174; trade unionist,
  113, 115–16, 147. *See also* Religion
"Church Forum" movement, 246
Church of Sea and Land, New York, 63
Church of the Ascension, New York, 237–49
Civilization: and Boasian anthropology,
  317–19; and evangelical traditions, 325; feminism and, 244; hierarchical visions of, 4, 5,
  79, 83, 86, 107, 133–34, 322–23; industrialization and, 246; A. Irvine's critiques of, 161,
  233, 236, 245–46, 325; and race, 240–42; waxwork depiction of, 75, 78–80, 86
Class autonomy: meaning of, 23; in *My Lady
  of the Chimney Corner*, 293, 297; wax museum depiction of, 85
Class conflict: in coal strike, 157–65; cultural,
  146–57; in early film, 209; and A. Irvine's
  gospel of work, 337; in A. Irvine's playlet,
  305–6; and religious sociability, 145; and
  trade unionists, 149–50
Class distinctions: conflict and, 12; A. Irvine's
  construction of, 7, 155–57, 228–37, 252–54,
  263, 267–76, 289–96; A. Irvine's early awareness of, 42; and missionary work, 61; popular
  theater and, 327; and religion, 36–38, 44, 47,
  60–63, 140–41, 147, 327. *See also* Working-
  class identity
Class politics: in New Haven, 144, 146–51; and
  trade union movement, 114–15
Cleaveland, Livingston Warner, 150–51
Comedy, in vaudeville, 92, 99
Commercial culture, and public sphere, 23–24,
  223, 325
Commons, John R., 68
Communist Party, 335
Congregationalists, liberal, 121–22; in New
  Haven, 140. *See also* Pilgrim Church; Second Congregational Church
Consumer display, culture of: A. Irvine's criti-
  cism of, 268, 272–73, 304–5; and public
  sphere, 326; in vaudeville, 203, 206, 207,

209; and working-class women, 211–12
Consumption, hierarchy of, 209
"Coon songs," 204, 236, 270
Cosmopoliton, 224
Crane, Stephen, 13, 23, 26, 101, 229, 327; *Maggie, A Girl of the Streets*, 16–19, 21
Cultural authority: A. Irvine and, 308; S. Poli
  and, 101, 192–93, 323; in vaudeville, 324
Cultural hierarchies: American chauvinism in,
  80; of art, 130; and intellectual critique of
  popular culture, 313; and evolutionary vernacular, 229; A. Irvine's discussions of,
  142–43, 161, 238; language of, 81; meaning of,
  23; national, 77–78; in vaudeville theater,
  99, 101, 198, 205; vaudeville criticism of, 93,
  96–97; in wax sculpture, 76–78;
  working–class formulations of, 5, 143
Cultural pluralism, 313
Cultural politics: of class, 17; of A. Irvine, 331;
  20th-century, 308–28
Cultural relativism, 297
Cultural studies, 11–12, 337–39
Culture: anthropological approach to, 321; and
  class identity, 12; defining, 1; ethnic, 116–20,
  186–91, 233, 270–71, 290–92, 313–14; industrial, 319; early 20th-century intellectual definitions, 309–21; A. Irvine's definitions of,
  155–56, 168–69; plebeian, in Ulster, 38–40;
  pluralist visions of, 340; popular concepts of,
  322–23; relativistic visions of, 310; trade
  unionist definitions of, 147; working-class,
  64–65, 115–21, 126–29, 136, 211–12, 236,
  269–70, 328. *See also* Cultural hierarchies
Culture industry, corporate consolidations in,
  336
Culver military academy, 298, 307
Curtis, Susan, 326
Curtius, Christopher, 73

Daly, Philip, 149, 150, 151, 152, 171
Dance halls, 211
Darby, John Nelson, 50
Darrow, Clarence, 279, 280, 281
Darwinian science, 24, 242, 310. *See also* Evolu-
  tionary science; Evolutionary thought
Davis, Gus, 95
Debs, Eugene V., 66, 173, 239, 240, 249, 262,
  263, 287, 332
De Leon, Daniel, 64

Index

cially ecumenical character of, 172; social service programs of, 168

Periodical press: authorship in, 224–25; H. James's criticism of, 256–57. *See also* Magazines

Piety: in American cultural history, 7–12; in cobbler's shop culture, 40; and military duty, 57; in S. Poli's theater, 106

Pilgrim Church (Fair Haven), 143. *See also* Second Congregational Church

Playlets, in vaudeville, 202, 299–300, 301, 325, 345, 348

Plymouth Brethren, 50, 51, 54, 64, 123

Poli, Rosa Leverone, 82–83, 330, 331

Poli, Sylvester Zeffarino, 3, 199; apprenticeship in Paris of, 73, 75–78; Catholicism of, 7–8, 190–91; Chevalier of the Crown of Italy awarded to, 328–29; children of, 330; civic leadership of, 192, 193; and corporate vaudeville, 194–98; early years, 72; Haymarket anarchist exhibit of, 83–86; military career of, 75; New Haven audience of, 179, 182–94; sells theatrical circuit, 330–31; social standing of, 189–90, 191; Theatrical Enterprises, 194, 199; wax exhibits of, 76–82, 83–87, 89; and World War I, 328–29

Poli's Eden Musée Theater (New Haven), 89

Poli's New England Theatres, 331

"Poli's New Theatre" (New Haven), 179, 180, 181

Poli theater (Troy, N.Y.), 88

Popular Front, 337

Popular realism, 71, 72; aesthetic based on, 130; ambiguity of, 84–85; caricature in, 100; cultural concepts associated with, 22; and cultural hierarchies, 322; dominant visual languages of, 76; vaudeville, 179; of wax museums, 72–83. *See also* Realism

Populism, American, 66, 173

Porter, Delia Lyman, 210–11

Porter, Edwin S., 209

Pragmatism, 310

Protestant clergy: and Anthracite Coal Strike, 158–59; and trade union movement, 116, 121–23; in Ulster, 36, 45; and water crusade, 147

Protestantism: and American labor movement, 116, 157–59; evangelical, 24, 43–44, 62, 244; "feminization," 300; liberal, 113–25, 326; in Ulster, 35–37, 43

Psychological Review of Reviews, 335

Public sphere: audiences in, 77–78; characteristics of debate in, 23; of cobbler's shop, 35; dilution of, 332, 333; enlightened discourse in, 246; evangelical values in, 9; Habermas's portrayal of, 25; in New Haven, 112

Quackenbos, Mary Grace, 228, 230, 274

Quinlivan, Frances Blanche, 335

Race, 2; assimilationist approaches to, 314; and class identity, 255–56; cultural hierarchies of, 79–80; evolutionary hierarchies of, 242, 340; evolutionary vernacular for, 234–35, 328; and hierarchy of civilization, 136; and Irish identity, 201, 266, 291; A. Irvine's approach to, 240, 255–56, 257; popular conceptions of, 236; socialist views on, 240–42, 264–65, 287; in wax museums, 75

Racism: Boas's approach to, 318; evolutionary, 136; in vaudeville, 183, 204

Ragtime, 203, 205

Realism: and film, 102; literary, 13–23; in periodical press, 225; vaudeville, 101–2; of wax museum, 71–72. *See also* Popular realism; Visual realism

Redfield, Robert, 318

Refinement: associated with Protestant pieties, 9; of churched elite, 156; hierarchical, 99, 212; in vaudeville, 182, 198, 201, 202

Reid, Fred, 47

Reilly, Joseph J., 116, 150

Religion: and challenge to elitism, 155; and class conflict, 125–29, 155–57, 159–62; class distinction, 36–38, 44, 47, 60–63, 140–41, 147, 327; and commercial culture, 24; in cultural debate, 1; and labor politics, 115–16, 120–21, 148, 162–63, 165–72; in vaudeville, 106, 209; and women, 144–45, 174; and working class, 129, 132, 146

Revivalism: in Britain and Ireland, 43; mid-century, 50; Moody-Sankey, 43–44, 126; popular, 68, and socialism, 263–64

Riis, Jacob, 17, 103, 142

Rockefeller, John D., 250, 300, 302

Roediger, David, 235

Roosevelt, Theodore, 158, 159, 245–46, 300

Ross, Stephen, 279

"Rube" sketch, in vaudeville, 91, 92, 96, 343, 349

Index

Library of Congress Cataloging-in-Publication Data

Oberdeck, Kathryn J.
The evangelist and the impresario : religion, entertainment, and
cultural politics in America, 1884–1914 / Kathryn J. Oberdeck.
p. cm. — (New studies in American intellectual and cultural history)
Includes bibliographical references and index.
ISBN 0-8018-6060-1 (alk. paper)
1. United States—Intellectual life—1865–1918. 2. Religion and culture—
United States—History. 3. Politics and culture—United States—History.
4. Working class—United States—History. 5. Irvine Alexander, 1863–1941.
6. Evangelistic work—Social aspects—Connecticut—New Haven—History.
7. Poli, Sylvester. 8. Vaudeville—Social aspects—Connecticut—New Haven—
History. 9. New Haven (Conn.)—Intellectual life. I. Title. II. Series.
E169.1.O16 1999
306'.0973—dc21   98-46628
                                                    CIP